Handbook of Foreign Language Communication and Learning
HAL 6

Handbooks of Applied Linguistics

Communication Competence
Language and Communication Problems
Practical Solutions

Editors
Karlfried Knapp and Gerd Antos

Volume 6

De Gruyter Mouton

Handbook of Foreign Language Communication and Learning

Edited by
Karlfried Knapp and Barbara Seidlhofer

In cooperation with
Henry Widdowson

De Gruyter Mouton

ISBN 978-3-11-026012-0
e-ISBN 978-3-11-021424-6

Library of Congress Cataloging-in-Publication Data

Handbook of foreign language communication and learning / edited by Karlfried Knapp, Barbara Seidlhofer, in cooperation with Henry Widdowson.
p. cm.
Includes bibliographical references and index.
ISBN 978-3-11-026012-0 (pbk. : alk. paper)
1. Languages, Modern – Study and teaching. I. Knapp, Karlfried. II. Seidlhofer, Barbara. III. Widdowson, H. G.
PB35.H287 2011
418.0071–dc22
2011013979

Bibliographic information published by the Deutsche Nationalbibliothek

The Deutsche Nationalbibliothek lists this publication in the Deutsche Nationalbibliografie; detailed bibliographic data are available in the Internet at http://dnb.d-nb.de.

Cover design: Martin Zech, Bremen
Cover image: xandert/morgueFile
Typesetting: Dörlemann Satz GmbH & Co. KG, Lemförde
Printing: Hubert & Co. GmbH & Co. KG, Göttingen
∞ Printed on acid-free paper

Printed in Germany

www.degruyter.com

Introduction to the handbook series

Linguistics for problem solving

Karlfried Knapp and Gerd Antos

1. Science and application at the turn of the millennium

The distinction between "pure" and "applied" sciences is an old one. According to Meinel (2000), it was introduced by the Swedish chemist Wallerius in 1751, as part of the dispute of that time between the scholastic disciplines and the then emerging epistemic sciences. However, although the concept of "Applied Science" gained currency rapidly since that time, it has remained problematic.

Until recently, the distinction between "pure" and "applied" mirrored the distinction between "theory and "practice". The latter ran all the way through Western history of science since its beginnings in antique times. At first, it was only philosophy that was regarded as a scholarly and, hence, theoretical discipline. Later it was followed by other leading disciplines, as e.g., the sciences. However, as academic disciplines, all of them remained theoretical. In fact, the process of achieving independence of theory was essential for the academic disciplines to become independent from political, religious or other contingencies and to establish themselves at universities and academies. This also implied a process of emancipation from practical concerns – an at times painful development which manifested (and occasionally still manifests) itself in the discrediting of and disdain for practice and practitioners. To some, already the very meaning of the notion "applied" carries a negative connotation, as is suggested by the contrast between the widely used synonym for "theoretical", i.e. "pure" (as used, e.g. in the distinction between "Pure" and "Applied Mathematics") and its natural antonym "impure". On a different level, a lower academic status sometimes is attributed to applied disciplines because of their alleged lack of originality – they are perceived as simply and one-directionally applying insights gained in basic research and watering them down by neglecting the limiting conditions under which these insights were achieved.

Today, however, the academic system is confronted with a new understanding of science. In politics, in society and, above all, in economy a new concept of science has gained acceptance which questions traditional views. In recent philosophy of science, this is labelled as "science under the pressure to succeed" – i.e. as science whose theoretical structure and criteria of evaluation are increasingly conditioned by the pressure of application (Carrier, Stöltzner, and Wette 2004):

> Whenever the public is interested in a particular subject, e.g. when a new disease develops that cannot be cured by conventional medication, the public requests science to provide new insights in this area as quickly as possible. In doing so, the public is less interested in whether these new insights fit seamlessly into an existing theoretical framework, but rather whether they make new methods of treatment and curing possible (Institut für Wirtschafts- und Technikforschung 2004, our translation).

With most of the practical problems like these, sciences cannot rely on knowledge that is already available, simply because such knowledge does not yet exist. Very often, the problems at hand do not fit neatly into the theoretical framework of one particular "pure science", and there is competition among disciplines with respect to which one provides the best theoretical and methodological resources for potential solutions. And more often than not the problems can be tackled only by adopting an interdisciplinary approach.

As a result, the traditional "Cascade Model", where insights were applied top-down from basic research to practice, no longer works in many cases. Instead, a kind of "application oriented basic research" is needed, where disciplines – conditioned by the pressure of application – take up a certain still diffuse practical issue, define it as a problem against the background of their respective theoretical and methodological paradigms, study this problem and finally develop various application oriented suggestions for solutions. In this sense, applied science, on the one hand, has to be conceived of as a scientific strategy for problem solving – a strategy that starts from mundane practical problems and ultimately aims at solving them. On the other hand, despite the dominance of application that applied sciences are subjected to, as sciences they can do nothing but develop such solutions in a theoretically reflected and methodologically well founded manner. The latter, of course, may lead to the well-known fact that even applied sciences often tend to concentrate on "application oriented basic research" only and thus appear to lose sight of the original practical problem. But despite such shifts in focus: Both the boundaries between disciplines and between pure and applied research are getting more and more blurred.

Today, after the turn of the millennium, it is obvious that sciences are requested to provide more and something different than just theory, basic research or pure knowledge. Rather, sciences are increasingly being regarded as partners in a more comprehensive social and economic context of problem solving and are evaluated against expectations to be practically relevant. This also implies that sciences are expected to be critical, reflecting their impact on society. This new "applied" type of science is confronted with the question: Which role can the sciences play in solving individual, interpersonal, social, intercultural, political or technical problems? This question is typical of a conception of science that was especially developed and propagated by the influential philosopher Sir Karl Popper – a conception that also this handbook series is based on.

2. "Applied Linguistics": Concepts and controversies

The concept of "Applied Linguistics" is not as old as the notion of "Applied Science", but it has also been problematical in its relation to theoretical linguistics since its beginning. There seems to be a widespread consensus that the notion "Applied Linguistics" emerged in 1948 with the first issue of the journal *Language Learning* which used this compound in its subtitle *A Quarterly Journal of Applied Linguistics*. This history of its origin certainly explains why even today "Applied Linguistics" still tends to be predominantly associated with foreign language teaching and learning in the Anglophone literature in particular, as can bee seen e.g. from Johnson and Johnson (1998), whose *Encyclopedic Dictionary of Applied Linguistics* is explicitly subtitled *A Handbook for Language Teaching*. However, this theory of origin is historically wrong. As is pointed out by Back (1970), the concept of applying linguistics can be traced back to the early 19th century in Europe, and the very notion "Applied Linguistics" was used in the early 20th already.

2.1. Theoretically Applied vs. Practically Applied Linguistics

As with the relation between "Pure" and "Applied" sciences pointed out above, also with "Applied Linguistics" the first question to be asked is what makes it different from "Pure" or "Theoretical Linguistics". It is not surprising, then, that the terminologist Back takes this difference as the point of departure for his discussion of what constitutes "Applied Linguistics". In the light of recent controversies about this concept it is no doubt useful to remind us of his terminological distinctions.

Back (1970) distinguishes between "Theoretical Linguistics" – which aims at achieving knowledge for its own sake, without considering any other value –, "Practice" – i.e. any kind of activity that serves to achieve any purpose in life in the widest sense, apart from the striving for knowledge for its own sake – and "Applied Linguistics", as a being based on "Theoretical Linguistics" on the one hand and as aiming at usability in "Practice" on the other. In addition, he makes a difference between "Theoretical Applied Linguistics" and "Practical Applied Linguistics", which is of particular interest here. The former is defined as the use of insights and methods of "Theoretical Linguistics" for gaining knowledge in another, non-linguistic discipline, such as ethnology, sociology, law or literary studies, the latter as the application of insights from linguistics in a practical field related to language, such as language teaching, translation, and the like. For Back, the contribution of applied linguistics is to be seen in the planning of practical action. Language teaching, for example, is practical action done by practitioners, and what applied linguistics can contribute to this is, e.g., to provide contrastive descriptions of the languages involved as a foundation for teaching methods. These contrastive descriptions in turn have to be based on the descriptive methods developed in theoretical linguistics.

However, in the light of the recent epistemological developments outlined above, it may be useful to reinterpret Back's notion of "Theoretically Applied Linguistics". As he himself points out, dealing with practical problems can have repercussions on the development of the theoretical field. Often new approaches, new theoretical concepts and new methods are a prerequisite for dealing with a particular type of practical problems, which may lead to an – at least in the beginning – "application oriented basic research" in applied linguistics itself, which with some justification could also be labelled "theoretically applied", as many such problems require the transgression of disciplinary boundaries. It is not rare that a domain of "Theoretically Applied Linguistics" or "application oriented basic research" takes on a life of its own, and that also something which is labelled as "Applied Linguistics" might in fact be rather remote from the mundane practical problems that originally initiated the respective subject area. But as long as a relation to the original practical problem can be established, it may be justified to count a particular field or discussion as belonging to applied linguistics, even if only "theoretically applied".

2.2. Applied linguistics as a response to structuralism and generativism

As mentioned before, in the Anglophone world in particular the view still appears to be widespread that the primary concerns of the subject area of applied linguistics should be restricted to second language acquisition and language instruction in the first place (see, e.g., Davies 1999 or Schmitt and Celce-Murcia 2002). However, in other parts of the world, and above all in Europe, there has been a development away from aspects of language learning to a wider focus on more general issues of language and communication.

This broadening of scope was in part a reaction to the narrowing down the focus in linguistics that resulted from self-imposed methodological constraints which, as Ehlich (1999) points out, began with Saussurean structuralism and culminated in generative linguistics. For almost three decades since the late 1950s, these developments made "language" in a comprehensive sense, as related to the everyday experience of its users, vanish in favour of an idealised and basically artificial entity. This led in "Core" or theoretical linguistics to a neglect of almost all everyday problems with language and communication encountered by individuals and societies and made it necessary for those interested in socially accountable research into language and communication to draw on a wider range of disciplines, thus giving rise to a flourishing of interdisciplinary areas that have come to be referred to as hyphenated variants of linguistics, such as sociolinguistics, ethnolinguistics, psycholinguistics, conversation analysis, pragmatics, and so on (Davies and Elder 2004).

That these hyphenated variants of linguistics can be said to have originated from dealing with problems may lead to the impression that they fall completely into the scope of applied linguistics. This the more so as their original thematic focus is in line with a frequently quoted definition of applied linguistics as "the theoretical and empirical investigation of real world problems in which language is a central issue" (Brumfit 1997: 93). However, in the recent past much of the work done in these fields has itself been rather "theoretically applied" in the sense introduced above and ultimately even become mainstream in linguistics. Also, in view of the current epistemological developments that see all sciences under the pressure of application, one might even wonder if there is anything distinctive about applied linguistics at all.

Indeed it would be difficult if not impossible to delimit applied linguistics with respect to the practical problems studied and the disciplinary approaches used: Real-world problems with language (to which, for greater clarity, should be added: "with communication") are unlimited in principle. Also, many problems of this kind are unique and require quite different approaches. Some might be tackled successfully by applying already available linguistic theories and methods. Others might require for their solution the development of new methods and even new theories. Following a frequently used distinction first proposed by Widdowson (1980), one might label these approaches as "Linguistics Applied" or "Applied Linguistics". In addition, language is a trans-disciplinary subject par excellence, with the result that problems do not come labelled and may require for their solution the cooperation of various disciplines.

2.3. Conceptualisations and communities

The questions of what should be its reference discipline and which themes, areas of research and sub-disciplines it should deal with, have been discussed constantly and were also the subject of an intensive debate (e.g. Seidlhofer 2003). In the recent past, a number of edited volumes on applied linguistics have appeared which in their respective introductory chapters attempt at giving a definition of "Applied Linguistics". As can be seen from the existence of the Association Internationale de Linguistique Appliquée (AILA) and its numerous national affiliates, from the number of congresses held or books and journals published with the label "Applied Linguistics", applied linguistics appears to be a well-established and flourishing enterprise. Therefore, the collective need felt by authors and editors to introduce their publication with a definition of the subject area it is supposed to be about is astonishing at first sight. Quite obviously, what Ehlich (2006) has termed "the struggle for the object of inquiry" appears to be characteristic of linguistics – both of linguistics at large and applied linguistics. Its seems then, that the meaning and scope of "Applied Linguistics" cannot be taken for granted, and this is why a wide variety of controversial conceptualisations exist.

For example, in addition to the dichotomy mentioned above with respect to whether approaches to applied linguistics should in their theoretical foundations and methods be autonomous from theoretical linguistics or not, and apart from other controversies, there are diverging views on whether applied linguistics is an independent academic discipline (e.g. Kaplan and Grabe 2000) or not (e.g. Davies and Elder 2004), whether its scope should be mainly restricted to language teaching related topics (e.g. Schmitt and Celce-Murcia 2002) or not (e.g. Knapp 2006), or whether applied linguistics is a field of interdisciplinary synthesis where theories with their own integrity develop in close interaction with language users and professionals (e.g. Rampton 1997/2003) or whether this view should be rejected, as a true interdisciplinary approach is ultimately impossible (e.g. Widdowson 2005).

In contrast to such controversies Candlin and Sarangi (2004) point out that applied linguistics should be defined in the first place by the actions of those who practically *do* applied linguistics:

> [...] we see no especial purpose in reopening what has become a somewhat sterile debate on what applied linguistics is, or whether it is a distinctive and coherent discipline. [...] we see applied linguistics as a many centered and interdisciplinary endeavour whose coherence is achieved in purposeful, mediated action by its practitioners. [...]
> What we want to ask of applied linguistics is less what it is and more what it does, or rather what its practitioners do. (Candlin/Sarangi 2004:1–2)

Against this background, they see applied linguistics as less characterised by its thematic scope – which indeed is hard to delimit – but rather by the two aspects of "relevance" and "reflexivity". Relevance refers to the purpose applied linguistic activities have for the targeted audience and to the degree that these activities in their collaborative practices meet the background and needs of those addressed – which, as matter of comprehensibility, also includes taking their conceptual and language level into account. Reflexivity means the contextualisation of the intellectual principles and practices, which is at the core of what characterises a professional community, and which is achieved by asking leading questions like "What kinds of purposes underlie what is done?", "Who is involved in their determination?", "By whom, and in what ways, is their achievement appraised?", "Who owns the outcomes?".

We agree with these authors that applied linguistics in dealing with real world problems is determined by disciplinary givens – such as e.g. theories, methods or standards of linguistics or any other discipline – but that it is determined at least as much by the social and situational givens of the practices of life. These do not only include the concrete practical problems themselves but also the theoretical and methodological standards of cooperating experts from other disciplines, as well as the conceptual and practical standards of the practitioners who are confronted with the practical problems in the first place. Thus, as Sarangi and van Leeuwen (2003) point out, applied linguists have to become part of the respective "community of practice".

If, however, applied linguists have to regard themselves as part of a community of practice, it is obvious that it is the entire community which determines what the respective subject matter is that the applied linguist deals with and how. In particular, it is the respective community of practice which determines which problems of the practitioners have to be considered. The consequence of this is that applied linguistics can be understood from very comprehensive to very specific, depending on what kind of problems are considered relevant by the respective community. Of course, following this participative understanding of applied linguistics also has consequences for the Handbooks of Applied Linguistics both with respect to the subjects covered and the way they are theoretically and practically treated.

3. Applied linguistics for problem solving

Against this background, it seems reasonable not to define applied linguistics as an autonomous discipline or even only to delimit it by specifying a set of subjects it is supposed to study and typical disciplinary approaches it should use. Rather, in line with the collaborative and participatory perspective of the communities of practice applied linguists are involved in, this handbook series is based on the assumption that applied linguistics is a specific, problem-oriented way of "doing linguistics" related to the real-life world. In other words: applied linguistics is conceived of here as "linguistics for problem solving".

To outline what we think is distinctive about this area of inquiry: Entirely in line with Popper's conception of science, we take it that applied linguistics starts from the assumption of an imperfect world in the areas of language and communication. This means, firstly, that linguistic and communicative competence in individuals, like other forms of human knowledge, is fragmentary and defective – if it exists at all. To express it more pointedly: Human linguistic and communicative behaviour is not "perfect". And on a different level, this imperfection also applies to the use and status of language and communication in and among groups or societies.

Secondly, we take it that applied linguists are convinced that the imperfection both of individual linguistic and communicative behaviour and language based relations between groups and societies can be clarified, understood and to some extent resolved by their intervention, e.g. by means of education, training or consultancy.

Thirdly, we take it that applied linguistics proceeds by a specific mode of inquiry in that it mediates between the way language and communication is expertly studied in the linguistic disciplines and the way it is directly experienced in different domains of use. This implies that applied linguists are able to demonstrate that their findings – be they of a "Linguistics Applied" or "Applied Linguistics" nature – are not just "application oriented basic research" but can be made relevant to the real-life world.

Fourthly, we take it that applied linguistics is socially accountable. To the extent that the imperfections initiating applied linguistic activity involve both social actors and social structures, we take it that applied linguistics has to be critical and reflexive with respect to the results of its suggestions and solutions.

These assumptions yield the following questions which at the same time define objectives for applied linguistics:

1. Which linguistic problems are typical of which areas of language competence and language use?
2. How can linguistics define and describe these problems?
3. How can linguistics suggest, develop, or achieve solutions of these problems?
4. Which solutions result in which improvements in speakers' linguistic and communicative abilities or in the use and status of languages in and between groups?
5. What are additional effects of the linguistic intervention?

4. Objectives of this handbook series

These questions also determine the objectives of this book series. However, in view of the present boom in handbooks of linguistics and applied linguistics, one should ask what is specific about this series of nine thematically different volumes.

To begin with, it is important to emphasise what it is not aiming at:

- The handbook series does not want to take a snapshot view or even a "hit list" of fashionable topics, theories, debates or fields of study.
- Nor does it aim at a comprehensive coverage of linguistics because some selectivity with regard to the subject areas is both inevitable in a book series of this kind and part of its specific profile.

Instead, the book series will try

- to show that applied linguistics can offer a comprehensive, trustworthy and scientifically well-founded understanding of a wide range of problems,
- to show that applied linguistics can provide or develop instruments for solving new, still unpredictable problems,

- to show that applied linguistics is not confined to a restricted number of topics such as, e.g. foreign language learning, but that it successfully deals with a wide range of both everyday problems and areas of linguistics,
- to provide a state-of-the-art description of applied linguistics against the background of the ability of this area of academic inquiry to provide descriptions, analyses, explanations and, if possible, solutions of everyday problems. On the one hand, this criterion is the link to trans-disciplinary co-operation. On the other, it is crucial in assessing to what extent linguistics can in fact be made relevant.

In short, it is by no means the intention of this series to duplicate the present state of knowledge about linguistics as represented in other publications with the supposed aim of providing a comprehensive survey. Rather, the intention is to present the knowledge available in applied linguistics today firstly from an explicitly problem solving perspective and secondly, in a non-technical, easily comprehensible way. Also it is intended with this publication to build bridges to neighbouring disciplines and to critically discuss which impact the solutions discussed do in fact have on practice. This is particularly necessary in areas like language teaching and learning – where for years there has been a tendency to fashionable solutions without sufficient consideration of their actual impact on the reality in schools.

5. Criteria for the selection of topics

Based on the arguments outlined above, the handbook series has the following structure: Findings and applications of linguistics will be presented in concentric circles, as it were, starting out from the communication competence of the individual, proceeding via aspects of interpersonal and inter-group communication to technical communication and, ultimately, to the more general level of society. Thus, the topics of the nine volumes are as follows:

1. Handbook of Individual Communication Competence
2. Handbook of Interpersonal Communication
3. Handbook of Communication in Organisations and Professions
4. Handbook of Communication in the Public Sphere
5. Handbook of Multilingualism and Multilingual Communication
6. Handbook of Foreign Language Communication and Learning
7. Handbook of Intercultural Communication
8. Handbook of Technical Communication
9. Handbook of Language and Communication: Diversity and Change

This thematic structure can be said to follow the sequence of experience with problems related to language and communication a human passes through in the course of his or her personal biographical development. This is why the topic areas of applied linguistics are structured here in ever-increasing concentric circles: in line with biographical development, the first circle starts with the communicative competence of the individual and also includes interpersonal communication as belonging to a person's private sphere. The second circle proceeds to the everyday environment and includes the professional and public sphere. The third circle extends to the experience of foreign languages and cultures, which at least in officially monolingual societies, is not made by everybody and if so, only later in life. Technical communication as the fourth circle is even more exclusive and restricted to a more special professional clientele. The final volume extends this process to focus on more general, supra-individual national and international issues.

For almost all of these topics, there already exist introductions, handbooks or other types of survey literature. However, what makes the present volumes unique is their explicit claim to focus on topics in language and communication as areas of everyday problems and their emphasis on pointing out the relevance of applied linguistics in dealing with them.

Bibliography

Back, Otto
1970 Was bedeutet und was bezeichnet der Begriff 'angewandte Sprachwissenschaft'? *Die Sprache* 16: 21–53.

Brumfit, Christopher
1997 How applied linguistics is the same as any other science. *International Journal of Applied Linguistics* 7(1): 86–94.

Candlin, Chris N. and Srikant Sarangi
2004 Making applied linguistics matter. *Journal of Applied Linguistics* 1(1): 1–8.

Carrier, Michael, Martin Stöltzner, and Jeanette Wette
2004 *Theorienstruktur und Beurteilungsmaßstäbe unter den Bedingungen der Anwendungsdominanz.* Universität Bielefeld: Institut für Wissenschafts- und Technikforschung [http://www.uni-bielefeld.de/iwt/projekte/wissen/anwendungsdominanz.html, accessed Jan 5, 2007].

Davies, Alan
1999 *Introduction to Applied Linguistics. From Practice to Theory.* Edinburgh: Edinburgh University Press.

Davies, Alan and Catherine Elder
2004 General introduction – Applied linguistics: Subject to discipline? In: Alan Davies and Catherine Elder (eds.), *The Handbook of Applied Linguistics*, 1–16. Malden etc.: Blackwell.

Ehlich, Konrad
1999 Vom Nutzen der „Funktionalen Pragmatik" für die angewandte Linguistik. In: Michael Becker-Mrotzek und Christine Doppler (eds.), *Medium Sprache im Beruf. Eine Aufgabe für* die *Linguistik*, 23–36. Tübingen: Narr.

Ehlich, Konrad
2006 Mehrsprachigkeit für Europa – öffentliches Schweigen, linguistische Distanzen. In: Sergio Cigada, Jean-Francois de Pietro, Daniel Elmiger, and Markus Nussbaumer (eds.), *Öffentliche Sprachdebatten – linguistische Positionen. Bulletin Suisse de Linguistique Appliquée/VALS-ASLA-Bulletin* 83/1: 11–28.

Grabe, William
2002 Applied linguistics: An emerging discipline for the twenty-first century. In: Robert B. Kaplan (ed.), *The Oxford Handbook of Applied Linguistics*, 3–12. Oxford: Oxford University Press.

Johnson, Keith and Helen Johnson (eds.)
1998 *Encyclopedic Dictionary of Applied Linguistics. A Handbook for Language Teaching*. Oxford: Blackwell.

Kaplan, Robert B. and William Grabe
2000 Applied linguistics and the Annual Review of Applied Linguistics. In: W. Grabe (ed.), *Applied Linguistics as an Emerging Discipline. Annual Review of Applied Linguistics* 20: 3–17.

Knapp, Karlfried
2006 Vorwort. In: Karlfried Knapp, Gerd Antos, Michael Becker-Mrotzek, Arnulf Deppermann, Susanne Göpferich, Joachim Gabowski, Michael Klemm und Claudia Villiger (eds.), *Angewandte Linguistik. Ein Lehrbuch*. 2nd ed., xix–xxiii. Tübingen: Francke – UTB.

Meinel, Christoph
2000 Reine und angewandte Wissenschaft. In: *Das Magazin*. Ed. Wissenschaftszentrum Nordrhein-Westfalen 11(1): 10–11.

Rampton, Ben
1997 [2003] Retuning in applied linguistics. *International Journal of Applied Linguistics* 7 (1): 3–25, quoted from Seidlhofer (2003), 273–295.

Sarangi, Srikant and Theo van Leeuwen
2003 Applied linguistics and communities of practice: Gaining communality or losing disciplinary autonomy? In: Srikant Sarangi and Theo van Leeuwen (eds.), *Applied Linguistics and Communities of Practice*, 1–8. London: Continuum.

Schmitt, Norbert and Marianne Celce-Murcia
2002 An overview of applied linguistics. In: Norbert Schmitt (ed.), *An Introduction to Applied Linguistics*. London: Arnold.

Seidlhofer, Barbara (ed.)
2003 *Controversies in Applied Linguistics*. Oxford: Oxford University Press.

Widdowson, Henry
1984 [1980] Model and fictions. In: Henry Widdowson (1984) *Explorations in Applied Linguistics* 2, 21–27. Oxford: Oxford University Press.

Widdowson, Henry
2005 Applied linguistics, interdisciplinarity, and disparate realities. In: Paul Bruthiaux, Dwight Atkinson, William G. Egginton, William Grabe, and Vaidehi Ramanathan (eds.), *Directions in Applied Linguistics. Essays in Honor of Robert B. Kaplan*, 12–25. Clevedon: Multilingual Matters.

Acknowledgements

In putting this volume together, we could rely on the help of several colleagues. We would like to thank Julia Hüttner for her competent editorial assistance during various stages of this project. Very special thanks go to Riccarda Schmidt for her indefatigable commitment to this book in general and especially for her careful copy editing, proof reading and the compilation of the name index. We also gratefully acknowledge the creative support by Barbara Karlson and Wolfgang Konwitschny of Mouton de Gruyter especially in the final production phase of this book.

Karlfried Knapp
Barbara Seidlhofer
Henry Widdowson

Contents

V. Evaluation in language learning and teaching

1. Introduction Developing foreign language communication: Principles and practices

Karlfried Knapp, Barbara Seidlhofer and Henry Widdowson

Although other volumes in this series make it abundantly clear that the scope of applied linguistics ranges widely over many kinds of language experience, it is a matter of historical fact that its name first became established as an area of enquiry concerned with the acquisition and use of foreign languages, particularly of English. Indeed, in the minds of many people applied linguistics is still predominantly associated with issues in foreign language pedagogy, and especially with the teaching of English as a foreign or other language. Over recent years, as the scope of applied linguistics has extended, and its socio-political significance been more fully recognised, this narrower definition of applied linguistics is no longer seen as appropriate, and has at times been deplored. But just as it would be a mistake to confine applied linguistics to its traditional concerns, so it would be a mistake to disregard or undervalue the extensive theory and research into foreign language education and pedagogy that has been carried out in its name. Issues relating to the learning and use of languages other than one's own have become of increasing importance in this present era of globalisation and international communication and so although this is only one area of applied linguistic activity, with no claim to priority over any other, it remains an area of crucial significance, with its relevance to everyday life undiminished, and if anything increased.

The purpose of this volume is to represent how thinking and research have developed in this area of foreign language communication and learning. We can think of applied linguistics generally as a mediation process whereby expertise in the linguistic disciplines based on theory and empirical research is brought to bear on problems that people experience with language in their everyday affairs. What this volume is concerned with is the experience people have of learning and using a language other than their own. One of the difficulties of this area of applied linguistics is that most foreign language learning is already mediated through teaching, itself claimed to be a legitimate area of expertise, and ideas about how to teach are often deeply entrenched in established tradition, accepted as received wisdom and common sense. Quite naturally, therefore, proposals for rethinking that come from elsewhere are treated with some scepticism, resisted as too abstruse and theoretical, not sufficiently grounded in the practical reality of classrooms. Conversely, from the expertise side, there has at times been a tendency to take the relevance of linguistics as self-evident, to suppose that research findings from controlled experimentation can, and should, be unilaterally transferred to the different contexts of language classrooms without adequate consideration of how well grounded they are in principle and how feasible in practice.

With this in mind, it is of particular importance that mediation in this area of applied linguistics should be based on reciprocal understanding. Theoretical ideas about language, approaches to linguistic description and the findings of research on language acquisition may carry a good deal of conviction within the different disciplinary communities of linguists, but their relevance in the practical domain of language education and pedagogy cannot just be assumed, but has to be demonstrated. Applied linguistics is not accountable to linguistics alone. On the other hand, if language teaching is to have any professional status, it cannot simply conform to established convention or follow the dictates of practical expediency. All language pedagogy, no matter how down to earth, is ultimately based on ideas about the nature of language and language learning. Deeply embedded as they often are in established practice, however, they may remain implicit and unrecognised. It is the purpose of applied linguistics to bring these ideas into the open, make them explicit so that teachers can subject them to critical appraisal and evaluate their current validity alongside other ideas. This does not mean that established practices are to be rejected out of hand as remnants of past thinking, but that if they are to be retained, their retention can be justified. The same applies to any new ideas that are proposed. They too need to be critically examined and their relevance assessed.

Innovation is no guarantee of validity: new ideas may be just as suspect as old ones.

It is a mistake, not always avoided in the past, to suppose that theory and research in language and language learning can unilaterally determine educational policy and pedagogic practice. Policy decisions about the role of foreign languages in education and procedures followed in classroom teaching obviously need to take all kinds of other factors into account. But these decisions and procedures can be informed by insights and findings from theory and research, referring to them without deferring to them. The essential function of applied linguistics is to draw attention to such insights and findings and develop a critical awareness of their potential relevance in the practical domain. How far this potential is or can be actually realized is a matter for local decision. Applied linguistics, conceived of in this way as a mediation process, is an essential component of foreign language teacher education. It releases teachers from the confines of convention and a dependence on fashion, enables them to think critically and independently for themselves, and thus provides them with the necessary incentive and authority as professional people. It substantiates their claim to be 'reflective practitioners' in that it indicates what lines their reflection might take, and gives them something to reflect about.

In line with the overall objectives of this series, this volume seeks to focus explicitly on different aspects of the mediation process by enquiring into how far the policies, principles and practices of foreign language teaching and learning are, or can be, informed by the theoretical considerations and the findings of empirical research that emerge from the linguistic disciplines. The contributions to this volume explore various aspects of foreign language communication and learning and subject them to critical appraisal with this aim in mind.

The contributions are arranged in sections which deal with these aspects along a scale of increasing specificity, beginning in Section I at a relatively abstract level with questions about the nature of a foreign language in general, its role in education and what factors are involved in its acquisition. In Section II, these questions are taken up and explored from various perspectives, each focusing on different aspects of the foreignness of the foreign language – linguistic, cognitive, cultural, political – and what implications these have for the way they are taught and learned. Section III then deals with factors that have to be taken into consideration in the design of the foreign language as a classroom subject, and Section IV with how these have been taken into account in different approaches to foreign language instruction that have been proposed. The contributions in the last section then address what is involved in the assessment of what learners have achieved and in the evaluation of curricula and courses designed to promote their learning.

Section I. The nature of foreign language learning

Most people in the world are multilingual, and most of this multilingualism is naturally acquired in the process of socialization. However, in some cases, especially in the modern industrialised nations states of the Western hemisphere, multilingualism is induced by instruction in particular languages. These are *foreign languages* – languages which are taught and learned, and not acquired. Which of these is selected to be taught depends on a number of factors. The foreign language may be one that has an important status as a means for international communication, or it may be one that has more local national or regional significance. The selection or non-selection of a foreign language taught in schools and other educational institutions has important social, political and economic implications.

Foreign language is a term used to refer to a language that is induced by teaching rather than naturally acquired. But the concept of foreignness is a complex one, and this complexity is explored in the first paper in this section, 'What makes a language foreign?'. Konrad Ehlich points out that *foreign* is a notion whose meaning is relative. Although languages conventionally are labelled as foreign by virtue of the fact that they are taught to non-native speakers at schools, there are different degrees of foreignness. These are, on the one hand, a consequence of formal features such as typological distance or lexical closeness, and on the other are determined by the role languages play as markers of national identity. Furthermore, linguistic foreignness is not only used as a means of demarcation between nations, but also for drawing up borders within nations, especially to speakers of immigrant or minority languages. Ehlich argues that this misuse of linguistic foreignness to sustain national identity is in conflict with recent trends of global communication and transnational migration and he therefore calls for new concepts for foreign language teaching informed both by the multilingualism most foreign language learners bring into the classroom and by the diversity of linguistic means that can be used in intra- and international communication.

Ehlich's argument for the need to unpack the notion of 'foreign language' leads him to question other concepts as well. Thus, although an individual able to communicate in more than one language is said to be multilingual, the definition of multilingualism implied here is vague with respect to the degree of ability and the number of languages involved – "more than one" may include just another one in addition to the respective mother tongue, but also three and many more. Also, the everyday concept of *mother tongue* as the one language acquired first needs clarification, as there are people who acquire several languages simultaneously from birth and as with the number of languages involved in multilingualism, its manifestations and functions vary considerably.

Multilingualism is also a theme in the next chapter of this section, 'Multilingualism and foreign language teaching'. Antje Wilton discusses the concept of multilingualism in relation to other concepts such as *bilingualism*, *trilingualism* and *polylingualism* and in relation to types of first and second language acquisition and foreign language learning. Whereas research into bilingualism is long established, research on trilingualism or newly emerging multilingual practices such as polylingualism has only recently begun to gain in significance. Thus, the field of multilingualism is faced with the need to reconsider established ideas and redefine its terms to take account of the changing multilingual situation of the modern world.

Wilton then proposes a dimension-oriented approach to multilingualism designed to reflect and represent its complex and diverse manifestations in history, as an individual and social phenomenon, and as realized in various kinds of interaction. She goes on discuss two newly emerging areas of applied linguistic research. One of these concerns receptive multilingualism, increasingly being regarded as a significant communicative resource for learners and therefore an ability to be explicitly taught as a legitimate educational objective in its own right. The second concerns attitudes to multilingualism. This she points out has important implications for public opinion on multilingual issues and thus on policies for the development and implementation of foreign language teaching.

The implications of induced multiligualism for educational policy are taken up in the third chapter in this section. In her contribution, 'Foreign language teaching and educational policy', Rosamond Mitchell addresses key trends in current educational policy, language policy and language teaching. In a broad-brush historical account, the relationships between language, culture and literacy are explored and the changing relations between mother tongue education and second and foreign language education discussed. The development of foreign language learning as a "mass social activity" and its relationship with formal schooling is presented, and the underlying models and constructs of the foreign language subject in schools related to general, educational philosophies of classical humanism, progressivism and reconstructionism.

As Mitchell points out, current educational policy and implementation is heavily influenced by the pre-eminence of English in Europe and the "expanding circle" countries in particular, and she goes on to discuss its impact, as evident in the growing demand for the teaching of English in primary education and the dominance of this language in the development of new teaching methods. The chapter then critically examines the negative consequences of the dominance of English as a foreign language world wide, focusing on policies that in effect bring about the marginalisation of foreign language education in countries where English is predominantly spoken as a native language.

Most of the research on how languages are learnt is based on studies of the natural acquisition or the guided instruction of a second language in the literal, numerical sense. One might therefore say that this research is in fact dealing with the development of bilingualism rather than multilingualism. However, the assumption is plausible that the processes and outcomes of acquiring or learning a particular language might be different if more languages than just the L1 were acquired or learnt before. There is in fact growing evidence that this is the case – evidence compiled in studies of multiple language learning leads to the conclusion that multilingualism is an appropriate term only if a learner develops competence in at least a third language.

Multilingualism in this sense is the topic of chapter 5, 'Learning and teaching multiple languages' by Britta Hufeisen and Ulrike Jessner. These authors provide a survey of the concepts, theoretical models, findings, and applications of research in this domain of language learning. "Multiple language learning" normally refers to the learning of more than two languages in tutored instruction (= third, fourth, or nth language learning, for which the term *Third Language Acquisition* (TLA) is used, but the term TLA could also refer to the untutored acquisition of a second, third or fourth etc. language (labelled equally as L3). The study of this subject and its practical relevance for teaching are motivated by the assumption that an L3 learner relies on a different kind and amount of previous knowledge than what an L2 learner is equipped with. The chapter presents empirical evidence supporting this assumption both from psycholinguistic and applied pedagogical perspectives and it also demonstrates the practical relevance of this field of study by sociolinguistic research that focuses on the frequency and societal context of TLA.

Drawing on such empirical work, theoretical models of multiple language learning have been developed, of which Herdina and Jessner's *Dynamic Model of Multilingualism*, Meißner's *Multilingual Processing Model* and Hufeisen's *Factor Model* are outlined. The authors also give examples of possible applications for teaching such as training learners to consciously employ metacognitive transfer strategies. They suggest that to fully take advantage of the range of linguistic knowledge an L3 learner brings to class, languages should not be taught separately and independent of each other, but that the teaching of all languages should be integrated into one curriculum.

Any form of teaching foreign languages has to take into account how languages are learnt. There has long been a general consensus among researchers that language teaching should take the innate mechanisms into account that are effective in naturalistic language acquisition and that the mental dispositions and processes that learners themselves bring into the classroom have not been adequately taken into account in language teaching practices. The question then arises as to which of the findings of almost forty years of second language acquisition (SLA) research provide reliable guidance for foreign language pedagogy and how far such findings might be made relevant in practice.

This is the question addressed by Vivian Cook in chapter 4 of this section, 'Second language acquisition and foreign language pedagogy'. Cook begins by providing a brief survey of the relationship between SLA research and language teaching and comes to the conclusion that teachers and methodologists typically use this research to justify current practice rather than to develop innovative modes of language teaching, Cook suggests how research concepts such as Universal Grammar (UG) and L2 learners' strategies of communication and learning could be taken up and made relevant for teaching. However, practical suggestions of this kind represent only one of the possible applications of insights from SLA research. Another one could be to use research findings to prompt a critical examination of commonly held and taken for granted assumptions. Examples of such assumptions would be that languages are best learnt through the spoken, not the written, language, that the foreign language rather than the first language should be used in the classroom, or that grammar should not be taught explicitly. But as Cook demonstrates with arguments mainly from the UG framework, these assumptions are not well founded. Finally, taking up a more recent strand of SLA research, Cook argues that L2 users are not, as they are often taken to be, deficient versions of native speakers, but language users in their own right, with distinctive modes of linguistic knowledge and behaviour, and that teaching therefore should involve not just the second language but the whole linguistic configuration in the learner's mind so that measures of success should be based on the learner's L2 use and not on monolingual target language norms.

A key finding of SLA research is that foreign language learning is much less under the control of teachers than previously thought but that the learners themselves are largely independent actors in the process of language acquisition – be it by subconsciously following innate processes of language acquisition or by consciously employing strategies of learning and communication. Consciousness is related to awareness, and therefore one has to ask how far the individual's awareness of language and the process of language learning has a bearing on the outcome of foreign language teaching.

It is this question that is addressed in the next chapter, 'Language awareness'. Here Willis Edmondson points out that language awareness studies as currently conceived do not form a coherent body of work, but rather a collection of different research interests and agendas sheltering under one umbrella. Among these, he identifies three strands of enquiry that impinge more or less directly on foreign or second language learning. These are the role of explicit or conscious knowledge of aspects of the target language, the role of knowledge of, and insight into, different aspects of the target language culture, and the role and relevance of awareness concerning the language acquisition process itself. They are distinguished as different types of awareness, namely *linguistic awareness*, *cultural* (or intercultural) *awareness*, and *language learning awareness*.

However, after a careful discussion of the concepts of consciousness, acquisition and awareness, Edmondson concludes that language awareness and explicit knowledge about the target language cannot be distinguished and that language awareness can best be seen as a corollary of, a prelude to, or a consequence of noticing the gap between what the learner knows and what the learner encounters. With respect to intercultural awareness, he distinguishes between a broad pedagogical concept, which adds a communicative function to foreign language skills to develop a degree of intercultural competence and a more specifically focused awareness of the cultural implications of linguistic features themselves which may help to explicate or avoid misunderstandings occasioned by the different presuppositions of people from different lingua-cultural backgrounds. Finally, Edmondson argues that language learning awareness may influence language processing, as it may promote and direct intentional learning and affect motivation.

Section II. Perspectives on foreign language learning and teaching

The contributions in Section I explore a range of different issues concerning the nature of multilingualism and the implications for education and pedagogy of the foreignness of foreign languages. These contributions make clear that this foreignness is not only a linguistic matter but involves cognitive, cultural and political factors as well. In this section, each of these factors is given primary focus.

What, first of all, does foreign language learning and teaching look like from a linguistic point of view? As Henry Widdowson points out in his chapter 'The linguistic perspective' it has generally been taken as self evident that linguistic theory and description necessarily determines the design of the foreign language subject. What teachers teach, it is supposed, is essentially the same as what linguists describe. Linguistic perspectives change, however, and the principles and methods that define one paradigm of enquiry are rejected as untenable or inadequate by the next, and so the very nature of language is represented in quite radically different ways. Approaches to language teaching have tended to follow suit. Influenced and informed by new developments, the subject has changed accordingly, with the earlier structuralist approach yielding place to communicative language teaching to correspond with a shift of focus from the formal properties of the linguistic code to the functioning of language in contexts of use. Following the same tradition of deference to linguistic authority, the current pedagogic trend is to have the language presented for learning replicate the *real* or *authentic* usage of native speakers, as recorded in a corpus.

The question that arises is the extent to which this conformity to linguistic models, themselves necessarily only a partial representation of experienced language, is pedagogically valid. Using Hymes' well-known model of *communicative competence* as frame of reference, this chapter critically explores this question by examining different aspects of language knowledge and ability and how they figure in the process not of using a familiar first language but in learning a foreign one. It is argued that the foreign language subject is very different from the object language of linguistic description and can only be effectively designed by taking into account the contexts and conditions of the learning process, and that its objective should be to provide an investment in communicative capability for future use rather than to get learners to try to replicate native speaker behaviour.

Communication is of course not only an exchange of linguistic tokens. A language, as Claire Kramsch points out in her chapter 'The cultural perspective', embodies the shared social conventions and values that constitute the culture of the community which speaks it. But although language is always culturally charged, there is no one-to-one correspondence between a language and a culture. Thus many near-native speakers of French do not identify with any particular French culture and many Armenians living in France or the U.S. feel that theirs is an Armenian culture even though they do not speak a word of Armenian. Moreover, culture manifests itself in various semiotic modalities: verbal, visual, musical.

All this, Kramsch observes, poses problems for foreign language pedagogy. Which kinds of culture is it appropriate to teach (high or popular, mainstream or ethnic) and which aspects (historical facts, norms of behaviour, myths, ideologies)? Or should it be the foreign culture only or in explicit association with that of the learners? Finally, to what extent should other semiotic systems be taught, of which language is only one? How these questions are resolved depends on different local factors including the needs and purposes of students, the symbolic power of the foreign language concerned, and the educational policies and the larger geopolitical agendas of nation-states and their governments. Having taken stock of these issues, Kramsch proposes ways of conceiving of culture as the meaning-making practice that lies at the very heart of the language learning and teaching enterprise.

It is not only the cultural component of the foreign language subject that is affected by political considerations, but such considerations also bear on fundamental questions about which foreign language should be taught at all. These are the central concern of Janina Brutt-Griffler's chapter 'The political perspective'. As she notes, the traditional notion that foreign language teaching and learning are value-neutral activities has been contested in recent years on the grounds that the promotion of one particular foreign language and its associated culture can impact negatively on the survival of others. The rapid globalising spread of English in particular has been seen as endangering the continuing existence of other languages and as a threat to linguistic diversity, thereby furthering the ideological and economic agenda of its native speakers. The teaching of English, therefore, can be seen as a hegemonic activity lending support to the cause of linguistic imperialism.

Brutt-Griffler uses empirical data on language spread to argue that the threat to the world's endangered languages stems from a very different source – locally dominant and particularly national, rather than international, languages. The issue of the political implications of the choice of the foreign language to be taught is, therefore, by no means confined to the case of English. As to the charge of linguistic imperialism, Brutt-Griffler argues that this is based on a misconceived notion of a static linguistic and cultural homogeneity which disregards the dynamic interplay of multiple and conflicting forces that re-align concepts of language, nation, culture and identity in the processes of transnationalism and diaspora. Again, these forces are relevant to the way the foreignness of any language or any culture is perceived and this, in turn, must have implications for how it is taught and learned.

In the final chapter in this section, 'The cognitive perspective', Jean-Marc Dewaele focuses attention on the psychological aspects of foreign language acquisition. Learners bring to the learning process a natural cognitive endowment, an innate knowledge of language – in effect their own agenda for acquisition. This endowment, however, is subject to change in the course of an individual's life, affected by experience and maturation, and so age is taken to be an important factor in determining the role of cognition in language learning. It is indeed commonly taken for granted that the speed of learning and the degree of competence attained are influenced by this variable and that beyond a certain critical point, the capability for language learning naturally decreases with age. This encourages the widely held assumption that to achieve high competence in an additional language, learning should start in the early years of life.

Dewaele submits this assumption to critical scrutiny by reviewing the best known and most recent findings on the effects of age on language acquisition and the *Critical Period Hypothesis* (CPH) in the fields of psycholinguistics, cognitive psychology, social psychology, and the neurosciences. He discusses the different factors that this research identifies as influencing foreign language acquisition including emotional states, attitudes, sensitivity to verbal stimuli, laterality, and the physical shape of the brain. On the basis of this discussion he concludes that CPH is open to question and that early exposure is only one in a long list of independent variables that affect ultimate success as a multilingual.

Section III. The design of foreign language teaching

The contributions in the section are centrally concerned with the general design features of the foreign language subject. Teaching is necessarily an intervention intended to further the learning process, so the question arises as to what form that intervention should take, and on what grounds. By reference to what principles does one decide which aspects of language are selected and ordered in a course, and what classroom activities are pedagogically appropriate?

It is the first of these questions that is addressed in Keith Johnson's chapter 'Foreign language course design'. The focus of attention here is on the *syllabus*, a general schematic construct which provides the frame of reference for the design of courses tailored for particular groups of learners. Constructing a syllabus involves two essential processes: the selection of aspects of language that constitute its content and the linear ordering of this content in some kind of graded sequence. As far as content is concerned, Johnson describes how this has been variously defined at different times with the traditional selection of linguistic forms in the structural syllabus giving way to a focus on the communicative use of these forms in the notional / functional syllabus favoured in the work of the Council of Europe and seen as more closely attuned to the actual needs of foreign language users. With regard to the ordering of content, Johnson considers how far this can be based on the findings of SLA research and needs to be informed by notions like *teachability* and *processability*.

A major issue in syllabus design has been the extent to which it should focus on units of language or kinds of language activity and whether it should be product or process oriented. Johnson discusses this distinction with reference to more recent proposals for task-based and lexical syllabuses, and concludes with an argument for a multidimensional syllabus which provides for the inclusion of non-systematic as well as systematic components and reconciles the allowance for communicative initiative on the part of learners with the requirement for linguistic control.

The chapter that follows – 'The methodology of foreign language teaching' by Ted Rodgers then looks at how the schematic construct of a syllabus might be implemented and provides a detailed review of various proposals that have been made for designing classroom activities. He traces the development and interpretation of several key themes across the history of language teaching methodology, with explicit reference to English, but with implicit relevance to the teaching of foreign languages in general. Methodology has for some time been interpreted as a description and comparison of various methods of language teaching, given distinctive names – *Audiolingualism*, the *Silent Way*, *Suggestopedia* and so on – and defined by prescribed recipe-like procedures for language instruction. Under the influence of more functional or communicative views of language learning, pedagogic proposals became less directive and formulaic. Although still given distinctive titles like *Communicative Language Teaching* (CLT), and later *Task-Based Language Teaching* (TBLT), they were less rigidly prescriptive in their specifications and were accordingly called 'approaches' rather than 'methods'.

More recently, some scholars have aspired to re-think methodology in even less restrictive ways in terms of *principles* of instructed language acquisition, moving still further from recommendations for specific activities or techniques and seeking to establish something more like general attitudes or perspectives which allow teachers themselves to devise actual classroom practices locally appropriate for the learning needs of their students and the socio-cultural contexts in which instruction takes place. Rodgers concludes his critical survey by observing that one of the key issues in methodology, whether conceived in terms of method, approach or principle, is how to reconcile two aspects of a language which naturally combine in normal use, but which seem to need separate attention in teaching, namely its formal properties, and especially its grammar, on the one hand, and on the other the way it functions as communication in contexts of use.

The development of methodological procedures from method to principle that Rodgers describes reflects a shift in the teacher/learner role relationship, and an increasing realisation of the need for teacher intervention to allow for learner initiative. In his chapter on 'Learner autonomy', Lienhard Legenhausen presents the key anthropological, socio-political, psychological and educational arguments which justify this as a matter of pedagogic principle. Such arguments invoke the basic human need for gaining control over the environment and the human right to greater political freedom and emancipation, and are supported by the tenet of constructivist psychology that new knowledge cannot in fact be transmitted or taught, but rather has to be constructed by the learners themselves.

Legenhausen goes on to describe the principles of autonomous language learning on three hierarchically ordered levels. Underlying principles include the view that language learning is a creative construction process and that all language learning is based on authentic communicative interaction. Derived from these are guiding principles according to which the foreign language class should be organised to foster awareness raising and to ensure that all communication is truly authentic. On the lowest level Legenhausen exemplifies procedural principles by which the higher level principles are implemented in the classroom. He also shows that the characteristics of the successful autonomous learner are identical to those known from the "Good Learner" research and presents evidence in support of the view that the autonomous classroom is more effective than the traditional one controlled by the imposition of teacher authority.

The last two contributions in this section are concerned with language abilities, with ways in which foreign language learners might be guided to act upon their knowledge in spoken and written modes of communicative behaviour. Martin Bygate in his chapter 'Teaching the spoken foreign language' is concerned with the first of these modes. After reviewing the way oral language performance has figured in language pedagogy in the past, he goes on to consider the complex nature of spoken language and the corresponding problems this poses for the development of oral language proficiency. As he indicates, one can think of spoken language in very different ways. It can be thought of as a linguistic product, and here recent work in corpus linguistics in particular has revealed the distinctive formal patterns of spoken text, the relative frequency of occurrence of certain grammatical features. Or one can conceive of spoken language in terms of socio-psychological processing whereby what is conceptualized in the individual mind is articulated into an appropriate stream of sound. Again, spoken language can be taken as the use of the spoken medium to realise an interactive mode of communication.

Bygate then goes on to review in detail how far different approaches and activities take account of these different ways of conceiving of spoken language. He identifies a range of controversial issues that point to future areas of research, among which are questions concerning the extent to which the foreign language learners should be required to conform to the norms of native speaker users in respect to accuracy, fluency and idiomaticity.

The next chapter, 'Teaching the written foreign language' by Bill Grabe and Fredricka Stoller then considers the pedagogic issues that arise in getting learners to cope with the foreign language in written mode, and in particular with the development of the writing ability. They make the point that there is an extraordinary range of settings and contexts in which instruction in foreign language writing occurs and that the difficulty in acquiring this ability, the purpose for acquiring it, and the required level of proficiency in it, all vary enormously from one situation to another. Thus learners already fluent in the spoken language will have different problems with the written language than those who are not. Some learner groups, those studying a foreign language for specific purposes, for example, may need to be able to write at an advanced level to meet their academic requirements, while others will never have to write anything except a simple essay, and may never have any further calls on their writing ability. Finally, there are adult learners who may not be literate in their own language(s) and thus will need basic writing skills.

What emerges from this discussion is that any pedagogic approach to the teaching of writing in a foreign language will depend on first establishing the capabilities, the linguistic experience and the purposes of the learners for whom instruction is to be designed. This will determine which aspects of writing should be the focus of attention, and what would be an adequate level of achievement, from the basic skill in managing the medium to the ability to make effective use of it as a mode of communication.

Section IV. Approaches to foreign language teaching

Foreign language pedagogy is essentially an enabling intervention which involves the specification of learning objectives and the design of classroom activities which will guide the learning process towards the achievement of these objectives. The contributions in this section of the volume discuss different approaches that can be taken to both of these aspects of teaching.

The first of these, 'The principles of approach' by Anthony Howatt, identifies two general and complementary traditions of foreign language pedagogy. The first (and older) of these two traditions is founded on the educational principle that a foreign language is a subject matter like any other and that it should be taught in a coherent and well-ordered manner with due regard to the intellectual and moral values reflected in both methods and materials. Howatt points out that although formal grammar used to be a conspicuous component of this approach, the key feature is not in fact grammar but an *engagement with text*, i.e. it is a tradition which rests on the assumption that literate forms of communication (whether transmitted in writing or in speech) are the proper objects of serious study.

The contrasting tradition starts from the basic principle that acquiring a new language is a natural process available to all normal human beings on condition that they are motivated to co-operate and are provided with the appropriate circumstances for acquisition. Spoken interaction lies at the heart of the approach, and this has often proved difficult to reproduce in the classroom. For much of the time it has had to rely on representations of interaction (*dialogues*) rather than on instances of genuine communication, and, for this reason, it might be called a *mimetic* (imitative) tradition. However, more recent teaching techniques, notably *tasks*, have offered a more sophisticated interpretation of *natural processes* than the old rote-learning routines of the *direct method*.

These two principles of approach have often been seen to be in incompatible opposition, but Howatt argues that some reconciliation is possible, and necessary, when they are interpreted in practice in the light of local needs and priorities. The point that principles of approach need to be adapted to suit different circumstances is also made in the next chapter by Michael Byram and Mari-Carmen Mendez, 'Communicative language teaching' (CLT). The authors stress that this is indeed an approach and not a method representing as it does a change in purpose and emphasis, and a change in the "object" that is taught and learnt. They explain the historical evolution of CLT in its various forms in Europe and North America, pointing out that the two strands have been surprisingly independent. On the one hand, in the USA the development can be traced from the critique by Hymes of Chomskyan, and ultimately Bloomfieldian, perspectives on language learning. In Europe, the origins can be traced to the work of anthropologists but also to the work of the Council of Europe and the *Common European Framework of Reference*.

Byram and Mendez then go on to critically examine the advantages and disadvantages of CLT and discuss a number of controversial issues including the role of grammar and the use of the native speaker as a model for language learners. They point to the need to understand the particular characteristics of language learners and their socio-cultural identities and raise the crucial question of whether and to what extent CLT in its more common forms needs to be adapted to specific situations to be made educationally and pedagogically compatible with local traditions.

The next two chapters are concerned with approaches that seek to develop a communicative ability in the foreign language by relating it to specific domains of use. As is pointed out in the first of these, 'Language for specific purposes vs general language' by Claus Gnutzmann, a good deal of foreign language teaching, especially for adults, is geared towards its use in professional contexts and this differs in many respects from the use of everyday language. Gnutzmann describes the typical linguistic features of language used for specific purposes (LSP), such as the specific selection, use and frequency of morphosyntactic features and the high degree of standardisation of vocabulary, and traces how this language has been described from register analysis, discourse analysis and contrastive textology to the more recent learner-centred approach represented by *content and language integrated learning* (CLIL).

But as Gnutzmann explains, LSP is not only distinctive with respect to its formal linguistic features – the use of standardised vocabulary, for example, and the frequency of passive constructions and nominalisations. There are also significant differences between the teaching and learning of LSP and general language, which mainly arise from the fact that the objectives of LSP have to be strictly based on the learners' needs, and since these are related to academic or professional domains, the learners quite often know more about the subject than the teacher. This can lead to a shift in the role relationship of teacher and learner with the former no longer the sole authority but dependent on the expert knowledge of the latter. Due to the impact of globalisation, the language most frequently used for LSP is English. So this language serves as a lingua franca across cultures in international LSP communication and this, as Gnutzmann observes, raises a number of issues concerning the nature of intercultural communication competence in an LSP context.

The next chapter, Dieter Wolff's 'Content and language integrated learning' (CLIL), concerns the making of the foreign language specific in classroom contexts. CLIL refers to any educational situation in which an additional language and therefore not the most widely used language of the environment is used for the teaching and learning of subjects other than the language itself. The advantage of integrating the foreign language with the content of other subjects in this way is that it allows for exposure time and for a more realistic context for communicative use.

As the chapter shows in more detail, CLIL exists in different variants determined by factors like the level of education (primary, secondary, tertiary), by the degree to which the teaching focuses on the language itself as well as on the subject, by the kind of subject and the extent to which it is language-dependent, and by the degree to which CLIL is integrated into the curricular and evaluative structure of an educational system. Furthermore, Wolff points out, CLIL requires a special emphasis on promoting reading comprehension and writing skills, and the discourse of CLIL lessons can be characterised, like much of LSP, by a relatively restricted set of communicative functions like *identify – classify/ define – describe – explain – conclude/argue*.

Though there is still little empirical research on the effects of CLIL, impressionistic evidence suggests that it has a positive impact on student motivation. However, as Wolff emphasises, there are still controversial issues that need further study. Among these are the possible negative effect on the acquisition of subject knowledge on the one hand and on the other, the reduction of conceptual and communicative capability in the first language quite apart from more practical problems concerning teacher training and the development of adequate teaching materials.

In the last chapter of this section, 'Computer assisted foreign language learning', attention shifts to approaches to methodology which exploit the possibilities of recent developments in electronic technology. In this chapter, Kurt Kohn illustrates how currently available technology allows for the innovative development of language learning tasks among which are autonomous content-based learning, collaborative learning in synchronous and asynchronous eGroups, customisation and authentication of cultural and subject related material, and online self-assessment and feedback. Kohn explains how the capability for fast data processing of the computer made it possible to develop a range of language practice tools – from vocabulary and grammar trainers to text programs – that helped support more extensive self-study activities and contributed to the promotion of more learner autonomy. Present-day technology not only makes available multimedia and web-based language learning contents and opportunities for online communication and interaction, but also more individualised environments that provide error feedback, learning material, and interactive tasks that are sensitive to the learner's level of proficiency and learning needs.

As a result of technological developments language learning today is witnessing a process of pedagogical diversification: whereas teachers previously had books and cassettes/tapes, they now have the additional resources of CD-ROMs and the web, and group work and individual self access can be enhanced by discussion forums, chats, blogs, wikis and podcasts. Kohn suggests that these developments call for a blended approach to pedagogy whereby traditional forms of language learning and teaching are integrated with the new potential of e-learning. But he also points out that the realisation of the full potential of blended learning depends on the adequacy of teacher training and reform to the institutional framework of language teaching at schools.

Section V. Evaluation in language learning and teaching

Whether as a result of natural acquisition in contexts of actual use, or of instruction in the contrived contexts of classrooms, or both, learners achieve a degree of proficiency in a foreign language, and there are occasions when there is a need to assess it. This need arises, for example, when an individual wants to enrol at a university in a foreign country, or apply for a job, or for citizenship in another country, where a degree of proficiency is specified as a necessary qualification. In such situations, there is the need for valid and reliable measures that give objective information about a certain standard and allow for comparisons between individuals. In the case where learning is induced by instruction, the question arises as to how far the design of instruction has been effective in the inducement. So whereas one kind of evaluation relates to the learner output, another relates to the teacher input. The next two chapters are concerned with the first of these.

Tim McNamara's contribution 'Principles of testing and assessment' addresses issues relating to the measurement of proficiency. As he makes clear, these issues are by no means confined to technical questions about the valid and reliable design of tests, but have much wider socio-political and ethical implications, and this makes an understanding of the nature of assessment and its procedures of particular importance. Making extensive reference to research in the field, McNamara explains how test scores form the basis for inferences about individuals and groups and examines the chain of reasoning that supports these inferences. He surveys procedures for the development and validation of tests in the various skill areas, and in relation to specific settings – academic, work-related and others, and identifies recent trends.

McNamara points out that whereas the *design of tests* and the significance of test scores for the measurement of proficiency are well documented, the *use of test scores* has been less well conceptualised, even among those who argue that their use should be analysed and defended as intrinsic to their validation. Such an understanding requires a more adequate theory of the social and policy settings in which tests are located. It is in the use of test scores, their significance of tests in a non-statistical, socio-political sense as a means of regulation and control where the most complex problems of assessment arise.

The chapter that follows, 'Issues in Certification' by Annelie Knapp, takes up the question of how test scores are standardised and certificated. She observes that a vast number of certification systems are currently available for a wide variety of languages. These differ considerably with respect to the underlying concept of *proficiency* and the procedures for measuring it, and many are problematical on theoretical and methodological grounds.

Knapp surveys the development of proficiency testing and of certification, how it started about fifty years ago in the academic field in the UK as well as the USA as a reaction to the enormous increase of overseas students from non-English speaking countries, and how this pioneering work triggered off the development of certificates for other – mainly European – languages, of more specialised, domain-specific certificates and ultimately led to the *Common European Framework of Reference for Languages* (CEFR). She describes in detail the best known certification frameworks such as TOEFL, TOEIC, IELTS, ALTE and the CEFR and goes on to highlight some key problems relating to the construct of language proficiency, the devising of grading scales and the models which should serve as benchmarks. A closer look at how certification is put into practice reveals other unresolved issues, such as determining the equivalence between certificates and test scores, factors affecting the implementation of tests, and economic pressures that impinge on the quality of tests and testing.

The final chapter in this section, and in the volume, 'Evaluating curricula, courses and textbooks', by Pauline Rea-Dickens and Richard Kiely, is, as its title indicates, concerned with the evaluation of the design of foreign language instruction, with what is taught rather than what is learned. They describe theory, policy and practice perspectives on language programme evaluation and explore current understandings of evaluation within language programmes, with particular reference to evaluation as a tool for learning. Taking an *English for Academic Purposes* (EAP) programme as an example, they illustrate how evaluation shapes the participation of programme stakeholders such as students, teachers and the institution hosting the programme. This case study sets out both the potential for evaluation to enhance opportunities for learning, and the challenges involved in facilitating take-up of these opportunities by students, teachers and institutional managers. The authors subsequently examine the background to these discourses of programme evaluation both in terms of theoretical perspectives in applied linguistics and in the management of educational and social programmes more generally.

Rea-Dickens and Kiely then go on to consider controversial and emergent issues in the field of language programme evaluation. These include the place of assessment of learning outcomes in the evaluation of curricula and programmes, the development of a stakeholder approach in evaluation theory and practice and the role of evaluation in programme management, as well as the development of autonomy and effective learning by the use of new technologies.

Envoi

Although, as was acknowledged at the beginning of this introduction, enquiry into the principles and practices of foreign language teaching and learning is only one area of applied linguistics, it is, as we trust the contributions to this volume make apparent, a complex and multi-faceted one that has to take into account a range of theoretical, ideological and practical issues. In so doing, it makes a connection with areas of applied linguistics represented in the other volumes of this series and engages with problems of particular current significance. Globalization creates both the possibility and the need for communication across linguistic and cultural boundaries. The ability to communicate in a foreign language so as to negotiate understanding, and avoid misunderstanding, between individuals and across communities has never been more crucial. We hope that the contributions in this volume will give some indication of what is involved in the teaching and learning of this ability, and of the central importance of foreign language education for the future of an increasingly globalized world.

I. The nature of foreign language learning

2. What makes a language foreign?

Konrad Ehlich

1. Introduction

This paper considers some aspects of a phenomenon which seems to need no further consideration: the characteristics of foreignness in connection with languages and with language in general. Recent developments in language teaching theory, in linguistics, in cultural anthropology, in sociology and in philosophy have paid attention to the notion of foreignness and to its implications for understanding a large variety of phenomena from processes of language learning to identity formation of Self in its difference and its relationship to the Other.

The paper starts with some observations on attention paid to foreignness and on its opposite, the neglect foreignness has experienced for a long period of time (sect. 2). It discusses the semantics of "foreign" as part of a larger group of expressions whose meaning is determined with regard to a specific relational centre (sect. 3). Foreignness with regard to languages is group-specific and constitutive for groups (sect. 4), and it is related to different degrees of distance constituting different language types, differences of proximity and "false friends". Foreignness is constructed in the establishment of linguistic variation (sect. 5). Constructing foreignness has become an essential part of the nation building processes of the 19th and 20th centuries to the effect that the distinction of linguistic foreignness ist one of the counter stones for national identity formation (sect. 6). Linguistic foreignness does not only occur in the form of distinction of the other nation(s) or state(s), but also within the own nation (sect. 7). The use of linguistic foreignness and linguistic identity in the context of the nation state is in conflict with more recent global tendencies of transnational migration processes. A world of permanent movement and change, characterized by linguistic encounters of speakers of different languages, of language contact and of linguistic change needs new concepts for foreign language teaching and learning (sect. 8). The linguistic constellation of our days needs new concepts for identifying language encounter and the acceptance of linguistic foreignness as a challenge for a new type of ethics of communication in the one world of our days. A "global language" or "*lingua franca*" cannot even superficially meet such demands and therefore does not provide a genuine alternative to the teaching of other languages. These demands are often in conflict with the present day neglect of foreign language learning which is doomed to oblivion of other languages by reference to one single global language (sect. 9).

2. 'Foreignness' – attention and neglect

It is the foreign languages that come to mind first when we think about foreignness in language. The expression 'foreign language' appears to be an unproblematic word of everyday communication. The teaching of foreign languages is professionalized – in schools and private institutions. All of this seems to be self evident to such a degree that even the large "Handbook of Foreign Language Teaching" [*Handbuch Fremdsprachenunterricht*, Bausch et al. 1991] does not contain a lemma "foreign language", and does not list the term in its extensive index.

In contrast to this neglect of 'foreign languages', the expressions 'foreign' and 'foreignness' themselves have received significantly more attention. It is the field of intercultural literary studies that, in drawing on basic insights of hermeneutics, has made the experience of foreignness in reading its main focus. The studies of Krusche since the 1980s (see Krusche 1980, 1985 and 2003 as well as the bibliography in Wierlacher 2001: 533–554) pursue the "experiential opportunities for readers from other cultures" (Krusche 1985) and attempt to develop an analytical grasp of the alienations of their reading processes by exploring the fundamental questions of foreignness itself (2003).

Wierlacher (1993) turned foreignness into a "cultural topic" in its own right and dedicated to it a well received collection of papers that accompanied the foundation of a special institute for the study of "cultural xenology" (*kulturwissenschaftliche Fremdheitsforschung*, cf. Wierlacher 1980, Wierlacher and Bogner 2003.).

Ricken and Balzer (2007: 56–57) even arrive at the following conclusion: "Like few other conceptual series, the concepts of 'difference', 'alterity' and 'alienity' indicate a categorical re-orientation of thinking emergent over the last decades and comprising cultural and social sciences alike."

A large German science foundation dedicated one of the focal points of a complex research programme to the 'own' and the 'other' – a comprehensive collection of papers reports on the various projects (Craanen and Gunsenheimer 2006). Amongst the comparatively few projects explicitly dealing with linguistic foreignness is one by Jürgen Trabant and Brigitte Jostes that creates the basis for the most recent investigations into the semantics of 'foreign' (*fremd*) (cf. Naguschewski and Trabant 1997, Jostes and Trabant 2001, Jostes 2001). Here the word 'foreign' is seen as a "key word of cultural sciences" and is investigated for methodological purposes instigated by this perspective. These works, especially Jostes (2004) and their basis, Trabant's reconstruction of Humboldt's thoughts on language (2007), have provided a blueprint for further research into the semantics of 'foreign'. König and Siemund (2001) continued this line of research with a semantics based on set theory. Münkler and Ladwig (2007, 2008) report on large sale projects on foreignness.

Even in the context of these projects, however, foreign languages as such play a much smaller role than they do, for instance, in Harald Weinrich's seminal, and much earlier, paper "The foreignness of foreign languages" [*Fremdsprachen als fremde Sprachen]* (1988, first published in 1985). In emphasising the foreignness of foreign languages, Weinrich warns against a negative perspective on foreignness, which he constrasts with his own "aesthetics of foreignness" (*Ästhetik der Fremdheit*).

Foreign has also been the topic of variety of sociological and philosophical analyses (cf. Hogrebe 1985, Horstmann 1986/1987, Waldenfels 1997, 2006). The interdisciplinary research efforts remain unsatisfactory, however.

In the following I attempt to find answers to my title question by exploring the semantics of 'foreign' first and then by illustrating the foreignness of foreign languages in an exemplary manner with regard to some prototypical linguistic contexts.

3. *foreign* – semantic and cognitive explorations

The semantics of the expression 'foreign' leads into some quandary as it is quite language specific even with regard to the European languages (the differences can be even greater in other cultures; for e.g. Arabic see Bauer 2001, Beshara 2009; for a general overview Waldenfels 2006).

Trabant (2000: 41) reports on the differences between French and German:

> Last year I had to give a talk in Paris on a topic which I had worked out in German as ‚Fremdheit der Sprache'. When I had to turn this into French, I had to re-think what I wanted to say. Not only was it difficult to render the word *Fremdheit*, and hence the title of my talk, but also the adjectives *fremd* and *étranger* did not coincide. Notwithstanding that difficulty, I think I succeeded in communicating my topic – since topics are parts of what Humboldt calls the 'objective domain in the middle, between all languages and independent of languages'. But I assure you that I had a lot of trouble keeping together in French that part of reality that is delineated differently in German. French and German have cut that realm of reality in different ways. There is a language-included difference of *thought* at stake. Or how should we call that experience? Anyhow, I had to *think* twice to re-make it into French." (2000: 14)

For German *fremd*, English dictionaries offer the translations *strange* in the sense of *unbekannt* ('unknown'), *ungewohnt* ('unusual'); *foreign* in the sense of *ausländisch* ('outlandish'), *fremdartig* ('different'); *exotic* as applying to non-native plants; and, last but not least, *outside* in the sense of *nicht dazugehörig* ('not-belonging'). If consulted in the other direction, they also yield *alien* in the sense of 'foreign', 'outlandish'. *Alien*, however, is also listed as a translation for *andersartig* ('different'), *zuwider* ('repugnant') and even a *nicht naturalisierten*

Bewohner des Landes ('non-naturalised inhabitant of a country', Langenscheidt, 44). In the Romance languages we find the terms *étrange* ('peculiar', 'odd', 'strange') in French, *stragnero* in Italian etc. These words derive from Latin *extraneus* – a direct derivation from *extra* ('outside') – which is also the basis for English *strange*.

Greek *xenos*, which applies to both a stranger and a guest, accounts for a very different perspective on foreignness. The Hebrew word *ger* applies to the 'classical immigrant' who, in times of (especially economic) necessity or famine, leaves the 'house of the fathers' to find more favourable, or at least bearable, conditions elsewhere.

Germanic *fremd*, Dutch *vreemd* and the Romance words deriving from Latin *extraneus* emphasise distance or remoteness. The Germanic word derives from *fram* ('(far) away from') (Kluge and Seebold: 32). Latin *extraneus* is in opposition to *intra*. This 'inner area', the 'origin' the expression *intra* refers to, is however not clearly specified, it appears to be self-evident. The origin negated by 'extraneus' is 'proprius', the *own* (see König and Siemund 2001).

The opposites for *extraneus* listed in the Latin dictionary comprise *proprius*, but also *meus* ('my'), *tuus* ('your'), and *suus* ('his', 'her', 'its') (Georges vol. I, col.: 306). These words offer some aspects of the underspecified origin, the *intra* of *extraneus*, but they also create a new problem: Two of these expressions, *meus* and *tuus*, are deictics and are thus tied to the speakers' own *linguistic action*.

The usage of *extraneus* provides some further indications as to *intra*, the origin. *Extraneus* is that which "has no relationship to the house or the family" (col. 2638), "has no relationship ... to our person, our country" (col. 2638) or "has no relationship to our republic" (col. 2639; in opposition to *domesticus*). *Extraneus* also has the meanings of 'foreigner' (in opposition to *romanus*), 'stranger', and maybe even 'non-human' as in "*extraneus ... humanitatis*" – an impossibility, however, according to Hieronymus and Tertullian (ibid.). As can be easily observed, these explanations also make use of a deictic expression: the plural speaker *origo* 'our'.

In contrast to deictic expressions, 'to be foreign' is not a linguistic structure in the first place. In relying on deictic crutches, as it were, the conceptual explanations of the dictionary quoted above awkwardly point at an entire complex of problems in understanding the concept of foreignness. What, then, is foreignness? *Foreign* is, without doubt, no deictic expression. Deictics are linguistic pointers – they unfold their functionality through the speaker's *linguistic action* whose 'I', 'here', and 'now' is the origin or *origo* (Bühler) from where the pointing occurs. Yet *foreignness* is not constituted through linguistic action alone. Nevertheless, foreignness bears a surprising structural analogy to that what deictics do. In both cases, a centre is established that serves as a reference point for that which does not belong to this centre. With deictics, this plays out as the opposition between distance and proximity – which, of course, is not an absolute 'distance' and 'proximity', but nearness or remoteness in reference to the *origo* always constituted anew by every speech action. The distinction between *proprius* and *extraneus*, between the 'own' and the 'other', is not constituted by speech action, but it is made in relation to a *categorisation* of the respective lifeworld. This categorisation process is a *mental* activity that arrives at a mental result. From a systematic perspective, foreignness therefore is the derivation of a specific self-perception.

In this context, the extensions of 'self' go beyond the single thinking and categorising ego. As can be seen from the explanations of *extraneus* in the Latin dictionary quoted above, the extension of 'self' starts with the *ego* and proceeds from there to the group the ego is a member of, then to the larger association to which the group belongs, and, finally, to the republic or the state, to which the association belongs. It is not difficult to continue this line of thought right through to the extraterrestrial *alien* that would indeed be *extraneus humanitatis*. The 'self', the origin from where 'foreign' derives its respective meaning, is thus extendable and gradable in a way very similar to the *origo* of deictics. The usage of the deictic expression 'I' for the conceptualisation of this origin is still quite awkward, because this usage avails itself of the parallel, but not identical structure of deictic reference. Since the distinction between the 'own' and the 'other' results from a mental process, such a parallel is destined to create categorical confusion.

Dividing the lifeworld (and then other systems too) into a categorical 'self' and thus another area excluded from the self (which is the aspect König/Siemund emphasise in terms of set theory) are mental activities. These mental activities are activities of inner perception that act as the basis for further categorisations and classifications that, in turn, retroact on the inner perception. Hence the category of foreignness is part of what the Cartesian "cogito" refers to. Foreignness is therefore a matter of "events of the mind" for the elucidation of which Wittgenstein, Hegel's "Phenomenology of Mind" and Husserl's phenomenology have provided insights based on the authors' respective prerequisites.

The categorisation of something as foreign designates it as 'not one's own'. It is a categorisation by negation. Both the linguistic *origo* and the mental origin, the self, have a specific negation. While the latter's negation cannot be employed for deictic purposes, the negation related to the *origo*, such as Latin *alter*, *alis*, *alius* can be employed to characterise a specific kind of foreignness. *Alius* is the negation of the speaker-*origo*, the negation of 'I', the 'non-I', so to speak. Here the procedure of the division of the lifeworld indeed avails itself of linguistic action.

The mental procedure of determining something as 'foreign' can be applied to different areas of reality. This is the fact responsible for the different semantic spectra yielded by our initial analysis above – from the 'exotic' plant to that which is foreign in an intellectual sense: things that are 'curious', 'odd' or 'peculiar'. The semantics of 'idiosyncratic' – 'blended in its own way' – is particularly interesting in this context, as it recognises the *proprium* of the other that is foreign to one's own mental perception.

To sum up: The expression 'foreign' belongs to a group of expressions whose semantics unfolds from a specific point of reference. One could call such expressions 'relationed expressions'. Deictics are a very important class of relationed expressions, as they are highly relevant for any linguistic system. Their point of reference, the *origo* is the very speech action in which they are uttered. However, the class of relationed expressions is not just made up of spatio-temporal deictics. As we have seen, the semantics of 'foreign' and 'foreignness' rely on a mental point of reference, the *proprium*, the 'self', which results from categorisation and classification processes.

This allows for the following conclusions as to the 'foreignness' of foreign languages: Foreignness does not apply to any language *per se*, but results from the distance of this language in relation to a group of speakers. The foreignness of a language results from an outside point of view. Hence the characterisation of a language as 'foreign language' is only *one* special instance of a frequent practice of social reality

4. Language and groups

The mental categorisation of something as 'foreign' is frequently applied to social life. The mental origin of this categorisation is the group one belongs to, be it the family or other types of groups beyond that.

Language is amongst the most prominent attributes of any group. Language is deeply involved in group formation, but in a way that is not always very transparent. The different forms of association, i.e. families, tribes, peoples, nations, states and supranational alliances, are tied to language in a fashion neither unequivocal nor easy to disentangle. Language is the medium of such associations and plays a major role in their reproduction and perpetuation. Or vice versa: The role language plays in this context is one of the three major functional domains of language: the *communitarian* function (Ehlich 2007a, B7).

The emergence, continuation, integration, and repulsion of human associations, their slow or rapid change has an impact on the language entertained within these social forms. *Linguistic* change and linguistic constants are tied to *social* change and social constants, but in a very indirect manner. Hence language frequently appears to be asynchronous with regard to social change. Linguistic change is usually much slower than social change, which can be quite instantaneous, for instance under conditions of revolution.

Since a certain language L_i is usually acquired during early childhood, speakers of L_i (and also linguists from the area where L_i is spoken) regard this language as a given, as 'natural', so to speak. The tacit assumption of the 'naturalness' or 'givenness' of L_i also applies to the communicative functions for which this language is employed. There is – at least in areas where only one language is spoken – very little opportunity for a critical reflection on this assumption. This leads to a situation where L_i is equated with language as such: $L = L_i$. For those who maintain this equation, the experience that other speakers speak the languages $L_a \ldots L_n$ apart from L_i is initially irritating. This irritation has always been part of the semantics of 'foreignness'. The expression 'foreign' indicates *distance*, and distance determines its meaning in a specific way. Alfred Schütz's characterisation of the confrontation of a stranger and an established group, albeit without specifically addressing questions of language, expresses this irritation.

Dealing with foreignness is one of the more problematic tasks imposed by lifeworlds. Lifeworlds with limited radii and sufficient distances to other lifeworlds rarely face this problem, but if they do, they usually encounter it even more fiercely.

Modern lifeworlds, however, are characterised by frequent instances of being disturbed by foreignness, as *foreignness* and *mobility* are mutually dependent. This also applies to language. However, such experiences of foreignness are not as recent as modern self-perception wishes to construct them. Linguistically homogenous areas of communication are only one specific form of communication, even though their stability helps to reduce the complexity and to increase the reliability of lifeworlds as a *conditio sine qua non* of societal existence.

Foreignness does not apply to any language *per se*, but results from the distance to a language L_j. Foreignness is therefore not 'foreignness *per se*', but 'foreignness for' a speaker S_i of L_i, $i \neq j$. Foreignness with respect to a language L_j always results from an external viewpoint.

5. Foreignness and degrees of distance

5.1. Distance

The distance between speaker S_i and the language L_j can be constituted in rather different ways. A monolingual speaker experiences a distance to all languages apart from L_i, the language he or she has spoken since the early days of acquisition. However, a distance can also exist with regard to partial areas of the communicative ranges of this language L_i that, in other partial areas, has been acquired by speaker S_i so that he or she can use and understand it. The divergence between language L_i available to S_i and other languages L_{n-i} is characterised by different 'degrees of distance'. Linguistics investigates two of these degrees according to the concepts of 'language typology' on the one hand and 'language variation' (with regard to distances within language L_i) on the other.

5.2. Typological aspects

All languages have certain things in common, but these commonalities are not easy to determine. (If one investigated only the sounds, one would ignore aspects of the writing system – and of the linguistic system of, say, sign languages. In phylogenetic terms, however, phonic systems do have some kind of precedence.) The prerequisites of any language based on sounds are the ability to articulate which is characteristic of the human species, and a corresponding ability to perceive. It appears that the human vocal tract allows for distinctions that are universally used, such as the one between vowels and consonants. But even this is at the point where, with respect to phonemic systems, commonalities between languages thin out quite quickly. The demands languages make on perception are by no means universal, as the phonology of the 20th century has made very clear (Trubetzkoy 1953).

There are many different ways in which linguistic systems of the world use the potentialities of sound. This pertains to *prosody* as well as to the *formation of segments*. The specific phonemic systems of languages allow for typological classifications. There are two dimensions of these classifications, one concerning historical system changes (for instance sound shifts or nasalations), the other concerning structural proximity or structural distance. The latter also applies to the combinatorics of the phonic elements (for instance syllable structure and its use for word formation and inflections). These differences in the phonemic systems constitute the fundamental typological difference between tone and non-tone languages, which accounts for intensive experiences of foreignness, especially on the level of perception. Chinese, one of the most important tone languages, will at best appear as sheer singsong to many speakers of Central European languages. Any such speaker asked to record in any way what he or she perceives of this language will very quickly give up. A language such as German, however, with a syllable structure allowing for up to three consonants at the beginning and up to four at the end ('*Strumpf*', '*impfst*') is, to speakers of some other languages, foreign to a degree hard to remedy even through serious training. Learners therefore have to 'open up' such complex clusters by adding epenthetic vowels: Hence a single syllable of the structure consonant + consonant + vowel + consonant is expanded to a structure consisting of two syllables: consonant + vowel + consonant + vowel + consonant (CCVC → CVCVC). This is the process that yields, for instance, a Turkish learner's '*schirib*' for German '*schreib*'. However, a German learner will have significant difficulties with Chinese tone contours such as '*bà*', '*bá*' and even '*bă*'. Tone contours are not a distinctive feature in German, which makes it difficult to memorise such 'irrelevant' information.

Thus, the foreignness of a foreign language is determined by *typological distance*. What has just been illustrated with regard to phonological structures, also applies to other parts of the linguistic structure. If a language differentiates aspects by verb conjugation (as most Slavonic languages do), its speakers will find languages that do not make such a distinction 'foreign'. And vice versa: Users of a verb system like the one German possesses, will have major problems just with the comprehension of the various forms of aspect of such languages.

Another example is the existence of articles, of determination, with regard to which even typologically 'related' languages differ. Even highly advanced Russian learners of German still have major trouble working out when to use an article, and which one.

Assigning languages to specific language types is an enterprise easily affected by a substantialist view of language. However, as linguistic structures change very slowly, it can be quite meaningful to characterise a language L_i as 'isolating', 'agglutinating' or 'synthetic'. Yet such typological assignments should not be made just on the basis of very few criteria such as inflection. These criteria should in fact be expanded to differentiated criteria grids (cf. Ehlich 2007a B1) that could be used to give a comprehensive picture of foreignness from the viewpoint of a point of reference.

For this purpose, it would be highly useful to have a reference language that is not part of the world's languages, a language that could serve as an absolute meta-language. However, the impossibility of obtaining such a meta-language seriously increases the difficulties of determining 'foreignness' and 'self' with respect to languages. Hence the only solution is that we have to look at each language with the eyes of speakers of many other languages. We do, however, not yet possess any systematic procedure to conduct these multiple changes of perspective. The determination of typological foreignness is thus always tied to the linguistic properties of reference languages – a prime opportunity for ethnocentrism to entrench itself in the analysis of foreignness.

Traditional grammatical categories and terminologies are a prominent example of this: They derive from the description of a very specific subgroup of languages, i.e. the highly inflective Indo-European languages Ancient Greek and Latin. Such languages constitute a distinctive language type. Nevertheless, the long process of grammatical category formation with respect to these two languages, a process that is still continuing more or less tacitly, has yielded categories that are likely to be assumed as being universal.

The most consequent employment of such 'universal' categories classifies their absence in another language as deficiency. This procedure yields descriptions of the kind that, for instance, Chinese 'possesses no verbal inflection' and 'no nominal inflection', etc. Phonological foreignness is thus compounded by 'structural remoteness'.

The work of a linguist in describing foreign languages is therefore hampered by its being tied to the typological features of his or her own language. Of course, it would be illusory to attempt a language-independent description of languages and ditto classifications of their respective proximity and distance, as this would just be a special instance of the, quite frequent, general illusion that science could, on principle, do without understanding, i.e. dispense with its hermeneutic obligation.

As can be seen from this, the characterisation of a language as 'foreign' is not just a mental activity of naïve speakers; it is at the very core of linguists' business. Talking about 'foreign languages' is, however, just the surface of this problem. The categorical systems linguists employ are, in fact, relationed systems in disguise. This fundamental problem of linguistics as such leads to bitter experiences when, finally, scientific consciousness has to come to terms with the fact that its work has been infused with basic ethnocentrism.

As there is no leaping 'outside' relationed systems, there is basically just *one* way of dealing with ethnocentrism in linguistics: the constant critical reflection of what happens in the process of categorising something as 'foreign'. Such reflection could avoid the attempt to deny or eliminate foreignness and thus to just affirm the *proprium*, the 'own'. Such reflection could ensure that negative consequences of categorisation processes could be controlled and sufficiently thwarted.

5.3. Modelling proximity – and 'false friends'

While explicit typological differences are very noticeable, so called 'closely related' languages seem to be a lot less 'foreign'. Languages that seem to be 'close' to each other are regarded as (relatively) easy to learn. The linguistics of the 19th Century employed the metaphor of kinship to model this proximity – a metaphor that allows for rendering different distances in an image based on everyday experience. As often happens with images, one soon lost sight of the metaphorical character of this conceptualisation, and even repressed it from consciousness in favour of a biologisation of languages according to family relations. 'Scientific racism' availed itself of this substantiation and contributed to it – a fact that was not immaterial with regard to the preparation and the carrying out of National Socialist crimes (Römer 1989).

In addition to kinship, there is a second metaphor: friendship. If the distance to a foreign language is comparatively small, this language seems to make a lot of 'special offers' to the learner, i.e. promises to spare him or her acquisitional steps. But many of those friends of the learning process that seem to reduce the burden of acquisition are in fact pseudo-helpers, or 'false friends'. Because of the small distance, identities or similarities are identified where there are none.

More precisely: The unbearable aspect of false friends is that they do away with the fundamental assumption of difference that accompanies the experience of linguistic foreignness. False friends invite conclusions that are not covered. Their general point of origin is a genuine similarity in a dimension of linguistic action, for instance in the phonic dimension. Inductive processes lead to the conclusion that formal identity must mean functional identity. The German word *Wetter* has Dutch *weer* as its equivalent. Both differ linguistically, but in a very transparent way: Dutch dropped the dental consonant between the vowels. Prefixation wit *Un-* yields German *Unwetter* ('storm'). This prefix has a parallel in Dutch (*on-*) which is applied to *weer* in the same way as German *Un-* to *Wetter*, yielding *onweer*. This is how far the similarities go. The likely conclusion is that the meaning of *onweer* is the same as *Unwetter*. But this is not the case: Dutch *onweer* means thunder and lightning, 'thunderstorm'. The Dutch equivalent of German *Unwetter*, however, is *noodweer*.

False friends simulate continuous proximity, although they can only ever represent partial proximity. Whenever things come to the crunch they deny the support they promised in the first place.

Nevertheless, an active acquisitional strategy that goes beyond the false friends is quite successful. Linguistic proximity has the potential to reduce the foreignness of a different language – a potential that immediately results in progress of learning.

5.4. Aspects of variation as constructions of linguistic foreignness

Languages that are typologically remote display significant differences across a wide range of linguistic dimensions. Their mutual foreignness is experienced immediately in the process of learning. To overcome this foreignness during the acquisition process, learners have to allow the foreign language to expand the range of what their consciousness accepts as language.

There is, however, a linguistic attitude that strongly works against this. Linguistic xenophobia expresses itself in the conceptualisation of foreignness as a negative – in the extreme as a classification of the foreign language speaker as someone who does not really speak at all. This can easily lead to a situation where such speakers' qualification as humans is at stake, too. The Greek concept of *barbaros* is an example of an extreme form of such a negation (see Nippel 2001) – barbarians are linguistically characterised by their '*brbr*', they are producers of incomprehensible sounds. From there it is only a small step to use such people as slaves who, because of the limitations of their language, do not qualify as human.

However, even minimal linguistic foreignness can be used as a means of discrimination, especially when groups have a strong need for demarcation. Then, linguistic boundaries may quickly become physically insurmountable. In the extreme, such differences may become a *Shibboleth*

> "Then said they unto him, Say now Shibboleth: and he said Sibboleth: for he could not frame to pronounce it right. Then they took him, and slew him at the passages of Jordan: and there fell at that time of the Ephraimites forty and two thousand". Bible, King James Version, Judges 12,6).

Small linguistic differences have had fatal results, not only in the Biblical story.

As we can see from these examples, 'foreignness' can result from the demarcation requirements of groups where small linguistic characteristics indicate whether or not someone is a group member. This is how foreignness can become a societal construct.

In contrast to what was mentioned before, the societal interest in the expansion of the extension of communication areas can also lead to processes of *linguistic integration*. It is mainly the *teleological dimension* of language, the realm of purposes of communication or the realm of illocutions that is involved in these expansions. Of course, such expansions leave residual needs for demarcation unsatisfied – desires that can be met through the maintenance of regional varieties or even the reconstitution of linguistic difference.

In situations of linguistic integration, group formation occurs in various ways. Youth language and thieves' argot are two clear examples where *social* groups or sub groups attempt to re-constitute linguistic foreignness against an established, expanded variety. By availing itself of devices of the established variety, thieves' argot suggests an impression of non-foreignness that makes the practice of foreignness even more efficient. The systematic violation of linguistic norms of the established variety becomes the basis for alternative norms.

Local and regional varieties also exploit the maintenance of their foreignness against the subsumptive force of expanded, comprehensive languages. They do so by maintaining life worlds that can serve as a refuge for alternative group formation against comprehensive forms of socialisation. Regional dialects are dialects only because they maintain their foreignness against comprehensive communicative alternatives. In the dialects, the socialising power of the comprehensive variety is communicatively put into perspective or even broken. Mutual foreignness between standard and dialect is dialect's lifeblood.

In such situations, the criterion of minimal distance is of special importance. To maintain a difference, even the smallest linguistic features can be used – which makes phonology a very suitable area for membership attributions. Group membership and exclusion receive special importance when socialising processes are processes of domination, i.e. processes that generalise social differences diachronically in history. The difference between urban and rural areas shows this quite clearly, where the village dialect constitutes an exemplary sociotope for the creation of foreignness.

The last type of variation to be discussed here involves the *gnoseological dimension* of language, i.e. its function with respect to the passing on of existing knowledge and the creation of new knowledge. Language reflects the increasing societal differentiation of knowledge, but in doing so, it becomes a foreign language to those who take no part in this differentiation. Even though modern societies have little tendencies towards arcane knowledge, it is the sheer abundance of knowledge that creates linguistic foreignness. This leads to a situation where, besides some 'general variety', there are 'languages for special purposes' as varieties that are only functional for certain groups. This kind of linguistic foreignness is one of the greatest communicative challenges to democratic societies.

As we have seen, inclusion and exclusion are pertinent features of language. Large parts of our communication history have been determined by the practice of inclusion and exclusion on the basis of the construction of linguistic foreignness. The fact that there are only some 6000 languages currently spoken shows, at the same time, that the number of languages is significantly smaller than the number of human associations.

Thus, language always and foremost integrates societal difference. This is, without doubt, a central function of language that results from communicative practices and, at the same time, influences them crucially. The production of 'common languages' or 'standard languages' makes available communicative potentials that act as a backdrop for variation – and thus intrinsic foreignness.

6. The nationalisation of language

There are some historical periods where the expansion of languages with respect to an extension of *teleological*, *gnoeseological* and *communitarian processes* is especially apparent. One such period is the establishment of the Greek *koiné* during the post-Alexandrine epoch, another is the expansion of Arabic since the mid 7th Century. Probably the most prominent example is the creation of so-called national languages that mark the communication of modern times. These processes reached their peak with the development and implementation of 'project nation' (Anderson 1983). During these developments, language not only gained in *teleological* and *gnoseological* range. Especially with respect to its *communitarian* dimension, language becomes the core construct of the new social and political association form of the nation state. In the construction of the new political order, language has a function that goes far beyond the communitarian requirements of the then eliminated dynastic identity formation. This new political order is – once again – one of inclusion and exclusion, but in an aggravated manner. Territorial domination and imperial expansion demand proofs of membership – for which language is a suitable candidate. These linguistic proofs of membership create, in turn, procedures of linguistic exclusion. Societal reality does not quite catch up with these ideological requirements. But up to now, language has always been at the centre of conflicts, be it in Belgium, on the Balkans, in the Basque Region or in the Baltic states, to mention just a few European examples (cf. Spolsky 2004, Naglo 2007).

As language is being determined according to its new communitarian function, it consolidates itself as *one* language within defined borders. The production and implementation of normative grammars goes hand in hand with the national functionalisation of languages. This implies a conceptualisation of human identity as being *monolingual* at the core. Thus, talking about 'foreign languages' acquires a new dimension, a new poignancy. The teaching of standardised languages, be it the 'own' language and one or more 'foreign' ones, becomes a means of domination. Success in the acquisition of foreign languages and mastery of one's own become proof of membership of such groups within the nation state that are especially involved in the exertion of its domination.

At the same time, the nationalisation of languages devalues all those languages that do not acquire national status. This applies to the so called *minority languages* in particular. Within the national framework, they are 'foreign' languages. France of the 19th and 20th century, and 20th century Spain under the rule of Franco are extreme examples of this. The characterisation of minority languages as 'foreign', undertaken before the backdrop of the 'national language', leads to an alienation of these 'minority' speakers from their languages. In conjunction with 'anthropological' monolingualism, the quite unshakable ideological foundation of the nationalised language, the linguistic marginalisation of national minority languages is subjectively subscribed to by their respective speakers themselves.

The *migrants* of the present, whose languages have no status in the immigration country, are subject to similar processes.

7. Linguistic foreignness and 'foreign languages' within the paradigm of national languages

The way Europe currently deals with languages as foreign languages is crucially determined by the phase of the nationalisation of languages. During this period the choice of particular linguistic varieties as standards massively changed the rank of other languages with respect to the 'people's' standards. This resulted in a long-term devaluation of the previous language of scholarship, Latin, and, of course, in the devaluation of smaller regional varieties. The functional ranges of the latter became successively smaller, they turned into languages of social proximity (Koch and Oesterreicher), 'domestic languages'.

The establishing of standard languages created a European image (not a reality) of what languages are about: All purposes of communication are served by standard languages of which each has its own territory. Within its own territory, any of these languages has exclusive rights to the innovative communicative sectors tied to the constitution of a nation: politics, literature, economic communication, law and administration. Whether or not religion is part of this programme, is denomination-dependent: in Protestant areas this is traditionally the case, but not in Roman-Catholic ones. However, religious communication, because of its being tied to tradition, has a tendency to create its own varieties even when it avails itself of the national language ('Luther-Deutsch' in Germany; the variety of the King James Version or the English Revised Version in England).

Those languages that were nationalised early and permanently compete with each other whenever they cross the borders of their respective territories. Such crossings, if they do not lead to diplomatically or militarily enforced border changes (for an example, see Glück: 1979 about the three divisions of Poland and their linguistic consequences), demand a more or less perfect command of the competing national language. This need is served by the introduction of extensive *foreign language teaching* in the European education systems – as well as in those systems structured according to the same model. This results in a – partially reciprocal – canon of modern European foreign languages. This canon was in competition with the 'old' canon of foreign languages consisting of Latin, Ancient Greek and, to a limited extent, Ancient Hebrew. This – still ongoing – competition over the schools' timetables will lead, in the long term, to the elimination of Europe's 'classical' languages of education.

The school canon of foreign European languages is determined by this competition of national language options. For languages outside this canon, the odds of making it into the school curriculum are therefore very small. Their teaching relies on private interest, private language teaching by expatriate native speakers and private educational institutions. The current Greek example, where quality school education with regard to language is only available in private institutions (the so-called *frontisteria* that absorb 2.4 % of private household spending) demonstrates that public systems may even be almost incompetent to teach foreign languages in general. Educational programmes for adults such as evening schools or the German *Volkshochschulen* may offer some remedy for the imbalance of the school canon, but they do not change the fact that the acquisition of languages outside this canon is a matter of individual motivation.

The production of European national languages resulted in a kind of linguistic taxonomy also of other elements of the nationalisation process, especially with respect to *national literatures*. To be able to read these literatures in their original languages became one of the central objectives of foreign language teaching. Within the German school system, it was only the *Realschulen* with their practical focus that made some feeble attempts at, for instance, the teaching of business correspondence in a foreign language.

Cultures that are not direct competitors in the imperial struggle of European national states have also almost no chance of supporting and maintaining their languages in this situation, as these languages appear to be devalued by this historical process. Especially European colonial expansion has tended to result in the partial, or sometimes total, elimination of numerous languages. Old 'civilised languages', i.e. languages supported by cultures with a long distinguished history, such as Arabic or Indian languages, became thus discredited, as is revealed by their expansive characterisation as 'remote', a characterisation that was also seen as 'naturally' grounded in typological distance. Thus, the criteria of proximity and distance directly mapped the factual hegemonic and colonial structures – a stranglehold from which linguistic determination of foreignness was only slowly able to free itself. The adoption of colonial languages in large areas of the decolonised world ratifies this discreditation *ex post* and to this day.

At the same time, the role of standard languages as national languages has had negative consequences for the value of those languages spoken within a homogenised national territory without being able to adapt to the national language via variety transformation. This led to a hierarchy of languages within *one* territory, a hierarchy that provoked policies of language elimination and, in resistance to these policies, policies of language maintenance. Most European national states feature such fault lines resulting from national language formation. This struggle is still going on and frequently has assumed a militant quality in post war Europe. There are numerous examples. In Spain, during the rule of Franco and afterwards, it is the unpacified competitors of Castilian, i.e. Catalan and Galician – as well as typologically distant Basque – that have successfully emancipated themselves as languages in their own right, i.e. independent from central domination. As a consequence, the entire spectrum of varieties is currently undergoing a revaluation.

The high rank of the national languages has consequences for the linguistic consciousness of their speakers: They naturally assume that speakers of other languages have to learn the national language – an obligation of the others, without being obliged themselves to learn the others speakers' languages. Even in areas where periods of hard and ongoing struggle resulted in comprehensive language laws providing for the coexistence of several standard languages, the mutual declarations of the foreignness of the respective 'other' remain relevant for the groups involved. South Tyrol, where both Italian and German coexist as standard, is a prime example of this (Naglo 2007). The recent history of former Yugoslavia can serve as an almost classical example for the demonstration of all facets of the constitution of foreignness: the non-reciprocity of the evaluation of languages and the motivation to learn the language of the other have resulted in an explosive maintenance of the criteria of linguistic foreignness.

Such explosiveness reveals itself in a broad range of different constellations. The most obvious one is the open language dispute in which the foreignness of the 'other' is over-emphasised, for instance the dispute between Flemish and

French speaking regions in Belgium or the dispute about monolingual German versus bilingual German – Slovenian place name signs in Austria (Carinthia, Burgenland). Much more subtle are cultural differences articulated within, or camouflaged by one linguistic variety as can be observed with respect to the standards of 'Austrian' versus 'Federal' German.

To date, there is no comprehensive theory of the interrelations between culture and language. A key challenge for such a theory would be to capture the relationship between the dynamics and – relative – statics in the elaboration, use and change of languages, a relationship whose theoretical analysis fell out of sight by Saussure's dichotomy of diachrony and synchrony. This relationship, however, does contain quite a few significant problems to be solved, such as the question what – apart from everyday conceptions of language and the presuppositions of linguistic analysis – actually entitles us to speak about *one* language in the context of linguistic change. The same applies to the concept of culture that readily assumes a homogenous whole where there is, in fact, an entire ensemble of cultures permanently changed by linguistic, cognitive and emotive practices. Determining culture within the realm of national languages covers up intracultural differences and simplifies intercultural ones (cf. Redder and Rehbein 1987). Neostupný's recommendation to apply the linguistic concept of *sprachbund* to cultures also ('kulturbünde'; Clyne 1996) is one step towards a differentiated conception allowing for a sublation of models developed within the horizon of nationhood. Such differentiations are necessary with respect to hybrid cultural products resulting from a fusion of elements of national cultures, and with respect to the overcoming of conceptual ethnocentrism. Within these contexts, the question of what makes a language foreign receives contradictory answers leading to a change in perspectives on language, categorically, and with respect to everyday communicative practice.

8. Migration, globalisation and foreign languages

The reality of the 21st Century transcends national borders whilst, in some parts of the world (for instance on the African continent and in former Yugoslavia) the implementation of 'project nation' has not yet been completed. The movements of populations termed 'migration' result in the bottom up dissolution of the constructs of national homogeneity. This has led to a situation where regions in which monolingualism was previously established in the form of a national standard have meanwhile become multilingual.

Hence, increasing parts of the population, and especially the younger generations, are individuals who are multilingual in different ways and to different degrees (cf., e. g., Clyne 2005 for the Australian situation). The institutions of most countries have not yet caught up with the challenges posed by this new situation.

As for foreign language teaching, this situation is still being dealt with in the paradigm of the national state which has led to a diffuse situation characterised by the distinction of *foreign language acquisition* versus *second language acquisition*. The acquisition of the 'second language' is thereby seen as a basically natural process induced by a multilingual lifeworld, while 'foreign languages' are institutionally taught. The interrelations between these two types of language learning have resulted in various mixed types of language acquisition whose structures are only barely understood. Individuals have many different options to acquire languages in multilingual constellations, and their biographies depend very much on which options they chose (cf. Scollon and Scollon 1994, Maies 2008).

Educational institutions tend to view these new multilingual constellations as 'problematic' and mostly overlook the fact that these constellations do offer opportunities for a re-interpretation of the relationship between the 'self' and the 'other'. Overcoming school's "monolingual habitus" (Gogolin 1994) requires – besides a drastic reform of the objectives of language teaching – the recognition of students' factual multilingualism. The fundamental distinction between native and foreign language teaching cannot be upheld. An obvious consequence, which would however be hard to sell to policy makers and institutions alike, is the transformation of a curriculum based on 'school subjects' into a comprehensive system where language teaching transcends the boundaries of individual languages.

Multilingualism demands a re-interpretation of the *communitarian* dimension of language. In contrast to membership attributions founded on monolingualism within a nation-based conception of language, the new situation entails the necessity and opportunity of multilingual affiliations (cf. House and Rehbein 2004, Krefeld 2002).

As a result of these developments, language, as a specific manifestation and foundation of culture, acquires new functions. Post-national processes dissolve the conception of culture as a homogenous entity based on a national language. The development of mass media and the acceleration of economically based cultural exchange have already been overtaken by the possibilities of the internet. However, within these developments a cultural supremacy of Anglophone and, in particular, US-American provenance has taken hold. Thus, globalisation appears as a new form of cultural and linguistic hegemony.

The adoption of English as a so called international *lingua franca* (cf. Knapp and Meierkord 2002) is a very good illustration of this problematic constellation. Some communicative domains such as academia or business have become more and more homogenised by this lingua franca. Hence communication in those regions of the world where English is no native language is characterised by a new dichotomy in which speakers experience that their native languages are becoming foreign to them in an increasing number of communicative domains. This results in a reduction of the functional range of these languages, as they are deprived of entire communicative domains. Thus, national languages suffer the same fate as those varieties that were reduced to domestic languages during the process of nationalisation.

But this process also affects the language used as lingua franca. For this usage results in linguistic change which turns the lingua franca variety of English into a language foreign to native speakers of English – a process that can be experienced as linguistic expropriation (see Graddol 2006 for a multi-faceted view of these processes).

9. Trans-nationalisation and practice in dealing with linguistic foreignness – a challenge for language teaching

Transnationalisation poses a substantial linguistic challenge especially to Europe as the birthplace of the 'project nation'. There are several possible strategies and models of how to deal with this linguistic challenge. One such strategy could consist of a radicalisation of nationalisation, i.e. the adoption of a single language for entire Europe, for instance the implementation of a current national language ('lingua franca' English, or even Chinese for the generation after the next one) or of an artificial language. Another possible strategy could be the communicative maintenance of a manageable array of languages aimed at the acquisition of several languages.

Foreignness will always need to be dealt with, as it is an essential part of human existence that cannot be conjured away. The central way we encounter foreignness is via language, and it is the foreign languages that offer a prime opportunity of dealing with foreignness. Foreignness is not just a disturbing aspect of language to be eliminated. The other, i.e. a stranger, is the starting point and the goal of any communication (see Humboldt's reflections on the dualis). This is why foreignness is a condition for the possibility of communication.

A world in the process of becoming a global society requires a new relationship towards foreignness. Language and languages do not just offer an opportunity for this new relationship (Weinrich 2004). They are, in fact, the societal domain destined to bring into being a new thinking that does not rely any more on the dichotomy of inclusion and exclusion, but that is able to conceive of the acceptance of the other, the stranger, as the condition of the possibility of the acceptance of the 'self' by the other. This is – in a non-trivial sense – a central aim of education. Foreign languages and their acquisition are thus becoming the programmatic domain that turns hermeneutics, the previous special discipline of theology, philosophy and philology, into an ordinary skill of multilingual people in multilingual constellations. It is this skill that will bring about 'familiar foreignness' (cf. Ehlich 2007b).

The teaching of foreign languages needs common endeavours in the field of language planning, teacher training and curriculum design. The qualifications of foreign language teachers will have to transcend the boundaries of the respective foreign language or languages they teach. The future of language teachers needs a thorough basis in linguistics and language theory and an increase in reflection on language and on foreignness as part of the *conditio humana*. The future language teacher does not see the scope of his/her activities in one single language, be it the "mother tongue", be it "English" or "French" or "Spanish" etc. He/she will be a specialist for language and language acquistion who helps the learners in their endeavour to successfully acquire new linguistic capacities that can be used as resources for communicative interaction in a non-monolingual lifeworld.

Consequently, the qualification of language teachers will change considerably, and these changes will make the job teaching languages even more challenging and fascinating than is has ever been.

The author thanks Winfried Thielmann (Munich/Chemnitz) for his translation of most parts of the German manuscript, and Karlfried Knapp, Barbara Seidlhofer and Winfried Thielmann for their comments on earlier versions of the text.

References

Anderson, Benedict
1983 *Imagined Communities. Reflections on the Origin and Spread of Nationalism*. London: Verso.

Bauer, Thomas
2001 Fremdheit in der klassischen arabischen Kultur und Sprache. In: Jostes and Trabant (eds.): 85–105.

Bausch, Karl-Richard, Herbert Christ, Werner Hüllen and Hans-Jürgen Krumm (eds.)
1989 *Handbuch Fremdsprachenunterricht*. 3rd edition. Tübingen: A. Francke Verlag/UTB.

Beshara, Helen Ayad
2009 *Der Fremdheitsbegriff und der Fremde im Deutschen und im Arabischen*. Dissertation. Ain Schams Universität Kairo.

Bühler, Karl
1934 *Sprachtheorie*. Jena: Fischer.

Clyne, Michael
1996 *Inter-Cultural Communication at Work*. Cambridge: Cambridge University Press.

Clyne, Michael
2005 *Australia's Language Potential*. Sydney: University of New South Wales Press.

Craanen, Michael and Antje Gunsenheimer (eds.)
2006 *Das 'Fremde' und das 'Eigene'. Forschungsberichte (1992–2006)*. Bielefeld: transcript.

Ehlich, Konrad
2007a *Sprache und sprachliches Handeln.* 3 vol. Berlin/New York: de Gruyter.
Ehlich, Konrad
2007b *Transnationale Germanistik.* München: iudicium.
Georges, Karl Ernst
1913 *Ausführliches lateinisch-deutsches Wörterbuch.* Reprinted 1988. Darmstadt: Wissenschaftliche Buchgesellschaft.
Glück, Helmut
1979 *Die preußisch-polnische Sprachenpolitik.* Hamburg: Helmut Buske.
Gogolin, Ingrid
1994 *Der monolinguale Habitus der multilingualen Schule.* Münster: Waxmann.
Graddol, David
2006 *English Next.* London: British Council.
Hogrebe, Wolfram
1985 Die epistemische Bedeutung des Fremden. In: Hermann Sturm (ed.), *Das Fremde. Ästhetische Erfahrung beim Graben, Reisen, Messen, Sterben.* Aachen: Rader Verlag.
Horstmann, Axel
1986/1987 Das Fremde und das Eigene – 'Assimilation' als hermeneutischer Begriff. *Archiv für Begriffsgeschichte* 30: 7–43.
House, Juliane and Jochen Rehbein (eds.)
2004 *Multilingual Communication. Hamburg Studies on Multilingualism 3.* Amsterdam/Philadelphia: John Benjamins.
Hüllen, Werner
1987 *Englisch als Fremdsprache.* Tübingen: Narr.
Jostes, Brigitte
2004 *Fremdheit. Historisch-anthropologische Erkundungen einer linguistischen Kategorie.* Humboldt-Studien. Paderborn/München/Wien/Zürich: Ferdinand Schöningh.
Jostes, Brigitte and Jürgen Trabant (eds.)
2001 *Fremdes in fremden Sprachen.* München: Wilhelm Fink Verlag.
Jostes, Brigitte
2001 Fremdes als Gegenstand des vergleichenden Sprachstudiums. In: Jostes and Trabant (eds.): 245–269.
Kluge, Friedrich and Elmar Seebold
1999 *Etymologisches Wörterbuch der deutschen Sprache.* 23rd edition. Berlin/New York: de Gruyter.
Koch, Peter and Wulf Oesterreicher
1985 Sprache der Nähe – Sprache der Distanz. Mündlichkeit und Schriftlichkeit im Spannungsfeld von Sprachtheorie und Sprachgeschichte. *Romanistisches Jahrbuch* 36: 15–43.
König, Ekkehard and Peter Siemund
2001 Identität und Alterität: Zur Semantik von *fremd* und ähnlichen Ausdrücken. In: Jostes and Trabant (eds.): 109–129.
Krefeld, Thomas
2002 Migration, Sprachbewußtsein und Wissenschaftsideologie – über dynamische Räume und ihre statische Beschreibung. In: Konrad Ehlich and Ve-

nanz Schubert (eds.), *Sprachen und Sprachenpolitik in Europa*, 145–170. Tübingen: Stauffenburg.

Krusche, Dietrich
1980 Die Kategorie der Fremde. Eine Problemskizze. In: Wierlacher (ed.): 47–56.

Krusche, Dietrich
1985 *Literatur und Fremde. Zur Hermeneutik kulturräumlicher Distanz*. München: iudicium.

Krusche, Dietrich
2003 *Zeigen im Text. Anschauliche Orientierung in literarischen Modellen von Welt*. Würzburg: Königshausen and Neumann.

Knapp, Karlfried and Christiane Meierkord
2002 *Lingua Franca Communication*. Frankfurt a. M.: Peter Lang Verlag.

Maas, Utz
2008 *Sprache und Sprachen in der Migrationsgesellschaft. Die schriftkulturelle Dimension*. Göttingen: Vandenhoeck and Ruprecht.

Messinger, Heinz
1994 *Langenscheidts Handwörterbuch Englisch, Teil 1: Englisch-Deutsch*. 6th edition. Berlin: Langenscheidt.

Münkler, Herfried and Bernd Ladwig
1997 Dimensionen der Fremdheit. In: Herfried Münkler and Bernd Ladwig (eds.), *Facetten der Fremdheit*, 11–44. Berlin: Akademie Verlag.

Münkler, Herfried and Karin Meßlinger (eds.)
1998 *Die Herausforderung durch das Fremde*. Berlin: Akademie Verlag.

Naglo, Kristian
2007 *Rollen von Sprachen in Identitätsbildungsprozessen multilingualer Gesellschaften in Europa*. Arbeiten zur Sprachanalyse 50. Frankfurt am Main: Peter Lang Verlag.

Naguschewski, Dirk and Jürgen Trabant (eds.)
1997 *Was heißt hier "fremd"? Studien zu Sprache und Fremdheit*. Berlin: Akademie Verlag.

Nippel, Wilfried
2001 Die "Barbaren" aus der Sicht der Griechen. In: Jostes and Trabant (eds.): 43–56.

Redder, Angelika and Jochen Rehbein
1987 Zum Begriff der Kultur. In: Angelika Redder and Jochen Rehbein (eds.) *Arbeiten zur interkulturellen Kommunikation*, 7–21. Bremen. OBST 38

Ricken, Norbert and Nicole Balzer
2007 Differenz: Verschiedenheit, Andersheit, Fremdheit. In: Jürgen Straub, Arne Weidemann and Doris Weidemann (eds.), *Handbuch Interkulturelle Kommunikation*, 56–69. Stuttgart/Weimar: Metzler.

Römer, Ruth
1989 *Sprachwissenschaft und Rassenideologie in Deutschland*. 2nd edition. München: Wilhelm Fink Verlag.

Scollon, Ron and Suzanne Wong Scollon
1995 *Intercultural Communication. A Discourse Approach*. Oxford, UK/ Cambridge, USA: Blackwell.

Spolsky, Bernard
2004 *Language Policy.* Cambridge University Press

Trabant, Jürgen
2000 How relativistic are Humboldt's "Weltansichten"? In: Martin Pütz and Marjolijn Verspoor (eds.), *Explorations in Linguistic Relativity,* 25–44. Amsterdam/Philadelphia: John Benjamins.

Trabant, Jürgen
2007 Über die Aktualität des Sprachdenkens Wilhelm von Humboldts. In: Brunhilde Wehinger (ed.), *Plurale Lektüren. Studien zu Sprache, Literatur und Kunst,* 13–27. Berlin: edition tranvía.

Trubetzkoy, Nikolai S.
1953 *Grundzüge der Phonologie.* Göttingen: Vandenhoeck and Ruprecht.

Waldenfels, Bernhard
1997 *Topographie des Fremden. Studien zur Phänomenologie des Fremden I.* Frankfurt a. M.: Suhrkamp.

Waldenfels, Bernhard
2006 *Grundmotive zur Phänomenologie des Fremden.* Frankfurt a. M.: Suhrkamp.

Weinrich, Harald
1988 Fremdsprachen als fremde Sprachen. In: Weinrich 1988: 195–220.

Weinrich, Harald
1988 *Wege der Sprachkultur.* München: Deutscher Taschenbuch Verlag.

Weinrich, Harald
2004 *Sprache, das heißt Sprachen.* Tübingen: Narr.

Wierlacher, Alois (ed.)
1980 *Fremdsprache Deutsch. Grundlagen und Verfahren der Germanistik als Fremdsprachenphilologie.* Vol 1. München: iudicium.

Wierlacher, Alois (ed.)
2001 *Kulturthema Fremdheit. Leitbegriffe und Problemfelder kulturwissenschaftlicher Fremdheitsforschung.* 2nd edition. München: iudicium.

Wierlacher, Alois and Andrea Bogner
2003 *Handbuch Interkulturelle Germanistik.* Stuttgart/Weimar: Metzler.

3. Multilingualism and foreign language learning

Antje Wilton

1. Introduction

A recent definition of a multilingual individual is given as follows:

> A multilingual individual is anyone who can communicate in more than one language, be it active (through speaking and writing) or passive (through listening and reading). (Wei 2008: 4)

This definition illustrates the core meaning of the prefix 'multi' as 'more than one'. In the case of multilingualism, more than one refers to the number of languages involved either as languages spoken by an individual, as languages present in a society, speech community or institution, or as languages used in a stretch of discourse or conversation.

The investigation of the manifold forms of multilingualism is an important field of research in Applied Linguistics. Recent global and, in many areas of the world, also more local developments are giving rise to the development of new and intensified forms of travel, communication, and migration. These new forms often result in differentiated patterns of language contact and multilingual language use.

As multilingualism and linguistic diversity are seen as more and more advantageous in many areas of the world, official policies emerge that aim to implement demands for language learning and linguistic diversity. This is particularly important in the growing European Union. The European Union officially and explicitly promotes the protection and use of minority and lesser known languages:

> Promoting linguistic diversity means actively encouraging the teaching and learning of the widest possible range of languages in our schools, universities, adult education centres and enterprises. Taken as a whole, the range on offer should include the smaller European languages as well as all the larger ones, regional, minority and migrant languages as well as those with 'national' status, and the languages of our major trading partners throughout the world. (Action Plan 2004–2006, http://ec.europa.eu/education/doc/official/keydoc/actlang/act_lang_en.pdf, p. 9)

More generally, the European Union encourages multilingualism by espousing a policy which requires citizens to learn at least three languages, i.e. two languages in addition to their respective mother tongue:

> The EU's language policy promotes multilingualism and aims for a situation in which every EU citizen can speak at least two foreign languages in addition to their mother tongue. (http://ec.europa.eu/education/languages/eu-language-policy/index_en.htm, 15. 12. 2008)

This is important with respect to multilingual education and foreign language learning: as many individuals do not find themselves in a situation in which the acquisition of three or even more languages is a natural result, demand for formal education in a variety of languages is increasing. The distinction between natural acquisition and formal learning (Krashen 1986) is an important one to make when talking about foreign languages and will be discussed in more detail below. Ideally, it is argued, foreign language learning should start at a very early age:

> It is a priority for Member States to ensure that language learning in kindergarten and primary school is effective, for it is here that key attitudes towards other languages and cultures are formed, and the foundations for later language learning are laid. (Action Plan 2004–2006, http://ec.europa.eu/education/doc/official/keydoc/actlang/act_lang_en.pdf, p. 7)

Very early language acquisition is often favoured because it is thought to lead to a desired native-like competence in the L2. Although studies have shown that there can be an advantage of younger language learners over older language learners in certain areas of competence such as phonology, it has also been argued that an early age of onset of foreign language acquisition alone does not necessarily lead to higher or even native-like proficiency. Many other factors have to be considered when ultimate proficiency in a foreign language is investigated (see Dewaele, Ch. 11, this volume). Thus, the demand for early foreign language acquisition as formulated in the Action Plan is mainly concerned with the shaping of positive attitudes of young children towards multilingualism and language learning in general. Nevertheless, the Action Plan also recognises the need to promote language learning in older children and adults as part of a policy to promote "a lifetime of language learning" (Action Plan 2004–2006, http://ec.europa.eu/education/doc/official/keydoc/actlang/act_lang_en.pdf, p. 8).

Early contact with a foreign language in many areas of the world amounts to early contact with English. In a study conducted for the British Council, Graddol (2006) argues that a command of English as the world's most popular foreign language is now rather a necessary basic skill than a specialised competence:

> [...] English seems to have joined this list of basic skills. Quite simply, its function and place in the curriculum is no longer that of 'foreign language' and this is bringing about profound changes in who is learning English, their motives for learning it and their needs as learners. (Graddol 2006: 72).

If a command of English is almost normal, the value of speaking additional languages is increasing, in particular for native speakers of English:

> The slogan 'English is not enough' applies as strongly to native speakers of English as for those who speak it as a second language. We are now nearing the end of the period where native speakers can bask in their privileged knowledge of the global lingua franca." (Graddol 2006: 118)

Thus, foreign language learning in various forms will be in increasing demand in the future (see Mitchell, Ch. 4, this volume), resulting in more and more multilingual individuals and societies. Both individuals and societies alike have to and are overcoming the stage of seeing multilingualism as a threat to personal as well as cultural identity which has been associated with monolingualism for several hundred years. This "monolingual bias" (cf. Auer and Wei 2007a: 1) led to an idealisation of monolingualism as the natural, even God-given state of affairs, and multilingualism

> was considered to be the consequence of some kind of disturbance in the 'language order', such as migration or conquest, which brought language systems into some kind of unexpected and 'unnatural' contact with one another, often leading to structural simplification [...] (Auer and Wei 2007a: 2)

It is not surprising that language contact was seen as a threat to the purity of the language, an idea which persists until the present day and still causes lively public debates in many (European) countries. Connected with the demand for a pure language is the belief that a language can in some way be fixed, and that it constitutes a closed, well-defined and stable system if detrimental influences can be controlled. Traditional linguistics was for a long time based on a similar presumption, viewing language contact and multilingualism as marginal to the study of language:

> By and large, the study of linguistics was equal to analysing single languages [...]. The fact that languages influence each other through language contact [...] was acknowledged of course from the very start of linguistics, but this contact was not seen in the context of multilingualism, and it was taken to be a secondary phenomenon which presupposed the existence and stability of the language systems in contact. (Auer and Wei 2007a: 1).

In contrast, current research in Applied Linguistics provides rich material to support and promote multilingualism as a beneficial development for societies and individual alike.

2. Multilingualism and related concepts

2.1. Bilingualism

Bilingualism is often regarded as the prototypical case of multilingualism, the meaning of 'multi' as 'more than one' being specified by using 'bi' in the sense of 'more than one, i.e. two'. Indeed, most research that focuses on the presence of more than one language in an individual, society, institution, or conversation investigates instances of bilingualism rather than multilingualism in a broader sense. Although research on aspects of societal bilingualism has a long history dating back to the seventeenth century, more modern research produced isolated studies of bilingual individuals and bilingual speech towards the end of the 19th century and became increasingly popular after the 1960s with the turn towards the "period of additive effects" (Baker 1993: 111–114) when the opinion prevailed among researchers that bilingualism has a positive influence on an individual's intelligence. Since then, much work has been done to show the cognitive advantages of bilingualism, the uniqueness of bilingual competence and the social and economic benefits of bilingualism. Crucial issues that have been addressed are the characteristics and types of bilingual acquisition such as simultaneous (BFLA, *Bilingual First Language Acquisition*) and sequential acquisition, the linguistic phenomena connected with the acquisition and use of two languages by individuals, the representation of two languages in the bilingual brain, cognitive processes connected with bilingual language use, interactional manifestations and practices of bilinguals such as language choice, as well as questions of identity, ideology, and language policy. Modern studies of bilingualism continue to extend the research focus and investigate e.g. the nature and effect of bilingualism in later life (Dewaele 2007; Bialystok 2008), the situation of bilinguals in monolingual environments (Jørgensen and Quist 2007; Gogolin 2003) or the development of biliteracy (García, Bartlett and Kleifgen 2007; Rivera and Huerta-Macías 2007).

The reason for such extensive research on bi- rather than multilingualism can been seen in the belief that the most important differences are to be found between the acquisition of a first and another language (e.g. Tracy 2007) and not between a second and third or following language. Indeed many important insights of multilingual acquisition and use have been gained from bilingualism studies. Elwert (1973), in describing his multilingual childhood and adolescence, uses the term and the concept of bilingualism and only occasionally uses the term multilingualism as a synonym:

> Unter Zweisprachigkeit wird nachstehend auch Mehrsprachigkeit mitverstanden, denn die Probleme bleiben grundsätzlich die gleichen, ob das nicht-einsprachige Individuum nur eine oder mehrere Sprachen mehr spricht als das einsprachige Individuum (Elwert 1973: 2).
> [In the following, bilingualism is used to include multilingualism, because the problems remain generally the same, whether the non-monolingual individuum speaks only one or several additional languages more than the monolingual individuum. *My translation, A. W.*]

His perception of himself as a bilingual rather than a distinctively multilingual individual seems to be shaped considerably by the research available to him at the time. Until today, this research has a notable focus, if not even a bias, towards investigating bilingualism as the relevant manifestation of any other kind of multilingualism:

> The bilingual bias refers to the tendency to view multilinguals as bilinguals with some additional languages rather than as speakers of several languages from the start. It also refers to the associated tendency of regarding bilinguals' acquisition and production processes as default processes for multilinguals. Taking the position that multilinguals are bilinguals with additional languages essentially reflects the underlying assumption that the additional languages are somewhat superfluous. The multilingual mind becomes a mind with two languages, to which some more languages can be added (or dropped), but the addition (or reduction) of languages is somewhat optional. (De Angelis 2007: 15)

This assumption is known as the *no-difference* position which is implicitly or explicitly assumed by many studies in the very influential field of second language acquisition (SLA)[1] (De Angelis 2007: 3). In SLA, 'second' generally refers to "any language that is learned subsequent to the mother tongue" (Ellis 1997: 3). This use of the term implies a certain focus in researching multilingual language acquisition in that it distinguishes clearly the languages involved into a first language (L1, mother tongue, native language) and a (or several) second language(s) (L2, non-native languages). The latter are acquired after the acquisition of the mother tongue has been completed or has progressed considerably. The result of such an aquisition process can then be termed sequential bilingualism, and it is this state that is of major interest to researchers in SLA.

It is noticeable that even within the literature explicitly claiming to research multilingualism, a bias towards bilingualism is prevalent. An informal perusal of anthologies or journals with multilingualism in the title reveals that they often contain articles on bilingualism rather than multilingualism. In some cases this might be due to a deliberately specific use of the term. Hoffmann (2001: 2) points out that in certain fields of sociolinguistic research, such as language contact and language planning and education, researchers

> [...] preferred to employ the term 'multilingualism' (rather than 'bilingualism') so as to distinguish clearly the macrolinguistic from the microlinguistic level of investigation. Moreover, multilingualism encompasses the idea that not only is more than one language involved, but also that any number of linguistic varieties may be present in the particular sociolinguistic situation under consideration.

In other cases, it seems that a transitional phase in the use of the terms is visible, as observed by Clyne (1997: 95) when he submitted an article for a journal:

> Although this journal is entitled the *International Journal of Bilingualism*, it describes its focus as 'the language behaviour of the bi- and multi-lingual individual'. Thus, while the general title continues the tradition of subsuming lingualism exceeding two under bilingualism [...], the journal's focus statement implies that people using more than two languages may be different to bilinguals.

The new orthographic form bi/multilingualism as e.g. used by Moyer (2008) shows how current discussion and research are in a transitional stage: on the one hand, it seems difficult to relinquish bilingualism as the prototype of multilingualism; on the other hand more and more researchers are aware of its restrictions and increasingly refer to multilingualism rather than bilingualism.

Finally, in some cases, research which set out to investigate a multilingual situation revealed that the subjects themselves exhibit bilingual rather than multilingual practices (Hoffmann 2001; Clyne 1997).

Despite these terminological inconsistencies and developments, it is true that much research is still concerned with a combination of two particular languages. Only recently has the investigation of multilingualism 'proper' gained sufficient ground (see section 6).

2.2. Trilingualism

Trilingualism, third language acquisition or additional language acquisition (De Angelis 2007: 11) is fairly new as a focused topic of its own. Researchers addressing this issue stress the point that the acquisition of a third language is different from the acquisition of a second language, and thus monolingualism, bilingualism, trilingualism, quadrilingualism etc. are each to be regarded as unique constellations and investigated as such (see Hufeisen and Jessner, Ch. 5, this volume). It is undisputed that they all share a considerable amount of features, but recent research provides increasing evidence that they are also distinctively different in many respects. A more detailed investigation of individual trilingualism, then, can serve to overcome the bilingualism bias described in the previous section (Cenoz and Jessner 2000; Cenoz 2003; Cenoz, Hufeisen and Jessner 2001a+b; De Angelis 2007; Jessner 2006). Many of those studies reveal that trilingual individuals often have one foreign language in their linguistic repertoire, and this observation will have increasing relevance to foreign language teaching:

> Trilingualism is likely to gain in prominence due to the exigencies of globalisation which will encourage people to have their first language, another language of significance in the region, and an international language. (Clyne 1997: 95–96)

Regionally significant languages as well as English as the most important international language are often introduced via formal educational systems, and although the status of English in many parts of the world is changing from a traditional foreign language to that of a basic skill (see section 1), the context of its acquisition as an international language is still that of formal instruction.

2.3. Plurilingualism

The term 'plurilingualism' is generally used to mean multilingualism, especially in the Romance languages and multilingualism research in French and Italian language contexts (cf. Lüdi 1995, 2002, 2004; Meißner and Picaper 2003; Wiater 2006 and others). Occasionally, the terms refer to the distinction between individual and societal multilingualism, with multilingualism denoting the individual and plurilingualism the societal phenomenon (cf. Auer and Wei 2007: 2 when referring to plurilingual states).

The plurilingualism approach taken by the Common European Framework (CEFR) emphasises yet another aspect in that it claims to go beyond multilingualism as the mere number of languages present in an individual or society by promoting plurilingualism as the individual ability to use several languages in a creative, flexible and immediate way, even if competence in some/one of the languages is minimal:

> Plurilingualism differs from multilingualism, which is the knowledge of a number of languages, or the co-existence of different languages in a given society. Multilingualism may be attained by simply diversifying the languages on offer in a particular school or educational system, or by encouraging pupils to learn more than one foreign language, or reducing the dominant position of English in international communication. Beyond this, the plurilingual approach emphasises the fact that as an individual person's experience of language in its cultural contexts expands, from the language of the home to that of society at large and then to the languages of other peoples [...], he or she does not keep these languages and cultures in strictly separated mental compartments, but rather builds up a communicative competence to which all knowledge and experience of language contributes and in which languages interrelate and interact. (http://www.coe.int/T/DG4/Linguistic/Source/Framework_EN.pdf)

Such a conceptualisation of an individual's linguistic competence is undoubtedly necessary to understand and promote modern forms of multilingualism and thus is the basis of much current research on multilingualism. The suggestion by the CEFR to term this modern conceptualisation plurilingualism, however, does not seem to have gained any ground in the research literature. Instead, the concept of multilingualism is broadened (see below).

2.4. Polyglot

Polyglot is not a widely used academic term, but rather a commonly used, positively associated term for an individual speaking several, in some cases even an exceptionally large number of languages. It implies linguistic competence in international contexts and a particular talent to learn and use many languages. The term is mostly used outside linguistics in the language learning industry and is often defined in dubious ways, mainly on websites dedicated to foreign language learning (e.g. www.polyglot.co.uk).

According to Baker and Prys Jones (1998: 7), a *Polyglot of Europe* Contest was held in Brussels in 1990, won by Derick Herning (Shetland) for his oral competence in 22 languages. Wikipedia gives a list of 16 polyglots who claimed of themselves or were reported to speak at least 10 languages, some of them even more than 50 (http://en.wikipedia.org/wiki/Polyglot_(person)).

In addition to referring to a multilingual person, polyglot can also be used to refer to a text or book which contains the same text in a number of languages, and many websites offering translation services and computer technology use it.

2.5. Polylingualism

As a very recent term, *polylingualism* emerged from studies investigating very dynamic language use in multilingual conversation, where traditional categories of language such as code, variety, and language do not seem to fit the observed linguistic behaviour of the interactants. Those traditional categories and the conversational practices such as codeswitching based on them presuppose separable systems which are combined in a particular way. In polylingual interactions, however, those categories do not adequately reflect the choices and combinations made by the interactants. Thus, Møller prefers to call such dynamic language use *polylingual*:

> I argue that terms like bilingual or multilingual are inappropriate in order to describe this verbal interaction because these terms presuppose that linguistic production is divided in categories in advance. Instead I suggest the term polylingual as more sufficient in describing the fluent use of linguistic features which are locally constructed as categories of linguistic features, regardless of how linguistic features are categorised in society at large. (Møller 2008: 217)

Such language behaviour is particularly common among young adolescents in urban environments, where many languages are present, but not available to every individual as distinct languages to be learned and used:

> The young speakers become acquainted with many different features from these languages, and they use some of them in their speech without learning all the other parts of the languages involved. The use of features from several different languages in the same production has become frequent, especially in in-group interaction, even when the speakers apparently know very little of several of the involved languages. (Jørgensen 2008: 168)

Indeed, it seems that multilingualism in its traditional sense as the (ideally optimum) mastery of several languages is neither necessary nor even desirable in such environments. Instead, language users exploit all the linguistic features available to them in order to achieve their communicative aims. This very creative, dynamic and increasingly common phenomenon is also referred to as *languaging* (Jørgensen 2008: 169–174). Jørgensen stresses that languaging as such is something common to all language users. Polylingual languaging is just a particular type of languaging, which is by no means chaotic or random. Instead, the choice of items or features is linked to criteria employed by the interactants to construct meaningful discourse, and to achieve a variety of different communicative aims. In that it is similar to other types of code mixing, and to choices made in other forms of languaging (see also the concept of *crossing*, Quist and Jørgensen 2007).

2.6. Multilingualism

In contrast to the prominent view of 'multi' meaning 'more than one' as shown in the above discussion of the related concepts of bilingualism and trilingualism, there are definitions which explicitly define 'multi' as 'more than two', albeit demanding only minimal knowledge in the languages additional to the first (mother) tongue. Here is one example:

> Als mehrsprachig darf schon der bezeichnet werden, der auf der Basis der Kenntnis der Muttersprache eingeschränkte Kenntnisse in wenigstens zwei weiteren Sprachen entweder in gleichen oder verschiedenen Diskursbereichen hat. (Bertrand and Christ 1990: 208)
> [A person can be called multilingual if on the basis of the knowledge of his/her mother tongue he/she has restricted knowledge in at least two further languages, either in the same or in different discourse areas. *My translation, A.W.*]

Implicitly, the authors deny bilingualism the status of 'true' multilingualism, or at least view the state of being bilingual as only a step towards becoming a multilingual person proper. This is evident in their pomotion of the concept of *Eingangssprache*, i.e. the first formally learned foreign language in addition to the mother tongue at school. In the learning process, the Eingangssprachen have a special function, because they

> […] führen den Lerner zum ersten Mal bewußt über die Muttersprache hinaus, und sie präsentieren einen neuen Bestand von sprachlichen Bezeichnungsmitteln, sie zeigen eine neue Form der Versprachlichung von Erfahrungen und führen in andere soziale Konventionen ein […]. Die Eingangssprache soll ihrerseits auf das Lernen weiterer Fremdsprachen vorbereiten. (Bertrand and Christ 1990: 209–210.)
> [[…] lead the learner beyond the scope of his mother tongue, and they present a new repertoire of linguistic means, they show a new form of verbalisation of experiences […]. The Eingangssprache should prepare the learner for the acquisition of additional foreign languages. *My translation, A. W.*]

Like the definition given by Wei (2008: 4) at the beginning of this chapter, the above definition highlights another important aspect in that it allows restricted knowledge in a language as a sufficient basis for multilingual competence. The authors stress that "unter Mehrsprachigkeit nicht zu verstehen ist, man müsse mehrere Sprachen gleichermaßen beherrschen." (Bertrand and Christ 1990: 208) [multilingualism does not require equal competence in several languages, *my translation, A.W.*]. This view is particularly important in understanding emerging concepts like receptive multilingualism (see section 4.1.).

For the purposes of this chapter it is more useful to take a broad view of who is to be called multilingual and to go along with Wei's definition of a multilingual individual. In doing that, we accept multilingualism as a broad concept describing the outcome of the acquisition of more than one language by an individual. On a societal level, multilingualism can be broadly defined as the presence of more than one language (or speech community) in a society. This broad concept encompasses the above terms and provides an umbrella term for a variety of phenomena. With regard to a particular individuum, society, situation or research context, the broad concept then can be defined more specifically, for instance to mean bilingualism or trilingualism or their variants such as diagonal or vertical multilingualism[2].

In the European context, individual multiligualism is to be achieved mainly by the learning of foreign languages. A foreign language generally is defined as a

> [...] second language that is not widely used in the learners' immediate social context but rather one that might be used for future travel or other cross-cultural communication situations, or one that might be studied as a curricular requirement or elective in school with no immediate or necessary practical application. (Saville-Troike 2006: 188)

Thus, foreign language learning is the learning of non-native languages for the purpose of cultural enrichment, communicative benefits, inherent interest and personal motivation. A foreign language differs from an additional language acquired as part of bilingual or multilingual first language acquisition in its functions for the individual and in the processes of its acquisition. According to the very popular Three-Circle-Model devised by Kachru (1992) for the categorisation of Englishes around the world, a foreign language has two decisive characteristics: it is predominantely learned in a formal context, usually in the language classroom in primary, secondary or tertiary education, and, as indicated in the definition above, it is learned for international communication rather than for communication within the speech community of the learner. Whereas the natural acquisition of several languages from birth is usually the result of particular language constellations in the immediate environment of an individual, the formal learning of a foreign language is a largely conscious process and the result of a decision taken by the learner. Some researchers stress the importance of the distinction between (natural) acquisition and (formal) learning because of the fundamental differences of the processes involved (Krashen 1986)[4]. The creation of a natural situation for language acquisition on a large scale involves much more effort than providing foreign language teaching. Thus, it is likely that the more languages an individual acquires, the more of those languages will be learned as foreign languages. Similarly, if multilingualism is officially promoted by an active language policy, the way to achieve this widespread multilingualism is through teaching foreign languages.

However, it has also been pointed out that any dichotomy in the attempt to distinguish features of language acquisition such as simultaneous/sequential and acquisition/learning does not reflect adequately the variety of possible combinations and learning situations of the individual learner (cf. Ellis 2008). For foreign language teaching and education, it is much more useful to see such distinctions as poles at the end of continua, and to recognise the multitude of ways in which multilingualism can be present/be established in an individual. Thus, education systems will increasingly have to take into account that many individuals entering the system are already bi- or multilingual and therefore already possess knowledge about language learning. This knowledge is based on the different processes of acquisition (simultaneous, sequential, a mixture of both etc.) and therefore differs considerably in its nature and its manifestations, for instance in shaping learning strategies.

It is clear, then, that a multilingual can have several native and non-native languages. It also seems clear that the more languages are involved, the more likely is it that at least one of them is acquired sequentially and therefore a non-native and often a foreign language. For this reason, many studies investigating multilingualism focus on the impact of prior knowledge of language(s) in the acquisition process of further languages. Very few studies in comparison have looked at multilingual first language acquisition, where all languages are acquired simultaneously (De Houwer 2009; Hoffmann 1985), possibly because such instances are much less common than the hybrid type of multilingualism discussed above.

3. Dimensions of multilingualism

3.1. Historical multilingualism

Multilingualism is an outcome of language contact in the broadest sense. Language contact can be caused by a number of circumstances, often involving the migration of groups of people, such as political developments, natural disasters, religious oppression, economical and educational advantages (cf. Wei 2007: 3–4). Language contact is an important aspect in the development of any modern national language and has established itself as an independent research framework in linguistics:

> Historical linguists have for a long time tended to overemphasise the purity of languages in their historical transmission from one generation to another and to underestimate the impact of contact between languages, but more recent scholarship has recognised contact to be almost ubiquitous and of primary importance in the development of languages and language varieties. (Schneider 2007: 11)

However, it is easier to focus on the results of language contact (i.e. by investigating structural aspects of the respective languages) than to assess the sociolinguistic processes and consequences of language contact for the multilingual practices of a society and/or the individuals living therein (Kremnitz 1990: 41–43). There is plenty of material available providing researchers with evidence of multilingual language use in written texts, exemplified by the bilingual Rosetta Stone engraved in ancient Egypt about 2200 years ago through to the many texts in European antiquity involving Latin and Greek and, from the dawn of medieval times, increasingly also the vernaculars of the emerging kingdoms of Europe. However, much less is known about the oral multilingual practices of those times, as investigations with modern sociolinguistic methods are obviously impossible (Adams and Swain 2002).

Furthermore, there seem to be few historical sources explicitly commenting on aspects of multilingual language use and the status of multilingualism in society. This appears to be the case at least for a number of European languages such as German, indicating that multilingualism is either not present or taken for granted and thus not worth commenting on. Furthermore, the history of a modern language is often seen and told as the history of its standard variety (cf. Mesthrie 2006) with an emphasis on codification and normative processes, including aspects of linguistic purism. The very popular depiction of the relationship between languages in language families and their subgroups in the shape of a family tree[3] is often criticised for not taking processes of language contact into account and thus giving a wrong picture of languages as living organisms genetically related rather than in contact with each other.

Until the rise of the nation state in the 19th century, language contact and multilingualism were in most cases the outcomes of natural develoments rather than of explicit language policy. During the Roman dominance in Europe, there seems to have been no such explicit language policy (cf. Kremnitz 1990: 45), although we find comments in the literature about the speech of the 'barbarians'. Latin was certainly the dominant language in Europe at the time, functioning as a lingua franca in an empire so vast and needing a large number of people from various cultural and linguistic backgrounds to control and maintain it that multilingualism among some parts of the population must have been inevitable. Indeed, for the educated citizen of Rome the study of Greek and literary Latin was an important part of education (for a history of foreign language learning see Mitchell, Ch. 4, this volume). As Latin continued to keep its position as the lingua franca in particular of the church and as the language of learning, multi- or at least bilingualism was a necessity for any scholar in the Middle Ages (cf. Kremnitz 1990: 41–43). With the technical, institutional and political changes of the Renaissance, language was discovered as a means to express cultural and national identity. Efforts to refine and establish the local vernacular as a codified standard language alongside or even instead of Latin are seen as expressions of a growing cultural and therefore also linguistic patriotism. This upgrading of native languages together with the process of standardisation resulted in a demarcation between languages (see Ehlich, Ch. 2, this volume). It often went hand in hand with mythical or racist views, attributing the speakers of a prestige language with certain inherent qualities, thereby disqualifying speakers of other languages (cf. Gardt 1999: 109). Linguistic patriotism in Europe is evident in the popular formation of linguistic societies such as the *Fruchtbringende Gesellschaft* in Germany or the *Accademia della Crusca* in Italy as early as the 17th century. It led to the conception of monolingualism as the ideal state for a society or nation as well as for the individual (cf. Gardt 1999: 108).

The concept of a language as an expression of national identity was also transported to other areas of the world through colonisation, a process which is most vividly expressed by Noah Webster:

> Let us then seize the present moment, and establish a *national language*, as well as a national government. Let us remember that there is a certain respect due to the opinions of other nations. As an independent people, our reputation abroad demands that, in all things, we should be federal; be *national*; for if we do not respect *ourselves*, we may be assured that *other nations* will not respect us. In short, let it be impressed upon the mind of every American, that to neglect the means of commanding respect abroad, is treason against the character and dignity of a brave independent people. (Webster [1789] 1997: 406)

One consequence of the close link between nation and national language was the development of the ideal of the native speaker. The concept of the native speaker gains in power only if there is a powerful concept of language to be a native speaker of. Thus, Davies (2003) argues that the standardisation of language has consequences for those who speak it and those who want to learn it, as learners seek the target of native-like competence:

> The point being made is that in the standard language situation it may be that access to the native speaker is more frequently sought because it is the standard and because therefore it is in demand [...] (Davies 2003: 65)

He argues further that the process of standardising a language is at the same time also a process of defining who is a native speaker:

> [...] you are a native speaker if you speak the standard language [...]. The fact of explicitness makes a reality of what was before a concept: the process of standardising is an operational definition of the native speaker. (Davies 2003: 65)

Although it is obvious that even those speakers who claim to speak the standard language as their native language differ from each other and from the standard in various ways, the ideal of native – or perfect – command of a national standard language equips the speaker with high prestige and potentially devalues all other forms of competence possible in a language, particularly if the language in question is not the first language of the speaker but his/her second or foreign language (cf. Braunmüller 2007: 27). In a multilingual context, the ideal of the native speaker finds its echo in the idea of the *balanced bilingual*, an ideal which like the concept of the ideal native speaker is increasingly thought to be unattainable and ill-suited to serve as a target for second or foreign language acquisition.

The importance of language contact and multilingualism for the history of a language should be viewed in a more differentiated fashion as the shared history of many languages. The development of a standard variety constitutes only one aspect in the history of a language. Many seemingly modern phenomena are present in various stages or throughout the historical developments of a language, as exemplified in the case of English:

> In this period (450 to 1100) a number of phenomena existed that we might mistakenly think of as post-colonial and post-modern: English was fragmented, had multiple norms, varied considerably, was used in multilingual settings and evinced a fair degree of borrowing in contact with other languages. (Mesthrie and Bhatt 2008: 13)

With the growing interest in learning and teaching new forms of multilingual communication such as intercomprehension, research into processes and results of language contact gains in importance. An important prerequisite for the teaching of intercomprehension strategies is the assessment of the degree of similarity between the languages (see section 4.1. below). Furthermore, language history as a history of language contact and multilingualism will be increasingly in demand in foreign language teaching to overcome stereotypes of languages as separate, unrelated entities:

> Die Bedeutung der Ähnlichkeit und der Unterschiede von Sprachen muss durch die Einbeziehung auch von Etymologien häufiger betont werden [...].Wenn derartige Sprachvergleiche bereits in den schulischen Fremdsprachenunterricht einbezogen werden, lassen sich Lernstrategien entwickeln, die für das *lifelong learning* in diesem Bereich konstitutiv sind. (Ahrens 2004: 12).
> [The importance of similarities and differences between languages must be stressed by reference to etymologies [...]. If such language comparisons are part of foreign language teaching in schools, language learning strategies for lifelong learning can be developed which are fundamental in this area. *My translation, A.W.*]

3.2. Societal Multilingualism

Viewed as a societal phenomenon, multilingualism does not necessarily imply that all individual members of the group are multilingual, but that several languages are present within a certain society. Thus, a multilingual society can indeed be composed of or contain a sizeable proportion of multilingual individuals, but a society can also encompass several monolingual groups of speakers, with each group speaking a different language. Both scenarios can exist naturally or be enforced by government policy, and both scenarios can result in an official recognition as a multilingual society (Switzerland, Belgium, Canada). More common, however, are societies which include smaller groups of multilingual speakers such as immigrant or autochthonous minorities. As almost all European states belong to this category, recognition of minorities and their languages becomes increasingly necessary in the promotion of a unified yet culturally and linguistically diverse Europe. Changing patterns of migration, which are documented for the European context in several studies (Fürstenau, Gogolin and Yağmur 2003; Schroeder 2002; Extra and Yağmur 2003), lead to different patterns of language use. According to these studies, even immigrants belonging to small (linguistic) minority groups value and use both (all of) their languages and gain access to or establish educational facilities in their language of origin outside and often unrecognised by the official education system – as documented for Germany by Gogolin (2004: 58). One example of a newly emerging immigration pattern is what is known as transmigration (Gogolin 2004: 56–57), in which immigrants do not give up the ties with their country of origin, but establish a pattern of travelling backwards and forwards between their country of origin and their country of migration. Such dynamic migration patterns lead to an increase of multilingual practices in multilingual speech communities, whose members regard their multilingualism as part of their identity rather than a conflicting repertoire of majority and minority languages.

Generally, the situation of languages that are spoken by a minority of people within a society can be described according to two different types of status (Kremnitz 1990: 93; Auer and Wei 2007a: 10–11). According to the first type, the immigrant or 'new' minority languages (see e.g. Martin 2007), the minority group speaks a language that is an official or majority language in a different state and is thus influenced by this language, i.e. it has the support usually provided by media, codification and standardisation processes (dictionaries, grammars, application in the educational system) and can benefit either from close geographical proximity to the country in which the language is spoken by a majority, from a continuous stream of migrants from this country or from contact with the county of origin by transmigration as described above. In contrast, an autochthonous minority language (see e.g. Gardner-Chloros 2007) is confined to a certain small territory and often lacks the resources to establish media representation, codification, standardisation and the use of the language in the educational system.

However, despite the fact that multilingualism is nowadays generally seen as positive, many societies in the modern global world still find it difficult to accept multilingualism as a valuable part of, and not as a threat to, their identity. Language as part of culture plays a vital role in the socialisation process of individuals, but also in the self-concept of groups and their sense of unity. In second language acquisition research, it has been shown that success in learning a second language is related to the level of identification of the learner with the target language group (cf. Schumann 1978). A strong social cohesion within the source language group, its size and status in relation to other groups can impede successful identification with the target language group, thus making the establishment of multilingualism more difficult for individuals as well as whole groups. In many cases, such parameters are still in operation, leading to an often reluctant acceptance of minority languages by the majority group.

3.3. Individual Multilingualism

It is estimated that the majority of people are multilingual, and that monolingualism is the exception rather than the norm (Wei 2007: 5). Naturally, this estimate depends on the definition of multilingualism: the broader the scope of the definition, the more people will be characterised by it. Minimal definitions of multilingualism encompass people with very low competence in one of the languages involved, even if this is the only additional language to the native one, and the person is in fact minimally bilingual. Other definitions require active competence, competence in several, not just one, languages in addition to the mother tongue or even native-like control of all (usually two) languages (cf. Bloomfield 1933). However, as we have seen above, this maximal definition and resulting balanced bilingualism is difficult to maintain with an increasing number of languages learned.

Another aspect has to be considered when trying to describe an individual as multilingual: implicitly it is assumed that a language is a precisely definable system with clear boundaries, distinct and recognisably different from other languages. This impression is enforced by the existence and promotion of standard modern languages. However, there are researchers who claim that

> Jeder Mensch ist mehrsprachig. Neben der Hoch- und Amtssprache eines Landes gibt es seit jeher eine größere Zahl von Regionalsprachen, Lokalsprachen, Dialekten, Milieusprachen und individuellen oder gruppenbezogenen sprachlichen Besonderheiten, die von Bewohnern eines Landes gesprochen werden (Wiater 2006: 7)
> [Every person is multilingual. Besides the standard and official language of a country there have always been a considerable number of regional and local languages, sociolects and individual or group specific lects spoken by the inhabitants of a country. *My translation, A.W.*]

In this definition, local, social and functional varieties are accepted as systems the mastery of which results in multilingualism. Together with the claim that even monolinguals exhibit bilingual grammars at certain stages of L1 acquisition (cf. Tracy 2007) and the claim that the human being is equipped to learn more than one (and also more than two) languages from birth (cf. Meisel 2007), individual multilingualism is seen as something inherently human and natural (see also Cook, Ch. 5, this volume)

In a bilingual individual the two languages can be combined in many different ways: a person might indeed be almost equally proficient in both languages, all four language skills, and many domains of language use. More common is the dominance or preference of one language over the other, be it because the second language was acquired later in life, because the second language is the lesser used one or the less prestigious one, or because it is the less useful one in a particular context. Language combinations in a multilingual person are even more complex (cf. Cenoz 2000; Hufeisen and Jessner, Ch. 5, this volume).

An important aspect in relation to the concept of lifelong learning is the variable nature of multilingualism in the course of a person's life. Multilingual biographies rarely show a continuous and stable use of all languages acquired in a lifetime. With an increasing number of languages, their combination and their dominance can vary greatly in different phases of life. Phenomena such as transient multilingualism (Hoffmann 2001; Harding and Riley 1986), changes in proficiency in a certain language due to changing conditions in the environment of the speaker and language acquisition in later stages of life such as late adulthood not only shape the self-perception of the multilingual person (Elwert 1973; Clyne 1997), but also the needs with respect to language learning. Educational systems providing language teaching for learners of all ages have to take the dynamics of individual multilingualism as a biographical feature into account.

3.4. Institutional Multilingualism

The presence of multilingual practices in an institution can be the result of external circumstances, for instance when local authorities, hospitals, police stations and courts see themselves in the need to extend their services to non-native speakers of the official language. Often, these institutions develop their own solutions by employing native speakers of the minority language(s) as staff or avail themselves of the services of professional – and often non-professional – interpreters (Bührig and Meyer 2004).

International companies usually employ English as the company's lingua franca. However, linguistic diversity exists within international companies and teams, but in its implicitness constitutes a problematical factor rather than a resource. Many companies are slow in realising that language diversity is a problem in international contexts, and many are even slower in recognising a potential in such diverse language constellations. This is reflected in the treatment of language diversity – or rather the lack of it – in management literature:

> However, compared to cultural diversity in international teams, which has been widely studied [...], language diversity has received relatively little specific attention in the management literature. Consequently, the importance of the language factor is often overlooked, as it is generally treated as just one ingredient of culture, while the actual process of interpersonal interaction that takes place through language is usually left unexamined. (Henderson 2005: 66–67)

The dominance of English in international work teams has a considerable impact not only on issues of information transfer, but also on team building and socialisation processes. Participants are often unaware that the use of English as a lingua franca veils the underlying different communication patterns shaped by the cultures and languages of those using the lingua franca. Native speakers of English often do not acknowledge the fact that they are talking to non-native speakers of English with often diverging levels of competence and instead of accommodating to their interlocutor's communicative abilities use their native speaker status to exercise dominance and power. On the other hand, non-native speakers create a social coherence and solidarity by their shared status of lingua franca users, thereby excluding native speakers from such socialisation processes (cf. Henderson 2005: 77–78).

The opposite case to using a shared language, the use of a non-dominant language by parts of the company or team, excludes the other employees or members and is thus viewed negatively by those excluded. However, in situations where a dominant language other than the company's lingua franca could be used, for instance when the French or German branch of an international company has a local meeting, two options present themselves: the participants can either continue to use the lingua franca to show their solidarity with the company or because they have developed the use of the lingua franca at work as a habit, or they can use the local language (French or German). Both options are chosen, with the first apparently more frequent than the second, and both options have negative as well as positive potential. It is very rare for companies to make an explicit statement concerning their language policy, if at all present, and even rarer for companies to claim practised multilingualism as part of their company profile. It is obvious, however, that for relations with the local population and production sites, companies value multilingual expertise in their managers.

As an educational institution with a long history of providing foreign language teaching (see Mitchell, Ch. 4, this volume), the school could be expected to be the prominent place of actively promoted multilingualism. However, there is still ample evidence for negative attitudes towards multilingual language use in schools. Children with a multilingual language background are in most cases taught by monolingual teachers, who often sanction and thus suppress their pupils' multilingual practices (cf. Gogolin 2003). In many foreign language classes, the language to be learned is the medium of instruction, and other well-known teaching models also promote the monolingual use of the foreign language (CLIL, immersion programmes and others). Even, and perhaps surprisingly, the popular and expensive international schools have no explicit language policies promoting multilingualism.

Originally established as monolingual English schools for the children of English-speaking diplomats and other expatriate parents, the schools did not seem to regard it as their responsibility to acknowledge and tackle problems arising out of the multilinguality of the students. Only gradually do the schools realise that their clientele has changed (cf. Cummins 2008).

However, international schools are seen by many resident parents as the opportunity for their child to become multilingual, i.e. competent in English as well as their mother tongue and thus adequately prepared for a global future. International schools are only beginning to acknowledge that they might have to provide support for those children who do not have an active command of English at the time of entering the school:

> Many English-medium international schools are beginning to move away from unquestioned use of English as the only legitimate language of instruction and interaction within the school. Gradually, other languages are being acknowledged as important cognitive tools, as crucial channels of communication within the family, and as resources for communication and cooperation within our global community. However, for many schools this journey is just beginning and some have not even realised the dysfunctional and discriminatory nature of 'education as usual'. (Cummins 2008: xi)

Thus, many international schools are in effect still monolingual schools facing the same problems like other monolingual schools, but because their language of education and administration is a desired prestige language, the fact that they do not actively promote multilingualism is often overlooked. There is the demand that international schools must move away from conformity and homogeneity to diversity, and to use this diversity as a resource. In companies and schools and no doubt other institutional forms, the active use of more than one language as a valued multilingual strategy is still an innovation.

3.5. Multilingualism in discourse

Turning to multilingualism as it manifests itself as a feature of communication or, more specifically, of a conversation, again the starting point is a broad definition of multilingual communication:

> Generally speaking, 'multilingual communication' can be characterised by the following features:
> - The use of several languages for the common purposes of participants
> - Multilingual individuals who use language(s) to realise these purposes
> - The different language systems which interact for these purposes
> - Multilingual communication structures, whose purposes make individuals use several languages. (House and Rehbein 2004: 1)

Those general features of multilingual communication can manifest themselves in various forms in actual conversation. First of all, it is possible that some of the languages involved in a conversation play a latent role rather than actually being used on the surface of the conversation. An example of such communication would be lingua franca communication, arising when interactants with different mother tongues choose to converse in a common language that is not the mother tongue for any of them (Seidlhofer 2007; Knapp and Meierkord

2002). Depending on the degree of competence in the common language, interactants might have to or choose to draw on their other languages to facilitate conversation, for instance by inserting lexical items, transferring meaning or grammatical structures from their first language into the lingua franca, or their first language is noticeable as an accent. Such phenomena are usually referred to as interference, and are by no means irrelevant or accidental. On the contrary, the systematic and persistent influence of mother tongues on the lingua franca may lead eventually to the establishment of new varieties of this lingua franca. This development is particularly significant in the case of English:

> Mutual negotiation results in a shared variety which is a second language for some and a first language, incorporating erstwhile L2-transfer features, for others. (Schneider 2007: 45).

Very similar to and often equated with lingua franca communication is communication between a native speaker and a non-native speaker in a respective language. This type of conversation is also referred to as learner discourse, exolingual communication (Lüdi 1987; Dausendschön-Gay, Gülich and Krafft 1995) or NS-NNS (native speaker-non-native speaker) communication. Research on NS-NNS communication focuses mainly on the particular strategies used by the interactants to create meaning (Long 1983a+b; Gass 2003; Gass and Varonis 1994) and the effect of such conversation on the learning process of the non-native speaker. Of special interest are also the linguistic and interactional modifications made by the native speaker to adjust to the perceived level of competence of the non-native speaker (e.g. *foreigner talk*, Hinnenkamp 1982; Jakovidou 1993).

However, despite the impact of individuals' other languages on the conversation, the communication types described above share the feature of a single language used for communication by the interactants. When two languages are actively used in the same conversation, again different forms and constellations emerge. If both interlocutors possess sufficient receptive skills in the other person's language, they can use their own language respectively (receptive multilingualism, cf Zeevaert 2007). A very common phenomenon of conversations among multilinguals with active knowledge in the same languages is code-switching. Having been viewed in earlier research by purists as contamination of the language, by psychologists as evidence of poor competence in either language or as interference and by teachers as mistakes, code-switching has received intensive attention in more recent studies, which have shown it to be a highly complex and creative feature of multilingual conversation and a unique competence of multilingual individuals (Auer 1998; Heller 1988 and many others). However, with respect to the (foreign language) classroom, such practices are often still viewed as undesirable (Gogolin 2003) and are subject to negative comments or even sanctions. This is particularly critical if the sanctions are aimed at multilingual children who come to the monolingual classroom and experience their natural code-switching abilities as damaging (Gogolin 2003), often because their teacher is not bilingual (Meißner 2004).

Another way of establishing multilingual discourse is to interpret from one language into the other(s). Depending on the situation, this can be and is done to various levels of professionalism: in highly formalised situations such as the court of law or a political meeting, trained professional interpreters take on this highly specialised task of transferring the utterances of one person in language X into language Y for the benefit of the audience, paying great attention to accuracy and fidelity and keeping to a pre-established, fairly rigid turn-taking structure (Knapp and Knapp-Potthoff 1985; Knapp-Potthoff and Knapp 1986). As situations become more informal, so do the forms of interpreting used in them, ranging from using semi- or unprofessional multilinguals as interpreters (e.g., members of a family, native speakers of minority languages, cf. Wadensjö 1998; Carr et al. 1997) down to spontaneous and only very loosely structured forms of everyday interpreting (*interactional translation*, Wilton 2009). Thus, ad-hoc interpreting is one form of discourse many multilinguals might find themselves in.

All the above types of multilingual discourse and the conversational practices used in them can be and are observed, described and evaluated. An interesting observation is made by Hoffmann (1991: 12–13), who states that in many studies on trilinguals, including her own, conversational and speech production data rarely show the use of all three languages of the individual, even when two trilinguals with the same language combinations interact with each other. This might be due to the particular type of trilinguals investigated in the studies, but recent studies on multilingual codeswitching (Stavans and Swisher 2006; Pittman 2008) support this observation. Such a "tendency for bidirectionality involving the dominant language" (Hoffmann 1991: 13) needs to be investigated further as a possible unique feature of multilingual conversation.

4. Contributions of Applied Linguistics

As seen from the above discussion, Applied Linguistics tackles a large and varied number of issues related to multilingualism, its characteristics and manifestations. For this section, two topics of current relevance have been selected to illustrate the insights and impact that research in AL can have on current issues in multilingualism.

4.1. Receptive Multilingualism

Leading researchers in the field of receptive multilingualism claim that it has not yet established itself as an independent research area:

> Receptive multilingualism cannot (yet) be regarded as an established field within research on multilingualism, even though the economic and political developments, usually denoted as globalisation, have led to a considerable increase in international communication. In fact, it has become clear, that communicative challenges connected to these developments are hardly solvable using traditional concepts of multilingualism. Therefore, new concepts have to be developed and discussed. (Zeevaert and ten Thije 2007: 1)

Braunmüller (2007: 27–28) attributes the low prestige of receptive multilingualism to the adherence to an ideal of native-like command of a language. Indeed, the idea persists that the command of a language requires the active application of productive skills. The sole use of receptive skills is still seen as imcomplete and insufficient. For example, Bausch argues that the model of receptive multilingualism does not meet the basic human need to "Sprachen nicht nur allein verstehend, sondern vor allem auch angemessen produzierend erwerben, lernen und gebrauchen zu wollen" (1989: 36, quoted in Scherfer 2002: 98 [acquire, learn and use languages not only for understanding, but above all for producing adequately. *My translation, A.W.*]). Others argue that the mastery of receptive skills does enable a person to act in a multilingual environment, because

> [...] the concept of receptive multilingualism requires more than minimal linguistic knowledge, and is neither a simple pidgin nor incomplete language learning. Instead, it represents the acquisition of receptive competencies in more than one given target language, and at the same time includes a set of specific foreign language learning strategies on the side of the hearer in receptive multilingualism. (Zeevaert and ten Thije 2007: 3–4)

Thus, receptive multilingualism requires active participation of the hearer, and negotiation skills of all interactants when the optimal form of conversation for mutual understanding has to be negotiated among the participants. An easy answer to the problem of the diverse language backgrounds of interactants could be the use of one lingua franca as described in section 3.5. above. This role is usually filled by English, and it is this dominance that leads researchers to propose alternative models of communication which do not eliminate, but exploit the linguistic diversity present in a certain area. It is therefore not surprising that receptive multilingualism is emerging as a field particularly applicable to the European context, stressing three main points:

- Multilingualism is a social phenomenon deeply embedded in European language history.

– Multilingual understanding does not necessarily require near-native language competency.
– English as a *lingua franca* is not the one and only solution for interlingual communication. (Zeevaert and ten Thije 2007: 3–4)

A feature that significantly shapes the kind of multilingual discourse chosen in a particular situation is the relationship between the languages involved. As Zeevaert (2007: 105, 110) explains, receptive multilingual communication can occur between speakers of remotely related or unrelated languages and between speakers of closely related languages. Typological proximity enables interactants to recognise features of the languages involved as similar, thus enabling and enhancing mutual understanding on the basis of linguistic relationships. Klein and Stegmann (2000) base their model of receptive reading and listening competence (*Sieben Siebe*, *Seven Sieves*) on the close relationship between Romance languages in Europe and develop strategies of systematic inference that serve as sieves to achieve understanding of a text. This method is known as intercomprehension, and is devised for teaching intercomprehension skills in a European context. Thus, the Sieben Siebe-model is currently being extended to the other two large language groups present in Europe, the Germanic and the Slavic languages, including the development of teaching materials and online courses (http://www.eurocomprehension.info/).

4.2. Multilingualism and attitudes

As multilingualism becomes a more and more public issue and thus permeates society as a relevant aspect of everyday life, attitudes towards multilingualism gain force. The present Commissioner for Multilingualism in the European Union, Leonard Orban, explicitly invites Europeans to voice their opinions on and experiences with multilingualism in the internet forum on his website. The practice of sharing one's opinion with others has recently been facilitated by the technical developments of the internet, providing chatrooms and in particular forums addressing almost any topic.

Today, the 'official', i.e. the politically correct and scientifically and academically supported view of multilingualism, is positive. In studies, policies and statements the overall message is the inevitability and desirability of mutliligualism for societies as well as individuals in a globalised future.

Seen from today's perspective, early studies attributing detrimental effects of bilingualism on intelligence and identity building of individuals were flawed in their methodology and hypotheses. Since then, a vast number of studies have shown bilingualism to be an enrichment for individuals – as well as societies – in many respects (see section 2.1.). This is not to deny that there are problems with bilingualism or multilingualism. However, research has also shown that many problems linked with multilingualism are not caused by the fact that more than one language is involved in the development of an individual or the communication practices of a society, but by the way in which multilingualism is viewed, implemented or restricted. Thus, it is those external factors that give rise to problems connected with multilingualism and not multilingualism itself.

Attitudes among the general public towards multilingualism constitute such an external factor. In the domain of everyday life the positive picture painted of multilingualism is slightly different, partly because stereotypes and prejudices prevail and partly because people form opinions on the basis of their own everyday experiences, and those might indeed be negative. Multilingual speakers of low prestige languages often have to face accusations of not being able to speak any language properly, of being late starters in language acquisition generally, of having split or unstable personalities and the like. Phenomena of language mixing such as codeswitching are seen as evidence of poor linguistic competence. If, however, two or more prestigious languages are involved, negative attitudes often turn into positive ones, which can be just as misguided: bi(multi)lingual children are more intelligent, learn their additional languages without effort, and are generally advantaged in later life. Codeswitching is then seen as an enviable skill.

Surprisingly, the negative effects thought to be connected with speaking two languages are now transferred to multilingualism. Even among those who have come to accept that bilingualism is on the whole a good thing, especially if it is introduced at a very early age (BFLA) and language separation is strictly adhered to (one-parent, one-language approach), some people still hold on to the belief that there must be a limit to the number of languages a human mind can master. This concern was already raised in connection with bilingualism, but is now transferred to tri- or multilingualism. People now believe that this limit does not lie between the first and the second, but between the second and third language: frequently one encounters such statements as "two languages are ok, three are too many", in particular if acquired simultaneously:

> Drei Sprachen finde ich persönlich etwas viel. 2 Sprachen sind (richtig gelernt) sicher eine Bereicherung. (http://www.elternforen.com/thema28931.htm)
> [Personally I think that three languages are too many. Two languages (learned properly) are definitely an enrichment, *My translation, A.W.*]

The more languages are involved, the more threatening the idea of confusion becomes: to many people the – simultaneous – acquisition of more than two languages will inevitably result in chaos, undesirable language mixing and inadequate language competence. Thus, people might find themselves in a truly multilingual environment and worry about its effect on their children:

> [...] Ich bin 32 Jahre, verheitatet mit einem Uruguayer, wir leben in Brasilien und haben einen einjährigen Sohn. Es wird viel über Zweisprachigkeit diskutiert, aber hier haben wir es leider mit 4 Sprachen zu tun: Ich spreche Deutsch mit unserem

> Sohn, mein Mann Spanisch, das wären unsere Muttersprachen. Dann sprechen mein Mann und ich Englisch miteinander und hier in Brasilien wird Portugiesisch gesprochen. das mein Sohn bald im Kindergarten lernen wird. Ist das nicht irgendwie zuviel??? Hat jemand mal davon gehört, ob sowas funktioniert? Sicher wäre es gut, die Sprachen zu reduzieren, aber im Moment weiß ich nicht wie [...] (http://www.elternforen.com/thema33662.htm)
> [[...] I am 32 years old, married to a Uruguayan, we live in Brazil and our son is one year old. There is much discussion on bilingualism, but unfortunately here we are faced with four languages: I speak German to our son, my husband Spanish, these are our mother tongues. My husband and I speak English to each other, and here in Brazil the language is Portuguese, which my son will learn soon in the kindergarten. Isn't that somehow too much??? Has somebody got an idea if this works? I'm sure it would be good to reduce the number of languages, but at the moment I don't know how [...], *My translation, A.W.*]

This quotation illustrates the potential for Applied Linguistics to take such individual perspectives seriously and use them as a staring point for research: the mother in the quotation above is aware of a lively public discussion of bilingualism, but does not find it useful to help her in her complex multilingual situation. Instead, she appeals to other parents and gets helpful advice and encouragement on the basis of their personal experiences. The growing academic interest in researching such complex forms of multilingualism is apparently matched by a public demand for research-based insights and guidelines on how to implement multilingualism effectively in everyday life. Thus, it is imperative that Applied Linguistics research follows the example of Leonard Orban and takes note of such opinions:

> [...] the Multilingualism Forum should be a discussion forum for you – and not just an exchange between you and me. I will certainly take your opinions on board when building my new strategy for multilingualism later this year. (http://forums.ec.europa.eu/multilingualism/en/)

Furthermore, Applied Linguistics research must continue to present a convincing force against counterproductive prejudices and stereotypes, which, as illustrated above, can themselves generate new forms.

In particular the prestige of languages strongly affects the attitudes towards multilingualism and also strongly affects the practices and policies concerning multilingualism. In a recent public discussion about the promotion of Turkish for children with a Turkish language background in German schools, one of the most frequent arguments brought up against this idea was the fact that Turkish is not a globally relevant language and therefore not important. If the idea that only a globally relevant language is worth being included in the curriculum plays a role in language planning and education, the individual speaker will be left alone with the difficulties and problems connected with maintaining a native language without the support of an educational system (see also Mitchell, Ch. 4, this volume).

5. Research perspectives

Applied Linguistics worldwide covers an impressively diverse range of topics. With respect to multilingualism and foreign language learning, many aspects are addressed and investigated. It is important to encourage more research in these areas and also to mention some desiderata. Thus, Applied Linguistics should

– define its concern more prominently as research on multilingualism in all its manifestations, i.e. recognise forms such as intercomprehension and receptive multilingualism as part of its focus, thereby trying to sort out terminological inconsistencies and biases wherever possible;

– promote the recognition of multilingualism as a multi-faceted and individual phenomenon which cannot be subsumed under a few general demands, standards and regulations among public bodies, polititians, educationalists and the general public. This includes avoiding unreflected views of its negative, but also of its positive effects.

– continue and enforce the investigation of multilingual biographies and multilingualism as a lifelong process: not only the initial acquisition process, but also the maintenance of multilingualism throughout life is an important aspect in view of the demand for 'lifelong learning'.

– continue and enforce research into multiliteracy and other related aspects;

– encourage research on the historical development and relationships of languages and its application in the teaching of multilingualism.

– promote a broad perspective of the teaching of foreign languages seen in the context of societal and political developments, as they influence if not determine the way languages are taught and which languages are taught and for what reason, thereby affecting all levels of the educational system (research, didactic methodology, organisation, educational policy, Gogolin 2004: 55).

Notes

1 For a comprehensive up-do-date discussion of research on second language acquisition see Ellis (2008).

2 Diagonal and vertical refer to types of multilingualism which combine knowledge of (a) standard language(s) and (a) non-standard variety(ies), either unrelated (diagonal) or related (vertical).

3 The well-know *Stammbaumtheorie* was developed by August Schleicher in the middle of the 19th century (Schleicher [1848/1850] 1983). This theory was strongly influenced by the natural sciences and thus postulated genetic relationship and growth and death of languages in analogy to living organisms:

> Der systematische Theil der Sprachforschung [...] hat [...] eine unverkennbare Ähnlichkeit mit den Naturwissenschaften. Diess stellt sich namentlich bei der Eintheilung der Sprachen in Klassen heraus. Der ganze Habitus einer Sprachenfamilie lässt

sich unter gewisse Geschtspunkte bringen, wie der einer Pflanzen- oder Thierfamilie. (Schleicher 1983: 28)

4 In this article, the terms 'acquisition' and 'learning' are used as synonyms and in a general sense covering both natural and formal processes unless otherwise indicated.

References

Adams, Jim N. and Simon Swain
2002 Introduction. In: Jim N. Adams, Mark Janse and Simon Swain (eds.), *Bilingualism in Ancient Society. Language Contact and the Written Text*, 1–20. Oxford: Oxford University Press.

Ahrens, Rüdiger
2004 Mehrsprachigkeit als Bildungsziel. In: Bausch, Königs and Krumm (eds.): 9–15.

Anstatt, Tanja (ed.)
2007 *Mehrsprachigkeit bei Kindern und Erwachsenen*. Tübingen: Attempto.

Auer, Peter (ed.)
1998 *Code-Switching in Conversation*. London: Routledge.

Auer, Peter and Li Wei
2007a Introduction: Multilingualism as a problem? Monolingualism as a problem? In: Auer and Wei (eds.): 1–12.

Auer, Peter and Li Wei (eds.)
2007b *Handbook of Multilingualism and Multilingual Communication*. Berlin/New York: Mouton de Gruyter.

Baker, Colin
1993 *Foundations of Bilingual Education and Bilingualism*. Clevedon: Multilingual Matters.

Baker, Colin and Sylvia Prys Jones
1998 *Encyclopedia of Bilingualism and Bilingual Education*. Clevedon: Multilingual Matters.

Bausch, Karl-Richard
1989 Thesen für den Fremdsprachenunterricht an unseren Schulen nach 1992. In: Eberhard Kleinschmidt (ed.), *Fremdsprachenunterricht zwischen Sprachenpolitik und Praxis*, 34–40. Tübingen: Narr.

Bausch, Karl-Richard, Frank G. Königs and Hans-Jürgen Krumm (eds.)
2004 *Mehrsprachigkeit im Fokus*. Tübingen: Narr.

Bertrand, Yves and Herbert Christ
1990 Vorschläge für einen erweiterten Fremdsprachenunterricht. *Neusprachliche Mitteilungen* 43: 208–213.

Bialystok, Ellen
2008 Cognitive effects of bilingualism across the lifespan. In: Harvey Chan, Heather Jacob and Enkeleida Kapia (eds.), *BUCLD 32: Proceedings of the 32nd Annual Boston University Conference on Language Development*, 1–15. Boston: Cascadilla Press.

Bloomfield, Leonard
1933 *Language*. New York: Holt.

Braunmüller, Kurt
2007 Receptive multilingualism in Northern Europe in the Middle Ages: A description of a scenario. In *Receptive Multilingualism*, Ludger Zeevaert and Jan D. ten Thije (eds.), 25–47. Amsterdam/Philadelphia: John Benjamins.

Bührig, Kristin and Bernd Meyer
2004 Ad-hoc interpreting and achievement of communicative purposes in doctor-patient-communication. In: Juliane House and Jochen Rehbein (eds.), *Multilingual Communication*, 43–62. Amsterdam/Philadelphia: Benjamins.

Carr, Silvana E., Roda Roberts, Aideen Dufour, and Dini Steyn (eds.)
1997 *The Critical Link: Interpreters in the Community. Papers from the First International Conference on Interpreting in Legal, Health and Social Service Settings. Geneva Park, Canada, June 1–4, 1995*. Amsterdam: John Benjamins.

Cenoz, Jasone
2000 Research on multilingual acquisition. In: Cenoz and Jessner (eds.): 39–53.

Cenoz, Jasone
2003 The additive effect of bilingualism on third language acquisition: A review. *The International Journal of Bilingualism* 7 (1): 71–88.

Cenoz, Jasone, Britta Hufeisen and Ulrike Jessner (eds.)
2001a *Looking beyond Second Language Acquisition: Studies in Tri- and Multilingualism*. Tübingen: Stauffenburg.

Cenoz, Jasone, Britta Hufeisen and Ulrike Jessner (eds.)
2001b *Crosslinguistic Influence in Third Language Acquisition: Psycholinguistic Perspectives*. Clevedon: Multilingual Matters.

Cenoz, Jasone and Ulrike Jessner (eds.)
2000 *English in Europe: The Acquisition of a Third Language*. Clevedon: Multilingual Matters.

Clyne, Michael
1997 Some of the Things Trilinguals Do. *International Journal of Bilingualism* 1:2, 95–116.

Cook, Vivian
1992 Evidence for multicompetence. *Language Learning* 42 (4): 557–592.

Cummins, Jim
2008 Foreword. In: Eithne Gallagher, *Equal Rights to the Curriculum*, x–xii. Clevedon: Multilingual Matters.

Dausendschön-Gay, Ulrich, Elisabeth Gülich and Ulrich Krafft
1995 Exolinguale Kommunikation. In: Reinhard Fiehler and Dieter Metzing (eds.), *Untersuchungen zur Kommunikationsstruktur*, 85–117. Bielefeld: Aisthesis.

Davies, Alan
2003 *The Native Speaker: Myth and Reality*. Clevedon et al.: Multilingual Matters.

De Angelis, Gessica
2007 *Third or Additional Language Acquisition*. Clevedon et al.: Multilingual Matters.

De Houwer, Annick
2006 Bilingual language development: Early years. In: Keith Brown (ed.-in-chief), *Encyclopedia of Language and Linguistics*, 2nd edition, vol. 1, 780–786. Oxford: Elsevier.

De Houwer, Annick
2009 *Bilingual First Language Acquisition.* Clevendon: Multilingual Matters.

Dewaele, Jean-Marc
2007 Becoming bi- or multi-lingual in later life. In: Auer and Wei (eds.): 101–130.

Ellis, Rod
1997 *Second Language Acquisition.* Oxford: Oxford University Press.

Ellis, Rod
2008 *The Study of Second Language Acquisition.* 2nd edition. Oxford: Oxford University Press.

Elwert, Theodor
1973 *Das zweisprachige Individuum und andere Aufsätze zur romanischen und allgemeinen Sprachwissenschaft.* Wiesbaden: Steiner.

Extra, Guus and Kutlay Yagmur (eds.)
2004 *Urban Multilingualism in Europe: Immigrant Minority Languages at Home and School.* Clevedon et al.: Multilingual Matters.

Fürstenau, Sara, Ingrid Gogolin and Kutlay Yagmur (eds.)
2003 *Mehrsprachigkeit in Hamburg: Ergebnisse einer Sprachenerhebung an den Grundschulen in Hamburg.* Münster / Berlin: Waxmann.

García, Ofelia, Lesley Baertlett and JoAnne Kleifgen
2007 From biliteracies to pluriliteracies. In: Auer and Wei (eds.): 207–228.

Gardner-Chloros, Penelope
2007 Multilingualism of autochthonous minorities. In: Auer and Wei (eds.): 469–491.

Gardt, Andreas
1999 *Geschichte der Sprachwissenschaft in Deutschland.* Berlin/New York: Walter de Gruyter.

Gass, Susan
2003 Input and interaction. In: Catherine Doughty and Michael Long (ed.), *The Handbook of Second Language Acquisition*, 224–255. Malden, Mass.: Blackwell.

Gass, Susan and Evangeline Varonis
1994 Input, interaction, and second language production. *Studies in Second Language Acquisition* 16 (3): 283–302.

Gogolin, Ingrid
2003 "Das ist doch kein gutes Deutsch!" – Über Vorstellungen von "guter" Sprache und ihren Einfluss auf Mehrsprachigkeit. In: Ines De Florio-Hansen and Adelheid Hu (eds.), *Plurilingualität und Identität. Zur Selbst- und Fremdwahrnehmung mehrsprachiger Menschen*, 59–71. Tübingen: Stauffenburg.

Gogolin, Ingrid
2004 Lebensweltliche Mehrsprachigkeit. In: Bausch, Königs and Krumm (eds.): 55–61.

Graddol, David
2006 *English Next.* Londo: British Council.

Harding, Edith and Philip Riley
1986 *The Bilingual Family.* Cambridge: Cambridge University Press.

Hinnenkamp, Volker
1982 *Foreigner Talk und Tarzanisch: eine vergleichende Studie über die Sprechweise gegenüber Ausländern am Beispiel des Deutschen und des Türkischen.* Hamburg: Buske.

Heller, Monica (ed.)
1988 *Codeswitching: Anthropological and Sociolinguistic Perspectives.* Berlin: Mouton de Gruyter.

Henderson, Jane Kassis
2005 Language diversity in international management teams. *International Studies of Management and Organization* 35 (1): 66–82.

Hoffmann, Charlotte
1985 Language acquisition in two trilingual children. *Journal of Multilingual and Multicultural Development* 6 (6): 479–495.

Hoffmann, Charlotte
2001 Towards a description of trilingual competence. *International Journal of Bilingualism* 5 (1): 11–17.

Hoffmann, Charlotte and Jehannes Ytsma (eds.)
2003 *Trilingualism in Family, School and Community.* Clevedon: Multilingual Matters.

House, Juliane and Jochen Rehbein
2004 What is 'multilingual communication'? In *Multilingual communication,* Juliane House and Jochen Rehbein (eds.), 1–17, Amsterdam/Philadelphia: John Benjamins.

Jakovidou, Athanasia
1993 *Funktion und Variation im Foreigner Talk.* Tübingen: Narr.

Jessner, Ulrike
2006 *Linguistic Awareness in Multilinguals: English as a Third Language.* Edinburgh: Edinburgh University Press.

Jørgensen, J. Normann
2008 Polylingual languaging around and among children and adolescents. *International Journal of Multilingualism* 5 (3): 161–176.

Jørgensen, J. Normann and Pia Quist
2007 Bilingual children in monolingual schools. In: Auer and Wei (eds.): 155–173.

Kachru, Braj
1992 Teaching world Englishes. In: Braj Kachru (ed.), *The other Tongue: English across Cultures,* 355–366. Urbana: University of Illinois Press.

Klein, Horst G. and Tilbert D. Stegmann
2000 *EurocomRom, Die Sieben Siebe.* Aachen: Shaker.

Knapp, Karlfried and Annelie Knapp-Potthoff
1985 Sprachmittlertätigkeit in der interkulturellen Kommunikation. In: Jochen Rehbein (ed.), *Interkulturelle Kommunikation,* 450–464. Tübingen: Narr.

Knapp, Karlfried and Christiane Meierkord (eds.)
2002 *Aspects of Lingua Franca Communication.* Frankfurt: Lang.

Knapp-Potthoff, Annelie and Karlfried Knapp
1986 Interweaving two discourses – The difficult task of the non-professional interpreter. In: Juliane House and Shoshana Blum-Kulka (eds.), *Interlingual and Intercultural Communication. Discourse and Cognition in Translation and Second Language Acquisition Studies*, 151–169. Tübingen: Narr.

Krashen, Stephen
1986 *The Input Hypothesis: Issues and Implications*. London: Longman.

Kremnitz, Georg
1990 *Gesellschaftliche Mehrsprachigkeit*. Wien: Braumüller.

Long, Michael
1983a Linguistic and conversational adjustment to non-native speakers. *Studies in Second Language Acquisition* 5 (2): 177–193.

Long, Michael
1983b Native speaker/non-native speaker conversation and the negotiation of comprehensible input. *Applied Linguistics* 4 (2): 126–141.

Lüdi, Georges
1987 Exolinguale Konversation und mehrsprachige Rede. Untersuchungen zur Kommunikation in Sprachkontaktsituationen. In: Els Oksaar (ed.), *Soziokulturelle Perspektiven von Mehrsprachigkeit und Spracherwerb*, 76–100. Tübingen: Narr.

Lüdi, Georges
1995 Eléments pour une histoire du plurilinguisme. Polyglossie et pratiques plurilingues chez les Romains. In: Antoni M. Badia i Margarit (ed.), *Estudis de Lingüística i Filologia*, 553–564. Barcelona: Publicacions de l'Abadia de Montserrat.

Lüdi, Georges
2002 Traces de contacts linguistiques et de plurilinguisme vécu dans les archives de l'ancien Évêché de Bâle entre 1450 et 1550. In: Jean-Claude Rebetez, *La Donation de 999 et l'Histoire Médiévale de l'Ancien Évêché de Bâle*, 455–474. Porrentruy: Fondations des Archives de l'ancien Évêché de Bâle.

Lüdi, Georges
2004 Pour une linguistique de la compétence du locuteur plurilingue. *Revue Française de Linguistique Appliquée* 10 (2): 125–135.

Martin, Peter
2007 Multilingualism of new minorities (in migratory contexts). In: Auer and Wei (eds.): 493–507.

Meisel, Jürgen
2007 Mehrsprachigkeit in der frühen Kindheit: Zur Rolle des Alters bei Erwerbsbeginn. In *Mehrsprachigkeit bei Kindern und Erwachsenen*. Tanja Anstatt (ed.), 93–113. Tübingen: Attempto.

Meißner, Franz-Joseph
2004 Sprachenlernen zusammendenken. Aufhören, Rücken an Rücken zu forschen, zu planen, zu lehren und zu lernen. In: Bausch, Königs and Krumm (eds.): 148–162.

Meißner, Franz-Joseph and Isle Picaper (eds.)
2003 *Mehrsprachigkeitsdidaktik zwischen Frankreich, Belgien und Deutschland = La Didactique du Plurilinguisme entre la France, la Belgique et l'Allemagne*. Tübingen: Narr.

Mesthrie, Rajend
2006 World Englishes and the multilingual history of English. *World Englishes* 25 (3/4): 381–390.

Mesthrie, Rajend and Rakesh M. Bhatt
2008 *World Englishes. The Study of New Linguistic Varieties.* Cambridge: Cambridge University Press.

Møller, Janus Spindler
2008 Polylingual performance among Turkish-Danes in late-modern Copenhagen. *International Journal of Multilingualism* 5:3, 217–236.

Moyer, Melissa
2008 Research as Practice: Linking Theory, Method and Data. In *The Blackwell Guide to Research Methods in Bilingualism and Multilingualism,* Li Wei and Melissa G. Moyer (eds.), 18–31. Malden/Oxford/Victoria: Blackwell Publishing.

Pittman, Julia
2008 Bilingual and trilingual codeswitching between Hungarian, Romanian and English in the speech of two Transylvanians living in North America. *International Journal of Multilingualism* 5 (2): 122–139.

Quist, Pia and J. Normann Jørgensen
2007 Crossing – negotiating social boundaries. In: Auer and Wei (eds.): 371–389.

Ribbert, Anne and Jan ten Thije
2007 Receptive multilingualism in Dutch-German intercultural team cooperation. In: ten Thije and Zeervaert (eds.): 73–101.

Rivera, Klaudia and Ana Huerta-Macías
2007 *Adult Biliteracy.* London: Routledge.

Saville-Troike, Muriel
2006 *Introducing Second Language Acquisition.* Cambridge: Cambridge University Press.

Scherfer, Peter
2002 Was ist und wie erlernt man Interkomprehension? In: Gerhard Kischel (ed.), *EuroCom Mehrsprachiges Europa durch Interkomprehension in Sprachfamilien*, 87–101. Hagen: Fernuniversität.

Schleicher, August
[1848/1850] 1983 Sprachvergleichende Untersuchungen. Frankfurt a. M.: Minerva.

Schneider, Edgar W.
2007 *Postcolonial English: Varieties Around the World.* Cambridge: Cambridge University Press.

Schroeder, Joachim
2002 Bildung im geteilten Raum. Schulentwicklungen unter Bedingungen von Einwanderung und Verarmung. Münster: Waxmann.

Schumann, John
1978 *The Pidginization Process: A Model for Second Language Acquisition.* Rowley, Mass.: Newbury House.

Seidlhofer, Barbara
2007 Common property: English as a lingua franca in Europe. In: Jim Cummins and Chris Davison (eds.), *Handbook of English Language Teaching*, 137–154. New York: Springer.

Stavans, Anat and Virginia Swisher
2006 Language switching as a window on trilingual acquisition. *International Journal of Multilingualism* 3 (3): 193–220.
ten Thije, Jan and Ludger Zeervaert (eds.)
2007 *Receptive Multilingualism*. Amsterdam: John Benjamins.
Tracy, Rosemarie
2007 Wie viele Sprachen passen in einen Kopf? In: Anstatt (ed.): 69–92.
Wadensjö, Cecilia
1998 *Interpreting as Interaction*. London/New York: Addison Wesley Longman.
Webster, Noah
[1789] 1997 *Dissertations on the English Language*. London: Routledge/Thoemmes Press.
Wei, Li
2007 Dimensions of bilingualism. In: Li Wei (ed.), *The Bilingualism Reader*, 3–24. London/New York: Routledge.
Wei, Li
2008 Research perspectives on bilingualism and multilingualism. In: Li Wei and Melissa G. Moyer (eds.), *The Blackwell Guide to Research Methods in Bilingualism and Multilingualism*, 3–17. Malden/Oxford/Victoria: Blackwell Publishing.
Wiater, Werner
2006 Vorwort. In: Werner Wiater (ed.), *Didaktik der Mehrsprachigkeit*, 7–9. München: Ernst Vögel.
Wilton, Antje
2009 *Lachen ohne Grenzen*. München: Iudicium.
Zeervaert, Ludger
2007 Receptive multilingualism and inter-Scandinavian semicommunication. In: ten Thije and Zeervaert (eds.): 103–135.
Zeervaert, Ludger and Jan ten Thije
2007 Introduction. In: ten Thije and Zeervaert (eds.): 1–21.

http://en.wikipedia.org/wiki/Polyglot_(person), 18. 12. 2008.
http://www.eurocomprehension.info/, 13. 02. 2009
http://www.polyglot.co.uk, 04. 11. 2008
http://forums.ec.europa.eu/multilingualism/en/, 02. 02. 2009
http://www.coe.int/T/DG4/Linguistic/Source/Framework_EN.pdf, 02. 09. 2009
http://ec.europa.eu/education/doc/official/keydoc/actlang/act_lang_en.pdf
http://ec.europa.eu/education/languages/eu-language-policy/index_en.htm, 15. 12. 2008
http://www.elternforen.com/thema28931.htm
http://www.elternforen.com/thema33662.htm

Recommended readings

Auer, Peter and Li Wei (eds.)
2007b *Handbook of Multilingualism and Multilingual Communication.* Berlin/New York: Mouton de Gruyter.

Baker, Colin and Sylvia Prys Jones
1998 *Encyclopedia of Bilingualism and Bilingual Education.* Clevedon: Multilingual Matters.

Hoffmann, Charlotte and Jehannes Ytsma (eds.)
2003 *Trilingualism in Family, School and Community.* Clevedon: Multilingual Matters.

ten Thije, Jan and Ludger Zeervaert (eds.)
2007 *Receptive Multilingualism.* Amsterdam: John Benjamins.

Wei, Li (ed.)
2007 *The Bilingualism Reader.* London/New York: Routledge.

Wei, Li
2008 Research perspectives on bilingualism and multilingualism. In: Li Wei and Melissa G. Moyer (eds.), *The Blackwell Guide to Research Methods in Bilingualism and Multilingualism*, 3–17. Malden/Oxford/Victoria: Blackwell Publishing.

4. Foreign language teaching and educational policy

Rosamond Mitchell

1. Introduction

This chapter sets out to review key trends in current policies and practices in foreign language education in school settings. Language education is a complex process, ranging from instruction in literacy practices directly reflecting the mother tongue spoken in the child's home, through instruction in 'high' varieties related to the home language variety, to instruction in quite unrelated varieties. In the contemporary world, the recipients of language education in a single setting may themselves be a homogeneous or heterogeneous group, in terms of their language and ethnic backgrounds. The language(s) spoken in the home may be part of the cultural heritage of autochthonous minorities, or may be languages spoken by new immigrant communities. Language education takes place in some settings where monolingualism is still the norm, but more usually in settings where a degree of multilingualism obtains.

Given these complexities, some commentators have ceased to distinguish between 'second' and 'foreign' language education (e.g. van Els 2005), and others have argued that language education policies should encompass all aspects of language development in a coherent way (e.g. Lo Bianco 1987). However, in this chapter we will maintain our focus on the teaching of languages which do not have a strong currency as medium of communication in the immediate environment of the learners. There are many other useful treatments of educational policies for autochthonous minority languages (e.g. Williams 2005; Nic Craith 2006; Grin 2003), and also concerning language policies for 'new' immigrant communities (e.g. Ager 1996; Nic Craith 2006; Extra 2007). Here we will concentrate on the clearest cases of 'foreign' language education, inevitably paying a good deal of attention to the teaching of English in 'expanding circle' countries (Kachru 1992) as well as in Europe, and also to attempts to sustain traditional foreign language education in 'inner circle' Anglophone countries.

Section 2 briefly traces the history of foreign language education and its relationship with the development of formal schooling and its transformation into a mass social activity. Section 3 explores some models and constructs offered by language policy experts and curriculum theorists to interpret attempts at the strategic direction and planning of foreign language teaching. Section 4 examines changing policy objectives, and in particular the impact of English on both the goals and the practices of foreign language education in 'expanding circle' contexts and in Europe. Particular attention is paid to the great recent growth of English teaching in primary education, and to the notion of content based language learning. Finally some attention is paid to the evolution of foreign language education policy in Anglophone countries, noting current tensions between the appeal to 'intercultural' objectives, and the meeting of perceived economic and security needs. In conclusion the chapter briefly suggests some roles for applied linguists in the continued evolution of policy as it seeks to influence practice.

2. Broad brush history

It is a truism that language and formal education are intimately related. Language is the major vehicle of human thought (Vygotsky 1986) and the prime means through which 'World 3 knowledge' (Popper 1972) is accumulated and transmitted by human societies, and thus inevitably the major vehicle of socialisation of all kinds. In addition, since the invention of literacy, language itself has been a major focus of educational effort and attention. Clearly, scribes needed to be trained even for early forms of literacy used for the most basic record keeping in early civilisations. With the rise of the 'religions of the book', sacred texts became a major educational focus, and remain so to this day to a significant extent (e.g. the widespread study of the Koran in religious schools).

There is also plenty of evidence that the development of literacy involved much more than the conversion into marks on paper or on stone of people's preexisting spoken language (Olsen 1994). The technology of literacy provides new perspectives on the nature of language, and gives rise quickly to new varieties of language, which are considered appropriate for committal to a permanent record. Educational effort then is invested in mastery of these distinctive written codes, which may achieve special religious, cultural and/or political significance. The teaching of literacy becomes a vehicle for promoting a particular world view, a body of 'cultural capital', a political ideology and/or a vision of citizenship within new nation states. Thus citizens and would-be citizens of the Roman Empire studied both Greek and a relatively standardised version of 'literary' Latin in organised schools, and expected to use Latin as a lingua franca with other citizens from highly diverse language backgrounds (Fotos 2005; Adams 2003: 690–693). In medieval Europe, the Catholic Church continued to promote Latin education which served multiple religious and secular purposes (e.g. legal systems and scholars made use of Latin, as well as churchmen). In eighteenth century England, a newly standardised variety of English was promoted through dictionaries, grammars etc. for use in schools (Crowley 1989). This variety was in turn heavily promoted in non-English speaking parts of the British Isles in the nineteenth century, through state-provided English-medium education for all, e.g. in Ireland and in Wales (Crowley 2000: 133–134), and in due course throughout the wider British empire, at least for prospective elite groups (Pennycook 1998). In revolutionary France, the teaching of French literacy was similarly promoted as a means of modernising and unifying the republican citizenry (Judge 2007; Balibar 1985). Today, the teaching of Putonghua/Mandarin in the school system throughout modern China is seen as vital to national unity (Zhou and Sun 2004; Zhou 2001).

Quite separately from historically documented educational efforts primarily associated with the promotion of literacy in 'standard' languages, the informal learning of languages other than the first language of early childhood must date back at least to the earliest origins of homo sapiens. Multilingualism, informally acquired, is a common and widespread feature of people's spoken language competence today, and this must have been true for past millennia. Some traces of informal language learning practices are surely to be found in the dual language texts and dialogues, documented in Europe from the thirteenth and fourteenth centuries onwards for the learning of languages such as French, Dutch and English (Beaune 1985: 296; Fotos 2005: 658; Howatt 1984: 6–7). However at the time of the European renaissance, with the decline of Latin as lingua franca in many legal and political domains, and the corresponding rise in status of languages such as French and Italian, a range of European languages received more systematic formal attention as 'foreign languages' in educational contexts. Grammars and textbooks were written targeting school age learners as well as adults, and these languages started to be taught in school settings (Howatt 1984: 19–31). By the eighteenth century, for example, German was taught in French military schools of the type attended by the young Napoleon (Balibar 1985).

In the course of the nineteenth century, 'modern' foreign languages gradually made their way onto the curriculum of 'academic' secondary schools and universities in Europe, alongside the established classical languages of Greek and Latin (see account in Howatt 1984). A strong lead came from Germany, where this same century saw the development and subsequent export of the so-called 'grammar-translation' method, where grammar rules are introduced one by one and illustrated with exemplar sentences and exercises including sentence-level translation (Fotos 2005: 661–662). The original aims of the grammar-translation method were to make language learning more practical and accessible; however in prestige educational institutions, foreign language education was frequently overloaded with metalinguistic and literary content, in emulation of classical languages. At the same time, the growth of international trade and industry, and mass migrations to colonise new territories, led to greatly increased demand for more practical foreign language teaching among adults. Private institutions such as the Berlitz schools proved open to experimentation and the adoption of more 'natural', skills-oriented teaching methods. At the end of the nineteenth century, the Reform Movement preached the primacy of spoken language, and the centrality of meaningful texts (rather than sentences) for the language classroom. These ideas in turn influenced secondary school curricula to some extent in the first half of the 20th century. However, grammar-translation approaches were substantially displaced only after World War 2, giving way to audiolingual, audiovisual and 'communicative' methods better suited to the new mass publics for foreign languages in the increasingly democratised and accessible secondary education systems of the developed world.

European imperial expansion from the fifteenth century onward led to the worldwide dissemination of Dutch, Portuguese, Spanish etc., with profound and lasting impacts on the world languages 'map'. Initially these impacts took place outside the framework of formal education, through military, trade and settlement activities (not least the slave trade). However the increasingly bureaucratic later empires, especially those of Great Britain and France, saw it as necessary to provide education for at least a small elite group in the languages of empire, thus laying the nineteenth century groundwork for 'second language education' (Graddol 2006: 84–85); this process is described e.g. for India by Dheram (2005). 'Modernisation' movements in a range of Asian countries beyond the formal colonial empires, yet responding to growing pressures from these, also started to promote organised foreign language teaching on a small scale. For example Japan introduced a new higher education system including English language study from the 1870s, and English was included in the curriculum for a new network of secondary schools from the 1890s (Butler and Iino 2005). Organised English instruction was offered for some prospective civil servants from the 1860s in imperial China (Adamson 2004), where missionaries also promoted English education.

The twentieth century saw an immense expansion and transformation of formal education systems around the world. In early-industrialised countries, the nineteenth century had already seen rising demand for basic literacy skills in national languages which led to the innovation of universal, state-supported primary education. In the twentieth century, these same societies saw the growth of universal secondary education and great expansion of higher education, to meet the needs of citizens in increasingly 'post-industrial' economies. The secondary school curriculum was accordingly transformed to meet the perceived needs of a new mass public rather than traditional elites. The study of foreign languages was transformed in the process. The association of language study with high culture (e.g. the literary canon) was broken; the analytically demanding grammar translation approach was challenged with more experiential pedagogies (audiolingual, situational, communicative), and specialised language teacher education programmes were developed to train cohorts of teachers in their use. Thus for example, the development of comprehensive secondary education in the UK during the 1960s and 1970s was accompanied by the extension of foreign language learning to (almost) all lower secondary students; the methods used changed accordingly from grammar-translation to situational teaching (Hawkins 1997). In Sweden after World War 2, the teaching of French and German, with 'elite', high culture connotations, was downplayed in favour of English with its more 'democratic' connotations (Cabau-Lampa 2007).

On a worldwide scale, the end of World War 2 and the demise of the British and French empires led to major changes in language education policies. In postcolonial settings, debates centred around the future role in education of ex-colonial languages (especially French and English), and vernacular languages (such as Arabic or Kiswahili). Foreign language education policies reflected political affiliations, with Russian being promoted as first foreign language in China in the 1950s (Mao and Min 2004; Adamson 2004), and in Eastern Europe until the end of the 1980s (Medgyes 1993). English on the other hand became established as first foreign language in Taiwan from the 1940s (Chen 2006), and in Japan from the 1950s (Butler and Iino 2005). Overall the post World War 2 trend was ultimately towards English, which has quickly replaced Russian in Eastern European school systems and elsewhere since the collapse of the Soviet Union from 1989 (Nyikos 1994; Neau 2003; Decke-Cornill 2003), and is also impacting strongly on other languages of regional significance, such as German in Eastern Europe (Raasch 1997; Lohse 2004; Hoberg 2002; Darquennes and Nelde 2006). The apparently unstoppable rise of English worldwide, in multiple roles as second language, foreign language, and lingua franca, has profoundly affected language education policies everywhere and will be considered in more detail in following sections.

3. State of the art: central concepts and theoretical approaches

Contemporary theorists generally see formal education as a key instrument created and used by modern nation states to achieve multiple goals of cultural transmission, economic advancement and social cohesion. From this point of view, language in its widest sense is central to educational policymaking. Lo Bianco (2008) sums up the goals of the 'secondary linguistic socialisation' provided by formal education to include:

- Promotion of national standard language literate capability, for all types of learner including majority language speakers, speakers of autochthonous minority languages, immigrants and children with special needs;
- Inculcation of socially valued 'elevated' linguistic registers and styles;
- Teaching disciplinary language conventions of particular fields and professions;
- 'Occasional' concessions to non standard dialects and minority languages;
- Teaching of prestige, strategic or status languages (Lo Bianco 2008: 113–114).

Among these goals, only the last concerns us centrally here, but planning for foreign language education will evidently be profoundly affected by policy making for the wider group of goals.

Theoretical discussions of language in education policy, or 'language acquisition management' (Baldauf, Li and Zhao 2008), refer to a number of dimensions which need to be taken into account in order to model and analyse particular settings. As can be seen from Table 1, for Baldauf, Li and Zhao, these dimensions include:

Table 1. Dimensions of language acquisition management (after Baldauf, Li and Zhao 2008, p. 235)

Access policy	Which languages are to be taught to whom, at what level, and for how long
Personnel policy	Requirements for teacher training, selection and employment
Curriculum policy	What curriculum is mandated and by whom
Methods and materials policy	What teaching methods and materials may be prescribed
Resourcing policy	How language acquisition programmes will be paid for
Evaluation policy	How learning outcomes are measured and reported, what uses are made of exam results etc
Community policy	To what extent policy is supported by 'bottom up' consultation with students, parents and local communities
Teacher-led policy	To what extent teachers can influence aspects of language in education policy

Kaplan and Baldauf (2005) apply this model systematically to the analysis of language in education policy in two contrasting settings, Japan and Sweden. Throughout this chapter we will make use of relevant aspects of the model, paying particular attention to access (choice of language) and its interrelations with curriculum and methodology. For reasons of space, only limited attention will be paid here to other key features such as personnel policy and evaluation policy.

The 'access' dimension is developed more fully by van Els (2005), with a discussion of status planning in second/foreign language education. Van Els argues for a strongly 'functionalist' view of status planning: for him, second/foreign languages only have a clear cut case for inclusion in the curriculum where a communicative need can be demonstrated for the learning public concerned (though he accepts that ancillary educational goals such as the development of intercultural understanding, or critical thinking, can also be addressed through foreign language learning). He argues accordingly for an analysis of communicative need in terms of competences, situations and functions, as exemplified in the longstanding Council of Europe research and development programme on foreign language education (Council of Europe 2001). Consistently with this perspective, Van Els favours obligatory inclusion of foreign language study in the curriculum where 'communicative need' can be demonstrated; he is concerned with the overall coherence of provision in the service of fully meeting the specified needs (which he calls 'articulation'); he believes choice of language(s) on offer should be controlled; and he acknowledges the place of lingua franca English as a "very suitable candidate for acceptance as second-language-for-all" (van Els 2005: 973).

Other theorists challenge such a functionalist approach to language acquisition planning however, in different ways. Firstly, North (2008) reminds us that while foreign language instruction can be timetabled, not all learners will necessarily benefit from it in similar ways; he describes how after a common period of instruction in lower secondary school, learners of English as a foreign language in a Swiss study were spread over three different levels of achievement in the CEFR (North 2008: 224). The actuality of institutionalised failure in classroom foreign language learning is a serious challenge to any simple view of needs and how to meet them.

Secondly, Cha and Ham (2008) argue that selection of foreign languages for inclusion in school curricula cannot be explained solely in functionalist terms relating to communicative need. They cite the example of Korea, which until recently has concentrated its foreign language educational effort almost exclusively on English and taught neither Chinese nor Japanese on any significant scale, despite important regional economic links with both countries. They also argue that many countries have adopted English as compulsory first foreign language for reasons of prestige and as a 'taken for granted' component of modern globalising curricula, rather than on account of substantive local and national needs. This view gains some support from analysis of foreign language evaluation systems in many contexts. It is not obvious that the high school leaving examinations in English common throughout Asia for example, are well adapted to certifying students' practical communicative proficiency in English. A functionalist perspective would see these examinations as ripe candidates for reform. Instead these tests survive presumably because they have a rather different social purpose, e.g. contributing to selection of students for different forms of higher education. Similarly the survival of foreign language education in Anglophone countries cannot be attributed today to any preoccupation with mass 'communicative need'; the rationales advanced in its support in such contexts most typically focus on cultural, intercultural and identity factors (Byram 2008).

Language planning theorists also take different views about the demonstrable effectiveness of language-in-education policy (LEP). Shohamy (2005) implies that such policies can be strongly effective:

> LEP serves as a mechanism for carrying out national language policy agendas. LEP are imposed by political entities in top-down manner, usually with very limited resistance as most generally schools and teachers comply. These policies are then reinforced by teachers, materials, curricula and tests. For bureaucrats, LEP offers a very useful opportunity for exercising influence as they can enforce various political and social ideologies through language (Shohamy 2005: 76).

Spolsky (2004) is considerably more sceptical about the long term impact of language policymaking:

> Looking at the language policy of established nations, one commonly finds major disparities between the language policy laid down in the constitution, and the actual practices in the society. Within social groups, it is also common to find conflicting beliefs about the value of various language choices. One is therefore faced regularly with the question of which the real language policy is. In many nations, one is hard pressed to choose between the complex multilingual ecology of language use, and a simple ideological monolingualism of constitutionally stated language management decisions (Spolsky 2004: 217–218).

Spolsky certainly acknowledges schools as an important location for language acquisition policy making (Spolsky 2004: 47–48). However he cites the cases of France and Ireland to illustrate the limits of formal language-in-education policy in either suppressing or reviving autochthonous minority languages. He does not discuss cases of success and failure in foreign language education policy explicitly; cases will be discussed later in this chapter, both of public enthusiasm for foreign language learning outrunning official policy and provision, and also of failed foreign language education initiatives.

The last theorist to be considered here is Clark (1987), who argues that the evolution of foreign language education policy can usefully be related to broad underlying educational trends. He identifies three broad educational philosophies, termed:

- Classical humanism
- Reconstructionism
- Progressivism (Clark 1987: 91–99).

'Classical humanism' is primarily concerned with the development of general cognitive abilities, and the transmission of valued "knowledge, culture and standards" (Clark 1987: 93) from one generation to another. 'Reconstructionism' is concerned with achieving a consensus on common societal goals, and bringing about desired social and economic change through the education system. 'Progressivism' is concerned with the development of the individual learner as a whole person, and with fostering their autonomy and capacity to learn. In the next section we begin by applying these concepts to the analysis of contemporary policy goals.

4. Areas of tension and controversy

4.1. Policy goals for FL education

The 'classical humanist' rationale for foreign language learning within formal education systems was internationally prominent until World War 2, and still maintains a foothold in some educational sectors, e.g. in academic high schools in parts of continental Europe where the study of pre-20th century foreign language literature, for example, is still prized. However in the 21st century this rationale is generally in retreat, on the defensive even within higher education systems: see e.g. Zhaoxiang (2002) and Yin and Chen (2002) for arguments in favour of the promotion of humanistic and literary education in English departments in Chinese universities.

'Reconstructionist' rationales have been strongly developed and expressed in support of the post World War 2 expansion of foreign language teaching around the world, most strikingly with respect to English. These arguments are commonly couched in economic terms, referring to the preparedness of nation states for the challenges of globalisation. Thus for example, a commission established by the Japanese prime minister in 1999 to articulate "Japan's goals in the 21st century" (Hashimoto 2007: 29) included the following argument in its final report:

> The advance of globalization and information-technology call for a world-class level of excellence. Achieving world-class excellence demands that in addition to mastering information technology, all Japanese acquire a working knowledge of English – not as simply a foreign language but as the international lingua franca. English in this sense is a prerequisite for obtaining global information, expressing intentions, and sharing values. (Prime Minister's Commission 2000, Chapter 1 IV (2), cited in Hashimoto 2007: 31).

Here, lingua franca English is clearly seen as an essential tool for success in the international knowledge economy; similar views have been expressed in similar debates e.g. in Thailand, Korea and other countries (Yim 2007). Graddol reports initiatives in countries as diverse as Colombia and Mongolia to promote universal bilingualism in the national language and English (2006: 89) essentially on economic grounds; in Japan, the Prime Minister's Commission initiated a public debate about the desirability of giving English legal recognition as an official language of the country (Matsuura, Fujieda, and Mahoney 2004), and similar discussions have taken place in Taiwan and Korea (Yim 2007). Even in the Anglophone world, a high status inquiry into the condition of foreign language learning within the United Kingdom at the millennium came up with a report which leaned heavily on economic arguments to promote reform:

> In a smart and competitive world, exclusive reliance on English leaves the UK vulnerable [...] The UK workforce suffers from a chronic shortage of people at all levels with usable language skills. Companies increasingly need personnel with technical or professional skills plus another language and often their only option is to recruit native speakers of other languages. Mobility of employment is in danger of becoming the preserve of people from other countries. (Nuffield Languages Inquiry 2000: 6).

The impact of 'reconstructionist' thinking can also be seen in the way the outcomes of foreign language learning are increasingly defined in school curricula. Since the 1970s there have been initiatives to spell out the precise skills and levels of language knowledge to be achieved (the UK 'Graded Objectives' movement and the USA ACTFL 'Oral Proficiency' scales are early examples, as are the 'Threshold Level' and related functional definitions of language competency published from the 1970s by the Council of Europe). Since the publication in 2001 of the Common European Framework of Reference for Languages (CEFR: Council of Europe 2001), school systems across Europe have increasingly made use of its defined set of six main 'levels' as targets for foreign language learning in various stages and types of foreign language education. For example, the French Ministry of National Education has recently committed itself to achievement of Level A1 on the CEFR in the first foreign language, by the end of primary school (Ministère de l'Education Nationale 2006), and identified higher levels of the Framework as objectives for secondary school foreign language learning. Similarly the Hungarian National Basic Plan for Education (2003, in Petneki 2007) defines school targets in terms of CEFR levels as follows, cf. Table 2:

Table 2. Notional outcomes of foreign language learning, Hungary

Language	10th school year	12th school year
First foreign language	A2–B1	B1–B2
Second foreign language	A1–A2	A2–B1

An instrumentalist focus on the achievement of defined skills and proficiency levels is however typically modified and contextualised, by the inclusion of 'progressivist' goals and values in curriculum rationales. For example, according to national planners the prime objective of foreign language education in Hungary is "language proficiency which is useful for everyday life" (National Basic Education Plan 2003, cited in Petneki 2007). Yet the stated wider goals include:

- (National) civilization and folklore;
- Membership in the European Union and the world;
- Teaching of environmental awareness;
- Education towards a communicative culture;
- Education for physical and mental health;
- Learning how to learn (National Basic Education Plan 2003, cited in Petneki 2007).

Similarly in Italy, foreign language education goals include:

- be aware of one's own cultural background;
- know the world where one lives in;
- communicate and interact with people belonging to different cultures;
- compare Italian and foreign cultural systems;
- deal with real situations and meaningful tasks;
- integrate theoretical and practical skills (Businaro 2007).

One major thrust in the 'progressivist' tradition of foreign language education is the concern for the development of intercultural understanding and intercultural communicative competence, a longstanding concern of the Council of Europe and also reflected very explicitly in the CEFR, and in the 'foreign language standards' of the American Council on the Teaching of Foreign Languages (ACTFL n.d.). In this tradition, foreign language education is seen as a vehicle for the promotion of a range of positive social values including citizenship, tolerance, and antiracism, as well as the capacity to communicate effectively across cultural and linguistic boundaries (Byram 1997; Starkey 2002). Another focus can be found in the 'language awareness' movement, which seeks to link foreign language education with the development of metalinguistic understanding, and advocates a comparative approach linking foreign language and L1 education (Hawkins 1987; Costanzo 2003; Hawkins 2005).

However, it is clear that the main 21st century drivers which determine basic factors in foreign language education policy such as the choice of language(s), the amount of time devoted to foreign language study, and the degree of investment in teachers and resources, are instrumental goals which prioritise the development of practical language skill. Goals of intercultural understanding and metalinguistic awareness are seen by many commentators as insufficient of themselves to justify sustained investment and universal commitment to foreign language education in the curriculum. To quote a Dutch perspective: "It is clear that language policy that aims at fostering foreign language learning on the basis of cultural interest and intercultural understanding is doomed to fail" (de Bot 2007: 274).

Test cases can be found in the recent expansion of foreign language learning into the primary school curriculum. Here, experimental courses focussing on 'taster' language experiences, multilingual experiences, learning how to learn etc, have typically given way to instruction focussing on the development of skill in a single language, e.g. in France (Ministère de l'Education Nationale 2006) and even in England (Department for Education and Science 2005). Assessment schemes generally focus also on measuring achievement in terms of language skills, and rarely incorporate measurement of attitudes, intercultural understanding, or language awareness.

4.2. Choice of language(s) in foreign language education: the pre-eminence of English

In the nineteenth century, French, German and English were all significant in formal foreign language education, at least in Europe, though with the pre-eminent place going to French (Wright 2006). In the contemporary European Union (25 states surveyed in 2005) the position seems more diverse, and five languages have a significant presence on the school curriculum: English, French, German, Spanish and Russian. However, English is now pre-eminent among these, being studied by 46 per cent of all primary age children, by 87 per cent of lower secondary school students, and by 90 per cent of all upper secondary school students (Eurydice 2005). By comparison, around a quarter of all secondary school students are learning French and German (Darquennes and Nelde 2006). Plans to sustain diversity in the foreign languages offered have encountered consumer resistance. For example in Hungary, after the political changes of the late 1980s and the collapse of Russian as first foreign language, there was considerable investment in both German and English as alternative foreign languages (Nyikos 1994). In the mid 1990s the number of school students learning German as first foreign language was running above 300,000 (Földes 2004). However in the 2000s there has been increasing pressure from students and parents for English provision; from 2011 it has been agreed that English will become the first foreign language throughout Hungary, with German relegated along with other languages to the second foreign language slot. 'Access' policy has thus been substantially affected by consumer demands. (See Dörnyei, Csizér and Németh 2006 for an empirically based longitudinal account of the evolution of Hungarian student attitudes.)

Within the European Union, there have been repeated policy attempts to promote both individual multilingualism, and societal plurilingualism, and to encourage member states to support these goals through their education systems, reviewed in Grin (2006) and Phillipson (2003). In 1995 the European Commission published a White Paper arguing for the need for communicative ability in at least two foreign languages in addition to the mother tongue (the '1 + 2' formula): "proficiency in several Community languages has become a precondition if citizens of the European Union are to benefit from the occupational and personal opportunities open to them in the border-free Single Market" (European Commission 1995: 47). In 1998 following French proposals the Council of Europe recommended more specifically that young people should have the opportunity to develop this 1+2 competence in school, and in 2002 the Barcelona European Council resolved in favour of teaching at least two foreign languages from a very early age. Only a small number of countries (Sweden, Luxembourg, Iceland, Estonia) have made learning a second foreign language compulsory for all students from primary school; around 20 European countries make the learning of two foreign languages compulsory for at least part of secondary education (Eurydice 2005).

Grin (2006) discusses anomalies in the 1+2 policy. He points out that as a means to promote international communication, a 1+2 strategy will fail unless the choice of foreign languages is restricted and directed (people need to know the same language(s) to communicate). Yet if any particular language is chosen, language learning effort will be invested in that language over others. Thus the 1+2 policy itself could undermine the plurilingualism and linguistic diversity it ostensibly seeks to support.

Cabau-Lampa (2007) provides a case study of the experience of Sweden, a country which has set out to make the learning of two foreign languages compulsory for all, during basic education (the nine-year *grundskola*). English has been well established as the first foreign language since the 1940s, and is now introduced to around a third of all children from Grade 1 (age 7). Until the 1990s, learning a second foreign language had however been largely reserved for 'academic' track students. In the early 1990s, as part of a general renewal of education and preceding the general policy recommendations of European bodies, it was decided that a second foreign language chosen from among French, German and Spanish should be studied from Grade 6 or 7 by all students (with exceptions, i.e. children opting to study a minority language such as Sami, or requiring remedial Swedish or English teaching). By the mid 2000s, around 65 per cent of all Grade 9 students were studying a second foreign language, with Spanish overtaking first French, then German to become the most popular of the three. However, Cabau-Lampa reports a range of obstacles to raising this percentage; most notably, student surveys show that foreign languages other than English are perceived as difficult, and not very relevant to everyday life and work. These views are growing in strength. For example, in 1997 44 per cent of students surveyed believed a second foreign language was 'important'; in 2003, only 24 per cent of students in a similar survey agreed with this. Cabau-Lampa remarks in her concluding comments: "The problem in Sweden is that all the parties interested in foreign language teaching want it to be reinforced, except those primarily concerned, i.e. the learners. The latter have made their choice: to put priority on English learning" (Cabau-Lampa 2007: 352).

Graddol (2006) demonstrates how this preference for English is worldwide. In China English is now part of formal education for all, from Grade 3 in primary school until university (where success in a College English test is a prerequisite for graduation in any discipline); English is more or less unchallenged in the 'first foreign language' slot throughout Asia. There is admittedly also a growing interest in learning Mandarin as a foreign language, following the economic rise of China; around 30 million people are now learning Mandarin internationally, with increasing interest in the East Asian region, e.g. in South Korea. Similarly Spanish has growing regional importance as a foreign language in Latin America, with a commitment by Brazil in 2005 to offer Spanish in all its secondary schools. These regional commitments seem likely on present trends to complement the teaching and learning of English, however, not to supplant it.

4.3. English as a lingua franca: a defining role in language education policymaking?

In the 21st century and in an era of globalisation, the present place of English as the pre-eminent world language/dominant lingua franca must be acknowledged, even if longer term questions can be raised about its status (Crystal 2003; Graddol 2006). There is an international belief that knowledge of English brings social, economic and 'knowledge' benefits, and as we have seen, English has come to dominate the 'foreign language' slot in school and university curricula around the world. It is displacing traditional 'first foreign languages' in many places, e.g. German in Sweden or Hungary (Cabau-Lampa 2006; Petneki 2007), or French in Cambodia (Neau 2003). For a selection of country case studies of the evolution of English language education policies, see e.g. Adamson (2004); Lam (2002); and Mao and Min (2004) on the People's Republic of China, Bohn (2003) on Brazil, Chen (2006) on Taiwan.

The perceived desirability of English has impacted on foreign language education policy internationally in a number of ways, some more predictable than others. Teacher supply has involved primarily the mass training of local specialists in English, but also the re-training of now redundant teachers of other foreign languages (such as teachers of Russian in Hungary), and the recruitment of native speakers to work alongside local teachers, often with much less professional training (as e.g. in the Japanese JET scheme). The language norms to be aimed at have come under scrutiny in both 'outer circle' and 'expanding circle' countries, with increasing debate about the potential of targeting instruction and assessment on local and/or lingua franca varieties of English, rather than American or British native speaker norms (McKay 2002; Elder and Davies 2006; Jenkins 2006; Holliday 2005). In this domain however, change on the ground is much more limited, with most formal instruction in English as a foreign language still predicated on progression towards native speaker norms.

Enthusiasm for English has had much more obvious impact on foreign language education strategies in terms of the dissatisfaction it has created with 'traditional' curriculum patterns, i.e. a few hours' formal instruction per week, spread over the period of secondary education. This educational model is increasingly seen as inappropriate, overly focussed on the formal language system rather than on the functional and communicative skills which are seen as the prime goal of English learning. Above all, it is seen as simply not effective in equipping enough learners with sufficiently advanced levels of English to function well in the international knowledge economy.

The first great policy change which has swept through educational systems since the 1990s is the general tendency to lower the starting age for foreign language learning, most usually as a way of responding to parental expectations and accommodating more time for English learning. The Eurydice survey in Europe (2005: 39) reports that "at least half of all pupils in primary education learn a foreign language in the majority of countries"; in all the countries surveyed except for Belgium and Luxembourg, English was the most commonly taught language, the starting age has been falling and numbers learning English have been steadily increasing.

In Asia similarly the 1990s and 2000s have seen a great increase in primary English learning. In China, for example, a formal policy was adopted from 2001 mandating the beginning of English instruction in Grade 3, despite major challenges to do with teacher supply and resourcing (Hu 2007; Li 2007). In Japan, the Ministry of Education published in 2003 an 'Action Plan to Cultivate Japanese with English Abilities', to tackle perceived stagnation of standards in English language learning. Among its provisions, elementary schools were to be allowed to experiment with a range of foreign language activities (in practice, English language activities) to enhance international education (Butler and Iino 2005). By 2006, over 90 per cent of Japanese elementary schools were reporting teaching some English language, and the Ministry of Education was proposing formal inclusion of English in the elementary school curriculum. English is compulsory in Korea from the third grade, with extensive government investment in materials development and teacher education. In Taiwan, English was made compulsory from the fifth grade in 2001, then from the third grade in 2003 (Chen 2006). However, Chen points out that many districts and schools start English teaching earlier than they are required to do, and offer more hours (e.g. Taipei schools start English teaching from Grade 1). All these Asian initiatives are officially supported by arguments about internationalization and globalization, plus popular beliefs about young children's aptitude for foreign language learning. They are well supported by parents; in the wealthier countries, the school offering is frequently supplemented by private supplementary classes. In Taiwan for example, a majority of primary school children are said to attend 'cram school' classes in English, and some countries have felt it necessary to restrict the extent of English provision at pre-school level.

The second change in provision triggered by dissatisfaction with 'drip feed' models of foreign language education has been the rise of more intensive programmes, and in particular the adoption of the target foreign language (again almost always English) as a medium of instruction. In second language contexts, there are longstanding traditions of L2 medium instruction which go back in many cases to the development of national education systems. Thus standard 'national' languages (English in the United Kingdom, French in France, Spanish in Andean nations etc. etc.) have been used as the main medium of instruction in educational provision for indigenous minority groups (e.g. speakers of Gaelic, Welsh, Breton, Quechua etc. etc.). In contexts where bilingualism has gained political recognition, L2 medium instruction has been used as a means to promote it, e.g. the provision of French immersion education for English speaking Canadians. What is 'new' is the intensification of foreign language instruction in languages without significant local communities of speakers, through engagement with other educational content.

Models and terminology for FL medium instruction vary in different parts of the world. In Europe the term 'content and language integrated learning' (CLIL) is commonly used to describe programmes where at least part of the school programme is delivered through the foreign language (Seikkula-Leino 2007; Wolff ch. 20, this volume), though the term 'bilingual education' is also commonly used e.g. in Germany. The European Union has been very active in the promotion of CLIL since the 1990s (Marsh 2002) and continues to support a range of projects in this area. The logic supporting CLIL has been the perceived need for enhanced foreign language competence and the inadequacy of traditional FL teaching models to deliver this:

> There is broad consensus within the European Union that a delivery gap exists between what is provided as foreign language education, and outcomes in terms of learner performance. Targets for requisite foreign language competencies are not yet being reached [...] calling for additional curricular time for foreign language learning within given curricula would have been largely unsuccessful. Existing demands on curricular time were then, as now, largely non-negotiable. Integrating language with non-language content, in a *dual-focussed learning* environment, emerged as a solution (Marsh 2002: 9–10).

The extent of actual provision in European schools is difficult to estimate, but a recent Eurydice report suggests between 3 and 30 per cent of children in Europe may experience some form of CLIL at some stage of their education (Eurydice 2006). A variant is the intensive foreign language year offered in many Hungarian secondary schools (Petneki 2007). Graddol argues that content based language instruction is difficult to implement in a 'top down' organised manner, because of the issues raised to do with personnel policy. That is, the status of language teachers is altered, as CLIL requires them to collaborate with or even be replaced by bilingual content teachers (Graddol 2006: 86).

In Asia, the intensification of EFL teaching is achieved partly by a growth in 'bilingual' education (i.e. English-medium education), but also by initiatives such as the creation of 'English villages' in Korea and Taiwan, where learners can supposedly take part in a short term total immersion experience. In Taiwan, the private provision of English-medium pre-school education has been very popular, though controversial, with state attempts to restrict the practice attracting "public outcry" (Oladejo 2006).

4.4. Foreign language education policies in 'inner circle' English-speaking countries

Foreign language education policies of historically Anglophone countries such as the USA, UK or Australia are also deeply affected by the rise of English as a world language and its widespread use as the pre-eminent language of business and finance, of science and technology, and of the leisure industries. In such countries, European languages (pre-eminently French and German) were historically taught as part of a 'classical humanist' educational experience for academic and social elites, initially alongside the classical languages of Greek and Latin, and then supplanting them. The 20th century 'democratisation' of education in these countries (e.g. the introduction of comprehensive secondary education in the UK in the 1970s) coincided with the post World War 2 spread of English as an increasingly unchallenged world language. Finding a relevant new place for foreign languages in the education systems of such countries has proved challenging, with intermittent policy initiatives from central governments generally meeting an equivocal or even indifferent response from the wider public and learners in the school systems. The rationales advanced in support of foreign language education in Anglophone contexts have varied, at times making instrumental, economic and even security-related arguments, but generally also appealing to progressivist and developmental reasons for foreign language learning. In these settings, decisions about the somewhat marginal activity of foreign language education can often be seen to be byproducts of other educational initiatives, sometimes unintended ones.

The evolution of foreign language education policy in England is reviewed in Hawkins (1997) and Mitchell (2007). Comprehensivisation in the 1970s was followed by a considerable expansion of foreign language teaching in the lower secondary school, with the focus on French, German and Spanish, and adoption of situational and audiovisual methodologies which were perceived to be more 'accessible' for the new learner public. There was government sponsored experimentation in the late 1970s with foreign language teaching at primary school level also, though this was not pursued when problems of teacher supply and continuity during transition to secondary school were seen to limit the programme's effectiveness (Burstall 1974). Increasing dissatisfaction with the general educational standards being achieved in a highly devolved educational system led to a great centralisation of English education and introduction of a National Curriculum from 1990. A byproduct was the emergence of 'languages for all' in the secondary school system, with study of a foreign language becoming compulsory for all students aged 11–16, as one of the so-called 'foundation subjects' of the new curriculum. This policy lasted just 10 years, with languages once more becoming optional from age 14, as a result of a more general relaxation of the National Curriculum after 2000. The percentage of 16 year olds taking a national examination in a language peaked at 78 per cent in 1999–2001, but once language study became optional at this level, many learners voted with their feet. In 2007, just 46 per cent of 16 year olds took a language examination (CILT 2007). The main decline was in numbers studying French and German, with Spanish rising somewhat in popularity, against the overall downward trend.

Alongside these wider changes, some special attention and resource was nonetheless given to the protection of foreign languages in English schools. In 2002 a so called 'National Strategy' for languages in England was published which included a substantial renewed commitment to promote foreign language teaching in primary schools, in partial compensation for the loss of compulsory instruction in the secondary school (Department for Education and Science 2002). This primary school initiative has been supported by an outline curriculum and considerable investment in resources and in teacher development, and has been widely adopted though it is not – yet – compulsory (Department for Education and Science 2005). In 2007 a further review proposed a range of measures intended to make foreign language study more attractive for upper secondary students, though these fall short of any return to compulsion (Dearing and King 2007).

Australia has a devolved education system where main responsibilities for schools lie with the states, and educational provision remains very diverse, with different starting ages and degrees of compulsion (Liddicoat et al. 2007). As an Anglophone country with substantial immigrant communities from increasingly diverse language and ethnic backgrounds, seeking to find a postcolonial role and build constructive links with Asia, language education policy has been of active if intermittent national concern for 20 years. The 1987 'National Languages Policy' was an attempt to deal in a coordinated way with all aspects from mother tongue English and ESL to foreign, immigrant and indigenous languages (Lo Bianco 1987). The 1990s saw specific central government initiatives providing funding and training to promote the teaching of four Asian languages, on economic and strategic grounds (Erebus Consulting Partners 2002). The current 'National Plan for Languages Education in Australian Schools 2005–2008' however lays prime stress on 'intercultural' language learning and the need to promote intercultural awareness and understanding.

At present the 10 most commonly taught foreign languages in Australian mainstream schools are a mix of international languages and languages of immigrant communities, cf. Table 3:

Table 3. Foreign languages in Australian schools, ranked by popularity (after Liddicoat et al. 2007, p. 32)

1	Japanese
2	Italian
3	Indonesian
4	French
5	German
6	Chinese
7	Spanish
8	Modern Greek
9	Arabic
10	Vietnamese

According to Liddicoat et al. (2007), the total number of school students participating in some form of foreign language learning in 2005 was 47.5 per cent. Most language study occurs in primary schools, and language enrollments decrease steadily from Year 7; numbers of senior secondary students learning languages remain low despite special policy efforts directed at this age group. There are concerns at national level about teacher quality and teacher supply.

The USA lacks a tradition of strong centralised educational policymaking, and at state and school district level, practice and exposure to foreign language learning vary greatly. In 1997, 31 per cent of elementary schools reported teaching a foreign language (to around 4 million out of 27 million students), while 86 per cent of secondary schools reported doing so (Branaman and Rhodes 1997); Spanish was much the most widely taught language at both levels, followed by French and German. The wider 'standards' movement in American education embodied in the 'Goals 2000: Educate America Act' led in the late 1990s to the articulation by the FL teaching profession of a set of 'National Standards for Foreign Language Teaching', intended as a tool to guide foreign language education in the changing context of publicly funded education, and addressing intercultural as well as communicative objectives (Phillips 2007). However, federal government interest in foreign language education has been substantially influenced by economic and especially security concerns, e.g. during World War 2 and in the post-Sputnik period (Muller 1986; Kramsch 2005). Following the terrorist attacks of September 2001, there was a revival of concern about the security value of languages (Edwards 2004). Consequently the Federal government has invested in a number of research and advanced teaching institutions with the aim of developing advanced specialist language capability in languages felt to be "critical for the nation in today's world" (Brecht 2007: 265), e.g. Arabic , Chinese, or various Turkic languages. These initiatives are controversial among professionals and have sparked debate once again about the rationale and goals of any expansion of foreign language education: functional and instrumental goals of a narrowly conceived 'communicative competence', or a more broadly based 'intercultural competence'? A selection of positions from this debate can be found in a recent 'Perspectives' section of *Modern Language Journal* (Blake and Kramsch 2007).

5. Contribution of applied linguistics: futures and solutions

In this chapter it has been acknowledged that foreign language education policies cannot be imposed by 'bureaucrats' and ideologists, but require a reasonable consensus among students, parents and the wider community to take root and deliver a measure of foreign language learning. Contexts have been identified where enthusiasm for foreign language learning has run ahead of formal educational provision (e.g. for English in pre-school education in Taiwan), and also contexts where existing provision has been abandoned by the student clientele (e.g. the decline of German learning in Hungary, or the failure to retain upper secondary school students in any kind of foreign language learning, in the UK or Australia). Unsurprisingly it seems foreign language education succeeds best where a social consensus supports it. Much the strongest social consensus, currently in favour of English, derives from visions of economic success associated with globalisation; however, intercultural and 'citizenship' arguments sustain a measure of commitment to other languages at least in the European context. A major failure of current policies, however, is to achieve the 'joined up' thinking argued for by Lo Bianco (2008) and others, which would connect foreign language learning with the actual domestic multilingualism of contemporary societies. This connects with a second major failure, i.e. the relative inefficiency of school based foreign language learning and the many students who are not succeeding under present instructional conditions.

Applied linguists as specialists and professionals are active commentators on the evolution of policy making as this chapter has shown. However they have no mandate to lead it. Decisions e.g. to lower the starting age for learning English as a foreign language, to protect and promote diversity in foreign language learning through a '1 + 2' policy, or to invest in the specialist teaching of languages deemed significant for national security, are ideological in nature relating to aspirations and visions for identity, and can only be realised through public debate and investment. Applied linguists can contribute to such debates as resource people and informed citizens, but cannot impose their own preferred 'expert' solutions.

Once the broad outlines of public policy are clear, however, applied linguists have many roles in shaping and supporting the evolution of foreign language education. Traditionally they have been centrally concerned as 'experts' with many elements of Baldauf's developmental model: with language teacher education, with curriculum design, with development of methods and materials for foreign language instruction and assessment. In the current context of globalisation these concerns are taking new forms and applied linguistics must adapt accordingly. Some suggestions follow as to the fresh areas where applied linguistics expertise will be needed:

- the integration of both linguistic and non-linguistic goals in FL curricula, teaching materials and assessment instruments (interdisciplinary subject content, intercultural understanding, citizenship, criticality …);
- preparation of new types of FL instructor, who can teach both content and language appropriately to learners of all ages;
- finding ways of working with more heterogeneous, multicultural and multilingual learner publics, and engaging more of them in successful learning;
- preparation of both teachers and learners to operate in a world of uncertainty, e.g. of many Englishes and lingua franca usages, and/or of policy inconsistencies and changes;
- reduction of boundaries between formal and informal learning, collective and individual learning.

References

ACTFL
n.d *Standards for Foreign Language Learning*. Alexandria, VA: American Council on the Teaching of Foreign Languages.

Adams, James N.
2003 *Bilingualism and the Latin Language*. Cambridge: Cambridge University Press.

Adamson, Bob
2004 *China's English: A History of English in Chinese Education*. Hong Kong: Hong Kong University Press.

Ager, Dennis
1996 *Language Policy in Britain and France: The Processes of Policy*. London: Cassell.

Baldauf, Richard B, Minglin Li and Shouhui Zhao
2008 Language acquisition management inside and outside the school. In: Bernard Spolsky and Francis M. Hult (eds.), *The Handbook of Educational Linguistics*, 233–250. Oxford: Blackwell Publishing.

Balibar, Renée
1985 *L'Institution du Français*. Paris: Presses Universitaires de France.

Beaune, Colette
1985 *Naissance de la Nation France*. Paris: Gallimard.

Blake, Robert and Claire Kramsch
2007 National language educational policy. Guest editors' Introduction. *Modern Language Journal* 91 (2): 247–249.

Bohn, Hilario I.
2003 The educational role and status of English in Brazil. *World Englishes* 22 (2): 159–172.

Branaman, Lucy and Nancy Rhodes
1997 Foreign language instruction in the United States: A national survey of elementary and secondary schools. Washington, D C: Center for Applied Linguistics.

Brecht, Richard D.
2007 National language educational policy in the nation's interest: Why? How? Who is responsible for what? *Modern Language Journal* 91 (2): 264–265.

Burstall, Clare
1974 *Primary French in the Balance*. Windsor: National Foundation for Educational Research.

Businaro, Barbara
2007 Foreign language teaching in Italian schools. Bolzano/Bozen: Free University of Bolzano/Bozen.

Butler, Yuko Goto and Masakazu Iino
2005 Current Japanese reforms in English language education: The 2003 'Action Plan'. *Language Policy* 4 (1): 25–45.

Byram, Michael
1997 *Teaching and Assessing Intercultural Communicative Competence*. Clevedon: Multilingual Matters.

Byram, Michael
2008 *From Foreign Language Education to Education for Intercultural Citizenship*. Clevedon: Multilingual Matters.

Cabau-Lampa, Beatrice
2007 Mother tongue plus two European languages in Sweden: Unrealistic educational goal? *Language Policy* 6 (3/4): 333–358.

Cha, Yun-Kyung and Seung-Hwan Ham
2008 The impact of English on the school curriculum. In: Bernard Spolsky and Francis M. Hult (eds.), *The Handbook of Educational Linguistics*, 313–327. Oxford: Blackwell Publishing.

Chen, Su-Chiao
2006 Simultaneous promotion of indigenisation and internationalisation: New language-in-education policy in Taiwan. *Language and Education* 20 (4): 322–337.

CILT
2007 *Language Trends Secondary Survey 2007: Data Report*. CILT the National Centre for Languages. Accessed 24. 06. 08. Available from http://www.cilt.org.uk/research/languagetrends/2007/trends2007_statistical_report.pdf.

Clark, John
1987 *Curriculum Renewal in School Foreign Language Learning*. Oxford: Oxford University Press.
Costanzo, Edvige
2003 Language education (educazione linguistica) in Italy: an experience that could benefit Europe? Strasbourg: Council of Europe, Language Policy Division.
Council of Europe
2001 *Common European Framework of Reference for Languages*. Cambridge: Cambridge University Press.
Crowley, Tony
1989 *The Politics of Discourse: The Standard Language Question in British Cultural Debates*. Basingstoke: Macmillan.
Crowley, Tony
2000 *The Politics of Language in Ireland 1366–1922: A Sourcebook*. London: Routledge.
Crystal, David
2003 *English as a Global Language*. 2nd ed. Cambridge: Cambridge University Press.
Darquennes, Jeroen and Peter Nelde
2006 German as a lingua franca. *Annual Review of Applied Linguistics* 26: 61–77.
de Bot, Kees
2007 Language teaching in a changing world. *Modern Language Journal* 91 (2): 274–276.
Dearing, Ron and Lid King
2007 Languages Review. Nottingham: DfES Publications.
Decke-Cornill, Helene
2003 'We would have to invent the language we are supposed to teach': The issue of English as Lingua Franca in language education in Germany. In: Michael Byram and Peter Grundy (eds.), *Context and Culture in Language Teaching and Learning*, 59–71. Clevedon: Multilingual Matters.
Department for Education and Science
2002 Languages for all, languages for life: A strategy for England. Nottingham: DfES Publications.
Department for Education and Science
2005 Key Stage 2 framework for languages. Nottingham: DfES Publications.
Dheram, Premakumari
2005 English language teaching in India: Colonial past vis-a-vis curricular reform. In: George Braine (ed.), *Teaching English to the World*, 59–70. Mahwah, New Jersey: Lawrence Erlbaum.
Dörnyei, Zoltán, Kata Csizér and Nóra Németh
2006 *Motivation, Language Attitudes and Globalisation: A Hungarian Perspective*. Clevedon: Multilingual Matters.
Edwards, J. David
2004 The role of languages in a post-9/11 United States. *Modern Language Journal* 88 (2): 268–271.

Elder, Catherine and Alan Davies
2006 Assessing English as a lingua franca. *Annual Review of Applied Linguistics* 26: 282–301.

Erebus Consulting Partners
2002 Evaluation of the national Asian languages and studies in Australian schools strategy: A report to the Department of Education, Science and Training.

European Commission
1995 White paper on education and training: Teaching and learning, towards the learning society. Brussels: European Commission.

Eurydice
2005 Key data on teaching languages at school in Europe. Brussels: Eurydice European Unit.

Eurydice
2006 Content and language integrated learning at school in Europe. Brussels: European Commission.

Extra, Guus
2007 From minority programmes to multilingual education. In: Peter Auer and Li Wei (eds.), *Handbook of Multilingualism and Multilingual Communication*, 175–206. Berlin: Mouton-deGruyter.

Földes, Csaba
2004 Deutsch als Europasprache aus ungarischer Sicht. In: W. Christian Lohse (ed.), *Die deutsche Sprache in der Europaeischen Union*, 109–128. Baden-Baden: Nomos.

Fotos, Sandra
2005 Traditional and grammar translation methods for second language teaching. In: Eli Hinkel (ed.), *Handbook of Research in Second Language Teaching and Learning*, 653–670. Mahwah, New Jersey: Lawrence Erlbaum.

Graddol, David
2006 *English Next*. London: The British Council.

Grin, François
2003 *Language Policy Evaluation and the European Charter for Regional or Minority Languages*. Basingstoke: Palgrave Macmillan.

Grin, François
2006 Peut-on faire confiance au modèle '1+2'? Une évaluation critique des scénarios de communication dans l'Europe multilingue. *Revista di Llengua i Dret* 45: 217–231.

Hashimoto, Kayoko
2007 Japan's language policy and the 'lost decade'. In: Amy B. M. Tsui and James W. Tollefson (eds.), *Language Policy, Culture and Identity in Asian Contexts*, 25–36. Mahwah, New Jersey: Lawrence Erlbaum.

Hawkins, Eric
1987 *Awareness of Language: An Introduction*. Cambridge: Cambridge University Press.

Hawkins, Eric
2005 Out of this nettle, drop-out, we pluck this flower, opportunity: re-thinking the school foreign language apprenticeship. *Language Learning Journal* 32: 4–17.

Hawkins, Eric (ed.)
1997 *Thirty Years of Language Teaching*. London: CILT Publications.

Hoberg, Rudolf (ed.)
2002 *Deutsch – Englisch – Europaeisch: Impulse für eine Neue Sprachpolitik*. Mannheim: Duden.

Holliday, Adrian
2005 *The Struggle to Teach English as an International Language*. Oxford: Oxford University Press.

Howatt, Anthony P. R.
1984 *A History of English Language Teaching*. 2nd edition Oxford: Oxford University Press.

Hu, Yuanyuan
2007 China's foreign language policy on primary English education: What's behind it? *Language Policy* 6 (3/4): 359–376.

Jenkins, Jennifer
2006 Current perspectives on teaching world Englishes and English as a lingua franca. *TESOL Quarterly* 40 (1):157–181.

Judge, Anne
2007 *Linguistic Policies and the Survival of Regional Languages in France and Britain*. New York: Palgrave Macmillan.

Kachru, Braj
1992 Teaching world Englishes. In: Braj Kachru (ed.), *The Other Tongue: English Across Cultures*, 355–366. Urbana: University of Illinois Press.

Kaplan, Robert B. and Richard B. Baldauf
2005 Language-in-education policy and planning. In: Eli Hinkel (ed.), *Handbook of Research in Second Language Teaching and Learning*, 1013–1034. Mahwah, New Jersey: Lawrence Erlbaum.

Kramsch, Claire
2005 Post 9/11: foreign languages between knowledge and power. *Applied Linguistics* 26 (4): 545–567.

Lam, Agnes
2002 English in education in China: policy changes and learners' experiences. *World Englishes* 21 (2): 245–256.

Li, Minglin
2007 Foreign language education in primary schools in the People's Republic of China. *Current Issues in Language Planning* 8 (2): 148–161.

Liddicoat, Anthony, Angela Scarino, Timothy Curnow, Michelle Kohler, Andrew Scrimgeour and Anne-Marie Morgan
2007 An investigation of the state and nature of languages in Australian schools. Canberra: Department of Education, Employment and Workplace Relations.

Lo Bianco, Joseph
1987 *National Policy on Languages*. Canberra: Australian Government Publishing Service.

Lo Bianco, Joseph
2008 Educational linguistics and education systems. In: Bernard Spolsky and Francis M. Hult (eds.), *The Handbook of Educational Linguistics*, 113–126. Oxford: Blackwell Publishing.

Lohse, W Christian, (ed.)
2004 *Die Deutsche Sprache in der Europäischen Union: Rolle und Chancen aus Rechts- und Sprachwissenschaftlicher Sicht.* Baden-Baden: Nomos.

Mao, Luming and Yue Min
2004 Foreign language education in the PRC: a brief overview. In: Minglang Zhou and Hongkai Sun (eds.), *Language Policy in the People's Republic of China*, 319–330. Dordrecht: Kluwer.

Marsh, David
2002 *CLIL/EMILE: The European Dimension.* Jyväskylä: UniCOM Continuing Education Centre.

Matsuura, Hiroko, Miho Fujieda and Sean Mahoney
2004 The officialization of English and ELT in Japan: 2000. *World Englishes* 23 (3): 471–487.

McKay, Sandra
2002 *Teaching English as an International Language.* Oxford: Oxford University Press.

Medgyes, Peter
1993 The national L2 curriculum in Hungary. *Annual Review of Applied Linguistics* 13: 24–36.

Ministère de l'Education Nationale
2006 Enseignement des langues vivantes: Rénovation de l'enseignement des langues vivantes étrangères. *Bulletin Officiel* 23.

Mitchell, Rosamond
2007 A future for foreign language education in an Anglophone context: policy debates in England. Paper presented to 2nd 'Cutting Edges' conference, Canterbury, June 2007.

Muller, Kurt E.
1986 *Language Competence: Implications for National Security.* New York: Praeger.

Neau, Vira
2003 The teaching of foreign languages in Cambodia: a historical perspective. *Language Culture and Curriculum* 16 (3): 253–268.

Nic Craith, Mairéad
2006 *Europe and the Politics of Language: Citizens, Migrants and Outsiders.* Basingstoke: Palgrave Macmillan.

North, Brian
2008 Levels and goals: Central frameworks and local strategies. In: Bernard Spolsky and Francis M. Hult (eds.), *The Handbook of Educational Linguistics*, 220–232. Oxford: Blackwell.

Nuffield Languages Inquiry
2000 Languages: The next generation. Final report and recommendations of the Nuffield Languages Inquiry. London: The Nuffield Foundation.

Nyikos, Katalin
1994 Retooling for communication: Hungary reorients its FL teaching. *Georgetown University Round Table on Languages and Linguistics*: 102–107.

Oladejo, James
2006 Parents' attitudes towards bilingual education policy in Taiwan. *Bilingual Research Journal* 30 (1): 147–170.

Olsen, David R.
1994 *The World on Paper: The Conceptual and Cognitive Implications of Writing and Reading*. Cambridge: Cambridge University Press.

Pennycook, Alastair
1998 *English and the Discourses of Colonialism*. London: Routledge.

Petneki, Katalin
2007 *School policy documents and multilingualism in Hungary*. Szeged: University of Szeged.

Phillips, June K.
2007 Foreign language education: Whose definition? *Modern Language Journal* 91 (2): 266–268.

Phillipson, Robert
2003 *English-Only Europe? Challenging Language Policy*. London: Routledge.

Popper, Karl R
1972 *Objective Knowledge: An Evolutionary Approach*. Oxford: Oxford University Press.

Raasch, Albert (ed.)
1997 *Sprachenpolitik Deutsch als Fremdsprache: Länderberichte zur Internationalen Diskussion* Amsterdam: Rodopi.

Seikkula-Leino, Jaana
2007 CLIL learning: Achievement levels and affective factors. *Language and Education* 21 (4): 328–341.

Shohamy, Elana
2005 *Language Policy: Hidden Agendas and New Approaches*. London: Routledge.

Spolsky, Bernard
2004 *Language Policy*. Cambridge: Cambridge University Press.

Starkey, Hugh
2002 Democratic citizenship, languages, diversity and human rights. Strasbourg: Council of Europe, Language Policy Division.

van Els, Theo
2005 Status planning for learning and teaching. In: Eli Hinkel (ed.), *Handbook of Research in Second Language Teaching and Learning*, 971–991. Mahwah, New Jersey: Lawrence Erlbaum.

Vygotsky, Lev Semenovich
1986 *Thought and Language*. Cambridge, Mass: M.I.T. Press.

Williams, Glyn
2005 *Sustaining Language Diversity in Europe: Evidence from the Euromosaic Project*. Basingstoke: Palgrave Macmillan.

Wolff, Dieter
2009 Content and language integrated teaching. See chapter 20 in this volume. Berlin: Mouton de Gruyter.

Wright, Sue
2006 French as a lingua franca. *Annual Review of Applied Linguistics* 26: 35–60.

Yim, Sungwon
2007 Globalization and language policy in South Korea. In: Amy B. M. Tsui and James W. Tollefson (eds.), *Language Policy, Culture and Identity in Asian Contexts*, 37–54. Mahwah, New Jersey: Lawrence Erlbaum.

Yin, Qiping and Shubo Chen
2002 Teaching English literature in China: importance, problems and countermeasures. *World Englishes* 21 (2): 317–324.

Zhaoxiang, Cheng
2002 English departments in Chinese universities: purpose and function. *World Englishes* 21 (2): 257–267.

Zhou, Minglang and Hongkai Sun (eds.)
2004 *Language Policy in the People's Republic of China.* Dordrecht: Kluwer Academic Publishers.

Zhou, Youguang G.
2001 Language planning of China. *Journal of Asian Pacific Communication* 11 (1): 9–16.

Recommended readings

Baldauf, Richard B., Minglin Li and Shouhui Zhao
2008 Language acquisition management inside and outside the school. In: Bernard Spolsky and Francis M. Hult (eds.), *The Handbook of Educational Linguistics*, 233–250. Oxford: Blackwell.
Presentation of a set of issues central to implementation of language in education policy, including FL education policy, with two country case studies (Japan and Sweden).

Beacco, Jean-Claude and Michael Byram
2003 *Guide for the Development of Language Education Policies in Europe: From Linguistic Diversity to Plurilingual Education.* Strasbourg: Council of Europe.
A sample Council of Europe document on 'plurilingualism' and how this might be implemented through the development of appropriate language education policies in Europe. The place of foreign languages and English in particular is discussed alongside other languages, with the goal of devising overall policies which will support linguistic diversity, the management of communication in Europe and 'democratic citizenship'.

Blake, Robert and Claire Kramsch (eds.)
2007 The issue: National language education policy. *Modern Language Journal* 91: 247–283.
Collection of short articles providing a wide range of perspectives on future directions for foreign language education in the USA, in the light both of recent educational focus on 'standards' in public education and national security requirements for advanced learning of particular languages.

Breidbach, Stephan
2002 European communicative integration: the function of foreign language teaching for the development of a European public sphere. *Language Culture and Curriculum* 15: 273–283.
Argument for the promotion both of English language learning and of plurilingualism as necessary aspects of language education policy for Europe.

Cha, Yun-Kyung and Seung-Hwan Ham
2008 The impact of English on the school curriculum. In: Bernard Spolsky and Francis M. Hult (eds.), *The Handbook of Educational Linguistics*, 313–327. Oxford: Blackwell.
A study of the historic rise and institutionalisation of EFL as a school subject, and a critique of 'functionalist' explanations.

Hu, Yuanyuan
2007 China's foreign language policy on primary English education: what's behind it? *Language Policy* 6: 359–376.
An account of the introduction of English to the primary school curriculum in China, representative of a general international trend, and a critical assessment of the policy.

Kramsch, Claire
2005 Post 9/11: foreign languages between knowledge and power. *Applied Linguistics* 26: 545–567.
An examination of the conflicting demands placed on foreign language educators and applied linguists by considerations of economics, national security and globalisation.

Lo Bianco, Joseph
2008 Educational linguistics and education systems. In: Bernard Spolsky and Francis M. Hult (eds.), *The Handbook of Educational Linguistics*, 113–126. Oxford: Blackwell.
An overview of the role of formal education in secondary linguistic socialisation, and the changing goals of education in trans-national times. A stimulating general backdrop to consideration of specific foreign language education issues.

Phillipson, Robert
2003 *English-Only Europe? Challenging Language Policy.* London: Routledge.
An argument for the strengthening of interventionist language policies within Europe to support and maintain multilingualism, including strong promotion of foreign language learning in schools.

Seikkula-Leino, Jaana
2007 CLIL learning: achievement levels and affective factors. *Language and Education* 21: 328–341.
A sample research paper on the implementation of content and language integrated learning in Finland, one of the pioneering European contexts for this approach to foreign language education.

Shohamy, Elana
2006 *Language Policy: Hidden Agendas and New Approaches*. London: Routledge.
A general overview of interactions between overt and covert language policies, including two chapters on language education policies, and language tests and their overt/covert contributions to policy creation and implementation.

van Els, Theo
2005 Status planning for learning and teaching. In: Eli Hinkel (ed.), *Handbook of Research in Second Language Teaching and Learning,* 971–992. Mahwah, NJ: Lawrence Erlbaum.
A clear expression of the 'functionalist' perspective on language acquisition planning, relating this to needs analysis and to current popular models of communicative competence.

5. Learning and teaching multiple languages

Britta Hufeisen and Ulrike Jessner

1. Introduction

"Learn your business partner's language" is often given as the external justification for learning foreign languages. In the case of business partners with differing linguistic backgrounds, it seems reasonable and logical to learn multiple languages simply in order to be able to communicate in more than one or two languages. In addition to these external professional requirements, there is the worldwide norm of societal and individual multilingualism and learning multiple languages. However, the process of becoming and the state of being multilingual is not only a matter of multilingual competencies and literacies or even dialectal competencies, but also requires a level of intercultural sensitivity, and an awareness of all three. The Council of Europe has specified the European goal of becoming multilingual in its request that each member state provide their citizens with the opportunity to learn at least two foreign languages besides their first language(s). Furthermore, one of the languages learned should preferably be a language of wider communication and the second one should be a neighbouring or minority language. This would mean, for instance, that somebody living in Germany should be competent in German, learn English, French or Spanish as the language of wider communication and Polish or Danish as the neighbouring language or Turkish or Russian as a minority language. This person might also indeed already be proficient in German and Turkish because he or she has a Turkish background. A second example would be that of an Austrian citizen who is proficient in German (and possibly a second language of minority communication) to learn Spanish or English as a language of wider communication, plus Croatian or Italian as a minority and/or neighbouring language.

In line with these political and educational developments, a significant amount of linguistic research in the field of multiple language learning has recently evolved both within Europe and worldwide. The aim of this chapter is to provide an introduction to this research. Its emphasis will be not so much on the learning of a first foreign language, but instead highlight the learning of a second and further foreign languages. Multilingualism research is taking place in diverse areas, including psycholinguistics (e.g. the effects of multiple language learning on the individual), sociolinguistics (e.g. the effects of multiple language learning on the community and/or society and the effects of growing up multilingually), and applied linguistics (e.g. the effects of multiple language learning on the structured process of instruction).

Therefore, this chapter will first introduce the terminological framework used in the literature on multiple language learning. This will be followed by an overview of research to date on theory and practice in learning and instruction. Finally, limitations of this research and challenges for future studies will be discussed as stimulation for furthering research in multilingualism.

2. Basic concepts

2.1. Defining multiple language learning

In this chapter, the main terms which are in use in research on multiple language learning will be discussed. Overall, such concepts differ from traditional research terminology concerned with bilingualism or the learning of two languages (i.e. classical Second Language Acquisition (SLA) research) or on bilingualism:

Multiple language learning very often refers to the learning of more than two languages in tutored instruction (= third, fourth, or nth language learning), for which the term Third Language Acquisition (TLA) is used, but the term could also refer to the learning of a second or third or fourth foreign language (= L3) in a natural context.

Being multilingual means being proficient in more than two languages, as is the case with citizens who grow up with three or more languages. This could include proficiency in languages such as Finnish, Swedish, and Sami in Northern Finland, languages such as Turkish, Kurdish and German in Germany; or an Italian dialect, standard Italian and Slovenian in the North East of Italy.

Becoming multilingual can evolve from being surrounded by more than two languages on a daily basis. Such a situation might be expected, for example, of an individual growing up in Switzerland who becomes proficient in Romansh, Italian and German. However, it could just as easily apply to a person who grows up with just one first language and then learns two or more languages in the course of his/her school career.

Within the framework of current research into multiple language learning, a differentiation is made between societal and individual multilingualism. However, this chapter will not go into detail about societal multilingualism and instead concentrate on individual multilingualism which has developed as a result of multiple language learning.

It is important to note that this viewpoint represents a contrast to earlier and common beliefs that the prefix 'multi' indicates 'more than one', with the consequence that multilingualism is often (erroneously) used as a synonym for bilingualism only and that multiple language learning is somehow identical to learning a first foreign language (= L2).

However, researchers of multilingualism take the strong stand that bilingualism, trilingualism, or quadralingualism should be regarded as specific subtypes of multilingualism. That is, the learning of a first foreign language learning (= L2 learning), a second (= L3 learning), a third (= L4 learning) a fourth (= L5 leaning) etc. all should be regarded as specific processes of multiple language learning. This means as well that first and second foreign language learning have a special status, which will be explained below.

Likewise, for these researchers, trilingualism (or second foreign language learning) are not to be treated simply as extended bilingualism and extended SLA but as specific subtypes of multilingualism and multiple language learning in their own right. The justification for a distinction between bilingualism and multilingualism is increasing empirical evidence which demonstrates that learning a third (or fourth, fifth etc.) language is a completely different process to learning a second language. It is crucial to take into account that the L3 learner relies on a different set of previous knowledge than that which the L2 learner is equipped with. This previous knowledge marks a different starting point for the onset of the learning of a subsequent further language. The result is often a faster and more carefully planned language learning process on the part of the learner, as will be discussed below in more detail.

So far, little attention in L3 research has been focused on specific variants within one language or language family. This would include dialectal variants and standard variants in combination with foreign languages or different social registers. In the course of time it is expected that these linguistic situations will be studied as well.

A number of researchers representing a multilingual standpoint argue that all types of language learning and acquisition – even L1 acquisition – should be classified as multilingual learning. In this view, the study of multiple language learning and of the multilingualism that results from this learning provides a prototypical theoretical umbrella for the study of language acquisition as a whole. These researchers believe that only the study of multilingualism can provide insights into the language acquisition processes as a whole (Herdina and Jessner 2002; Flynn, Foley and Vinnitskaya 2004; Cenoz, Hufeisen and Jessner 2003).

2.2. Describing multiple language learning scenarios

The process of acquiring or learning three or more languages is characterised by diversity and complexity. This complexity mainly concerns the routes and the influential factors in TLA. In SLA, one can distinguish between two kinds of routes: that is, growing up with two languages in the family or the community, or learning an L2 in a tutored instruction setting once the primary L1 acquisition has been finished. In TLA, the number of routes of acquisition mulitplies, as described by Cenoz (2000). With respect to three languages, she describes at least four prototypical types of the succession of languages:

- Simultaneous acquisition of L1/L2/L3: A child may grow up with three (or more) languages simultaneously (e.g. Oksaar 1978; Gatto 2000; Gatto and Stanford 2000; Hoffmann 1985; Hélot 1988), this could also be called triple first language acquisition.
- Consecutive acquisition of L1>L2>L3: A monolingual speaker starts learning his/her L2 in grade 5 and his/her L3 in grade 7, both in a tutored fashion.
- Simultaneous acquisition of L2/L3 after acquiring the L1: A monolingual speaker starts learning his/her L2 and L3 simultaneously in grade 6 at secondary school.
- Simultaneous acquisition of L1/L2 before learning the L3: A child who is growing up bilingually starts learning another language at school at an early age (Cenoz and Lindsay 1994).

There is a wide variety of possible combinations of TLA that match these four prototypical scenarios.

Other concrete scenarios could include the following:

- An adolescent student starts learning yet another foreign language in grade 12 after she has already learned/started learning a first foreign language in school starting in grade 5.
- A child who grows up with two migrant languages may start learning the community language in kindergarten and commence learning the standard variety of the host country and typical foreign languages at school.
- A university student who has already learned two foreign languages at school starts learning a new language at the age of 27.
- A child who grows up with a dialect might acquire the standard variant in kindergarten and start learning foreign languages at school.
- An employee – 45 years old – after having used her L2 English in professional circumstances, begins to learn a new foreign language.
- A learner has learned a first and a second foreign language after having acquired the L1, but he or she does not continue learning or using the L2 until 20 years for professional reasons. It would be interesting to study the maintenance state of this possibly forgotten L2 and the process of relearning this L2.

These various scenarios show the multitude of possible language combinations and the complexity of multilingualism as a linguistic phenomenon. They also show that much more complex possible research methods have to be used in order to study these complex phenomena effectively and systematically.

3. Research on multiple language learning

3.1. The early years

Although L3 has only recently received more systematic attention by a small but increasing part of the linguistic community, researchers such as the German Maximilian Braun who wrote about multilingualism as early as 1937 defined multilingualism as the "active and passive comprehensive proficiency in two or more languages [our translation]" (Braun 1937: 115). He differentiated between learning and acquisition and believed that it was determination and aptitude that guided the language learning process and its success. Later on Vildomec (1963) published a monograph on multilingualism, in which he dealt with the learning styles of his multilingual subjects in a kind of anecdotal way. Some years later Naiman et al. (1978) worked on the language learning strategies of the good language learner, that is the experienced language learner.

In the late 60s and early 70s, typical research questions were concerned with interferences between the three or more languages of a learner (Stedje 1976, 1977; Zapp 1979, 1983). Data usually consisted of production data of learners at school and university and usually concentrated on the negative effects of the interactions of the various languages in the learners' minds. Such research usually resulted in warnings for the foreign language classroom teacher to make sure that the multiple languages the students had in their heads be carefully separated and that no connection among them be allowed, made or even emphasised. It was only during the late 80s and early 90s that the positive aspects of the existence of several languages in the minds of the learners was investigated and exploited in search of new pedagogical concepts. For example, Thomas (1987) and Ringbom (1987) found that learners who were already competent in two languages learned an Lx as their L3 more effectively than monolingual learners learning the same Lx as their L2. They also drew attention to individual learner phenomena, such as determination, motivation, aptitude, attitude and learning style.

3.2. Current research

Over the last 15 years, interest in third language learning has grown considerably, along with general interest in multilingualism (for detailed overviews on TLA research, see Cenoz, Hufeisen and Jessner 2001a, b, 2003b; De Angelis 2007). Recent research has looked into the differences and similarities between the processes of learning a second versus those of learning a third language.

The biannual L3 conferences on Third Language Acquisition and Multilingualism, the first of which took place in 1999 in Innsbruck, Austria, have continuously attracted an increasing number of participants, which led to the founding of the International Association of Multilingualism in 2003. In addition, the

International Journal of Multilingualism was launched in 2004 as well as a book series in 2006 in order to provide adequate channels for publications in this area. Over the past few years a variety of methodological approaches have been developed to investigate multilingual phenomena (described in more detail below).

With respect to TLA, the following main areas of research can be characterised:

(a) sociolinguistic studies which investigate multilingual communities and children growing up multilingually;
(b) psycholinguistic studies which deal with the multilingual individual learner, and
(c) applied studies which take into account the specifics of the learning context, the conditions and products of such learning, and the possible consequences for the foreign language learning classroom.

3.2.1. Sociolinguistic perspectives

L3 research from a sociolinguistic perspective focuses on linguistic situations as can be found in regions where minority languages exist. For example, Turkish migrants in Germany might use Turkish and German in daily life and be learning English as their L3 in tutored instruction. In some European regions, minority languages are used as autochthonous languages. For example, in the Basque Country, about one third of the population is bilingual in Spanish and Basque and the younger generations tend to study English as a third language. Likewise in Catalonia, most people are bilingual in Spanish and Catalan, and again English is learned as a third language. In the northern part of the Netherlands, the citizens of Friesland use Frisian and Dutch on a daily basis and children learn English as their third language from an early age at school. In Austria, where the majority of the population speaks German as a dominant language, there are two bilingual enclaves: one in Carinthia, where Croatian and German are used together, and the other one in Burgenland, where Hungarian and German are used on a daily basis. Here again, the bilingual children come into tutored contact with English as their third language.

On the other hand, in Cyprus, although there are two official languages, this does not necessarily mean that all the citizens are bilingual. The same applies to Switzerland with its four official languages French, German, Italian and Romansh. Not all citizens speak all four languages; some might be competent in two of the official languages and learn L3 and L4 in school, others might have a migrant language background, speak a Swiss German dialect in daily life, use standard German as L3 in official situations and learn L4 and L5 at school.

These examples show how manifold the linguistic situations may become once the minority languages, dialectal variants and other migrant and heritage languages which are part of an individual learner's repertoire are included in the study of multiple language learning. With this variety in mind, one can see that in a number of European countries, English is learned as an L3 (or L4, L5 or L6 respectively), although from a standard language point of view it appears to be the first foreign language in tutored instruction (Cenoz and Jessner 2000; Jessner 2006). Hoffmann (2000) introduced the term 'multilingualism with English' to refer to this phenomenon both as a societal and individual phenomenon.

Apart from English as L3, there are also other typical L3s, such as German, which are the focus of L3 research. As mentioned above, German might be learnt by children with a Turkish or Kurdish language background in Germany. French might be learnt by Belgian immigrants from Africa who come to Europe with a previous multilingual background. Yet another example is provided by bilingual immigrant children living in an Arabic and/or Berber family from Morocco who then acquire Dutch as a third language in the Netherlands.

Nevertheless, English and German represent the languages which so far have formed the focus of much TLA research (for an overview see Jessner 2008).

Among the topics of L3 research, the prestige of language variants is studied with respect to language choice: Prestige influences the speaker's willingness to maintain a migrant, heritage or minority language in a new environment, as well as his or her attitudes towards learning additional languages. Whether a language is maintained in a new environment depends very much on the prestige of this language in this context. For instance, in a Polish family in an Austrian or German context the younger generation might decide not to maintain the Polish language but to acquire other, seemingly more prestigious languages at school and university such as Spanish or Italian.

Lasagabaster and Huguet (2007) published a large-scale questionnaire study on the attitudes of pre-service teachers towards third language learning and/or multilingualism in a number of officially bilingual contexts in Europe such as Ireland, Malta, Wales, Friesland, Basque Country, Catalonia, and Galicia. The researchers concluded from their comparative study that the widespread favourable attitudes towards minority languages reflect changes in linguistic policies over the previous two decades which had been aimed at the protection and revitalization of the minority languages. They added that trilingual education and the presence of three languages in the curriculum was becoming more commonplace.

Aronin and Ò Laoire have studied multilingual situations and contexts in countries such as Israel and Ireland with respect to the effects on an individual learner's repertoire. They investigated, for instance, the linguistic situation of Russian immigrants in Israel and how these speakers adapt to the linguistic situation in Israel, which includes Hebrew, English and Arabic as the languages of communication. They describe these situations as instances of 'individual mutilinguality'. These examples again illustrate how diverse the scope of research can be (Aronin 2006; Aronin and Ò Laoire 2003; Aronin and Singleton 2008).

3.2.2. *Psycholinguistic perspectives*

Psycholinguistic research in the domain of L3 is concerned with the multilingual individual and individual processes of multiple language learning and use. Examples include studies focussing on the tri- respectively multilingual learner, developmental patterns of TLA, language maintenance, attrition and loss, as well as the characteristics of multilingual production and their underlying cognitive mechanisms. Over the last few years the main fields of psycholinguistic research on L3 learning have included cross-linguistic influence and linguistic and language learning awareness. These two areas will be discussed briefly in the following sections.

Cross-linguistic influence: Interaction in the sense of cross-linguistic influence between languages in TLA is a more complex phenomenon than cross-linguistic influence in SLA, which in traditional studies was viewed as being influenced by the mother tongue.

In a multilingual system, cross-linguistic influence not only takes place between the L1 and the L2, but also between the L2 and the L3, and the L1 and the L3. Cross-linguistic influence can result in processes and products such as positive and negative transfer of linguistic units, transfer of L2 language learning strategies into L3 learning or language loss of the L2 due to the recent learning of the L3 (recency effect, e.g. Hammarberg 2001). Alternatively, in a migration context, both the L2 or the L3 or the L2 and the L3 can jeopardise the maintenance of the L1, and as a consequence, result in language attrition (see also Jessner 2003).

A number of studies have provided evidence that the L2 fulfils a particular role during the learning of further foreign language. It appears that L3 learners and users do not simply fall back on their L1 in their L3 production and reception, but rather on their L2. The L2 seems to take over the role of a source, default and supplier language during production of the L3, especially when the L3 learner has not yet reached a high level of competency in the L3 (Hufeisen 1991). In research specifically on the learning of an L3 of Indo-European origin, results showed that L3 learners whose L1 is typologically unrelated to the L2 and/or L3 tended to transfer linguistic and language learning knowledge from their L2 and not from their L1 (e.g. Bartelt 1989; Hufeisen 1991; Cenoz 2001; Wei 2003). This finding has been corroborated by studies which have investigated learners whose complete language repertoire consists of Indo-European languages (Singleton 1987; Dewaele 1998; De Angelis and Selinker 2001; De Angelis 2005a, b).

Several factors related to linguistic and language learning awareness have been identified as salient in cross-linguistic processes in TLA which are:

Psychotypology: It appears that perceived linguistic distance between languages is more influential on cross-linguistic influence than the factual linguistic distance. In other words, learners who believe their L2 and L3 to be related find many parallels between the two. They will then find it easier to learn the L3 than those learners who cannot detect any similarities between their L2 and their L3, even though linguistically there may be many (Hammarberg 2001).

Recency of use: The longer an L2 has not been used by the speaker, the lower is its cross-linguistic influence on the L3 (Hammarberg 2001).

Level of proficiency in the target language: The higher the language proficiency level in the L3 the weaker the cross-linguistic influence of L2 on L3 is (Hammarberg 2001).

The foreign language effect or the tendency of L3 language learners to activate the first foreign language: Especially in the early stages of L3 learning, learners do not only tend to activate their L2 as opposed to L1-related knowledge for production and reception tasks in the L3, but also in connection with L3-specific learning strategies (Hufeisen 1991).

Furthermore, the activation of languages is related to what Grosjean (2001) refers to as language mode. The concept of language mode (2001) deals with the variable conditions in multiple speech situations. The language choice in a certain situation is governed by the language mode, that is, it depends on the language mode how many languages are activated in a speech situation. Depending on variables including the speaker's language mixing habits, the usual mode of interaction, the presence of monolinguals, etc. the speaker can be in mono-, bi- or trilingual mode.

The learners' perception of correctness of an L3-target word (De Angelis and Selinker 2001; see also Hall and Ecke 2003).

Hammarberg (2001), Cenoz (2003b) and Jessner (2006) discovered that L3 learners tended to activate all their languages during L3 performance. Jessner (2006) found, for instance, that the majority of bilingual (German and Italian) students from South Tyrol activated German and Italian in order to counteract lexical deficiencies during production in their L3 English for various reasons. German, the dominant language in most cases, acted as a kind of springboard for the detection of lexical deficits, whereas Italian was used as a confirming agent after the cognate in the target language was activated.

In a recent Canadian study, Tremblay (2006) found that L2 exposure can influence the learners' ability to use their L2 knowledge in order to overcome their lexical deficits in L3. A higher level of L2 proficiency, on the other hand, appears to correlate with a lower level of frequency with which the L2 intrudes during L3 production.

As mentioned above, to date most studies have concentrated on either German or English as an L3. It is only recently that other languages such as L3 French or L3 Italian have received attention (see list in Jessner 2008).

Linguistic and language learning awareness: Today it is widely assumed that life with two or more languages can lead to linguistic and cognitive advantages (Cummins 1991). In a number of studies carried out in the Basque Country and in Catalonia (Cenoz 1991; Cenoz and Valencia 1994; Sanz 1997; Muñoz 2000; Sagasta 2003) it was found that bilingual children outperformed monolinguals in the acquisition of English as a foreign language. These cognitive advantages are linked in the learner to a heightened level of metalinguistic awareness, creative or divergent thinking, communicative sensitivity and greater experience of language learning.

In a survey of several L3 studies on overall linguistic proficiency, Cenoz (2003a) could show a positive effect of bilingualism on TLA and further, that this effect is related to metalinguistic awareness, language learning strategies and communicative ability, particularly in the case of typologically close languages.

Linguistic awareness is defined as a conscious sensitivity towards languages and their relationship among each other. Language learning awareness is defined as conscious knowledge about the foreign language learning process and the ability to apply this knowledge to the current foreign language learning process. Jessner (2006) defines linguistic awareness in multilinguals as an emergent property of multilingual proficiency and as consisting of at least two dimensions in the form of cross-linguistic awareness and metalinguistic awareness. Cross-linguistic awareness refers to the learner's implicit and explicit awareness of the links between the language systems. She also points out that metalinguistic and metacognitive awareness play an important role in the development of language learning strategies of multilingual learners and users (Moore 2006). Due to their experience in learning languages, multilingual learners use different and often also more strategies compared to monolingual students learning their first foreign language (cf. McLaughlin 1990).

Mißler (2000) carried out a large-scale study on language learning strategies of multilingual students in a German context by using a German version of the Strategy Inventory for Language Learning, originally developed by Oxford (1990). Mißler found that an increase in languages in a learner's language repertoire corresponded to an increase in language learning experience. This experience was mirrored by the number of foreign language learning strategies these learners knew and used. Ender (2007) applied Mißler's methodology to her reading study of multilingual learners of French at Innsbruck University in Austria and found that expert learners outperformed other learners who did not exploit their prior language knowledge or their repertoire of language learning strategies in the same way. Kemp (2007) detected a threshold effect for the use of grammar learning strategies, such that diversification in and augmentation of strategy use occurs to a greater extent during acquisition of an L3.

Other supporting evidence comes from another large-scale study in Germany by Müller-Lancé (2003) in his investigation of L3 learners of Romance languages. He developed a strategy model of multilingual learning. In it he distinguishes between productive (or retrieval) and receptive (or inferencing) strategies, which turn out to depend mainly on formerly acquired lexical competences in other foreign languages.

3.2.3. Pedagogically applied studies

L3 research in pedagogically applied investigations are usually conducted in school and university settings and very often involves action research projects. Research concentrates on issues of how the instruction and learning process of an L3 can be made more efficient and effective by dealing with the topic of learners' knowledge of their other languages as part of the curriculum. Another goal is to develop and teach specific learning strategies based on the assumption that L3 learning takes place against the background of one completed or at least an ongoing L2 learning process. Three of these applied projects will be introduced in the following section.

EuroCom – European Intercomprehension: The idea behind this project is that etymological similarities and parallels between languages of the same language family can be used as a tool to ease the learning process of languages in cases where one language of a respective language family has already been learned. For example, if learners have learned French as their L2 or L3, it is assumed that the learning of additional languages of the Romance language family such as Portuguese, Catalan or Rumanian should be eased. The method of instruction and learning is based on seven linguistic techniques which compare the languages in question and facilitate the continual construction of hypotheses about the new target languages (see also the discussion of Meißner's model below). The aim is enable the learner to acquire receptive knowledge of the target languages very rapidly in order to be able to read texts. Such *intercomprehension projects* have been undertaken with the Romance languages (Klein and Stegmann 2000), the Germanic languages (Hufeisen and Marx 2007a; Ribbert and ten Thije 2007) and the Slavic languages (Zybatow 1999). Klein (2004) tested this concept with students at secondary school who were 14 to 15 years-old. She found that the students were intrigued by the idea of learning several languages at the same time and by trying to apply the specific seven techniques as tools for the deciphering of new texts.

DaFnE: Another recent project developed the idea of creating synergies in the learning of German as an L3 after learning English as an L2, which is a very common order of language learning worldwide. The project was funded by the

European Centre for Modern Languages of the Council of Europe in Graz and was titled *DaFnE* (*Deutsch als Fremdsprache nach Englisch* = German as a foreign language after English). In the framework of this project several methodological questions were investigated, including: how much L2-English students need to know in order to use their L2 linguistic background in the learning process of German as L3, which linguistic domains are close enough in these two languages so that German could be taught through English; how texts in textbooks can be constructed and filled with international and English words so that the text can be understood very easily, without a minimal knowledge of German. In the early stages of the project, several textbooks were written whose aim was to include English. Later textbooks included more languages than only English. Several pilot studies in various European countries were also undertaken to test instruction according to DaFnE principles (Hufeisen and Neuner 2003).

EaG. Yet another project – EaG (L3 English after L2 German) – was based on the fact that many Eastern European students at German-speaking universities have encountered difficulties in their degree programmes: They are expected to read English textbooks and attend courses in English. However, they mostly have high levels of competencies in German but not in English. With this in mind the EaG project tried to combine the concepts of EuroCom and DaFnE and also introduced a curriculum for autonomous self-study which used L2 German as a bridge language as a way to facilitate the development of receptive competencies in English as the L3. This project, conducted at the Technical University of Darmstadt, demonstrated that the students who had been instructed according to EaG principles found it much easier to follow their regular programme of studies than those students who had not been sensitised to L3 acquisition by means of EaG (Hufeisen and Marx 2007b).

4. Models

Parallel to these chiefly empirical research activities, attempts have been made to develop theoretical models of multiple language learning. Three models designed to meet various theoretical criteria will be discussed in greater detail below: Herdina and Jessner's Dynamic Model of Multilingualism, Meißner's Plurilingual Processing Model, and Hufeisen's Factor Model. Other models which focus on multilingual speech production, such as Clyne's plurilingual processing model (2003) or Hammarberg's language function model (2001) will not be considered in further detail.

4.1. Herdina and Jessner's Dynamic Model of Multilingualism

The language development of multilingual speakers is a complex and dynamic process. In sciences such as meteorology, mathematics, ecology, physics and psychology dynamic systems theory (DST) has been applied to complex problem solving for some time now but only recently has applied linguistics started using it as a conceptual metaphor (see de Bot, Lowie and Verspoor 2007; Freeman and Cameron 2008).

The Dynamic Model of Multilingualism (DMM; Herdina and Jessner 2002; Jessner 2008), applies DST to multilingual acquisition since both complexity and variability of multilingual development lend itself to the use of this thinking metaphor. In the DMM a holistic perspective to multilingualism, which presents a necessary presupposition of a DST perspective, is taken. Such a view assumes that the changing parts of a system are dynamically interrelated and that they not only influence each other's development but also the development of the system. Hence the multilingual speaker is described as a unique but competent speaker-hearer who is not compatible to a monolingual speaker's language contained within a multilingual's repertoire.

A holistic approach was originally developed by Grosjean (1985) and followed by Cook (1999, 2003). Yet, in both their approaches the relationship between the dynamics of language development and holism have not been discussed.

In accordance with DST the multilingual system is characterised by features such as, non-linearity, reversibility and complexity. Due to the perceived communicative needs of a multilingual individual, language choice and hence the development of the multilingual system changes over time, which can also result in language attrition and/or loss. Sometimes reactivation takes place after a certain period of time or languages simply are no longer used and can be replaced by others. Variability in the process depends on sociological, psychological and individual factors; but the context of learning, be it natural or instructed play an additional role. In this way, DMM represents an autonomous model of multilingualism, serving both as a bridge between SLA and bilingualism, and as a model which explicitly focuses on more than two languages.

In consequence, multilingual proficiency (MP) can be defined as the dynamic interaction between the various language systems (LS_1, LS_2, LS_3, LS_n, etc.), crosslinguistic interaction (CLIN) and the M(ultilingualism)-factor or effect, as can be seen in the following generalised formula:

$LS_{1/}LS_{2/}LS_{3/}LS_n$ + CLIN+M-factor = MP.

The model language systems are seen as interdependent and not, contrary to the perception of traditional transfer research, as autonomous, as they are perceived in traditional transfer research. This means that the behaviour of each individual language system in a multilingual system largely depends on the behaviour of previous and subsequent systems and it would therefore not make sense to look at the systems in isolation. The concept of crosslinguistic interaction also integrates cognitive transfer, as discussed by Cummins (e.g. 1991) in his Interdependence Hypothesis and by Kecskes's (e.g. 2000 with Papp) common underlying conceptual basis. In both concepts, however, the outcome of the interdependence between the two language systems is a resulting additive overlap. The M-factor, which is described as an emergent property of the multilingual system, is responsible for the catalytic effects of third language learning (for a critical overview of studies on the effects of bilingualism on TLA, the reader is referred to Cenoz 2003). The skills and abilities which have been identified as responsible for the detected differences between second and third language learning, particularly in the case of a second foreign language, lead to an increase in metalinguistic and metacognitive awareness, as well as a heightened communicative sensitivity (see Hufeisen below). From a DST perspective multilingual systems are not comparable to monolingual systems as the former include components which monolingual systems lack, as even those components shared by both systems have a different level of significance within the multilingual system.

4.2. Meißner's Multilingual Processing Model

At the core of Meißner's multilingual processing model, which he situates at the interface of constructivist learning theory and multilingualism pedagogy (EuroComDidact, cf. Meißner 2002), is a spontaneous learner grammar. This model describes and explains the processes at work during the beginning stages of reading in an unknown language (ideally belonging to a language family that is familiar to the learner). The precondition for the application of these processes is that a learner is proficient in at least one foreign language (such as Russian) when learning another, closely related one (such as Polish or Ukrainian). The learner's is to employ specific strategies to quickly and systematically understand a text in the as yet unknown language. These underlying processes, which facilitate the understanding of the new language, are based on the assumption that learners will systematically employ their knowledge of previously learned languages in the attempt to make sense of the new text and to construct hypotheses about structure(s) in the new language. In doing so, it is expected that the learner will continually formulate and re-formulate hypotheses about the new language, thereby constructing a *spontaneous hypothesis learner grammar*. This hypothesis-led construction process works especially well when the languages involved are related to each other and when the learner grammar is initially based to a greater extent on previously learned language systems, rather than on the target language system. This element is the main difference to Selinker's notion of interlanguage (Meißner 2003: 40). In Meißner's view, it is only in the course of the language learning process that the spontaneous grammar is continuously revised and developed in the direction of the target language's structures and lexicon. The previously learned foreign language closest in genetic type to the new target language takes over the role of a *bridge language*. This bridge language functions as a matrix against which the new structures and lexicon are contrasted and compared. The existence of such (a) bridge language(s) is the precondition for the establishment of a spontaneous grammar. In addition, the following conditions hold: there must be an etymological relationship between the languages, the learner needs to be proficient in the bridge language(s), and finally, the learner needs to receive instruction in how to use the knowledge of previously learned languages as bridge languages. Only when these three conditions are met can the spontaneous grammar be established and continue to develop. In this process, the grammar undergoes four distinct stages (note that the model applies to receptive and not to productive skills):

In the first stage, after the first encounter with the new target language, a first spontaneous grammar of the language is hypothesised or constructed. Initial and rudimentary understanding is facilitated by the bridge language (for example, for a native speaker of Arabic, L2 English would help with the initial decoding of L3 German). The spontaneous hypothesis grammar is revised continuously, thereby being extended or enlarged dynamically as the target language input is systematically compared to previous hypotheses about the target language.

In the second stage, an interlingual correspondence grammar is created via the spontaneous grammar, which in turn constructs interlingual correspondence rules. These rules switch between previous linguistic knowledge of the bridge language(s) and the increasing knowledge of the new target language system. Over time, these rules come to resemble the target language's more and more closely. Noteworthy features of this interlingual correspondence grammar include instances of transfer between the source language(s) and the target language.

In the third stage, a multilingual inter-system is constructed which stores and saves all successful (as well as unsuccessful) interlingual transfer processes. This inter-system consists of transfer bases which provide the learner with a general framework for decoding and understanding the new language. The Multilingual Processing Model contains six such transfer bases: communicative strategy transfer, transfer of interlingual processing procedures, transfer of cognitive principles, transfer as pro- or retroactive overlap, learning strategy transfer, and lastly, transfer of learning experiences.

In the fourth and final stage, learning experiences in the target language are stored as a collection of metacognitive strategies.

Over the course of time, the learner gradually constructs a multilingual knowledge system containing both positive and negative correspondence rules.

These rules can be used when the learner is confronted with written or spoken texts. The rules can then be altered, revised and extended when another language system is introduced.

4.3. Hufeisen's Factor Model

This model describes the factors which constitute the conditions for the initial stages that learners go through in their language learning processes. Each of these factors consists of a group of aspects which share similar features, and accompanying each transfer from one language to another (from L1 to L2, from L2 to L3), a new bundle of factors is added to the factor complex. The following factors and their features are distinguished which apply to the L2 learning process in this model:

- *Neurophysiological factors* constitute the basis and the precondition for general language learning/acquisition, production and reception capability. If one of these factors is lacking or is flawed, language acquisition will be difficult, deficient or will fail (Gopnik, Kuhl and Meltzoff 1999).
- *Learner external factors* include features such as sociocultural and socioeconomic surroundings, culture-specific learning traditions, and the type and the amount of input the learner is exposed to. Lack of sufficient or qualitatively adequate input will result in difficult or deficient language acquisition/learning.
- *Emotional factors* exert an enormous influence on the language learning process. They include features such as anxiety, motivation, or acceptance of the new target language by the learner. For instance, a feeling of anxiety can result in a retarded or obstructed language learning process (cf. Dewaele 2002).
- *Cognitive factors* include language awareness, linguistic and metalinguistic awareness, learning awareness, knowledge of one's own learner type and the ability to employ learning strategies and techniques.
- *Linguistic factors* consist of the learner's L1(s).

The focus of Hufeisen's model lies on the salient differences between learning an L2 and learning an L3. In fact, it is these differences which constitute the justification for the rejection of (extended) L2 models for L3 learning. This model makes the assumption that, in the initial stages of learning an L2, the learner is completely inexperienced and therefore unfamiliar with the process of learning an additional language. An L3 learner, by contrast, is expected to already be acquainted with the 'foreign language learning process' and has (consciously or subconsciously) already collected individual techniques and strategies to deal with this type of learning situation, albeit with differing degrees of ultimate success. It is quite likely that the learner has already intuitively discovered his/

her learner type and can act accordingly to further his/her own L3 language learning success. This state of affairs serves as justification for a further L3-specific set of factors which do not yet apply to the L2 learning process:

Foreign/second language learning-specific factors, such as individual second language learning experiences, (explicit or subconscious) foreign language learning strategies and interlanguages of other previously learned languages.

The linguistic factor-bundle will then expand accordingly, from merely the L1(s) to L1(s) and L2, which will then probably take over the role of a bridge language on the way to the L3 (Hufeisen 1991). In fact, recent studies show that the L2 takes over the role of bridge language even if the L1 and the respective target language L3 are closer to each other than the L2 and the L3 (Hufeisen 2000). In other words, L3 learners have specific language knowledge and competencies at their disposal which are simply non-existent for L2 learners.

The Factor model not only attempts to illustrate the prototypical language learning process but can also be used in the analysis of concrete and specific learning situations. Factors interact with each other such that if one factor or factor complex changes, there is a corresponding impact on the whole learning situation. Each learner develops his or her own specific factor complex in which certain factors turn out to be predominant, thereby exerting a strong influence on the given learning situation. Other factors might weaken in significance and become less relevant during an individual's learning process.

5. Teaching first, second, third and further languages

What concrete applications can be extracted and employed from the above theories and empirical data in contexts of language instruction? Given that the models in question illustrate various features and strategies of the L3/Ln learning process, it seems logical to exploit the foreign language specific factors in the learning and instruction process which have been introduced in chapter 4.3. Various studies have provided evidence that such specific strategies can be both taught and learned and then employed in learning contexts (see Marx 2005 and Neuner-Anfindsen 2005). Students can be taught how to read and decipher texts by systematically referring back and forth to their whole language repertoire in order to compare and make educated guesses about new language content (see Meißner's spontaneous hypothesis grammar above). They can be taught how to cultivate a sensitivity for the similarities and parallels between their new and previous languages; in other words, how to establish for themselves a multilingual mode of thinking, so that they are not simply restricting themselves to the target language mode during their learning process. By taking advantage of this kind of multilingual set of mind they can discover their individual learner style or type which will in turn guide the organisation of their learning process in the direction of maximum benefit for their learning efforts (for example, the creation of systematic vocabulary, grammar, etc. tables if they have a cognitive approach to learning).

Other applied multilingual language tools might include creating a personal vocabulary notebook or a foreign language portfolio containing words and phrases from all the languages in their individual language repertoire. Previously learned languages can be acknowledged and used within the classroom context by teachers and students alike as bridge languages. The explicit acknowledgement of the existence of previous languages, plus recognition of their status as useful pedagogical tools will naturally ease the new language learning process. Both students and teachers need to be made explicitly aware that the benefits of such a multilingual approach in the classroom will outweigh any 'dangers' (i.e. interferences).

With regard to language education, there is also an urgent need for common language curricula (Hufeisen and Lutjeharms 2005), which namely do not preserve a separation of languages in school and university. The learning curve within the framework of L3 instruction and learning will be steeper and faster, because the learners are now more competent in the foreign language learning process.

Textbooks are needed which refer explicitly to previously learned languages and that emphasise similarities with other languages. In this way cross-linguistic comparison strategies will be strengthened. A prototypical L3 textbook could quite probably begin at a very high level from a very early stage on simply because there would be no need for the usual easy beginner exercises. Researchers recommend starting with complex texts from the outset. These challenges will encourage the learners to employ their already acquired knowledge about language and languages and – more importantly – about the language learning process itself.

The implication of such a curricular design would be a greater initial focus on receptive as opposed to productive skills, on language learning strategies in contrast to concrete language input, and finally, on the learners' own activities in their search for hypotheses about the new target language L3 rather than on the introduction or explanation of linguistic facts.

It is important to emphasise, however, that introducing the concept of multiple language acquisition and learning to the school curriculum should not be the responsibility of L3 or Ln teachers alone. This responsibility must be shared by all language instructors (including instructors of any given L1) and, of course, by the respective school boards and education ministries. Theoretically, it is the L2 instructors who could act as agents to lay the foundation of foreign language learning for their learners. It would, therefore be crucial that they do not teach the language in question in the typically isolated fashion as is often the case today: In Germany, teachers of English as a typical L2 usually refer neither to the L1s in a given learner group nor do they prepare the way for the later L3 learning process.

The concept of learning multiple languages in a compound fashion will certainly only be successful if education authorities acknowledge the fact that multilingualism does not simply entail establishing a single foreign language in the curriculum while at the same time ignoring opportunities for students to learn other foreign languages at a later stage. This requirement holds true especially in countries where English has become the standard foreign language and is viewed more or less synonymously with the notion of a or even the foreign language to learn.

Neither does the concept of multlilingualism in school contexts demand that English always be the language learned first. Learners who know another language besides English as their first foreign language seem not only to be better prepared to add English to their foreign language repertoire but also to then learn other languages on top of that (Raasch 2003). However, countries which in the past have had a strong tradition of migrant and foreign language instruction and learning, such as Scandinavian countries, are now seeing a trend towards increasing lesson hours in English. As a result, English slowly seems to be taking on the role of a second as opposed to a foreign language. At the same time, the number of hours of instruction in other foreign languages is being reduced. In the worst case, lessons in other foreign languages besides English are abandoned completely so that further foreign languages – if any – can only be learned on a voluntary basis (such as in Norway). This trend has progressed even further in Britain, where universities have simply erased the university entrance requirements for knowledge of a foreign language. This change in the curriculum basically means that individuals can take up and finish a university degree with just one language at their disposal and without any foreign language learning experience. This development, needless to say, does not help to foster the European notion of cultural and linguistic diversity.

At present it seems unlikely, however, that any other language besides English will gain prominent status as the L2 in any national curriculum. An etymological approach to English language teaching (Jessner 2006: ch. 5) is suggested to serve as a new didactic tool for encouraging the learning of other languages, even in countries where English predominates as the L2. According to such an approach the enormous number of Romance elements in the English language should be emphasised, not only to raise multilingual awareness in the language classroom but also to foster multilingual learning in students over the long term. Thus English could function as an ice-breaker in multilingual learning contexts, an idea which can be seen related to European Intercomprehension described above.

6. Controversial issues and questions for future research

6.1. Research into the learning of multiple languages

More research is needed in areas of the world where societal and individual multilingualism is viewed, acted upon and engaged in differently compared to the (Anglo-)/European-centred approaches discussed above. Such studies should, for example, focus on the impact of cultural factors of the foreign language learning process and on innovative research methods.

Indeed, factors such as L1 cultural learning styles seem to have such a significant impact on successful foreign language learning that they overshadow other factors designed to encourage success. Ouédroago (2005), for example, documents that methodological and strategic language learning approaches which include factors such as language awareness, learning strategies, or learning awareness do not work well in countries like Burkina Faso (Africa). The oral learning style of this culture does not value or emphasise such cognitive aspects as highly as is typical in the language classrooms of the Western hemisphere.

Kärchner-Ober (in press) reports that her learners in Malaysia experienced greater difficulties than she had anticipated when they were encouraged to apply previous language learning knowledge. This is due to proficiency levels of the languages used in Malaysia not being sufficiently developed which, hence, means that they cannot be used as a tool in a subsequent foreign language learning process.

As well, the application of previously learned knowledge as an act of self-initiated learning is not part of her Asian students' learning tradition. What she finds is that her learners have developed competencies or proficiency levels in their various languages that are limited to specific domains. The linguistic goal for these speakers is to be able to function appropriately in different everyday situations in Malaysia, however they are not fully competent, proficient, or fluent in any one of these various languages. She calls this situation *multi-semilingualism*. It should be noted that this phenomenon manifests itself in a very positive fashion as the language competencies in question match exactly the individual and societal needs of the learners/speakers.

It is clear that there are still many more and very specific aspects of individual multilingualism that merit further research, as for example the neurolinguistic perspectives (outlined in the work by Franceschini (Franceschini, Zappatore and Nitsch 2003). Future research on multilingual awareness could include the study of individual learning biographies as a means to isolate and measure the influence of factors or factor complexes from a sociolinguistic and psycholinguistic perspective. By triangulating perspectives, methods and results, it would then be possible to systematically determine whether different learning environments and conditions require respectively differing theories, or whether it is at all possible to create a single theoretical framework or model which comprises all types of foreign language learning and acquisition. In fact, there is a need for future research to develop specific L3 methods. The following crucial questions still need to be answered: Does research in multilingualism and multiple language acquisition necessitate specific types of data collection? Is it even possible or feasible to answer all research questions in multilingualism, or is it likely that influential variables involved in the learning process cannot ever be adequately controlled for, thus rendering the research findings unreliable?

6.2. Research in multiple languages teaching

Specific teaching methods, those which take a learner's multilingual past, present and possible future into consideration, will have to be developed and studied. The need then arises for targeted research methods designed to measure the success rate of these teaching methods. It needs to be tested in carefully controlled experiments whether new teaching instruction materials which take the learners' previous languages and language learning experiences into account actually have advantages over traditional materials.

Further investigation is also needed in order to verify the assumption that language learners who have English as their first foreign language tend to learn later foreign languages to a significantly lower degree than those learners whose first foreign language is not English. Does the learning of English obstruct the learners' interest in learning additional foreign languages and if so, why exactly?

Finally, further research in multilingual education and pedagogy should be directed at establishing norms for the teacher training process and to consider the following questions: What types of teachers does this new type of foreign language instruction require? Is it possible or even useful to offer joint courses such as language acquisition theory to future language teachers, irrespective of the language they teach? Would language teachers profit from joint introductions to multilingual teaching methodology? To what degree should future L1 teachers be involved in this awareness-building process and how can teachers of immigrant and minority languages be incorporated into this same process?

Answers to the above questions would have a far-reaching impact on local, regional and national education policies. Further clarity in these areas would, as a next stage, aid in positively influencing the in-service-training of foreign language teachers working in schools, universities and other educational institutions.

References

Aronin, Larissa
2006 Dominant language constellations: An approach to multilingualism studies. In: Muiris Ó Laoire (ed.), *Multilingualism in Educational Settings*, 140–159. Baltmannsweiler: Schneider Hohengehren.

Aronin, Larissa and Muiris Ó Laoire
2003 Exploring multilingualism in cultural contexts: Towards a notion of multilinguality. In: Charlotte Hoffmann and Jehannes Ytsma (eds.), *Trilingualism in Family, School and Community*, 11–29. Clevedon: Multilingual Matters.

Aronin, Larissa and David Singleton
2008 Multilingualism as a new linguistic dispensation. *International Journal of Multilingualism* 1: 1–16.

Baker, Colin
2001 *Foundations of Bilingual Education and Bilingualism*. Clevedon: Multilingual Matters.

Bartelt, Guillermo
1989 The interaction of multilingual constraints. In: Hans W. Dechert and Manfred Raupach (eds.), *Interlingual Processes*, 151–177. Tübingen: Narr.

Bialystok, Ellen, Fergus I. M. Craik, Raymond Klein and Mythili Viswanathan
2004 Bilingualism, aging, and cognitive control: Evidence from the Simon task. *Psychology and Aging* 19: 290–303.

Braun, Maximilian
1937 Beobachtungen zur Frage der Mehrsprachigkeit. *Göttingische Gelehrte Anzeigen* 199 (4): 8–130.

Cenoz, Jasone
2000 Research on multilingual acquisition. In: Cenoz and Jessner (eds.): 39–53.

Cenoz, Jasone
2001 The effect of linguistic distance, L2 status and age on crosslinguistic influence in third language acquisition. In: Cenoz, Hufeisen and Jessner (eds.) 2001b: 8–20.

Cenoz, Jasone
2003a The additive effect of bilingualism on third language acquisition: A review. *The International Journal of Bilingualism* 7 (1): 71–88.

Cenoz, Jasone
2003b Crosslinguistic influence in third language acquisition: Implications for the organization of the multilingual mental lexicon. *Bulletin VALS-ASLA* 78: 1–11.

Cenoz, Jasone, Britta Hufeisen and Ulrike Jessner (eds.)
2001a *Looking beyond Second Language Acquisition: Studies in Tri- and Multilingualism*. Tübingen: Stauffenburg.

Cenoz, Jasone, Britta Hufeisen and Ulrike Jessner (eds.)
2001b *Crosslinguistic Influence in Third Language Acquisition: Psycholinguistic Perspectives*. Clevedon: Multilingual Matters.

Cenoz, Jasone, Britta Hufeisen and Ulrike Jessner
2003a Why investigate the multilingual lexicon? In: Jasone Cenoz, Britta Hufeisen and Ulrike Jessner (eds.) 2003b: 1–9.

Cenoz, Jasone, Britta Hufeisen and Ulrike Jessner (eds.)
2003b *The Multilingual Lexicon*. Dordrecht: Kluwer.
Cenoz, Jasone and Ulrike Jessner (eds.)
2000 *English in Europe: The Acquisition of a Third Language*. Clevedon: Multilingual Matters.
Cenoz, Jasone and Diane Lindsay
1994 Teaching English in primary school: A project to introduce a third language to eight-year-olds. *Language and Education* 8: 201–210.
Cenoz, Jasone and Jose F. Valencia
1994 Additive trilingualism: Evidence from the Basque Country. *Applied Psycholinguistics* 15: 197–209.
Clyne, Michael
2003 *Dynamics of Language Contact*. Cambridge: Cambridge University Press.
Cook, Vivan
1993 Wholistic multi-competence: Jeu d'esprit or paradigm shift? In: Bernhard Kettemann and Wilfried Wieden (eds.), *Current Issues in European Second Language Acquisition*, 3–9. Tübingen: Narr.
Cook, Vivian
2003 The changing L1 in the L2 user's mind. In: Vivian J. Cook (ed.), *Effects of the Second Language on the First*, 1–18. Clevedon: Multilingual Matters.
Cummins, Jim
1991 Language learning and bilingualism. *Sophia Linguistica* 29: 1–194.
De Angelis, Gessica
2007 *Third or Additional Language Acquisition*. Clevedon: Multilingual Matters.
De Angelis, Gessica and Larry Selinker
2001 Interlanguage transfer and competing linguistic systems. In: Cenoz, Hufeisen and Jessner (eds.) 2001b: 42–58.
De Bot, Kees
1992 A bilingual production model: Levelt's Speaking Model adapted. *Applied Linguistics* 13: 1–24.
De Bot, Kees
2004 The multilingual lexicon: Modelling selection and control. *International Journal of Multilingualism* 1 (1): 17–32.
De Bot, Kees, Wander Lowie and Marjolin Verspoor
2007 A dynamic systems theory to L2 acquisition. *Bilingualism: Language and Cognition* 10 (1): 7–21.
Dentler, Sigrid, Britta Hufeisen and Beate Lindemann (eds.)
2000 *Tertiär- und Drittsprachen. Projekte und empirische Untersuchungen*. Tübingen: Stauffenburg.
Dewaele, Jean-Marc
1998 Lexical inventions: French interlanguage as L2 versus L3. *Applied Linguistics* 19: 471–490.
Dewaele, Jean-Marc
2002 Psychological and sociodemographic correlates of communicative anxiety in L2 and L3 production. *International Journal of Bilingualism* 6: 23–28.

Dewaele, Jean-Marc
2007 The effect of multilingualism, sociobiographical, and situational factors on communicative and foreign language anxiety of mature language learners. *International Journal of Bilingualism* 11 (4): 391–409.

Dörnyei, Zoltan
2005 *The Psychology of the Language Learner: Individual Differences in L2 Acquisition.* Mahwah, New Jersey: Erlbaum.

Ellis, Nick
2005 At the interface: Dynamic interactions of explicit and implicit language knowledge. *Studies in Second Language Acquisition* 24 (2): 143–188.

Ender, Andrea
2007 *Wortschatzerwerb und Strategieneinsatz bei mehrsprachigen Lernenden. Aktivierung von Wissen und erfolgreiche Verknüpfung beim Lesen auf Verständnis einer Fremdsprache.* Hohengehren: Schneider.

Flynn, Suzanne, Claire Foley and Inna Vinnitskaya
2004 The cumulative–enhancement model for language acquisition: Comparing adults' and children's patterns of development in first, second and third language acquisition of relative clauses. *International Journal of Multilingualism* 1 (1): 3–16.

Franceschini, Rita, Daniela Zappatore and Cordula Nitsch
2003 Lexicon in the brain: What neurobiology has to say about languages. In: Cenoz, Hufeisen and Jessner (eds.) 2003b: 153–166.

Gardner, Robert, Paul Tremblay and Anne-Marie Masgoret
1997 Towards a full model of L2 learning: An empirical investigation. *Modern Language Journal* 81: 344–362.

Gatto, Daniela
2000 Language proficiency and narrative proficiency of a trilingual child. In: Dentler, Hufeisen and Lindemann (eds.): 117–142.

Gatto, Daniela and Louis M. Stanford
2000 Error patterns in the storytelling of a trilingual child. In: Alan K. Melby and Arle R. Lommel (eds.), *LACUS FORUM XXVI: The Lexicon*, 131–142. Fullerton, California: The Linguistic Association of Canada and the United States.

Gopnik, Alison, Patricia Kuhl and Andrew Meltzoff
1999 *The Scientist in the Crib. Minds, Brains, and how Children Learn.* New York: William Morrow and Comp.

Graddol, David
2004 The future of language. *Science Magazine* 303: 1329–1331.

Green, David
1986 Control, activation and resource: A framework and a model for the control of speech in bilinguals. *Brain and Language* 27: 210–223.

Grosjean, Francois
1985 The bilingual as a competent but specific speaker-hearer. *Journal of Multilingual and Multicultural Development* 6: 467–477.

Grosjean, Francois
2001 The bilingual's language modes. In: Janet Nicol (ed.). *One Mind, Two Languages: Bilingual Language Processing*, 1–22. Oxford: Blackwell.

Haarmann, Harald
1980 *Multilingualismus (1). Probleme der Systematik und Typologie*. Tübingen: Narr.

Hall, Christopher and Peter Ecke
2003 Parasitism as a default mechanism in L3 vocabulary acquisition. In: Cenoz, Hufeisen and Jessner (eds.) 2003b: 71–86.

Hammarberg, Björn
2001 Roles of L1 and L2 in L3 production and acquisition. In: Cenoz, Hufeisen and Jessner (eds.) 2001b: 21–41.

Haugen, Einar
1956 *Bilingualism in the Americas*. Alabama: American Dialect Society.

Hélot, Christine
1998 Bringing up children in English, French and Irish: Two case studies. *Language, Culture and Curriculum* 1 (3): 281–287.

Herdina, Philip and Ulrike Jessner
2002 *A Dynamic Model of Multilingualism: Perspectives of Change in Psycholinguistics*. Clevedon: Multilingual Matters.

Hoffmann, Charlotte
1985 Language acquisition in two trilingual children. *Journal of Multilingual and Multicultural Development* 6 (6): 479–495.

Hoffmann, Charlotte
2000 The spread of English and the growth of multilingualism with English in Europe. In: Cenoz and Jessner (eds.): 1–21. Clevedon: Multilingual Matters.

Hufeisen, Britta
1991 *Englisch als erste und Deutsch als zweite Fremdsprache – Empirische Untersuchung zur zwischensprachlichen Interaktion*. Frankfurt: Peter Lang.

Hufeisen, Britta
2000 How do foreign language learners evaluate various aspects of their multilingualism? In: Dentler, Hufeisen and Lindemann (eds.): 23–39.

Hufeisen, Britta
2005 Multilingualism: Linguistic models and related issues. In: Britta Hufeisen and Robert Fouser (eds.), *Introductory Readings in L3,* 31–45. Tübingen: Stauffenburg.

Hufeisen, Britta and Madeline Lutjeharms (eds.)
2005 *Gesamtsprachencurriculum – Integrierte Sprachendidaktik – Common Curriculum. Theoretische Überlegungen und Beispiele der Umsetzung*. Tübingen: Narr.

Hufeisen, Britta and Nicole Marx (eds.)
2007a *EuroComGerm – Die Sieben Siebe. Germanische Sprachen lesen lernen*. Aachen, Shaker.

Hufeisen, Britta and Nicole Marx
2007b How can DaFnE and EuroComGerm contribute to the concept of receptive multilingualism? Theoretical and practical considerations. In: Jan ten Thije and Ludger Zeevaert (eds.), *Receptive Multilingualism. Linguistic Analysis, Language Policies and Didactic Concepts*, 307–321. Amsterdam: John Benjamins.

Jessner, Ulrike
2003 On the nature of crosslinguistic interaction in multilinguals. In: Cenoz, Hufeisen and Jessner (eds.) 2003b: 45–55.

Jessner, Ulrike
2006 *Linguistic Awareness in Multilinguals: English as a Third Language*. Edinburgh: Edinburgh University Press.

Jessner, Ulrike
2008 Teaching third languages: Findings, trends and challenges. *Language Teaching* 14 (1): 15–56.

Kärchner-Ober, Renate
in press *"The German Language is Completely Different from the English Language." Gründe für die Schwierigkeiten des Lernens von Deutsch als Tertiärsprache nach Englisch bei malaysischen Studenten mit verschiedenen nicht-Indo-Europäischen Erstsprachen. Eine datenbasierte, sozio-ethnografische Studie*. Tübingen: Stauffenburg.

Kecskes, Istvan and Tunde Papp
2000 *Foreign Language and Mother Tongue*. Mahwah, New Jersey: Erlbaum.

Kemp, Charlotte
2007 Strategic processing in grammar learning: Do multilinguals use more strategies? *International Journal of Multilingualism* 4 (4): 241–261.

Klein, Silvia H.
2004 *Mehrsprachigkeitsunterricht an der Schule. Protokoll einer 25-stündigen EuroComRom-Unterrichtsreihe mit Präsentations-CD für Lehrer* (Editiones EuroCom vol. 22). Aachen, Shaker.

Klein, Horst and Tilbert Stegmann
2000 *EuroComRom – Die sieben Siebe: Romanische Sprachen sofort lesen können*. 2nd edition. (Editiones EuroCom vol. 1). Aachen: Shaker.

Krashen, Stephen
1973 Lateralization, language learning, and the critical period: Some new evidence. *Language Learning* 23: 63–74.

Krashen, Stephen
1981 *Second Language Acquisition and Second Language Learning*. Oxford: Pergamon Press.

Lambert, Wallace
1977 The effects of bilingualism on the individual: Cognitive and sociocultural consequences. In: Peter Hornby (ed.), *Bilingualism: Psychological, Social and Educational Implications*, 15–28. New York: Academic Press.

Larsen-Freeman, Diane and Lynne Cameron
2008 *Complex System and Applied Linguistics*. Oxford: Oxford University Press.

Lasagabaster, David and Angel Huguet (eds.)
2007 *Multilingualism in European Countries*. Clevedon: Multilingual Matters.

Levelt, Willem
1989 *Speaking: From Intention to Articulation*. Cambridge: Cambridge University Press.

Mansour, Gerda
1993 *Multilingualism and Nation Building*. Clevedon: Multilingual Matters.

Marx, Nicole
2005 *Hörverstehensleistungen im Deutschen als Tertiärsprache. Zum Nutzen eines Sensibilisierungsunterrichts in "DaFnE"*. Baltmannsweiler: Schneider Hohengehren.
McLaughlin, Barry
1990 The relationship between first and second languages: Language proficiency and language aptitude. In: Birgit Harley, Patrick Allen, Jim Cummins and Merrill Swain (eds.), *The Development of L2 Proficiency*, 158–174. Cambridge: Cambridge University Press.
Meißner, Franz-Joseph
2002 EuroComDidact. In: Dorothea Rutke (ed.), *Europäische Mehrsprachigkeit. Analysen – Konzepte – Dokumente*, 45–64. Aachen: Shaker.
Meißner, Franz-Joseph
2004 Transfer und Transferieren. Anleitungen zum Interkomprehensionsunterricht. In: Horst G. Klein and Dorothea Rutke (eds.), *Neuere Forschungen zur Europäischen Interkomprehension*, 39–66. Aachen: Shaker.
Mißler, Bettina
2000 Previous experience of foreign language learning and its contribution to the development of learning strategies. In: Dentler, Hufeisen and Lindemann (eds.): 7–22.
Müller-Lancé, Johannes
2003 *Der Wortschatz romanischer Sprachen im Tertiärspracherwerb*. Tübingen: Stauffenburg.
Munoz, Carmen
2000 Bilingualism and trilingualism in school students in Catalonia. In: Cenoz and Jessner (eds.): 157–178.
Naiman, Neil, Maria Fröhlich, Hans H. Stern and Angie Todesco
1978 *The Good Language Learner*. Clevedon: Multilingual Matters.
Neuner-Anfindsen, Stefanie
2005 *Fremdsprachenlernen und Lernerautonomie. Sprachlernbewusstsein, Lernprozessorganisation und Lernstrategien zum Wortschatzlernen in Deutsch als Fremdsprache*. Baltmannsweiler: Schneider Hohengehren.
Oksaar, Els
1977 On becoming trilingual. In: Carol Molony, Helmut Zobl and Wilfried Stölting (eds.), *Deutsch im Kontakt mit anderen Sprachen*, 296–307. Kronberg: Scriptor.
Ouédroago, Dieudonné
2005 Mehrsprachigkeit und Deutschunterricht in Burkina Faso. Welche Strategien zur Verbesserung der Lehr- und Lernmethoden? Paper read at the International Conference for Teachers of German, August 2005, Graz/Austria.
Oxford, Rebecca
1990 *Language Learning Strategies*. Boston: Heinle & Heinle.
Raasch, Albert
2003 Europäische Sprachenpolitik – bottom up. Persönliche Erfahrungen und subjektive Perspektiven. In: Rüdiger Ahrens (ed.), *Europäische Sprachenpolitik – European Language Policy*, 257–266. Heidelberg: Universitätsverlag Winter.

Peal, Elizabeth and Wallace Lambert
1962 The relation of bilingualism to intelligence. *Psychological Monographs* 76: 1–23.

Ribbert, Anne and Jan ten Thije
2007 Rezeptive Mehrsprachigkeit und interkulturelle Kommunikation am Arbeitsplatz. In: Shinichi Karneyama and Bernd Meyer (eds), *Mehrsprachigkeit am Arbeitplatz*, 109–127. Frankfurt a. M.: Lang.

Ringbom, Hakan
1987 *The Role of L1 in Foreign Language Learning*. Clevedon: Multilingual Matters.

Safont, Maria Pilar
2003 Metapragmatic awareness and pragmatic production of third language learners of English: A focus on request acts realisations. *The International Journal of Bilingualism* 7 (1): 43–69.

Sagasta, Pilar
2003 Acquiring writing skills in a third language: The positive effects of bilingualism. *The International Journal of Bilingualism* 7 (1): 27–42.

Sanz, Christina
1997 L3 acquisition and the cognitive advantages of bilingualism: Catalans learning English. In: Lourdes Díaz and Carmen Pérez (eds.), *Views on the Acquisition and Use of a L2*, 449–456. Barcelona: Universitat Pompeu Fabra.

Schmid, Stephan
1993 Learning strategies for closely related languages: On the Italian spoken by Spanish immigrants in Switzerland. In: Bernhard Kettemann and Wilfried Wieden (eds.), *Current Issues in European Second Language Acquisition*, 405–419. Tübingen: Narr.

Sharwood Smith, Michael
1994 *Second Language Learning*. London: Longman.

Singleton, David
1987 Mother and other tongue influence on learner French. *Studies in Second Language Acquisition* 9: 327–346.

Stedje, Astrid
1976 Interferenz von Muttersprache und Zweitsprache auf eine dritte Sprache beim freien Sprechen – ein Vergleich. *Zielsprache Deutsch* 1: 15–21.

Stedje, Astrid
1977 Tredjespråksinterferens i fritt tal – en jämförelse studie. In: Rolf Palmberg und Håkan Ringbom (eds.), Papers from the Conference on Contrastive Linguistics and Error Analysis. Stockholm and Åbo, 7–8 February, 1977, 141–158. Åbo: Åbo Akademi.

Thomas, Jacqueline
1987 The role played by metalinguistic awareness in second and third language learning. *Journal of Multilingual and Multicultural Development* 9: 235–247.

Tremblay, Marie-Claude
2006 Crosslinguistic influence in third language acquisition: The role of L2 proficiency and L2 exposure. *CLO/OPL Ottawa* 34: 109–119.

Viereck, Wolfgang
1996 English in Europe: Its nativisation and use as a *lingua franca,* with special reference in German-speaking countries. In: Reinhard Hartmann (ed.), *English in Europe*, 16–23. Oxford: Intellect.
Vildomec, Veroboy
1963 *Multilingualism*. Leyden: Sythoff.
Wei, Longxing
2003 Activation of lemmas in the multilingual mental lexicon and transfer in third language acquisition. In: Cenoz, Hufeisen and Jessner (eds.) 2003: 57–70.
Zapp, Franz Josef
1979 Verzahnung von Zweit- und Drittspracherwerb. In: Walter, Gertrud und Konrad Schröder (Hg.), *Englisch*, 9–14. München/Wien: Oldenburg.
Zapp, Franz Josef
1983 Sprachbetrachtung im lexikalisch-semantischen Bereich: eine Hilfe im Zweit- und Drittspracherwerb. *Der fremdsprachliche Unterricht* 17: 193–199.
Zybatow, Lew
1999 Die sieben Siebe des EuroComRom für den multilingualen Einstieg in die Welt der slawischen Sprachen. *Grenzgänge* 6 (12): 44–61.

Recommended Readings

Munoz, Carmen (ed.)
2006 *Age and the Rate of Foreign Language Learning*. Clevedon: Multilingual Matters.
Moore, Danièle
2006 *Plurilinguismes et Ecole*. Paris: Didier.
de Bot, Kees and Sinfree Makoni (eds.)
2005 *Language and Ageing in Multilingual Societies*. Clevedon, UK: Multilingual Matters.

6. Developing links between second language acquisition research and language teaching

Vivian Cook

1. SLA research and language teaching

Teaching is only successful if it promotes learning in students. This statement seems such a truism that it hardly needs to be made. Teaching feeds off learning; any teaching activity needs to activate some learning process or strategy in the student's mind or else it won't teach anything. Yet in practical terms this obvious fact is often ignored in language teaching. The measure of a good lesson for many teachers, and indeed school inspectors, is one where the activities work and the students are happy, with little tangible evidence that the students have learnt anything.

The corollary of the truism is that the more teachers know about how people learn second languages the better they will teach. About the 1960s and 1970s, people began to take this view seriously by developing SLA research to underpin language teaching. This new discipline soon had its own journals such as *Second Language Research* and its own conferences such as the annual European Second Language Association (EUROSLA) meeting. Initially SLA research was largely initiated by applied linguists involved with language teaching, such as Robert Lado, Rod Ellis and Stephen Krashen, who saw it as feeding back into language teaching. Later SLA research tried to establish itself as an independent discipline, drawing on psychologists like Nick Ellis or linguists like Lydia White. Yet, despite the vast strides in SLA research, few people have been interested in maintaining the bridge to language teaching and only a fraction of the research has been applied to classroom teaching.

The first central concept in SLA research was that learners had a language of their own, given the name 'interlanguage' by Selinker (1972). The language the L2 learners spoke was neither the same as the second language that they had as target nor as the first language they already knew but was a system in its own right, created partly out of the L2 and the first language (L1), but also out of many other processes going on in their minds. SLA research swung away from seeing learners as passive recipients of whatever teachers liked to give to them to seeing them as active learners and creators. In 1960s teaching such as the audiolingual method, the teacher built up knowledge in the student's mind piece by piece (Lado 1964); the students had little say in what they did; anything that went wrong was the fault of the teaching. In most teaching since the 1970s the learners build up knowledge in their minds by trying to process language meaningfully and to use learning strategies etc: learning is their responsibility. The SLA concept of interlanguage turned the focus on the individual learner; teaching was helping the student to learn, not force-feeding them with information. The present perfect tense for example *I have lost my pen* would have formerly been taught say by a drill in which the student practiced the sentence with a large variety of vocabulary changes *I have lost my wallet/car-keys/...*, forcing the structure into the student's mind. Now it is taught by putting the student in a position where they have to communicate something using the present perfect. They learn it because they need to understand or to use it, the structure growing in their minds out of their interaction with the world. The idea of an independent self-directing interlanguage gives the students freedom to speak for themselves rather than parroting sentences supplied by the teacher in one way or another via drills, substitution exercises, fill-in exercises etc.

The change to a learner perspective led to a realisation that the stages of development that students go through are not necessarily the same as those that are followed in teaching. SLA research discovered that the interlanguage of learners goes through common stages of development, to a large extent independent of their first languages, whether in terms of grammar, vocabulary or pronunciation. One current version of the stages idea is Processability Theory (Pienemann 1998), which claims that all learners start by producing single content words, *beer, plane,* etc. Then they learn how to put words in the right order within one sentence, i.e. Subject before Verb in English *John like beer, Plane leaving*. Next they learn how to move parts of the sentence around so that they can ask questions *Does John like beer?, When is plane leaving?* Finally they learn to use the right order in embedded sentences such as reported speech *I asked if John liked beer.*

The Processability Model sequence is clearly at odds with the sequences embedded in many language teaching syllabuses and coursebooks. In the classroom students have been encouraged to use full sentences from the beginning, not isolated content words. One lesson for teaching called the *Teachability Hypothesis* was that "an L2 structure can be learnt from instruction only if the learner's interlanguage is close to the point when this structure is acquired in the natural setting" (Pienemann 1984: 201). In other words, teachers should not waste time on teaching things for which the students are not ready. Emphasising, say questions in the early stages may be useless as students cannot yet handle the word order movement on which they are based. Students are following a built-in schedule, not the one laid down by the teacher or the coursebook.

The switch in focus from the teacher to the learner as creator of their own language also led to SLA research looking at the choices that students make in their minds for using and learning the language. One branch is research into communication strategies – how do students compensate when they know less of the language than they need for getting an idea across to someone? The research tries to list all the strategies available to students (Tarone 1988) like *generalisation* – when a more general word can be used rather than a more particular one, such as *animal* for *rabbit*, and the *analytic strategy* in which the meaning of the word is conveyed in separate parts, not knowing the word *parrot*, a student says *talk uh bird*, conveying the meaning in the two parts. For teaching this provided a way of looking at tasks and of seeing how students can practice the strategies involved. Hence it supported making the students interact communicatively in the classroom – unthinkable under audiolingualism as the students would make 'mistakes' when not under the teacher's eagle eye – and was a major precursor for task-based learning.

Looking at learners more closely also revealed the extent to which they differed.

We have just seen how learners decide on strategies to use; hence they vary in the ways that they tackle learning and communicating. But there are a host of other dimensions on which students vary. One popular field was motivation: how does your motivation for learning a language affect your success in learning it? A continuing strand has been the idea that there are two main types of motivation: integrative, which involves wanting to take part in the society that uses the target language; and instrumental, which means using the language for some purpose like passing an examination or getting a job. From Gardner and Lambert (1972) on, this has been extensively investigated in many countries, showing some variations between different situations (Gardner 1985).

However the overall message is that learners need either high integrative or instrumental motivation to succeed. The lesson for teachers was partly that such deep-rooted motivation has a considerable amount of inertia; trying to change the student's long-term motivation was going against years of experiencing the attitudes of their schools, their parents and their societies towards second language learning.

An overall conclusion for teaching of the centrality of the learner and of learning was that much less is under the teachers' control than had previously been thought. The learner has an independent human mind that goes its own way regardless of the teacher; one of the characteristics of Good Language Learners was found to be that they knew what was best for them and would compensate for the type of teaching they received by adding stuff to suit themselves (Stern 1975). The language input that the students receive in the class, the tasks they carry out, are all adapted by them to suit their own needs. To a large extent the teacher has to fall in with the learners' strategies and spend time on teaching the things that are teachable and on providing the sustenance the learner needs.

This section has presented a selection of the bank of ideas about second language acquisition that teachers can draw on; Rod Ellis' mammoth *Study of Second Language Acquisition* (1994) for instance manages to take up 824 pages without even going into phonology or vocabulary. Many of the changes in thinking about language teaching over the last decades can be traced to the overall ideas about the nature of the learner developed in SLA research. Yet SLA research is typically used by teachers and methodologists to justify existing teaching methods and approaches, rather than to suggest changes to existing ways of teaching or to innovate new ways, as we see with task-based learning (Skehan 1998).

2. Some SLA research concepts and the classroom

Let us now select a few key SLA ideas which can be linked to teaching out of this vast array. As always, these should be treated, not so much as diktats by the applied linguist that teachers have to obey, as suggestions that may or may not turn out to be useful.

2.1. Universal Grammar

Two key concepts of the Universal Grammar school of linguistics are parameter-setting and vocabulary acquisition. Parameter-setting explains how human languages vary within a common framework. The grammar of a particular language reflects certain highly abstract principles that apply to any language because they are already built-in to the human mind. These do not need to be accounted for in language acquisition precisely because they are not so much learnt as inevitably forming part of our knowledge of any language whether first or second. The principles themselves cannot vary between languages; the differences between languages come from different settings for parameters. What distinguishes people who know English from those who know Chinese is the settings for these parameters. Take the pro-drop parameter which dictates whether you must have a pronoun subject in the sentence or not. In Chinese you can say:

Zou lu. ('walks road')

without a subject pronoun. But the English equivalent is impossible without a subject:

**Walks down the road.*

And has to be:

He/she/it walks down the road.

Chinese has a pro-drop setting for the parameter, English a non-pro-drop setting, as does every human language, whether German (non-pro-drop), Japanese (pro-drop), French (non-pro-drop), and so on for all the world's languages (although by far the majority of them are in fact pro-drop apart from English, German and French).

Acquisition of a language means acquiring the appropriate parameter settings for the language involved. In terms of second language acquisition, an English learner of Chinese has to switch from a pro-drop setting to a non-pro-drop setting; and vice versa for English learners of Chinese. And so on, for all languages that are learnt as second languages. This form of syntax goes with a particular theory of acquisition. Language acquisition is effectively parameter-setting from input: to set the parameter the learner needs to encounter language examples to demonstrate which way to set it. UG-related work emphasises how the mind creates language for itself out of what it hears using its inbuilt properties. The details of the situation and of the language encountered are more or less immaterial, short of total language deprivation.

The pro-drop parameter has been extensively researched in L2 acquisition. It turns out that resetting the parameter is more difficult for people learning non-pro-drop English from pro-drop backgrounds than it is for English people learning pro-drop languages such as Spanish (White 1986); the setting is also affected by so-called 'reverse' transfer in that people's L1 may be affected by the L2 setting (Tsimpli et al. 2004). Recent UG research into SLA has been concerned with the extent to which L2 learners start off with the same built-in knowledge of language as L1 monolingual children, for example the hypothesis that "the initial state of L2 acquisition is the final state of L1 acquisition" (Schwartz and Sprouse 1996: 41), and the extent to which they can acquire the same knowledge as a monolingual native speaker – the 'end-state' of acquisition. The nature of the initial state has become extremely murky with at least four hypotheses being advanced for it (Cook and Newson 2007). The consensus on the end-state is that, while some exceptional people can at least pronounce the L2 like a native (Bongaerts, Planken, and Schils 1997), most L2 learners could not pass for native speakers (whether this matters or not will be discussed later).

The more interesting implication comes from the current version of Universal Grammar called the Minimalist Program (Chomsky 1995). This maintains that parameter-setting is related to lexical items; the fact that *walk* needs a subject is part of our lexical knowledge. Since the principles of language are universal and built-in to the mind, all we learn when we acquire a language are the vocabulary items: language acquisition is just vocabulary acquisition. So when we learn the verb *walk* we learn that it has to have a subject, and so on. For language teaching this means on the one hand no need to teach core syntactic principles as they are already there (just as well as no course-book has ever covered them), on the other an increased need to teach vocabulary with a particular set of syntactic properties that demonstrate the type of sentence each item may occur in: for example the 'arguments' of the verb *walk* call for a subject but not for an object; *like* needs an animate subject and an object; *give* an animate subject, a direct object and an indirect object.

If the crucial aspect of acquisition is the provision of appropriate examples, then language teaching has to provide them. Give the learners a proper range of sentences and their mental parameters can be set; one of the justifications for the use of authentic language is indeed that it covers the full range of input features necessary for parameter-setting better than any selection by teacher, coursebook writer or syllabus designer can do. Most L2 learners of English speak first languages where it is not necessary to supply pronoun subjects in the sentence. Hence they need evidence to show them that English is a non-pro-drop language. The opening sentence of the coursebook *New Headway* (Soars and Soars 2002) is *Hello I'm Sandra*, neatly showing that a subject pronoun is necessary in English; a few pages later comes *It's a photograph*, showing that a dummy *it* has to fill in the subject slot; Unit 8 introduces *There's a CD player,* showing the need for a dummy subject *there* in existential sentences. Though it is unmentioned in the grammatical inventory for the course (or indeed probably any course): one of the main teaching points in this typical EFL grammatical progression is the correct pro-drop setting for English. While this coursebook does provide some appropriate input, this is the accidental by-product of covering other things rather than a deliberate policy.

Taking into account the complexity of words is perhaps more difficult. It is certainly possible to display the word in different grammatical contexts so that it is clear that *go* can be followed by prepositions such as *up* and *down,* but not usually by an object noun phrase, has a variety of written and spoken forms *go, goes, went,* and has a number of meanings such as 'travel', 'reach', 'start' etc. The teacher builds up the range of information for a vocabulary item in the student's mind. Yet mostly language teaching has seen its duty as repeating the new word a few times and listing it in a mini-lexicon – the word-list for *Headway* lists *go* with four phrases such as *go shopping*. The main moral for language teaching is to teach the complexity of words in terms of meanings, relationships with other words and syntactic potentials rather than as single items learnt in conjunction with single meanings.

2.2. L2 learners' strategies

This section is concerned with the strategies through which language is used and learnt, already mentioned briefly. The term 'strategy' is used in a variety of ways, the common factor being a deliberate choice by the learner to process or learn language in a particular way. The influential early idea of strategies came from Selinker's original paper on interlanguage (Selinker 1972), which he saw as made up of a complex of five central processes that are part of the 'latent psychological structure', including strategies of L2 learning, such as *simplification strategies*, when the learner 'simplifies' English so that say all verbs may occur in the present continuous, yielding sentences such as *I'm hearing him* and communication strategies, such as when the learner omits communicatively redundant grammatical items and produces *It was nice, nice trailer, big one*, leaving out *a*. The twin ideas of communication and learning strategies gave an impetus to a whole generation of researchers.

A distinctive flavour of communication strategies research was that it defined communication strategies in terms of failure; a communication strategy was something you resorted to when communication was actually breaking down rather than using to initiate the communication in the first place, in Tarone's words 'a mutual attempt of two interlocutors to agree on a meaning in situations where requisite meaning structures do not seem to be shared' (Tarone 1988). The research tended to yield longer and longer lists of potential strategies that learners could use, such as word-coinage – *heurot* for *clock* in French – or circumlocution – *when you make a container* for *pottery*. The approach seemed to be purely descriptive, rather like a plane-spotter's log of aircraft seen at Glasgow airport.

This led researchers at the University of Nijmegen (Poulisse 1990) to prune the lists by suggesting that the multifarious communication strategies actually came down to trying to compensate for a word that is not known in the second language through two core 'archistrategies':

- *the conceptual,* broken down into:
  - analytic *talk uh bird* for *parrot*,
  - holistic *table* for *desk*
- *the linguistic,* consisting of:
  - morphological creativity *ironize* for *iron*
  - L1 transfer *middle* for *waist*.

This model was tested on Dutch learners of English through experiments and other elicitation techniques to yield not only some idea of the relative importance of different strategies – holistic strategies came out way ahead – but also the discovery that a person's L2 strategies largely reflect their strategies for finding a word they didn't know in their first language. In other words, communication strategies driven by ignorance of a word are the same in the second language as in the first; in the second language we need to resort to them more often because we know fewer words. Teachers may not need to specifically teach communication strategies, simply encourage students to make use of those they already prefer.

Learning strategies research followed a similar path of first assembling examples of learning strategies into lists and then looking for more general explanations. A typical example of the first stage was a list of some 31 learning strategies, divided into three groups (O'Malley and Chamot 1990):

- *metacognitive strategies*, such as advance organisers for planning the lesson in advance,
- *cognitive strategies*, such as repetition through imitating speech,
- *social strategies*, such as cooperation through working with other students

Research into classrooms established that cognitive strategies outnumbered metacognitive by at least two to one and that social strategies were hardly mentioned. This led to the development of a teaching approach called *Cognitive Academic Language Learning Approach* (CALLA) (Chamot et al. 1999).

The most influential phase of this research came with the research instrument called the Strategy Inventory for Language Learning (SILL) (Oxford 1990). This required learners to rate sentences about themselves on 5-point scales going from 'Never true of me' to 'Always true of me'. Strategies were divided into

- *direct strategies* such as memory, cognitive and compensation
- *indirect strategies* such as metacognitive, affective and social

that is to say, the definition of strategies was broad and intended to cover the student as a whole. SILL has been used all over the world with thousands of students. A typical study is Shmais (2003), who administered it to 120 university students of English in Palestine; the most popular set of strategies were the metacognitive, with not much separating the others; sophomores use more memory strategies.

The inherent issues about applying strategies research to teaching are whether talking about them explicitly helps students to actually use them and whether there are dangers in imposing group solutions on people's idiosyncratic individual choice of strategies. The *Tapestry* coursebook series, for example (Benz and Dworak 2000), deliberately opts for organising teaching around the SILL scheme of:

- *language learning strategies* such as 'Practice speaking English with classmates as often as possible' (Unit 1)
- *academic power strategies* such as 'Learn how to address your teachers' (Unit 1).

It is then possible to use strategies research as an organising principle in language teaching.

This is a different question from whether strategies should be presented explicitly to the students, just as using grammar for teaching syllabuses is different from explaining it to the students. My coursebook *Meeting People* (Cook 1982) for instance included an exercise in which the students discussed the Good Language Learner strategies proposed by Stern (1975). Presenting strategies as a set of choices open to the students rather than as a predetermined set imposed upon them recognises that they are an individual matter and that students may profit more by choosing among the strategies for themselves rather than being forced to do the same things as everybody else.

The overall issue that strategies raise for teaching is the extent to which students should go their own way independently of teachers. Interlanguage was originally a declaration of independence for the L2 learner, recognising that they are creating a language of their own, not necessarily the one aimed at by the teacher. Communicative language teaching to some extent allowed students to think for themselves in creating their own communicative interactions; task based learning has been concerned more with the provision of tasks to be handled the teacher's way than with student-prompted tasks. Only perhaps in the autonomous learning theory is there a full expression of the idea that it is the students' right to decide what they do: in the words of Holec (1987), "Learners gradually replace the belief that they are 'consumers' of language courses with the belief that they can be 'producers' of their own learning program and that this is their right." (cf. also Legenhausen, Ch. 14 this volume).

3. Checking language teaching assumptions against SLA research

At another level we can use SLA research as a way of testing some of the assumptions that modern language teaching so takes for granted that they are barely mentioned. The source of many of them is the revolution in language teaching that took place in the late nineteenth century, whose consequences we are still living with. We shall look at three of the principles that have come down from this time and see whether they can be justified from SLA research:

3.1. Students learn best through spoken, not written language

The Reform movement of the 1880s emphasised the spoken language as a reaction against the largely writing-based grammar/translation method; indeed the reformers were among the founders of phonetics as a science, such as Henry Sweet (Howatt 2004). The long-standing tradition in linguistics since Aristotle is to see the spoken language as primary (Cook 2004). The main argument concerning language learning is usually that children learn to read and write some time after they learn to speak and listen. Historically this led at the most extreme to forms of audiolingualism where the written text was banned from the classroom during the early stages of acquisition. Communicative teaching and task-based learning still follow this tradition by treating the written language as a subsidiary aid to speech by getting students to fill in words in exercises, tick boxes to show comprehension, etc. (Cook 2004), rather than giving it the same respect for its natural forms as the spoken language. Tasks and communicative exercises have been seen as primarily spoken exchanges, using written language incidentally.

The objection from SLA research is then, not just that teaching minimises writing, but that it ignores the specifics of written language. Coursebooks for instance simply use the target punctuation without explanation, say goose-feet quotation marks in French ⟨le verbe «avoir»⟩, the initial upside-down Spanish question marks ⟨¿⟩ and exclamation marks ⟨¡⟩, and the hollow punctuation mark ⟨。⟩ and listing comma ⟨、⟩ of Chinese. The only teaching method to take a stand against the spoken language was perhaps the short-lived Reading Method in the 1930s (Mitchell and Vidal 2001). While writing is wide-spread in all classrooms and few stick to a purely oral approach, methodologists tend to see it as the servant of speech rather than having its own characteristics that need to be taught, and are progressively being revealed in research on the acquisition of L2 writing systems (Cook and Bassetti 2005); at best writing is taught at a global discourse level rather than as a practical skill comparable to pronunciation. Compare the amount of time any teacher currently devotes to teaching pronunciation with that spent teaching spelling; yet bad spelling arguably carries more stigma in real life uses than foreign accent. Regardless of whether teachers reject the over-riding role of spoken language, they can still take advantage of the precise details about the acquisition of second language writing systems now starting to be provided, not only at the level of global comparisons of meaning-based writing like Chinese with predominantly sound-based writing like English but also in terms of the types of spelling mistake people make and the ways they can be remedied.

3.2. Teachers and students should use the second language rather than the first language in the classroom

In an extreme reaction to the grammar/translation method's use of the first language in activities such as translation, the nineteenth century reform movement suggested the second language should be used almost exclusively in the classroom rather than the first (Howatt 2004), leading to the Direct Method and such patented spin-offs as the Berlitz Method, most extremely to the ban on the first language in the audiolingual and audiovisual classrooms. In the later communicative and task-based learning approaches, it is still hard to find any discussion of the role of the first language in the classroom, apart from the occasional advice to try to prevent the students using it in group work: "If they are talking in small groups it can be quite difficult to get some classes – particularly the less disciplined or motivated ones – to keep to the target language" (Ur 1996: 121). The recent Focus-on-Form (FonF) literature has argued for the use of grammatical explanation (Doughty and Williams 1998) but has never discussed which language should be used to explain it, implicitly accepting the second language as the norm. This L2 priority still seems embedded in many educational contexts. In the UK National Curriculum "The target language is the normal means of communication" (DES 1990). None of the 19 Local Education Authority advisors surveyed in the UK, 'expressed any pedagogical value in a teacher referring to the learner's own language' (Macaro 1997: 29). The justifications advanced usually rely on a compartmentalised view of bilingualism – Weinreich's coordinate bilingualism (Weinreich 1953) – in which the L2 user ideally separates the two languages completely in their minds. But an argument is also sometimes advanced that this is how children acquire their first language. SLA research however provides a corrective to these views by repeatedly emphasising in the past few years how the two languages are intimately connected in the mind, their lexical, syntactic and phonological systems interwoven.

3.3. Teachers should avoid explicit discussion of grammar

Another theme common to many methods from the nineteenth century onwards was that the role of overt grammar should be minimised and the rules learnt inductively from cunningly provided examples. Again this was maintained through the audiolingual and communicative methods. Grammatical explanation has tended to creep in by the back door of late in the Focus-on-Form movement, where grammar is used as a follow-up to the task rather than as its starting point (Willis and Willis 1996), in the tradition of Sweet (1899); as Long (1991: 45–46) puts it, 'focus on form [...] overtly draws students' attention to linguistic elements as they arise incidentally in lessons whose overriding focus is on meaning or communication'. The main reason put forward for avoiding explicit grammar is that children don't learn their L1 like this; parents rarely explain any aspect of language to them. While the issue of the role of explicit grammar in L2 learning is far from settled in SLA research, it seems at least plausible that it can be beneficial for many academic learners in classrooms – as shown by the many successful graduates in English from European universities who were trained through explicit grammar teaching.

The chief justifications for these principles is then how children learn their first language: L2 teaching should try to replicate the conditions of L1 acquisition. A keyword is 'natural': many methods of language teaching are claimed to be natural in mimicking the ways in which children acquire a first language. This does not mean that people necessarily agree on what *is* natural: the audiolingualists thought it was natural to associate stimulus and response, leading to their reliance on mechanical drills (Lado 1964); the supporters of Total Physical Response thought natural acquisition was reacting to imperatives – the 'golden tense' – leading to the students physically carrying out actions in the class (Asher 1977); the devotees of the Natural Approach saw acquisition as listening to comprehensible input, leading to exercises based on listening for meaning

(Krashen and Terrell 1983). But the main basis for these was not research about second language acquisition so much as the belief that the way you learn a first language is 'natural', meaning that a second language was best learnt in a similar fashion – hence the advantage of 'acquisition' over 'learning' in the Krashen framework (Krashen 1985).

What became apparent fairly shortly from SLA research was that L2 learners differ from L1 children in innumerable ways. One is the question of age: L2 acquisition can take place at any age, not just during the first few years of life. So L2 learners vary in terms of all the variations concomitant on age – physical, cognitive, social and emotional development. The reason why grammar explanations are not addressed to small children may just be that they are incapable of understanding them. Another difference is the situation in which the languages are learnt. L1 acquisition mostly involves a tight family situation, even if there are cultural variations, whereas second language acquisition situations can vary almost endlessly from prisoners in prisoner of war camps to children in primary school classrooms. Yet another crucial difference is literacy: most L2 learners have either acquired or are in the process of acquiring their first writing system. Literacy changes the way that we think (Luria 1976), even the structure of our brains (Petersen et al. 2000). Expecting literate students to depend on the spoken language ignores how minds are transformed by literacy. Overall, second language acquisition differs from first language acquisition because of the very presence of the first language in the learner's mind; general ideas about language such as 'learning how to mean' (Halliday 1975) do not need to be re-learnt for a second language. Hence basing L2 teaching on L1 acquisition may not work as there are two types of mind involved, one the property of an immature L1 learner without a previous language, the other of a more mature L2 learner with a previous language and probably literacy.

A more sophisticated justification for the three principles was based largely on methodologists' interpretation of learning theories in psychology. The most striking was the use of behaviourist theory in audiolingual teaching. Behaviourists had claimed that language was taught by associating stimulus and response, most famously in B.F. Skinner's 1957 book, *Verbal Behaviour* (Skinner 1957). Learning consisted of building up these associations till children could use them automatically – the same process involved in learning any activity, such as learning to drive a car. So audiolingualism concentrated on developing such skills through drill activities and repetitions of dialogues, as described in Rivers (1964), audiovisualism on the links between visual context and language (Guberina 1964). Audiolingualism also bequeathed to language teaching the idea that language consisted of four behavioural skills (Lado 1964), tacitly taken for granted in virtually all language teaching to this day; the emphasis on the spoken language led to the introduction of oral before written language, which coupled with the idea that non-productive skills were somehow 'passive', led to the well-known teaching sequence for the four skills of listening, speaking, reading and writing.

But the underlying rationale was a general theory of language learning that saw it as no different from any other form of human learning and that had, as Chomsky (1959) pointed out, been based on evidence from rats rather than human beings, let alone on first language learning. Not that this extrapolation from general learning theories to second language acquisition ceased with audiolingualism; such modern psychological theories as emergentism (Hulstijn 2000), connectionism (Blackwell and Broeder 1992) and chaos theory (Larsen-Freeman 1997) have been generalised to second language acquisition with scant evidence from SLA research itself and in the teeth of the claim that language is not in principle learnable solely by 'discovery procedures' from language input (Chomsky 1957). Unless we are totally convinced that all human learning follows the same route, i.e. deny the uniqueness of language that is basic to most linguistics, second language teaching cannot be based on ideas for which there is little or no direct SLA evidence. Arguments about L2 acquisition need to be based on research into L2 acquisition, not on parallels with other cases of language or non-language development.

So SLA research can be a liberating factor for teachers. Despite the support for the traditional three assumptions from most educational establishments, teachers can now feel freer to do what many have already done despite the advice from many educational establishments – use written language heavily with beginners, use the L1 in the classroom when it works better than the L2, and explain grammar in the first language. There may of course be other pedagogic reasons for sticking to the principles – using the L1 for example should not be an escape route to cover up the teacher's lack of L2 proficiency. But the major impact of SLA research is perhaps to say that the traditional teaching assumptions are not licensed by current SLA research. They should at least be thought out from scratch for the twenty-first century rather than taken for granted and justified from some common-sense view of language acquisition.

4. Two languages in one person

We will now develop a more idiosyncratic approach, which is not standard in the field as yet. The central fact of SLA research to me is that two languages coexist in the same mind, a first and a second. According to this view, we should not be looking at the L1 or the L2 in isolation but at the whole language system that the L2 user possesses.

4.1. Influence of the first language on the second

From the 1950s till the 1970s, the relationship of the L1 and the L2 was discussed in terms of the malign influence of the learner's first language on the second through interference or negative transfer; if only we could forget our first language when we learn a second! Contrastive Analysis pinpointed the differences between the first and second language and saw them as leading to errors in the learners' production (Lado 1957). Lado describes how Spanish learners add an *e* before English consonant clusters starting with /s/ so that *school* /sku:l/ becomes /esku:l/ in order to conform to Spanish syllable structure; how a Chinese learner of English finds *the man with a toothache* difficult because modifying phrases such as *with a toothache* precede the noun in Chinese; and so on. The later Error Analysis approach worked backwards from the mistakes that people make to their causes, chief among which was the first language. Corder (1971) points out how a learner sentence *I am told: there is bus stop* shows the learner's use of articles differs from that of English, leading back to the guess that the learner's L1 grammar lacks articles. Error Analysis was useful for teaching in suggesting the teacher had to think where mistakes could have from in the interlanguage processes rather than having a knee-jerk reaction that they were transfer from the L1. Banning the L1 from the classroom did not so much prevent interference as banish it to the privacy of the student's mind.

The overall belief was that the first language provided an obstacle to learning a second rather than an aid. Since the early 1970s this position has been in retreat, with more emphasis on the factors that learners have in common than on the peculiarities projected from their first languages. While the first language is undeniably a major influence for good or for bad on the acquisition of a second, it is only one among many other influences. Doubtless a certain number of mistakes are L1 transfer; many however are not and reflect universal processes of language acquisition and use.

In some areas of SLA research, the concept of L1 interference is still very much alive. Many of the writing system papers in Cook and Bassetti (2004) concern how the phonology of the first language or the characteristics of the first writing system affect the writing of a second; Dutch learners for example tend to spell ⟨cupboard⟩ as ⟨capboard⟩ because of their adaptation of the spoken English vowel /ʌ/ to Dutch /ɑ/ (Van Berkel 2005). Being at an early stage of development, L2 writing systems research can still get some mileage out of the L1 transfer research question, which has been done to death in other areas in dozens of books and thousands of theses. There is no need for further documentation of the influence of the second language on the first for every possible pair of first and second languages for every aspect of language.

A more intriguing development is the impact of the second language on the first. On the one hand the first language may change through attrition from the second language in the same mind. Schmid (2002) for instance found Germans living in the USA used more SVO sentences in speaking German than monolinguals. The first language may itself be transformed by the second language so that the person no longer speaks in the same way as a monolingual native speaker. Cook et al. (2003) showed that L1 speakers of Spanish, Greek and Japanese used slightly different cues for choosing the subject of an L1 sentence if they spoke English; Porte (2004) found that expatriate native speaker teachers are not immune to these effects, thus showing their native speaker status has a sell-by date rather than being good for the rest of their lives. In the dynamic systems model, the language system in the L2 user's mind is seen as constantly changing rather than ever achieving a static fixed form (De Bot, Lowie and Verspoor 2005). For language teachers and students then it may be a relief to discover they are not alone in feeling their first language is changing slightly may give them a defence against their friends and relatives who point out that are sounding slightly odd, as in the case of the reverse transfer of pro-drop settings.

4.2. Relating two languages in one mind

As well as the relationships between the two languages over time, research has looked at how the two languages relate at a particular moment in time. In particular a rich vein has explored the relationships between the two sets of vocabulary in the mind. One question has been whether the L2 user's lexicon is organised as two distinct stores, one for each language, or as a single store including both languages, or as two separate stores that overlap in some areas. While the answer often depends on the methods for measuring vocabulary, the consensus seems to be for a combined store accessed through two different routes (De Groot 2002); if, say an L2 user of English and French meets the written word *chat*, they perceive it as a word in the language of the particular context and then look it up in their mental lexicon where the two meanings of *cat* and *talk* are stored, one of which gets more activated because of the context. Several experiments have shown that both languages are invoked when an L2 user hears a word, only one being stronger than the other; a French L2 user of English has both meanings for the word *coin* activated even when they are reading their first language (Beauvillain and Grainger 1987). Learning an L2 vocabulary is not then done in isolation from the first. Without advocating direct translations, nevertheless the teacher needs to be aware that the first and second language words are interconnected in all sorts of ways not learnt and stored in complete separation.

The most dramatic relationship between the two languages in the same mind is demonstrated when they are both used simultaneously. Francois Grosjean (2001) claims that L2 users have two modes of using language – the monolingual mode in which they use one or the other language exclusively and the bilingual mode in which they use both at once in code-switching, as in a Greek student's *Simera piga sto shopping centre gia na psaksw ena birthday present gia thn Maria* ('Today I went to the shopping centre because I wanted to buy a birthday present for Maria'). Code-switching is by definition unavailable to monolinguals. It shows a complex ability to switch virtually instantaneously from one grammar to another grammar, one set of vocabulary to another, even one pronunciation system to another, with hardly any effect on fluency. Obviously code-switching takes place in very particular circumstances, notably when the listener shares both languages, and has strict rules of occurrence according to the situation, the topic, the social role, the overlap between the grammars of L1 and L2 and so on (Muysken 2000).

According to the view of code-switching known as the Matrix Model (Myers-Scotton 2002), the matrix language selects the overall syntax along with the grammatical morphemes as a frame for the system, the other fits vocabulary from the embedded language into this frame. For example the Russian/English sentence *On dolgo laia-l na dog-ov* ('He barked at dogs for a long time') shows matrix Russian grammatical morphemes and structure but an embedded English content word *dog* (Schmitt 2004). Code-switching is a normal ability of L2 users in real-life situations and can be utilised even by children as young as two years old (Genesee 2003). In a sense code-switching in the classroom has been prevented by the reluctance to see the bilingual mode of language as natural. Students need to see that this is a normal, and highly clever, thing that bilinguals can do.

The view that the two languages are always in a constantly changing relationship in the mind has consequences both for the practice of language teaching and for the learner's final goal. Language teaching has tried to treat the learner as a tabula rasa with no other language available; at best the L1 is a hurdle to be surmounted. The classroom has been treated as an ersatz monolingual situation in which only the second language should occur and teachers feel guilty if they use the L1 (Macaro 2001); if only the target language is proper, the students are effectively denied their whole experience previous to the class and the lives they lead outside the class. The lesson is that, however much you deny it or attempt to eradicate it, the first language is constantly there in the students' minds: the classroom is an L2 using situation with both languages present, albeit sometimes invisibly. Hence it may be better to consider rationally how this can be accommodated and exploited in language teaching (Cook 2001). As Swain and Lapkin (2000) put it, 'To insist that no use be made of the L1 in carrying out tasks that are both linguistically and cognitively complex is to deny the use of an important cognitive tool.'

In terms of the goals of teaching, the lesson is that L2 users are never going to be monolingual native speakers of the L2; they will always be different and will be capable of a range of activities that monolinguals cannot do, such as code-switching, and thinking and using language in distinctive ways. Hence while it is possible to compare L2 users with native speakers, it is not possible to say that the goal of language teaching is to speak like a native speaker, particularly for a global language like English where perhaps the majority of communication is between non-native speakers. The native speaker is on the one hand unattainable, on the other a limitation of L2 users to what monolingual native speakers can do. Language teaching has to train the learner to be a fully effective L2 user rather than a poor imitation of a native.

5. Conclusion

Cook (2008) outlines three ways in which SLA research can contribute to language teaching. Let us look at these three in the context of what we have been saying here.

5.1. Understanding the students' contribution to learning

It is the student who learns, not the teacher, obvious as this sounds when spelt out. The implication for teaching is that more stress has to be placed on what the students bring to the learning task, not on the teacher laying down what has to be done and what the student has to know. The Universal Grammar model sees the teacher as the provider of language input on which the student's mind can get to work. The strategies approach sees the teacher as providing opportunities for the student to tackle learning in different ways through tasks etc. SLA research is providing more and complex accounts of how the learner's mind works that the teacher can use to gain insight into their students and to affect their own behaviour.

5.2. Understanding how teaching methods and techniques work

If we start from what happens in classrooms, i.e. the sheer techniques of teaching, there is also much to be gained from SLA research. A technique implies certain ways of learning and processing, a certain type of student and a certain classroom situation. A structure drill for example was seen as a classic way of teaching oral structures and identified as an application of behaviourist learning theory. But it is also a communicative interaction in which people exchange information; it has strong implications for how the learner's memory stores and processes information; it involves particular kinds of learning strategy – all of which have been massively studied in recent years. SLA research provides multiple viewpoints on everything that goes on in the classroom. It can take us beyond the task itself to seeing what processes of processing and learning are used in the tasks teachers use in the classroom.

5.3. Understanding the goals of language teaching

Much of the contribution of SLA research however applies not to the question of what the teacher should do next in the classroom but to the general questions of why we are teaching and what we are teaching. As seen earlier, some SLA research starts to raise the issue of the kind of person we want the learner to be and how we imagine the new language will function in the L2 users' minds and what they will do with it. They may need to do things no native can do, like code-switching; they may need to talk to their fellow native speakers if their goal is English as Lingua Franca. Or, if they are learning English to be part of a multilingual community, say in Toronto, they need English for dealing with the public officialdom, with other non-native speakers in different communities, and with the monolingual English-speaking community.

SLA research certainly does not have magic solutions for language teaching. But it can provide some general ideas and some particular ones that may contribute to the totality of language teaching. The usefulness of SLA research for language teachers has hardly yet been tapped. As the discipline develops, it will surely provide suggestions that are more classroom related and thus fulfil the ambitions of its founders to base language teaching on a firm foundation of knowledge about second language acquisition.

References

Asher, James J.
1977 *Learning Another Language through Actions: The Complete Teachers' Guide-Book.* Los Gatos, Calif.: Sky Oaks Publications.

Beauvillain, Cécile and Jonathan Grainger
1987 Accessing interlexical homographs: some limitations of a language-selective access. *Journal of Memory and Language* 26: 658–672.

Benz, Cheryl and Kara Dworak
2000 *Tapestry: Listening and Speaking*. Boston: Heinle and Heinle.

Blackwell, Alan and Peter Broeder
1992 Interference and facilitation in SLA: A connectionist perspective. Seminar on PDP and NLP, San Diego, UCSD, May. Reported in Broeder and Plunkett 1994.

Bongaerts, Theo, Brigitte Planken and Eric Schils
1997 Age and ultimate attainment in the pronunciation of a foreign language. *Second Language Research* 19: 447–465.

Broeder, Peter and Kim Plunkett
1994 Connectionism and second language acquisition. In: Nick Ellis (ed.), *Implicit and Explicit Learning of Languages*, 421–453. London: Academic Press.

Chamot, Anna U., Sarah Barnhardt, Pamela B. El-Dinary and Jill Robbins
1999 *The Learning Strategies Handbook.* White Plains, NY: Addison Wesley Longman.

Chomsky, Noam
1957 *Syntactic Structures*. The Hague: Mouton.
Chomsky, Noam
1959 Review of B.F. Skinner Verbal Behavior. *Language* 35: 26–58.
Chomsky, Noam
1995 *The Minimalist Program*. Cambridge, MA: MIT Press.
Cook, Vivian J.
1982 *Meeting People*. Oxford: Pergamon.
Cook, Vivian J.
2001 Using the first language in the classroom. *Canadian Modern Language Review* 57 (3): 402–423.
Cook, Vivian J.
2004 Written language and foreign language teaching. In: Cook and Bassetti (eds.), 424–442.
Cook, Vivian J.
2008 *Second Language Leaning and Language Teaching*. 4th edition. London: Hodder.
Cook, Vivian J., Elisabet Iarossi, Nektarios Stellakis and Yuki Tokumaru
2003 Effects of the second language on the syntactic processing of the first language. In: Vivian J. Cook (ed.), *Effects of the Second Language on the First*, 214–233. Clevedon: Multilingual Matters.
Cook, Vivian J. and Benedetta Bassetti (eds.)
2004 *Second Language Writing Systems*. Clevedon: Multilingual Matters.
Cook, Vivian J. and Mark Newson
2007 *Chomsky's Universal Grammar: An Introduction*. 3rd edition. Oxford: Blackwell.
Corder, S. Pit
1971 Idiosyncratic dialects and Error Analysis. *International Review of Applied Linguistics* 9 (2): 147–159.
De Bot, Kees, Wander Lowie and Marjolijn Verspoor
2005 *Second Language Acquisition: an Advanced Resource Book*. New York: Routledge.
De Groot, Annette
2002 Lexical representation and lexical processing in the L2 user. In: Vivian J. Cook (ed.), *Portraits of the L2 User*, 29–64. Clevedon: Multilingual Matters.
Department of Education
1990 *English in the National Curriculum (No.2)*. London: Her Majesty's Stationery Office.
Doughty, Catherine and Jessica Williams (eds.)
1998 *Focus on Form in Classroom Second Language Acquisition*. Cambridge: Cambridge University Press.
Ellis, Rod
1994 *The Study of Second Language Acquisition*. Oxford: Oxford University Press.
Gardner, Robert
1985 *Social Psychology and Second Language Learning*. London: Edward Arnold.

Gardner, Robert and Wallace Lambert
1972 *Attitudes and Motivation in Second-language Learning.* Rowley, Mass.: Newbury House.
Genesee, Fred
2003 Portrait of the bilingual child. In: Vivian J. Cook (ed.), *Portraits of the L2 User,* 161–179. Clevedon: Multilingual Matters.
Grosjean, Francois
2001 The bilingual's language modes. In: Janet Nicol (ed.), *One Mind, Two Languages,* 1–22. Oxford: Blackwell.
Guberina, Petar
1964 The audiovisual, global and structural method. In: Barnet Libbish (ed.), *Advances in the Teaching of Modern Languages Vol. 1,* 1–17. Oxford: Pergamon.
Halliday, M. A. K.
1975 *Learning How to Mean.* London: Edward Arnold.
Holec, Henri
1987 The learner as manager: managing learning or managing to learn?. In: Anita Wenden and Joan Rubin (eds.), *Learner Strategies in Language Learning,* 145–157. Englewood Cliffs, New Jersey: Prentice-Hall.
Howatt, Anthony
2004 *A History of English Language Teaching.* 2nd edition. Oxford: Oxford University Press.
Hulstijn, Jan
2000 Emergentism and second language acquisition. plenary, EUROSLA Krakow, September.
Krashen, Stephen
1985 *The Input Hypothesis: Issues and Implications.* New York: Longman.
Krashen, Stephen and Tracy Terrell
1983 *The Natural Approach.* New York: Pergamon.
Lado, Robert
1957 *Linguistics across Cultures.* Ann Arbor: University of Michigan Press.
Lado, Robert
1964 *Language Teaching: A Scientific Approach.* New York: McGraw-Hill.
Larsen-Freeman, Diane
1997 Chaos/complexity science and second language acquisition. *Applied Linguistics* 18: 141–165.
Long, Michael H.
1991 Focus on form: a design feature in language teaching methodology. In: Kees de Bot, D. Coste, Ralph Ginsberg and Claire Kramsch (eds.), *Foreign Language Research in Cross-Cultural Perspective,* 39–52. Amsterdam: Benjamins.
Luria, Aleksandr R.
1976 *Cognitive Development: Its Cultural and Social Foundations.* Boston: Harvard University Press.
Macaro, Ernesto
1997 *Target Language, Collaborative Learning and Autonomy.* Clevedon: Multilingual Matters.

Macaro, Ernesto
2001 *Learning Strategies in Foreign and Second Language Classrooms.* London: Continuum.
Mitchell, Cheryl B. and Kari E. Vidal
2001 Weighing the ways of the flow: twentieth century language instruction. *Modern Language Journal* 85 (1): 26–38.
Muysken, Pieter
2000 *Bilingual Speech: A Typology of Code-Mixing.* Cambridge: Cambridge University Press.
Myers-Scotton, Carol
2002 *Contact Linguistics: Bilingual Encounters and Grammatical Outcomes.* Oxford: Oxford University Press.
O'Malley, J. Michael and Anna U. Chamot
1990 *Learning Strategies in Second Language Acquisition.* Oxford: Oxford University Press.
Oxford, Rebecca L.
1990 *Language Learning Strategies: What Every Teacher Should Know.* Rowley, Mass.: Newbury House.
Petersen, Karl M., Alexandra Reis, Simon Askelöf, Alexander Castro-Caldas and Martin Ingvar
2000 Language processing modulated by literacy: a network analysis of verbal repetition in literate and illiterate subjects. *Journal of Cognitive Neuroscience* 12 (3): 364–382.
Pienemann, Manfred
1984 Psychological constraints on the teachability of languages. *Studies in Second Language Acquisition* 6 (2): 188–214.
Pienemann, Manfred
1998 *Language Processing and Second-Language Development: Processability Theory.* Amsterdam: John Benjamins.
Porte, Graeme
2003 English from a distance: code-mixing and blending in the L1 output of long-term resident EFL teachers. In: Vivian J. Cook (ed.), *Effects of the L2 on the L1,* 103–119. Clevedon: Multilingual Matters.
Poulisse, Nanda
1990 *The Use of Compensatory Strategies by Dutch Learners of English.* Berlin: Mouton de Gruyter.
Rivers, Wilga M.
1964 *The Psychologist and the Foreign Language Teacher.* Chicago: Chicago University Press.
Schmid, Monika
2002 *First Language Attrition, Use, and Maintenance. The case of German Jews in anglophone countries.* Ph.D., University of Düsseldorf.
Schmitt, Elena
2004 No more reductions: to the problem of evaluation of attrition data. In: Monika Schmid, Barbara Kopke, Merel Keijzer and Lina Weilemar (eds.), *First Language Attrition,* 299–316. Amsterdam: John Benjamins.

Schwartz, Bonnie and Rex Sprouse
1996 L2 cognitive states and the Full Transfer/Full Access model. *Second Language Research* 12 (1): 40–72.

Selinker, Larry
1972 Interlanguage. *International Review of Applied Linguistics* 10 (3): 209–231.

Shmais, Wafa A.
2003 Language learning strategy use in Palestine. *TESL-EJ* 7 (2): 1–17.

Skehan, Peter
1998 *A Cognitive Approach to Language Learning*. Oxford: Oxford University Press.

Skinner, Burrhus F.
1957 *Verbal Behaviour.* New York: Appleton-Century-Crofts.

Soars, Liz and John Soars
2002 *New Headway English Course: Beginner.* Oxford: Oxford University Press.

Stern, Hans H.
1975 What can we learn from the good language learner?. *Canadian Modern Language Review* 31: 304–318.

Swain, Merrill and Sharon Lapkin
2000 Task-based second language learning: the uses of the first language. *Language Teaching Research* 4 (3): 251–274.

Sweet, Henry
1899 *The Practical Study of Language*. London: Dent (Oxford: Oxford University Press reprinted 1964).

Tarone, Elaine
1988 *Variation in Interlanguage.* London: Edward Arnold.

Tsimpli, Ianthi, Antonella Sorace, Caroline Heycock and Francesca Filiaci
2004 First language attrition and syntactic subjects: a study of Greek and Italian near native speakers of English. *International Journal of Bilingualism* 3: 257–278.

Ur, Penny
1996 *A Course in Language Teaching,*. Cambridge: Cambridge University Press.

van Berkel, Ans
2004 The role of the phonological strategy in learning to spell in English as a second language. In: Cook and Bassetti (eds.), 97–121.

Weinreich, Uriel
1953 *Languages in Contact.* The Hague: Mouton.

White, Lydia
1986 Implications of parametric variation for adult second language acquisition: an investigation of the pro-drop parameter. In: Vivian J. Cook (ed.), *Experimental Approaches to Second Language Acquisition*, 55–72. Oxford: Pergamon.

White, Lydia
2003 *Second Language Acquisition and Universal Grammar.* Cambridge: Cambridge University Press.

Willis, Jane and Dave Willis (eds.)
1996 *Challenge and Change in Language Teaching.* Oxford: Heinemann.

Recommended Readings

Cohen, Andrew
1990 *Language Learning: Insights for Learners, Teachers and Researchers.* New York: Newbury House/Harper Row.

Cook, Vivian J.
2008 *Second Language Learning and Language Teaching.* 4th edition. London: Hodder.

Dörnyei, Zoltan
2005 *The Psychology of the Language Learner: Individual Differences in Second Language Acquisition.* Mahwah, New Jersey: Lawrence Erlbaum Associates.

European Second Language Association (EUROSLA) at http://eurosla.org/

Howatt, Anthony
2004 *A History of English Language Teaching.* 2nd edition. Oxford: Oxford University Press.

Lantolf, James (ed.)
2002 *Sociocultural Theory and Second Language Learning.* Oxford: Oxford University Press.

Lightbown, Patsy and Nina Spada
2006 *How Languages are Learned.* Oxford: Oxford University Press.

Myles, Florence and Rosamond Mitchell
2004 *Second Language Learning Theories.* 2nd edition. London: Edward Arnold.

Odlin, Terence (ed.)
1994 *Pedagogical Grammar.* Cambridge: Cambridge University Press.

Second Language Acquisition Bibliography (SLABIB) at http://homepage.ntlworld.com/vivian.c/Vivian%20Cook.htm

Singleton, David
1999 *Exploring the Second Language Mental Lexicon.* Cambridge: Cambridge University Press.

Skehan, Peter
1998 *A Cognitive Approach to Language Learning.* Oxford: Oxford University Press.

VanPatten, William and Jessica Williams
2006 *Theories in Second Language Acquisition.* Mahwah, New Jersey: Lawrence Erlbaum Associates.

7. Language awareness

Willis Edmondson

1. Introduction

The term 'language awareness' is not easy to pin down precisely. One major reason for this is that there is considerable uncertainty regarding how broadly the term 'language' is to be conceived inside this collocation. Are for example such things as 'cultural awareness' or 'gender awareness' part of Language Awareness[1] or not? This chapter will be concerned only with those topics investigated under the rubric Language Awareness that impinge more or less directly on 'the nature of foreign language learning', given that the section of this book in which this chapter appears bears this rubric.[2]

An overview of the development of Language Awareness as a field of enquiry will be presented in the next part (2). Three topics covered by language awareness studies will then be focussed on, and their relationship to the nature of language learning will be explored. They are, briefly, the role and relevance of explicit knowledge concerning different aspects of a language to be learnt, the role and relevance of understanding relevant aspects of the culture in which the target language functions, and the role and relevance of knowledge of and insight into the nature of language learning itself. Each of these three topics will be handled in subsequent sections of the paper. This means then that part 3 of this chapter deals with linguistic awareness, part 4 with cultural awareness, and part 5 with language learning awareness. The brief sixth and final section of the paper seeks to summarise, and considers the role and relevance of the discipline of Applied Linguistics inside these three research domains.

2. Language Awareness and foreign language learning

The roots of the Awareness Movement are to be located in educational discussion and debate which developed in Great Britain in the 1970s. The Bullock report of 1975 was of particular importance. Initially a concern with the teaching of foreign languages inside the British educational system was at the core of the Awareness Movement. However, the link with modern languages turned out to be a tenuous one, and as awareness of Awareness grew, so did the concerns of foreign language teaching recede, as broader educational concerns took over. Language awareness was put forward as a goal for school learners in the national syllabus in Britain to remedy three educational problems that had allegedly become more and more apparent during the sixties and seventies: widespread illiteracy in English (particularly amongst school children of West Indian extraction), the generally low level of foreign language achievement inside the school system, and perceived divisive prejudices and a cultural narrowness among children and young people, reflected in racist attitudes and social unrest. The second issue – foreign language achievement – as I say went on to receive much less attention than the other two issues, possibly because it is an overtly pedagogic concern, while the other two are also social issues of political weight. Indeed, the fact that English was a foreign/second language for the children least profiting from the British educational system (West Indians, for example) was scarcely attended to. Thus, Hawkins who was among the first who put language awareness on the agenda, in his key publications (e.g. Hawkins 1984) does not focus on English as a foreign/second language, and as Brumfit points out (Brumfit 1992: 27), the interest in language awareness initially shown by teachers of French, German and Spanish in Great Britain was not shared at all by teachers of English.

So a real concern with English as a foreign language was absent, and the level of foreign language achievement inside schools ultimately did not receive a great deal of attention, either. The goals most commonly associated with instruction in language awareness were rather related to what is now known as intercultural learning. Consider the following three citations:

> "[...] More serious still is the (linguistic) parochialism and prejudice that is endemic in our society [...]. The chief aim (of the language awareness programme) will be to challenge pupils to ask questions about language, which so many take for granted [...]". The goal was that pupils should "be able to step outside their mother tongue and see it in some sort of perspective" (Hawkins 1987: 2, 4, 16 respectively).

It is important to recognise that in the light of these goals the Awareness movement was seen as relevant right across the curriculum. Thus, from the beginning, Awareness was a multi-facetted concept, bridging various tensions or dichotomies between for example teaching language and teaching literature, between teaching language skills and teaching cultural values, between first and foreign language teaching, between English as a mother-tongue and English as a second language, between subject-related targets and general educational goals.

There was initially no research into, and no theory of Awareness as such – the initial thrust of the movement lay in the direction of teaching materials, curriculum initiatives, and teacher training programmes. Furthermore, as already noted, the links with foreign language achievement did not carry particular weight inside the Awareness Movement. In fact, James and Garrett list improved mastery of foreign languages (the "performance domain" in their terms) as the last and by implication the least important area of application for Language Awareness (James and Garrett 1991: 17).

My claim is then that Language Awareness was from the start linked with broad educational and/or intercultural issues, often lacking a specific focus.

This tendency has, I suggest, grown rather than diminished since the establishment of the field. Public statements of the Association for Language Awareness and of the *Journal of Language Awareness* suggest the following broad areas of research and discussion inside Language Awareness studies:

(a) Mother tongue learning, foreign language learning and teacher education are relevant domains.
(b) The role of explicit knowledge about language in language learning and in language teaching is of special interest.
(c) A sensitivity to the manipulative uses of language and to such things as reporting bias is mentioned, and seems to overlap considerably with inter alia Critical Discourse Analysis in the sense of Fairclough, Pennycook, et al. (cf. e.g. Fairclough 1992).
(d) Literary awareness is explicitly mentioned.
(e) The role of language use and attitudes in interpersonal interaction, in work relations, in community life, and in the family are areas worthy of research.
(f) Professional areas such as the law or marketing, in which language plays a considerable role, are deemed of interest[3], and 'salient social issues' such as ageism, racism and sexism are singled out as worthy of attention[4].

Language Awareness covers then a very broad range of issues. However, types of awareness not specific to the central business of language acquisition will not be handled in this chapter, however intensively they might be pursued inside the Awareness movement, or indeed however seriously they may be taken by some educationalists. They will not be discussed here, as *critical awareness*, *literary awareness*, *gender awareness*, and additional currently politically correct stances which might be subsumed under the epithet *social awareness* may well be educationally desirable goals, but they are extrinsic to the goals of foreign language instruction. In the light of this stance, the sense in which *cultural awareness* is relevant to language learning will need to be carefully argued (see section 4 below).

This paper will focus then on three areas, namely perception of and acquaintance with different aspects of the foreign language firstly as a system, secondly as a cultural mediator, and thirdly as a cognitive achievement, i.e. awareness of the foreign language as a system, awareness of the cultural weight carried by that system, and awareness of the mechanisms, strategies and procedures activated in its acquisition. For each topic we shall be concerned to identify the concept, to examine its relevance for language acquisition and/or language education, and to refer to pedagogic materials, goals, and practices which seek to further it.

3. Linguistic awareness[5], explicit L2 knowledge and acquisition/learning

It was noted above that according to both the Journal and the Association of Language Awareness the role of explicit L2 knowledge in acquisition and in teaching strategy is an issue of especial interest inside language awareness research. Why? How does having explicit knowledge of aspects of the grammar of L2 relate to being aware thereof? Might they perhaps be the same thing? For to say "I am aware that the inflected verb goes at the end of subordinate clauses in German" logically implies the claim that the speaker also knows this fact. The opposite is also the case: if you know this rule, and can say so, you are aware of it. But if linguistic awareness of language is the same thing as explicit knowledge of language, then the concept is redundant, and it cannot in itself offer us any insight into language learning.

To clarify this central issue, let us first of all assume that explicit knowledge is conscious knowledge, and that the expressibility criterion holds for consciousness. This means that if you cannot say what it is you claim to know consciously, then that claim does not hold good, and the knowledge concerned is not explicit knowledge[6]. We will also assume that to be aware of something is also to be conscious of it: this I take to be uncontroversial. We need then to examine the sense in which awareness entails consciousness, and ask whether having explicit knowledge of aspects of L2 involves consciousness in the same sense. The terms to be related therefore are consciousness, explicit knowledge, awareness, and language acquisition/learning.

A useful starting-point for distinguishing different senses in which we might refer to aspects of language acquisition as "conscious learning" is provided by Schmidt (1994), who makes the following distinctions:

3.1. Consciousness as intentionality

Conscious learning in this sense is learning which occurs when the intention to learn is present. In psychological learning theory, non-intentional learning would then be *incidental* learning (Schneider and Kintz 1967; Eysenck and Keane 2000)[7]. Conscious learning and incidental learning may of course co-occur. The notion of linguistic awareness does not appear to overlap with intentionality. It seems however indisputable that one is aware of one's intentions, and can deliberate thereon. Thus intentions may link with decision-making, and strategy-use. Conscious learning as intentionality may therefore link with language learning awareness (cf. section 5 below). Incidental learning is of course something of which one is by definition not aware.

3.2. Consciousness as attention

Attention concerns the allocation of cognitive resources, and it therefore would seem to be a matter of definition that no learning can take place without attention being paid – at least not inside a cognitive theory of learning! Psychologists distinguish however between *focussed* attention, and *peripheral* attention, whereby only the former is conscious (cf. e.g. Eysenck and Keane 2000: chapter 5)[8]. In Second Language Acquisition theory, however, the notion that non-conscious attention to linguistic form can occur, potentially triggering acquisition, is in dispute. For the purposes of this discussion, we need not resolve this dispute: we are interested in attending that is conscious, and will wish to discover whether and how awareness relates to it.

Attention is important in acquisitional theory as it links with various hypotheses concerning the phenomenon of 'noticing'. Noticing is seen as the result of focussed or directed attention, and in the Second Language Acquisition (SLA) literature, three kinds of noticing with different degrees of importance or relevance for acquisition are mentioned:

1. A gap is perceived between what the learner knows and what the learner encounters. This may trigger the restructuring of interlanguage knowledge and/or the acquisition of new linguistic knowledge (Schmidt and Frota 1986).
2. A gap is noticed between that which one wants to say, and the linguistic means at one's disposal for saying it. This may trigger the development or application of communicative strategy (cf. e.g. the introduction to Kasper and Kellerman 1997).
3. A gap is recognised between what one is saying, or what one is planning to say, and relevant explicit L2 knowledge in one's possession. This is essentially a consequence of self-monitoring, and may trigger self-correction (cf. e.g. Krashen 1981 on monitoring; Edmondson 2003 on its acquisitional effects).

Where then does awareness fit in here? I suggest that this discussion of attention and noticing relates less to awareness itself than to becoming aware. This is so because you can attend to something, or you can notice it, but you cannot 'aware' it. In fact, one might rather become aware of something, as a result of noticing or attending to it. I shall develop this claim later.

3.3. Consciousness as awareness

Schmidt (1994) makes three distinctions regarding consciousness as awareness:

- To be aware of the fact that one is learning is not the same as being aware of what it is that is being learnt.
- Further different is an awareness of the results of learning.

- The conscious knowledge or awareness of the results of learning should further be distinguished from explicit instruction, intended presumably to bring about such conscious learning gains.

These distinctions are intuitively enlightening, but do not help us discover what is specific about awareness – awareness is rather presented as one type of consciousness.

3.4. Consciousness as control

Control concerns the amount of effort and weight of cognitive resources needed to access knowledge. The term 'control' is in fact rather misleading, as the search may fail. In other words the conscious mind commands, but the cognitive system is not under its control. The opposite of controlled language processing is of course automatic language processing, where this problem of access by definition does not arise.

These terms refer then to activating language knowledge, rather than acquiring it. Learners are perhaps commonly aware that their processing is non-automatic, and the cognitive burden of painful, controlled production may in some learners at least trigger strategies which further fluency. In this sense then awareness in this domain might be said to enhance acquisition. Also, becoming aware of their own increasing fluency in certain circumstances – I am thinking particularly of the illusion-of-fluency phenomenon during a stay-abroad programme (cf. Freed 1995; Edmondson 2000a) – may well trigger increased self-/confidence and motivation in some learners, which in turn may be reflected in different kinds of acquisition enhancement. Following this type of argumentation we can then establish informal links between the controlled/automatic dimension of processing, consciousness-as-awareness, and direct or indirect acquisitional development. These issues do not however impact on our discussion of linguistic awareness, but touch rather on language learning awareness (cf. section 5 below)

The above discussion of consciousness, acquisition and awareness, which was based on Schmidt (1994), has not revealed that which is distinctive about language awareness as opposed to explicit knowledge about the language to be learnt, nor what distinctive role or roles awareness may play in acquisition. This difficulty is not diminished if we look for help elsewhere in the second language acquisition literature[9]. For example in Skehan (1998), Schmidt's (1994) article is also discussed (1998: 56), and in the course of this discussion Skehan remarks that "awareness of the learning itself [...] confers advantages". But when Skehan moves on to "relate this discussion" to noticing (cf. for example Model 3.6. on page 57), the term 'awareness' is not to be found, nor indeed, except in rather trivial contexts, is the term 'awareness' invoked again in the book. Rather similarly, the only relevant references to Language Awareness that I have been able to find in the 888 pages of the Second Language Acquisition handbook of Doughty and Long (2003) occur in the chapter on implicit and explicit learning by DeKeyser, where the term is used as a synonym for consciousness when implicit learning is defined (DeKeyser 2003: 314).

In the discussion of attention and noticing above, it was suggested that noticing seems akin to becoming aware, and so being aware of something might well be seen as a result of noticing it, or attending to it. This view will now be adopted here. The argument is then that awareness is a state of arousal or sensitivity which leads to the heightened or more frequent perception of relevant features of the environment. Furthermore, the link with noticing (specifically of acquisitionally-relevant 'gaps', as specified above) is a dual one: noticing may trigger heightened awareness, which in turn will enable further noticing. So the link between awareness and acquisition can now be put as follows: salient or non-salient features of the Input are 'noticed' under propitious conditions which may or may not be teacher-induced. This can then under further conditions yet to be specified lead to these features of the target language being 'registered' in the brain such that the system is, as it were, cognitively attuned to noticing similar features in the future. This 'registration' and 'tuning' we call awareness. Looping now occurs, i.e. noticing stimulates Awareness, which stimulates noticing.

Where now does consciousness fit in with this view of awareness? At the beginning of this section of the paper it was assumed that to be aware of something is to be conscious of it. This is still a valid semantic assumption, but does not apply to the sense of awareness now being proposed, as it does not make much sense to say that a propensity for noticing (which is how language awareness is now understood) is or is not 'conscious'. One may of course be conscious that noticing takes place, and one can consciously recognise aspects of the language when in contact with them. Furthermore, as we have argued, the activation of explicit knowledge may be part of the noticing-awareness-acquisition syndrome. But I shall now wish to say that the conscious/unconscious dimension does not apply to language awareness as such, but to its workings and effects. Following this, of course, one may be aware of one's own awareness – but this leads us once more to language learning awareness (cf. section 5 below).

It was observed above too that SLA theorists are divided as to whether or not noticing is always conscious, i.e. whether the noticer is always conscious of that which is noticed, or whether one can notice something without noticing that one is doing so. Inside the view of awareness being developed here, it is plausible to suggest that as linguistic awareness develops, noticing effects may in fact become more and more unconscious. Initial noticing would however appear to be necessarily conscious, if awareness is to follow.

We turn finally in this section to pedagogic concerns. The link between acquisitional insight and pedagogic postulate is indirect. The situation is especially complex in this instance because linguistic awareness is, on my account, a type of corollary of, a prelude to, or a consequence of noticing, but as such would appear to have no obvious behavioural manifestations save noticing itself, proficiency gains, and the availability of different kinds of explicit knowledge, such that there would seem to be no means of distinguishing empirically between noticing and awareness. So though I have argued for an interpretation of the term awareness that is distinctive, awareness has additionally to be behaviourally discernible if it is to be subject to empirical research, and I do not believe that this is the case, given the current state of our knowledge. Therefore teaching goals and practices that relate to awareness may equally relate to the explicit, direct, or deductive teaching of grammar, to a focus on form or indeed forms (Long 1991), to consciousness-raising (e.g. in the sense of Sharwood Smith 1997), or to didactic strategies which claim to enhance noticing.

With this rider, pedagogic tendencies, findings and recommended practices – all of which might be related to issues in linguistic awareness as discussed above – include the following:

Skehan reports on several psychometric studies in which different learning groups were taught a specific grammatical feature via different methodologies, and then tested afterwards, either on proficiency or on 'noticing', or both (Skehan 199: 62–66). Relevant instructional variables were explicit rule-giving versus highlighting of the target grammatical feature during tuition, encouraging effective input processing versus requiring much output practice, *rule-oriented* instruction versus *meaning-oriented* instruction, and *traditional* (explicit rule-giving) versus *consciousness-raising* treatments. Skehan's tentative conclusions are that "merely having to comprehend" is not likely to lead learners to "engage with form" and that developing learning tasks which are both "meaningful" and which encourage "a focus on form and specific forms" is an important goal.

This leads us then to suggest links between language awareness and task-based teaching, because a major focus inside task-based research is developing tasks combining meaning and form as recommended by Skehan, and engendering relevant noticing. Thus, how far different kinds of 'focussed tasks' are effective in terms of increasing comprehension, production, and/or acquisition is one of the central issues dealt with in Ellis's extensive review of task-based learning and teaching (Ellis 2003). One tendency that emerges from this research is that comprehension tasks are more likely to enable/require relevant noticing of grammatical features than production tasks (a totally predictable, but nonetheless important finding), but that on the other hand simply flooding learners with input, even if it is 'focussed', or 'enhanced', does not seem to be enough in terms of enabling noticing or awareness.

Tasks which are specifically designed to combine relevant noticing and a degree of communicative authenticity include the Dictogloss (cf. e.g. Wajnryb

1990; Kowal and Swain 1994), "Interpretation Tasks" in the sense of Ellis (1995), and "Grammar Consciousness-Raising" à la Fotos (1994). These tasks are discussed from theoretical and pedagogical perspectives in Schlak (1999). Eckerth proposes a type of reconstruction task involving linguistically deviant but semantically interpretable messages, which are worked on by learners in pairs. He establishes empirically that advanced learners working on these tasks indeed notice and become aware of previously insecure aspects of L2, and acquire relevant explicit L2 grammatical knowledge, as shown in both immediate and delayed post-tests (Eckerth 2003). Edmondson (2002b) proposes ten general pedagogic principles, focussing on the roles of consciousness/awareness, and claims that these principles derive from SLA research.

It needs to be stressed once more, however, that the shift from research into language learning/acquisition to the recommendation of teaching strategy or indeed content is complicated by many variables, such that it is impossible to even predict with any certainty that specific learning effects are concomitant on the adaptation of the practice recommended. Thus in the course of his marathon run through task-based teaching and learning, Ellis comes to the conclusion that "It may be impossible to claim that one task is better than another on psycholinguistic grounds" (Ellis 2003: 127). In Edmondson (2005a) it is in fact argued that any contact with the target language has the potential for triggering acquisitionally-relevant cognitive activity. This view is termed the Dr. Pangloss perspective, and is supported by learner interview data.

The shift from acquisitional theory to pedagogic practice is complex, therefore. However, it seems highly likely that for most if not all learners a heightened degree of awareness of the nature of the language and of the skills being targeted will benefit language acquisition and performance. For which items or aspects of L2 this is particularly true, and for which it is not true at all, and how it might be appropriate to encourage the development of the required awareness are however important issues requiring further research.

4. Cultural awareness and language learning

Cultural awareness implies sensitivity to cultural aspects of the L2 (see also Kramsch, Ch. 8, this volume). Explicit knowledge about elements of L2 culture, transmitted or acquired via for example Cultural Studies, or what is known as *Landeskunde* in a German context, may feed into cultural awareness, and may also be occasioned by it, in the context of relevant communicative experience. The term cultural awareness is seen here as containing an intercultural component. I would argue that the concept of awareness, when applied to acquisitionally-relevant aspects of L2 culture, necessarily implies a perception of difference (or sameness) vis à vis other cultures, most obviously that encapsulated in one's L1. We might say, therefore, that the issue is once more 'gap-noticing' (or 'difference-detecting') as discussed in the context of noticing. So intercultural awareness is the topic to be discussed. We wish to establish whether and in what sense this type of awareness plays an active role in acquisitionally-relevant perceptions, cognitive processes, and linguistic and other behaviours. However the term 'intercultural awareness' is commonly used to indicate much more than the perception of a cultural difference between L1 and L2. It will be necessary then to distinguish between 'narrow' and 'broad' notions of intercultural awareness, and to restrict the discussion to interpretations that impinge on second language acquisition. I shall turn to this in a moment. First of all we should try to come to grips with the term 'culture'.

This is notoriously difficult, and I shall not attempt a watertight definition here, as there is none, save in the biological sense of the term. The difficulty is enhanced in the present context by two conditions. On the one hand I impose the requirement that only those cultural or intercultural perceptions are relevant which impinge on and relate to the contextualised use and interpretation of language, while on the other hand the concept of cultural awareness is to be distinguished from the concept of linguistic awareness discussed above. This is not easily achieved. For example the perception that in German *Ist der Stuhl frei?* is normative, and that the utterance topicalises the speaker's wishes, while in English *Is this chair taken?* seems equally normative, though the query addresses the situation the speaker does not want – this perception concerns both a difference in language use, and a difference in cultural behavioural norms, precisely because they are one and the same thing. I shall therefore leave the dividing-line between pragmatic and socio-cultural aspects of language use undefined. It can of course now be argued that a 'pragmatically extensive' view of linguistic awareness might well make the intercultural awareness under discussion spurious. We shall simply accept this as a possible argument, and proceed to ignore it. Let us now return to the distinction between the 'narrow' and 'broader' views of cultural or intercultural awareness. Here the delimitation issues are, I suggest, of more weight.

These two views are compared in Edmondson (1994), and contrasted in Table 1, which is adapted from Edmondson and House (1998). The 'narrow' interpretation of intercultural awareness[10] stresses that a language is embedded in cultural traditions, values and attitudes, and may help to explicate misunderstandings occasioned by the different cultural presuppositions operating for persons from different linguo-cultural backgrounds, even if they are using a common language. The second (or 'broader') interpretation however goes beyond this, and links directly with the origins of Awareness, and the motivation behind the early work of Hawkins, as sketched above.

Table 1 Intercultural awareness and foreign language teaching: two models

Communicative Model	Educational Model
Awareness concerns the target language culture	Awareness may concern any and all cultures.
Teaching goals are therefore specific to the language studied.	Teaching goals are not language-specific.
Teaching goals are also specific to foreign language teaching.	Pedagogic goals spread right across the curriculum.
Cultural awareness addresses communication skills in L2.	Cultural awareness also concerns communication skills in L1.
Classroom communication 'mimics' communication outside the class.	Communication inside the multicultural class is important.
The targetted external behaviours focus on language skills.	The targetted external behaviours focus on attitude and affect.
Awareness contributes to the goals of foreign language teaching.	Foreign language teaching contributes to intercultural awareness.

Table 1 suggests that the 'educational model' is extrinsic to foreign language learning. This suggestion may however be rejected if the educational model simply embraces, subsumes and maybe expands the communicative. Indeed, it would on the face of it be most odd if proponents of the broad view did not seek to relate intercultural awareness to language acquisition, but this is to the best of my knowledge not explicitly attempted. There is in fact much tension and uncertainty here. Lothar Bredella for example states in Bredella 2000a that "literary texts in the foreign language classroom must contribute to language learning" (2000a: 376), but in Bredella 2000b 'language learning' is not mentioned at all, while in Bredella 1999 the author assigns priority to intercultural educational goals in foreign language teaching, as opposed to goals focussing on language skills[11]. In Kramsch (1993) close links between cultural awareness and language proficiency are postulated, and the book richly demonstrates such links in pedagogic practice[12]. The author appears then to be operating with the communicative model. However by 1996 Kramsch is taking a clear educational stance, explicitly aligning herself with a view of intercultural awareness which has affinities with the work of Fairclough et al. – Kramsch herself proposes the term "critical intercultural literacy" (Kramsch 1996) as a primary goal for foreign language instruction. This tension between communicative and intercultural goals is further reflected in the Common European Framework (CEFR: 103–105). In section 5.1.1.3 of this document we read of the desirability of perceiving similarities and differences between the "world of origin" and the "world of the target community". We read further that intercultural awareness "is also enriched by an awareness of a wider range of cultures than those carried by the learner's L1 and L2. This wider awareness helps to place both in context". Section 5.1.2.2 then goes on to deal with intercultural skills and intercultural know-how (the latter presumably deriving from intercultural awareness), but in fact focuses on communicative behaviour likely to diminish misunderstanding. It seems then that the document essentially adopts a communicative stance, but pays lip-service to the educational stance as a source of further 'enrichment' or 'contextualisation'.

Consider finally Byram (1997). The purpose of this monograph is "to explore the issues which arise if we wish to evaluate and/or assess a person's ability to relate to and communicate with people who speak a different language and live in a different cultural context". The key term here is 'relate to', which I take to be the educational goal, and which is mentioned before the communicative goal. Notice too that Byram does not refer to relating to people in or through communicating with them, but of relating to them, and communicating with them. A model for 'Intercultural Communicative Competence' is developed. Factors such as self-knowledge and strategies for discourse management feed into 'intercultural competence' (the ability to 'relate'). This competence is distinct from various linguistic competencies in a foreign language, which together make up communicative competence. Logically enough, then, communicative and intercultural competence come together in 'Intercultural Communicative Competence'. On this view, the function of foreign language skills is to add a communicative dimension to intercultural competence. The proposal is not that intercultural goals add 'depth' or 'enrichment' to the cultural/communicative goals of foreign language instruction, but rather the opposite.

The educational model in Table 1 is then indeed different in kind. Intercultural awareness in this broad sense does not inherently relate to foreign language learning as such, but can be incorporated into the goals of foreign language teaching on socio-political, ideological, and/or educational grounds. There are however, it seems to me, potential dangers inherent in the pedagogic implementation of broader intercultural educational goals. The most obvious problem is who is to describe or indeed prescribe which features of which culture(s) which groups of learners might be sensitivised to (see for example the discussion in Kramsch (2000) on the place of feminism in the teaching of French literature). There was until quite recently a widespread vogue in German language teaching materials for portraying Germans as unfriendly, racist and materialistic, which was apparently deemed politically correct at the time and may have contributed to learners' intercultural awareness, but probably did not encourage positive motivation and learning attitudes (cf. e.g. Ammer 1988; Földes 1995). The central issue is, then, as Kramsch (2000) puts it: "Who has a right to speak for whom and to describe whom in whose terms?"[13]

In discussing the appropriateness of the goal of intercultural communicative competence, Byram points out that in some educational contexts, the language to be learnt may to all intents and purposes be of no communicative relevance whatsoever, as the likelihood that the school learners will ever be in a position to use the target language is small (cf. Table 1 in Edmondson and House 1998, which makes the same point). In such learning contexts, Byram argues, intercultural goals assume importance, as it were, by default:

> "[...] it is particularly important that learning focused on a language which may never be used outside school – such as German or Russian – should give a high priority to the acquisition of skills, attitudes and knowledge which are transferable to situations both within and beyond national frontiers where cultural awareness and sensitivity is required. The acquisition of another language, or even part of one, may be less important and less feasible in the time available than the application of such transferable competencies, including the knowledge of how to manage communication in intercultural interactions" (Byram 1997: 29).

This suggests then that when foreign language teaching has in itself no practical purpose, it can be exploited for other educational goals. This seems on the face of it a slightly perverse argument, but it can well be argued that education in schools is not geared towards the transmission of skills and competencies that are of future practical value, but is geared rather towards the acquisition of representative spheres of knowledge and of skills that provide a basis for future learning and training[14].

Following this line of argument, we might now suggest that the narrow interpretation of intercultural awareness is appropriate when the development of practical communicative skills is not merely the nominal but the demonstrably real and relevant purpose of instruction, for example in TESOL classes in America, or German as a Second Language classes for immigrants in Germany. Such awareness can be seen as an extension of linguistic awareness, most obviously along its pragmatic/social parameters. Furthermore, relevant cultural information may of course engender interest, and indirectly affect learning outcomes via impacting on different aspects of motivation. Cultural input inside the communicative model may in some learning contexts take a tangible form: cultural awareness may be a matter of survival. Consider for example courses preparing students and other learner groups for a period of residence or study abroad (cf. e.g. J. A. Coleman 1996, 1997; Edmondson 2000a; and the brief overview in Jordan 1997: 101–105). Such courses are designed to be of immediate practical help, focussing on language skills, and practical matters such as registration formalities at the beginning of term at your new university. As Edmondson (2002a) points out, when such practical communicative needs and cultural adjustments are of prime importance, the broader goals of intercultural awareness recede into the background.

If however foreign language instruction in an institutional setting has educational goals that embrace, go beyond or indeed are superordinate to foreign language learning, then a broader view of intercultural awareness may well be appropriate. It is further true of course that the posited opposition between learning contexts in which the target language is of practical communicative utility, and other contexts in which this does not hold at all marks two extremes on a cline, such that some merging of the two models in Table 1 may be appropriate in pedagogic practice.

Interculturally relevant teaching concepts and materials are proposed inter alia in Byram and Esarte-Sarries (1991), Byram and Fleming (1998), Phipps and Gonzalez (2004), Kramsch (1993), Pulverness (2001), Utley (2004), Cankova and Gill (2001), House (1998, 2003).

5. Language learning awareness

Language learning awareness is a state of cognitive sensitivity concerning one's own language learning proclivities, styles, preferences, strengths and weaknesses[15] It differs from the two kinds of awareness discussed so far in two major respects. Firstly, it can affect learning behaviour directly; impinging on the learning process itself, as it can influence decision-making, learning goals, and strategic attack (cf. the remarks above on consciousness as intentionality). The second difference between linguistic or cultural awareness and the type of awareness under discussion here is that in this case the object of awareness does not lie outside of the learner's domain of experience as something that is by definition alien (the 'foreign' language, the 'foreign' culture), but lies as it were 'within'.

This second difference has consequences regarding the links between awareness and explicit knowledge. Clearly the learner has, in one sense at least, privileged access to knowledge regarding his or her own learning. Such knowledge, we may assume, is gained largely through introspection, self-observation, and reflection over past learning experience. It may therefore be consciously deliberated upon, and talked about, and is in this sense 'explicit', but it is essentially subjective knowledge. At least three riders are however called for:

(i) Some external source – for example a teacher – may offer relevant observations which trigger a gain in knowledge and/or experience (a comment such as *You seem to be quite interested in grammar*, advice on learning strategies, or feedback on learner performance are obvious – albeit contrived – examples).

(ii) Explicit knowledge about aspects of language learning, obtained for example from a course on second language acquisition, is also likely to influence the learner's self-perception and/or learning behaviour. This type of explicit input can of course be pedagogically purposed.

(iii) Learner motives and goals interact with language learning awareness, and these may be affected by explicit knowledge concerning for example the instrumental utility of language skills for different educational/professional purposes. Edmondson (1997) documents instances in which adult learners recalling their language learning histories regret or indeed resent that they were not aware at the time of learning of what they later came to appreciate regarding the goals and purposes of foreign language acquisition (cf. too Edmondson 1996).

So language learning awareness may influence language processing, as it may promote and direct *intentional* learning. It is further argued in Edmondson (1997) that such an awareness can affect attitudes, motives, and determination – i.e. the major components of the construct motivation. The role of awareness in motivational studies has not, however, to the best of my knowledge been explicitly researched, even if it has been implicitly assumed (cf. for example Crookes and Schmidt 1991; Dörnyei 2002; Riemer 2003). One clear link is provided by the resultative hypothesis (Ely 1986), which says that knowledge of learning effects can influence learning motivation. This is commonly interpreted as meaning that high achievement leads to increased effort, and even greater learning success, while low achievement is a negative motivator – in this case then achievement spirals downwards. However, there are further options – high achievement can stimulate complacency and laziness, while low achievement can stimulate determination. The resultative hypothesis interacts therefore with self-perception, learning goals and other factors. On the basis of written self-reports (learner autobiographies), Edmondson (2004) posits different types of individual motivational profiles regarding how learners react to external negative motivators. The claim here is that language learning awareness co-determines these different motivational-attitudinal profiles (see also Riemer 2000).

There has been little research into language learning awareness as such. Research into learner strategies and into the so-called 'good language learner' is however relevant. For my purposes here learner strategies are both potentially conscious and intentional (cf. footnote 7 above), i.e. intended by the learner to impact directly or indirectly on his/her language acquisition and/or proficiency.

A major research finding in this area is that there is no deterministic link between the use of a specific strategy, and the achieving of a specific cognitive, acquisitional, or communicative outcome. The careful formulation of Gillette (1987) still holds: "There appears to be no single set of strategies appropriate for recommendation to all learners". This is, I suggest, because the effectiveness of learner strategies is both individually-based and context-specific. It follows that it is not the case that the good language learner uses particular strategies in particular ways – the original OISE study (Naiman, McGrath and Lamb 1978) failed to establish a clear link between learning success and strategic profile.

The relevance of this discussion here is that language learning awareness would seem to be precisely the point at which strategy use and the optimal support of individual learning achievement meet, rather than for example in teacher-led courses of strategy-training or instruction, though such courses may well of course target individual learning awareness.

One general conclusion that does emerge from research into good language learners is that they seem to be rather aware persons. They are interested in grammar, and constantly look for patterns and regularities. They also analyse the target language as a means of communication, they monitor their own progress, they are in a word 'active' learners (cf. overviews in for example Skehan 1998: 263; Lightbown and Spada 1993: 34; Edmondson 2000b).

There are then solid grounds for believing that language learning awareness can increase the individual learner's competence and proficiency both directly via for example influencing learner strategy, and indirectly by for example affecting learning goals and motivation. There is furthermore a conceptual link between language learning awareness and the Autonomy Movement, i.e. the pedagogic thesis that the more the foreign language learner is involved in pedagogic decision-making, the greater the likelihood that the resultant pedagogy will be effective (cf. e.g. Sinclair, McGrath and Lamb 2000; Benson 2001, see also Legenhausen Ch. 15, this volume). The Autonomy Movement is grounded in general educational theory, rather than in SLA research, and seeks to impact directly on pedagogical practice and teacher training, though some experts in this field focus rather on teacher-free learning opportunities such as free-access learning materials and tandem-learning. But whatever degree of autonomy is advocated, it is evident that for example cooperating with learners in order to negotiate syllabus requirements and methodological principles presupposes a large degree of self-awareness and relevant learning experience on the part of the learners, and it is equally obvious that free access to learning opportunities presupposes learning purpose and proficiency on the part of the learning group exposed to these facilities. In other words, language learning awareness is called for, if autonomy is not to become a synonym for helplessness.

Materials are available which seek to help learners discover their own learning styles and preferences (cf. e.g. Oxford 1990: 41–42; Wenden 1991). The Hamburg web-site *Wie man Sprachen lernt* (*How languages are learnt*) offers several hundred pages of information and suggestions for language learners, the majority of which material targets language learning awareness[16]. A large number of schedules claiming to target learning style and self-assessment are offered on the internet, and some of these are doubtless helpful to a learner seeking a stimulus to self-awareness (cf. e.g. the questionnaire offered by the University of Leeds[17]).

Further materials related to language learning awareness and giving suggestions for encouraging it in language classrooms are to be found in for example

Wenden (1986), Chamot and Kupper (1989), Ellis and Sinclair (1989), Vann and Abraham (1990), O'Malley and Chamot (1990), Yang (1996), Chamot et al. (1996), Oxford and Leaver (1996), Rampillon and Zimmermann (1997), Cohen (1998), Edelhoff and Weskamp (1999).

Finally, I wish to mention a rather different but related type of awareness, which does not fit easily into the tripartite division followed in this paper, because although it is explicitly concerned with learning styles and learning sets (and is therefore correctly placed in this section of the paper), it is also explicitly concerned with intercultural encounters, on which criterion it might well have appeared in the previous section. The issue is that faced by language teachers of a particular cultural background who find themselves teaching in an entirely different sociocultural context, where quite different concepts of learning and of instruction hold and indeed quite different goals may operate for the teaching of the language in question. The targeted awareness concerns then 'cultures of learning', and the term 'sociocultural awareness' is sometimes used to describe the set of qualities that might best enable professional success in such a set of circumstances (cf. e.g. H. Coleman 1996; Dogancay-Aktuna 2005). The issue is essentially one of methodological adaptation, involving concrete pedagogical issues such as the acceptability of group work, the desirability of 'active' learner participation, or whether, indeed, it is acceptable to put questions to the learners without having given them the answer beforehand! (This last example is taken from van Lier 1996.) This type of awareness seems relevant not only to experienced teachers going to teach overseas (who are, of course, essentially in exactly the same position as the students going overseas to study, mentioned in the intercultural section of this paper), but also to SLA researchers, who are also often unwittingly committed to a philosophy of learning which may be both culturally determined, and culture-specific in its validity (this danger may be most apparent in task-based research – cf. Edmondson 2005a, 2006).

6. Summary

This chapter has sought to distinguish between awareness and other cognitive/affective conditions and states, and to argue and where possible to document the relevance of three kinds of awareness for the furthering of learning/acquisition in a foreign or second language setting. The first type of awareness dealt with – linguistic awareness – is closely linked with the issue of the relevance of explicit knowledge concerning the structure and use of the target language. It was claimed that linguistic awareness can play a role in perception, storage and production, but it is clear that individual learner differences and the nature of the area of language which is the object of awareness are – inter alia – relevant variables affecting potential acquisitional gains. However, the basic issue is one of acquisitional theory, i.e. how does learning take place. The second, culturally-oriented view of awareness was interpreted in two major ways. The first interpretation links with linguistic awareness, but focusses on language as a means of social interaction, rather than language as a closed linguistic system. It is extremely difficult, however, to distinguish sharply between a broadly-based linguistic awareness and (inter)-cultural awareness on this interpretation. The second, broader interpretation of intercultural awareness focusses on the content and goals of foreign language instruction, and seeks to suborn them, in that intercultural goals may be given priority over acquisitional goals in teaching programmes. This may, however, be pedagogically justified in specific learning contexts. The third sense developed was that of language learning awareness, and this was linked to the question of individual achievement in language learning, i.e. with what degree of success different persons might under similar conditions acquire/master aspects of L2.

It can be seen in retrospect that these three interpretations map on to distinct and salient features of language acquisition. Ellis (1985: 276), for example distinguishes between cognitive qualities which are shared by all learners, being biologically determined (metacognitive skills belong in this category on the view I am seeking to develop here), cognitive skills, proclivities and preferences which distinguish one person from another (the insights of language learning awareness are to be located in this module), and what we may refer to rather globally as learning context, the social situation in which the learning process is situated. My claim is clearly that the main thrust of cultural/intercultural aspects of awareness is to be located here. On this argument then the three aspects of language awareness mentioned address the central components of language acquisition – admittedly to different degrees and in different ways.

This may explain why there is no unified theory of the role of language awareness in language acquisition and teaching, or indeed in applied linguistics. What all three views developed here do have in common of course is the claim that the experience of language is heightened by the conscious reflection on and/or perception of what is involved. Furthermore, as has been pointed out at various points above, there are links between the three interpretations, specifically between the first two and language learning awareness. We might suggest further that an extension of language learning awareness from oneself to others – for example speakers of the language one is seeking to learn who are learning one's own L1 – that such a 'transfer' of learning awareness would seem likely to lead to insights and perceptions compatible with the broader goals of intercultural awareness.

How we conceive the role of applied linguistics regarding the three complexes discussed in this chapter depends of course on which concept of Applied Linguistics one accepts. My own belief is that Applied Linguistics cannot usefully be conceived of as a coherent discipline that has its own research agenda, and maps onto different research domains, making a contribution of some kind, before moving on (cf. Edmondson 2005b). I suggest on the contrary that issues such as language teaching, language acquisition, and effective language use are far too complex and important to be dealt with piecemeal. The uncertainty about the nature of awareness, and of what one should or might be aware of, brought out at the beginning of this paper already suggested a tension in the collocation 'language awareness' between cognition and perception on the one hand (the central concern is awareness), and the concerns of linguistics on the other (the central concern is language). This tension is also present of course in the rubric 'foreign language learning' (the reference is once more to the title of Section I of this volume). The point is in a nutshell that you cannot for research purposes separate the language and the awareness, nor can you separate the language and the acquisition. Furthermore, of course, the notion of an applied linguistics in the context of the nature of foreign language learning would seem to imply at least some impingement on pedagogic issues. Applied linguists can then in my view research into language awareness in all the senses discussed above, but will wish to redefine themselves and their research interests accordingly.

Notes

1 Capitalised Language Awareness denotes a concept or movement, non-capitalised language awareness is a cognitive capacity or possession that different people may have to different degrees, while 'language awareness' in single quotation marks is a term cited, but not used. It is conceded that in what follows these distinctions may become blurred.
2 In referring to foreign language learning I do not wish to exclude second language acquisition, i.e. the development of language skills and abilities in non-institutional second language settings. I shall distinguish between foreign and second language settings, but 'learning' and 'acquisition' will be used interchangeably, save that they will on occasion be collated ('learning/acquisition'), or the umbrella term 'language development' will be preferred.
3 Issues of cultural awareness have, for example, been raised and discussed regarding the provision of medical care (cf. e.g. Adams 1995).
4 My sources here are: ⟨www.lexicallynet/ala⟩ and ⟨http://www.multilingual-matters.com/multi/journals/journals_la.asp⟩.
5 'Linguistic awareness' is here an ad hoc term used to denote an awareness of language per se, i.e. an awareness of features of a language which are systematic and significant in that they impinge on language use. The term has nothing to do with knowledge of linguistics.
6 Of course one can have an argument about degrees of expressibility, and whether or not reflection is so to speak permitted. 'Potential expressibility' might then be a better descriptor.

7 A word of caution is appropriate regarding taking over terms and concepts from general psychological learning theory, and assuming their relevance for SLA. This caveat is widely accepted regarding the adoption of behaviourist learning theory in the past, but is often ignored when newer and more fashionable psychological theories arise. For example the fact that incidental learning occurs when subjects learn colours does not mean that incidental learning occurs regarding for example word-order rules for German.

8 'Attention' can be further sub-differentiated. Tomlin and Villa (1994) report for example on three types or stages of attention: alertness, orientation, and detection. Again the difficulty of mapping psychological concepts onto second language acquisition theory arises. Tomlin and Villa's central thesis is however that 'attention' and/or 'noticing' can occur without awareness, i.e. without the conscious assignment of cognitive resources. You cannot have awareness without attention, but you can attend without awareness, i.e. subconsciously.

9 Clearly, the whole of this literature cannot be surveyed here. It may be therefore that I select the least helpful sources in order to further my case. Be warned.

10 Terminology is a problem whenever the adjective 'intercultural' crops up (cf. Freudenstein 1994, who pointedly asks – is everything intercultural, or what?). In the literature I shall refer to in what follows, 'intercultural learning' is often the dominant term. I have elsewhere argued against the promulgation of this collocation (Edmondson 1994; Edmondson and House 1998), but shall assume here that it means something like the development of intercultural awareness.

11 Cf. "Mit Recht hat der interkulturelle Fremdsprachenunterricht allgemeine Erziehungsziele in den Mittelpunkt gerückt [Intercultural foreign language teaching has quite correctly placed general educational goals at its centre]" (as opposed to "fachspezifischen Lernzielen"), Bredella 1999. The central point here is these different goals are set up as alternatives, to be weighed one against the other.

12 "[...] If, however, language is seen as social practice, culture becomes the very core of language teaching. Cultural awareness must then be viewed both as enabling language proficiency and as being the outcome of reflection on language proficiency." (Kramsch 1993: 8).

13 Related and much discussed issues are the role of stereotypes in portraying a country (cf. e.g. Harden and Witte 2000; Löschmann and Stroinska 1998), and the desirability or otherwise of employing native-speakers of L2 as foreign language teachers (cf. e.g. Widdowson 1994).

14 Edmondson (1999) develops this type of argument, and comes to the radical conclusion that the teaching of practical foreign language skills should – with some caveats – be removed from the school curriculum.

15 In educational psychology, the term 'metacognition' denotes a form of higher-level planning. It is, according to Flavell, with whom the term is most commonly associated: "one's knowledge concerning one's own cognitive processes and products and anything related to them." (Flavell 1987). "Thinking about thinking" is also a widespread (informal) paraphrase. One also comes across references to 'metacognitive awareness' in the educational literature. Some overlap with language learning awareness can therefore be contrived.

16 Access: ⟨www1.uni-hamburg.de/fremdsprachenlernen/⟩

17 Access: ⟨http://www.leeds.ac.uk/languages/courses/fl/documents/learning.pdf⟩

References

Adams, Diane L. (ed.)
1995 *Health Issues for Women of Color: A Cultural Diversity Perspective*. Thousand Oaks: Sage Publications.

Ammer, Reinhard
1988 *Das Deutschlandbild in den Lehrwerken für Deutsch als Fremdsprache*. München: iudicium.

Bausch, Karl-Richard, Herbert Christ and Hans-Jürgen Krumm (eds.)
1994 *Interkulturelles Lernen im Fremdsprachenunterricht*. Tübingen: Narr

Benson, Philip
2001 *Teaching and Researching Autonomy in Language Learning*. London: Longman

Bredella, Lothar
1999 Zielsetzungen interkulturellen Fremdsprachenunterrichts. In: Lothar Bredella and Werner Delanoy (eds.), *Interkultureller Fremdsprachenunterricht*, 85–120. Tübingen: Narr.

Bredella, Lothar
2000a Literary texts. In: Byram (ed.) 2000, 375–382.

Bredella, Lothar
2000b Literary texts and intercultural understanding. In: Byram (ed.) 2000, 383–387.

Brumfit, Christopher
1992 Language awareness in teacher education. In: James and Garrett, 24–39.

Bullock, Alan (Chairman)
1975 *A Language for Life. Report of the Committee of Inquiry*. London: HMSO.

Byram, Michael
1997 *Teaching and Assessing Intercultural Communicative Competence*. Clevedon: Multilingual Matters.

Byram, Michael (ed.)
2000 *Routledge Encyclopedia of Language Teaching and Learning*. London/ New York: Routledge.

Byram, Michael and V. Esarte-Sarries
1991 *Investigating Cultural Studies in Foreign Language Teaching: a Book for Teachers*. Clevedon: Multilingual Matters.

Byram, Michael and M. Fleming
1998 *Foreign Language Learning in Intercultural Perspective*. Cambridge: Cambridge University Press.

Cankova, Michaela and Simon Gill
2001 *Intercultural Activities*. Oxford: Oxford University Press.

CEFR: The Common European Framework of Reference, Council of Europe. Published (inter alia) by Cambridge University Press, Pdf-version online at: http://www.coe.int/t/dg4/linguistic/Source/Framework_EN.pdf

Chamot, Anna U., Sarah Barnhardt, Pamela El-Dinary and Jill Robbins
1996 Methods for teaching learning strategies in the foreign language classroom. In: Oxford, Rebecca (ed.) 1996, 175–188.

Chamot, Anna U. and Lisa Kupper
1989 Learning strategies in foreign language instruction. *Foreign Language Annals* 22 (1): 13–24.

Cohen, Andrew
1998 *Strategies in Learning and Using a Second Language*. London/NewYork: Longman.

Coleman, Hywel (ed.)
1996 *Society and the Language Classroom*. New York: Cambridge University Press.

Coleman, James A.
1996 *Studying Languages: Survey of British and European Students – the Proficiency, Background, Attitudes and Motivations of Students of Foreign Languages in the United Kingdom and Europe*. London: Centre for Information on Language Teaching and Research.

Coleman, James A.
1997 Residence abroad within language study. (State of the art article). *Language Teaching* 30 (1): 1–20.

Crookes, Graham and Richard W. Schmidt
1991 Motivation: reopening the research agenda. *Language Learning* 41 (4): 469–512.

DeKeyser, Robert
2003 Implicit and explicit learning. In: Doughty and Long (eds.), 313–348.

Dogancay-Aktuna, Seran
2005 Intercultural communication in English language teacher education. *ELT Journal* 99 (2): 99–107.

Dörnyei, Zoltán
2002 The motivational basis of language learning tasks. In: Peter Robinson (ed.), *Individual Differences and Instructed Language Learning*, 137–158. Amsterdam: John Benjamins.

Doughty, Catherine J. and Michael Long (eds.)
2003 *The Handbook of Second Language Acquisition*. Oxford: Blackwell.

Eckerth, Johannes
2003 *Fremdsprachenerwerb in aufgabenbasierten Interaktionen*. Tübingen: Narr.

Edelhoff, Christoph and Ralf Weskamp (eds.)
1999 *Autonomes Fremdsprachenlernen*. Ismaning: Hueber.

Edmondson, Willis J.
1994 Was trägt das Adjektiv 'interkulturell' zu unserem Verständnis vom Lernen im Fremdsprachenunterricht bei? In: Bausch, Christ and Krumm (eds.), 48–55.

Edmondson, Willis J.
1996 Subjective theories of second language acquisition. In: Jürgen Klein and Dirk Vanderbeke (eds.), *Anglistentag 1995 Greifswald. Proceedings*, 453–464. Tübingen: Niemeyer.

Edmondson, Willis J.
1997 Sprachlernbewußtheit und Motivation beim Fremdsprachenlernen. *Fremdsprachen Lehren und Lernen* 26: 88–110.

Edmondson, Willis J.
1999 Die fremdsprachliche Ausbildung kann nicht den Schulen überlassen werden! *PRAXIS des neusprachlichen Unterrichts* 46 (2): 115–123.

Edmondson, Willis J.
2000a Grammatik und Kommunikation bei Auslandsaufenthalten. In: Beate Helbig, Karin Kleppin and Frank G. Königs (eds.), *Sprachlehrforschung im Wandel. Beiträge zur Erforschung des Lehrens und Lernens von Fremdsprachen. Festschrift für Karl-Richard Bausch zum 60. Geburtstag*, 363–382. Tübingen: Stauffenburg-Verlag.

Edmondson, Willis J.
2000b What we know about effective language learning, and some implications for language teaching. In: Pauli Kaikkonen and Viljo Kohonen (eds.), *Minne Menet, Kielikasvatus?*, 11–25. Universität Jyväskylä.

Edmondson, Willis J.
2002a Literatur und Interkulturelles Lernen: ein Perspektivenwechsel. In: Hans Barkowski and Renate Faistauer (eds.), *... in Sachen Deutsch als Fremdsprache*, 355–374. Hohengraben: Schneider.

Edmondson, Willis J.
2002b Wissen, Können, Lernen. Kognitive Verarbeitung und Grammatikentwicklung. In: Wolfgang Börner and Klaus Vogel (eds.), *Grammatik und Fremdsprachenerwerb. Kognitive, psycholinguistische und erwerbstheoretische Perspektiven*, 51–70. Tübingen: Francke.

Edmondson, Willis J.
2003 Output als autonomes Lernen: Spracherwerb und Sprachproduktion aus kognitiver Sicht. *Fremdsprachen Lehren und Lernen* 32: 196–213.

Edmondson, Willis J.
2004 Individual motivational profiles: the interaction between external and internal factors. *Zeitschrift für Interkulturellen Fremdsprachenunterricht* [Online] 9 (2), 21 pp. Accessible at http://www.ualberta.ca/~german/ejournal/Edmondson2.htm

Edmondson, Willis J.
2005a Learning from different tasks: the Dr. Pangloss perspective. In: Andreas Müller-Hartmann and Marita Schocker-v. Ditfurth (eds.), *Aufgabenorientierung im Fremdsprachenunterricht/Task-Based Language Learning and Teaching. Festschrift für Michael K. Legutke,* 53–66. Tübingen: Narr.

Edmondson, Willis J.
2005b Prejudice and practice in applied linguistics (Review article). *International Journal of Applied Linguistics* 15: 389–396.

Edmondson, Willis J.
2006 Taking tasks to task. Aufgabenbasierte Forschung und Lernaufgaben im Fremdsprachenunterricht. In: Johannes-Peter Timm (ed.), *Fremdsprachenlernen: Kompetenzen, Standards, Aufgaben, Evaluation. Festschrift für Helmut Johannes Vollmer*, 139–156. Tübingen: Narr.

Edmondson, Willis J. and Juliane House
1998 Interkulturelles Lernen – ein überflüssiger Begriff. *Zeitschrift für Fremdsprachenforschung* 9 (2): 161–188.

Ellis, Gail and Barbara Sinclair
1989 *Learning to Learn English*. Cambridge: Cambridge University Press.

Ellis, Rod
1985 *Understanding Second Language Acquisition*. Oxford: Oxford University Press.

Ellis, Rod
1995 Interpretation tasks for grammar teaching. *TESOL Quarterly* 29: 87–105.
Ellis, Rod
2003 *Task-Based Language Learning and Teaching*. Oxford: Oxford University Press.
Ely, Christopher M.
1986 Language learning motivation: A descriptive and causal analysis. *Modern Language Journal* 70 (1): 28–35.
Eysenck, Michael W. and Mark T. Keane
2000 *Cognitive Psychology. A Student's Handbook*. Hove: Psychology Press.
Fairclough, Norman (ed.)
1992 *Critical Language Awareness*. London: Longman.
Flavell, John H.
1987 Speculations about the nature and development of metacognition. In: Franz E. Weinert and Rainer H. Kluwe (eds.), *Metacognition, Motivation, and Understanding*, 21–29. Hillsdale, NJ: Lawrence Erlbaum.
Földes, Csaba
1995 Zum Deutschlandbild der DaF-Lehrwerke: von der Schönfärberei zum Frustexport? Ein Diskussionsbeitrag. *Deutsch als Fremdsprache* 32 (1): 30–32.
Fotos, Sandra
1994 Integrating grammar instruction and communicative language use through grammar consciousness-raising tasks. *TESOL Quarterly* 28: 323–351.
Freed, Barbara F.
1995 What makes us think that students who study abroad become fluent? In: Barbara F. Freed (ed.), *Second Language Acquisition in a Study Abroad Context*, 123–148. Amsterdam/Philadelphia: Benjamins.
Freudenstein, Reinhold.
1994 Alles interkulturell – oder was? In: Bausch, Christ and Krumm (eds.), 56–62.
Gillette, Barbara
1987 Two successful language learners: an introspective report. In: Claus Faerch and Gabriele Kasper (eds.), *Introspection in Second Language Research*, 268–279. Clevedon: Multilingual Matters.
Harden, Theo and Arnd Witte (eds.)
2000 *The Notion of Intercultural Understanding in the Context of German as a Foreign Language*. Bern: Peter Lang.
Hawkins, Eric
1984 *Awareness of Language*. London: Longman
Hawkins, Eric
1987 *Awareness of Language: An Introduction (revised edition)*. Cambridge: Cambridge University Press.
House, Juliane
1998 Kontrastive Pragmatik und interkulturelle Kompetenz im Fremdsprachenunterricht. In: Wolfgang Börner und Klaus Vogel (eds.), *Kontrast und Äquivalenz*, 62–88. Tübingen: Narr.

House, Juliane
2003 Teaching and learning pragmatic fluency in english as a foreign language. In: Alicia Martínez Flor, Esther Usó Juan and Ana Fernaandez Guerra (eds.), *Pragmatic Competence and Foriegn Language Teaching*, 133–160. Castellón: Universitat Jaume.

James, Carl and Peter Garrett
1991 *Language Awareness in the Classroom*. London: Longman.

Jordan, Robert R.
1997 *English for Academic Purposes. A Guide and Resource Book for Teachers*. Cambridge: Cambridge University Press.

Kasper, Gabriele and Eric Kellerman (eds.)
1997 *Communicative Strategies: Psycholinguistic and Sociolinguistic Perspectives*. London: Longman.

Kowal, Maria and Merrill Swain
1994 Using collaborative language production tasks to promote students' language awareness. *Language Awareness* 3: 73–91.

Kramsch, Claire
1993 *Context and Culture in Language Teaching*. Oxford: Oxford University Press.

Kramsch, Claire
1996 The cultural component of language teaching. *Zeitschrift für Interkulturellen Fremdsprachenunterricht* [Online] 1 (2), 13 pp. Accessible: ⟨http://www.spz.tu-Darmstadt.de/projekt_ejournal/jg_01_2/beitrag/kramsch2.htm⟩

Kramsch, Claire
2000 The cultural politics of language study. In: Beate Helbig, Karin Kleppin and Frank G. Königs (eds.), *Sprachlehrforschung im Wandel*, 459–471. Tübingen: Stauffenburg.

Krashen, Stephen
1981 *Second Language Acquisition and Second Language Learning*. Oxford: Pergamon.

Lightbown, Patsy and Nina Spada
1993 *How Languages are Learned*. Oxford: Oxford University Press.

Long, Michael H.
1991 Focus on form: A design feature in language teaching methodology. In: Kees de Bot, Ralph Ginsberg and Claire Kramsch (eds.), *Foreign Language Research in Cross-Cultural Perspective*, 39–52. Amsterdam: Benjamins.

Löschmann, Martin and Magda Stroinska (eds.)
1998 *Stereotype im Fremdsprachenunterricht*. Tübingen: Peter Lang.

Naiman, Neil, Maria Fröhlich, Hans H. Stern and Angie Todesco
1978 *The Good Language Learner*. Toronto: Ontario Institute for Studies in Education.

O'Malley, J. Michael and Anna. U. Chamot
1990 *Learning Strategies in Second Language Acquisition*. Cambridge: Cambridge University Press.

Oxford, Rebecca L.
1990 *Language Learning Strategies: What Every Teacher Should Know*. Rowley, Mass.: Newbury House.

Oxford, Rebecca L. (ed.)
1996 *Language Learning Strategies Around the World: Cross-Cultural Perspectives*. Honolulu, Hawaii: University of Hawaii Press.

Oxford, Rebecca L. and Betty Lou Leaver
1996 A synthesis of strategy instruction for language learning. In: Oxford (ed.) 1996, 227–246.

Phipps, Alison and Mike Gonzalez
2004 *Modern Languages: Learning and Teaching in an Intercultural Field*. London: Sage.

Pulverness, Alan
2001 *Changing Skies*. Addlestone: Delta Publishing.

Rampillon, Ute and Günther Zimmermann (eds.)
1997 *Strategien und Techniken beim Erwerb fremder Sprachen*. Ismaning: Hueber.

Riemer, Claudia
2000 Zur Rolle der selbstevaluativen Wahrnehmung des Lernenden. In: Wolfgang Börner and Klaus Vogel. (eds.), *Normen und Fremdsprachenunterricht*, 229–249. Tübingen: Narr.

Riemer, Claudia
2003 "Englisch war für mich nur Teil meines Stundenplans" – Motivation zum Englischlernen in Zeiten der Globalisierung. In: Nicole Baumgarten, Claudia Böttger, Marcus Motz and Julia Probst (eds), *Übersetzen, Spracherwerb und interkulturelle Kommunikation: das Leben mit mehreren Sprachen*. Themenheft der *Zeitschrift für interkulturellen Fremdsprachenunterricht* [Online] 7 (2). Available at: www.ualberta.ca/~german/ejournal/Riemer1.htm.

Schlak, Torsten
1999 Grammatikaufgaben im Fremdsprachenunterricht. *Fremdsprachen Lernen und Lehren* 28: 220–229.

Schmidt, Richard
1994 Deconstructing consciousness in search of useful definitions for applied linguistics. In: Jan H. Hulstijn and Richard Schmidt (eds.) *Consciousness in Second Language Learning. AILA Review* 11: 11–26.

Schmidt, Richard and Sónia Frota
1986 Developing basic conversational ability in a second language: A case study of an adult learner of Portuguese. In: Richard Day (ed.), *Talking to Learn: Conversation in Second Language Acquisition*, 237–326. Rowly, Mass.: Newbury House.

Schneider, Frank W. and B. L. Kintz
1967 An analysis of the incidental-intentional learning dichotomy. *Journal of Experimental Psychology* 73 (1): 85–90.

Sharwood Smith, Michael
1997 "Consciousness-raising" meets "Language Awareness". *Fremdsprachen Lehren und Lernen* 26: 24–32.

Sinclair, Barbara, Ian McGrath and Terry Lamb (eds.)
2000 *Learner Autonomy, Teacher Autonomy: Future Directions*. London: Longman.

Skehan, Peter
1998 *A Cognitive Appoach to Language Learning*. Oxford: Oxford University Press.
Tomlin, Russell and Victor Villa
1993 Attention in cognitive science and second language acquisition. *Studies in Second Language Acquisition* 16: 183–203.
Utley, Derek
2004 *The Culture Pack: Intercultural Communication Resources for Trainers*. Cambridge: Cambridge University Press.
Van Lier, Leo
1996 Conflicting voices: language, classrooms, and bilingual education in Puno. In: Kathleen M. Bailey and David Nunan (eds.), *Voices from the Language Classroom: Qualitative Research in Second Language Education*, 363–387. Cambridge: Cambridge University Press.
Vann, Roberta J. and Roberta G. Abraham
1990 Strategies of unsuccessful language learners. *TESOL Quarterly* 24 (2): 177–198.
Wajnryb, Ruth
1990 *Grammar Dictation*. Oxford: Oxford University Press.
Wenden, Anita L.
1986 Incorporating learner training in the classroom. *System* 14 (3): 315–325.
Wenden, Anita L.
1991 *Learner Strategies for Learner Autonomy*. London: Prentice-Hall Intemational.
Widdowson, Henry G.
1994 The ownership of English. *TESOL Quarterly* 29: 377–88.
Yang, Nae-Dong
1996 Effective awareness-raising in language learning strategy instruction. In: Oxford, Rebecca (ed.) 1996, 205–210.

Recommended Readings

Andrews, Stephen
2006 The evolution of teachers' language awareness. *Language Awareness* 15 (1): 1–19.
Brumfit, Christopher
1992 Language awareness in teacher education. In: Carl James and Peter Garrett, *Language Awareness in the Classroom*, 24–39. London: Longman.
Fairclough, Norman (ed.)
1992 *Critical Language Awareness*. London: Longman.
Harley, Birgit
1994 Appealing to consciousness in the L2 classroom. *AILA Review* 11: 57–68.
Schmidt, Richard
1994 Deconstructing consciousness in search of useful definitions for applied linguistics. *AILA Review* 11: 11–26.

Schmidt, Richard
1995 Consciousness and foreign language learning: A tutorial on the role of attention and awareness in learning. In: Richard Schmidt (ed.), *Attention and Awareness in Foreign Language Learning*, 1–65. Honolulu: University of Hawaii Press.

Schmidt, Richard
2001 Attention. In: Peter Robinson (ed.), *Cognition and Second Language Instruction*, 3–32. New York: Cambridge University Press.

Svalberg, Agneta
2007 Language awareness and language learning. *Language Teaching* 40: 287–308.

VanPatten, Bill and Teresa Cadierno
1993 Input processing and second-language acquisition: a role for instruction. *Modern Language Journal* 77 (1): 45–57.

II. Perspectives on foreign language learning and teaching

8. The linguistic perspective

Henry G. Widdowson

1. Introduction

It would seem to be self-evident that the discipline of linguistics should have insights to offer which are relevant to the understanding and effective promotion of foreign language communication and learning. Just what these insights might be and how their relevance might be demonstrated are issues which fall squarely within the scope of applied linguistics, seen as an area of enquiry which brings disciplinary expertise to bear on problems relating to language experience 'in the real world' (Brumfit 1995). How such enquiry might be conducted, and indeed just what is distinctive about applied linguistics itself, have, however, been matters of considerable contention (see Seidlhofer 2003 Section 5; Widdowson 2005). Even if one accepts that in principle applied linguistics is a process of reciprocal mediation whereby practice makes reference to theory and theory is made relevant to practice (Widdowson 1990) just how that principle can be effectively acted upon is beset with difficulties. For one thing, those concerned with the practice of foreign language teaching have been persistently suspicious of theory, tending to think that it is remote from the immediate classroom reality they have to cope with. The suspicion is exacerbated by a counter tendency on the part of linguists to claim the authority to determine how foreign language pedagogy should be designed.

There is one linguist, however, who would appear to endorse the language teacher's suspicion, and at the same time to imply that there is little point in taking linguistic perspectives on foreign language learning at all.

> I am, frankly, rather sceptical about the significance, for the teaching of languages, of such insights and understanding as have been attained in linguistics and psychology. (Chomsky 1966: 152–153)

It needs to be noted, however, that Chomsky made these comments in an address to language teachers where he makes it clear that he speaks as a linguist, and that, having no expertise in pedagogy, it is not actually for him to pronounce on this significance. Later in the same address, we find the following:

> It is possible – even likely – that principles of psychology and linguistics, and research in these disciplines, may supply insights useful to the language teacher. But this must be demonstrated, and cannot be presumed. It is the language teacher himself who must validate or refute any specific proposal. There is very little in psychology or linguistics that he can accept on faith. (Chomsky 1966: 155)

So it is not that Chomsky denies the possibility of the relevance of linguistics to pedagogic practice, indeed he thinks it likely. He simply disclaims any authority to say what it is. This is something that the language teacher has to determine.

It is interesting to compare Chomsky's position here with that which is adopted in Halliday, McIntosh and Strevens (1964), a book that was taken at the time of its publication as a kind of applied linguistics manifesto. The very conjunction, in its title, *The Linguistic Sciences and Language Teaching*, implies that it can be presumed that linguistics does have useful pedagogic insights to supply. This is made explicit in the following statement:

> He [the language teacher] is not teaching linguistics. But he is teaching something which is the object of study of linguistics, and is described by linguistic methods. It is obviously desirable that the underlying description should be as good as possible, and this means that it should be based on sound linguistic principles. (Halliday, McIntosh and Strevens 1964: 66)

Here the linguist does assume the authority to determine relevance on the grounds that since the object language the linguist is describing and the language subject the teacher is teaching are one and the same thing, 'it is obviously desirable' that pedagogic prescriptions for learning should conform to descriptions 'based on sound linguistic principles'. Such a presumption has proved very persuasive and has generally, in Chomsky's words, been taken on faith in foreign language pedagogy over the past fifty years. The question that needs to be considered is how far this obvious desirability has been convincingly demonstrated.

2. Linguistic descriptions and lessons from the past

The presumption to be considered then is that what is taught as a foreign language subject should be 'based on sound linguistic principles' and so be determined by linguists, since they know what these principles are, and teachers do not. The first, and most obvious, difficulty with this injunction is that linguists do not agree among themselves about what these principles are, which are sound and which are not. Not only are there radical differences of opinion about 'linguistic methods' but also about the object of description these methods should apply to.

2.1. Methods of description

As far as methods are concerned, there is, for example, a fundamental disagreement about how you go about obtaining valid data for description. Generative linguists, for example, following established tradition, rely on the 1st person data of introspection, with linguists using themselves as representative informants. Such a procedure is not, of course, available to linguists primarily concerned with describing hitherto unrecorded languages. They have to acquire their data from a 2nd person source by elicitation. Over recent years, with the computer making possible the collection and analysis of language corpora, linguists have been able to draw on the observed 3rd person data of actually occurring language. Which of these different linguistic methods, then, is to be preferred as leading to the best description, and therefore, presumably, as serving as the best basis for foreign language pedagogy?

It is important to note that 1st person introspection, 2nd person elicitation and 3rd person observation are not three different ways of getting at the same data but yield quite different kinds of data, and so whatever insights they have to offer to language pedagogy these insights will necessarily be of different kinds as well. Thus introspection will give you language in the abstract, something you know as a mental construct. With elicitation, you will get actually performed language behaviour, but particular behaviour that has been induced, and from which this underlying knowledge can only be indirectly inferred. So what you are able to elicit may not reflect what the informant knows – a problem which is, of course, all too familiar in language testing (see McNamara, Ch. 22 this volume). Observation will also give you behavioural data, but naturally occurring and not induced. With the development of corpus linguistics, there has been a marked tendency to prefer observed 3rd person data over any other, even to the extent of claiming that provide for the best possible linguistic description which invalidates all others.

We will take up the question of the relative pedagogic relevance of these different kinds of data in later discussion, but for the moment, we need to note that each kind has its limitations. Thus 1st person data exemplifies competence, but tells us nothing about how this is acted upon, how it is put to use in actual performance. The 3rd person data of corpora, on the other hand, do exemplify aspects of performance: they tell us what linguistic forms a selection of language users have produced, a cross section of behaviour. But they obviously cannot reveal what users might have used, or what they are capable of using, nor can they tell us about the pragmatic functions that the use of these forms performs. In spite of claims that corpus data carry, as one publisher puts it, a 'real language guarantee' (presumably as distinct from other kinds of data that do not), there is a good deal of the psychological and sociological reality of language that it does not, and cannot, capture. The fact of the matter is that each method of accessing linguistic data reveals some aspects of the reality of language as experienced by its users and none reveals all. Again, the question is: which aspects of the language experience of users would seem to be most relevant for foreign language learners?

2.2. Linguistic perspectives and structuralist language teaching

Although as was indicated earlier, teachers have often expressed suspicion of linguistics, and have indeed quoted Chomsky's scepticism to support it, there has, nevertheless, been a marked tendency to accept on faith that linguistic descriptions should determine the language of their subject. Generally speaking, teachers have been readily persuaded to go along with the different ways in which their subject has been formulated for them, and so to defer to linguistic authority rather than take it upon themselves to 'validate or refute' the pedagogic relevance of the linguistic insights and descriptions on offer. Thus as linguistic thinking has changed, so fashions in foreign language teaching have followed suit, often with little in the way of a critical appraisal of pedagogic suitability.

A case in point is the so-called oral/structural approach, widely promoted and practised as the mainstream orthodoxy in foreign language teaching from the middle of the last century (see Howatt 2004 and Ch. 17 this volume). This was informed by two principles assumed to be axiomatic in the linguistics of the time. The first was that languages were essentially formal constructs, systems of grammatical rules that determined the syntactic structure of sentences and it was these that it was the business of linguistics to describe. There were, of course, differences of descriptive focus. Linguists like Fries, for example, were concerned with categorising the various and manifold structural forms that overtly realised these rules, (Fries 1952; Fries and Fries 1985) and linguists like Chomsky more concerned with identifying the covert underlying rules of the system that explained the relationships between structures not immediately apparent from their surface forms (Chomsky 1957, 1965). In both cases, however, the focus of attention was on the formal properties of the linguistic code. That was the object of linguistic description, and accordingly that became what was taught as the foreign language subject: structures and sentence patterns[1].

But structures and sentence patterns are abstractions. If they are to be taught they have to be actualised, made manifest in some way. And here we come to the second principle of linguistic study in the 1950s – and one that has its origins with Henry Sweet and the Reform Movement in the 19th century (see again Howatt 2004) namely that language was primarily a spoken phenomenon, and written language a secondary and derived version. Therefore, if one carries this principle over into pedagogy, primacy should also be given to speech in language teaching. So it comes about that in the structural approach, the linguistic forms, the sentence patterns are manifested, presented and practised, by oral means. But here, unfortunately, we find that the two principles are in practice incompatible. When language naturally occurs as a spoken phenomenon, it does so as the realisation of linguistic forms for some communicative purpose: it is a mode of language use. Speaking sentence patterns is only the use of the vocal organs to give some perceptible substance to abstract linguistic forms. It is simply the use of the oral medium to manifest these forms, and this bears little if any resemblance to spoken language as such. Primacy is thereby shifted from the spoken mode to the oral medium as if it were the same thing. The only justification for giving primacy to the oral medium would be on the psychological grounds that linguistic forms, and the underlying rules they exemplify, are more effectively internalised by learners by means of spoken rather than written manifestations. I know of no language learning theory or empirical research, in or outside the classroom, that lends any substance to this belief.

Although the primacy of structure and of spoken language can both be adduced as separate linguistic principles, considered to be sound, at least at the time, their disparity becomes apparent when they are adopted together in language pedagogy. And further disparity follows when a third feature is added.

Linguistic structures are, as we have noted, abstractions and so need exemplification, and this is what a linguistic description provides. Exemplification, of course, requires the use of lexis of one kind or another. But since examples in a linguistic description are designed to exemplify the formal properties of structures, it may not much matter which words are used so long as they serve this purpose. But in the classroom, the structures which are presented and practised have to demonstrate meaning as well and here, obviously, the choice of words does matter. So far we have been dealing with the oral and the structural features of the oral/situational approach. The Indian scholar N. S. Prabhu refers to this approach as the structural-oral-situational approach: S.O.S. (Prabhu 1987). It is the second S, the situation feature, that accounts for meaning.

The general procedure was to lexicalise structures that could be set in correspondence with situations devised to demonstrate their meaning. So, for instance, the teacher might hold up a book and produce the structure *This is a book*, or point to a book and say *That is a book* thereby exemplifying the proximal/distal distinction between the two demonstratives; or walk to the door and exemplify the meaning of the present continuous tense by saying *I am walking to the door* at the same time. And so on. In spite of what has often been asserted, such procedures do not focus on form rather than meaning, for there clearly is a focus on meaning, the focus is on meaning in form, encoded or semantic meaning. There is no warrant in linguistic descriptions of the structuralist kind we are considering for this kind of exemplification. It is a pedagogic invention. Like the insistence on oral manifestation, it is grafted on to the structuralist principle to further the language learning process.

But of course the result is a use of language which bears little resemblance to the way language is naturally used. The situation can be said to provide a context for the structure, but the relationship between structure and context is the very opposite to that which normally obtains. In the S.O.S. approach, the situation/context has to exactly duplicate the structure, or otherwise it does not serve its exemplificatory purpose. In normal language use, however, the context and structure are complementary to each other: it is just what is not evident in the context that the structure is used to signify (for further discussion see Widdowson 2003 Ch. 9).

The main point to be made is that linguistic description based on the structuralist principle abstracts formal features out of language as it is actually used and, though it might be thought to be 'as good a description as possible' a pedagogy that uses it as a model cannot, as linguists can, deal with these forms in isolation. It has to bring in other features to give some substance to these abstractions, to make them actual in substance and meaning. Thus we arrive at the pedagogic hybrid S.O.S. Though this may be justified on the grounds that it facilitates language learning, it bears little resemblance to how structures, formal properties of the language, are realised in speech (or in writing) in relation to contexts of actual use.

A consideration of the relationship between structuralist linguistic descriptions and its influence on S.O.S. raises a fundamentally problematic issue in applied linguistics and foreign language pedagogy. This is the relationship between two kinds of reality: on the one hand, language as it naturally occurs, which can be seen as the eventual objective of learners, and which one might expect linguistic descriptions to account for, and on the other hand language which is designed as a subject to activate the learning process, which obviously cannot be accounted for by linguistic descriptions as such. In this sense, it is not at all the case that the teacher 'is teaching something which is the object of study of linguistics'.

2.3. Linguistic perspectives and the communicative approach

S.O.S. was subsequently challenged by a different approach, the co-called communicative approach (see Rodgers, Ch. 13 this volume). But again what motivated the challenge was a shift in thinking about linguistic methods and principles, rather than any critical evaluation of the pedagogy of the approach. Although S.O.S. was, and continues to be, discredited as ineffective, reliable evidence of its ineffectiveness is actually hard to come by. Its downfall was essentially occasioned by a change in linguistic fashion.

There was in some linguistic circles a dissatisfaction with methods and principles of description that focused on the formal properties of a language (and some linguists – J. R. Firth, for example – never subscribed to them anyway: see Widdowson 2007). Such an approach was thought to be altogether too abstract, and Chomsky's formalism was even more abstract than the structuralism of his predecessors in that it did not simply categorise structures, but looked for covert structural relations that were not apparent on the surface. Such abstract formalism seemed to be aridly reductionist in that it excluded from consideration altogether the essential nature of language as a means of communication. As Labov put it:

> [...] it is difficult to avoid the common-sense conclusion that the object of linguistics must ultimately be the instrument of communication used by the speech community; and if we are not talking about *that* language, there is something trivial in our proceeding. (Labov 1972: 187)

The object of formalist descriptions was clearly not language as an instrument of communication. What they described, in various ways, was the linguistic code that language users were assumed to know but not how they drew on this knowledge as a resource for actual communicative use. A different definition of the object of linguistic description was called for: one that focused on function rather than form, on communicative rather than linguistic competence. And as the focus of attention in linguistics shifted, the pedagogic focus shifted accordingly. The problem with S.O.S., it was assumed, was not that it was dependent on a linguistic description but on the wrong kind of linguistic description. Now that another and apparently more valid kind was in the offing, it promised to provide the basis of a more effective approach to pedagogy.

The change in orientation in thinking came in part from a functional approach to grammatical description, particularly associated with Halliday (for example Halliday 1973) and in part from two other disciplinary directions: the philosophical enquiry into pragmatics (especially Austin 1962; Searle 1969) and the sociolinguistic study of language in its social context (especially Hymes 1972; Labov 1972). These scholars were also accordingly seen as providing the theoretical linguistic credentials for communicative language teaching (CLT). But although their ideas are frequently invoked, it is not always clear just how their interpretation provides a coherent rationale for this approach to foreign language teaching.

The development of CLT has been well documented (see Byram and Mendez, Ch. 18 this volume). One of the most authoritative introductions to the thinking behind this approach is Brumfit and Johnson (1979). The first section of this book is entitled 'The linguistic background', and this consists of extracts from papers by Hymes (1972) on the one hand and Halliday (1973) on the other. These scholars are, then, represented as providing the theoretical bearings in reference to which the principles of a communicative approach to language teaching were to be established. But although Brumfit and Johnson provide a commentary which clarifies the points these scholars are making in these extracts, and point out how they represent a fresh perspective on language description, this does not amount to an explicit explanation of just how CLT principles can be derived from these particular theoretical ideas. The linguistic background, in this sense, remains in the background: it sets the scene for pedagogic action by presenting a general change of linguistic orientation from form to function.

But if one pays attention to what Hymes and Halliday actually say in these extracts, it becomes clear that they conceive of language functions in very different ways. In his now well-known formulation of communicative competence[2], Hymes points to four kinds of judgement that somebody competent in a language is able to make about any particular instance of it. The first of these is:

1. Whether (and to what degree) something is formally possible.

This component of competence has to do with the formal properties of the language code itself. This is usually equated with grammatical rules of the kind that Chomsky specifies in his model of generative syntax. But what is formally possible in a language relates to all levels of encoding and not only to grammar. Thus the phonological rules of a language will determine which sounds and which combinations are recognised as possible and which are not. Similarly, at the morphological level, there are constraints on word formation, so that, if we take English as the code in question, words like *lesscare* or *easyun*, though perfectly possible phonologically, are (unlike *careless* and *uneasy*) morphologically impossible. Again, it is easy to think of words which are impeccably well formed at the phonological and morphological levels, but which are lexically impossible – like *beautiless* (as distinct from *beautiful*) or *unsad* (as distinct from *unhappy*). And, of course, a sentence can be grammatically possible even if its constituents consist of impossible lexical items, as is regularly illustrated by the citing of nonsense verse like Lewis Carroll's *Jabberwocky*:

> *Twas brillig and the slithy toves*
> *Did gyre and gimble in the wabe.*

It needs to be noted that, as Hymes defines it, this first component of communicative competence has to do not only with whether a particular instance of a language is identified as formally possible or not, but with the recognition of 'degrees' of possibility, the extent to which it conforms to encoding conventions at different levels. It is important to stress this recognition of the relativity of the possible because it provides for creativity. Competence in a language is not just a matter of conforming to its encoding conventions at all levels at once, but of exploiting possibilities across levels, using the virtual resources for meaning making which are inherent in the language code itself.

And this is where Halliday comes in. For these formal resources for making meaning are what he refers to as 'meaning potential'. Though this is something inherent in the formal encoding of a language, and therefore a semantic property, it is, for Halliday, functionally motivated. That is to say, a language is encoded in the way it is because it has developed to serve the social and communicative needs of its users. The encoding is a semantic record, abstracted out of previous pragmatic use. Since what is encoded in a language reflects the functions that it has evolved to serve, a description of the possible is a matter of identifying how such functions have become abstracted and formally systematised in the language. Hence the name *Systemic/Functional Grammar.* So when Halliday talks about functions, he is talking about the possible in Hymes' terms, about the meaning potential of a language inherent in it as a system – a potential that is there in principle. He is not talking about how this potential gets communicatively realised in contexts of use.

But Hymes notion of function is not restricted to the possible. In his model of communicative competence, what is semantically encoded in linguistic forms, that is to say what is possible, is one aspect of their language that its users know about and which their linguistic competence enables them to determine. But this is only one component of a more general communicative competence which enables them to make other judgements as well:

2. Whether (and to what degree) something is *feasible* in virtue of the means of implementation available;
3. Whether (and to what degree) something is *appropriate* (adequate, happy, successful) in relation to the context in which it used and evaluated;
4. Whether (and to what degree) something is in fact done, actually *performed*, and what its doing entails.
(Hymes 1972: 281)

Communication has to do with how possible forms are appropriately used 'in relation to context' (as stated in 3 above). Function is indeed a function of this relationship, not an intrinsic semantic property. In other words, Hymes is concerned not with how communicative functions are internalised as semantic abstractions but with how they are pragmatically realised in contexts of actual use.

In accordance with the usual assumption that what linguists describe and what teachers teach is, or should be, essentially the same thing, CLT was in effect the adoption into foreign language teaching of what was taken to be a new perspective in linguistic description. But in respect to the crucial concept of function there are two perspectives, not one, and the question naturally arises as to how this difference was dealt with in pedagogic proposals.

One of the most influential set of proposals was that of Wilkins (1976). He argued that if, as seemed obviously desirable, communicative competence was to be the objective for learning (as it was the object of linguistic description) then the design principles of a foreign language syllabus, previously based on structuralist ideas, needed to be radically changed. The new design comprised three kinds of 'notional' content: 'semantico-grammatical categories', 'categories of modal meaning', and 'categories of communicative function'. As the name suggests, the semantico-grammatical categories have to do with what is encoded internally, with what Hymes refers to as the possible. But Wilkins explicitly associated these categories with Halliday's ideational function, and here we find the very confusion between the two concepts of function that was referred to earlier. In Halliday's scheme of things, the term 'ideational' refers to one of the language-external social and communicative functions that language has evolved to serve and which are subsequently encoded internally in the grammar in what

Halliday calls 'transitivity systems'. It is in these systems that the semantico-grammatical categories are to be found: there are no ideational categories as such in the grammar. Though Wilkins himself does not make the connection, his proposed categories of modal meaning are also related to Halliday's grammar, this time to what are called 'mood systems', which are the internal encodings here of another language-external social function, namely the interpersonal function.

So the first two of Wilkins' categories, the semantico-grammatical and the modal, have to do with the possible, with what is semantically encoded in the language, and so fall within the domain of Halliday's functional/systemic grammar. But the categories are not explicitly and systematically derived from this grammar, and so this part of the linguistic background seems to have no particular relevance as far as this account of CLT principles is concerned. This would appear to be borne out by Wilkins' comment that "Halliday's three-fold division of 'functions' does not parallel the division into three types of meaning that is proposed here" (Wilkins 1976: 21). No explanation is given why not, but one must surmise that there are pedagogic grounds for not following Halliday by deriving these modal and semantico-grammatical categories of the syllabus from the mood and transitivity systems that correspond with them in a systemic/functional grammar. What these grounds might be, however, is not made explicit. The question again arises as to how far an approach to linguistic description can or should be carried over into the design of the language subject, and what the criteria are for deciding one way or the other.

What, then, of Wilkins' third kind of category of 'communicative function'? Unlike the other kinds of category, these are not accounted for by grammatical systems at all. They are not semantically but pragmatically defined, and deal not with what is encoded but with how language functions externally in context. In other words, they have to do not with the possible but with the appropriate in Hymes' scheme. It was this kind of external pragmatic function that attracted most interest and came to be seen as the defining feature of this new approach to foreign language teaching. The semantic-grammatical categories of internal encoded functions inspired much less enthusiasm. They did not seem all that different from the structures that were taught in the old fashioned S.O.S. approach – dressed up a little differently but still focused on the semantics of the language code. There was a quite widespread assumption that if teachers got learners to activate the categories of communicative function, the semantic-grammatical categories would somehow take care of themselves. Again, we find those designing the language subject not so much conforming to models of description as applying them selectively, but without much sign of the critical process that Chomsky alluded to whereby teachers 'validate or refute' linguistic insights in reference to pedagogic criteria.

3. New proposals, old assumptions

As we saw earlier with the notions of structuralism and the primacy of the spoken language, one main difficulty with linguistic insights is that they come from different perspectives which are often incompatible. Faced with this difficulty, the natural tendency on the part of those concerned with foreign language teaching is to resolve it by selecting those that seem relevant or especially appealing and disregarding the others. The two concepts of function we have been discussing are a case in point. One can accept the validity of describing the formal properties of a language as historically motivated by the communicative functions it has evolved to serve, so that its internal systems, a reflex of these functions, constitute a meaning potential. One can also accept that this semantic potential can only be realised when language is put to pragmatic use. The question is, how do these two functions of language operate in concert, how does the potential get realised, how, in reference to Hymes' model do the possible and the appropriate inter-relate?

3.1. Selective focus on aspects of communicative competence

In the Hymes scheme, the possible is an intrinsic component of communicative competence, and there is no indication that it is less significant than any other. It would follow that an approach to teaching that focused on the possible – the formal properties of sentences – would be developing communicative competence in part. But only, of course, in part, and the question obviously arises as to how this relates to the other parts, and in particular to the appropriateness factor. But by the same token, focusing on the use of language in context and preferring the appropriate at the expense of the possible, is also only dealing with communicative competence in part. Since there is no indication of the relative significance of the four factors in the Hymes model, there is no reason for supposing that a focus on the possible should be considered any less communicative than a focus on the appropriate. Indeed, the fact the possible comes first in the list of components, one might be led to suppose that it somehow has primacy over the others.

The model gives no indication of relationships across these different factors either. And this is a crucial omission. For if these are 'components' of competence, they can only be components to the extent that they relate: the whole is not a sum but a function of its parts. There has to be some interdependency across the different kinds of knowledge that the model identifies, so if the knowledge of what is formally possible is to be an aspect of communicative competence then this must be relatable to a knowledge of the contextual conditions in which possible forms are appropriately used. The formally possible, therefore, has to be conceived of as, to use the Halliday term, meaning potential – a semantic resource for the making of appropriate pragmatic meaning. The two factors of the possible and the appropriate are interdependent and communication is a function of the relationship between them.

Interpreted in this way, an approach which seeks to develop communicative competence, as CLT claims to do, needs to give equal weight to the two concepts of function discussed earlier – the semantic functions of the possible and the pragmatic functions that are realised as contextually appropriate – and devise ways of demonstrating their relationship so that learners become aware of how it works: how what is possible provides for, and constrains, appropriate use, and how contextual appropriateness in its turn constrains what features of meaning potential get realised.

So far we have been considering the factors of the possible and the appropriate as constituent parts of communicative competence in the Hymes' scheme. What of the other two: the feasible and the actually performed? Where do they fit in, and how can they be interpreted as having pedagogic relevance? We will consider the feasibility factor a little later, but first, we will turn our attention to the fourth: the actually performed.

3.2. Real language and the authenticity doctrine

With what is actually performed we come to the most recent approach to linguistic description and the most recent linguistic influence on foreign language pedagogy. This approach involves the analysis of corpus data by computer. It is this that is now is assumed by many to be the best possible description, and accordingly to provide most satisfactorily for the needs of foreign language pedagogy. The object of description in corpus linguistics is not the abstract systems of the code, whether defined in functional terms or not, but language as it has actually occurred. Attention shifts from linguistic knowledge to language behaviour, from competence to performance. The only data that is taken into account is the 3rd person data of observation, now not dependent however on fallible human perception, but made reliably detailed and precise by objective electronic means.

John Sinclair, a prime mover in the development of corpus linguistics, was the first to point out the significance of this new approach to description, and did so in the following terms[3]:

Now that we have the means to observe samples of language which must be fairly close to representative samples, the clear messages are:

a) We are teaching English in ignorance of a vast amount of basic fact. This is not our fault, but it should not inhibit the absorption of the new material.
b) The categories and methods we use to describe English are not appropriate to the new material. We shall need to overhaul our descriptive systems.

c) Since our view of the language will change profoundly, we must expect substantial influence on the specification of syllabuses, design of materials and choice of method.
(Sinclair 1985: 252)

It is of interest to note – and of particular significance in the light of the present the discussion – that no distinction is made between the messages which relate to language teaching (a and c) and the message that relates to linguistic description (b). The implication is that the overhauling of descriptive systems necessarily involves changing the specification of syllabuses and design of materials (see Johnson, Ch. 12 this volume). The assumption is, as before, that what is described as the linguistic object should determine what is prescribed as the language subject: if the methods for describing the language change, then it follows that the choice of method in teaching it should change accordingly. Reference is made here to English, but the principle would presumably apply to the description and teaching of any language.

Corpus linguistics shifts attention to the fourth of Hymes' factors, the actually performed, and away from the first, the formally possible. But this does not, as was noted earlier, just mean a change of method for dealing with data but a reconceptualisation of what constitutes data in the first place. With corpus linguistics, the object and objective of description change quite radically. Its concern is exclusively with observed 3rd person data of observation, and any other data are not counted as valid. Its purpose is no longer to account for linguistic forms in the abstract but for those forms, and only those forms, that have been produced as texts, attested as actual behaviour. But new though this material may be, it is still material that consists of linguistic forms. They are forms of performed texts and not of possible sentences but they are forms all the same. Although as naturally occurring use, the production of these texts must have been appropriate to context at the time, many features of this context are not recoverable from the textual data alone, and so what made the text appropriate is not the kind of objective 'basic fact' that a corpus reveals. So although it is claimed that "the language of the corpus is, above all, real" (McCarthy 2001: 128), the reality is, in fact, limited.

It is indeed limited to only one aspect of communication as represented by the Hymes model, and in this respect is just as partial as a formalist description. The pedagogic question, therefore, arises once more as to how it can be related to the other factors to develop communicative competence in learners. The foreign language teacher is faced with the problem of establishing some kind of pedagogically coherent connection between the actually performed, the contextually appropriate and the formally possible – aspects of communicative competence that models of linguistic description only deal with in isolation. And here the feasibility factor comes in as well. For whatever connection is made, it has to be such as to result in language that is pedagogically feasible in that it can be accessed and processed by learners. How then can these different aspects of communicative competence be brought together to constitute a feasible subject for foreign language teaching and learning?

Unfortunately, pronouncements from corpus linguists do not encourage teachers to address this crucial question. The traditional and simplistic assumption that linguistic description should determine what is taught still prevails. Corpus linguistics, the argument goes, is the best possible description because it describes real language and so it is 'obviously desirable' that real language should be the subject to teach. Teachers have not been teaching it in the past, but that is not their fault since until corpus linguistics came along to reveal patterns of actually occurring usage, nobody knew what real language was really like. But now that the real thing is available, they have no excuse for not teaching it. So it is that Sinclair, as a corpus linguist, feels able to advise them that they should 'present real examples only' to their learners. This is the first of a number of precepts that it is assumed can be directly derived from corpus descriptions. As Sinclair puts it:

> The precepts centre on data, and arise from observations about the nature of language. They are not concerned with psychological or pedagogical approaches to language teaching. (Sinclair 1997: 30)

It would seem reasonable to ask how a precept for language teaching can avoid being 'concerned with pedagogical approaches'. It might be asserted that this precept overrides all pedagogic approaches (or at least those currently in practice), but though disclaiming any concern with pedagogy, Sinclair is nevertheless clearly pronouncing a pedagogic precept.

3.3. The reality of language: samples and examples

This then is the precept: *Present real examples only.*

Since the linguistic basis for this precept is made so explicit, it brings into particularly sharp relief the issue of pedagogic relevance that is central to the present discussion. In reference to the Chomsky quotation cited at the beginning of this chapter, here we have a 'specific proposal' emanating from linguistics which claims to 'supply insights useful to the language teacher'. It is, therefore, one that calls for critical consideration, to see on what grounds the teacher might 'validate or refute' it.

The first question that might be asked is: What is meant by 'real'? As has already been pointed out, language is real for the user when it is realised as appropriate to context. The textual data of the corpus is separated out from contextual connections and cannot as such therefore capture this reality. To restore such reality to any sample of text taken from the corpus, one would have to recover the particular contextual conditions which made it pragmatically appropriate when it was actually used. This would not only pose insurmountable problems for description, but more significantly for the present discussion, there would be little if any pedagogic point in trying to do so since these conditions obviously cannot be replicated in language classrooms. If this sample of text is to be appropriately re-used, a context for it has to be contrived so that it can be made real for learners. Otherwise, the sample loses its textual character and simply reduces to a linguistic form, an instance of the possible. The point is that in reference to the Hymes scheme as a model of communication, a corpus description accounts for the actually performed but not as it is related to the factor of the appropriate defined in terms of the attendant contextual conditions that make performance a reality for the original users. If this aspect of communication is to be realised for learners, therefore, contextual conditions have to be contrived in some way to establish the relationship. However real textual extracts taken from a corpus might have been for the original producers, this reality is not intrinsic to the text and so cannot travel with it. In this sense, it is not only that teachers cannot follow the precept by presenting real language only, they cannot present 'real language' at all.

What they do present has to be made appropriate to contexts that learners can engage with so that they can make sense of the language, appropriate it, make it their own. It also has to be language they can learn from. And here we come to a second question that teachers might ask about this precept: what is meant by 'example'?

The obvious point to be made here is that an example is always an example of something, the token of a type, and so must always involve some inference of typicality. An item of language, or of anything else if it comes to that, does not signal its own exemplification: this needs to be inferred. So a sample of textual data from a corpus has in some way to be interpreted as evidence of something typical for it to serve as an example. You can present any number of real samples of usage by random selection but they are of little help to learners if they cannot realise them as examples.

This obvious point can perhaps best illustrated by reference to another area of linguistic description, namely lexicography. It is now taken as 'obviously desirable' that dictionaries for language learners, like any other dictionaries, should be corpus-based and incorporate the facts of attested native speaker usage. One way of doing this is to give primacy not to the core semantic meaning of words but to the meanings which most frequently occurred in the corpus data, again favouring the actually performed factor over the encoded possible, and to use samples of corpus data to illustrate these meanings in dictionaries.

A dictionary entry typically consists of two parts: first an explanation is given of what a word denotes, that is to say the semantic meaning encoded in its form, and this is then complemented by an exemplification of this meaning, traditionally in a sentence invented for the purpose. In accordance with the current orthodoxy of the real, however, exemplification is now provided not by invented sentences but by samples of actual text. The question is: how far do they actually exemplify. Here are entries from three learner dictionaries, with the exemplification section, as is customary, in italics:

> **quaff** (v[Tn]) (*dated or rhet*) drink (sth) by swallowing large amounts at a time, not taking small sips: *quaffing his beer by the pint.*
> (*Oxford Advanced Learner's Dictionary* (*OALD*) 1989)
>
> **quaff** (*obj*) *v* to drink (something) quickly or in large amounts. *In Shakespeare's play 'King Henry IV', Falstaff and Bardolph are often seen quaffing in the Boar's Head Tavern.[I] He's always quaffing these strange herbal medicines, which he thinks will make him more healthy.*[T]
> (*Cambridge International Dictionary of English* (*CIDE*) 1995)
>
> **quaff** ... If you quaff an alcoholic drink, you drink a lot of it in a short space of time; an old-fashioned word. *By the time he had quaffed his third, he was winking playfully at a plump woman who sat across from him.*
> (*COBUILD Dictionary* 2001)

How far then, does the italicised second part in these entries complement the first and serve as effective exemplification?

In *CIDE* and *OALD* there is no indication in the definition (as there is in the *COBUILD Dictionary*) that the word 'quaff' relates to alcoholic drink, but one might suggest that this can be inferred from the examples given in *OALD* , where we have reference to beer, and in *CIDE*, where a tavern is mentioned. The obvious difficulty here, however, is that the learner cannot know how typical these are as textual occurrences: that is to say, whether these are examples of collocational regularities or just random tokens of text, or indeed if they are typical, what they are typical of. Thus learners cannot know whether the word's collocation with beer in this particular example is to be extended to cider or wine, or any other alcoholic beverage, or to any other beverage, alcoholic or not, in indeed to anything drinkable in general. The difficulty is compounded in the case of *CIDE* since this provides a second sample which directly contradicts the meaning of the word which might have been inferred from the first, and which is quite explicitly specified in the *COBUILD Dictionary.* The only way of avoiding such contradiction is for the learners to infer that this second sample demonstrates an ironic use. But how are they to make such an inference, particularly since in the *CIDE* entry (unlike those in *OALD* and the *COBUILD Dictionary*) there is no indication that the word is old fashioned, or 'dated or rhet.'?

So the real language samples of these entries do not seem to function as a reliable complement to extend the range of semantic meaning in the definition. But nor do they actually exemplify this meaning either. In *CIDE*, the occurrence of 'quaff' in the examples does not demonstrate what it means: Falstaff and Bardolph could have been seen doing all manner of things: eating, gambling, arguing, fighting, indulging in riotous or indecent behaviour. All we can tell from the example is that they were 'verbing'. The same point applies to the second sample in *CIDE*: in quaffing strange herbal medicines, he might be 'verbing' in all manner of ways – buying them, selling them, praising them, sipping them, injecting them. Nothing in the sample indicates that quaffing means to drink something, let alone in large amounts. This is also the case with the *COBUILD* example: 'by the time he had quaffed his third'. His third what? There is no way of knowing by reference to the example alone. Indeed the learner might even think that here we have a kind of formulaic phrase analogous to 'taken his seat', 'changed his mind', 'seen the light'; 'quaffed his third'.

The problem is that learners are presented with data but what these data are evidence of is left to them to work out for themselves. The citing of a particular occurrence tells learners how the word has been used on one occasion, but they do not know how typical this occurrence is.[4]

So the essential point is that such samples of real language data do not of themselves serve as examples of language to learn from. As token instances of text, they are in themselves often of little use to learners. If learners are to make use of them they have to be given guidance as to just how they are representative as examples, what types they are tokens of.

These dictionaries, then, would appear to be faithfully following the Sinclair precept, but it seems clear that in presenting real samples they are not really providing examples. The point is that a sample is an element of linguistic description which can be directly drawn from the corpus data and whatever reality it has is a linguistic reality. An example is a pedagogic construct that has to be made real by contrivance of some kind. The distinction is crucial, and seems obvious, but it is disregarded by the current authenticity orthodoxy:

> Contrived simplification of language in the preparation of materials will always be faulty, since it is generated without the guide and support of a communicative context. Only by accepting the discipline of using authentic language are we likely to come anywhere near presenting the learner with a sample of language which is typical of real English. (Willis 1990: 127)

It can be readily agreed that in the preparation of teaching materials, and the design of classroom activities more generally, there needs to be a communicative context to provide guide and support for learning. But this cannot simply be carried over from actual use but has to be designed to be appropriate to the learning context. As we have seen, a sample of language cannot be seen as typical of real English until it is converted into an example, and this calls for contrivance. One can only conclude that from the pedagogic point of new. it is in fact the exclusive use of authentic language that 'will always be faulty'.

4. Pedagogic and psychological perspectives

As we have seen, the argument for authenticity is based on observations about language that has actually been produced by its users, and specifically by a selected group of its native speaking users who are ratified as a reliable source of data. This, then, is a precept from a linguistic perspective only and psychological and pedagogic considerations are explicitly excluded. The question arises as to how the precept would look in the light of such considerations.

4.1. Language goals and learning processes

The essential problem with the linguistic perspective that we have been considering is that it focuses entirely on ends rather than means, and relates to the foreign language subject only in respect to what is taken to be the eventual goal of learning, and not to the learning process that must be followed to get there. The assumption that the language of the subject, the language to be taught and learned, can be derived from language description has a long history. It informs the contrastive analysis hypothesis, for example, which was based on the belief that the specification of the formal differences between languages would provide the basis for establishing learning difficulty (Lado 1957). It turned out that on the evidence of the language actually produced by learners that there was no such predictable correlation and attention shifted to a consideration of the learning process itself by error analysis (Corder 1981) and subsequently to the development of a vast new area of research into second language acquisition (SLA) (Ellis 1993; Cook, Ch. 6 this volume).[5]

SLA research, though informed by linguistic theory, notably that of Chomsky, proceeded quite independently of the changes of the subject inspired by different approaches to linguistic description. Thus the proposals referred to earlier for reformulating syllabus content in terms of notions and functions are based on a way of conceiving of language as the goal and not on the process of learning. Course design specifications for foreign language learning, of the kind exemplified by the Threshold Level specifications of the Council of Europe, and the subsequent Common European Framework for Languages, owe very little to research in second language acquisition. They are essentially concerned not with acquisition but levels of attainment. The two lines of enquiry, syllabus design concerned with the language as goal, the specification of objectives, on the one hand and SLA, with its concern for language learning as process, ran parallel to each other as independent developments.

And indeed still do. And here we return to the Sinclair precept: Present real examples only. This, as is explicitly acknowledged, arises from observations about the nature of language and has nothing to do with psychological considerations about the nature of language learning. Thus the tradition of keeping the two things separate is maintained. But in teaching a subject, the goal and the process have somehow to be reconciled – there is no point in having a goal without knowing how it might be achieved, or in engaging in a process without knowing what its outcome is supposed to be. So it is pertinent to ask how far this language based precept is consistent with precepts that might be based on psychological considerations concerning the process of second language acquisition.

What emerges from SLA research is that the learning process is constrained by certain psychological factors. Thus the acquisition of the grammatical features of a second language appears to follows a certain order, to some extent predetermined, and to proceed from one interlanguage stage to another. This natural order necessarily sets conditions on learnability. It would follow from this that it is pointless to present learners with real language if they are not at a stage of learning which would enable them to process it, if the sample could not be realised or made real as an example. The precept that would arise from observations about language learning, then, would be to present learnable examples only, and these are, to say the least, unlikely to correspond with samples of real language. And even if they did, they would be subject to modification by the developmental process that defines learning itself, whether this is taken to pass through determinate stages of interlanguage or not. The real language precept is based on a cumulative view of language learning, assuming that what is acquired is retained and stored intact, so that if unreal rather than real language is acquired it will get embedded in the learners' competence and be difficult to eradicate. As Sinclair puts it:

> [...] it should not ever be necessary for students to 'unlearn' anything they have been taught. They cannot be taught everything at once, and because our knowledge of the textual detail of language has been so vague, they have been taught half-truths, generalities which apply only in some circumstances. (Sinclair 1991: 499–500)

From a psychological or pedagogic perspective, however, this makes no sense at all. Both psycholinguistic research and pedagogic experience make it obvious that the acquisition of competence is not cumulative but adaptive: learners proceed not by adding items of linguistic knowledge, but by a process of continual revision and reconstruction. In other words, learning is necessarily a process of recurrent unlearning and relearning, whereby encoding rules are modified, extended, re-aligned or abandoned altogether to accommodate new language data. The whole learning process is a matter of continual cognitive adaptation as the learner passes through different transitional stages, each of which is an adapted version of the one preceding it. In this sense, learning can only progress by unlearning. So even if you presented real language only, as input, its reality would not survive, for it would be converted into processible data for learning, and the more real or authentic the input, the more difficult is the conversion likely to be.

4.2. Applied linguistics, linguistics applied

Over recent years, those concerned with the teaching of foreign languages, and especially English, have been taken to task for misrepresenting the language by disregarding the facts of usage, and the English of textbooks has been criticised as faulty in that it does not correspond with corpus findings (e.g. Mindt 1997; Römer 2004). The criticism is only valid, however, if it is assumed that what is actually performed in Hymes' scheme must take precedence over all other factors, and that the facts of linguistic description override pedagogic and psychological considerations about what language is appropriate and feasible for the purpose of furthering the learning process.

Although the authenticity doctrine has been promoted, and questioned, in reference particularly to the teaching of English as a foreign language (see Seidlhofer 2003 Section 2) it raises matters of principle about how, and how far, linguistic perspectives can be interpreted as applying to foreign language teaching in general. The assumption that the findings of linguistic description can define what is taught as a language subject typifies what I have called elsewhere 'linguistics applied' (Widdowson 1980, 2000) This involves the unilateral and non-negotiable application of a linguistic solution to a language problem and is distinct from 'applied linguistics' conceived of as a bilateral or multilateral process of mediation which considers how far linguistic insights or findings are consistent with other factors that have to be taken into account and what adjustments and compromises may be necessary to arrive at a negotiated settlement. With reference to this distinction, proposals that the language of the foreign language subject should be determined by linguistic descriptions, including the real language precept, belong to linguistics applied. The argument of this chapter is that these proposals need to be subjected to the kind of applied linguistic enquiry presented here which seeks to take account of other factors relevant to the definition of the foreign language subject.

It is important to stress, however, that to question the claim of linguistics applied is not at all to deny the potential of a linguistic perspective on language pedagogy. The different ideas about the nature of language, and the different approaches to linguistic description documented here all provide insights into the alternative ways in which the goals of learning can be defined, and of course the setting of such goals is an integral part of the language subject. The point is simply that it must also be integrated with the other part of the subject that has to do with how the process towards these goals is most effectively activated. Linguistics can offer all manner of insight for pedagogy to ponder on about what is formally possible in a language, what is communicatively appropriate, what is actually performed. But these have to be related to what it is feasible to teach, what can be readily processed and internalised by learners in the learning process, and for this we need to look for insights elsewhere.

5. Coda: Foreign language communication and learning

The title of this volume is *Foreign Language Communication and Learning*. The discussion of this present chapter has been concerned only with linguistic perspectives on foreign language learning, and has essentially been a critical commentary on the quotation from Halliday, McIntosh and Strevens (1964) claiming that the language of the pedagogic subject and the object of linguistic description are essentially one and the same thing. The object language that Halliday et al have in mind, and which is the concern of the other linguists whose approaches have been referred to, from Fries to Sinclair, is indeed conceived of as some kind of object, some definite entity identified as what is known and used as a first language. It is taken for granted that there is such a thing as 'the' English language, 'the' German language and so on, and they are essentially the property of their native speakers. So if any communication is described it is first language and not foreign language communication. The assumption is that anybody not producing language in conformity to this first language norm is by definition a learner who has not, or not yet, learned the language properly. A great deal of attention has, of course, been paid in SLA research to what learners do with the language and learner language has been, and is being, extensively collected in corpora (Granger 2003). But little data is available on what foreign users do with the language when they put it to communicative use outside the classroom. Again, there is a considerable literature on the different strategies that learners resort to (e.g. Faerch and Kasper 1983; O'Malley and Chamot 1989) but even when these are identified as communication strategies, they are strategies used by learners in classroom conditions, and it cannot be assumed that these will be the same as these learners employ when they find themselves in a user role.

So the position is that we have an abundance of descriptive data of the first language produced by native speaker users, and of the second language produced by foreign learners, but an almost total absence of data on the language produced by foreign language users. There are, however, indications of an increasing awareness of the need to explore how language that is learnt is put to actual use (as distinct from being put to the test) in the process of what Phipps calls 'languaging'[6]:

> the process of struggling to find a way of articulating the full, embodied and engaged interaction with the world that comes when we put the languages we are learning into action. We make a distinction between the effort of using languages that one is learning in the classroom contexts with the effort of being a person in that language in the social and material world of everyday interactions. (Phipps 2006: 12)

And, as far as English is concerned, research is currently being undertaken into how the language is put into action 'in the social and material world of everyday interactions', notably in the development of the VOICE corpus of English as a lingua franca (Seidlhofer 2001[7]). But English is, of course, only one language used in foreign language communication. How are others put to actual use in foreign language communication?

This would seem on the face of it to be a crucial and obvious question to ask. If you are concerned with teaching foreign language communication, it would be as well to find out how it is actually achieved. With the conventional fixation on native speaker norms as defining the one and only proper language, however, the question simply does not arise: there is, in this view, no such thing, or should be no such thing, as foreign language communication sui generis, but only communication by foreigners using the first language, second hand as it were, as best they can. It is this linguistic perspective that, as we have seen, creates problems for pedagogy, most obviously in the case of the 'real' language doctrine. But if we shift perspective and focus on the language actually performed not by native but foreign uses of a language, the situation changes radically. The objection raised against the real language doctrine was that it is a normative imposition: the language presented is neither appropriate to the classroom context nor feasible as something to learn from. But what is actually performed in foreign language communication is a realisation of what has been learned. Foreign language communicators are not borrowing somebody else's language but using the language of their own learning. Their communication is their learnt language put to use. This being so, a description of foreign language communication as the achievement of a goal would also provide indications of what learning processes are involved in achieving it, what aspects of the language taught, and what strategies, are carried over, exploited and extended in contexts of communicative use. Linguistic description in this case would indeed have insights to offer of direct relevance to pedagogy, in that it would show foreign language communication and learning as closely related, each providing an appropriate context for the other.

Notes

1 My purpose here is to indicate general trends of linguistic influence and not to go into detail about the development of this approach. For a comprehensive survey, see Howatt, Ch. 17 this volume.

2 This is not the only model of communicative competence that has been proposed. Canale and Swain (1980), for example, also distinguish four components: the grammatical, the sociolinguistic, the discoursal and the strategic, but how these relate to the Hymes scheme, or to each other, is not clear. Bachman (1990) has a model, designed for language testing which also has four major components, but which are further divided into no less than fourteen. This, of course makes the issue of how components relate as part of the actual communicative process even more problematic. For further discussion, see Widdowson 2003 Ch 12.

3 Since I am being critical here, I wish to make it clear that I fully recognise and unreservedly admire John Sinclair's innovative work in corpus linguistics. My criticism concerns only the claims that are made for the pedagogic relevance of corpus findings.
4 It should be noted that the entries discussed here have since been revised. The most recent editions of both the Oxford Advanced Learner's Dictionary (2005) and the Cambridge International Dictionary of English, renamed the Cambridge Advanced Learner's Dictionary (2008), now present no 'examples' at all, real or otherwise, perhaps in recognition of the limitations pointed out here. The most recent COBUILD dictionary (2009) does give an 'example', but replaces the earlier one with 'He's quaffed many a glass of champagne in his time'. This of course satisfactorily avoids the criticism made of the earlier one. If it is a real sample, however, it has obviously been carefully selected, and perhaps modified, to serve its purpose as an example, thereby lending support to my argument here.
5 This is not to dismiss the potential value of contrastive analysis in pedagogy, but again, only to point to the need for such linguistic insights to be critically evaluated. For a well balanced account of contrastive analysis and its relation to error analysis, see James 1980, Ringbom 1999, and for a re-evaluation of Lado 1957, see Kramsch 2007.
6 See also Swain and Deters 2007 about the process of languaging among language learners.
7 For further details see the webpage: http://www.univie.ac.at/voice/

References

Allen, John P. B. and Paul van Buren (eds.)
1971 *Chomsky: Selected Readings*. Oxford: Oxford University Press.

Austin, John L.
1962 *How to Do Things with Words*. London: Oxford University Press.

Bachman, Lyle
1990 *Fundamental Considerations in Language Testing*. Oxford: Oxford University Press.

Brumfit, Christopher J.
1995 Teacher professionalism and research. In: Cook and Seidlhofer (eds.): 27–41.

Brumfit, Christopher J. and Keith Johnson
1979 *The Communicative Approach to Language Teaching*. Oxford: Oxford University Press.

Bruthiaux, Paul, Dwight Atkinson, William G. Eggington, William Grabe and Vaidehi Ramanathan (eds.)
2005 *Directions in Applied Linguistics*. Clevedon: Multilingual Matters.

Canale, Michael and Merrill Swain
1980 Theoretical bases of communicative approaches to second language teaching and testing. *Applied Linguistics* 1 (1): 1–47.

Chomsky, Noam
1957 *Syntactic Structures*. Mouton: The Hague.

Chomsky, Noam
1965 *Aspects of the Theory of Syntax*. Cambridge, Mass.: M.I.T. Press.
Chomsky, Noam
1966 Linguistic theory. In: Robert G. Mead (ed.), *Reports of Working Committees for Northeast Conference on Teaching Foreign Languages*, 43–49. Wisconsin: George Banta Co. Inc. (Reprinted in Allen and van Buren eds.)
Cook, Guy and Barbara Seidlhofer (eds.)
1995 *Principle and Practice in Applied Linguistics*. Oxford: Oxford University Press.
Corder, S. Pit
1981 *Error Analysis and Interlanguage*. Oxford: Oxford University Press.
Ellis, Rod
1993 *The Study of Second Language Acquisition*. Oxford: Oxford University Press.
Faerch, Claus and Gabriele Kasper (eds.)
1983 *Strategies in Interlanguage Communication*. London: Longman.
Fries, Charles C.
1952 *The Structure of English, an Introduction to the Construction of English Sentences*. New York: Harcourt Brace.
Fries, Peter H. and Nancy M. Fries (eds.)
1985 *Toward an Understanding of Language: Charles C. Fries in Perspective*. Amsterdam: John Benjamins.
Granger, Sylviane
2003 The international corpus of learner English: A new resource for foreign language learning and teaching and second language acquisition research. *TESOL Quarterly* 37 (3): 538–546.
Halliday, Michael A. K.
1973 *Explorations in the Functions of Language*. London: Arnold.
Halliday, Michael A. K., Angus McIntosh and Peter Strevens
1964 *The Linguistic Sciences and Language Teaching*. London: Longman.
Howatt, Anthony P. R.
2004 *A History of English Language Teaching*. 2nd edition. Oxford: Oxford University Press.
Hymes, Dell
1972 On communicative competence. In: John Pride and Janet Holmes (eds.), *Sociolinguistics: Selected Readings*, 269–293. Harmondsworth: Penguin Books.
James, Carl
1980 *Contrastive Analysis*. Longman: Harlow.
Kramsch, Claire
2007 Re-reading Robert Lado 1957, *Linguistics across Cultures*. Classic book review. *International Journal of Applied Linguistics* 17 (2): 241–247.
Labov, William
1972 *Sociolinguistic Patterns*. Phialdelphia: University of Pennsylvania Press.
McCarthy, Michael
2001 *Issues in Applied Linguistics*. Cambridge: Cambridge University Press.

Mindt, Dieter
1997 Corpora and the teaching of English in Germany. In: Wichmann, Fligelstone, McEnery and Knowles (eds.): 40–50.
O'Malley, J. Michael and Anna U. Chamot
1989 *Learning Strategies in Second Language Acquisition*. Cambridge: Cambridge University Press.
Phipps, Alison
2006 *Learning the Arts of Linguistic Survival: Languaging, Tourism, Life*. Clevedon: Multilingual Matters.
Prabhu, N. S.
1987 *Second Language Pedagogy*. Oxford: Oxford University Press.
Quirk, Randolph and Henry G. Widdowson (eds.)
1985 *English in the World*. Cambridge: Cambridge University Press.
Ringbom, Hakan
1999 Contrastive and error analysis. In: Spolsky (ed.): 495–489.
Römer, Ute
2004 A corpus-driven approach to modal auxiliaries and their didactics. In: Sinclair (ed.): 185–199.
Searle, John R.
1969 *Speech Acts*. Cambridge: Cambridge University Press.
Seidlhofer, Barbara
2001 Closing a conceptual gap: The case for a description of English as a lingua franca. *International Journal of Applied Linguistics* 11 (3): 133–158.
Seidlhofer, Barbara (ed.)
2003 *Controversies in Applied Linguistics*. Oxford: Oxford University Press.
Sinclair, John M.
1985 Selected issues. In: Quirk and Widdowson (eds.): 248–254.
Sinclair, John M.
1991 Shared knowledge. In: James Alatis (ed.), *Linguistics and Language Pedagogy: The State of the Art*, 489–500. Georgetown: Georgetown University Press.
Sinclair, John M.
1997 Corpus evidence in language description. In: Wichmann, Fligelstone, McEnery and Knowles (eds.): 27–51.
Sinclair, John M. (ed.)
2004 *How to Use Corpora in Language Teaching*. Amsterdam: John Benjamins.
Spolsky, Bernard (ed.)
1999 *Concise Encyclopedia of Educational Linguistics*. Amsterdam: Elsevier.
Swain, Merrill and Ping Deters
2007 "New" mainstream SLA theory: Expanded and enriched. *Modern Language Journal* 91: 820–836.
Wichmann, Anne, Steven Fligelstone, Tony McEnery and Gerry Knowles (eds.)
1997 *Teaching and Language Corpora*. London: Longman.
Widdowson, Henry G.
1980 Models and fictions. *Applied Linguistics* 1 (2): 165–170.
Widdowson, Henry G.
1990 *Aspects of Language Teaching*. Oxford: Oxford University Press.

Widdowson, Henry G.
2000 On the limitations of linguistics applied. *Applied Linguistics* 21 (1): 3–25.
Widdowson, Henry G.
2005 Applied linguistics, interdisciplinarity, and disparate realities. In: Bruthiaux, Atkinson, Eggington, Grabe and Ramanathan (eds.): 12–25.
Widdowson, Henry G.
2003 *Defining Issues in English Language Teaching*. Oxford: Oxford University Press.
Wilkins, David
1976 *Notional Syllabuses*. Oxford: Oxford University Press.
Willis, Dave
1990 *The Lexical Syllabus*. London: Collins.

Recommended readings

Aronoff, Mark and Janie Rees-Miller (eds.)
2001 *The Handbook of Linguistics* Oxford: Blackwell.
Brown, Keith R. (ed.)
2006 *Encyclopedia of Language and Linguistics*. 2nd edition. Amsterdam: Elsevier.
Davies, Alan and Catherine Elder (eds.)
2004 *The Handbook of Applied Linguistics*. Oxford: Blackwell.
Halliday, Michael A. K., Angus McIntosh and Peter Strevens
1964 *The Linguistic Sciences and Language Teaching*. London: Longman.
Hidalgo, Encarnación, Luis Querada and Juan Santana (eds.)
2007 *Corpora in the Foreign Language Classroom.* Amsterdam: Rodopi.
Kaplan, Robert B. (ed.)
2002 *The Oxford Handbook of Applied Linguistics.* Oxford: Oxford University Press.
Knapp, Karlfried, Gerd Antos, Michael Becker-Mrotzek, Arnulf Depperman, Susanne Göpferich, Joachim Grabowski, Michael Klamm, Claudia Villiger (eds.)
2007 *Angewandte Linguistik. Ein Lehrbuch.* 2nd edition. Tübingen: Francke.
Seidlhofer, Barbara (ed.)
2003 *Controversies in Applied Linguistics.* (Section 5). Oxford: Oxford University Press.
Wichmann, Anne, Steven Fligelstone, Anthony McEnery and Gerry Knowles (eds.)
1997 *Teaching and Language Corpora*. London: Longman.
Widdowson, Henry G.
2000 On the limitations of linguistics applied. *Applied Linguistics* 21 (1): 3–25.
Widdowson, Henry G.
2003 *Defining Issues in English Language Teaching*. Oxford: Oxford University Press.

9. Cultural perspectives on language learning and teaching

Claire Kramsch

1. Introduction

In his 1999 novel *The Ground Beneath her Feet* Salman Rushdie portrays two adolescents from Bombay, she Vina Apsara, he Ormus Cama, out to invent a music that would be neither pure Western music – "the great weapon of cultural imperialism" – nor pure Indian music, the local product, but an impure music they could call their own in that "impure Bombay, where West, East, North and South had always been scrambled, like codes, like eggs". In a memorable passage, not devoid of his usual irony, Rushdie writes:

> What's a 'culture'? Look it up. 'A group of micro-organisms grown in a nutrient substance under controlled conditions.' A squirm of germs on a glass slide is all, a laboratory experiment calling itself a society. Most of us wrigglers make do with life on that slide; we even agree to feel proud of that 'culture'. Like slaves voting for slavery or brains for lobotomy, we kneel down before the god of all moronic micro-organisms and pray to be homogenized or killed or engineered; we promise to obey. But if Vina and Ormus were bacteria too, they were a pair of bugs who wouldn't take life lying down. One way of understanding their story is to think of it as an account of the creation of two bespoke identities, tailored for the wearers by themselves. The rest of us get our personae off the peg, our religion, language, prejudices, demeanour, the works; but Vina and Ormus insisted on what one might call auto-couture. And music [...] was the key that unlocked the door for them, the door to magic lands. (Rushdie 1999: 95)

In the culturally multiple and mixed urban context of India, Vina and Ormus 'tailor' their own culture, adapting to their own needs what society supplies them with. Rushdie acknowledges that most people's 'personae' are taken from the available models provided by social circumstances; but Vina and Ormus insisted on creating for themselves identities that were not 'bespoke', i.e., ready-made or made to order, but tailored to their needs. The term *autocouture* combines *auto-,* the Latin for self or agency, and *couture,* the French for fashion in the garment industry. It is also a pun on the homonym *haute couture*, the French for designer clothes or high fashion. By replacing *culture,* i.e., what is handed down by history, tradition and societal conventions, with the homonym *couture,* and coining their own oxymoron *autocouture*, the two youngsters coin for themselves a new multicultural identity that is as distinguished as *haute couture* and that will express itself through music.

This story can serve as a parable for what we could call the problem of culture in foreign language learning and teaching. On the one hand, language is usually seen to be indissociable from the culture of the speech community that speaks that language, whether it is highbrow culture or everyday culture; it is also inseparable from the way speakers of the language identify with that community. On the other hand, in our global times, when ways of life intermingle, speech communities have become more diverse, and identities are increasingly hybrid and changing, the concept of culture has lost some of its explanatory power. There are many fluent speakers of Mandarin who do not belong to any Chinese national community, many near-native speakers of French who do not identify with any particular French culture. Similarly, many Armenians living in the U.S. feel that theirs is an Armenian culture even though they do not speak a word of Armenian. Moreover, culture manifests itself in various semiotic modalities: verbal, visual, musical, electronic.

Hence the problem for the language teacher. Which aspects of culture should be taught in a language class: facts of geography and history, national symbols, small cultures or ways of life, norms of interaction and interpretation, attitudes and beliefs, myths and ideologies? Which kinds of culture: national, regional, professional culture, high culture or popular culture, mainstream or ethnic culture, civic or heritage culture? And whose culture should be taught: the culture of a target country or of a heritage community, or the hybrid culture of multilingual individuals who straddle various national cultures? Finally, to what extent should other semiotic systems be taught, of which language is only one?

These questions affect different language teachers differently, depending on the needs and purposes of their students. Where foreign languages are learned for professional opportunity, physical survival, intelligence gathering purposes, or even for mere philological or linguistic interest, culture may be perceived as a less important component of language study. By contrast, where they are learned for intercultural understanding, for social survival in an immigration context, for reconnecting to one's linguistic and cultural heritage, or for general humanistic purposes, culture becomes central to the language learning enterprise. Which aspects of culture and whose culture will be worth teaching will also depend on the symbolic value of the language taught and on the educational priorities of the educational institution. For example, the teaching of a language of global transaction like English will be more likely to teach small cultures of daily life than the history, literature and institutions of any particular nation-state. At prestigious private institutions, the foreign culture taught might be that of the humanistically educated elite, while in public schools the foreign culture might often be a culture of tourism.

In sum, while culture has always been an indissociable part of language teaching, the links between the language taught and the sociocultural context in which it is used have become much more diversified than they used to be. These links are now defined by a host of individual, institutional, and ideological factors that render the task of the foreign language educator particularly complex. The role of the applied linguist is to describe and explain this complexity and to suggest ways in which it can be turned into an educationally fruitful experience.

2. Historical background

There are roughly two different ways of looking at culture in language study, depending on one's disciplinary and political orientation, and on whose interests are being served: modernist and late modernist (see Giddens 1991). These two perspectives on culture coexist today in the theory and practice of language learning and teaching.

2.1. Modernist perspectives

Until the 1970's, culture was seen as the literate or humanities component of language study. In the 70's and 80's, following the communicative turn in language pedagogy, culture became synonymous with the way of life and everyday behaviours of members of speech communities, bound together by common experiences, memories and aspirations. In both cases, speech communities were seen as grounded in the nation – the national context in which a national language was spoken by a homogeneous national citizenry.

2.1.1. A humanistic concept

As a humanistic concept, culture is the product of a canonical print literacy acquired in school; it is synonymous with a general knowledge of literature and the arts. Also called 'big C' culture, it is the hallmark of the cultivated middle-class. Because it has been instrumental in building the nation-state during the 19th century, big C culture has been promoted by the state and its institutions, e.g., schools and universities, as national patrimony. It is the culture traditionally taught with standard national languages. Teaching about the history, the institutions, the literature and the arts of the target country embeds the target language in the reassuring continuity of a national community that gives it meaning and value. As Rushdie reminds us in the quote above, national cultures are always bound up with notions of the 'good' and 'proper' way of life which is why they elicit pride and loyalty. Because they are imbued with moral value, language learners who have grown up with other values find it often difficult to understand foreign cultures on their own terms. They find refuge in cultural stereotypes, or in literary fiction. The fact that foreign languages are still taught for the most part in departments of foreign language and literature and that the curriculum for foreign language majors still puts a heavy emphasis on the study of literature is a reminder that language study was originally subservient to the interests of philologists and literary scholars, not anthropologists or sociologists. With the advent of communicative language teaching, the humanistic concept of culture has given way to a more pragmatic concept of culture as way of life. But the prestige of big C culture remains, if only as *lieux de mémoire* in Internet chatrooms named, for example, *Versailles, Madison Avenue* or *Unter den Linden* – cultural icons of symbolic distinction.

2.1.2. *A sociolinguistic concept*

With the focus now on communication and interaction in social contexts, the most relevant concept of culture since the 80's has been that of 'little c' culture, also called "small cultures" (Holliday 1999) of everyday life. It includes the native speakers' ways of behaving, eating, talking, dwelling, their customs, their beliefs and values. Research in the cultural component of language learning has been deeply interested in cross-cultural pragmatics and the sociolinguistic appropriateness of language use in its authentic cultural context. To study the way native speakers use their language for communicative purposes, the convention one language = one culture is maintained and teachers are enjoined to teach rules of sociolinguistic use the same way they teach rules of grammatical usage, i.e., through modelling and role-playing. Even though everyday cultural practices are as varied as a native speaker's use of language in everyday life, the focus is on the typical, sometimes stereotypical, behaviours, foods, celebrations and customs of the dominant group or of that group of native speakers that is the most salient to foreign eyes. Striking in this concept of culture is the maintenance of the focus on national characteristics and the lack of historical depth.

The sociolinguistic concept of culture takes on various forms depending on whether the language taught is a foreign, second, or heritage language. In foreign language (FL) classes taught outside of any direct contact with native speakers, culture is mostly of the practical, tourist kind with instructions on how to get things done in the target country. FL learners learn about the foreign culture as an exotic curiosity; they try to adapt to it or temporarily adopt it as their own when they travel to the country.

In second language (SL) classes taught in the target country or in institutions run by native speakers abroad (e.g., *British Council, Goethe Institut, Alliance Française*), culture can also take the form of exposure to debates and issues of relevance to native speakers in the target country, or of discussions about living and working conditions for immigrants. In the same manner as children are schooled into becoming proper citizens, so are immigrants acculturated into the habitus of nationally defined native speakers, they acquire a national home they can be loyal to and a national identity of which they can be proud. Culture as a process of nurturance and socialisation is achieved mainly through schooling in its written, literate tradition.

But culture as nurture is never very far from culture as control. In the name of culture, as Rushdie sarcastically puts it, "we pray to be homogenised, or killed, or engineered". Up until recently, national cultures have been seen to assimilate immigrants into a homogeneous melting pot that not only erases their differences in origin, but eliminates their foreignness through educational training, i.e., social engineering (according to Rushdie's metaphor, it homogenises or pasteurises the foreign bacteria). In return, nation states give immigrants the honor to die on the battlefield for their adoptive country. Second language learners outside the target country are applauded and assisted by the respective nation states' institutions in their efforts to learn the national language, e.g., the British Council, the French Office of the Francophonie, the Goethe Institute, in the hope of strengthening the economic ties between the two countries. As the motto goes: 'Learn English, buy British'.

In heritage language (HL) classes taught to native speakers who wish to connect with their ancestral roots, culture is the very *raison d'être* of language teaching. It is not, however, without presenting major difficulties when the heritage community has either lost much of its original everyday culture (e.g., Native American languages, see Hinton 1994), or when its speakers belong to a community that historically no longer exists (e.g., Western Armenian or Yiddish). The teaching of culture in HL classes is very much linked to identity politics (Taylor 1994).

2.1.3. *Intercultural education*

The term 'intercultural' emerged in the eighties in the fields of intercultural education and intercultural communication. Both are part of an effort to increase dialogue and cooperation among members of different national cultures within a common European Union or within a global economy (for a review, see Kramsch 2001). Intercultural education as a component of a humanistic education is pursued with particular intensity in the Scandinavian countries (e.g., Hansen 2002), in Germany (for a review see Königs 2003) and in France (Zarate 2001; Moore 2001).

In foreign language study, the concept of intercultural competence has emerged in recent years in Europe alongside the concept of communicative competence (e.g., Bredella 1992; Byram 1997; Byram and Fleming 1998; Zarate et al. 2004); it characterizes a form of language competence that is less focused on approximating a native speaker linguistic or pragmatic norm than it is based on the subjective experience of the language learner engaged in the process of becoming bi- or multilingual and struggling with another language, culture and identity. Here too, culture is a modernist notion tied to the characteristics of native members of a national community who speak the national language and share in its national culture.

In sum: A modernist definition of culture as membership in a national community with a common history, a common standard language and common imaginings is rooted in the nation-state, as is the notion of native speaker and that of speech community. These notions denote stable entities or structures that have a social reality independent of the speakers who refer to them. This modernist definition of culture has been challenged by a lingua franca like English that knows no national boundaries and by global social actors who, like Vina and Ormus, defy the supremacy of the native speaker as well as the notion of neatly bounded speech communities.

2.2. Late modernist perspectives

Today, in the early years of the 21st century, the changed geopolitical landscape has changed the nature and the role of culture in language teaching (Risager 2006) in five major ways.

First, culture has become in many respects denationalised. For many people around the world, the equation one native language = one native culture has become obsolete. The typical language learner is no longer, for example, a monolingual NS of English learning German as an L2 at an American college in the US, but a Yoruba speaking Nigerian raised in French schools in Montreal learning German in Texas, or a Czech with a school knowledge of English, French and German, now an immigrant to the US and learning Japanese in California. She may flirt in French, study in English, eat Czech, listen to German music and wear Japanese kimonos. And who are heritage language speakers? If, as Joshua Fishman defines it, heritage language refers to a language "with which individuals have a personal connection" (Valdes 2001: 37), one could argue that Spanish serves as the heritage language of a Hispanic American learning Italian, or that Cantonese is the heritage dialect of a Chinese-American learning Mandarin Chinese.

Second, for many language learners culture has become deterritorialised. Learners of Yiddish or Western Armenian are learning a language that is no longer associated with an identifiable speech community. It lives off the memories of an imagined community, it becomes the locus of rituals and condensation symbols, an object of nostalgia or desire – a utopia like the "magic lands" that Rushdie's young protagonists want to reach through music. The cultural and the linguistic intersect here with identity politics and, as Charles Taylor argues in his 1994 essay on *Multiculturalism*, with the demand for recognition and the claim to equal worth. For example, the Armenian genocide is equally worth commemorating as the Jewish Holocaust or the American Civil War. Learning Armenian as a heritage language is, ultimately, the claim for a right to be remembered by history.

Third, culture has become dehistoricised and thus easier to appropriate. Contributing to the dehistoricisation of culture is not only immigration and diaspora, but technology. Through video and television and the advances of electronic communication, internet chatrooms and other modes of computer-mediated technology, foreign cultures have been taken out of their lived historical contexts. Thus, for example, the disenfranchised Hong Kong Chinese high school students studied by Eva Lam (2000), who have created for themselves on the Internet an alternative community of like-minded speakers of English as a lingua franca even though they actually live in various countries with different histories. The community they have built is reduced to the size of their computer screen or their palm pilot, it lives from stories told and chatty exchanges in the here-and-now of these students' imaginations.

Fourth, culture has become more fragmented. Paradoxically, the increased facility of access and appropriation has led not to a greater contact with global diversity, but to an increased fragmentation into class or occupation-specific, gender-, age or interest-specific groups. The more distant, foreign, or hostile the people or the information we can have access to, the more we tend to access only those we are familiar and comfortable with. Forms of communication like instant messaging have become more and more in-group and thus, incidentally, more vulnerable to market forces that are always on the look-out for consumer targets or market niches. Salman Rushdie's ironic narrator stance towards his protagonists and their "insistence" on "what one might call *auto-couture*" suggests that such a self-made culture might easily be preyed upon by the global marketing and fashion industry.

Fifth, culture has become a discourse, i.e., a social semiotic construction. In these dispersed cultures, languages fraternise, as do the multiple types of music in Vina and Ormus' repertoire. Whether they are fully mastered or not, whether they are even spoken at all or just heard and listened to during childhood, languages leave emotional traces of past experience, a personal connection that colours the way a new language is apprehended and used. Language as discourse has become part of the embodied aspect of culture, but less the culture of institutional memory and ratified history than the discursive, biographical memory of the language user. A portable culture, that lives from retellings through verbal narratives, film, music and other meaning making practices. The two youngsters in Rushdie's novel are exemplars of a generation of multilingual, hybrid, mobile youth, adept at switching and combining semiotic modalities, genres and styles, filled with desire and the need to identify with utopian futures, creating their own cultural communities across the globe in a mixture of different semiotic practices.

A late modernist definition of culture attempts to account for these new realities. If culture is no longer bound to the territory of a nation-state and its history, then we have to see it as a dynamic process, constructed and reconstructed in various ways by individuals engaged in struggles for symbolic meaning and for the control of identities, subjectivities and interpretations of history. Culture cannot be directly read into behaviours and events, it has a meaning that depends on who does the reading and from which position in society. After reviewing the notion of culture historically, we now turn to the various ways culture is being theorised in various fields relevant to applied linguistics.

3. State of the art: central concepts and theoretical approaches

The diversification of the notion of culture in the last fifteen years has made it necessary for applied linguistics to draw on multiple fields of research to explain the relation of culture to the learning and teaching of foreign languages. Each of these fields has proposed key concepts that are summarised in italics at the beginning of each section.

3.1. A view from sociolinguistics

Culture as social habitus, produced and reproduced through the interaction between individuals within a social order. Social conventions, etiquette, politeness, turns-at-talk, interactional rituals, symbolic power.

The first contact FL learners establish with a foreign culture is through face-to-face encounters with speakers who don't seem to share the same ways of using language in conversation. Thus a large branch of research in applied linguistics is devoted to cross-cultural pragmatics (e.g., Blum-Kulka, House and Kasper 1989) and the analysis of topic management and repairs between interlocutors from different (national) cultures (Moerman 1988; Markee 2000; Gardner and Wagner 2004). The work of Pierre Bourdieu has been influential in helping language educators like Bonny Norton (2000) integrate issues of social and cultural identity and symbolic power into second language acquisition research. It is now generally accepted that culture is a form of symbolic power that both enables and constrains individuals through dispositions or habitus acquired by the body in the course of primary socialisation in the family and at school. This habitus can change in contact with other linguistic markets or fields, such as when one learns another language and has to adopt the conceptual metaphors (see section 3.4. below) embedded in that language, but changes in the habitus take a long time to develop.

3.2. A view from sociocultural theory

Culture as socially distributed cognition within a given social speech community. Culture as the way language mediates our relation to the world, as participation, activity, collaborative task, and, ultimately, as inner speech.

Sociocultural theory, based on the work of Soviet psychologists Vygotsky and Leontiev in particular but also that of activity theory represented by Lave and Wenger (1991), is a theory of cognitive and linguistic development that is having a great impact on the way culture is conceived in language acquisition. Culture here is seen as ways in which cultural artifacts like language, but also other symbolic systems, mediate the acquisition or apprenticeship of knowledge and the integration of individual speakers into the ways of thinking and speaking of a given speech community. Through participatory activities and various mediational means, knowledge that exists in distributed form on the social plane gets internalised onto the psychological plane and ends up as the learner's inner speech (Lantolf 2000). Culture is thus both a process of acculturation and socialisation and an historically sedimented and institutionalised state of mind and body in the individual. In turn, the culture of any given group is constantly challenged, changed, and diversified through the various appropriations that non-native speakers (NNS) make of it. This is particularly true of the way native speakers (NS) of English have to adapt to the foreign conceptual metaphors brought by new immigrants in multicultural societies like the U.S. It is in this spirit that Pavlenko has studied how emotions are conceptualised in L1 and L2 and how bilinguals' emotion concepts may be distinct from those of monolingual speakers (2005). Wierzbicka has explored the mutual influence of emotion, language, and cultural scripts by individuals who know more than one language (1994).

3.3. A view from linguistic anthropology

Culture as socialisation, understood as both a process and a product. Culture as membership in a speech community, with shared assumptions about the world and one's place in it. Culture is shared lifeworld, common history, subjective memories and language ideologies.

Linguistic anthropology, represented by scholars like Ochs and Schieffelin (1988), Gumperz (1982), and Hanks (1996), has provided us with a range of useful concepts to understand the relationship of language and culture as a process of co-construction between participants in the communicative practices of everyday life. Unlike sociocultural theory, it is not a theory of cognitive development but of acculturation into a community of practice. As Elinor Ochs has shown (1996, 2002) language learning is primarily a means of socialisation, of learning how to match stances, acts, identities and activities to behave in ways that are congruent with those of a group. Language is also a way of establishing a subject-position vis-à-vis others and vis-à-vis oneself, both affectively and epistemically. In short, language learning is "becoming a speaker of culture" (Ochs 2002). Gumperz, Hanks and others have shown how culture is reproduced through contextualisation cues like code-switching, and through indexicals, evaluative markers and markers of space and time in discourse. As in the cognitive perspectives discussed below, culture for linguistic anthropologists is embodied in language.

Currently, linguistic anthropology is a dynamic field of research that takes culture not as a given, but as co-constructed representations, subjectivities. Schieffelin, Woolard and Kroskrity call these representations, mediated by language, *language ideologies.*

> Language ideologies are cultural representations, whether explicit or implicit, of the intersection of language and human beings in a social world. Mediating between social structures and forms of talk, such ideologies are not just about language. Rather, they link language to identity, power, aesthetics, morality, and epistemology. Through such linkages, language ideologies underpin not only linguistic form and use but also significant social institutions and fundamental notions of person and community (Schieffelin, Woolard and Kroskrity 1998: 3).

In its social constructionist view of culture, linguistic anthropology has affinities to some of the work done in cultural studies (see 3.5 below).

3.4. A view from cognitive science

Culture as cognitive structures of expectation. Culture as embodied idealised cognitive models (ICM) about the world, as the reciprocal influence of language and thought, language and emotion.

A recent strand of research in the cultural aspects of language learning and teaching comes from cognitive science. The cultural component of language and language use can be seen as the mental categories, metaphors and prototypes of members of a speech community that share common memories of the past, a common understanding of the present and common imaginings of the future.

Sociolinguistic research has made ample use of 'mental structures of expectation', variously called frames, scripts, or schemata (for a review see Tannen 1993; Cook 1994) to explain how speakers interpret spoken utterances and written texts in their native language. Classical schema theory sees schemata as relatively static mental representations of typical instances of things, texts or events. These representations, also called plans or maps, are located in the brain. Old schemata can be destroyed, new ones can be constructed or new connections made between existing schemata. But when it comes to learning a language different from the one of the speech community one grew up in, it is not clear how, according to schema theory, language learners deal with conflicting representations triggered by their different languages, nor how they manage to understand themselves 'in terms of' the other.

The work of cognitive linguists like George Lakoff sheds some light on this issue. It shows how the language we use to categorise people and events shapes our understanding of the world through idealised cognitive models (ICM) or conceptual metaphors, that we make of the world in order to apprehend it (Lakoff 1987). Thus for example, the ICM of a *car* for an American may be an efficient, speedy mode of transportation, as well as a status symbol, a symbol of freedom or an icon of the American way of life. Growing up in a given society, we acquire the ICMs of the members of that society together with their language but we actualise these ICMs through the choices we make in the language we use. Lakoff and Johnson (1980) have explored the conceptual metaphors that we acquire together with our native language and that we often actualise in our daily lives, for example the metaphor *life is a journey* when we speak of *taking a step in the right direction* or *he was nearing the end of his life*. Those metaphors are closely linked to the cultural metanarratives that societies live by, such as, for example, the freedom/redemption narrative typical of the American immigrant's story making it against all odds in the promised land (Pavlenko and Lantolf 2000). Fauconnier and Turner (2002) have coined the phrases "mental space" and "conceptual blend" to characterise the way the mind creates new knowledge by blending two mental representations, e.g., a new sportscar and an actress, into a composite conceptual space, such as in: *My (Dodge) Viper is my Sharon Stone. It's the sexiest vehicle on the road.*

Such an approach potentially avoids the essentialisation of cultures as it locates culture in the discourse of the speaking subject (Bhabha 1994) and in the way speakers make sense of their cultural reality through the metaphoric choices they make. These choices are not impervious to (stereo)types nor to the pressures from the group, but they are clearly social constructions of reality, not social reality itself (for the danger of taking conceptual metaphors for structural realities, see section 4 below).

These insights from cognitive linguistics can be applied to the way language learners make sense of the linguistic and conceptual metaphors specific of a given society (Littlemore and Low 2006). For instance, an American in Europe, seeking to go speedily, efficiently and punctually from one place to another, learns to see cars in terms of trains and to look up train schedules rather than rent-a-car agencies. After several train rides, his memory of transportation becomes grounded in a bodily experience – the embodied habitus of a train rider. He has not forgotten the meaning of a car for an American, but has blended the properties of cars and those of trains. Blended space theory can make us better understand this paradox, because it views schemata as nonpropositional structures connecting concepts and percepts, i.e., mind and body (Johnson 1987: 173–193). These structures are dynamic, imaginative mental creations, or conceptual integration networks, rather than static representations. Through these mental networks, our body/mind apprehends metaphorically one event in terms of another, integrates both in a conceptual blend that becomes relevant to us, because it is grounded in our bodily experience.

Closely related to work done in cognitive linguistics is research in cross-cultural psychology. Dan Slobin (2000) has used the various narrative renditions of the same cartoon story by native speakers of different languages to show how the syntactic choices that speakers have to make says something about the way they think as they speak, e.g., the culturally specific way in which they conceive of path and motion and the orientation of the body in space. Indeed, linguistic relativity, i.e., the way different languages orient their speakers to different ways of thinking, has been the object of a flurry of new research in recent years (for a review, see Kramsch 2003).

3.5. A view from cultural studies

Culture as symbolic power focuses on the way culture becomes entangled with social control, social identity, and dominant discourses such as the fetishisation of communication in a communication culture.

In the field of cultural studies, culture has been conceptualised in depth by scholars like Foucault (1970), Giddens (1991), Bhabha (1994), Cameron (2000), and Butler (1997) who have associated culture with symbolic power and identity. Culture as power does not reside in one or the other individual or group, it is diffuse, it both enables and disables. In a global world like ours, there is no centre of power to storm like the Bastille, the privilege of native speakers can also be their demise as more and more non native speakers appropriate for themselves the native speaker's language, and as Bakhtin would say, reaccentuate it to suit their interests and purposes. Youth thrown together by globalisation and migration construct for themselves stylised identities that offer them symbolic survival (Rampton 1995; Lam 2000). Nor is culture any longer just a national concept. Multinational corporations have disseminated the culture of fast capitalism, or neoliberal entrepreneurship around the world, with new ways of viewing communication. Cameron (2000) for example, building on Foucault's notion of discourse, i.e., ways of talking and thinking typical of a given culture, demonstrates how a therapeutic discourse of 'good communication' has permeated our entrepreneurial culture and is attempting to technologise and standardise everyday communication, to make it easier but also more homogeneous. Butler shows how we can reclaim the political promise of the performative by becoming aware of the possibility of resignifying words through active reflexion on the power of language to create social realities. In this respect, as Kramsch (1997) has argued, the privileged subject position is that of the NNS, who is both of the L1 and the L2 and is not hostage to either of them.

3.6. A view from discourse stylistics

Culture as style focuses on the way the individual uses the resources offered by the speech community to produce, reproduce or subvert the orders of discourse imposed upon him. The struggle with style includes the struggle against the dominance of existing genres, the language practices imposed by those in control of the technologies of the word, and the fight against the forces of convention and conformism.

The traditional goals of foreign language education – acquisition of one national standard code, communication skills and approximation in speech and behaviour to one target national culture –, have become complicated by the multiplicity of language varieties and cultural identities that coexist within one and the same nation, not to speak of the varieties of directly or vicariously experienced histories and ideologies. What needs to be taught now is the ability to interpret verbal behaviour through but also beyond the individual code, the ability to give meaning to stylistic choices like: code-switches, intertextual references and grammatical metaphors, emotional responses and evocations of worldviews. Discourse stylistics offers a way of moving from a structuralist to a post-structuralist approach to the study of culture in discourse. Linguists like Tannen who research the intricacies of conversational style and its links to an individual's cultural habitus (see section 3.1. above) usually favour a structuralist approach, as do critical discourse analysts like Fairclough, Wodak, van Dijk and others. Others who come from a literary tradition, like Fowler, Toolan, Widdowson and others, favour the flexibility and openness of a post structuralist approach without losing sight of the benefits of structural analyses of texts. There is as yet no study of the style of bilingual writers who write in one language but with memories of another, and whose writings bear traces of other languages even though they may write in only one language (see, however, Kellman 2000).

There has recently been a surge of interest, both in the US and in Europe, for language learners' memoirs and linguistic autobiographies like those of Eva Hoffman, Alice Kaplan, Richard Rodriguez in the US, Nancy Huston, Andrei Makine, Claude Esteban in France, Werner Landsburgh, Yoko Tawada in Germany. What is noteworthy is not only the fact that these testimonies are used as legitimate data by psycholinguists and other SLA researchers, but that they express, often in metaphoric terms, emotional and cultural realities that cannot be captured by factual communication alone. Applied linguists often give these texts structuralist readings that do not do justice to their literary nature.

The six views on culture discussed above do not exclude one another. For example a view of culture as social habitus (3.1.) does not preclude thinking of it as socially distributed cognition (3.2.) or as socialisation (3.3.). Each view comes from a different field of research (e.g., sociology, psycholinguistics, sociolinguistics, cognitive linguistics) that has its own theoretical concepts, its own methods of inquiry and modes of analysis. Applied linguists studying language and culture are careful to specify which field they draw on to make sure that the concepts are understood within their proper conceptual framework.

4. What does all this mean for FL education?

Culture as educational challenge highlights the pedagogic tension between modernist and late modernist perspectives on language and culture, between content and context, between individual and group identities and needs, and between learning to talk and learning to talk about talk.

In FL education, there is a tension between modernist and late modernist views of culture and the teaching of culture. On the one hand, culture is associated with stable territorially bound speech communities, of which the language learner needs to understand the cognitive schemata, conceptual metaphors, conversational styles, socialisation patterns and dominant ideologies prevalent in the members of these speech communities. On the other hand, culture is associated with hybrid, blended conceptual spaces, code-switchings by learners for whom the L2 is in fact a L3 or L4, untranslatable affective and epistemic stances, voices from elsewhere, and the very real power struggles to be listened to and accepted despite concerted efforts by the insider to stigmatise and exclude the outsider. In the first case, learners are called upon to learn, understand and memorise cultural content. In the second case, they are challenged to analyse and interpret, make connections and discover patterns in a cultural context and relate their findings to their own subject position. The first can be tested in the usual objective manner; the second is a matter of subjective interpretation and the ability to make a persuasive argument.

Given the institutional constraints of FL education – content-based lesson plans, textbooks' intrinsically structuralist nature, imperatives of accountability through measurement of learning outcomes –, it is no surprise that much of FL education favours a modernist approach to the teaching of culture in language classrooms. In the teaching of foreign languages, the most influential theory has been Byram and Zarate's theory of intercultural communicative competence (Byram and Zarate 1997), based on Zarate's influential work on the teaching of culture (Zarate 1986) and Byram's early work on social studies in foreign language education (Byram 1989). Their notion of culture is based on the national characteristics of native citizens of European nation states striving to understand each other across national boundaries within a united Europe. Similar work in intercultural education has been done in Germany by Hans Jürgen Krumm (2003), Ingrid Gogolin (1994) and others who coined the term 'interkulturelles Lernen' (see section 5 below) and in France by Zarate et al. (2004) who have highlighted the notions of 'médiation' and 'plurilinguisme' and 'pluriculturalisme' as foundational principles of FL education in Europe.

In the teaching of second languages to immigrants, the work of Bonny Norton (2000) in Canada represents a milestone as it turns educators' attention to the emotional and subjective aspects of language learning. Her work like that of Aneta Pavlenko (2005) and Pavlenko and Blackledge (2004) in the U.S. and Ingrid Gogolin (1994) and Adelheid Hu (1999) in Germany is part of a larger focus placed today on the relation of language and identity. Particularly for immigrants learning the dominant language of the host country, issues of identity are linked to the legitimate right to be heard and listened to. They complexify the notion of communicative or intercultural competence, by introducing the notions of symbolic power and the right to speak. As Bourdieu wrote, social acceptability cannot be reduced to grammaticality alone. "A person speaks not only to be understood but also to be believed, obeyed, respected, distinguished" (Bourdieu 1977: 648). Real communicative competence is the right to speak the language of authority; it implies the "power to impose reception" (Bourdieu 1977: 648).

In this perspective the concepts offered by sociolinguistic and sociocultural theory have direct implications for language teachers. The explicit teaching of speech act realisation and topic management in the style of the NS has become standard fare of FL textbooks since Kramsch first applied them to the teaching of French, German, and English (1981, 1984, 1985). The application of Bourdieu's notion of habitus was instrumental in spawning research on the teaching of foreign concepts and constructs both in the language classroom (see, e.g., Kramsch 1983) and on-line (see, e.g., the innovative cross-linguistic and cross-cultural project *Cultura* developed at M.I.T by Gilberte Furstenberg and her colleagues, Furstenberg et al. 2001).

Sociocultural theory has been equally influential on the teaching of culture in FL education in the U.S.. Vygotsky's work, reinterpreted in the Soviet Union by Leontiev in the light of activity theory, then in the United States by Lantolf and his colleagues in the light of sociocultural theory, has been given in the U.S. a fairly modernist interpretation. Culture is seen as the stable environment that constitutes the implicit knowledge that NSs have and that NNSs will internalise "with the help of more capable peers". By drawing on the affordances they find in that environment, learners will acquire the knowledge they need to participate and collaborate with others in the completion of joint tasks and activities. This approach has given additional support to a pedagogy of pair and group work within the currently favoured task-based methodology; it has reinforced a concept of culture as the non-problematic context of activities whose meaning can be negotiated through collaboration on common tasks.

However, the concept of culture has become complex as linguists have challenged the traditional duality NS-NNS, and the stable external reality of culture.

Some linguists like Vivian Cook (1999 see also Ch. 5, this volume) have acknowledged that language learners are not deficient approximations of monolingual NSs, but bilingual speakers in their own right. Teachers are encouraged to recognise their status as *multicompetent* speakers by taking their models not from monolingual NSs, but from bilingual speakers, by bringing bilingual users' situations and roles into the classroom, and by deliberately using the students' L1 in teaching activities. But the NS/NNS divide is so entrenched in FL study (indeed, it constitutes the raison d'être for the study of a foreign language and culture), that few scholars advocate making fruitful use of the students' native language and culture in the foreign language classroom (see, however, Blyth 2000). In second language learning by immigrants, teachers are more eager to make the NNSs understand and adapt to the ways of the NSs than vice versa, and the notion of multicompetency has not yet found its way in the majority of lesson plans for immigrants learning the language they need to survive in their host country.

If culture is not some stable entity external to the speaking subject, but is constructed and shaped minute by minute by speakers and hearers in their daily verbal and non-verbal transactions, then teaching culture in language classes is a matter of raising learners' awareness of the cultural representations associated with their and others' utterances. The cultural representations of learners of an L2 might be different from those of native speakers even though they mouth the same words. These differences must then be brought explicitly to the fore through a detailed analysis of the discursive features of speech. The challenge for language teachers is to find the right balance between having the students talk about cultural representations and having them talk and enact their own cultural representations. In foreign language study, there is increased pressure right now to rehabilitate the reflective component and the contrastive analysis (i.e., translation) exercises that had been all but discarded thirty years ago with the communicative revolution in language teaching (see LoBianco, Liddicoat and Crozet 1999; Liddicoat and Crozet 2000).

In the teaching of the host country's language to immigrants, it is the language socialisation paradigm that is gaining in popularity among language educators, not the critical reflection paradigm. Little effort is made by textbook writers to acknowledge the social and cultural changes brought about in the mainstream culture by the integration of NNSs. At a time when immigration societies are redesigning their citizenship tests to reflect not just civic facts but the dominant cultural values of the host country, a socialisation paradigm of language learning and teaching might present ethical dilemmas for the language teacher.

If learning another language means learning new linguistic and conceptual metaphors, then, as Littlemore and Low (2006) propose for the teaching of English, various exercises can raise the learners' awareness of figurative speech and its associated concepts in the minds of native and non-native speakers, including contrastive analyses of the conceptual metaphors in the L1 and the L2. They can also facilitate new ways of thinking of one's body in relation to one's environment. However, teachers should beware of falling into the structuralist trap. As Littlemore and Low warn, "teachers need to be acutely aware that using a conceptual metaphor is not the same as believing it. Saying 'I didn't catch what you said' does not commit you to believing the conduit metaphor" (2006: 97), nor subscribing to the folk notion that COMMUNICATION IS TRANSFER or that to argue in English is to become aggressive because, after all, ARGUMENT IS WAR. Hence the cautious use that should be made of conceptual metaphors as an explanatory principle that can be taught inductively or deductively in language classes.

In sum: New ways of looking at language competence – as multi-competence, as socialisation, as window to thought and culture, as stylistic choice, as marker of identity – prompt us to revisit the traditional teaching of culture in foreign language education. Culture is now seen as individual emotions, memories, habits of thought and behaviours, historical narratives, expressed differently through different languages and shared by a variety of speech communities. The relationship of language and culture has become akin to "global flows and local complexities" (Risager 2006). The national community is only one of the many cultures an individual participates in. Others are ethnic culture, youth culture, educational culture, professional culture, gender culture etc. Recent trends point toward a late modernist approach to the teaching of culture, more akin to literary interpretation than to the memorising of facts. They seem to favour more critical reflection on issues of power and identity, on the nature and subject position of the multilingual individual, and on the indeterminacy of meaning. In general, they suggest a need for what Mary Louise Pratt has called "cultural translation", i.e., "a process by which communication occurs across boundaries but preserves the distances it works to overcome" (Pratt 2002: 34) – an unresolvable contradiction indeed, that Pratt sees as the essence of cultural mediation, and that Kramsch has called "the third place" in language learning and teaching (Kramsch 1993).

5. Controversial issues

Considering the rather expansive boundaries of the domain 'language and culture', it is not surprising that there have been some virulent controversies about the theory and the practice of including culture in language learning and teaching (for controversies in applied linguistics, see Seidlhofer 2003). Virulent because it has become clear in this 21st century that all culture is political, i.e., engages group identity and individual symbolic survival. In these controversies, applied linguists have debated the best way to teach communicative competence across cultures (Edmondson and House 1998, 2000 vs. Hu 1999, 2000), structuralist vs. post-structuralist approaches to the study of social and cultural identity (Norton vs. Price in Seidlhofer 2003) and the nature of empirical evidence when researching culture in language (Widdowson vs. Fairclough in Seidlhofer 2003). Foreign language educators debate what culture to teach in language classes, if at all (Atkinson 1999, 2000 vs. Siegal 2000), whether to teach similarities or differences, even conflicts, between the source and the target culture (Kramsch 1995 a, b vs. Bernhardt 1995; Byrnes 1995), and in general how to deal with the moral and political dimensions of culture in language teaching. One example of these controversies will suffice here, taken from Kramsch et al. (2007).

Communication across cultures has been an object of controversy in Germany between discourse analysts (Edmondson and House 1998) and educational linguists (Hu 1999). For Edmondson and House (1998), as for many researchers in pragmatics, conversation and discourse studies, entities like culture, power, identity are constructed across turns-at-talk and in the minute-by-minute negotiation of face, stance and footing. Since, in their view, communication is the raison d'être of language learning, language instruction should focus on the study of culture in discourse, i.e., the cross-cultural dimension of discourse pragmatics and the misunderstandings or successful understandings brought about by the discursive management of language itself. Language teachers should teach non-native speakers how to recognise and adopt the discursive behaviour of the native speakers whose language they are learning, in order to find out ultimately how they think, what they value, and how they see the world. In short, foreign language instruction should focus on communicative competence and the cultural dimensions of discourse competence, not on intercultural competence.

Hu (1999) argues that the concept of culture as used by Edmondson and House is too restricted and essentialistic. To assume that 'German culture' speaks through the discourse of a speaker of standard German is an inappropriate assumption in our days of hybrid, changing, and conflicting cultures. For Hu, concepts like 'communication', 'language' and 'culture' cannot be taken at face value but must be problematised. Hence the usefulness of the term intercultural, that covers intra- as well as interlingual communication between people who don't share the same history, values, and worldviews. An intercultural pedagogy takes into account the students' culturally diverse representations, interpretations, expectations, memories, and identifications, that are, in turn, thematised, brought into the open through personal narratives and multilingual writings, and discussed openly in class. Hu's perspective on culture, like that of many educators working with immigrants, is close to the late modernist perspective discussed above.

This German debate about intercultural learning is part of a larger debate about which kind of education, specifically foreign language education, should be provided by secondary and post-secondary institutions in an age of globalisation. In Germany, the debate about culture in education, or *Bildungsdebatte*, can be divided into roughly two camps (see Kramsch and Wellmon 2008). One decries the instrumentalisation of education and appeals, either implicitly or explicitly, to a revitalisation of the humanistic ideal of education or *Bildungsideal.* The concept of *Bildung*, associated with an organic view of education through a process of autonomous reflection and self-discovery, goes back to 18th century views on the development of the human personality. By contrast with *Ausbildung* (or training) that referred to the acquisition of skills to be used in the workplace, 'Bildung' was the realisation of freedom through the self's own labour. It implied the creation of a sovereign and self-legislating subject. A liberal arts education or culture was the hallmark of an educated, i.e., cultivated, *(gebildete)* person. One of the major proponents of 'Bildung' was Wilhelm von Humboldt, Prussian Minister of Education under Napoleonic occupation and founder of the Humboldt University in Berlin in 1810. For Humboldt, the university exemplified the tension of 'Bildung' between the self and the world, not just because it is a privileged site of education but because of its institutional structure. He argued that, while a state university is not autonomous because it pursues the goals and needs of the State, nevertheless it does so from a place that is not immediately aligned with the exigencies of political necessity or utilitarian desire. As a locus of 'Bildung', the university is not simply the realisation or manifestation of sovereignty or the pursuit of an unsullied truth, but neither is it simply the production of functional, economically fit citizens for the immediate purposes of the State. It is a space in which the complex relationship of subject and world, individual and society is played out and reflected upon.

The other side in the 'Bildungsdebatte' argues that Germany must abandon, or at least drastically reevaluate its commitment to its humanistic educational tradition in the face of economic globalisation. Throughout the 19th and the 20th century, namely, a liberal education became a status symbol, the cultural capital of the middle-class educated ('gebildete') elite, that carefully discriminated between those who had education and those who had (merely) vocational training. In the 20th century the German literary and cultural canon was appropriated by German politicians for nationalistic and hegemonic purposes. According to Spiewak (2003), the ideal of a Humboldtian education cannot meet the specialised demands of a global economy. Germany's lingering commitment to a humanistic 'Bildungs'-tradition, he suggests, is partly responsible for Germany's current educational crisis. German universities do not need more Humboldtian idealism; they need practical, competence-focused education that prepares students for a global economy by endowing them with functional strategies to adapt to the social, economic and cultural demands of a changing world.

What this debate, carried out in the major news media as well as in professional and academic circles, reveals is that the engagement with the world beyond the self that Humboldt had envisaged as being the primary mission of the university has become inordinately more complex now that the world has become global. Today the challenge is not so much the creation of autonomous, sovereign subjects engaging with the world, as it is the uncertainty of what that world consists of. Who are we preparing our students to engage with? In an age of bewildering globalisation, the nation-university pair has been replaced by much more complex global flows, relationships which we have only begun to perceive, much less reflect upon.

Germany's current educational crisis and the tension between a humanistic education and a more pragmatic, market-oriented skills training mirrors debates in U.S. German Departments about the teaching of language and culture (see Kramsch et al. 2007). American universities, built on the German university model of teaching and research, inherited both its strengths and its division between 'Ausbildung' and 'Bildung'. The labour of foreign language departments in American academia is often divided between language instruction and literary-cultural studies. The former tends to emphasise the development of communicative competence or language skills for professional purposes, while the latter tends to emphasise literary analysis or the cultivation of an intellectual canon (see Kern 2002; Byrnes 2002). Just as Germany's current 'Bildungsdebatte' poses the question of education in terms of market-oriented skills or intellectual-personality development, so do American German Departments pose the question "why study German" as an either/or: either we as members of German Departments focus on the teaching of German as a global language (a language that affords our students access to a global community-market as consumers and economic actors) or we tend to cultivate a German cultural tradition from Goethe to Grass and Hegel to Habermas – a tradition unsullied by economic interests associated with linguistic competence. There is an assumption that the teaching of German as a functional tool for communication is incompatible with the more humanistic study of a German literary-cultural tradition. This apparent disconnect manifests itself in a division of labour with a very clear hierarchy: the teaching of language at the bottom and the teaching of culture at the top. In graduate programs, graduate student instructors labour in language classrooms, while faculty members engage in literary and cultural analysis. To this day, the division of labour at American research universities between language teachers and literature scholars has hardly been up for debate (but see MLA Ad Hoc comittee on Foreign Languages 2007).

6. Applied linguistics research perspectives

If applied linguistics has been defined as "the theoretical and empirical investigation of real-world problems in which language is a central issue" (Brumfit 1995: 27), the field straddles by definition not only several disciplines, but also several research paradigms. Among these, some take a structuralist, others a more post structuralist view of language and culture. As a field that has theorised both the theory and the practice of language learning and teaching, applied linguistics can help reframe problems that tend to get locked into irreducible positions, such as the culture/nurture, individual/society, mind/body, theory/practice dichotomies. For example:

1. The long tradition of dialogue and interaction in applied linguistics can help highlight the dialogic construction of culture in each of its theoretical strands.
2. It can help educational institutions bridge the gap between their theoretical mission and the problems in the real world through the production of complexity, reflexivity, imagination based on real-world issues.
3. It can contribute its long tradition of bridging 'pure' disciplines for the mutual benefit of both theorists and practitioners, in particular between the humanities and the social sciences.
4. In education, since its intrinsic mission is to bring together the research and teaching missions of academic institutions, it can help bridge the gap between the teaching of language and the teaching of literature/culture in foreign language and literature departments.

In terms of research methodology, culture in applied linguistics has been researched as the small culture of everyday life, as the shared 'ways with words' of a speech community, or as the long term historical and ideological heritage of an ethnic or national community. Up to now, applied linguistics has adhered mostly to a positivistic research approach of the modernist kind. But the nature of the real world makes such a modernist approach less useful than it used to be. The question is: Can applied linguistics broaden its research approaches to the teaching of language and culture to include interpretive, hermeneutic, post-structuralist modes of analysis without foregoing the insights that structuralism has gained the field? The increased interest in ethnographic approaches to conversation analysis, as well as in discourse stylistics, language ideologies, cognitive semantics and linguistic anthropology seem to suggest a move in that direction.

References

Atkinson, Dwight
1999 TESOL and culture. *TESOL Quarterly* 33 (4): 625–654.

Atkinson, Dwight
2000 The author responds .... *TESOL Quarterly* 34 (4): 752–755.

Bakhtin, Mikhail
1981 *The Dialogic Imagination.* Austin, TX: University of Texas Press.

Bernhardt, Elizabeth B.
1995 Response to Claire Kramsch. *ADFL Bulletin* 26 (3): 15–17.

Bhabha, Homi k.
1994 *The Location of Culture.* London: Routledge.

Blum-Kulka, Shoshona, Juliane House and Gabi Kasper (eds.)
1989 *Cross-Cultural Pragmatics: Requests and Apologies* (*Advances in Discourse Processes* Vol. 31). Norwood, NJ: Ablex.

Blyth, Carl (ed.)
2000 *The Sociolinguistics of Foreign Language Classrooms: Contributions of the Native, the Near Native, and the Non-Native Speaker.* Boston: Heinle.

Bourdieu, Pierre
1977 The economics of linguistic exchanges. *Social Science Information* 16 (6): 645–558.

Bredella, Lothar
1992 Towards a pedagogy of intercultural understanding. *Amerikastudien* 37: 559–594.

Brumfit, Christopher
1995 Teacher professionalization and research. In: Guy Cook and Barbara Seidlhofer (eds.), *Principle and Practice in Applied Linguistics*, 27–41. Oxford: Oxford University Press.

Butler, Judith
1997 *Excitable Speech. The Political Promise of the Performative.* London: Routledge.

Byram, Michael
1989 *Cultural Studies in Foreign Language Education*. Clevedon, UK: Multilingual Matters.

Byram, Michael
1997 *Teaching and Assessing Intercultural Communicative Competence.* Clevedon, UK: Multilingual Matters.

Byram, Michael and Geneviève Zarate
1997 Defining and assessing intercultural competence: Some principles and proposals for the European context. *Language Teaching* 29: 14–18.

Byram, Michael and Michael Fleming (eds.)
1998 *Language Learning in Intercultural Perspective. Approaches through Drama and Ethnography.* Cambridge: Cambridge University Press.

Byrnes, Heidi
1995 Response to Claire Kramsch. *ADFL Bulletin* 26 (3): 13–15.

Byrnes, Heidi
2002 The cultural turn in foreign language departments: Challenge and opportunity. *Profession 2002*: 114–129.

Cameron, Deborah
2000 *Good to Talk? Living and Working in a Communication Culture*. London: Sage.

Cook, Guy
1994 *Discourse and Literature.* Oxford: Oxford University Press.

Cook, Vivian
1999 Going beyond the native speaker in language teaching. *TESOL Quarterly* 33 (2): 185–210.

Edmondson, Willis and Juliane House
1998 Interkulturelles Lernen: ein überflüssiger Begriff. *Zeitschrift für Fremdsprachenforschung* 92: 161–188.

Edmondson, Willis and Juliane House
2000 Begrifflichkeit und interkulturelles lernen. Eine Antwort auf Hu 1999. *Zeitschrift für Fremdsprachenforschung* 11 (1): 125–129.
Fauconnier, Gilles and Mark Turner
2002 *The Way We Think. Conceptual Blending and the Mind's Hidden Complexities.* New York: Basic Books.
Foucault, Michel
1971 *L'ordre du Discours.* Paris: Gallimard.
Furstenberg, Gilberte, Sabine Levet, Kathryn English and Katherine Maillet
2001 Giving a virtual voice to the silent language of culture: The Cultura project. *Language Learning and Technology* 5 (1) (January 2001): 55–102. Also accessible at:http://web.mit.edu/french/culturaNEH/
Gardner, Rod and Johannes Wagner (eds.)
2004 *Second Language Conversations.* London: Continuum.
Giddens, Anthony
1991 *Modernity and Self-Identity. Self and Society in the Late Modern Age.* Stanford: Stanford University Press.
Gogolin, Ingrid
1994 *Der monolinguale Habitus der multilingualen Schule.* Münster: Waxmann.
Gumperz, John J.
1982 *Discourse Strategies.* Cambridge University Press.
Hanks, William
1996 *Language and Communicative Practices.* Boulder, CO: Westview Press.
Hansen, Hans Lauge (ed.)
2002 *Changing Philologies. Contributions to the Redefinition of Foreign Language Studies in the Age of Globalisation.* Copenhagen: Museum Tusculanum Press.
Hinton, Leanne
1994 *Flutes of Fire. Essays on California Indian Languages.* Berkeley: Heyday books.
Holliday, Adrian
1999 Small cultures. *Applied Linguistics* 20 (2): 237–264.
Hu, Adelheid
1999 Interkulturelles Lernen. Eine Auseinandersetzung mit der Kritik an einem umstrittenen Konzept. *Zeitschrift für Fremdsprachenforschung* 10 (2): 277–303.
Hu, Adelheid
2000 Begrifflichkeit und interkulturelles Lernen. Eine Replik auf Edmondson und House 1999. *Zeitschrift für Fremdsprachenforschung* 11 (1):130–136.
Johnson, Mark
1987 *The Body in the Mind. The Bodily Basis of Meaning, Imagination, and Reason.* Chicago: University of Chicago Press.
Kellman, Steven G.
2000 *The Translingual Imagination.* Lincoln, NE: University of Nebraska Press.
Kern, Richard
2002 *Literacy and Language Teaching.* Oxford: Oxford University Press.

Königs, Frank
2003 Teaching and learning foreign language in Germany: A personal overview of developments in research. *Language Teaching* 36 (4): 235–251.

Kramsch, Claire
1981 *Discourse Analysis and Second Language Teaching*. Washington, D.C.: Center for Applied Linguistics.

Kramsch, Claire
1983 Culture and constructs: Communicating attitudes and values in the foreign language classroom. *Foreign Language Annals* 16 (6): 437–448.

Kramsch, Claire
1984 *Interaction et Discours dans la Classe de Langue*. Paris: Hatier-Credif.

Kramsch, Claire
1985 *Reden, Mitreden, Dazwischenreden. Managing Conversations in German.* Boston: Heinle.

Kramsch, Claire
1993 *Context and Culture in Language Teaching*. Oxford: Oxford University Press.

Kramsch, Claire
1995a Embracing conflict versus achieving consensus in foreign language education. *ADFL Bulletin* 26 (3): 6–12.

Kramsch, Claire
1995b Reply to Heidi Byrnes and Elizabeth B. Bernhardt. *ADFL Bulletin* 26 (3): 17.

Kramsch, Claire
1997 The privilege of the non-native speaker. *PMLA* 112 (3): 359–369.

Kramsch, Claire
2001 Intercultural communication. In: Ronald Carter and David Nunan (eds.), *The Cambridge Guide to Teaching English to Speakers of Other Languages*, 201–206. Cambridge: Cambridge University Press.

Kramsch, Claire
2003 Language, thought, and culture. In: Alan Davies and Catherine Elder (eds.), *Handbook of Applied Linguistics*, 235–261. Oxford: Blackwell.

Kramsch, Claire, Tes Howell, Chantelle Warner and Chad Wellmon
2007 Framing foreign language education in the U.S. The case of German. Special issue of *Critical Inquiry in Language Studies* 2/3: 151–178.

Kramsch, Claire und Chad Wellmon
2008 From *Bildung durch Sprache* to language ecology: The uses of symbolic competence. In: Sabine Duff, Werner Hüllen and Frederike Klippel (eds.), *Visions of Languages in Education*. Münchener Arbeiten zur Fremdsprachenforschung, 215–226. Munich: Langenscheidt.

Krumm, Hans-Jürgen
2003 Einheit in der Vielfalt. Mehrsprachigkeit und europäische Identität. In: Ernst Klett Sprachen (ed.), *Sprachbuch*, 69–80. Stuttgart: Klett.

Lakoff, George
1987 *Women, Fire and Dangerous Things. What Categories Reveal about the Mind.* Chicago: University of Chicago Press.

Lakoff, George and Mark Johnson
1980 *Metaphors We Live by.* Chicago: University of Chicago Press.

Lam, Wan S. E.
2000 L2 literacy and the design of the self: A case study of a teenager writing on the internet. *TESOL Quarterly* 34 (3): 457–480.

Lantolf, James (ed.)
2000 *Sociocultural Theory and Second Language Learning*. Oxford: Oxford University Press.

Lave, Jean and Etienne Wenger
1991 *Situated Learning. Legitimate Peripheral Participation.* Cambridge: Cambridge University Press.

Liddicoat, Anthony J. and Chantal Crozet (eds.)
2000 *Teaching Languages, Teaching Cultures*. Melbourne: Language Australia.

Littlemore, Jeannette and Graham Low
2006 *Figurative Thinking and Foreign Language Learning*. New York: Palgrave Macmillan.

Lo Bianco, Joseph, Anthony J. Liddicoat and Chantal Crozet
1999 *Striving for the Third Place*. Melbourne: Language Australia.

Markee, Numa
2000 *Conversation Analysis.* Mahwah, NJ: Lawrence Erlbaum.

MLA Ad Hoc Committee on Foreign Languages
2007 Foreign Lanuages and Higher Education: New structures for a changed world. *Profession* 2007, 234–245.

Moerman, Michael
1988 *Talking Culture. Ethnography and Conversation Analysis.* Philadelphia: University of Pennsylvania Press.

Moore, Daniele (ed.)
2001 *Les Représentations des Langues et de leur Apprentissage.* Paris: Didier-Crédif.

Norton, Bonny
2000 *Identity and Language Learning*. London: Longman.

Ochs, Elinor
1996 Linguistic resources for socializing humanity. In: John J.Gumperz and Stephen Levinson (eds.), *Rethinking Linguistic Relativity*, 407–437. Cambridge: Cambridge University Press.

Ochs, Elinor
2002 Becoming a speaker of culture. In: Claire Kramsch (ed.), *Language Acquisition and Language Socialization. Ecological Perspectives*, 99–120. New York: Continuum.

Ochs, Elinor and Bambi Schieffelin
1988 *Language Socialization across Cultures.*

Pavlenko, Aneta
2005 *Emotions and Multilingualism*. Cambridge: Cambridge University Press.

Pavlenko, Aneta and James Lantolf
2000 Second language learning as participation and (re)construction of selves. In: Lantolf (ed.), 155–178.

Pavlenko, Aneta and Adrian Blackledge (eds.)
2004 *Negotiation of Identities in Multilingual Contexts.* Clevedon, UK: Multilingual Matters.

Pratt, Marie Louise
2002 The traffic in meaning: translation, contagion, infiltration. *Profession* 2002 (1): 25–36.
Rampton, Ben
1995 *Crossing. Language and Ethnicity among Adolescents.* London: Longman.
Risager, Karen
2006 *Language and Culture: Global Flows and Local Complexity.* Clevedon, UK: Multilingual Matters.
Rushdie, Salman
1999 *The Ground Beneath Her Feet.* London: Jonathan Cape.
Schieffelin, Bambi B., Kathryn A. Woolard and Paul V. Kroskrity (eds.)
1998 *Language Ideologies. Practice and Theory.* Oxford: Oxford University Press.
Seidlhofer, Barbara (ed.)
2003 *Controversies in Applied Linguistics.* Oxford: Oxford University Press.
Siegal, Meryl
2000 Comments on Dwight Atkinson's "TESOL and Culture". A reader reacts. *TESOL Quarterly* 34 (4): 744–752.
Slobin, Dan
2000 Verbalized events. A dynamic approach to linguistic relativity and determinism. In: Susanne Niemeier and Rene Dirven (eds.), *Evidence for Linguistic Relativity*, 108–138. Amsterdam: John Benjamins.
Spiewak, Martin
2003 Humboldts Totengräber. *Die Zeit* 19: 1.
Tannen, Deborah
1993 What's in a frame? Surface evidence for underlying expectations. In: Deborah Tannen (ed.), *Framing in Discourse*, 14–56. Oxford: Oxford University Press.
Taylor, Charles
1994 *Multiculturalism and "The Politics of Recognition".* Princeton, NJ: Princeton University Press.
Valdes, Guadalupe
2001 Heritage language students: Profiles and possibilities. In: Joy K. Peyton, Donald A. Ranard and Scott McGinnis (eds.), *Heritage Languages in America. Preserving a National Resource*, 37–80. Washington, D.C.: CAL Eric.
Wierzbicka, Ana
1994 Emotion, language, and cultural scripts. In: Shinobu Kitayama and Hazel Markus (eds.), *Emotion and Culture: Empirical studies of mutual influence*, 133–196. Washington, DC: American Psychological Association.
Zarate, Geneviève
1986 *Enseigner une Culture Étrangère.* Paris: Hachette.
Zarate, Geneviève (ed.)
2001 *Langues, Xénophobie, Xénophilie dans une Europe Multiculturelle.* Caen: Centre Regional de Documentation Pedagogique de Basse-Normandie.
Zarate, Geneviève, Aline Gohard-Radenkovic, Denise Lussier, Hermine Penz
2004 *Cultural Mediation in Language Learning and Teaching.* Strasbourg: Council of Europe. European Centre for Modern Languages.

Recommended Readings

Bibliography

Kovecses, Zoltan
2006 *Language, Mind and Culture. A practical Introduction*. Oxford: Oxford University Press.

Handbooks, overviews, general literature

Andersen, Hanne Leth, Karen Lund and Karen Risager (eds.)
2006 *Culture in Language Learning*, 11–26. Aarhus, DK: Aarhus University Press.
Byram, Michael (ed.)
2000 *Routledge Encyclopedia of Language Teaching and Learning*. London: Routledge.
Kramsch, Claire
2006 Culture in language teaching. In: Keith Brown (ed.), *Encyclopedia of Language and Linguistics*, 2nd edition, 322–329. Oxford: Elsevier Science.
Van Deusen-Scholl, Nelleke and Nancy H. Hornberger (eds.)
2008 *Encyclopedia of Language and Education*. 2ndedition. Vol.4 *Second and Foreign Language Education.* Heidelberg: Springer Science and Business Media, LLC.

Journals

Journal of Multilingual and Multicultural Development
Language and Intercultural Communication
Language Awareness
Language, Culture and Curriculum

10. The political perspective

Janina Brutt-Griffler

1. Introduction

The present chapter considers the topic of political perspectives on foreign language learning and teaching. It considers the main politically-inspired approaches, explores the traditions from which they emerge, examines their underlying assumptions, and assesses the degree to which they can be empirically verified. As political approaches have focused largely on English, so must this chapter, but it takes up as well issues of minority/endangered languages, foreign language teaching in mother tongue English-speaking nations, and questions of general linguistic relevance. The inclusion of a chapter devoted to political perspectives on language learning and teaching reflects a largely contemporary preoccupation with questions rooted in the exploration of language in society and the nature of language itself.

The study of language has been and continues to be a highly contested subject. Since the 1960s, concerns have been raised about linguistic inquiries that focus on grammatical and structural features alone, divorcing language from its actual use by speakers in social contexts. Language is not an isolated system of communication as it is sometimes conceived, but it is constitutive of and constitutes social relations that are embedded in the very linguistic system. In the words of Saville-Troike (2003), "what language is cannot be separated from how and why it is used, and [...] considerations of use are often prerequisite to recognition and understanding of much linguistic form" (Saville-Troike 2003: 3). This formulation of language and language use affords a richer understanding of, for example, the Japanese linguistic markers of politeness or the Javanese system that inscribes the social roles for the interlocutors. A critical perspective allows the user of the language and the learner to become sensitised to the linguistic forms that to some extent reflect societal relations and values in the speech communities. It might reveal the embeddedness of gender or class relations, for example, emerging out of, contributing to, or sparking calls for linguistic change aimed at societal change. Thus an early focus of feminist activism included calls to end the defining of women in the English-speaking communities by their marital status by the widespread use of *Miss* or *Mrs.* through the substitution of the unmarked *Ms*.

At the national and international level, a political perspective can inform a historical and societal process of the favouring of one variety of a language as a standard or official language. At the supranational level, a political perspective can provide a window into international or global languages that serve as lingua francas and their distributions as means of international communication. Political perspectives can also provide a useful assessment of educational practice, including the allocation of resources to promote language learning in schools and communities, determination of the relevance of best practices to language learners, and transitions between the home literacy practices and those in academic institutions.

In providing a brief overview of this body of scholarly work, this contribution seeks to explore a set of issues that political perspectives have brought to the fore in applied linguistics. As will be shown, a significant effort and creative energy has been spent on the critique of the role of the English language worldwide. While this contribution takes English as its principal case study, it does so in relation to its impact both real and imagined on the teaching and learning of other foreign languages. The central thrust of the critique of Foreign Language Teaching – and English Language Teaching in particular – as an inherently political undertaking concerns not language endangerment as such but the separate claim that the spread of certain languages is inherently harmful to the interests of other languages and cultures. In that sense, whether it leads to language shift or language endangerment, FLT is dangerous in and of itself, because it fosters *cultural imperialism* or *linguistic imperialism* if the wrong languages are taught to the wrong people. Though of comparatively recent vintage, such a perspective has become influential enough that alongside the traditional fields of study in applied linguistics there has grown a large and vibrant subfield that concerns itself exclusively with minutely examining the ideological content of FLT in its myriad of manifestations.

2. Historical background

Perhaps the most politicised of all areas of investigation in applied linguistics today, the study of English as a foreign language, began from an apparently largely apolitical set of concerns. Starting in the 1970s, scholars in English applied linguistics set out to investigate questions connected to intercultural communication among English speakers globally. Smith (1976) defined EIL as a language of L2 users who do not need to adopt the culture of mother tongue speakers to use English effectively. Smith's (1987) work helped to ignite the longstanding controversy as to whether the "ownership" of English is vested in its mother tongue speakers, with numerous scholars rejecting such a proposition on historical and linguistic grounds (Kachru 1996; Widdowson 1994). Subsequent interdisciplinary work on English language spread and use underscored the legitimacy of English in postcolonial contexts and based much of its conceptual work on the notion of 'indigenisation' in the context of 'other' local languages and cultures. This new understanding helped to inaugurate a productive sociolinguistic paradigm known as *World Englishes* (Kachru 1985).

This paradigm gave rise to a body of work on the linguistic description of new varieties of English (e.g., Butler 1981; Kachru 1985), literary work on postcolonial literatures (e.g., Ashcroft, Griffiths and Tiffin 1989), and sociohistorical studies of English in the former British Empire (e.g., Bolton 2003; Brutt-Griffler 2002). Importantly, the World Englishes paradigm initiated a new discourse into the discipline of English applied linguistics, including the recognition that English is an 'indigenous' language in some postcolonial contexts as, for example, Hindi in India, thus blurring the ideological and linguistic notions of English as a 'foreign' versus 'native' language (cf. Mufwene 2004). For many scholars working within this framework, English has often been viewed as an essential linguistic equaliser in a multilingual context where other ethnic languages compete for dominance.

In the 1980s and early 1990s, a rival paradigm to that of World Englishes emerged clustered around issues of English as a linguistic and cultural threat to other languages (Skutnabb-Kangas 1988; Phillipson and Skutnabb-Kangas 1986; Phillipson 1992; Skutnabb-Kangas and Phillipson 1995; Nettle and Romaine 2000; Kontra et al. 2002). Focused on questions of linguistic human rights, linguistic imperialism, and more recently language endangerment, this body of work departs from the notion that languages such as English could ever be 'indigenised' in 'foreign' contexts. Rather, it has conceptualised language spread as the encroachment of dominant languages on other, leading to such catastrophic outcomes as the displacement of indigenous and smaller languages. In the view of these scholars, applied linguistics does not simply have the mission of understanding the processes underway, but the overtly political imperative of intervening to prevent both the inherent injustice of *linguicism* (Skutnabb-Kangas 2000) and averting an ongoing language extinction that presumably threatens the majority of the world's living languages.

While the notions of linguicism, language endangerment, and linguistic human rights have raised consciousness about a number of sociolinguistic issues, including the often unequal allocation of resources in foreign language learning, more recent approaches have brought a greater degree of refinement to the role of English and its use among the growing number of bi- and multi-lingual speakers. Taking languages as highly complex linguistic systems with a range of variation at all levels of linguistic description (phonology, syntax, pragmatics), most recent perspectives explore the user's linguistic choices during an interaction for the purpose of self-presentation and negotiation of one's identity and ethnicity (Brutt-Griffler and Davies 2006; Rampton 2006). This view of language carries important implications for bi-lingual and multi-lingual speakers who may choose to draw on language resources (mother tongues, English, and foreign languages) to transcend the ascribed social categorisations of gender, class and ethnicity (cf. Blommaert 2008). In analysing English use in Africa, Mazrui suggests the notion of "English as an exit visa" that relates to language as a "possible instrument of temporary 'escape' from ethnic-based cultural constraints" (2006: 65). The focus on speakers' subjectivity challenges the traditional notion of social categories that have tended to ascribe a definite relation between language competence and a speaker's geopolitical space.

A growing acceptance of new varieties of English helped conceptualise a new and highly productive paradigm of *English as a lingua franca* (ELF) in Europe (Seidlhofer 2004). Pölzl and Seidlhofer (2006) claim that successful English as lingua franca communication involves a "trade-off between achieving a satisfactory degree of mutual intelligibility while retaining a 'comfortable' measure of personal identity" (Pölzl and Seidlhofer 2006: 152). Highlighting the importance of context in which ELF communication takes place, the authors conclude from a study of Arabic ELF speakers that ELF is a "global phenomenon locally realized" (Pölzl and Seidlhofer 2006: 152).

Leading proponents of this paradigm insist on the importance of empirical descriptions of language and language use that go beyond ideological debates (Seidlhofer 2001). Innovative empirical work has been pursued in such domains as ELF lexicogrammar (Seidlhofer 2004), phonology and attitudes towards ELF (Jenkins 2000, 2007), and discourse and discourse processes (House 2002; Mauranen 2003). This new research paradigm provides applied linguists with the much needed empirical data to better understand the controversies surrounding English language and foreign language use and pedagogy.

3. State of the art: central issues

3.1. What are the stakes?

"The world is about to be hit by a tidal wave of English," writes the *Independent* (Burleigh 2004), describing Graddol's (2004) startling projection in a study for the British Council that half of the world's population will either speak or be in the process of learning English by 2015. The same report contains an even more surprising warning: that, paradoxically, this unprecedented English spread poses a substantial risk to Great Britain's citizens and economy if urgent steps are not taken to promote the study of foreign languages. The same recognition lies behind a major language policy initiative of the Bush Administration in the US called the National Security Language Initiative (NSLI) that includes a significant allocation of federal resources to teaching foreign languages deemed strategically important (e.g., Arabic, Chinese, Hindi, Swahili, and Turkish) (AL-Batal 2007: 270). These two English speaking nations rank relatively low in foreign language abilities among their citizens. In Britain, a recent EU survey found that 30 % can speak a second language, while the corresponding figure for the United States, according to a U.S. Senate Resolution, comes in at only 9 % among the native born (Blake and Kramsch 2007: 247).

Though it has been more common to focus on the purported linguistically homogenising forces of globalisation, the actual impact is considerably more complex. Nations like Britain and the US are beginning to exhibit something of an awakening to an urgency to increase the linguistic capital of their citizens. Byrnes (2002) notes that "the greater ethnic and linguistic diversity of nations, and the demands for more democratisation around the world may not simply be that societies require a multilingual citizenry but that this citizenry of the future requires upper levels of language abilities" (Byrnes 2002: 35). Byrnes' observation resonates with a trend among some applied linguists toward promoting *advanced language proficiency* and developing foreign language programs aimed at younger learners (cf. Donato and Tucker 2007).

Another group of applied linguists emphasises a very different and alarming set of stakes: what Nettle and Romaine call "the biolinguistic diversity crisis" that includes "the extinction of languages [...] as part of the larger picture of worldwide near-total ecosystem collapse" (Nettle and Romaine 2000: 17). Scholars of what has come to be called 'language endangerment' project that anywhere from fifty to ninety percent of the world's more than 5,000 languages will disappear in the twenty-first century (Nettle and Romaine 2000; Crystal 2000). A growing literature implicates the complicit role of the applied linguistics profession in the impending catastrophe. According to Nettle and Romaine "Many smaller languages are dying out due to the spread of a few world languages such as English, French, Chinese, and so on" (Nettle and Romaine 2000:18).

Somewhat strangely, perhaps, the field of applied linguistics, implicated as much in the spread of all of them, has tended in recent years to approach those languages very differently. It has shown almost a positive zeal in its promotion of the importance of learning languages like French, Spanish, and Chinese. As to the promotion of English, when Ridge (2002) broached the subject during his plenary at a recent international applied linguistics conference, he felt virtually compelled to apologise, so much has its spread been encased in what he so aptly characterised as the "hermeneutics of suspicion." Such are the contours of the early twenty-first century controversies that have occupied applied linguists with respect to language use and practice. The different positions represented in the literature have given rise to very different understandings of the implications for foreign language teaching, specifically which languages should be taught, how they should be taught, and to whom.

3.2. The statistics of language use: which languages are being acquired?

Parallel to – though often separated from – the charged political debate about the English juggernaut overwhelming other foreign languages, a much more complicated picture has emerged from empirically-grounded research over the past decade. It shows that as the dominant foreign language being learned globally, English does have formidable rivals, which, paradoxically, are not 'foreign' languages at all but the 'national' languages in most of the world. Indeed, the main linguistic contest today is not that between English and disappearing mother tongues (which, while they account for a numerical majority of the world's languages, are only spoken by a tiny fraction of its population), but between English and national languages that are themselves foreign languages to many, and sometimes most, of their speakers. And despite the confident projections of both proponents and critics of English spread, the outcome in this competition is by no means foreordained.

Because there has been much more interest in political advocacy than empirical study, only the most rudimentary estimates of the number of language speakers and learners are available, some of the best provided by a Christian missionary organisation that has, somewhat oddly, become a favourite of those concerned with cultural imperialism. According to Ethnologue, there are 508 million English speakers worldwide, including L2 speakers. In Graddol's (2000) data, there are 375 million native English speakers world wide, 375 million speakers for whom English is a 'second' language and about 750 million speakers of English as a 'foreign' language. Such numbers derive from the potential impact of the widespread introduction of English as a subject in countries such as China and India. Graddol (2006) shows that more people are learning English in China than in any other country; 176.7 million were studying formally in 2005. In societies in which the vast majority of the population resides in rural areas and attains only low levels of education, government policy statements do not equate to achieved results.

To begin to gauge the pervasiveness of the national-language-as-foreign-language phenomenon requires a more detailed examination of a far lesser-known phenomenon that is nevertheless an everyday reality for much of the world's population. Table 1 provides a statistical picture of 15 national languages and the corresponding numbers of both native speakers and second language speakers for each of these languages.

In addition to these nearly 850 million second language speakers of these 15 national languages alone – or more than the highest estimates of the number of English speakers – there are some other large categories to consider. For instance, *Ethnologue* lists alongside the 206 million first-language speakers of all varieties of Arabic another 246 million second-language speakers of all Arabic varieties. Recent estimates put the total number of Swahili speakers throughout East and Central Africa at more than 70 million – all but some two million sec-

Table 1 First and second language speakers of 15 national languages

Nation	National Language*	First Language Speakers (millions)	Second Language Speakers (millions)
Chinese	Mandarin Chinese	867	178
Indonesia	Indonesian	23	140
India	Hindi	180	120
Russia	Russian	117	110
Philippines	Tagalog	14	40
Bangladesh	Bengali	100	40
Iran**	Farsi	22	40
Pakistan	Urdu	11	40
Thailand	Thai	20	40
Tanzania	Swahili	1	30
Turkey	Turkish	46	20
South Africa	Zulu	9	16
Nigeria	Hausa	18	15
Myanmar	Burmese	32	10
Azerbaijan	Azerbaijani (North)	6	8
			Total = 847

* Some nations may have more than one national "or official" language; the language given here is the most widely spoken.

** Estimate taken from various sources.

ond-language speakers. In Congo – a nation of 66 million – it is estimated that as many as half may now speak Swahili, and the number has been increasing, meaning that Swahili has already far outgrown that of a national language, Lingala (7 million L2 users alongside its 2 million L1 users). Alongside national languages in many nations, there are languages having some official status at the regional level that can account for similarly large numbers of L2 speakers, including, to name just a few, Cantonese in China (34 million L2 speakers) and in India, six languages alone – Assamese, Cebuano, Kannada, Malayam, Tamil, and Telugu – count perhaps as many as 50 or 60 million L2 speakers combined. In total, then, there are significantly more than 1 billion speakers of national or of other locally politically dominant languages as second languages.

There are also significant differences in the attainment of proficiency. In the case of English, learners who have obtained low level proficiency must be counted in to obtain the more arresting totals. In contrast, proficiency is in general much higher in national languages, both because they are spread across all social classes of society and because they tend to be the language of instruction in the schools, rather than being taught as a subject. These languages are also generally used in all domains of society rather than being limited to a few. Finally, there is in evidence in many cases a tendency for some speakers to abandon their mother tongues in favour of the national language, while there is no evidence of any significant trend of this kind in the case of English, however much English might come to dominate certain domains such as academic publishing. To disguise such trends behind the prevalent notion that such national languages are 'second' rather than 'foreign languages' is itself to bring to bear a political distinction in a political argument, one rooted in the political philosophy of nationalism, which views the dominance of the nation-state as normative and beneficial, while seeing in the transnational a threat.

Alongside the transnational ('globalisation') and the national (the attempt to create or consolidate unified national languages), there is a third force driving L2 acquisition: *urbanisation* in the postcolonial world. Given the breakdown of the *colonial rural production system*, the lack of sustainability of which has driven an exodus from the countryside to the cities, the urban population of the global South grew from 304 million to 2 billion between 1950 and 2000 (McFalls 2003: 30).

Wholly responsive neither to the nation-building project of the postcolonial state nor to that of ethnic maintenance centred in rural areas, the nonurban population who comprised the majority within postcolonial societies of Africa and Asia may be and often are actuated by instrumental views of language. As such, they frequently demonstrate a preference for languages that impart an urban, rather than a national or ethnic, identity. Concomitant with the process of urbanisation in Africa, as Mufwene (2004: 211) has pointed out, urban lingua francas, including Lingala in Congo, Isicamtho in South Africa, chiHarare in Zimbabwe, Town Bemba in Zambia, and Wolof in Senegal, have encroached upon "the function of most indigenous languages as markers of ethnic identity" and are used to deemphasise ethnicity and signal new urban cultures.

Though, as will be discussed below, the alleged encroachment of 'dominant' languages, particularly English, is generally assumed to serve (or stem from) Western interests, Western governments have actually been most proactive in recent years in instituting language policies aimed at increasing foreign language proficiency in their populations. The efforts of the two largest of these political entities, the European Union and the United States, have both produced increases in foreign language education, though to very different levels of both numbers of students and levels of proficiency attained.

A recent large scale national study carried out by the Modern Language Association of America shows a steady increase in foreign languages enrolments at the tertiary level; modern languages enrolments in 2006 have risen by 12.9 % in comparison to 2002. The most striking increases were in Arabic (126.5 %)

and Chinese (51.0 %). Spanish is the most taught language in the US, with a 10.3 % increase since 2002. French remained second, increasing by 2.2 % and German came in third with a 3.5 % increase (Modern Language Association 2007: 2). Importantly, this study also analysed the enrolments in the upper-level classes attempting to determine the levels of attainment in foreign language competency. When four-year colleges and universities were analysed, eight languages showed approximately 20 % of students enrolled in upper-level courses. Advanced language courses may be electives or requirements in the major/minor academic concentration at the university. The five top languages enrolling the highest percentage of advanced learners were, in order, Russian, Portuguese, Korean, French and Spanish. The study also found 31.2 % more students enrolled in the so called less commonly taught languages in 2006 than in 2002. The highest numbers among the Middle Eastern and African languages were for Aramaic, Swahili, and Persian.

Trends at the secondary level also show an upward trajectory. Data collected by the National Centre for Education Statistics reveal an increase in foreign language teaching at the secondary level from 37.5 % to 43.6 % of all students from 1990 to 2000, with all of the gain coming from Spanish and to a much lesser extent from less commonly taught languages like Japanese. While the percentage and absolute numbers of students learning French (comprising 18.8 % of the total) and German (4.9 %) have declined, Spanish (70.9 %) has assumed the preeminent position as the foreign language of choice in American secondary schools – the same phenomenon is evident at the university level, with the highest number of students in Spanish classes (Modern Language Association 2007: 9).

European participation rates are far more impressive. A comprehensive European Commission report concludes that "almost all pupils in general secondary education learn at least one foreign language" throughout the EU. In only two nations, Ireland and the UK, do fewer than 90 % of lower secondary (ISCED level 2) students take at least one foreign language, with an even higher rate among higher secondary (ISCED level 3), while in the majority of EU member states more than half of all primary school students study a foreign language (39–45), a rate that is steadily rising with the implementation of the EU's 'two plus one' language policy (i.e. being able to use two languages in addition to the mother tongue (Commission of the European Communities 1995: 47). The Council of Europe, a supranational organisation comprising 43 states, has energetically promoted the learning of modern languages and articulated its policy of *plurilingualism* that is

> Not simply a linguistic policy choice at an important point in the history of Europe ... [but] also a matter of helping learners [...] to construct their linguistic and cultural identity through integrating into it a diversified experience of otherness; to develop their ability to learn through this same diversified experience of relating to several languages and cultures (Council of Europe 2001: 134).

Its policy has been translated into a *Common European Framework of Reference* (CEFR) to guide language learning at all levels and has exerted a positive impact on curricula and, in particular, on language assessment (Little 2007).

English, French and German remain the most studied languages, with English being the overwhelming first option, as "at least 90 % of pupils" in the "great majority of [EU] countries" take English according to European Commission statistics (Eurydice 50; also see Wastiau-Schlüter 2005). Available evidence is also overwhelmingly supportive of the notion that Europeans are learning languages to a much higher level of proficiency, as already 56 % of EU citizens report the ability to hold a conversation in a foreign language (Eurobarometer 2006).

4. Controversial issues

Tollefson (2007) has called attention to the advent of an activist orientation among certain scholars in applied linguistics that contrasts with the theoretical and empirical that others take. Those adhering to such an approach see a significant part of their work as aimed at consciousness raising in the interests of particular policy goals. In claiming, as Nettle and Romaine (2000) do, that "Many smaller languages are dying out due to the spread of a few world languages such as English, French, Chinese, and so on" (Nettle and Romaine 2000: 144), a number of influential scholars have linked foreign language teaching to language endangerment. In this model, minority languages are endangered by the principal modern languages, the major European languages (English, French, German, Spanish and Portuguese) combined with emergent rivals like Chinese, Japanese, and Arabic. They write, "Some have used the terms 'language murder' and 'language suicide,' suggesting that languages do not die natural deaths, English, as Glanville Price puts it, is a 'killer language'" (Price 2000: 141). To bolster this point, they cite the case of Africa, in which English spread, they assert, "is leading to the top-down displacement of numerous other tongues" (Nettle and Romaine 2000: 144). Similarly, Phillipson (2003: 6, 176) writes about the threat posed by English, including in southern Africa, "to other languages and cultures", even portending, perhaps, language attrition and "a loss of cultural vitality". Implicating the learning of English in "postethnicity," he contrasts with it the use of African languages, which, he implies, carry the "wellsprings of ethnic identification" (Phillipson 1999: 104). In common with the mainstream of the language rights and language endangerment literature, he assumes that English currently represents the greatest threat to 'indigenous' languages in Africa.

Such arguments have exerted a significant impact upon a world awakened to the very real threats posed by environmental degradation in the form of global warming and species loss. Thus, Bradley and Bradley (2002: xii) contend, "The globalisation of English and the spread of other national languages are not so different from the spread of new genetically modified plant varieties controlled by multinational companies". Such assertions, in which the role of "other national languages" goes unanalysed tend to assign fault to English, under the rubric of linguistic imperialism (see section 4.2.3.), while largely ignoring the far more significant opposite trend. Given the importance of this issue, the lack of an empirical approach to substantiating claims is all the more regrettable.

4.1. Underlying assumptions of the language endangerment paradigm

The claims of the relation of English spread to language endangerment rely on a number of contradictory claims:

1) English is an "elite lingua franca" in Asia and Africa (Phillipson 1992);
2) "indigenous" peoples are marginalized and powerless (Phillipson 1999; Skutnabb-Kangas 2000; Nettle and Romaine 2000);
3) yet, somehow they are shifting, not to local lingua francas and national languages, but to English – the language of the powerful and privileged.

Such arguments, including those found in Nettle and Romaine, also involve an ideologically-driven conflation of language endangerment and the thesis of 'linguistic imperialism' to which it is closely conceptually linked. Specifically,

1) The overgeneralisation that "peripheral rural communities" are home to "traditional languages" and "traditional peoples" (Nettle and Romaine 2000). The postcolonial rural environment reflects not the *pre*colonial, but the *colonial*, past, and thus does not perpetuate a language ecology rooted in *tradition* but in *recent history*.
2) Though they claim that rural populations constitute "the stewards of most cultural and linguistic diversity," rural areas and their inhabitants are not the isolated regions, and thus safe havens for indigenous languages, that Nettle and Romaine (2000) conceive them to be. Given the urban-rural continuum rather than divide that characterises the majority of "postcolonial" African and Asian contexts, rural areas are inextricably linked to urban through continuous patterns of migration, bringing languages into constant contact, as evidenced by the spread of urban vernaculars to rural areas (Makoni, Brutt-Griffler, and Mashiri 2007; McLaughlin 2001).
3) Despite their claim that English poses a threat to endangered languages in Africa via its "top-down displacement of numerous other tongues," those languages actually have, in general, no institutional representation (of the kind referenced in "top-down displacement"). Their disappearance, therefore, has nothing to do with such processes, which would rather concern the status of the large local or 'indigenous' languages that are not endangered.

4.1.2. Language endangerment: the empirical evidence

The empirical evidence for the hypothesis that English spread is a causal factor in language endangerment globally is thin. According to *Ethnologue*, the source for Nettle and Romaine's statistical analysis of language endangerment, 50 % of languages that might disappear in the next century by their estimate have fewer than 10,000 speakers each. The speakers of those approximately 3000 languages combined account for some 0.1 % of the world's population. These statistics actually serve to demonstrate the lack of relation of the spread of English as a world language to language endangerment, since the latter has nothing to do with the bilingual proficiency of 99.9 % of the world's population. Even if we took the higher figure of a language needing 100,000 speakers to be considered safe, and that, by that count, 82 % of the world's languages are endangered, that would still mean that language endangerment would have nothing to do with the bilingual competency of 94 % of the world's population who do not speak any of those languages. Granting the very tentative and approximate nature of these statistics, there is no hard statistical evidence that the spread of English is endangering the languages of the world.

To substantiate such a hypothesis would require evidence that English is spreading as a national language – that monolingual speakers of English are appearing on a large scale throughout the world. On the contrary, what is emerging from any investigation of the question is that speakers are shifting to local, 'indigenous' dominant languages, often languages of wider communication, not world/international languages.

Though much of the scholarship on language loss makes a facile equation between 'dominant' and European languages (cf. Mufwene 2004), an analysis of the world's largest languages show that 'locally dominant' is very unlikely to be a European language outside Europe. Table 4 shows the distribution of the world's largest languages – those with 10 million or more speakers.

Table 2 The distribution of the world's largest languages, in millions

	Total	European	Non-European
100 million or more:	10	4	6
50–100	12	3	9
10–50	43	8	35
Total	65	15	50

(*Ethnologue*)

In addition, of the nearly 200 languages with between 1 and 10 million speakers, around 85 % are non-European, depending on how one classifies 'European' and what counts as a 'language' versus a 'dialect' (Ethnolgue)

The political narrative of language endangerment/linguistic imperialism suggests, if it does not positively assert, that "halting the spread" of English, as Phillipson (2003) puts it, should serve to safeguard the world's smaller languages. On the contrary, as Mufwene (2002) has remarked, "We should not overrate the importance of European languages has regarding language endangerment" (Mufwene 2002: 17). There is a dearth of evidence that the 4 percent of the world's population classified as 'indigenous' that speaks 60 % of the world's languages held to be endangered are shifting to monolingual English speakers anywhere outside the principal English-speaking nations.

A case in point is South Africa, often cited as a model of progressive language policy for its 11 official languages. None of those languages are, however, endangered. On the contrary, they all have more than 1 million speakers, putting them among the 5 % of the world's largest languages. On the other hand, *Ethnologue* lists some 24 other languages spoken in South Africa, 15 of which are indigenous. Some, like Xiri, are listed as "nearly extinct." Their speakers, however, are shifting not to English, but to other African languages. As one expert notes, "One of the main reasons [for their pending extinction] is that bilingual Khoisan speakers shift to the dominant language of the area and stop teaching their mother tongue to their children" (The Khoisan Language-Family,http://www.nvtc.gov/lotw/months/september/khoisan.html). Ironically, then, the erosion of Khoisan languages is, if anything, accelerated by the institutional representation of dominant local languages – just the opposite of what Nettle and Romaine assert.

4.1.3. English and language endangerment in Europe

The same point is evident from an examination of the language map of Europe, where the necessity for language policy posed by the creation and expansion of the European Union has precipitated a spirited debate on the role of English (cf. Ammon 2006). At the centre of the anti-English opposition has been, once again, the linguistic imperialism/language rights paradigm, spearheaded by Robert Phillipson (2003). His sequel to the influential *Linguistic Imperialism* (1992) is the just as ominously titled *English-only in Europe?* In this book, Phillipson (2003) renews the attack on the dangers of English spread: failure to "halt the spread of English" might result in language attrition and "a loss of cultural vitality" (Phillipson 2003: 200). While it is not clear what Phillipson means by the phrase "loss of cultural vitality" the question of a "threat to other languages" is much more susceptible of investigation. Insofar as linguists consider having a large base of native speakers ensures the vitality of any language, Europe's languages can only come under threat from English to the degree that it erodes their base of native speakers. To date, English has not appeared in the European Commission's annual survey as a mother tongue in any EU nation outside the

UK and Ireland (European Commission 2005). In reality, this is a moot point. Every European national language belongs to the top 5 % of languages whose future is deemed secure by even the most pessimistic analysis (Ethnologue).

Moreover, EU unification has created the opportunity for greater language diversity. As the European Commission report (2005) on "Europeans and Languages" attests, "due to the free movement of labour and the possibility to study in another Member State, in most of the countries there are people of other EU nationalities speaking another EU language as their mother tongue"(European Commission report 2005: 3). So minority languages in Europe – in another EC report termed 'languages with kin states' (e.g., German in Poland) – are under no threat either (Research Centre on Multilingualism 2005). Given basic demographic realities driving immigration, the same is true with languages of non-European origin. In fact, both the number of languages present in Europe and the number of speakers of diverse languages is increasing – at least compared to its totals over the last few centuries. By those measures – which are not at all insignificant – globalisation is intensifying linguistic diversity in Europe.

If, therefore, English (or for that matter any other 'big' national language) is threatening any languages in Europe, it is only those minority languages that the EC report on "Regional and minority languages in the new Member States" classifies as "stateless" or "unique" languages – those that nowhere have an associated state in which they serve as a national language (Research Centre on Multilingualism 2005). The report lists 22 such languages in Europe, with numbers of speakers ranging from several million to fewer than 1000. Of these, seven have more than 1 million speakers, placing them among the most spoken 5–6 % of the world's languages, and another four have between half a million and one million speakers – all regarded as having secure futures. Three languages are either extinct or are so near extinction already that English can hardly be said to matter to their future. That leaves four languages with between 100,000 and 500,000 speakers, and 5 with between 10,000 and 100,000, all of whose futures remain in considerable doubt, according to the team of experts from the European Commission, all of which are threatened by other national languages than English.

4.1.4. *English and language endangerment: some conclusions*

Where English is 'endangering' languages is only thereby, perforce, where it is spoken as a 'national' language (the US, UK, Australia, New Zealand, and perhaps a few exceptional areas with idiosyncratic histories like Papua New Guinea) – but not in Africa, in Asia, in Latin America, and not even in Europe outside the British Isles and Ireland. The threat posed by English spread to indigenous languages, then, turns out to be an issue 'internal' to that handful of countries, not places to which English is spreading as a second language or lingua franca.

Thus, though the global spread of English is said to be displacing indigenous languages, destroying language and cultural ecologies, even threatening biodiversity, if not life on the planet, it is not, ironically, English as a world language but national languages, would-be national languages, or other locally dominant languages that are displacing the world's rapidly disappearing languages. Statements such as Nettle and Romaine's assertion that "Many smaller languages are dying out due to the spread of a few world languages such as English, French, Chinese, and so on" turn out be misleading. Part of the confusion is terminological, for where these languages are implicated in language death it is precisely not as world languages, but as national languages. Given the small number of nations in which these large languages are thus prime culprits in language endangerment, the focus on the teaching of them as foreign languages as the source of the problem is misplaced.

Indeed, much of the actual language endangerment has remained almost invisible to linguists because of the political categories in which they frame the issue. The language endangerment paradigm presumes that the two primary sociolinguistic forces driving language shift are those of the linguistic/cultural imperialism of exogenous origin (see section 4.2.3.) and the ethnic impulse of indigenous origin. Absent the former, and thereby left to itself, it reasons, the latter must prevail. The assumption that, for example, the peoples of Africa are uniformly, or even primarily, concerned with preserving ethnic affiliations through the use and promotion of language boundaries that mark ethnicity fails to capture the actual sociolinguistic dynamic. Rather, the southern African context in particular features:

- closely related – partially or even fully mutually intelligible – languages within a southern African regional language continuum rather than an ecology of independent systems;
- a situation in which precolonial identities have been reconstructed to the point that their reconstitution is impossible, while neither colonial ethnic identities tied to cultural imperialist and colonialist agendas (Ranger 1989) nor the postcolonial nation-state's attempt to superimpose a unified identity exert a particularly strong hold;
- a sociopolitical crisis of government and a concomitant (or, perhaps, precipitating) economic collapse has pushed basic survival strategies to the forefront of everyday experience. Further aggravating the endemic problems is the perception, or the reality – as in much of the global South – that urban location provides a privileged socioeconomic status – one that the recent urban removals enforced by Zimbabwe's Mugabe regime has made even more precarious.

In the complex realities of a nation in which the state has resorted to mass scale urban removals, many people in the region's cities are increasingly opting to use urban vernaculars, an amalgam of one or more African language and English (Makoni, Brutt-Griffler and Mashiri 2007). To reductively attribute the sprinkling of English lexis and, less often, structural elements within the emerging languages or existing languages to a language from indigenous to dominant misses the significance of the process at work. First, that overstates and overvalues the actual influence of English on indigenous languages, subsuming even cases in which English influence is non-existent or minimal under the category of English dominance and encroachment. Such an approach in effect trivialises the 'indigenous' languages said to be the objects of preservation efforts, since it downplays differences among them in comparison to their overarching distinctness from 'exogenous' languages – as we find in the use of the notion of African languages in Nettle and Romaine (2000) and in Phillipson (1999). To say that language shift from one 'indigenous' African language to another which is lexically and structurally English-influenced amounts to a shift from an indigenous language to English would be akin to arguing that English is really linguistically subsumed under the French that exerted an enormous impact on it – certainly far greater than that of English on African languages. Speakers of English-influenced vernaculars in Africa are no more anglophone than English speakers are francophone. Such arguments seem to construct the object of language preservationism in terms of maintaining (an impossible and nonexistent) indigenous purity rather than variety, as though the real object were to protect indigenous languages from contamination (cf. Mufwene 2002). In such terms, those speakers who shift to vernaculars are already lost to cultural purity, and so are really no longer indigenous at all, a self-contradictory argument which, if anything, only points to the reductionist nature of the categories employed.

When the complexities of the sociolinguistic contexts in which language endangerment is taking place are restored, the neat and tidy political narrative of language endangerment gives way. There is little empirical evidence of the much-trumpeted global threat to languages from English, a notion that serves, instead, to camouflage the encroachment of national and locally dominant languages, together with those conveying urban identity in parts of the postcolonial world. The lack of representation of an evidenced-based assessment of such forces underscores the degree to which the field of Foreign Language Teaching (FLT) has become politicised over the last decade and a half, beginning with the assertion of its culpability in what a coherent and highly visible group of critics call 'cultural and linguistic imperialism'.

4.2. History of the term 'cultural imperialism'

Indeed, the notion of cultural imperialism has become so integral a part of the discourse of the field of applied linguistics that its etymology and underlying assumptions are seldom examined. The term 'imperialism' in its modern usage emerged in the late nineteenth and early twentieth centuries as a description by British liberal opponents of colonialism of the underlying economic purposes of the partitions of Africa and Asia among the European powers. Economists mapped the geography of the production of colonial-produced raw materials that fed the unprecedented buildup of manufacturing in the major industrialised economies in Europe and North America. Their understanding was adopted by Lenin, who added a political dimension that described the system as the apotheosis of capitalism (Lenin 1916), the term thereafter being most commonly associated with Marxian or quasi-Marxian political economy. This association was made all the closer by the accession to effective power over the colonial empires of labour and social democratic parties in the major European powers, as such parties dropped their opposition to the suzerainty of the vast majority of Asia and Africa. On the other side, as anti-colonial movements emerged they seized on the theory of imperialism to buttress the revolutionary content of their struggle. The notion of an anti-imperialist struggle was central to the process of decolonisation by means of both political settlements and armed struggle.

The notion that a distinct and fundamental cultural purpose underlay colonialism arose in the 1960s and 1970s, that is, after most of the historical process of decolonisation was complete. The notion grew, in part, out of the study of US media penetration into much of the world with a message favourable to US political interests. This critique tapped into the opposition engendered by the rapid infiltration of American (and other Western) material culture and the political outlook it seemed to support throughout much of the 'developing world' Despite the colonising role of Western Europe and the US, the 'first world' was able to successfully promote the image of a disinterested, perhaps even altruistic, promoter of economic development, democratisation, and social progress in the parts of the world it had so recently despotically oppressed. Latin American commentators, in particular, attacked the 'media imperialism' that facilitated such goals. The idea proved attractive in newly postcolonial societies in which public opinion was often seen to be effectively manipulated externally, as opposed to being responsive to the sorts of internal processes at work in the major industrialised nations.

At the same time, issues of 'Westernisation' ran much deeper in postcolonial societies subject to what political theorists like Frantz Fanon saw as deep divisions between 'traditional' rural areas and 'Westernised' urban populations (Fanon 1963). Though the latter can be traced to pragmatic accommodations by imperial regimes, the cultural implications were recognised as potentially profound. For some, they portended the destruction of indigenous culture under the irresistible force of the Western. More than simply 'media imperialism' aimed at very particular political goals, theorists began to conceive this process as 'cultural imperialism'. Gienow-Hecht (2002) writes:

> In this interpretation, 'culture' suggests a natural and static heritage of traditions that are akin to a certain country. It also serves as a tool of social control as important as controlling material resources. Hence, cultural imperialism implies the efforts of one country to undermine another country's cultural heritage by imposing its own.

4.2.2. *Critics of the theory of cultural imperialism*

As used by most of its critics, 'cultural imperialism' was meant to denote not just the 'attempt' to dominate. It presupposed the 'accomplishment' of that goal. Indeed, cultural imperialism suggests that, as in the paradigm underlying received understandings of the development of the world economy, Western industrial interests built the global economic system in its own image, so too had they constructed the modern world culturally. Modernity, as such, becomes essentially a product of Western agency in which the rest of the globe figures as recipient of economic and political structures, ideas, science, technology and culture. Opponents of the theory noted the remarkably similar conclusions to which both critics and champions of Western culture arrived: the unquestioned dominance of the West. They noted too that the notion of cultural imperialism employed a binary of the determining and the determined. The remarkably simplistic notion of cultural transfer could not stand up to close scrutiny. Appiah characterises the theory's assumptions cogently: "Talk of cultural imperialism 'structuring the consciousnesses' of those in the periphery treats people [...] as blank slates on which global capitalism's moving finger writes its message, leaving behind another cultural automaton as it moves on." To critics like him, therefore, "It is deeply condescending" (Appiah 2006: 3).

Indeed, the theory of cultural imperialism denies that the colonised "can decide for themselves what they do and do not approve of" (Appiah 2006: 3). Affected by a sort of ideological "false consciousness" – termed 'hegemony' – which makes the victims of cultural imperialism virtually oblivious to the replacement of their autonomous indigenous with Western cultures, so much so that they may act as its agents and champions, the peoples of the postcolonial world are often not the best judges of what they should want or what is best for them. Instead, those who claim to be guardians of their interests are those who remain free from cultural imperialism by virtue of their participation in the very global structures responsible for it. If, then, the notion of cultural imperialism too arose in the West, like the culture that colonialism sought to spread, it is free from the taint of that origin. Ironically, such a notion depends on a conception of precisely the sorts of cultural universals that the theory of cultural imperialism precludes.

Far from admitting such universals, the theory of cultural imperialism posits that certain ideas belong to certain cultures and can only be destructive of others. This cultural essentialism precludes the usefulness of ideas originating in one culture to another, the possibility that, as Appiah (2006) puts it, other cultures can "adapt products to suit their own needs" (Appiah 2006: 4). And yet, paradoxically, the very process of decolonisation that produced, in its turn, the critique of cultural imperialism was a perfect example of just such creative adaptation. As Appiah notes, "It's no accident that the West's fiercest adversaries among other societies tend to come from among the most Westernised of the group" (Appiah 2006: 5). He adds, "In fact, one way that people sometimes respond to the onslaught of ideas from the West is to turn them against their originators" (Appiah 2006: 5). These contradictions in the theory of cultural imperialism led to refinements that attempted to sharpen the analytically blunt instrument by conceiving processes of *transculturation* that sought "to circumvent the simplistic active-passive, dominator-victim dualism" (Gienow-Hecht 2002).

4.2.3. Linguistic imperialism *as a form of cultural imperialism*

The version that emerged in applied linguistics as 'linguistic imperialism' however, essentially reproduced the older notion of cultural imperialism, and linguistic analysis has in general remained considerably less nuanced than that in other social sciences (see Brutt-Griffler and Davies 2006). Much of the literature on linguistic imperialism tends to reproduce the determined/determining binaries. Thus Nettle and Romaine divide the world into the 'traditional' (indigenous) and the modern (Western); they unconsciously divide humanity into *we* and *they*:

> An elimination of the linguistic diversity on such a massive scale would do the evolution of the human mind a great disservice. Thousands of languages have arrived at quite different, but equally valid, analyses of the world; there is much to learn from these languages, if *we* only knew about *them* and understood *them*.

In the same way, they dichotomise 'current ways of thinking' in the West – which they also contrast to what they refer to as "Western scientific knowledge" with the "quite different, but equally valid, analyses of the world" that "thousands of languages have arrived at" (Nettle and Romaine 2000: 70). The implication is clear: Western languages and cultures claim ownership over science, and indigenous languages "quite different [...] analyses of the world." Ironically, if anything embodies 'cultural imperialism' it would seem to be the 'appropriation' of the products of human thought as Western achievements. To give but one example to the contrary, where would science be without mathematics, and where would the latter be without the concept of zero and the system of algebra, both, as indicated by the words English uses for them, transmitted into European culture from Arab? Is the concept of zero, which made its way into European cultures and languages from the Arabic, forever an exogenous notion, the product of "quite different analyses of the world"? Is science ever reducible to culture – the universal to the particular?

Moreover, advocates of the notion of linguistic imperialism tend to express themselves in sweepingly categorical terms. Phillipson (2003), for instance, writes: "the advance of English, while serving the cause of international communication relatively well, and bringing success to its users, can represent a threat to other languages and cultures." He warns that, "English has acquired a narcotic power in many parts of the world, an addiction that has long-term consequences that are far from clear." And he thus cites approvingly "language policy measures introduced in France, Poland, Hungary, and Sweden to halt the advance of English" as "an attempt to manage a threatening condition through applying various types of preventive action, and sanction" (Phillipson 2003: 200).

Given the opaqueness of his discussion, it is unclear what Phillipson means by English representing a threat to "other languages and cultures." It could be interpreted as a quasi-chauvinistic argument – that knowing a foreign language redounds negatively on the 'native' culture.

To be sure, the opposite argument can just as easily be made: cultural vitality in, say, Europe is strengthened by the growing knowledge of other languages – currently according to Eurobarometer, more than half of Europeans can converse in at least two languages, a figure that reaches almost 70 % of young Europeans (European Commission 2005: 5). Phillipson, an advocate of multilingualism, would surely agree. Paradoxically, such arguments as to the threat of FLT seem to vanish when the language in question is not English. Hence, the dangers are not those of FLT in general, then, but English in particular. In this he is far from unusual. The explanation for the current political climate in applied linguistics that manifests itself as a tendency to extol the teaching of all languages other than English results from ideological trends that have exerted a large impact on the field in recent decades. Adherents of such views have been successful to a degree in framing a debate in which there is a tremendous disproportion in the discussions of the threat posed by English as compared to the dearth of those devoted to the threat posed by national languages, particularly national languages outside of Europe, and virtually none of the role of urban lingua francas in Africa.

4.2.4. *Language rights*

Phillipson's (1992) explanation is that this question is not really about the cultural interests of individuals at all. It is, rather, about "cultural inequalities between English and other languages" (Phillipson 1992: 47). The argument of language rights advocates seems to be not about the rights of speakers but of languages as such (cf. Mufwene 2004). Though they use the language of human rights, they have essentially altered the classical liberal political terms in which that doctrine is couched, substituting a communitarian focus on corporate rights. It is not persons that are to be protected, but languages and cultures. Ostensibly, the latter are being protected from the encroachment of dominant languages and cultures – though in this view it is theoretically difficult to conceive how such reputedly predatory languages and cultures can act other than through their speakers, yet another contradiction inherent in this standpoint. Precisely because languages and cultures are not themselves social actors, but conceptual stand ins for their speakers, in practice they can only be insulated from the actions of their speakers. The rights of languages become the constraints on their speakers. English spread can only be "halted," as Phillipson advocates, by preventing people from learning it.

Some appear untroubled by the notion that the rights that appertain to a given individual is based on the first language they speak, since the locus of rights inhere in groups defined on the basis of language. Such investigators agree with Phillipson, Skutnabb-Kangas and others that the social good to be derived from protecting languages outweighs the constraints on individual rights. Others have objected that, because the elite cannot be prevented from having access to all languages, the brunt of such protections fall on society's disempowered. In other words, all the more in the case of a discussion taking place in English, those who engage in it are always effectively discussing the rights of others. For if left to decide the issue for themselves, speakers appear insistent on learning English. This preference has been very accurately measured for Europe. Eurobarometer 2006 shows that 68 % of Europeans identify English as one of the two "most useful" foreign languages to learn (Phillipson 1992: 30); and 77 % list English as being one of the two foreign languages children should learn (Phillipson 1992: 32–33). According to Graddol (2006) data, 60.3 % of all school students in EU are studying English. (The numbers are weighed down by English not being an appropriate foreign language for the UK and Ireland. Hence the actual numbers for the non-English speaking EU nations are above 70 % and 80 % respectively).

Europeans are far from alone in this determination. English as a world language developed not in Europe, but in the postcolonial world, and it has been imposed back on Europe. Hence, as the EU is finding today, English is not so much being chosen as forced upon Europe – and not by the Anglophone nations, but by the rest of the world, principally Asia. The vast majority of people from the global South, unlike speakers of French, Spanish, and German, face the condition that their languages will not be among the handful of those that will otherwise comprise international languages. Even more, most people in the global South live in areas that do not even have a national language, since nation-states were themselves an external imposition crossing existing linguistic and ethnic lines. The choice to speak English is thereby a pragmatic one, and may not be driven by a cultural imperialist or ideological agenda. It should occasion no surprise, and has nothing to do with cultural imperialism, if the global South should prefer to learn one language to learning many, and should prefer that that language be an external language, rather than a dominant regional language like Mandarin Chinese or Hindi, which unify other ethnic groups in opposition against them in a way that English does not.

4.3. Linguistic diversity and 'globalisation'

Political perspectives in applied linguistics also inform issues pertaining to linguistic diversity in society. The prevalent notion that linguistic (and thereby cultural) diversity is *decreasing* due to transnationalism (Nettle and Romaine 2000; Phillipson 2003; Bradley and Bradley 2002) oversimplifies the complexity of the processes underway. Such arguments rely on a very particular set of assumptions – that language diversity consists of many more or less uniform language-using communities each speaking its own language – hence, on the number of discrete languages that can be counted and recorded. What is not explained is why that conception alone describes linguistic diversity and why what Nettle and Romaine (and others) call "biolinguistic diversity" only functions in these particular conditions. Two other, perhaps equally significant, measures of linguistic diversity are increasing: the numbers of multilingual speakers – or the range of linguistic proficiencies of individual speakers – in many parts of the world and the number of languages represented in most of the large cities of the world.

A cursory glance at statistics of language use notices how significantly linguistic diversity precisely in the major English-speaking nations is actually increasing rather than decreasing, and, to a great measure, as a result of transnational migrations. Statistics from the largest such nations are particularly telling. In the United States, 10.8 million children ages 5–17 speak a language other than English at home, according to the National Centre for Education. This figure represents 20 % of all school children (National Centre for Education 2008). The distribution of bilingual speakers in the US is however uneven, as evidenced by the Census Bureau's 2004 American Community Survey. For example, in three states, Texas, New Mexico, and California, these comprise one third of the total – including more than 40 % in California. In one fifth of American states, the non-English mother tongue population comprises more than a fifth of the population, including in all of the nation's five most populous states (California, Texas, New York, Florida, and Illinois) (U.S. Census Bureau 2006). In major urban centers in the US, the school-age population is approaching or has reached a preponderance of non-English mother tongue speakers. The proportion of 5 to 17 year-olds who use a language other than English at home is 48 % in New York City, 55 % in San Francisco, 66 % in Los Angeles and 72 % in Miami. Perhaps even more revealing is the picture from a

Midwestern city like Minneapolis. Not only does 35 % of the school age population report using languages other than English at home, but the variety of the languages is itself remarkable: about one third Spanish, another one third Hmong, with the remaining one third made up of unspecified African languages (15 %), Vietnamese (3.6 %), Laotian (2.5 %), Arabic (2 %) and 26 other languages and undifferentiated language groups (Modern Language Association 2006). According to the 2000 US Census, more than 4 million children were reported as living in households in which no one over the age of 14 speaks any English (US Census Bureau 2006).

Two other English speaking countries (Canada and the UK) show an equally diverse population linguistically. The 2001 Canadian Census found that the mother tongues of 39.9 % of the population of Toronto were languages other than English and French, with the corresponding number for Vancouver coming next at 37.6 %. The census returned more than 100 different mother tongues in nationwide use (Canada 2001 Census 2006). In the United Kingdom, 9 % of students in primary and secondary schools in 2002 in England had a mother tongue other than English. A recent study reports 30 % of London schoolchildren being non-English home users, with a total of more than 300 languages represented (Baker and Eversley 2000). As immigration continues to change the demographics of the world, these numbers will grow, with demographers projecting another 150 million international migrants to the US alone by 2050. But even if global English spread were a cultural imperialist project, it could only fail. In what meaningful ways are we seeing the spread of Anglo-American culture? Is, for instance, the notion of a spirit of empirical research a specifically Anglo-American invention? Is universalism an Anglo-American cultural trait? Is the entrepreneurial spirit Anglo-American? Is the corporation a purely Anglo-American form? On the contrary, what is developing in opposition to national culture is not the dominance of a *foreign* culture, but a transnational one. And that ultimately is the most pointed threat to nationalism of all, thereby sparking the degree of opposition we see to transnationalism, including its linguistic and cultural components. National cultures, so often portrayed as a sort of social state of nature due to their association with ethnicity as the alleged primordial condition of human society, are indeed threatened by globalisation.

4.3.1. Language, nation and culture

The threat to the nation-state and the culture that is imagined to underlie it does not come from English spread. On the contrary, the obverse is true, the erosion of the nation-state (which has produced such transnational entities as the EU) is driving the spread of English as a world language. It appears that cause and effect are here conflated. Rather than a medium that spreads Anglo-American culture, English as a world language is the expression of the contradictions inherent in the construct of national culture that English is alleged to threaten. We see this most clearly, paradoxically, in the very nations which would seem to have the most to gain from the global spread of English, and so nations in which we would expect the dominance of English to be most complete: the United States, Canada, and the UK. Witness the stunning growth of multilingualism in each, introducing a cultural hybridity that destabilises the notion of Anglo-American culture.

The framework of language endangerment fails to capture the sociolinguistic realities of the world because of its flawed conceptual basis. The literature on language endangerment and language rights conceives the encroachment of dominant languages on indigenous. What goes unnoticed is that when framed in this manner the analysis makes subtle resort to the worldview of an earlier period – imperialism. So often conflated with the globalisation that marks its dissolution, imperialism was constructed on notions of space and place: the idea that certain people should speak certain languages in certain places. Languages, like the people who spoke them, were to be confined to definite geographical boundaries in the effort to uphold the national and ethnic privilege from which imperialism took root. Europe could not dominate the world without enforcing the boundaries that kept the colonised people in the colonial world, and equally the European in the imperial centres. It could not maintain its position other than by reifying an allegedly essential national and ethnic distinction between Europeans (and by extension, European languages) and the indigenous peoples (and their languages). Even the transplanted European and colonial retained their essential identity in, as it were, exile. An Englishman, for example, maintained that identity though he might have spent his whole life in India – and vice versa. Though globalisation has done much to undermine, perhaps fatally, notions of space and place, when we ask of languages, as we ask of people, "Where are you from?" we attempt to reconstruct notions of 'belonging' – that certain languages belong to certain places and to certain people (see Brutt-Griffler 2005). In other words, we conjure up the imperialist worldview that certain people should speak certain languages in certain places.

5. Contribution of applied linguistics: possible solutions

The ongoing debates on the socio-political dimension of English and foreign languages in applied linguistics have begun exploring forces of transnationalism and their impact on language, including such processes as language endangerment, cultural and linguistic imperialism, and heritage language learning. The discourse of linguistic inequalities raised concerns about the 'attrition' of some functions of 'official national languages' such as German, French, and Italian (i.e., languages of large communities) in light of English language dominance in higher education in EU institutions (see Ammon 2006; Truchot 2002). Ammon, for instance, suggests that the promotion of English in Germany might equally have an undesirable impact on the 'international standing of German' and the teaching of the language to foreigners (Ammon 2006: 324–326). Maintaining several working languages and specifying conditions under which official national languages would be used is part of his solution to a set of complex questions.

The heritage language movement that has gained momentum in recent years owes much to these debates. They helped foreground the linguistic and educational needs of a growing number of students in 'migrant' communities worldwide (Cummins 2005; de Bot and Groter 2005; Wiley 2005). It has even been suggested that heritage language education constitutes an emerging new field (Brinton, Kagan and Bauckus et al. 2008). While a consensus on the category 'heritage speaker' is lacking, the debates have called attention to the linguistic resources of the local communities. At the same time, they have reinforced the necessity of promoting students' home languages and their academic proficiency in English in schools (cf. Cummins 2005; Valdes 2004). Educators such as Cummins put forward a set of instructional and 'attitudinal strategies' to draw out and build onto such community resources. Here he advocates the need to overcome 'monolingual instructional assumptions'; instructional practice should include literacy practices that draw on bilingual strategies and make use of the L1. Instruction should help students develop "cross-linguistic transfer" and "bring their two languages into productive contact" (Cummins 2005: 588). This can be achieved with a variety of student-authored dual language books, multimedia projects and sister class projects where students from different language backgrounds collaborate. In educational contexts, heritage language education needs to develop the positive value of the home language and attend to "the messages children receive about the value and status" of their languages (Cummins 2005: 590).

This area of research has also yielded a number of research projects focusing on examining the nature of language competence among young multilingual learners and the relationship between 'dominant' and minority languages in the classroom. Brutt-Griffler and Collins' (2007) cultural ethnography in an English speaking context (US) suggests that English language education can be the basis of bilingual education. Classroom discourse analysis shows that instructional practices in the English language arts classroom incorporate students' knowledge of concepts and lexicon from their first language. It suggests the transcendence of the binary of English versus other languages in the classroom and underscores the growing reality of bilingualism (see also Rampton 2006). At the same time, bilingual students' performance can be uneven across different cultural groups. To further understand potential causes for such uneven performance, new studies point to diasporic connections and relate the role of linguistic and cultural capital that communities bring with them to their 'new' host countries. Brizić (2006), for example, offers a compelling study of immigrant children from Turkey and former Yugoslavia living in Austria showing the additional challenges among the children whose parents' L1 and L2 literacy reflects social and linguistic inequalities that are in the country of origin (Brizić 2006: 358). As such, a "fortification of the children's linguistic self-confidence in the L2 and L1" and the involvement of parents is an important factor in successful language development among bilingual learners.

Taking a step into the future, political perspectives will no doubt continue to mirror the intellectual trends that produce them. We might expect, for instance, that a strand within applied linguistics will put increasing focus on the transnational or diasporic scope and depth in order to tune into the 'differences in agentivity' among language users, learners, parents, and educators. On the other hand, from a larger societal standpoint, applied linguists continue facing the challenging task of impacting institutional language policy decisions and allocating resources to expand language education. Political perspectives here again reassert their relevance. Their proponents will continue to attempt to raise awareness about language in society and the role of language education therein; they will at times stimulate a dialogue between the profession and various governmental and legislative bodies, with the ultimate goal of exerting impact on language policy decisions and educational change.

References

Alatis, James and Carolyn A. Straehle
1997 The universe of English: Imperialism, chauvinism, and paranoia. In: Larry E. Smith and Michael L. Forman (eds.), *World Englishes 2000*, 1–20. Honolulu: University of Hawaii.

Al-Batal, Mahmoud
2007 Arabic and national language educational policy. *Modern Language Journal* 91: 268–271.

Ammon, Ulrich
2006 Language conflicts in the European Union. *International Journal of Applied Linguistics* 16: 319–338.

Appiah, Kwame Anthony
2006 The case for contamination. *The New York Times*, January 1: 1–6.

Ashcroft, Bill, Gareth Griffiths and Helen Tiffin
1989 *The Empire Writes Back*. London: Routledge.

Baker, Philip and John Eversley (eds.)
2000 *Multilingual Capital*. London: Battlebridge.

Bisong, Joseph
1995 Language choice and cultural imperialism: A Nigerian perspective. *ELT Journal* 49: 122–132.

Blake, Robert and Claire Kramsch
2007 Guest editors' introduction. *Modern Language Journal* 91: 247–249.
Blommaert, Jan
2008 Multi-everything London. *Journal of Language, Identity, and Education* 7: 81–89.
Bolton, Kingsley
2003 *Chinese Englishes: A Sociolinguistic History*. Cambridge: Cambridge University Press.
Bradley, David and Maya Bradley (eds.)
2002 *Language Endangerment and Language Maintenance*. London: Routledge.
Brinton, Donna M., Olga Kagan and Susan Bauckus (eds.)
2008 *Heritage Language Education: A New Field Emerging*. New York: Routledge.
Brizić, Katharina
2006 The secret life of languages. Origin-specific differences in L1/L2 acquisition by immigrant children. *The International Journal of Applied Linguistics* 16: 340–362.
Brutt-Griffler, Janina
2002 *World English. A Study of its Development*. Clevedon: Multilingual Matters Press.
Brutt-Griffler, Janina
2005 Globalisation and applied linguistics: Postimperial questions of identity and the construction of applied linguistics discourse. *International Journal of Applied Linguistics 15* (1): 113–115.
Brutt-Griffler, Janina and James Collins
2007 English as a multilingual subject: Theoretical and research perspectives. In: Viv Ellis, Carol Fox and Brian Street (eds.), *Rethinking English in Schools*, 158–173. London/New York: Continuum International Publishing Group.
Brutt-Griffler, Janina and Catherine Evans Davies (eds.)
2006 *English and Ethnicity*. New York, NY: Palgrave Macmillan Ltd.
Burleigh, James
2004 English to be spoken by half the world's population within 10 years. *Independent*, December 9.
Butler, Susan (ed.)
1981 *The Macquarie Dictionary*. Sydney: Macquarie Dictionary Company Limited.
Byrnes, Heidi
2002 Toward academic-level foreign language abilities: Reconsidering foundational assumptions, expanding pedagogical options. In: Betty Lou Leaver and Boris Shekhtman (eds.), *Developing Professional-Level Language Proficiency*, 34–58. Cambridge: Cambridge University Press.
Council of Europe
2001 *Common European Framework of Reference for Languages: Learning, Teaching, Assessment*. Cambridge: Cambridge University Press.
Cummins, Jim
2005 A proposal for action: Strategies for recognizing heritage language competence as a learning resource within the mainstream classroom. *The Modern Language Journal* 89: 585–592.

De Bot, Kees and Durk Gorter
2005 A European perspective on heritage languages. *The Modern Language Journal* 89: 612–616.
Donato, Richard and Richard G. Tucker
2007 K-12 language learning and foreign language educational policy: A school-based perspective. *The Modern Language Journal* 91: 256–258.
Fanon, Frantz
1963 *The Wretched of the Earth*. Transl. Constance Farrington. New York: Grove Weidenfeld.
Gienow-Hecht, Jessica C. E.
2002 Cultural imperialism. In: Alexander DeConde, Richard D. Burns and Fredrik Logwall (eds.), *Encyclopedia of American Foreign Policy* 1, 397–408. New York: Scribner.
Graddol, David
2000 *The Future of English* [digital edition updated from 1997 version] British Council http://www.britishcouncil.org/learning-elt-future.pdf.
Graddol, D
2006 *English Next.* http://www.britishcouncil.org/learning-research-english-next.pdf.
House, Juliane
2002 Developing pragmatic competence in English as a lingua franca. In: Karlfried Knapp and Christiane Meierkord (eds.), *Lingua Franca Communication*, 245–269. Frankfurt a. M.: Lang.
Jenkins, Jennifer
2000 *The Phonology of English as an International Language*. Oxford: Oxford University Press.
Jenkins, Jennifer
2007 *English as a Lingua Franca: Attitude and Identity.* Oxford: Oxford University Press.
Joseph, E. John
2006 *Language and Politics*. Edinburgh: Edinburgh University Press.
Kachru, Braj B.
1985 Standards, codification, and sociolinguistic realism: The English language in the outer circle. In: Randolph Quirk and Henry G. Widdowson (eds.), *English in the World: Teaching and Learning the Language and Literatures*, 11–30. Cambridge: Cambridge University Press.
Kachru, Braj B.
1996 The paradigms of marginality. *World Englishes* 15: 241–255.
Kontra, Miklos, Robert Phillipson, Tove Skutnabb-Kangas and Tibor Varady (eds.)
1999 *Language: A Right and a Resource. Approaching Linguistic Human Rights.* Budapest: Central European University Press.
Lenin, Vladimir
1917 *The Highest Stage of Capitalism*. Petrograd: Zhzn i Znaniye Publishers.
Little, David
2007 The Common European Framework of Reference for Languages: Perspectives on the making of supranational language education policy. *The Modern Language Journal* 91: 645–653.

Makoni, Sinfree, Janina Brutt-Griffler and Pedzisai Mashiri
2007 The use of "indigenous" and urban vernaculars in Zimbabwe. *Language in Society* 36: 25–49.
Manley, Michael
1991 *The Poverty of Nations*. London: Pluto Press.
Mauranen, Anna
2003 The corpus of English as a lingua franca in academic settings. *TESOL Quarterly* 37 (3): 513–527.
Mazrui, Alamin M.
2004 *English in Africa: After the Cold War*. Clevedon: Multilingual Matters Press.
McLaughlin, Fiona
2001 Dakar Wolf and the configuration of an urban identity. *Journal of African Cultural Studies* 14: 153–172.
McFalls, Joseph A.
2003 Population: A lively introduction. *Population Bulletin* 58 (4): 3–39.
Mufwene, Salikoko S.
2002 Colonisation, globalisation, and the future of languages in the twenty-first century. *International Journal on Multicultural Societies* 4: 165–197.
Mufwene, Salikoko S.
2004 Language birth and death. *Annual Review of Anthropology* 33: 201–222.
National Center for Education
2008 http://nces.ed.gov/programs/coe/2008/section1/indicator07.asp.
Nettle, Daniel and Suzanne Romaine
2000 *Vanishing Voices: The Extinction of the World's Languages*. New York: Oxford University Press.
Phillipson, Robert
1992 *Linguistic Imperialism*. Oxford: Oxford University Press.
Phillipson, Robert
1999 Political science. In: Joshua Fishman (ed.), *Language and Ethnic Identity*, 94–108. New York: Oxford University Press.
Phillipson, Robert
2003 *English-only Europe? Challenging Language Policy*. London: Routledge.
Phillipson, Robert and Tove Skutnabb-Kangas
1986 *Linguicism Rules in Education*. Roskilde: Institute VI, Roskilde University Centre (3 volumes).
Pratt, Mary L.
2003 Building a new public idea about language. *Profession 2003*: 110–119.
Price, Glanville (ed.)
2000 *Languages in Britain and Ireland*. New York: Blackwell.
Pölzl, Ulrike and Barbara Seidlhofer
2006 In and on their own terms: The "habitat factor" in English as a lingua franca interactions. *International Journal of the Sociology of Language* 177 (1): 151–176.
Rampton, Ben
2006 *Language in Late Modernity: Interaction in an Urban School*. Cambridge: Cambridge University Press.

Ranger, Terence
1989 The invention of tradition in colonial Africa. In: Eric Hobswbwan and Terence Ranger (eds.), *The Invention of Tradition*, 211–262. Cambridge: Cambridge University Press.

Ridge, Stanley
2002 English, ideology and need. Plenary at AILA. Applied Linguistics in the 21st Century: Opportunities and creativity. 13th World Congress of Applied Linguistics. 16–21 December 2001, Singapore.

Saville-Troike, Muriel
2003 *The Ethnography of Communication: An Introduction*. 3rd edition. Malden, MA: Blackwell.

Seidlhofer, Barbara
2001 Closing a conceptual gap: The case for a description of English as a lingua franca. *International Journal of Applied Linguistics* 11: 133–158.

Seidlhofer, Barbara
2004 Research perspectives on teaching English as a lingua franca. *Annual Review of Applied Linguistics* 24: 209–239.

Seidlhofer, Barbara, Angelika Breiteneder and Marie-Luise Pitzl
2006 English as a lingua franca in Europe: Challenges for applied linguistics. *Annual Review of Applied Linguistics* 26: 3–34.

Skutnabb-Kangas, Tove
1988 Multilingualism and the education of minority children. In: Tove Skutnabb-Kangas and Jim Cummins (eds.), *Minority Education: From Shame to Struggle*, 9–44. Clevedon: Multilingual Matters. First published in Phillipson and Skutnabb-Kangas 1986: 42–72.

Skutnabb-Kangas, Tove
2000 *Linguistic Genocide in Education – Or Worldwide Diversity and Human Rights?* Mahwah/London: Lawrence Erlbaum Associates.

Skutnabb-Kangas, Tove
2004 Do not cut my tongue, let me live and die with my language. *The Journal of Language Identity and Education* 3: 127–134.

Smith, Larry E.
1976 English as an international auxiliary language. *RELC Journal* 7: 38–43.

Smith, Larry E.
1987 *Discourse Across Cultures: Strategies in World Englishes*. New York: Prentice Hall.

Tollefson, James
2007 Scholarship and activism on language. *Language Research Bulletin* 22, ICU, Tokyo.

Truchot, Claude
2002 *Key Aspects of the Use of English in Europe*. Strasbourg: Language Policy Division, Council of Europe. Retrieved March 3, 2008, from http://www.coe.int/T/E/Cultural_Cooperation/education/Languages/Language_Policy/Policy_development_activities/Studies/TruchotEN.pdf.

Wastiau-Schlüter, Patricia (ed.)
2005 Foreign language learning: A European priority. Eurydice in Brief. Brussels. Retrieved March 3, 2008, from http://www.eurydice.org/Documents/Eurydice_en_bref/EN/4_pages_languae_EN.pdf.

Widdowson, Henry G.
1994 The ownership of English. *TESOL Quarterly* 28: 377–381.
Wiley, Terrence G.
2005 The reemergence of heritage and community language policy in the U.S. national spotlight. *The Modern Language Journal* 89: 594–601.
Valdes, Guadalupe
2004 Between support and marginalization: The development of academic language in linguistic minority children. In: Janina Brutt-Griffler and Manka M. Varghese (eds.), *Bilingualism and Language Pedagogy*, 10–40. Clevedon: Multilingual Matters.

Recommended readings

Berns, Margie, Kees de Bot and Uwe Hasebrink
2007 *In the Presence of English. Media and European Youth*. New York: Springer.
Canagarajah, Suresh
1999 *Resisting Linguistic Imperialism in English Teaching*. Oxford: Oxford University Press.
Crystal, David
2000 *Language Death*. New York: Cambridge University Press.
Duchene Alexandre and Monica Heller
2007 *Discourses of Endangerment: Interest and Ideology in the Defense of Languages*. London: Continuum.
Edwards, Viv
2004 *Multilingualism in the English-Speaking World: Pedigree of Nations*. Malden, MA: Blackwell.
Gnutzmann, Claus and Frauke Intemann (eds.)
2005 *The Globalisation of English and the English Language Classroom*. Tübingen: Narr.
Joseph, E. John
2006 *Language and Politics*. Edinburgh: Edinburgh University Press.
Pennycook, Alistair
1998 *English and the Discourses of Colonialism*. London: Routledge.
Pennycook, Alistair
2001 *Critical Applied Linguistics: A Critical Introduction*. Mahwah, NJ: Lawrence Erlbaum.
Seidlhofer, Barbara (ed.)
2003 *Controversies in Applied Linguistics*. Oxford: Oxford University Press.
Simpson, Andrew
2008 *Language and National Identity in Africa*. Oxford: Oxford University Press.
Widdowson, Henry G.
2003 *Defining Issues in English Language Teaching*. Oxford: Oxford University Press.
Wright, Sue
2004 *Language Policy and Language Planning*. New York: Palgrave.

11. The cognitive perspective: Age effects and/or critical periods?

Jean-Marc Dewaele

1. Introduction

There is a strong feeling among multilinguals that age of onset of acquisition (AoA) of an additional language is a crucial factor in ultimate performance in that language. Testimonies like the following one by a quadrilingual (English L1, German L2, French L3, Korean L4) are quite frequent in the database on multilingualism and emotions filled out by more than 1500 participants (Dewaele and Pavlenko 2001–2003): "I'm always more comfortable communicating in English. I think I started with German too late to really ever feel satisfied with my communicative competence even though I've lived in Germany for 5 years."

The participant who started learning German at the age of 15 links her perceived deficit in German to her late AoA. She sees this deficit as something permanent that no amount of authentic interactions in German will overcome.

Is there actually hard scientific evidence underlying this widespread belief that a later AoA hinders ultimate attainment? Is there a point in life from which it becomes quasi impossible to reach full competence in an additional language? Few topics in applied linguistics have attracted as much sustained attention. The critical period hypothesis (CPH) is traced back to the book *Speech and Brain-Mechanisms* published in 1959 by the neurologists Penfield and Roberts. The term "critical period" (CP) was coined by Lenneberg in 1967 in his book *Biological Foundations of Language*. The basic idea is that children lose the cerebral flexibility to learn languages from mere exposure to the language after puberty. Foreign language learning is still possible after puberty, but they have to be "taught and learned through a conscious and laboured effort" (Lenneberg 1967: 176). Lenneberg does not make explicit claims about the possibility of successful naturalistic acquisition of the L2 after puberty. The debate has been raging ever since on the validity of the hypothesis, the definition of the term "critical period", its possible causes and its effects in the foreign language. The wealth of research on the CPH illustrates the fascination of the scientific community for the neurobiological substrate of language learning and ultimate attainment. Several contributions and edited volumes on the topic have been published recently (Abello-Contesse et al. 2006; García Mayo and García Lecumberri 2003; Indefrey and Gullberg 2006; Muñoz 2006; Singleton and Ryan 2004). The implications of the findings are massive outside the academic field.

Parents, teachers and politicians need to know whether children can benefit from early exposure to a foreign language. Proficiency in a foreign language confers not only an intellectual edge to the learner but it is also an important economical advantage, as multilingualism, or, more cynically, proficiency in the new lingua franca, English, becomes an essential commodity in the global marketplace.

The common view that 'younger is better' in learning a foreign language has led to the introduction of early foreign language teaching in Italy, Spain, France, Germany, Ireland and Scotland. No such unanimity exists within the applied linguistic community, with some authors claiming that "the idea of a critical period specifically for language development may well have had its day" (Singleton and Ryan 2004: 227). Others have pointed out that we need to look at the evidence without pre-conceptions: "the mere fact that an idea is popular among lay-people does not mean that is has to be wrong either" (DeKeyser 2006).

The present chapter will present an overview of a selection of some of the most famous and the more recent findings on age effects and the CPH within the "core" field of linguistics (i.e. grammar, morphosyntax, syntax, phonology) as well as in contiguous research areas (cognitive psychology, social psychology, neurolinguistics, neuroanatomy) that considered the effect of AoA on foreign language anxiety, attitudes, language choice for the expression of emotions, physiological reactions to verbal stimuli, language choice for complex cognitive operations, laterality, and the physical shape of the brain. Inevitably, some studies straddle across categories.

In the next section some controversial issues in CPH research will be discussed including issues of causes and effects, and of measurement, counterevidence for the CPH, and AoA and rate of foreign language learning. Future perspectives for research on CPH will be presented in the final section, with a call for epistemological and methodological diversity and the constitution of international interdisciplinary AoA networks.

A notorious difficulty in reviewing studies on the CPH lies in the decision to label a particular work either as 'pro' or 'contra' CPH. Results are often inconclusive and could be interpreted either way, depending on the researcher's perspective. Rather than classifying the literature in black or white terms, we have preferred to present the research along a continuum: at one end, studies that claim to have evidence of a critical period, on the other end, studies that report age effects, but not necessarily in line with the strict interpretation of the CPH. As age ranges by which participants are categorised as 'early/young' or 'late/older' vary considerably in the literature, we will specify the exact age ranges. Finally, a distinction is usually made between L2 learners, bilinguals and/or multilinguals and bilingual and/or multilingual learners. The term 'learner' refers to any individual acquiring a new language: the L2 learner is acquiring a second language, the bilingual and/or multilingual learner is acquiring an additional language (third, fourth, fifth ..., see also Hufeisen/Jessner, Ch. 12, this time). When authors use the term 'bilingual/multilingual', they typically focus on individuals who are typically no longer actively learning an L2, but have become legitimate L2 users (cf. Cook 2002).

2. State of the art

Excellent critical overviews of the research on the CPH can be found in DeKeyser and Larson-Hall (2005) and Hyltenstam and Abrahamsson (2003), who defend the existence of the CPH, and in Birdsong (2004, 2005, 2006), who is much more critical of the CPH. The present overview does not claim to be exhaustive but it will focus more on some of the latest developments in the field.

2.1. AoA and grammar

The seminal works on the CPH date from the late 1970s and the 1980s. Most of these studies showed that a low AoA is linked to higher scores on grammaticality judgment tasks (Harley 1986; Patkowski 1980). One of the most widely cited (and most often replicated) works in CPH research is the study by Johnson and Newport (1989). The authors used oral grammaticality judgement tests with 46 Korean and Chinese learners of English, all of whom had lived in the United States for 5 years or more. About half of the participants had arrived in the US at age 16 or younger, the others had immigrated at a later age. Separate correlation analyses of AoA with test scores on 276 short sentences representing 12 basic grammar structures in English were performed for both groups. A strong AoA effect emerged when all participants were considered (a correlation of $r = -.77$ between AoA and L2 test scores): in other words, a decline in scores with increasing AoA. Separate analyses on the groups of younger and older arrivals revealed a very strong negative correlation AoA and L2 proficiency in the young group ($r = -.87$) but a non-significant negative relationship emerged in the group of late arrivals ($r = -.16$) (Johnson and Newport 1989: 79).

Johnson (1992) replicated the previous study with the same participants, using a written format. The patterns that emerged were very similar to those obtained with orally presented stimuli, even though correlations between AoA and test scores were slightly lower than in the previous study ($r = -.54$ for the complete sample; $r= -.73$ for those who arrived at age 16 or younger).

A comparable picture emerged from a study by Johnson and Newport (1991) on the link between AoA and oral grammaticality judgements concerning subjacency in L2 English among 21 native speakers of Chinese with a first exposure to English ranging from ages 4 to 38. Those who had arrived before adulthood obtained significantly better scores ($r = -.63$).

DeKeyser (2000) replicated the Johnson and Newport (1989) study with a sample of 57 Hungarian-speaking immigrants who had resided for at least 10 years in the US. Age of arrival ranged between 1 and 40. A strong negative correlation (r = –.63) was found between AoA and score on the grammaticality judgement test which the author interprets as a clear indication that "early age confers an absolute, not a statistical, advantage – that is, there may very well be no exceptions to the age effect. Somewhere between the ages of 6–7 and 16–17, everybody loses the mental equipment required for the implicit induction of the abstract patterns underlying a human language, and the critical period really deserves its name" (2000: 518).

McDonald (2000) found strong AoA effects in a study on early L2 learners of English (14 Spanish and 14 Vietnamese L1 speakers who moved to the US at or before age 5) who all scored significantly higher on grammaticality judgement tasks than late L2 learners (10 Vietnamese L1 speakers who moved to the US between the ages of 6 and 10 and 14 Spanish speakers who arrived in the US after the age of 14)[1]. Most participants were undergraduate students. The native Spanish early learners' scores were not significantly different from those of a native English control group (n = 14). However, the native Vietnamese early learners performed less well on the grammaticality judgement task than the native English speakers. McDonald concludes that "native language appeared to make a difference for early acquirers, whereas a later age of acquisition caused a more general problem" (2000: 395). McDonald notes that there is a continuous linear increase with AoA in the problems language learners have in decoding surface structure. She argues that older learners may lack memory capacity to decode all but the simplest types of structures (2000: 417).

McDonald pursued this line of enquiry in a 2006 study with late 50 L2 learners of heterogeneous linguistic backgrounds (age of arrival: 12 and over) who rated their current English usage as superior to the current usage of their L1. These L2 learners and a control group of 50 English native speakers (all were undergraduate students) performed measures of English working memory, decoding, speed, and a grammaticality judgement task. Compared to the control group, the late L2 learners scored lower on all measures. Arrival age was found to correlate with L2 judgement accuracy, even beyond the critical age. She discovered that her native speakers suffered from similar processing difficulties (albeit to a lesser degree) during grammaticality judgement in a high noise or memory stress condition. MacDonald concludes that her explanation of processing conditions is superior to the CPH in accounting for the grammatical performance of late L2 learners (2006: 398).

The study by White and Genesee (1996) is often cited as counter-evidence against the CPH. Researchers collected data through face-to-face interviews in English L2 using pictures with four AoA groups of 89 immigrant participants (0–7, 8–11, 12–15, and 16+) and a control group of 16 native speakers of English. The dependent variables were subjacency and empty category principles. The authors found that the "near-native group" among the L2 subjects in their study consisted of individuals who were "virtually indistinguishable" from native speakers "both in terms of their accuracy and their speed", i.e. who have attained a "native-like" or ultimate L2 proficiency (1996: 258). Although admitting that there are age-related effects on L2 proficiency in that younger learners are generally more likely to achieve near-native proficiency than older learners, White and Genesee determined that of 31 of their L2 subjects who started learning English as adults (i.e. whose initial age of exposure to the L2 was 16+) almost one third achieved native-like proficiency ratings (1996: 259).

A similarly critical perspective towards the CPH can be found in Birdsong and Molis (2001) who used the same grammaticality judgement tests as in the Newport and Johnson study. Birdsong and Molis' participants were Spanish natives in the US. A non-significant correlation was found between AoA and L2 performance in the group of early arrivals (age 16 and younger) because this subgroup performed at ceiling. In contrast, the performance of late arrivals was significantly negatively correlated with AoA. In a meta-analysis of the CPH literature on morphosyntax and pronunciation, Birdsong (2005) concluded that in all analyses of pooled data from early and late arrivals, AoA effects persist indefinitely across the span of surveyed AoA (i.e., there is no cut-off point). He further observed that in analyses of disaggregated samples significant AoA effects emerge for late learners, suggesting a postmaturational decline in attainment. Finally, he notes that AoA effects are inconsistent in studies who focused on early-arrival data alone. Thus, instead of the critical age of acquisition factor, other factors such as frequency of target language use need to be taken into account. Bialystok and Miller (1999) had already argued that AoA affects proficiency "through all ages tested rather than defining a point of critical period" (1999: 127). Factors such as the relation between the two languages and the syntactic structure being tested are more crucial for language proficiency than the critical age factor (Bialystok and Miller 1999: 144).

DeKeyser and Larson-Hall (2005), in their critical analysis of the Birdsong and Molis (2001) study, argue that the strong AoA effect in the older group might be linked to a very short length of residence of some members, "which means their test results were not representative of ultimate attainment" (2005: 90). The high correlation in the older group in the study by Birdsong and Molis (2001) could be due to the presence of two outliers, i.e. two of the five oldest members of the groups had very low scores (DeKeyser and Larson-Hall 2005: 90). DeKeyser and Larson-Hall (2005) also refuse to regard the evidence presented by White and Genesee as a refutation of the CPH. They argue that if no significant correlation was found between AoA and performance, it is because "not much correlation with any variable can be expected in a group that, by definition, can show almost no variation" (2005: 95).

Studies linked to the Barcelona Age Factor project (BAF) (and thus tutored Second Language Acquisition (SLA)), focussing on grammaticality judgements, have reported that earlier exposure (ages 8–9) to English L3 in a classroom did not result in better performance but that length of exposure to English had a positive effect on performance (García Mayo 2003; Muñoz 2006). Researchers looked at age effects on the rate of acquisition and "ultimate attainment" among Catalan-Spanish native speakers who were learners of English in a school context. One cohort of participants started learning English in primary school at the age of 8, a second group started in secondary education at age 11, a third group started at age 14 and a fourth group started after the age of 18 (Muñoz 2006). Data were collected three times from the first two groups and two times for the older groups. Comparisons could thus be made between participants of the same age, excluding cognitive maturity effects. The first group was tested at the ages of 10; 9, 12; 9 and 16; 9. The second group was tested at ages 12; 9, 14; 9 and 17; 9. The third group was tested a ages 15; 9 and 19; 1. The fourth group was tested at ages 28; 9 and 31; 4 (Muñoz 2006: 15). The general findings are that older starters progress more quickly but that after a similar number of hours of exposure (i.e. 200 hours at time 1, 416 hours at time 2 and 726 hours at time 3) (Muñoz 2006: 15), the differences between the groups are usually limited, with older starters having a slight advantage. Exposure needs to be intense to have any effect, and AoA "seems to be more relevant for skills that can be acquired implicitly, whereas age at learning can be seen as a factor explaining the rate of learning of most skills" (Muñoz 2006: 34). The group of instructed learners who started learning at age 8–9 had a significant weaker performance than the group who started at age 11–12.

In sum, the literature seems to suggest that there are consistent age effects for grammaticality judgment tasks in situations of untutored acquisition. However, not all the findings conform to a strict interpretation of the CPH: the AoA at which L2 learners start to deviate from L1 control groups in grammatical judgement varies considerably, AoA effects have been found beyond the CP and some late learners attain native-like performance.

2.2. AoA and phonology

Research on the effect of CP on phonological variables has been abundant and many studies report consistent and significant AoA effects, and even a CP. Scovel (2006) reviewed his own work and other recent research on AoA and foreign accent and concludes that there is a biologically-based critical period "which makes it virtually impossible for anyone acquiring a second language after about the age of twelve to speak that new language without a foreign accent" (2006: 43). Scovel, as we see, leaves the door open for possible exceptions to the CPH in phonology by using the word "virtually".

The classic studies that reported findings supporting the CPH in phonology date from the mid-seventies. Seliger, Krashen and Ladefoged (1975) used self-reports on pronunciation from immigrants to the US and Israel asking them whether they would be viewed as native in their English or Hebrew. More than 80 % of those who had arrived in the country before the age of 10 believed they could pass for native speakers, while only 7 % of participants who arrived at the age of 16 or older claimed to be native-like.

In support of the CPH are also the studies by Oyama (1976, 1978) who analysed the accents of 60 Italian immigrants to the US using a reading task and spontaneous speech. The participants' AoA ranged from 6 to 20 years. Pronunciation error rates correlated highly with AoA after length of residence had been partialed out. Patkowski (1980) replicated this design using a spontaneous speech task with 67 immigrants from various backgrounds and found a significant negative correlation between AoA and accent rating. A similar picture emerged from the study of Flege, Munro and MacKay (1995) who looked at accents in sentence production by 240 Italian immigrants to Canada with a minimum of 15 years of residence in Ontario. Age of arrival accounted for 60 % of the variance. Ioup and Tansomboom's (1987) study confirmed the effect of AoA on the acquisition of Thai tone by children and adult native speakers of English. While the children did well, the adults performed poorly. Using a similar design, Tsukada et al. (2005) found significant age effects in the production and perception of English vowels by 72 native Korean learners of English. Native Korean adults and children differing in length of residence in North America were compared to age-matched native English speakers. The native Korean children were found to discriminate English vowels more accurately than native Korean adults but their scores hovered below those of the native English children. Acoustic analyses also showed that native Korean children produced significantly larger between-vowel contrasts in a picture-naming task than native Korean adults but differed from age-matched native speakers.

However, a number of researchers have found evidence of native-like pronunciation among older L2 learners, which they interpret as counter-evidence for the CPH.

Bongaerts et al. (1997) studied spontaneous speech samples and reading aloud from 22 Dutch native speakers learning English and 5 native British English speakers. Native British English speakers rated each participant's speech for accent. Results showed that the 10 learners of English could not be distinguished from native speakers despite the fact that their AoA began at age 12, which the authors interpret as evidence that older L2 learners can attain native-like pronunciation. A similar study was conducted by Abu-Rabia and Kehat (2004) who question the CPH hypothesis after presenting the case of 10 successful late-starters of Hebrew who attained a native-like pronunciation. In a design similar to that used by Bongaerts et al. (1997), Muñoz and Singleton

(2007) analysed the accent of 12 advanced late L2 learners of English (Spanish and/or Catalan as L1) with an average AoA of 22.5 and an average length of residence of 10 years, plus a native-speaker control group. Native speakers of English judged the accents of participants retelling a film extract. While a significant difference emerged between native speakers and L2 learners in terms of foreign accent ratings, two of the learners scored within the native-speaker range, thus "beating" the CP (2007: 187). The authors do note that these two learners did stand out from the others: they were the youngest at time of testing and had English as their home language.

Flege et al. (2006) designed a longitudinal study of 1.2 years to evaluate the influence of AoA (adult vs. child) and length of residence in an L2-speaking country (3 vs. 5 years) on degree of foreign accent in English L2. Participants were Korean adults and children living in the US, and age-matched groups of native English adults and children. Native speaker listeners rated the sentences by the immigrants for overall degree of perceived foreign accent. The native Korean children received significantly higher ratings than the native Korean adults did, but lower ratings than the native English children. The native Korean children spoke English with detectable foreign accents, even those who had arrived at a young age and had been enrolled in English-medium schools for an average of 4 years. No significant differences emerged for the native Korean children and adults between the start and the end of the research period. Length of residence was not significantly correlated with the ratings. The authors argue that their findings are inconsistent with the hypothesis that adult-child differences in L2 speech learning are due to the passing of a CP. They suggest that the children's milder foreign accents could be due to the greater L2 input typically received by immigrant children than adults.

A similar research design was used by Munro and Mann (2005) to examine the link between AoA (ranging from age 3 to 16) and the degree of perceived accent in the speech of 32 native speakers of Mandarin who learned English as an L2. A group of native speakers of English rated speech samples of variable length and linguistic context (single words, sentences, short paragraph, and self-generated picture narration). The authors failed to find a cut-off point in the AoA that could be interpreted as a CP. Accentedness deviated from ratings by native speakers in a highly linear manner with AoA. These deviations began at an AoA of about 5, with some participants bottoming out with an AoA of 7, whereas ratings close to those of native speakers were given to others whose AoA was greater than 5.

Fullana (2006), a phonological study linked to the BAF project, showed that older classroom starters (ages 11 and 14, and adult beginners) performed significantly better than younger starters (age 8) in discrimination of English vowels and consonant contrasts. This confirms earlier findings reported by García Lecumberri and Gallardo (2003) based on a sample of three groups of 20 Basque-

Spanish bilingual children who had started learning English at school at age 4, 8 and 11. Older starters were found to be significantly better at discriminating sounds, vowels and consonants. They also scored higher on intelligibility and lower on foreign accent. In a follow-up study, Gallardo and García Lecumberri (2006) looked at the effect of AoA on phoneme perception in the L3 English of 30 primary and secondary students from the Basque country. The students' AoA for English was 4, 8 and 11, they all had had 560 hours of exposure to English, and their age at testing was 10, 13 and 16. Onset ages 4 and 8 did not make a difference in performance but those who started at age 11 did obtain better results. The authors do point to the potential effect of age at testing, and the difference in cognitive development. They conclude that, contrary to the CPH, the early starters in a formal learning environment, i.e. before the fixing of phonetic categories at age 5 or 6, did not seem to have had an advantage in the medium term.

Scovel (2006) reflects on the interpretation of findings that seem to support the existence of a CP for phonology in untutored acquisition and the decision to introduce foreign language classes very early. He insists that "the existence of a critical period for the ability to sound like a native speaker does *not* imply, [...] that the best time to initiate foreign language instruction is childhood" (2006: 43). Scovel attacks "the folk belief in 'the earlier the better' in foreign language education" arguing that "even if accentless speech were the only goal of these language programs, exposure to a new language before puberty is a necessary but insufficient criterion for growing up into a successful bilingual" (2006: 43–44).

In sum, age effects seem particularly strong in the acquisition of L2 phonology in untutored contexts. However, the fact that some exceptional late L2 learners reach native speaker levels has been interpreted by some researchers as evidence against the CPH. Also, there seems to be some evidence that in tutored L2-acquisition older starters can achieve a more native-like pronunciation than younger ones.

2.3. AoA and proficiency

A similar rather mixed picture emerges if one looks into the overall range of L2-proficiency reached by L2-starters of different ages. Trofimovich and Baker (2006) analysed variation in the production of five suprasegmentals (stress timing, peak alignment, speech rate, pause frequency, and pause duration) in six English declarative sentences by 30 adult Korean learners of English and 10 adult native English speakers. The learners' AoA (range: 17.5–33 years) was found to be significantly linked to the learners' L2 speech rate, duration and frequency of pausing. Participants who arrived in the US in their early twenties produced L2 speech at a faster rate and with fewer pauses and hesitations than participants who arrived in their late twenties and early thirties. However, AoA was not linked to their accentedness in English L2.

Harris (2004) looked at self-perceived proficiency in English L2 of 52 immigrants of Spanish-speaking origin as a background variable in her study on variation in electrodermal activity by using skin resistance measurement when participants were exposed to emotion terms in the L1 and L2 (see below, Chap. 2.4). She found that early age of arrival in the US was a better predictor of increased English proficiency and decreased Spanish proficiency than either age of significant exposure or length of stay. Age of arrival was strongly negatively correlated with self-rated proficiency in English and positively correlated with decreased proficiency in Spanish (2004: 231).

Dewaele and Pavlenko (2001–2003) developed a web questionnaire to investigate self-reports on bilingualism and emotion in different languages from a wide range of participants. It contained a question on AoA in their different languages, allowing this information to be used as an independent variable in a series of studies, as well as self-reported proficiency levels in different languages. One of studies to come out of this project is Dewaele (2007a) where variation in self-perceived oral proficiency ratings of 475 English L2 users were analysed. Early starters (i.e. those who started between birth and age 2, and those who started between age 3 and 12 either in tutored or untutored conditions) were found to rate their oral proficiency in English significantly higher than participants who started learning English after age 12. There was a linear decrease in self-reported proficiency across the AoA groups. A larger-scale study on 1459 multilinguals revealed that AoA was one of the significant predictors of self-perceived oral proficiency in the L2, the L3, the L4 but not the L5 (Dewaele 2006a).

Hakuta, Bialystok, and Wiley (2003) used self-reported proficiency data from Chinese and Spanish immigrants in the 1990 US census to test the CPH. The authors tested two models: one that assumed that 15 is the critical age, another that assumed the critical age was 20. They predicted a sharp drop in self-reported proficiency at either point. However, they did not find a discontinuity in their data; instead, they found that success in SLA steadily declines throughout life spans. However, the Hakuta, Bialystok and Wiley (2003) study has been strongly criticised on methodological grounds (DeKeyser and Larson-Hall 2005; Stevens 2004). The original authors acknowledge some of the methodological limitations of their 2003 study but argue that additional analyses addressing these concerns did not uncover additional evidence in support of the CPH (Wiley, Bialystok and Hakuta 2005).

Another often cited 'anti-CP' study is Ioup et al. (1994) based on data from two adult native speakers of English learning Egyptian Arabic. The first participant of the study, Julie, was first exposed to the acquisition of Egyptian Arabic in a naturalistic setting as an adult and had subsequently become highly fluent in it. The second participant, Laura, had received formal training and had also attained a high level of proficiency. Eight out of a panel of 13 native speakers identified the two participants as native speakers of Egyptian Arabic. Julie,

Laura and a control group of 11 Egyptian Arabic native speakers were asked to discriminate among regional Arabic dialects. While Julie and Laura achieved 100 % accuracy in this task, two Egyptian Arabic native speakers scored only 85 % on this task. Laura performed less well on a discrimination task of regional Egyptian dialects but Julie scored close to the native speakers. Both Julie and Laura scored like native speakers on a translation task and a grammaticality judgement task. Laura (but not Julie) experienced more difficulties in a sentence interpretation task. The authors conclude that both Julie and Laura could pass for native speakers of Egyptian Arabic. They suggest that the ultimate proficiency in L2 depends more on the manner of acquisition (formal or naturalistic) than the initial AoA but also that linguistic competence of an L2 speaker is interwoven with such factors as individual linguistic aptitude and talent. More specifically, the authors hypothesise an explicit positive link between aptitude and proficiency scorings whereby successful learners scoring high in terms of auditory, linguistic or memory ability will generally find themselves "at the high end of a proficiency continuum" (1994: 76).

Hirsh et al. (2003) considered the role of AoA in picture naming with a group of 40 L2 users (Spanish L1, English L2), who had started learning the L2 at school at the age of 10) and a group of 33 English monolinguals. The Spaniards were students spending a year in Cardiff as part of the Socrates scheme. Speed of picture naming in a given language was predicted by AoA for that language, that is, L2 values predicted L2 performance for the Spaniards and L1 values predicted L1 performance for the monolinguals. The researchers note that: "no matter what one's language background is, monolingual or bilingual, a crucial determinant of naming times in English is the age at which those word forms were learnt in English. […] AoA effects are more likely to be due to the relative order in which items are acquired within a language" (2003: 124). The authors underline that AoA is an important factor in speech production regardless of whether the words were learned during the CP. The strong, independent effect of AoA of the L2 is interpreted as evidence that the point at which one acquires a word in an L2 can influence one's speech production performance in that L2. The authors conclude that "any theory of the mechanism through which age of acquisition takes its effects must not rely on a critical period" (2003: 125).

Two further studies from Spanish researchers reported that younger starters in English L2 classes lagged behind older starters. Cenoz (2003) analysed oral and written proficiency measures based on data from the REAL group (Research in English Applied Linguistics – University of the Basque Country). She reports that after a similar number of hours of exposure (600 hours) the older starters outperform the younger ones in most measures of proficiency, with the exception of the mechanics of writing (2003: 86). Muñoz (2006) analysed data from six different AoA groups in the BAF project and also found significantly higher morphological accuracy rates for older starters.

In sum, the patterns that emerge from the research suggest age effects on measures of proficiency in untutored L2 learning. Researchers showing late learners performing at native speaker level argue that these exceptions refute the CPH. This interpretation is rejected by DeKeyser and Larson-Hall (2005) who warn against generalisations of limited findings. The patterns for AoA and phonological variables from the BAF project are comparable to the ones reported previously for other variables gathered within the same project, namely that older starters perform better than younger starters.

2.4. AoA and affective variables

A number of studies have investigated the effect of AoA on variables linked to foreign language anxiety, attitudes, emotions and physiological reactions to verbal stimuli.

AoA has been considered as an independent variable in a series of studies by the cognitive psychologist Cathy Harris and her colleagues. Harris (2004) used electrodermal monitoring (i.e. fingertip electrodes) to compare reactivity for emotion words and emotional expressions in the L1 and the L2 of 31 early Spanish-English bilinguals who had grown up in the US and learnt English before the age of 7, and 21 late Spanish-English bilinguals who were first exposed to English during middle childhood (ages 13+). The early bilinguals showed stronger reactions to both Spanish and English taboo words. No such difference was obtained for the late bilinguals, which suggests that AoA of the L2 modulate speakers' physiological reaction to emotional language. Harris, Gleason and Ayçiçegi (2006) observed that if the L2 is acquired in early childhood, and to greater proficiency than L1, it will be experienced as more, or equally emotional to L1. Although this could be interpreted as support for the CPH, the authors themselves do not attribute the difference to AoA but rather to the emotional contexts of learning (Harris, Gleason and Ayçiçegi 2006: 277). A language is experienced as emotional when it is acquired and used in an emotional context, which is typically the case for early learning and less so for late learning or instructed learning.

In a series of studies on the communication of emotion in multilinguals' different languages, we have attempted to measure the effect of multiple independent variables linked to participants' linguistic history (including AoA), sociobiographical and psychological characteristics on language choice, perception of languages and proficiency, and foreign language anxiety. Dewaele (2004a) focused on language choice for swearing among 1039 multilinguals in up to five languages. AoA was found to be significantly linked to language preference for swearing in the L2: early acquirers of the L2 reported swearing more in that language. No AoA effect emerged in the L3, the L4, nor the L5. A similar pattern emerged for perceived emotional force of swear words and taboo words in the languages of the same participants (Dewaele (2004b). Early acquirers of the L2 judged swear words and taboo words in that language to be stronger. The relationship weakened and then vanished in the languages learnt later (2004b: 218). Dewaele (2006b) uncovered similar patterns for the language choice for the expression of anger. Early starters used the L3 significantly more frequently to express anger in five different situations compared to those who started learning later. The pattern remained significant in 3 out of 5 situations for the L4 and 2 out of 5 for the L2 (2006a: 138).

Dewaele, Petrides and Furnham (2008) focused on communicative/foreign language anxiety in a sub-sample of 464 multilinguals. Ratings were collected on a 5-point Likert scale for communicative anxiety in the first language, and foreign language anxiety in the L2, L3, and L4 in five different situations (speaking with friends, colleagues, strangers, on the phone, and in public). Strong AoA effects emerged for the L2 and L3, with early starters reporting lower levels of foreign language than late starters. The relationship looks like a inverted stretched "L", with those who started learning the L2 and L3 between birth and age 2 scoring higher on the foreign language anxiety scale than the next group with an AOA ranging between 3 and 7. A steady increase was observed across the older AoA groups, with the oldest AOA group (25+) reporting the highest levels of foreign language anxiety in the L2 and L3. The effect was typically stronger in more stressful situations (telephone conversations and public speech).

Cenoz (2003) included attitudes towards English L3 and motivation to learn English in her research design. The group of primary school starters were found to score significantly higher on both dimensions compared to two group high school starters. In other words, younger starters liked English more and were more motivated to learn it. However, Tragant (2006), who selected 759 instructed learners from the pool of participants in the BAF project, found that a smaller proportion of early starters answered "yes" to the question whether they liked learning English.

In sum, the general trend in research on AoA and affective variables shows a link between an early start in a foreign language and stronger emotional bonds with that language (including lower levels of foreign language anxiety).

2.5. AoA and cognitive processes: mental calculation

Dewaele (2007b) looked at the effect of different independent variables, including AoA, on frequency of a particular language choice for mental calculation in the population of 1454 multilinguals reported earlier. A significant link was found between the dependent variable and AoA in the L2 and in the L3 but not in the L4 and L5. Those who had started learning their L2 and L3 earlier were more likely to use that language for mental calculation. We speculated that if a language is around at the time that mental calculation is being learnt, the probability of it being involved in this cognitive operation is higher. Family members communicating with children in another language than the school language may, for example, rehearse timetables with them in both the L1 and the L2. Once the skill of mental calculation has been acquired, and can be performed in the L1 – or the L2, it is unlikely to be radically affected by the L3, when that language appears on the curriculum, typically in secondary education. It is possible that AoA is not necessarily the immediate neurobiological cause of the effect discovered on frequency of choice of the L2 for mental calculation, but rather an indirect effect, linked to environmental factors (Dewaele, 2007b).

2.6. AoA and the brain

Research on the effect of early and late bilingualism on the brain has become more and more sophisticated in recent years. Early research focused on laterality in the bilingual brain (Vaid and Genesee 1980). These studies exploited the contralateral sensory organisation of the brain. Research had shown that monolinguals have a right ear, or a right visual field advantage when presented with linguistic input, which suggests a greater involvement of the left hemisphere. The question was whether bilinguals would exhibit the same pattern, or whether they would use the right hemisphere more in language processing. Vaid and Genesee (1980) proposed an integrative model of bilingual laterisalisation in which they included language acquisitional factors, such as AoA. They assumed that early bilinguals (having mastered the L1 and L2 in similar contexts before age 6) would display a hemispheric involvement similar to that of monolinguals, while late bilinguals (having mastered the L2 after age 12) would show more right hemisphere involvement. Pursuing the same research question, Vaid and Hall (1991) carried out a meta-analysis of 59 laterality studies of bilinguals. Eleven studies with monolingual control groups showed no significant differences between bilinguals and monolinguals in lateralisation. However, among bilinguals, AoA appeared to be significantly linked to lateralisation: early bilinguals were found to be less left lateralised than late bilinguals. In a first recent meta-analysis of 28 studies of bilinguals and monolinguals, Hull and Vaid (2005a) did find the expected result, i.e. that bilinguals (especially early bilinguals) were less left lateralised than monolinguals. A second meta-analysis of 69 studies comparing early and late bilinguals (Hull and Vaid 2005b) corroborated the finding of AoA: early bilinguals involved both hemispheres in language processing, whereas late bilinguals were more left lateralised. Electrophysiological research has also shown the importance of AoA in the development and functioning of neural subsystems underlying language (Hull and Vaid 2005b). However, there is no consensus in the literature on the exact causes of variation in neural activation across languages (i.e. AoA and/or proficiency levels) (Vaid 2007).

Recent research has also focused on the grey matter, a major component of the central nervous system, in the brain of bilinguals. Grey matter consists of nerve cell bodies and short nerve cell extensions and is composed of unmyelinated neurons (DeMyer 1988). Its function is to route sensory or motor stimulus to interneurons of the central nervous system for creation of response to stimulus. Hercules Poirot, the famous (fictional) bilingual Belgian detective, always proudly refers to his logical thought processes as to "his little grey cells". Recent research suggests that being bilingual, may have given Hercules an edge over his monolingual peer in the novels, Japp, the hapless Scotland Yard detective. Indeed, the early acquisition of L2 seems to be linked to structural changes in the brain. Mechelli et al. (2004) looked at 25 English-speaking monolinguals, 25 early (AoA > 5 years) bilinguals and 33 late (AoA: 10–15 years) bilinguals speakers of English and a second European language. The early bilinguals who had practised the L2 regularly since their acquisition and the late bilinguals had used the L2 regularly for at least 5 years. Voxel-based morphometry[2] revealed greater grey matter density in the left anterior parietal cortex in the bilingual group compared to the monolingual group (the difference was significant in the left hemisphere and was a trend in the right hemisphere). This particular area of the brain "has been shown by functional imaging to become activated during verbal-fluency tasks" (2004: 757). The same differences appeared between the early and the late bilinguals (significant in both hemispheres). A negative correlation was found between AoA and a proficiency measure based on reading, writing, comprehension and speaking tests in a group of 22 Italian native speakers with English as an L2 (AoA: 2–34 years). The researchers also discovered that grey-matter density correlated significantly with L2 proficiency and with AoA in exactly the same left inferior parietal region. The authors conclude that: "Early bilinguals probably acquire a second language through social experience, rather than as a result of a genetic predisposition. Our findings therefore suggest that the structure of the human brain is altered by the experience of acquiring a second language" (2004: 757). One important implication of this finding for the debate on the CPH is that early exposure to an L2 and a regular use of that L2 are linked to higher levels of proficiency, and that this superior performance is linked to a clearly identifiable neurological substrate. de Bot (2006) proposes an alternative view to Mechelli et al.'s (2004) findings, considering the monolinguals as the exception rather than the bilinguals. de Bot argues that the expansion of grey matter among bilinguals is natural given the fact that the human brain is equipped to deal with multiple languages. However, because monolinguals do not exploit this capacity, the synaptic density of the inferior parietal lobes decreases due to synaptic pruning (2006: 130).

Not all brain research into AoA uncovers significant differences between early and late bilinguals. Frenck-Mestre et al. (2005) used functional magnetic resonance imaging to investigate the network of cortical and subcortical regions that contribute to articulation in English-French bilinguals. Half of participants were bilingual from birth and half had learned French after the age of 12. Overt articulation was found to result in the bilateral activation of the motor cortex, basal ganglia and cerebellum, and also the supplementary motor area, in both English and French. The threshold and extent of the network involved in articulation was identical for the early and late bilinguals with the exception of greater variation in the left putamen for the latter group. The authors interpret their findings as an indication that AoA does not result in fundamental differences in the neural substrates that subserve language in bilinguals.

In sum, research on AoA, and possible CP effects in the bilingual brain, is as inconclusive as the research on linguistic variables. Some researchers did uncover significant age effects, others played the differences down. Given that this type of research is still in its infancy, and is typically based on small samples, its findings should be handled with caution.

3. Controversial issues in CPH research

3.1. CP: causes and effects

DeKeyser and Larson-Hall (2005) points out that it is important to have a clear definition of CP because "Far too often [...], the idea of a CP is rejected because of specific interpretations of it, rather than because of the core idea" (2005: 89). Scovel (2006: 35) makes a similar point: "SLA researchers have sometimes employed different terms with sometimes different meanings to explain the emergence of foreign accents and other constraints in SLA". DeKeyser and Larson-Hall (2005) use the relatively broad interpretation of the term proposed by Lenneberg (1967) that does not refer to the causes: (CP is) "automatic acquisition from mere exposure" that "seems to disappear after this age" (1967: 176). DeKeyser and Larson-Hall (2005) add that the young child learns implicitly through mere exposure, and that this mechanism is severely limited in older adolescents and adults (2005: 89). They emphasise that the hypothesis applies to both first and second language acquisition (SLA), and that it does not apply to rate of acquisition but rather to ultimate attainment in grammar and pronunciation. Researchers like Paradis (2004) have suggested that CP effects are caused by the decline of procedural memory for late L2 learners which forces these learners to rely on explicit learning instead: "It is the acquisition of implicit competence that is affected by age both biologically (gradual loss of plasticity of the procedural memory for language after about age 5) and cognitively (greater reliance on conscious declarative memory for learning in general and, consequently, for learning a language from about age 7)" (Paradis 2004: 59).

Paradis (2004) points out that the upper age limit varies with respect to the component of the implicit language system that is being acquired through exposure to language interaction. This is, in chronological order, prosody, phonology, morphology, and syntax (2004: 59). Since the learning of vocabulary is subserved by declarative memory, it is not susceptible to the CP (2004: 59).

All researchers agree that in SLA there are age effects, or "general age factors" (Singleton 2003), but they disagree on the existence of cut-off points (i.e. the term 'critical'), the effect of confounding variables and the exact cause of the age effects. Birdsong (2005) argues that the decline in attained L2 proficiency "is not linked to maturational milestones, but persists over the age spectrum, this is progressive loss, not decisive loss" (2005: 125). He also insists that "any number of exogeneous and endogeneous variables may come into play that can flatten the slope of decline and result in significant numbers of nativelike attainers" (2005: 125).

DeKeyser and Larson-Hall (2005) are also very careful in their defence of the CP for SLA: "There appears to be a qualitative change in language learning capacities somewhere between the age of 4 and 18 years. That still leaves the question of how this qualitative change should be characterised" (2005: 99–100). They also point out that this CP is not the only maturational effect to play a role: "individuals go through gradual physical and psychological changes of all kinds all through their life-span" (2005: 103). These changes are superimposed on the CP phenomenon "and add an extra layer of difficulty to the analysis" (2005: 103).

A final point is that, as de Bot (2008: 122) points out, "an early start does not mean that much in itself. When a language is not used after that early start, it may disappear completely".

He refers to the work of Ventureyra (2005) who found that 26 Koreans who had been adopted and moved to France between the ages of four and eight had completely lost their L1 Korean. In other words, "studying the early/late distinction can only be done when the rest of the language development history is taken into account" (2008: 122).

3.2. What would constitute counter-evidence to the CPH?

One of the burning issues in the CPH debate is the question of what constitutes counter-evidence to the CPH hypothesis (cf. Birdsong 2005; Hyltenstam and Abrahamsson 2000). Long (1990) stated that it would be enough "to produce learners who have demonstrably attained native-like proficiency despite having begun exposure well after the closure of the hypothetised sensitive periods" (1990: 274). Following this line of reasoning, researchers (Abu-Rabia and Kehat 2004; Birdsong 1992, 1999, 2003; Bongaerts 1999; Bongaerts et al. 1997; Van Boxtel, Bongaerts and Coppen 2003) have indeed come up with cases of non-native speakers who scored at native-speaker level. The proportions of non-native speakers scoring at native-speaker level are always small as well as the size of the samples. It remains to be seen whether this is indeed sufficient evidence to reject the CPH, as a majority of these already highly proficient L2 users remain below native speaker range. One major difficulty lies in determining the native language norms: which sociolect should be chosen, which variant of the language is to serve as touchstone? Is it possible to have a control group that matches the experimental group perfectly? How much attention should be paid to intra-individual variation (cf. McDonald 2000, 2006)? What do we do with the inevitable outliers (who might in fact have been bored with the test and performed below their level of competence)? If we accept that there is a 'native-speaker' range: how do we decide on the cut-off points? If these native speakers have knowledge of foreign languages, would this (even limited) multilingualism affect their grammatical intuitions in the L1? A second problem is more of an ideological nature: if we accept, as Grosjean (1989) puts it, that bilinguals are not the sum of two monolinguals, can we consequently engage in comparisons between a language which is the L2 or L3 of multilinguals with that language such as it produced by monolinguals of that language?

Researchers (e.g. Bialystok and Hakuta 1999; Birdsong 2004, 2005, 2006; Flege 1999) have argued that a distribution of end-state performance, to be consistent with the CPH, should incorporate a point of inflection, corresponding to the start of a decline in learning ability, i.e., the offset of the period of peak sensitivity. Birdsong (2006) proposes three basic patterns: firstly, a stretched L; secondly, an upside down mirror image of the stretched L, resembling a stretched "7"; and thirdly a stretched "Z" (see figure 1).

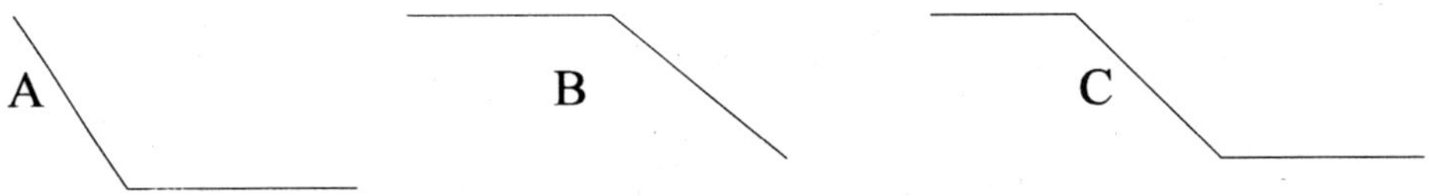

Figure 1. Three patterns of bounded age effects (from Birdsong 2006: 15)

The first pattern (A) shows an age-related decline "ceasing at a point of articulation that coincides with the end of maturation" (2006: 15). The second pattern (B) shows a flat portion where success is guaranteed, followed by a steady decline. The third pattern (C) "begins with a period of ceiling effects, followed by a decline that ceases at the end of maturation after which the age function flattens and no further age effects are seen" (2006: 16). Birdsong points out that there is evidence in the literature (DeKeyser 2000) about the left portion of pattern but that there is no evidence for the right segment of the stretched L, i.e. a flat function or floor effect, because later learners show a random array of scores or a continuous decline in performance with increasing AoA (2006: 17).

Evidence has been found for pattern B (Birdsong and Molis 2001), where the left segment represents the "window of opportunity", with scores at ceiling, followed by an unbounded decline in ultimate attainment with advancing AoA (2006: 17). Johnson and Newport (1989) claim to have found evidence of the third pattern (C). However, Birdsong argues that "the crucial flattening feature of the function, whose beginning should coincide with the end of maturation, is in fact not present in the data" (2006: 16).

3.3. AoA and rate of foreign language learning

It is also important to distinguish between AoA and rate of foreign language learning. One could wonder for example whether the organisation of the English foreign language curriculum might explain the results from the BAF project showing a faster rate of acquisition for older starters and usually a higher rate of performance compared to younger starters. Muñoz (2003) observes that if schools do not provide the amount of exposure in the L2 that children get in their L1, the natural advantage of young children for implicit learning might be lost. It is also possible that the exposure to English in the primary schools in Spain was just not of the same quality and intensity as the exposure that later starters got in secondary education. The finding of an inversed age effect, i.e. older starters performing better, might therefore be an artefact of the research design linked to the quality of English foreign language teaching in primary schools. Although all groups had had similar number of hours of instruction in English, there is no way to find out how much English was actually used by teachers, how good that English was, how much English was produced by learners, how much contact with English older starters might have had outside the classroom. Depending on the answers to these questions, the picture and conclusions might change dramatically. Ideally, to investigate the age effect, all other variables should be kept constant, especially the ones linked to exposure. DeKeyser and Larson-Hall (2005) point out that the observation 'earlier is better' typically applies to kinds of learning that are typically not provided at school. It is therefore imperative, in their view, to adapt instruction to age of the learner rather than starting to teach foreign languages at a younger age (2005: 88).

4. Future research perspectives

Research on AoA within the core applied linguistic field has been intense, fuelled by a need to take political decisions (when to introduce a foreign language at school) and by mere curiosity about the fact that AoA may be one of these crucial individual differences between learners. Methodological choices have been found to affect the outcomes of investigations into age effects: What in/dependent variables have been selected? How have they been defined? How have they been measured? How have they been statistically analysed? Have measures been compared with an L1 norm? Who constituted the L1 control group and the experimental group? What kind of language instruction did the experimental group have? How much contact did they have with the target language outside the school? How prestigious was the target language in the eyes of the learners? As Singleton (2005) pointed out, the CPH is a coat of many colours: different applied linguists have made different methodological decisions, they have been able to only partially control the independent variables in their research design, and as a consequence results are often hard to compare and interpret. One potential way forward is to form research networks where similar research designs would be adopted, comparable data would be collected from around the world and analysed and interpreted in a uniform way. Muñoz (2006) has shown that this is possible on a national scale with the BAF project. Lasagabaster and Huguet (2006) successfully applied this network idea for research on foreign language learning motivation across Europe. Such an interdisciplinary network on AoA effects would perfectly placed under the umbrella of AILA.

As we have shown, the study of AoA effects has moved to contiguous areas of research, namely cognitive psychology, neurolinguistics and neuroanatomy. The unique methodologies used by these researchers may allow them to pinpoint maturation phenomena with greater precision. Since AoA and language learning are linked to a neurological substrate, it makes perfect sense to pursue this way of enquiry with vigour, using the latest technologies. Caution is needed in interpreting the findings because, as Hagoort (2006) points out: "As everyone involved in cognitive neuroscience of language realises, it is far from trivial to relate to each other the levels of linguistic description, processing architecture, and neural hardware" (2006: 92).

That said, not only different methodologies, but also different epistemological approaches would benefit research in AoA. So far the dominant epistemological stance in AoA research has been the 'etic' perspective (i.e. a description of a behaviour according to the researcher's point of view) (Pike 1967). In other words, a participant produces language samples that are analysed in a clinical way by the researcher. The self-assessment or the opinion of the participant is irrelevant in this etic perspective. A different approach can be adopted where the researcher aims at producing an 'emic' account of behaviour, i.e. a focus on the participant's point of view. In AoA research this would imply an elicitation of judgements on participant's past linguistic experiences and descriptions of habitual linguistic behaviour, including affect and emotion (a small number of studies have been carried out in this perspective, including Bialystok and Hakuta 1999; Cenoz 2003; Seliger, Krashen and Ladefoged 1975).

One could finally argue that the CPH debate is basically a version of the nature versus nurture debate. Defenders of the CPH insist on the existence of maturation and its consequences on how languages are learnt and to what level of attainment. Critics of the CPH downplay the importance of maturation, reject the idea of 'critical periods', and point to a host of social factors that determine the language learning. As nature and nurture are inextricably linked (Uylings 2006), and factors interact, it is very difficult to extricate the different effects. The result is that according to one's beliefs in the matter, one can argue that the glass is half full or half empty. Researchers love to show that a different interpretation of the data of a colleague could lead to a different conclusion (Bialystok 2002; Birdsong 2005; DeKeyser 2005), or that the existence of confounding variables or methodological problems might explain the results.

To conclude, it is important to point out that early exposure is only one in a long list of independent variables that affect ultimate success as a multilingual. Factors such as motivation, quality of the input, amount of authentic interactions in the foreign language have a much stronger effect on ultimate attainment. It may therefore seem excessive to completely overhaul language teaching programmes by introducing foreign languages at a younger age (cf. Scovel 2006). The evidence suggests that an earlier exposure is insufficient in itself. There is an additional potentially vicious side-effect, as happened in the United Kingdom in 2002, namely that to 'compensate' for the earlier introduction of foreign languages, 14- to 16-year-old students were allowed to drop foreign languages from their curriculum. This resulted in a massive drop of students taking foreign languages. The result could be catastrophic for the UK: if the result of the earlier exposure is similar to that obtained in Spain, and if language instruction stops at puberty, generations of schoolchildren will leave school without even a basic competence in a foreign language. This is surely not what applied linguists, working in good faith on extremely complex issues, had intended.

Notes

1 The author considers that arrival age is generally comparable to AoA.
2 This technique compares "the density or volume of gray or white matter in stereotactically normalised structural MRI (Magnetic Resonance Imaging) brain images" (Green, Crinion and Price 2006: 108–109).

References

Abello-Contesse, Christian, Rubén Chacon-Beltran, Maria Dolores Lopez-Jiménez and Maria Mar Torreblanca-Lopez (eds.)
2006 *Age in L2 Acquisition and Teaching.* Bern: Peter Lang.

Abu-Rabia, Salim and Simona Kehat
2004 The Critical Period for second language pronunciation: Is there such a thing? Ten case studies of late starters who attained a native-like Hebrew accent. *Educational Psychology* 24: 77–98.

Bialystok, Ellen
2002 On the reliability of robustness: A reply to DeKeyser. *Studies in Second Language Acquisition* 24: 481–488.

Bialystok, Ellen and Kenji Hakuta
1999 Confounded age: Linguistic and cognitive factors in age differences for second language acquisition. In: David Birdsong (ed.), *Second Language Acquisition and the Critical Period Hypothesis*, 161–181. Mahwah, NJ: Erlbaum.

Bialystok, Ellen and Barry Miller
1999 The problem of age in second language acquisition: influences from language, structure, and task. *Bilingualism: Language and Cognition* 2 (2): 127–145.

Birdsong, David
1992 Ultimate attainment in second language acquisition. *Language* 68: 706–755.

Birdsong, David
1999 Introduction: Whys and why nots of the Critical Period Hypothesis for second language acquisition. In: David Birdsong (ed.), *Second Language Acquisition and the Critical Period Hypothesis*, 1–22. Mahwah, NJ: Erlbaum.

Birdsong, David
2003 Authenticité de prononciation en français L2 chez des apprenants tardifs anglophones: Analyses segmentales et globales. *Acquisition et Interaction en Langue Etrangère* 18: 17–36.

Birdsong, David
2004 Second language acquisition and ultimate attainment. In: Alan Davies and Catherine Elder (eds.), *Handbook of Applied Linguistics*, 82–105. London: Blackwell.

Birdsong, David
2005 Interpreting age effects in second language acquisition. In: Judith F. Kroll and Annette M. D. de Groot (eds.), *Handbook of Bilingualism: Psycholinguistic Approaches*, 109–127. Oxford: Oxford University Press.

Birdsong, David
2006 Age and second language acquisition and processing: A selective overview. *Language Learning* 56 (1): 9–49.

Birdsong, David and Michelle Molis
2001 On the evidence for maturational constraints in second-language acquisition. *Journal of Memory and Language* 44 (2): 235–249.

Bongaerts, Theo
1999 Ultimate attainment in foreign language pronunciation: The case of very advanced late foreign language learners. In: David Birdsong (ed.), *Second Language Acquisition and the Critical Period Hypothesis*, 133–159. Mahwah, NJ: Erlbaum.

Bongaerts, Theo, Chantal Van Summeren, Brigitte Planken and Erik Schils
1997 Age and ultimate attainment in the pronunciation of a foreign language. *Studies in Second Language Acquisition* 19: 447–465.

Cenoz, Jasone
2003 The influence of age on the acquisition of English: General proficiency, attitudes and code-mixing. In: Maria Pilar García Mayo and Maria Luisa García Lecumberri (eds.), *Age and the Acquisition of English as a Foreign Language*, 77–93. Clevedon: Multilingual Matters.

Chandler, Paul M.
2006 Critical period or language learning difficulties: Are there two types of adult foreign language learners? In: Abello-Contesse, Chacon-Beltran, Lopez-Jiménez and Torreblanca-Lopez (eds.), 59–77.

Cook, Vivian
2002 Background to the L2 user. In: Vivian Cook (ed.), *Portraits of the L2 User*, 1–28. Clevedon: Multilingual Matters.

de Bot, Kees
2006 The plastic bilingual brain: Synaptic pruning or growth? Commentary on Green, et al. *Language Learning* 56 (1): 127–132.

de Bot, Kees
2008 The imaging of what in the multilingual mind? *Second Language Research* 24 (1): 111–133.

DeKeyser, Robert
2000 The robustness of critical period effects in second language acquisition. *Studies in Second Language Acquisition* 22: 499–533.

DeKeyser, Robert
2006 A critique of recent arguments against the critical period hypothesis. In: Abello-Contesse, Chacon-Beltran, Lopez-Jiménez and Torreblanca-Lopez (eds.), 49–58.

DeKeyser, Robert and Jenifer Larson-Hall
2005 What does the Critical Period really mean? In: Judith F. Kroll and Annette de Groot (eds.), *Handbook of Bilingualism: Psycholinguistic Approaches*, 88–108. Oxford: Oxford University Press.

DeMyer, William E.
1988 *Neuroanatomy*. New York: John Wiley and Sons.

Dewaele, Jean-Marc
2004a Blistering barnacles! What language do multilinguals swear in?! *Estudios de Sociolingüística* 5: 83–106.

Dewaele, Jean-Marc
2004b The emotional force of swearwords and taboo words in the speech of multilinguals. *Journal of Multilingual and Multicultural Development* 25 (2/3): 204–222.

Dewaele, Jean-Marc
2006a L'effet de variables objectives et affectives sur la maîtrise orale de multilingues adultes. *Etudes de Linguistique Appliquée* 422: 441–464.

Dewaele, Jean-Marc
2006b Expressing anger in multiple languages. In: Aneta Pavlenko (ed.), *Bilingual Minds: Emotional Experience, Expression, and Representation*, 118–151. Clevedon: Multilingual Matters.

Dewaele, Jean-Marc
2007a Interindividual variation in self-perceived oral communicative competence of English L2 users. In: E. Alcón Soler and M. P. Safont Jordà (eds.), *The*

Intercultural Speaker. Using and Acquiring English in the Foreign Language Classroom, 141–165. Berlin: Springer Verlag.

Dewaele, Jean-Marc
2007b Multilinguals' language choice for mental calculation. *Intercultural Pragmatics* 4 (3): 343–376.

Dewaele, Jean-Marc and Aneta Pavlenko
2001–2003 Web questionnaire Bilingualism and Emotions. University of London.

Dewaele, Jean-Marc, Dino Petrides and Adrian Furnham
2008 The effects of trait emotional intelligence and sociobiographical variables on communicative anxiety and foreign language anxiety among adult multilinguals: A review and empirical investigation. *Language Learning* 58 (4): 911–960.

Flege, James Emil
1999 Age of learning and second-language speech. In: David Birdsong (ed.), *Second Language Acquisition and the Critical Period Hypothesis,* 101–131. Mahwah, NJ: Erlbaum.

Flege, James Emil, Murray Munro and Ian MacKay
1995 Factors affecting degree of perceived foreign accent in a second language. *Journal of the Acoustical Society of America* 97: 3125–3134.

Flege, James Emil, David Birdsong, Ellen Bialystok, Molly Mack, Hyekyung Sung and Kimiko Tsukada
2006 Degree of foreign accent in English sentences produced by Korean children and adults. *Journal of Phonetics* 34 (2): 153–175.

Frenck-Mestre, Cheryl, Jean-Luc Anton, Muriel Roth, Jyotsna Vaid and François Viallet
2005 Articulation in early and late bilinguals' two languages: evidence from functional magnetic resonance imaging. *Neuroreport: For Rapid Communication of Neuroscience Research* 16 (7): 761–765.

Fullana, Natalia
2006 The development of English FL perception and production skills: starting age and exposure effects. In: Muñoz (ed.) 2006, 41–64.

Gallardo, Francisco and Maria Luisa García Lecumberri
2006 Age effects on single phoneme perception for learners of English as a Foreign Language. In: Abello-Contesse, Chacon-Beltran, Lopez-Jiménez and Torreblanca-Lopez (eds.), 115–131.

García Lecumberri, Maria Luisa and Francisco Gallardo
2003 English FL sounds in school learners of different age. In: Maria Pilar García Mayo and Maria Luisa García Lecumberri (eds.), *Age and the Acquisition of English as a Foreign Language*, 115–135. Clevedon: Multilingual Matters.

García Mayo, Maria Pilar
2003 Age, length of exposure and grammatically judgments in the acquisition of English as a foreign language. In: Maria Pilar García Mayo and Maria Luisa García Lecumberri (eds.), *Age and the Acquisition of English as a Foreign Language*, 94–114. Clevedon: Multilingual Matters.

Green, David, Jenny Crinion and Cathy J. Price
2006 Convergence, degeneracy and control. *Language Learning* 56 (1): 99–125.

Grosjean, François
1989 Neurolinguists, beware! The bilingual is not two monolinguals in one person. *Brain and Language* 36, 3–15.

Hagoort, Peter
2006 What we cannot learn from neuroanatomy about language learning and language processing. Commentary on Uylings. *Language Learning* 56 (1): 91–97.

Hakuta, Kenji, Ellen Bialystok and Edward Wiley
2003 Critical evidence: a test of the critical-period hypothesis for second-language acquisition. *Psychological Science* 14: 31–38.

Harley, Birgit
1986 *Age in Second Language Acquisition*. Clevedon: Multilingual Matters.

Harris, Catherine L.
2004 Bilingual speakers in the lab: Psychophysiological measures of emotional reactivity. *Journal of Multilingual and Multicultural Development* 25 (2/3): 223–247.

Harris, Catherine L., Jean B. Gleason and Ayse Ayçiçegi
2006 Why is a first language more emotional? Psychophysiological evidence from bilingual speakers. In: Aneta Pavlenko (ed.), *Bilingual Minds: Emotional Experience, Expression, and Representation*, 257–283. Clevedon: Multilingual Matters.

Hirsh, Katherine W., Catriona M. Morrison, Silvia Gaset and Eva Carnicer
2003 Age of acquisition and speech production in L2. *Bilingualism: Language and Cognition* 6 (2): 117–128.

Hyltenstam, Kenneth and Niclas Abrahamsson
2000 Who can become native-like in a second language? All, some, or none? On the maturational constraints controversy in second language acquisition. *Studia Linguistica* 54: 250–166.

Hyltenstam, Kenneth and Niclas Abrahamsson
2003 Maturational constraints in SLA. In: Catherine J. Doughty and Michael H. Long (eds.), *The Handbook of Second Language Acquisition*, 539–588. Malden, MA/Oxford, UK: Blackwell.

Hull, Rachel and Jyotsna Vaid
2005a Clearing the cobwebs from the study of bilingual brain: Converging evidence from laterality and ERP studies. In: Judith F. Kroll and Annette de Groot (eds.), *Handbook of Bilingualism: Psycholinguistic Approaches*, 480–496. Oxford: Oxford University Press.

Hull, Rachel and Jyotsna Vaid
2005b Language lateralization in bilinguals: a meta-analytic tale of two hemispheres. Unpublished ms. Rice University, cited in Vaid, Jyotsna (2007).

Indefrey, Peter and Marianne Gullberg
2006 Introduction. *Language Learning* 56 (1): 1–8.

Ioup, Georgette, Elizabeth Boustagui, Manal el Tigi and Martha Moselle
1994 Reexamining the critical period hypothesis: A case study of successful adult SLA in a naturalistic environment. *Studies in Second Language Acquisition* 16: 73–98.

Ioup, Georgette and Amara Tansomboom
1987 The acquisition of tone: a maturational perspective. In: Georgette Ioup and Steven H. Weinberger (eds.), *Interlanguage Phonology*, 333–349. Cambridge, MA: Newbury House.

Johnson, Jacqueline S. and Elissa L. Newport
1989 Critical period effects in second language learning: The influence of maturational state on the acquisition of ESL. *Cognitive Psychology* 21: 60–99.

Johnson, Jacqueline S.
1992 Critical period effects in second language acquisition: The effect of written versus auditory material on the assessment of grammatical competence. *Language Learning* 42: 217–248.

Lasagabaster, David and Angel Huguet (eds.)
2006 *Multilingualism in European Bilingual Contexts*. Clevedon: Multilingual Matters.

Lenneberg, Eric H.
1967 *Biological Foundations of Language*. New York: Wiley.

Long, Michael H.
1990 Maturational constraints on language development. *Studies in Second Language Acquisition* 12: 251–285.

McDonald, Janet L.
2000 Grammaticality judgements in a second language: Influences of age of acquisition and native language. *Applied Psycholinguistics* 21: 395–423.

McDonald, Janet L.
2006 Beyond the Critical Period: Processing-Based explanations for poor grammaticality judgement performance by late second language learners. *Journal of Memory and Language* 55 (3): 381–401.

Mechelli, Andrea, Jenny T. Crinion, Uta Noppeney, John O'Doherty, John Ashburner, Richard S. Frackowiak and Cathy J. Price
2004 Structural plasticity in the bilingual brain. *Nature* 431: 757.

Muñoz, Carmen
2003 Variation in oral skills development and age of onset. In: Maria Pilar García Mayo and Maria Luisa García Lecumberri (eds.), *Age and the Acquisition of English as a Foreign Language*, 161–181. Clevedon: Multilingual Matters.

Muñoz, Carmen
2006 (ed.) *Age and the Rate of Foreign Language Learning*. Clevedon: Multilingual Matters.

Muñoz, Carmen and David Singleton
2007 Foreign accent in advanced learners: Two successful profiles. *EUROSLA Yearbook* 7: 171–190.

Munro, Miles and Virginia Mann
2005 Age of immersion as a predictor of foreign accent. *Applied Psycholinguistics* 26 (3): 311–341.

Oyama, Susan
1976 A sensitive period for the acquisition of a non-native phonological system. *Journal of Psycholinguistic Research* 5: 261–84.

Oyama, Susan
1978 The sensitive period and comprehension of speech. *Working Papers on Bilingualism* 16: 1–17.

Paradis, Michel
2004 *A Neurolinguistic Theory of Bilingualism*. Amsterdam/Philadephia: Benjamins.

Patkowski, Mark S.
1980 The sensitive period for the acquisition of syntax in a second language. *Language Learning* 30: 449–472.
Penfield, Wilder and Lamar Roberts
1959 *Speech and Brain-Mechanisms*. Princeton, NJ: Princeton University Press.
Pike, Kenneth Lee
1967 *Language in Relation to a Unified Theory of Structure of Human Behavior*. 2nd edition. The Hague: Mouton.
Scovel, Thomas
2006 Age, acquisition and accent. In: Abello-Contesse, Chacon-Beltran, Lopez-Jiménez and Torreblanca-Lopez (eds.), 31–48.
Seliger, Herbert W., Stephen Krashen and Peter Ladefoged
1975 Maturational constraint in the acquisition of second language accent. *Language Sciences* 36: 20–22.
Singleton, David
2003 Critical Period or general age factor(s)? In: Maria Pilar García Mayo and Maria Luisa García Lecumberri (eds.), *Age and the Acquisition of English as a Foreign Language*, 3–22. Clevedon: Multilingual Matters.
Singleton, David
2005 The Critical Period Hypothesis: A coat of many colours. *International Review of Applied Linguistics* 43: 269–286.
Singleton, David and Lisa Ryan
2004 *Language Acquisition: The Age Factor*. 2nd edition. Clevedon: Multilingual Matters.
Stevens, Gillian
2004 Using census data to test the critical-period hypothesis for second-language acquisition. *Psychological Science* 15 (3): 215–216.
Tragant, Elsa
2006 Language learning motivation and age. In: Muñoz (ed.), 237–267.
Trofimovich, Pavel and Wendy Baker
2006 Learning second language suprasegmentals: Effect of L2 experience on prosody and fluency characteristics of L2 speech. *Studies in Second Language Acquisition* 28 (1): 1–30.
Tsukada, Kimiko, David Birdsong, Ellen Bialystok, Molly Mack, Hyekyung Sung and James Flege
2005 A developmental study of English vowel production and perception by native Korean adults and children. *Journal of Phonetics* 33: 263–290.
Uylings, Harry B. M.
2006 Development of the human cortex and the concept of "critical" or "sensitive" periods. *Language Learning* 56 (1): 59–90.
Vaid, Jyotsna and Fred Genesee
1980 Neuropsychological approaches to bilingualism: A critical review. *Canadian Journal of Psychology* 34: 417–445.
Vaid, Jyotsna and D. Geoffrey Hall
1991 Neuropsychological perspectives on bilingualism: Right, left and centre. In: Allan G. Reynolds (ed.), *Bilingualism, Multiculturalism and Second Language Learning*, 81–112. Hillsdale, NJ: Lawrence Erlbaum.

Vaid, Jyotsna
2007 The bilingual brain: What is right and what is left? In: Jeanette Altarriba and Roberto R. Heredia (eds.), *An Introduction to Bilingualism: Principles and Processes,* 151–169. Hillsdale, NJ: Lawrence Erlbaum.

Van Boxtel, Sonja, Theo Bongaerts and Peter-Arno Coppen
2003 Native-like attainment in L2 syntax. *EUROSLA Yearbook* 3: 157–181.

Ventureyra, Valérie A. G.
2005 A la recherche de la langue perdue: étude psycholinguistique de l'attrition de la première langue chez des Coréens adoptés en France [In search of the lost language: a psycholinguistic study of first language attrition among Korean adoptees in France]. Unpublished PhD Thesis, Ecole de Hautes Etudes en Sciences Sociales (EHESS), Paris. Cited in de Bot (2008).

White, Lydia and Fred Genesee
1996 How native is near-native? The issue of ultimate attainment in adult second language acquisition. *Second Language Research* 12: 233–265.

Wiley, Edward W., Ellen Bialystok and Kenji Hakuta
2005 New approaches to using census data to test the Critical-Period Hypothesis for Second-Language Acquisition. *Psychological Science* 16: 341–343.

Recommended readings

Francis, Norbert
2005 Research findings on early first language attrition: implications for the discussion on critical periods in language acquisition. *Language Learning* 55 (3): 491–531.

Muñoz, Carmen
2008a Symmetries and asymmetries of age effects in naturalistic and instructed L2 learning. *Applied Linguistics* 29(4): 578–596.

Muñoz, Carmen
2008b Age-relatet differences in foreign language learning. Revisiting the empirical evidence. *International Review of Applied Linguistics* 46 (4): 197–220.

Newman-Norlund, Roger D., Scott H. Frey, Laura-Ann Petittoand Scott T. Grafton
2006 Anatomical substrates of visual and auditory miniature second-language learning. *Journal of Cognitive Neuroscience* 18 (12), 1984–1997.

Shafer, Valerie L. and Karen Garrido-Nag
2007 The neurodevelopmental bases of language. In: Erika Hoff and Marilyn Shatz (eds.), *Blackwell Handbook of Language Development,* 21–45. Malden, MA: Blackwell Publishing.

Slabakova, Roumyana
2006 Is there a critical period for semantics? *Second Language Research* 22 (3): 302–338.

III. The design of foreign language teaching

12. Foreign language syllabus design

Keith Johnson

1. Introduction

Syllabus design is central to the course design process. Designing a course involves a host of issues associated with the implementation of syllabuses for use in specific language teaching programmes. These include inter alia how a selected syllabus will need to be adapted to a specific learning level and to a local context; how and in what form information will be gathered to provide the specifications of language and content which the syllabus will contain; how lesson units will be structured, and by means of what methodology the syllabus content will be carried to the learner. Because syllabus design plays such an important role in course development, this chapter, which focuses on syllabuses, will in fact be addressing many of the issues which relate to the development actual language teaching programmes.

The decades since the 1970s have been interesting ones in the area of syllabus design. The structural syllabus, as conceived by applied linguists working within structural linguistics and audiolingual methodology, came to be questioned, and the answers led in various directions. One direction resulted in developments of the structural syllabus to take account of new work in the areas of corpus linguistics and SLA where growing understanding of what learning sequences learners themselves follow (morpheme acquisition orders) provoked a reconsideration of the procedures used for selection and ordering of items in the traditional structural syllabus. Another direction led to a number of proposals for entirely different syllabus types. Some of these were developed to focus attention on areas of language use other than grammatical competence, the notional/functional syllabus being a case in point. In other developments, the teaching of grammatical competence remains an aim, but alternative modes (other than the structural syllabus) of reaching it are explored. The procedural and task-based syllabuses are examples. This chapter begins with a short description of the 'traditional' structural syllabus, then considers recent developments to it before turning attention to other syllabus types.

2. The 'traditional' structural syllabus

The behaviourist notion of 'shaping' plays an important role in the early conception of the structural syllabus. According to this principle, complex behaviours are broken down into small parts which are incrementally taught, until the entire behaviour is covered. Language, as a complex behaviour is approached in this way. The 'small parts' language is divided into are given various names according to the framework being used (Palmer, 1917/1968 for example has 'ergons'), but the most commonly accepted notion is that of 'sentence patterns' – typical configurations of sentence/phrase types associated with structures. Three sentence patterns associated with the copula BE are for example *This is + NP, Is this + NP, This isn't + NP.* Wilkins (1976) uses the term 'synthetic' to describe the syllabus type of which this is an example – the learner is presented with 'small parts' which are built up incrementally, by a process of synthesis to create a whole.

Halliday, McIntosh and Strevens (1964), and Mackey (1965) provide two of the few discussions in the 1960s of the criteria used in structural syllabus design for the selection and ordering of items. According to Mackey it is the 17th Century Moravian educational reformer Comenius who gives early importance to what Mackey calls 'gradation'. One of Comenius's main principles was that 'knowledge must necessarily come in successive steps, and that proficiency could be obtained only by degrees' (Mackey 1965: 204). For Mackey there are two main processes involved in gradation. The first is grouping, which answers the question 'what goes with what?' The principles at work here are that "related things should be taught together; opposites should also be taught together" (Mackey 1965: 205). The second is sequencing – 'what comes before what?'. According to Mackey, the principles of gradation were forgotten after the death of Comenius till the 19th Century, and Harold Palmer in 20th Century, who "included 'gradation' as a major division of his work" (Mackey 1965: 206).

2.1. Major criteria

Some of the major criteria used for gradation in structural syllabus design are described below; for a more detailed consideration, see White (1988).

2.1.1. Simplicity criterion

According to this criterion, the syllabus moves progressively from simple to complex. A fundamental tool for identifying simple and complex was contrastive analysis of the learner's mother and target languages. This procedure will identify what is simple and what is complex for a learner, following Lado's (1957) dictum that "those elements that are similar to the [learner's] native language will be simple for him, and those areas that are different will be difficult". Mackay (1965) lists four other relevant factors – ease of demonstrability; brevity (shorter items being easier to teach); regularity; and learning load.

2.1.2. *Sequencing or grouping*

This involves placing items sharing some similarities close to each other on the syllabus. For example, many course books start with the copula BE. in sentence patterns like: *Helen is a painter*; *Is Helen a painter?*; *Helen isn't a painter.* They then move to the present continuous (*Helen is phoning her mum*; *Is Helen phoning her mum?*; *Helen isn't phoning her mum*) because the tense involves auxiliary BE. The rationale is that once BE has been taught, large elements of the present continuous will have been mastered.

2.1.3. *Frequency*

According to the frequency criterion, the most often used forms are introduced first. An example of a frequency study which had implications for syllabus design is George (1963) who finds that the 'simple' tenses far outstrip the 'continuous' ones; in the case of the simple present referring to present action versus the present continuous, the ratio is 24:1. This finding suggests the simple tense should be taught before the continuous ones.

2.1.4. *Utility*

'Most useful' is often interpreted as meaning 'most frequent'; Palmer (1917/1968) for example notes that units "may be classified according to their degree of frequency or rareness, i.e. according to their degree of utility". But various other considerations may be brought into play. The example given above regarding BE and the present continuous might be said to illustrate that a sentence pattern may not be frequent itself, but may be useful as a 'stepping stone' to learning other, more frequent patterns. It is a characteristic of many structural books that much initial instruction focuses on the copula BE, practising sentences like *Helen is a painter; Is Helen a painter?; Helen isn't a painter.* Teachers may complain that sentences like these have low occurrence in real life and hence do not deserve early and extensive coverage. But, it may be counter-argued, once these patterns have been mastered, various more frequent sentence patterns are already partially learned. A second sense of 'useful' relates to the classroom teaching process. Patterns like *Open the door* and *What's this?* often occur early in courses because they are so useful in the classroom; once the imperative has been learned, many classroom actions can be practised, and the *what* question facilitates classroom vocabulary practice – the teacher can point at objects and ask what they are.

2.1.5. Teachability

It naturally happens that structures which are easy to convey tend to be taught before ones that are difficult to teach. Thus the some/any distinction often occurs early in courses because it is easy to explain and practise. Other grammatical items, like the indefinite article, also mentioned earlier, can be extremely difficult to teach, and are either postponed or (most often) ignored and left for learners to 'acquire' in some unspecified way. These comments refer to the notion of teachability in terms of ease of explanation of demonstration by the teacher. A different sense of the term is discussed later below.

2.2. Gradation and psychological reality

Like a number of writers on the topic of structural syllabus design, Mackey (1965: 206) considers the psychological grounds of gradation, an issue that is also tackled at length by McDonough (1980). The latter notes that the two components felt to be important for learning difficulty are 'complexity' and 'difference'. As regards complexity, he comments that "psychologists have objected that there is no reason to assume that linguistic complexity is in itself a cause of learning difficulty because many constructions that appear complex in terms of counts of elements or underlying rules are used by native speakers with no hesitation or greater difficulty in execution that apparently simple ones, in appropriate contexts". He cites Herriot (1969) and Wason and Johnson-Laird (1972) as evidence. Further evidence is provided by some transformational psycholinguists who attempted to measure complexity in terms of how many transformations were involved in a sentence. Hence *You like coffee* would be considered simpler than *Do you like coffee?* (because the latter involves an interrogative transformation), which in turn is simpler than *Don't you like coffee?* (which involves an added negative transformation). But, as Fodor and Garrett (1966) conclude: "a theory which associates complexity with derivational history is not confirmed".

The component of 'difference' refers to contrastive analysis and the belief that both errors and learning difficulty were largely to be accounted for in terms of transfer from L1 to target language. But a number of pieces of research at the beginning of the 1970s cast serious doubt over the importance of contrastive information. In his study of errors, George (1971) found that mother-tongue interference accounted for only a third of errors. The morpheme acquisition studies undertaken a little later, Dulay and Burt (1973) and Dulay and Burt (1974) for example, reach similar conclusions and are lead to hypotheses regarding universal orders of acquisition for morphemes in second language acquisition.

McDonough (1980: 312) looks in detail at how one textbook, Alexander (1974), introduces the simple present tense and suggests that despite careful grading and staging, learning difficulties can nevertheless occur. A particular problem he draws attention to is how introduction of related but different patterns in close proximity can lead to false generalisations being made. George's (1971) example is with the patterns *This is a book* and *This is Seta* which might lead to productions like **This is book*. McDonough's overall conclusion is that too little is known about learning processes to make confident statements regarding difficulty in relation to syllabus construction.

2.3. The structural syllabus and SLA

Though the traditional structural syllabus held sway for a long time, problems emerged with it. One issue relates to conflicting criteria. Palmer notes this early on (1917/1968), his example being that "it is quite impossible to reconcile the principle of frequency with that of concreteness" (Palmer [1917] 1968: 88). A further example, given earlier in discussion of George's (1963) research, is that while a simplicity criterion may suggest that the continuous tenses should be taught before the simple tenses (the latter having particularly complex interrogative and negative forms), a frequency criterion might suggest teaching the simple present first. In addition, design cannot be based entirely on any 'abstract' linguistic grading procedure, but will inevitably involve factors related to the specific learners and their educational circumstances. As Halliday, McIntosh and Strevens (1964: 210, cited in White 1988) put it: "for an intelligent approach to sequencing it is almost essential to have practical teaching experience with the pupils for whom a given course is intended, because here above all the teaching programme must be sensitive to the precise needs of the pupils, both in general terms and in close detail". For reasons such as these, many regard structural syllabus design as less of a science and more of an art.

Pienemann's (1985) objection to the structural syllabus is that it is not based on learning theory criteria; "there is", as he puts it, "a serious lack of arguments from a learning theoretical point of view" (Pieneman 1985: 26); and later: "properties of language learning were neglected in material grading, although grading is regarded as the basic motor for tutoring the learning processes" (Pieneman 1985: 28). In that paper, Pienemann discusses the implications for syllabus design of the morpheme acquisition order studies of Dulay and Burt (1973 and 1974 for example) which suggest that learners have their own order for learning structures – what amounts to an *internal syllabus*. The issue for syllabus design is what implication the existence of an internal syllabus has for the value of an external syllabus. There are a number of possible implications.

One is to argue that since learners have their own internal syllabuses, external ones are of little use and should not be used. If learners are provided with exposure to language, the argument runs, the expectation is that they will utilise their internal acquisition order to make sense of how the language works. This type of solution is behind various syllabus types to be considered later in this chapter.

A second possible stance (less often discussed in the literature and not mentioned by Pienemann) would be simply to ignore the existence of an internal syllabus and to continue working with an external one. One of a number of possible arguments for this view would be to point out that many of the morpheme studies were done in a naturalistic target language context where the target language was being spoken in the environment. It might be said that this situation is so different from one where the target language is foreign, heard only in the classroom, that parallels cannot be drawn.

A third possible answer is Pienemann's own. He suggests that information about acquisition orders should lead to a reformulation of external syllabuses, to reflect what is known about internal ones. In Pienemann (1985) he investigates this possibility by looking at three word order rules in German, which for ease of explication might be called Rules A, B and C. Acquisition order studies show, Pienemann argues, that these rules are acquired in the order: A first, then B, then C. In his own study, Pienemann takes two groups of learners of German as a foreign language. One group has learned Rule A but not Rule B, while the second group has learned both A and B. Both groups are taught Rule C. The finding is that although both groups can pass a formal test on Rule C after it has been taught, only the group that has learned Rule B actually uses Rule C in language use outside class. This leads to the conclusion that if one wishes to teach Rule C properly, it is necessary to have taught Rules A and B first. Pienemann generalises this finding into the hypothesis that learners will only really master a structure if their learning stage is nearing that item in their internal syllabus. Pienemann calls this the 'teachability hypothesis'. It "predicts that instruction can only promote language acquisition if the interlanguage is close to the point when the structure to be taught is acquired in the natural setting" (1985: 36). Pienemann later develops a Processability Theory (Pienemann 1998) which claims to be able to predict the order in which linguistic structures emerge in second language acquisition, based on the gradual development of a set of the procedural skills. According to the model, and following the same principles as his teachability hypothesis, the lower level processing procedures are requisite for the functioning of higher level ones.

There are differences of opinion as to how much a syllabus based on internal acquisition orders would differ from a traditional one. Hatch (1978) suggests that the differences would be small, and that finding out about natural orders would, from the point of view of language teaching syllabus design at least, not be worth the effort. Rogers (1994), on the other hand, analyses seven textbooks teaching German as a foreign language, finds that they do not follow what is known about natural acquisition orders of German, and argues that for the orders to be adequately reflected would therefore require a degree of change to the syllabuses.

There are many practical problems associated with attempts to apply what is known about the internal syllabus to structural syllabus design, not the least being the incomplete state of our knowledge regarding what the internal syllabus consists of. But the work of applied linguists like Pienemann constitutes a genuine attempt to utilise SLA research for the purposes of syllabus design. At the very least it reminds applied linguists that a central concern in syllabus development must be the state of knowledge the consuming learner is at.

2.4. Structural syllabuses and corpus linguistics

Other developments in traditional structural syllabus design have taken place as a result of the growth of corpus linguistics. McEnery and Wilson (1996), among others, suggest a role for corpora in syllabus design, and Leech, Rayson and Wilson (2001) provide possible tools for using corpora in this way. This role relates to the fact that corpora can provide information regarding frequency. The work of George (1963) mentioned earlier was painstakingly compiled 'manually' and cannot but be restricted in its scope given the amount of effort involved in calculating frequency statements without machine help. Now that computer-based corpora are available, that information is much more easily accessed.

As Cook (1998) among others notes, in the early days of corpus linguistics there was a tendency for somewhat grandiose claims to be made for the role of the new field in this area (and indeed in language teaching in general). Since information about frequency is useful to the syllabus designer, there is indeed a valid role for corpus linguistics to play. But it needs to be remembered that frequency, as shown earlier in this chapter, is but one criterion the syllabus designer uses for selection and gradation. One of the arguments used by Cook (1998) for a cautious approach to the value of corpus linguistics in language teaching questions the centrality of frequency as a criterion in syllabus design. Another, more general sort of argument is put forward by Widdowson (1980, and more recently 2000, 2003) as part of his view that the proper practice of applied linguistics involves the principled utilisation and modification of information provided by the linguist for applied means, rather than the wholesale adoption of linguistics for language teaching. Widdowson expresses this distinction by use of the terms 'linguistics applied' (an unsatisfactory procedure where the starting point are findings from linguistic enquiry which are applied in language teaching in an indiscriminate way) and 'applied linguistics' (a more satisfactory procedure where the starting point are problems identified in language teaching and solutions sought wherever they may occur, including linguistics).

3. The lexical syllabus

Corpus linguistics is particularly powerful and appropriate for the analysis of lexical items, and it is therefore no surprise that the growth of corpus linguistics should be associated with proposals for the development of lexical syllabuses, which use the vocabulary item as the unit of organisation. Sinclair and Renouf (1988) begin their discussion of this proposal by noting that though there has been research on word frequency in relation to course design (Gougenheim et al., 1956 is mentioned inter alia), courses differ considerably in terms of lexical systematisation. Renouf (1984) analysed portions of nine major EFL courses and finds huge variation in terms of number of words introduced and number of repetitions of words (to reinforce learning). Sinclair and Renouf consider various issues related to the development of lexical syllabuses. They propose (Sinclair and Renouf 1988: 148) three criteria for lexical selection, to focus on:

- the commonest word forms,
- their central patterns of usage,
- the combinations which they typically form.

In relation to the first, they provide a list of the commonest 200 word forms according to the Birmingham Corpus. Though it is naturally not their proposal that any beginner course should cover only these forms, they make the point that teaching these forms early will be enormously cost-effective for learners. For example, they point out that the most frequent word, *the*, is approximately 4 % of all text, with the next two frequent items, *and* and *of* account for another 4 %. The most frequent ten words on their list add up to 17 % of all text.

As regards central patterns of usage, they point out that computers may be more efficient at identifying frequent usages that human observers. The latter might for example assume that the most frequent uses of *see* are to do with visual perception. In fact corpus evidence suggests that the two most frequent uses are in phrases like *I see* and *you see*, where the meaning approximates to *understand*.

A point which Sinclair and Renouf's paper touches on but does not develop at length is the extent to which a lexical syllabus can me made to cover information which is currently associated with structural syllabuses. They note that

> "if the analysis of words and phrases has been done correctly, then all the relevant grammar, etc., should appear in a proper proportion. Verb tenses, for example, which are often the main organizing feature of a course, are combinations of some of the commonest words in the language" (Sinclair and Renouf 1988: 155).

It is a point that suggests itself in earlier discussions (in Palmer [1917] 1968, for example where consideration of structures is closely associated with key lexical items), and it leads to subsequent proposals in Willis (1990) that a syllabus can consist of a corpus. Willis (1990) and Willis (1994) provides a number of examples of how what is traditionally regarded as grammar teaching may be viewed in lexical terms. The passive voice is, for example, normally seen (and taught) as a transformation from the active. Another conceptualisation is to view it as BE plus adjective/past participle. Further examples from Willis (1994) are the 'second conditional' and reported statements.

4. Notional/functional syllabuses

In the mid to late 1960s awareness was increasing among applied linguists of the problem of over-emphasis on structural competence and insufficient attention paid to other dimensions of communicative competence, particularly appropriateness. Newmark (1966) is a clear example of this awareness, and his paper speaks of the student who may be entirely 'structurally competent', yet who is unable to perform even the simplest communicative task.

In his seminal paper, Hymes (1970) provides the theoretical framework in which this issue can be addressed. He describes four parameters of communicative competence: *the possible, the feasible, the appropriate* and *the performed.* He argues that Chomskyian linguistics placed too much attention on the first of these, and there is no doubt that language teaching had done the same. Of the three remaining parameters it was the appropriate that caught the attention of applied linguists interested in language teaching, and a good part of what came to be called communicative language teaching (CLT) may be seen as an attempt to bring the teaching of appropriateness into the language classroom. On the syllabus design dimension, developments here are closely associated with the work of the Council of Europe, who set up a team to introduce new programmes for the teaching of foreign languages in all member countries. In his 1972 paper, one member of the team, Wilkins, discusses three possible syllabus types – the structural, the situational and the notional. He looks first at the situational syllabus as an alternative to the structural. In situational syllabuses, language items closely associated with the situations learners are likely to find themselves in are identified and taught in 'units identified by situational labels' Wilkins discusses a number of problems with the situational syllabus, chief among which is that "the diversity of linguistic forms in any one situational unit makes the task of generalizing grammatical learning a difficult one and without it the learner may acquire no more than a set of responses appropriate to that one situation" (Wilkins 1972: 84). Interestingly, this is a main objection later to be levelled at Wilkins' third syllabus type, which he calls the notional, and to which we now turn.

The two major categories that Wilkins' notional syllabus introduces for the purposes of syllabus design are[1]:

1. Semantico-grammatical categories (described by some as 'notions'). These are "categories which, in European languages at least, interact significantly with grammatical categories" (Wilkins 1972). Examples from Wilkins' (1973) list are *point of time; frequency, dimensions; location.*
2. Categories of communicative function ('functions'). These relate "to uses of language where there is at best an very untidy relationship between the function of the utterances and the grammatical categories through which these functions are realised" (Wilkins 1972). Examples from Wilkins' (1973) list are *greeting; inviting; expressing disapproval; requesting information.*

The Council of Europe's proposal was that notions and functions would form the basis for syllabuses that listed these, rather than (initially at least) grammatical structures.[2] This in turn would lead to language lessons focusing not on structures, but on notional, conceptual or functional areas, hence providing semantic and communicative dimensions to the teaching. Figure 1 below gives an example of the contents page of a functionally organised textbook of the type which became widespread from the late 1970s onwards.

1. Talking about yourself
2. Meeting people
3. Asking about things
4. Asking for things
5. Inviting
6. Making arrangements
7. Asking the way
8. Asking for help
9. Asking for permission

Figure 1. Part of the contents page of Johnson and Morrow (1979), showing areas to be covered in the first nine teaching units

4.1. Needs analysis

Because the notions and functions that a language is able to describe are a very high number, the development of notional/functional syllabuses led to problems of selection which go beyond those faced by the structural syllabus, and again the Council of Europe's work in this area was important. Richterich, a member of the Council's team, approached the issue by developing a framework for looking at learners' language needs, defined as "the requirements which arise from the use of a language in the multitude of situations which may arise in the social lives of individuals and groups" (Richterich 1972: 32). The procedure of needs analysis became important to notional/functional syllabus design. In the

Council's model, the notion of 'situation' was broken down into the following sub-components:

Settings: Subdivided into *Geographical setting*: the country in which the user wants to use the target language, and *Place* e.g. at the airport, in the hotel, in the office.

Topics: What the user wants to talk about. E.g. 'leisure activities' or 'business matters'.

Roles: The most important of the various sorts identified are *social roles*. E.g. 'stranger to stranger', 'customer to shopkeeper', 'doctor to patient'.

4.2. The common core and the T-Level

Needs analysis is particularly suited to LSP (language for specific purpose) teaching, which flourished under notional/functional (n/f). This flourishing occurred partly because increasing numbers of learners had need of this type of specific training, but also because n/f provided a clearer way of differentiating course content according to learning purpose than could be achieved in the structural syllabus.

It may be easy to identify important situations for the LSP student, but this may be quite impossible for general teaching programmes, where learners will not have specific purposes for learning and where situations for use cannot therefore be readily identified. The Council of Europe's answer to this problem lies in the concept of the 'common core'. All learners, whatever their eventual uses of the FL, will (the argument runs) need a certain common core of notions and functions. In the functional area, these are particularly uses associated with general socialising, like *greeting*, *requesting information*, *inviting*. The Council of Europe therefore incorporated the notion of the common core into their unit/credit framework. The framework identifies five levels of proficiency (*threshold, basic, general competence, advanced* and *full professional*). Each level had a common core unit, plus additional specialised units. Van Ek developed a specification for the common core of the Threshold Level. His document, called *The Threshold Level*, appeared in two forms: van Ek (1975) for the adult learner, and van Ek (1978) for the secondary school student. These specifications were landmark documents in course design and were followed by designers both inside and outside Europe. Because n/f specifications are initially non-language-specific (being stated in conceptual and behavioural terms), they may be used for various languages. Hence the Threshold Level has been developed for other languages – the French *Niveau-Seuil*, German *Kontaktschwelle*, Spanish *Nivel Umbral* and Italian *Livello Soglia* for example.

4.3. N/f syllabuses: uses and criticisms

N/f syllabuses are particularly useful in some situations. One very large audience was the one for which, arguably, this syllabus type came into existence – learners who because of earlier teaching practices had developed grammatical but not communicative competence. To meet this audience, many books at the upper intermediate level and above were developed to 'activate' grammatical knowledge in relation to categories of use. This led to an implicit teaching strategy in which structural teaching was undertaken at the early stages, employing a traditional structural syllabus. At a second stage a communicative dimension was added, recycling grammar in relation to notional/functional categories. This strategy, though widespread, was rarely explicitly stated. One exception is Yalden (1983) who talks in terms of a 'proportional syllabus' where structural orientation is gradually replaced over time by a communicative one.

Because it permits specific focus on functions identified as important through needs analysis, LSP is a common application for n/f. So-called 'urgency courses' are another. In this increasingly common sort of course the learner has an urgent need to learn a language, usually for study or work purposes. Through needs analysis, n/f is able to identify and meet urgent learner requirements.

In the 1970s and early 1980s, n/f syllabuses dominated syllabus design in language teaching. Ministries of Education world-wide adopted this syllabus type. But as time passed criticisms grew. According to Paulston (in Wilkins, Brumfit and Paulston 1981: 93), Wilkins' approach "is quite atheoretical; it says nothing about how languages are learned" (this in spite of the fact that Wilkins (1976) spends considerable time associating n/f with what he calls an 'analytic' as opposed to a 'synthetic' mode of learning – see the following section). A second area of criticism concerns the so-called lack of generativity of n/f. There is the danger that n/f will simply provide a kind of elaborate phrasebook, without any real generative capacity for communication. As Widdowson (1978) puts it: "[in n/f] learners are being provided with language teaching programmes which attempt to develop communicative behaviour in dissociation from a knowledge of system and its meaning potential which can alone ensure that what is learned really is a capacity for communication, and not simply a collection of form/function correlates". For an interesting attack and defence of n/f, see Wilkins, Brumfit and Paulston (1981).

It is now rare to find textbooks which are organised exclusively along n/f lines, and the problem of generativity has led some to return to a predominantly structural syllabus (where generativity is not an issue). But even in such cases it has become commonplace for materials to include an n/f dimension (see discussion of the notion of the multidimensional syllabus later in this chapter).

5. 'Analytic' and 'Type B' syllabuses

In his 1976 book, Wilkins draws a distinction between what he calls 'synthetic' and 'analytic' approaches to syllabus design. These labels refer to what is supposed to be the learner's processes involved in each. In a traditional structural syllabus, the learner is provided with items of the language in an incremental fashion, one by one. The learner's task is one of synthesis, combining the 'pieces of information' provided by teaching to form an overall knowledge of how the language operates. In an 'analytic' syllabus, the learner is given language in a less pre-digested form; this may for example be in large stretches of discourse containing many exemplars of many linguistic forms. Here the learner's task – to achieve that same overall knowledge of how the language operates – is to analyse the input into components (an analysis which need not necessarily of course be done on a conscious level). Where in relation to this distinction n/f syllabuses lie is arguable. Wilkins places them firmly in the 'analytic camp' because a truly functionally organised course will not provide structurally systematic coverage of the language; but Johnson (1979) questions the analytic status of n/f.

A broader distinction, involving analytic/synthetic but going beyond it, is developed in White (1988), who speaks of Type A and Type B syllabuses. White (1988:44) describes Type A (associated with Wilkins' synthetic) as interventionist, external to the learner, other directed, determined by authority, based on content as perceived by the expert, with objectives defined in advance. Type B on the other hand are internal to the learner, inner directed, negotiated between learners and teachers, based on content as perceived by the learner, with objectives described afterwards. Long and Crookes (1992) utilise White's distinction, and identify three forms of Type B syllabus – the process, procedural and task syllabus. These are now considered in turn.

6. The process syllabus

One of the characteristics of Type A syllabuses is that they are *product syllabuses*, 'based on the pre-specification of content' (White 1988: 94), whether this be stated in structural, notional-functional or other terms. The *process syllabus* on the other hand, focuses on the "processes of learning and procedures of teaching – in other words [on] methodology". Therefore although the n/f syllabus constituted a major departure from the structural syllabus, the two are similar in the respect that they provide specifications of the 'product' which learners are intended to master.

The process/product distinction comes into language teaching from general educational studies. White (1988) traces the concept of the 'process curriculum' back to the 1960s and a course by Bruner in which "the [...] aims [...] centre around the processes of learning rather than the products [...]" (Bruner 1960). The modern day process syllabus in language teaching is associated with Breen, whose 1984 paper provides seminal discussion. He acknowledges that learners "need plans in order to have a sense of direction and continuity in their work" (Breen 1984: 51); therefore there is a central role for 'syllabus as plan'. But he argues that the plan's value may not reside in what it actually shows or represents (its content, that is), so much as on how it is used in the classroom. Different uses are possible; for example, rather than standing as a prescription of content and its order of presentation, the syllabus might provide a check list by which learner progress can be measured.

Breen's criticism of the product syllabus is essentially one of those mentioned above as a criticism of n/f (one version of the product syllabus). It is that a "repertoire of communication" is specified, whereas the process syllabus deals with a "capacity for communication" (Breen 1984: 51). In the latter, the emphasis is "upon the capabilities of applying, reinterpreting, and adapting the knowledge of rules and conventions during communication by means of underlying skills and abilities" (Breen 1984: 52). The view that communication involves, in Breen and Candlin's (1980: 91) words, "convention-creating as well as convention-following", leads towards a syllabus in which mastery of a discrete repertoire of rules is replaced by the creative reinterpretation of conventions in communicative acts. A further claim for the process model is that it concerns the process of learning. Breen makes comparison between syllabuses and maps, and argues that in a product syllabus the designer "draws the map beginning at the destination". The process syllabus on the other hand would "prioritise the route itself" (Breen 1984: 52), and would hence presumably take due account of present learner position as much as of final destination. A further useful distinction, found in Breen (1983), related to the process/product one is between a syllabus of 'ends' and of 'means'. According to Breen, the process syllabus does not supplant the product version, but is seen as creating a framework for it; the process syllabus interrelates "with a syllabus of subject-matter [product]" (1984: 59). Product syllabuses are in fact reinterpreted by learners and teachers once actual classroom teaching begins.

Breen (1984) provides some indication of what a process syllabus would contain. Four levels or elements are recognised. The first, *decisions for classroom language learning*, concerns matters of participation, procedure and subject-matter, and provides answers to the questions: 'who does what with whom, on what subject-matter, and with what resources, when, how, and for what learning purpose(s)?'. What is selected at this level becomes the second level of *alternative procedures*, adopted by a particular set of learners, and perhaps stated in a 'working contract' drawn up between them and their teacher. At the third level *alternative activities* are specified, and these break down into actual *tasks* (Level 4). Breen's examples of tasks include 'agreeing a definition of a problem' and 'organising data'. The model also has a place for on-going evaluation and 'thereby, a cyclic process through the levels from level 1 to 4 and from level 4 to level 1 again' (Breen 1984: 57).

White (1988) indicates that in the general educational literature process approaches are not without their critics, and the problems which writers like Taylor and Richards (1979) note with the process curriculum in general are likely to hold for language teaching process syllabuses in particular. These problems include the heavy demands process teaching is likely to make on teacher competence, as well as the issue of how objective assessment may be made in the absence of predetermined outcomes. Further, Hirst (1975), cited in White (1988), argues that the process syllabus is still, like its product counterpart, concerned with ends rather than means even if these are not specified in a behavioural manner. The sentiment is echoed by Johnson (1993) who suggests that processes, once listed, become products. Long and Crookes (1992) identify four particular problems which lead them away from the process syllabus in the direction of task syllabuses. These are firstly that the process syllabus is not based on prior needs analysis; secondly that evaluations of task difficulty and sequencing are not undertaken; thirdly that no provision is made for form focus; and fourthly that the process syllabus is not based on any language learning theory (Long and Crookes, 1992: 40–41).

7. Procedural and task-based syllabuses

The second syllabus type Long and Crookes discuss is Prabhu's 'procedural syllabus'. Though Breen (1984: 60) sees his process and Prabhu's procedural syllabus as "different in function and nature", White (1988) classifies both together as "Type B syllabuses". Prabhu (1986) sees many of the developments in syllabus design which occurred in Europe during the 1970s (he is thinking specifically of the n/f syllabus), as attempts to bring new dimensions to language teaching, particularly associated with the Hymesian notion of appropriateness. He notes that in the Indian context the problem at that time was not the lack of an appropriateness dimension to language teaching, but the failure to teach grammar in a successful way. The structural syllabus was, in other words, failing to do its job properly. His aim is to find a way of improving the teaching of structure.

Prabhu's starting point is the idea – at first sight paradoxical – that in order to teach grammatical structures one should focus not on form but on message. If classroom activities succeed in concentrating on what is being said rather than on how it is being said, then ultimately the structures will become absorbed. The relationship of this idea to what happens in L1 acquisition is clear. Prabhu's argument continues by claiming that one cannot really focus on meaning if at the same time one is following a linguistically proscribed syllabus; learners cannot be expected to concentrate on what is being said if the syllabus is at every point dictating what grammatical items are to be used. Covert linguistic focus is for Prabhu an unsatisfactory procedure, yet one commonly followed in language teaching (including, it may be argued, CLT). In this procedure, the teacher uses strategies to pretend that message focus exists, while all participants know that the true focus is on form. For example, the teacher may decide to practise the simple past tense by asking students to describe what they did at the weekend – pretending that the interest is on students' activities and lives whereas it is really on a tense.

Prabhu's argument leads him to propose a language teaching programme which is not based on a language syllabus. He has instead a programme, or syllabus, of tasks. This task-based syllabus tells the teacher what kinds of activities will be undertaken in class each day but not what language items will arise. The syllabus therefore provides a framework for classroom activity, fulfilling the role of 'syllabus as plan' mentioned earlier in relation to Breen, but avoiding prescription of linguistic items. He calls this task-based syllabus 'procedural'. It was developed and experimented with in Southern India, particularly Bangalore and Madras. Figure 2 below illustrates part of Prabhu's procedural syllabus. Each lesson (43–52 in the syllabus) focuses on the use of maps and plans:

43. making the plan of a house (and labelling parts), following instructions; oral, then written, response
44. task presented on paper
45. charting movements from one part of the house to another; giving directions (e.g. *cross the living room, then turn right; go through the second door*); oral, then written, directions
46. competition between groups (house plans supplied; each group demanding instructions from another)
47. map of a few streets, with places marked; giving directions from one place to another; oral, then written, directions
48. tasks presented on paper
49. map of a district/state with different towns and roads marked; questions on possible routes from one town to another; oral, then written, responses
50. map of a district/state, with distances indicated; choice of the shortest route and its distance; oral, then written, responses
51. map of district/state, with roads and railway lines indicated; stating routes involving both rail and road (also, perhaps, places to be walked to); oral, then written, responses
52. task presented on paper

Figure 2. Part of the Bangalore 'procedural' syllabus (from RIE 1980)

For the fullest discussion of the procedural syllabus, see Prabhu (1987).

Prabhu's is arguably the earliest version of a task-based syllabus. Since then this syllabus type has grown considerably in various directions, into Long and Crookes (1992) third syllabus type, which they call the 'task syllabus'. In order to understand how these later versions relate to Prabhu, it will be useful to identify three characteristics of his 'procedural' version:

1. *Rationale*: Prabhu's work may be seen as a significant contribution to a larger debate concerned with *form and message focus* in language teaching (Doughty and Williams 1998). It may be argued that communicative methodology placed strong emphasis on message focus, attempting to create in the classroom conditions where focus would be on 'getting messages across' rather than on the structure of the language. As shown above, it is central to Prabhu's rationale that he views message focus in communicative language teaching as a bogus form of form focus. He therefore seeks to create entire message focus through a concentration on tasks. The literature he refers to in defence of this position is L1 acquisition (where there mostly message focus) and other-subject (content) teaching where the same condition holds Prabhu (1986).
2. *Needs analysis*: No concern is given in Prabhu's work to the process of needs analysis. Tasks, that is, are not selected because they have been identified by needs analysis as ones which will be undertaken by learners in real life. Though Prabhu does not discuss the question of selection of tasks at much length, the criteria he has in mind are related to cognitive challenge and learner interest. He would further associate himself with the arguments against n/f and needs analysis described earlier, that what language teaching must provide is a 'capacity for communication' rather than a set of situationally-bound phrases. He would note that language employs a relatively small set of ('generative') structures that can be employed in any situation. Therefore whatever tasks are utilised, these structures will make an appearance over time.
3. *Selection and grading*: Prabhu pays relatively little attention to the question of task grading. As noted above, selection of tasks is made in terms of learner interest and although mention is made of cognitive complexity as a mode of grading, this is not substantially developed as a theme in Prabhu's work.

8. Other versions of task-based syllabuses

Task-based approaches have multiplied since Prabhu's time, and in the variety of versions that have been developed the three issues described above have made important appearance. One of the more fully articulated versions is developed in Long (1985) and Long and Crookes (1992). In order to differentiate this approach from Prabhu's we shall deal in turn with each of the three points mentioned above:

1. *Rationale*: Long and Crookes clearly base their rationale within SLA research, in two specific respects. The first relates to the focus on form/message issue. A number of applied linguists have noted that if total attention is given to message focus, learners are naturally likely to feel that stasis has been reached if the message they are communicating has been understood. They are therefore likely to fossilise into the use of forms which though inappropriate nevertheless convey meanings – Johnson (1996) example is the sentence *Give me beer* which if said in a bar is, though unacceptable, likely to result in a beer being served. Since beer is indeed served, the learner will not have the motivation to improve their language. Indeed, one explanation for the phenomenon of fossilisation (Vigil and Oller, 1976) is based on this argument. For this reason, it has therefore come to be argued that more 'message focused' approaches to teaching (a category including task-based teaching) are likely to benefit from the injection of some degree of form focus, something which Prabhu does not allow[3]. There have been various suggestions as to how some degree of form focus may be added. Wesche and Skehan (2002) describe a number of positions. One of these is Samuda's (2001) notion that it is possible to 'seed' tasks with specific structures, while still maintaining the naturalness of the task. The second is found in Skehan (1998) who claims that teachers will be able to draw on findings in task-based research which suggest likely directions to follow (resulting in 'pedagogically desired lines of progress').

   There have been other suggestions for form focus in the literature. Willis (1996) has opportunities for form focus after tasks; H. Johnson (1992) introduces form-focused work into the tasks themselves, and Johnson (1996) proposes separate components of teaching – form and message focused – running side by side (a proposal touched on at the end of in this chapter).

   In their discussion on this issue, Long and Crookes, and Long (1991) draw a distinction between *focus-on-forms* and *focus-on-form*. The former is what occurs in the structural syllabus, where the forms (structures) of the language constitute the main organising principle. This is not seen as a beneficial procedure. But like others mentioned above (and unlike Prabhu), Long and Crookes do recognise the necessity for some form focus, and their conceptualisation of tasks does allow for form focus – in the "use of pedagogic tasks and other methodological options which draw students' attention to aspects of the target language code" (1992: 43).

   A second set of ideas which provide the background to Long and Crookes' view relate to the role of interaction in SLA. The respective roles of input interaction and output in SLA have come in for considerable attention in the past few decades, leading to the development of an Input Hypothesis (Krashen 1985), an Output Hypothesis (Swain 1993; de Bot 1996) and an Interaction Hypothesis, which Long (1996) associates himself with. Central to this view is that (in the words of Skehan 1992: 181) "the construction of opportunities for interaction has a vital place in language teaching". Tasks for Long and Crookes are vehicles providing the possibility for 'organising learning opportunities'. It is a rationale different from that of Prabhu.

2. *Needs analysis:* Long (1985) also views the task as a vehicle for 'expressing learner needs'; it is a unit for needs analysis which shares common elements with the Council of Europe's 'activity' unit, mentioned earlier. Long notes that 'the things people will tell you they do if you ask them and they are not applied linguists' are what we have come to call tasks. Examples (from Long and Crookes 1992: 44) are "buying a train ticket, renting an apartment, reading a technical manual, solving a math problem, reporting a chemistry experiment, taking lecture notes". These real life tasks are turned into pedagogic tasks which form the basis of classroom teaching. Long (1985) notes that many job specifications are made in terms of tasks already, and where this is the case, the ESP needs analysis is done already.
3. *Task grading*: In addition, Long develops a concept of task grading: "Grading is determined by the degree of difficulty of the pedagogical tasks themselves (from simple to complex), as well as such normal considerations as variety, pace and duration. 'Difficulty' here, however, does not mean difficulty in terms of the linguistic demands [...] rather it refers to the difficulty of pedagogical tasks in such aspects as the number of steps involved in their execution, the number of parties involved, the assumptions they make about presupposed knowledge, the intellectual challenge they pose [...] and so on" (1985: 93).

   Long exemplifies with a 'selling an airline ticket task', where the more options involved (for example, providing aisle, central and window seating options) the more complex the task will be.

   The notion of grading made in terms which go beyond linguistic complexity to consider cognitive and affective complexity has become a major theme in the rapidly growing task-based teaching literature, and much of the discussion relates to issues of processing (in Bialystok, 1982; Johnson 1996 and elsewhere). A central notion is that cognitive processing demands will often make a learner unable to 'perform his competence' (the phrase is from Ellis 1985), and that therefore manipulation of operating conditions (Johnson's 1996 phrase is ROCs, for *real operating conditions*) will make tasks more or less complex for the learner to undertake. As Skehan (1992: 189) notes: "it may be possible to predict systematic influences of performance conditions on the nature of the language used".

Much research effort has been put into determining the conditions which will control task difficulty. Crookes (1989) looks at the variable of planning time, and concludes that providing time to plan had no effect on accuracy, but did have effect on variety of lexis and degree of risk taking. In a series of studies, Skehan and Foster (1995 for example) consider learner task performance along three parameters:

- *accuracy* the proportion of error free clauses
- *fluency* various measures are used, including number and length of pauses,
- *complexity* the amount of subordination

They also look at different task types – in the 1995 paper at personal, narrative, decision-making. In the same vein, a series of studies by Bygate (see Bygate 2005 for useful discussion) consider the variable of task repetition and the effects this has on performance.

Though it is early days, a likely application of studies like these is in the area of task-based syllabus design. Information provided by research about what makes tasks complex to perform may result in clearer ideas about how tasks may be graded – providing in other words fresh criteria for undertaking something which (as we have seen in this chapter) has been central to syllabus design throughout history – gradation.

9. Content-based instruction

Task-based teaching may be seen as a version of what has come to be called content-based instruction (CBI). This is defined by Brinton, Snow and Wesche (1989) as "the integration of particular content with language-teaching aims". A major reason for the interest in this type of teaching in recent decades relates to the form/message focus debate discussed earlier. One characteristic of various types of task-based syllabuses is that they are syllabuses stated in 'other-than-linguistic terms'. The same may be said of CBI. As will be shown, there are various models of CBI, but a basic notion is that they centre round syllabuses which are based on 'other-than-linguistic' content – syllabuses of geography, history, mathematics, science. In this way, their starting point is akin to Prabhu's, that "in order to teach grammatical structures one should focus not on form but on message"; or, in Krashen's words this time (speaking in Palfreman 1983), that "subject teaching is language teaching". The variant of that position, also discussed earlier, that despite the importance of message, there needs to be room for form focus too, is also represented in some versions of CBI.

Brinton, Snow and Wesche (1989) do not in fact mention task-based teaching as a source of CBI. The historical roots which they do mention relate to the period 1960–90 and are three. The first is the 'Language across the curriculum' movement which was stimulated by a governmental report in the UK (Bullock 1975). The Bullock Report provides a thorough review of teaching in English as an L1 and concludes that it should cross over all subject matter domains. This attempt to relate L1 and other subject teaching was influential in North America, and led to a number of publications dealing with strategies for cross-curricular teaching. The second is the development of LSP, already touched upon above. The third are the immersion programmes which began in Canada in the 1960, an early one being the celebrated 'St Lambert experiment' which developed a French immersion programme in the Montreal suburb of St Lambert in 1963. According to Brinton, Snow and Wesche (1989), 240,000 Canadian children were participating in bilingual immersion programmes by 1987. These spread to the Unites States in the early 1970s (the first being the Spanish Immersion Programme in Culver City, California) such that in the 1980s there were over twenty-five such programmes in the US, teaching a variety of languages.

Brinton, Snow and Wesche (1989) identify three main prototype models of CBI:

1. *Theme-based*: The teaching is organised round unrelated topics (e.g. heart disease, noise pollution), or around one major topic (e.g. marketing). In this model, students for whom the language of instruction is an L2 ('L2 students') are mixed together with L1 students;
2. *Sheltered*: In this model, L2 students are taught separately from L1 students. This means that the teacher is able to introduce speech modifications to make the input comprehensible. The example given for this model is a University of Ottawa course entitled *Introduction to Psychology*.
3. *Adjunct*: Here there are two programmes, a content-based one and a parallel language programme. They "complement each other in terms of mutually co-ordinated assignments".

Brinton, Snow and Wesche (1989) note that despite differences between the various approaches, there are common elements, particularly:

- a view that being based on other-than-linguistic content facilitates learning to occur;
- the use of authentic materials (though these may be adapted or supplemented by the teacher);
- the occurrence of some degree of accommodation (such as simplification) in order to meet learners' language level.

Wesche and Skehan (2002) provide a useful overview of CBI. In their conclusion they note that CBI "perhaps offer[s] as close to a comprehensive environment for second language development as is possible in the classroom" (Wesche and Skehan: 227). They argue that it is particularly useful for two types of clientele. The first is the very young learner who will willingly accept the native-speaker teacher as a language model. The other is the older learner who already has a degree of grammatical competence but who needs to be able to use this in communicative contexts. This second is identical to the 'activation' role discussed earlier in relation to n/f.

An initiative which has been responsible for the recent development of CBI, especially though not inclusively within Europe, goes under the name of CLIL (for Content and Language Integrated Learning, see Wolff Ch. 20, this volume). Details of this initiative can be found on the CLIL Compendium website (http://www.clilcompendium.com), where CLIL is described as referring "to any dual-focused educational context in which an additional language, thus not usually the first language of the learners involved, is used as a medium in the teaching and learning of non-language content". There are now a considerable number of European institutions which engage in CLIL, and this increase in interest is attested by a number of recent publications, Deller and Price (2007) for example. Part of the aim of the CLIL Compendium group, which is supported by the Directorate-General for Education and Culture of the European Commission, is to identify and research the variables involved in CLIL teaching.

10. The multidimensional syllabus

This chapter has so far dealt with syllabuses as if they were, and had to be, mutually exclusive; that a course designer has to select one parameter (the structure, the situation, the task, the function etc.) as the unit of organisation for a course, to the exclusion of all others. But this is not of course the case. There are various ways in which different syllabus specifications may be combined to create what is sometimes referred to as the 'multidimensional syllabus' (Johnson 1982; Stern 1992). In order to discuss the multidimensional syllabus, it is beneficial to introduce a distinction which although sometimes difficult to apply in practice nevertheless has its uses. It is between a *syllabus inventory* and a *syllabus*. The former is a collection of lists made according to various parameters – functions, topics, structures etc. – and is hence multidimensional by its very nature. A clear example of a syllabus specification is the Council of Europe's *T Level* document where the parameters are settings, topics, roles, notions, functions and exponents. It is nowadays the rule rather than the exception to find materials where syllabus specifications (in the contents page) show various specifications – functions, structures, topics and the like.

Course designers often select one of the parameters on the syllabus specification to be their unit of organisation. From the *T Level* they might for example select the setting, the topic or the function, to produce a setting-based (situational) syllabus, or a topic-based syllabus, or a functional syllabus. Because one parameter is selected as unit of organisation, it does not mean that the other parameters are ignored. Hence if course writers select the function their unit of organisation, they can ensure that each functional unit deals with materials related to the settings, topics, roles and notions on the specification; these lists would in effect operate as check lists. Because such a course would be based on one unit of organisation, it would be an example of the uni-dimensional syllabus (based on a multidimensional syllabus inventory).

But equally clearly multidimensional specifications can lead to syllabuses where the unit of organisation shifts at different points in the course. One example in the early days of n/f is Morrow and Johnson (1979). These are functionally based materials, with each teaching unit covering a functional area. But since it is recognised that functional organisation leads the learner to encounter structural diversity (a number of different grammatical structures occurring in the same functional unit), a number of structurally-oriented units are interspersed to bring together grammatical points which might otherwise not receive sufficient coverage. A more frequent type of multidimensionality in recent times involves shifts of focus within each teaching unit. Thus sections of a unit will focus on a structure, others on a function, and still others perhaps in a syllabus of learning procedures.

There are several advantages to basing courses on a multidimensional syllabus. Sinclair and Renouf (1988) note that this serves to show that "language has many facets, and corresponds partially to many different patterns of organization" (Sinclair and Renouf 1988: 144). There is also the potential pedagogic advantage of providing variety, with the shift of focus changing at regular points. But there are also disadvantages. Johnson (1982: 68) notes that over-frequent shifts of focus may confuse the learner. Sinclair and Renouf (1988), who consider this issue from the point of view of teaching structures and lexis, note that "it is exceptionally difficult to teach an organized syllabus of both grammar and lexis at the same time" (Sinclair and Renouf 1988: 143). The variety may, they say, be bewildering, "and the actual coordination minimal".

11. Conclusion: Systematic and non-systematic components in course design

There are few if any educational domains where so much attention has been paid to course design as in the domain of second or foreign language teaching. The developments that have occurred in this area over the past few decades have resulted in syllabuses very much more complex and rich than those of the past. This complexification and enrichment comes hand in hand with increasingly developed insights into what is involved in both language use and language learning.

A theme that has occurred more than once in this chapter is the form versus message distinction. By way of conclusion, two further related distinctions will be considered because they together raise the issue as to the extent to which it is desirable entirely to map out course content – the issue, one might say, of the limits of (linguistically specified) course design. The two distinctions relate more directly to practice types than to syllabus design, but have implications for the latter. The first is *part versus whole* – part practice being focused on selected (linguistic) items, whole (holistic) practice on language use involving the combination of a number of linguistic skills in real time. The second is *control versus freedom* – controlled practice being where input and output are under the control of the teacher, course book, syllabus; versus free practice where learners are given rein to say or write what they please. It is possible to put forward a pedagogically sound case that a course design should allow for all these sorts of practice. If so, then a means has to be found of incorporating not just part and controlled practice, but whole and free practice too, the latter in components which are not linguistically pre-specified (mapped out linguistically in advance).

We have already considered some ways of combining these various components, suggesting how control may be injected into a freer sort of practice (form focus put into task-based work, for example). Mention has also been made of the adjunct version of CBI where content teaching is linked to language teaching; the former may be regarded as relatively linguistically uncontrolled while the latter may involve a degree of control. Some versions of the multidimensional syllabus may also manage the mixture; a combination of structural and task-based teaching for example might manage this.

Johnson (1981, 1996, 2004) considers the issue in terms of what he calls 'systematic' and 'non-systematic' components to language courses, and puts forward a number of possible ways of combining the two. Johnson (2004) describes a *Contiguous Component Solution*. This is similar in many respects to the adjunct version of CBI. In it, the teaching programme has two components. One is a component of form-focused language work, possibly following a traditional structural syllabus. Component 2 contains nothing but message-focused activities or tasks. The two components would run contiguously; for example, Component 1 might be used on Mondays, Wednesdays and Fridays, and Component 2 on Tuesdays and Thursdays. There would be the possibility of altering the relative proportions according to learner level. The feature of this solution which distinguishes it from adjunct CBI is that no attempt is made to relate the two components in terms of content. The content covered in Component 1 would neither feed into nor come out of what occurs in the non-systematic Component 2. The components would follow quite separate programmes, and the expectation would be that over a long period of time (that is, not the next day, nor even the next week) language learned in Component 1 would begin to make its appearance in Component 2, 'seeping' (to use Tarone's (1983) term) from form-focused practice into message-focused activities. One characteristic of this procedure is that it avoids hypothesising too direct a link between input and uptake which many find the major objection to the standard presentation → practice → production sequence. The notion of two linguistically unrelated components reflects the expectation that a more circuitous path exists linking what is taught and practised with what becomes internalised and proceduralised.

Whether this Contiguous Component Solution or some other one is adopted, the case remains strong that courses should not be 'linguistically designed' from beginning to end. The complexification and enrichment in course design mentioned at the beginning of this section brings with it the danger of course 'over-specification'. But good course design involves understanding not just what (and how) to design, but also what not to design.

Notes

1 Wilkins' later book (1976) introduces a third category type, *Categories of modal meaning*. These have been less influential on developments in syllabus design and are hence not discussed here.

2 Unfortunately there are differences in the way terminology is used. Wilkins uses the term 'notional' to refer to syllabuses stated in terms of either semantico-grammatical categories or categories of communicative function, or both. 'Notional syllabus' is therefore an 'umbrella term' for this type of syllabus in general. But many call 'semantico-grammatical categories' notions, and in this terminology a 'notional syllabus' would be one expressed in semantico-grammatical terms only. Similarly 'categories of communicative functions' are called functions. The 'umbrella term' in this case would be 'notional/functional syllabuses'. One also finds 'semantic' and 'communicative' used in this umbrella sense.

3 The exception is if the learners themselves request form focus by asking questions (e.g. about grammar).

References

Alexander, Louis G.
1974 *Target English.* Harlow: Longman.

Bialystok, Ellen
1982 On the relationship between knowing and using linguistic forms. *Applied Linguistics* 3 (3): 181–206.

Breen, Michael P.
1983 Prepared comments on paper by Keith Johnson. In: Keith Johnson and Don Porter (eds), *Perspectives in Communicative Language Teaching*, 58–66. London: Academic Press.

Breen, Michael P.
1984 Process syllabuses for the language classroom. In: Christopher J. Brumfit (ed.), *General English Syllabus Design*, 47–60. Oxford: Modern English Publications with the British Council. ELT Documents 118.

Breen, Michael P. and Christopher N. Candlin
1980 The essentials of a communicative curriculum in language teaching. *Applied Linguistics* 1 (2): 89–112.
Brinton, Donna M., Marguerite A. Snow and Marjorie Wesche
1989 *Content-Based Second Language Instruction.* Rowley, Mass.: Newbury House.
Bruner, Jerome S.
1960 *The Process of Education.* Cambridge, Ma.: Harvard University Press.
Bullock, Alan
1975 *A Language for Life: Report of the Committee of Inquiry Appointed by the Secretary of State for Education and Science under the Chairmanship of Sir Alan Bullock.* F.B.A. London: Her Majesty's Stationery Office.
Bygate, Martin
2005 Oral second language abilities as expertise. In: Keith Johnson (ed.), *Expertise in Second Language Learning and Teaching*, 104–127. Basingstoke: Palgrave Macmillan.
Cook, Guy
1998 The uses of reality: a reply to Ronald Carter. *ELT Journal* 52: 57–64.
Crookes, Graham
1989 Planning and interlanguage variability. *Studies in Second Language Acquisition* 11: 367–383.
de Bot, Kees
1996 The psycholinguistics of the output hypothesis. *Language Learning* 46: 529–555.
Deller, Sheelagh and Christine Price
2007 *Teaching Other Subjects through English.* Oxford: Oxford University Press.
Doughty, Catherine and Jessica Williams
1998 *Focus on Form in Classroom Second Language Acquisition.* Cambridge: Cambridge University Press.
Dulay, Heidi and Marina K. Burt
1973 Should we teach children syntax? *Language Learning* 23 (2): 245–258.
Dulay, Heidi and Marina K. Burt
1974 Natural sequences in child second language acquisition. *Language Learning* 24 (1): 37–53.
Ellis, Rod
1985 *Understanding Second Language Acquisition.* Oxford: Oxford University Press.
Fodor, Jerry A. and Merrill Garrett
1966 Some reflections on competence and performance. In: John Lyons and Roger J. Wales (eds.), *Psycholinguistics Papers*, 135–182. Edinburgh: Edinburgh University Press.
George, Herbert V.
1963 A verb-form frequency count. *English Language Teaching* 18 (1): 31–37.
George, Herbert V.
1971 *Common Errors in Language Learning.* Rowley, Mass.: Newbury House.
Gougenheim, Georges M., Paul Rivenc, René Michéa and Aurélien Sauvageot
1956 *L'Élaboration du Français Elementaire: Étude sur l'etablissement d'un vocabulaire et d'une grammaire de base.* Paris: Didier.

Halliday, Mak A. K., Angus McIntosh and Peter Strevens
1964 *The Linguistic Sciences and Language Teaching.* Harlow: Longman.

Hatch, Evelyn
1978 Apply with caution. *Studies in Second Language Acquisition* 2 (2): 123–143.

Herriot, Peter
1969 The comprehension of active and passive sentences as a function of pragmatic expectations. *Journal of Verbal Learning and Verbal Behaviour* 8: 166–169.

Hirst, Paul
1975 *The Curriculum and its Objectives: A Defence of Piecemeal Curriculum Planning.* The Curriculum, Studies in Education 2. Windsor: NFER Publishing Company.

Hymes, Dell
1970 On communicative competence. In: John Gumperz and Dell Hymes (eds.), *Directions in Sociolinguistics*, 35–71. New York: Holt, Rinehart and Winston.

Johnson, Helen
1992 Defossilizing. *ELT Journal* 46 (2): 180–189.

Johnson, Keith
1979 Communicative approaches and communicative processes. In: Christopher J. Brumfit and Keith Johnson (eds.), *The Communicative Approach to Language Teaching*, 192–205. Oxford: Oxford University Press.

Johnson, Keith
1981 'Systematic' and 'non-systematic' components in a communicative approach to language teaching. In: René Richterich and Henry G. Widdowson (eds.), *Description, Présentation et Enseignement des Langues*, 60–72. Paris: Credif/Hatier.

Johnson, Keith
1982 *Communicative Syllabus Design and Methodology.* Oxford: Pergamon Institute of English.

Johnson, Keith
1993 Review of White, R.V and Arndt, V. 'Process Writing'. *ELT Journal* 47 (1): 89–91.

Johnson, Keith
1996 *Language Teaching and Skill Learning.* Oxford: Blackwell Publishers.

Johnson, Keith
2004 From communicative activity to task: A short but significant journey. *The Journal of Asia TEFL* 1 (1): 185–195.

Johnson, Keith and Keith E. Morrow
1979 *Approaches.* Cambridge: Cambridge University Press.

Krashen, Stephen D.
1985 *The Input Hypothesis: Issues and Implications.* London: Longman.

Lado, Robert
1957 *Linguistics across Cultures: Applied Linguistics for Language Teachers.* Ann Arbor/Michigan: University of Michigan.

Leech, Geoffrey, Paul Rayson and Andrew Wilson
2001 *Word Frequencies in Written and Spoken English: Based on the British National Corpus.* London: Longman.

Long, Michael H.
1991 Focus on form: a design feature in language teaching methodology. In: Kees de Bot, Daniel Coste, Ralph Ginsberg and Claire Kramsch (eds.), *Foreign Language Research in Cross-Cultural Perspective*, 39–52. Amsterdam: John Benjamins.

Long, Michael H.
1985 A role for instruction in second language acquisition: task-based language training. In: Kenneth Hyltenstam and Manfred Pienemann, *Modelling and Assessing Second Language Acquisition*, 77–100. Clevedon: Multilingual Matters.

Long, Michael H.
1996 The role of the linguistic environment in second language acquisition. In: William C. Ritchie and Tej K. Bhatia (eds.), *Handbook of Second Language Acquisition*, 413–468. San Diego: Academic Press.

Long, Michael H. and Graham Crookes
1992 Three approaches to task-based syllabus design. *TESOL Quarterly* 26 (1): 27–56.

Mackay, William F.
1965 *Language Teaching Analysis*. London: Longman.

McDonough, Steven
1980 Psychological aspects of sequencing. *International Review of Applied Linguistics* 18 (4): 311–320.

McEnery, Tony and Andrew Wilson
1996 *Corpus Linguistics*. Edinburgh: Edinburgh University Press.

Morrow, Keith and Keith Johnson
1979 *Communicate 1 and 2*. Cambridge: Cambridge University Press.

Newmark, Leonard
1966 How not to interfere with language learning. *International Journal of American Linguistics* 32 (1): 77–83.

Palfreman, Jon
1983 *A Child's Guide to Languages*. Horizon. UK: BBC Television.

Palmer, Harold E.
[1917] 1968 *The Scientific Study and Teaching of Languages*. Oxford: Oxford University Press.

Pienemann, Manfred
1985 Learnability and syllabus construction. In: Kenneth Hyltenstam and Manfred Pienemann (eds.), *Modelling and Assessing Second Language Acquisition*, 23–75. Clevedon: Multilingual Matters.

Pienemann, Manfred
1998 *Language Processing and Second Language Development: Processability Theory*. Amsterdam/Philadelphia: John Benjamins Publishing Company.

Prabhu, N. S.
1986 *The Bangalore Project*. Interview with Keith Johnson. Reading: Centre for Applied Language Studies, University of Reading.

Prabhu, N. S.
1987 *Second Language Pedagogy: A Perspective*. Oxford: Oxford University Press.

Renouf, Antoinette J.
1984 Corpus development at Birmingham University. In: Jan Aarts and Willem Meijs (eds.), *Corpus Linguistics: Recent Developments in the Use of Computer Corpora in English Language Research*, 3–39. Amsterdam: Rodopi.

Richterich, René
1972 Definition of language needs and types of adults. In: John L. M. Trim, René Richterich, Jan van Ek, and David A. Wilkins, *Systems Development in Adult Language Learning*, 29–88. Strasbourg: Council of Europe.

RIE
1980 *Newsletter 1 (Special Series).* Regional Institute of English South India, Bangalore.

Rogers, Margaret
1994 German word order: a role for developmental and linguistic factors in L2 pedagogy. In: Martin Bygate, Alan Tonkyn and Eddie Williams (eds.), *Grammar and the Language Teacher*, 132–159. New York: Prentice Hall.

Samuda, Virginia
2001 Guiding relationships between form and meaning during task performance: the role of the teacher. In: Martin Bygate, Peter Skehan and Merril Swain (eds.), *Researching Pedagogic Tasks: Second Language Learning, Teaching and Testing*, 119–140. London: Pearson Education.

Sinclair, John M. and Antoinette J. Renouf
1988 A lexical syllabus for language learning. In: Ronald Carter and Michael McCarthy (eds.), *Vocabulary and Language Teaching*, 141–160. London: Longman.

Skehan, Peter
1992 Second language acquisition strategies and task-based learning. In: Peter Skehan and Chafe Wallace (eds.), *Thames Valley University Working Papers in English Language Teaching*, 178–208. ELT Department, Thames Valley University.

Skehan, Peter
1998 Task-based instruction. In: William E. A. Grabe, *Annual Review of Applied Linguistics 18: Foundations of Second Language Teaching*, 268–286. Cambridge: Cambridge University Press.

Skehan, Peter and Pauline Foster
1995 Task type and task processing conditions as influences on foreign language performance. In: Peter Skehan (ed.), *Thames Valley University Working Papers in English Language Teaching*, 139–188. ELT Department, Thames Valley University.

Stern, Hans H.
1992 *Issues and Options in Language Teaching.* Oxford: Oxford University Press.

Swain, Merrill
1993 Three functions of output in second language learning. In: Guy Cook and Barbara Seidlhofer (eds.), *Principles and Practice in Applied Linguistics: Studies in Honour of H. G. Widdowson*, 125–144. Oxford: Oxford University Press.

Tarone, Elaine
1983 On the variability of interlanguage systems. *Applied Linguistics* 4 (2): 141–163.

Taylor, Philip H. and Colin Richards
1979 *An Introduction to Curriculum Studies.* Windsor: NFER Publishing Company.

van Ek, Jan A.
1975 *The Threshold Level.* Strasbourg: Council of Europe.

van Ek, Jan A.
1978 *The Threshold Level for Schools.* Harlow: Longman.

Vigil, Neddy A. and John W. Oller
1976 Rule fossilization: a tentative model. *Language Learning* 26 (2): 281–295.

Wason, Peter C. and Philip N. Johnson-Laird
1972 *The Psychology of Reasoning.* London: Batsford.

Wesche, Marjorie B. and Peter Skehan
2002 Communicative, task-based, and content-based language instruction. In: Robert B. Kaplan (ed.), *Oxford Handbook of Applied Linguistics*, 207–228. Oxford: Oxford University Press.

White, Ronald V.
1988 *The ELT Curriculum.* Oxford: Blackwell Publishers.

Widdowson, Henry G.
1978 The acquisition and use of language system. In: Albert Valdman (ed.), *Studies in Second Language Acquisition*, 15–26. Indiana University Linguistics Club 2/1.

Widdowson, Henry G.
1980 Models and fictions. *Applied Linguistics* 1 (2): 165–170.

Widdowson, Henry G.
2000 On the limitations of linguistics applied. *Applied Linguistics* 21 (1): 3–25.

Widdowson, Henry G.
2003 *Defining Issues in English Language Teaching.* Oxford: Oxford University Press.

Wilkins, David A.
1972 Grammatical, situational and notional syllabuses. Reprinted in: Christopher J. Brumfit and Keith Johnson (eds.), *The Communicative Approach to Language Teaching*, 82–90. Oxford: Oxford University Press, 1979.

Wilkins, David A.
1973 An investigation into the linguistic and situational common core in a unit/credit system. In: John L. M. Trim, René Richterich, Jan van Ek and David A. Wilkins, *Systems Development in Adult Language Learning*, 129–146. Oxford: Pergamon Institute of English.

Wilkins, David A.
1976 *Notional Syllabuses.* Oxford: Oxford University Press.

Wilkins, David A., Christopher J. Brumfit and Christina B. Paulston
1981 Notional syllabuses revisited. *Applied Linguistics* 2 (1): 83–100.

Willis, Dave
1990 *The Lexical Syllabus: A new Approach to Language Teaching.* London: Harper Collins.

Willis, Dave
1994 A Lexical approach. In: Martin Bygate, Alan Tonkyn and Eddie Williams (eds.), *Grammar and the Language Teacher*, 56–66. New York: Prentice Hall.
Willis, Jane
1996 *A Framework for Task-based Learning*. London: Longman.
Yalden, Janice
1983 *The Communicative Syllabus: Evolution, Design and Implementation*. Oxford: Pergamon Institute of English.

Recommended readings

Breen, Michael P.
1984 Process syllabuses for the language classroom. In Christopher J Brumfit (ed.), *General English Syllabus Design*, 47–60. Oxford: Modern English Publications with the British Council. ELT Documents 118.
Brinton, Donna M., Marguerite A. Snow and Marjorie B. Wesche
1989 *Content-Based Second Language Instruction*. Rowley, Mass.: Newbury House.
Doughty, Catherine and Jessica Williams
1998 *Focus on Form in Classroom Second Language Acquisition*. Cambridge: Cambridge University Press.
Graves, Kathleen
1999 *Designing Language Courses: A Guide for Teachers*. Florence, KY: Heinle ELT.
Johnson, Keith
1982 *Communicative Syllabus Design and Methodology*. Oxford: Pergamon Institute of English.
Long, Michael H. and Graham Crookes
1992 Three approaches to task-based syllabus design. *TESOL Quarterly* 26 (1): 27–56.
McDonough, Jo and Christopher Shaw
2003 *Materials and Methods in ELT: Second Edition*. Oxford: Blackwell (particularly Part 1).
Pienemann, Manfred
1985 Learnability and syllabus construction. In: Kenneth Hyltenstam and Manfred Pienemann (eds.), *Modelling and Assessing Second Language Acquisition*, 23–75. Clevedon: Multilingual Matters.
Prabhu, N. S.
1987 *Second Language Pedagogy: A Perspective*. Oxford: Oxford University Press.
Richards, Jack C.
2001 *Curriculum Development in Language Teaching*. Cambridge: Cambridge University Press.

Sinclair, John M. and Antoinette Renouf
1988 A lexical syllabus for language learning. In: Ronald Carter and Michael McCarthy (eds.), *Vocabulary and Language Teaching*, 141–160. London: Longman.
Wesche, Marjorie B. and Peter Skehan
2002 Communicative, task-based, and content-based language instruction. In: Robert B. Kaplan (ed.), *Oxford Handbook of Applied Linguistics*, 207–228. Oxford: Oxford University Press.
White, Ronald V.
1988 *The ELT Curriculum.* Oxford: Blackwell Publishers.
Wilkins, David A.
1976 *Notional Syllabuses.* Oxford: Oxford University Press.
Yalden, Janice
1983 *The Communicative Syllabus: Evolution, Design and Implementation.* Oxford: Pergamon Institute of English.

13. The methodology of foreign language teaching: Methods, approaches, principles

Theodore S. Rodgers

1. Methodology defined

As one dictionary (The *Oxford Advanced Learner's*) defines it, methodology is 'a set of methods and principles used to perform a particular activity'. The activity we are concerned with is foreign or second language teaching. That seems straightforward enough. However, the concept of methodology would seem to be problematic. We might note, to begin with, that the term itself is not used with any consistency in the applied linguistic literature devoted to issues in foreign language teaching.

The Cambridge Guide to Teaching English to Speakers of Other Languages (Carter and Nunan 2001), for example, there is, in its 25 thematic chapters, no separate and explicit treatment of methodology as such at all. Another overview appearing a year later from the same publisher goes to the opposite extreme: *Methodology in Language Teaching: An Anthology of Current Practice* (Richards and Renandya 2002) gives prominence to methodology, but uses it indiscriminately as an umbrella term to cover almost every topic in language education imaginable.

Earlier literature on the teaching of foreign or other languages acknowledges the notion of methodology but interprets it in somewhat diverse ways. Methodology is variously taken as comprising:

a) various generic techniques for teaching of the basic skill areas of reading, writing, listening and speaking (Harmer 1997; Ur 1997),
b) a universal set of techniques for teaching any linguistic material in any skill e.g. Presentation, Practice, Production (PPP) (Rivers 1968) or Observe, Hypothesise, Experiment (Lewis 1993),
c) an eclectic, teacher-personalised collage of techniques and methods (Hammerly 1991),
d) learning to put into practice certain general principles of good language teaching derived from research or observation (Brown 1994; Kumaravadivelu 1994),
e) conscious modelling by less experienced teachers of the practices of expert or experienced teachers whatever these may be (Freeman 1992, Revell and Norman 1997).

Abstracting common features from these different views, methodology might be defined as the variety of ways teachers use to activate the learning process –

the techniques, activities, etc. locally appropriate to particular teaching/learning situations. Such a definition can be related to Keith Johnson's contribution to this volume (ch. 12) which deals with syllabus design by saying that methodology broadly conceived is the way a syllabus may be implemented, thus drawing a general distinction between syllabus and methodology, the former being a static construct, the latter a dynamic process.

But this variety of ways of activating the learning process are not just random practices but are informed by some beliefs or assumptions, whether made explicit or not, about what constitutes effective learning and how it can be most effectively induced. So this way of thinking of methodology is consistent with the dictionary definition we began with: methodology can be understood as a set of principles underlying practice. Defined in this general way, methodology is to be distinguished from specific sets of procedures/techniques which constitute a method or methods tied to particular prescriptions of how language should be organised for instruction.

The dictionary entry also refers to a set of methods, and methodology has also been defined along these lines as comprising:

f) descriptions and demonstrations of various methods and their features, e.g. Silent Way, Natural Approach, Suggestopedia, Total Physical Response, etc. (Larsen-Freeman 2000; Richards and Rodgers 2001)

Methodology, then, can be taken as a general cover term for classroom activities directed at the inducement of language learning. This can be understood in two ways: either as a set of general principles that in one way or another inform the variety of local practices, or as a set of methods that prescribe particular techniques of instruction. Either way, we can take methodology as referring to a range of pedagogic practices, some of which become specified as prescribed methods.

2. Methods

Although ideas about language teaching and learning have a long history, it is in the mid-19th century that these most prominently took the form of specific methods, that is to say a specification of prescribed procedures or techniques. (Howatt 2004; Kelly 1969) What appears to distinguish post-1840 methods from earlier proposals and practices are factors like the following:

a) represented as unique and distinctive, labelled with the definite article and the term 'method' (e.g., The Prussian Method, The Direct Method, The Grammar Translation Method, The Berlitz Method, The Audio-Lingual Method),
b) represented as an innovation or discovery,

c) often associated with a 'guru' – a major father figure – as self-proclaimed founder of 'the' method,
d) specification of a set of instructional directions and exercises to be rigorously followed in the implementation of the prescribed method,
e) vigorous and committed promotion by its believers.

Novel features of methods were often, indeed, novel at the time, and many of the features of earlier methods were re-cycled in the pedagogy of a century later. Focus on oral language, the use of inductive rather than deductive presentation, involving gestures on the part of teachers, and physical movement on the part of the student, the use of conversational dialogs, the rationalised specification of selection and sequencing of language forms, the featuring of 'natural' language use – all these were promoted as unique contributions to language instruction by 19th century method creators. And all of these features appear again, with recognisable similarities if in different combinations, in methods introduced a century later.

The mid-years of the 20th century was dominated by a set of classroom practices which became known as 'The Audio-lingual Method'. The major features of audiolingualism were lessons built around dialogues featuring particular grammatical features and intensive practice of those features through teacher-directed pattern practice.

The period of the 1970s and 1980s was marked by a set of methods which emerged out of disaffection with audiolingualism and were often somewhat idiosyncratic in name and procedure. These were typically associated with one 'founder spokesman', usually (coincidentally or not) a white male of middle years. To emphasise the liveliness of method invention and promulgation during this period of one hundred years or more, Richards and Rodgers (2001) give brief surveys of 18 methods (and approaches) Each of these was typically associated with a specific set of activities which marked the brand. Although many of the activities, even if not crediting their original sources, were subsequently taken up and indeed still appear in teacher preparation programs and in standard second language student texts, they were extracted as separate elements and not as parts of the whole package that defines the method as such.

2.1. Some major methods

One educational website lists some thirty second language teaching 'methods'. Activity types for all of these cannot be described even if it were instructive to do so.

Below are given some thumbnail descriptions of learning activities recommended (or prescribed) for several of the more widely-discussed methods from the middle 1800's to the present time (see also Neuner and Hunfeld 1993;

Ortner 1998). Although widely discussed, it is difficult to determine how many of the methods comprised mainline language teaching practices in their time or with what fidelity teachers claiming to teach according to these methods actually followed these prescribed practices.

2.1.1. *Presentation, practice and production (PPP)*

This is not so much a specific method as a more generally prescribed formulaic procedure offered as a 'standard' practice for prospective language teachers in their pre-service training.

'Presentation' represents the introduction to a lesson, and necessarily requires the creation of a realistic (or realistic-feeling) situation requiring the target language to be learned. The language elements are provided in small familiar chunks. A target language 'model' is then presented on which choral practice is based. This is a very teacher-orientated stage where error correction is important.

'Practice' usually begins with what is termed 'mechanical practice' by means of drills and repetitive exercises, and gradually moving into more demanding procedures like information gap activities, dialog creation and controlled role-plays. Practice is seen as the necessary first stage in ensuring accurate knowledge of the new language.

'Production' is seen as the culmination of the language learning process, whereby the learners act upon their linguistic knowledge, where they perform their competence and become users of the language. The teacher's role here is to provide occasions where the students can actively apply the language they have been practising. The teacher typically does not correct or become involved unless students directly appeal to him/her to do so.

PPP has by no means met with universal approval. Indeed it has sometimes been roundly condemned:

> [...] any paradigm based on, or remotely resembling, Present-Practice-Produce (PPP) is wholly unsatisfactory, failing as it does to reflect either the nature of language or the nature of learning. It is not sufficient to suggest that such a paradigm represents one of a number of ways in which language is learned; the fact is that the PPP paradigm is, and always was, nonsense. (Lewis 1996: 11)

Lewis offers an alternative formula:

The OHE Cycle – *Observe, Hypothesise, Experiment* (Lewis 1991).

Other proposals for three stage procedures include:

The ITB Model – *Into, Through and Beyond* (Brinton and Holten 1997).

The ESA Model – *Engage, Study, Activate* (Harmer 1998).

2.1.2. The Grammar-Translation Method

The principal characteristics of learning via the Grammar-Translation Method were these:

1. The goal of foreign language study is to learn a language in order to read its literature or in order to benefit from the mental discipline and intellectual development that result from foreign language study.
2. Reading and writing are the major focus; little or no systematic attention is paid to speaking or listening.
3. Vocabulary selection is based solely on the reading texts used, and words are taught through bilingual word lists, dictionary study, and memorisation.
4. The sentence is the basic unit of teaching and language practice. Much of the lesson is devoted to translating sentences into and out of the target language.
5. High standards of accuracy are emphasised.
6. Grammar is taught deductively; that is, by presentation and study of systematically presented grammar rules, which are then practised through translation exercises.
7. The student's native language is the medium of instruction. It is used to explain new items and to enable comparisons to be made between the foreign language and the student's native language.

2.1.3. The Direct Method

The Direct Method originated in Europe in the 19th century and is still used widely in commercial language schools. Typical activities and practices include:

1. Classroom instruction is conducted exclusively in the target language.
2. Only everyday vocabulary and sentences are taught.
3. Oral communication skills are built up in a carefully graded progression, chiefly organised around question-and-answer exchanges between teachers and students.
4. Grammar is taught inductively.
5. New teaching points are introduced orally.
6. Concrete vocabulary is taught through demonstration, objects, and pictures; abstract vocabulary is taught by association of ideas.
7. Both speech and listening comprehension are focused on.
8. Correct pronunciation and grammar are emphasised.

2.1.4. *The Audio-Lingual Method*

Dialogues and drills form the basis of audio-lingual classroom practices. Dialogues provide the means of contextualising key structures and illustrate situations in which structures might be used. Various kinds of drills are used to practice the patterns demonstrated in the dialogues. Brooks (1964: 156–161) includes the following Audio-Lingual-Method-drill types:

1. *Repetition.*
2. *Inflection.* One word in an utterance appears in another form when repeated.
3. *Replacement.* One word in an utterance is replaced by another.
4. *Restatement.* The student rephrases an utterance.
5. *Completion.* The student hears an utterance that is complete except for one word then repeats the utterance in completed form.
6. *Transposition.* A change in word order is necessary when a word is added.
7. *Expansion.* When a word is added it takes a certain place in the sequence.
8. *Contraction.* A single word stands for a phrase or clause examples.
9. *Transformation.* A sentence is transformed by being made negative or interrogative.
10. *Integration.* Two separate utterances are integrated into one.
11. *Rejoinder.* The student makes an appropriate rejoinder to a given utterance.
12. *Restoration.* The student is given a sequence of words that have been culled from a sentence and uses these words to restore the sentence to its original form.

2.1.5. *Total physical response*

Imperative drills are the major classroom activity in Total Physical Response. They are typically used to elicit physical actions and activity on the part of the learners. An example would be:

Wash
wash your hands.
your face.
your hair.

Other class activities include role plays and slide presentations, where role plays centre on simulation of everyday situations and the carrying out of classroom available actions.

2.1.6. *Suggestopedia*

Physical surroundings and atmosphere in classroom, including art and music, are vital to make sure that students feel relaxed and confident (See Lozanov 1979; Schiffler 1991). An early lesson of Suggestopedia usually consisted of three phases: deciphering, concert session (memorisation séance), and elaboration.

1. *Deciphering*: The teacher introduces the grammar and vocabulary of a target text, preferably in a playful manner.
2. *Concert session (active and passive):* In the active session, the teacher reads the text at a normal speed, sometimes intoning some words, and the students follow. In the passive session, the students relax and listen to the teacher reading the text calmly. Music ('Pre-Classical') is played background.
3. *Elaboration*: The students demonstrate what they have learned via original texts, dramas, songs, and games.

2.1.7. *The Silent Way*

Perhaps typical of the period was the method labelled by its founder 'The Silent Way'. For a decade, Silent Way received official status as the preferred method of teaching languages to Peace Corps volunteers chosen to work in various, mostly 'third world', situations. The Silent Way was based on the premise that the teacher should be silent as much as possible in the classroom and the learner should be encouraged to think through and verbally produce, independently, as many solicited language utterances as possible. It was primarily aimed at oral production of beginning second language learners. The Silent Way and its accompanying paraphernalia – Fidel pronunciation charts, Cuisenaire rods, vocabulary charts, books, worksheets, audio and video tapes, etc. were actively promoted by the head guru, Caleb Gattegno, in a number of presentations and publications (e.g. Gattegno 1972). It was similarly supported by several educational enthusiasts reared within the previous audio-lingual tradition (e.g. Stevick 1980; Oller and Amato 1983).

2.2. Methods appraised

Recently there seems to be a broadly articulated opinion that although there was once an age of 'Language Teaching Methods' that age is now over, and that it is not only possible but desirable to conceive of methodology with no methods in mind. Brown (1994) opined that "[t]he era of methods is over"; and Kumaravadivelu (1994, 2001) noted that the profession is now in post-method "condition" and required post-method "thinking".

What motivated the fall from grace of methods and brought about the anti-method sentiments that are recorded in, for example, Brown (2002), Richards

(1984), Richards and Rodgers (2001)? The reasons were, broadly speaking, of two kinds, one related to their pedagogic applicability, the other to their theoretical underpinning.

With regard to the first kind of reason, it was argued that methods tended to be too prescriptively rigid. On the micro-level of local classroom reality, no account was taken of the variable socio-cultural and individual characteristics of teachers and students, so there was an imposition of conformity on a naturally dynamic process. On the macro-level, methods were not sensitive to the larger educational, social and political contexts in which learning and teaching are inevitably set. On the educational front, they were offered as 'stand-alone' pedagogical entities rather than as one of many inter-related sub-components comprising curriculum. Curriculum design, development, dissemination and assessment are not viewed as relevant and necessary elements in the planning of instruction. In short, the adoption of a prescribed method left little room for any necessary adaptation.

With regard to the second kind of reason, methods were typically unsupported by any explicit theorising or evidence of empirical data. They tended to be based on implicit belief, and to represent personal pedagogic preferences and not much else. With the emergence of applied linguistics, it was thought that proposals for language teaching could and should be put on a more explicit and principled theoretical and empirical footing.

Although we might concede that there is a case against methods along these lines, it should also be recognised that many of the ideas implicit in their procedures have found their way into current thinking. Thus, for example the notion that students should talk more than the teacher, that non-verbal clues, artefacts and media are useful aids to language learning, that cognition and problem solving are supportive of learning and retention were all major premises of the Silent Way. Other ideas, as we shall see, have been incorporated into subsequent methodological assumptions.

This is not to suggest that the similarities between several current methodology proposals and those of the earlier methods represent some sort of intentional continuity or deliberate development in language pedagogy. Some forty years ago Mackey observed that "while sciences have advanced by approximations in which each new stage results from an improvement, not a rejection, of what has gone before, language teaching methods have followed the pendulum of fashion from one extreme to the other" (Mackey 1965: 139). Despite some current disagreement regarding the onward and upward characterisation of the path of scientific progress and, despite some disclaimers that current post-method thinking has disarmed the pendulum of fashion (e.g. Kumaravadivelu 1994), we are nevertheless witnessing some unwitting re-cycling into current thinking of a number of instructional suggestions from former methods since abandoned or ignored.

It is also worth noting that some of the ideas, at least those that were followed in the design of methods, implicitly and instinctively informed by pedagogic experience, have subsequently been endorsed by theoretical research. As evidence for this, PPP is a case in point. Although dismissed as totally invalid (e.g. Lewis 1996) and theoretically uninformed ("there is no *evidence* in its favour, or *theory*", Skehan 1996: 18), recent research in cognitive psychology would seem to provide substantial evidence in its support (de Keyser 2007).

But there is a further point that might be made in favour of methods. Their formulaic nature as a set of directions for teaching may, as we have seen, have its pedagogic shortcomings, but it also has the advantage of providing specific guidelines and with them a sense of security, for trainee teachers. So methods can be used as training to provide a basis on which later initiatives can develop, as a preliminary phase in teacher education. It might also be added that the common belief in a method has a solidarity effect: it creates a sense of professional community, with a shared purpose, ideology, and idiom and this provides adherents with a cohort of like-minded colleagues with whom they can share enthusiasm, ideas and experiences.

Nevertheless, all that being said, the main charge against methods as the imposition of a set of prescribed procedures remains. And the recognition of the need to be more flexible, more adaptable to variable pedagogic conditions brings with it a move from the notion of method to the notion of approach.

3. Approaches

The generally accepted distinction between method and approach has been formulated as follows:

> A method refers to a specific instructional design or system based on a particular theory of language and of language learning. It contains detailed specifications of content, roles of teachers and learners and of teaching procedures and techniques. It is relatively fixed in time and there is generally little scope for individual interpretation. Methods are learned through training. The teacher's role is to follow the method and apply it precisely according to the rules.

An approach, on the other hand, is a more general set of beliefs and principles that can be used as a basis for language teaching.

> Each of these approaches (or at least those that have been more fully elaborated and adopted) has a core set of theories and beliefs about the nature of language, of language learning, and a derived set of principles for teaching a language. None of them however leads to a specific set of prescriptions and techniques to be used in teaching a language. They are characterised by a variety of interpretations as to how the principles can be applied. [...] They allow for individual interpretation and application. They can be revised and updated over time as new theories and new practices emerge. (Richards and Rodgers 2001: 244–245).

Many of the current anti-method proposals can thus be considered 'approaches' under this broad definition. The most popular of the approaches which came to supplant methods were Communicative Language Teaching (CLT) and its offshoots – Task-Based Language Teaching (TBLT) and Content-Based Instruction (CBI). I will now review these approaches and the proposals for instruction and the particular activities, exercises and tasks that came to be associated with these approaches.

3.1. Communicative language teaching (CLT)

In spite of certain differences of perspective on communicative language teaching (cf. Brumfit and Johnson 1979; Legutke and Schocker-v. Ditfurth 2003; Savignon 2003; Widdowson 1978; see also Byram and Mendez, ch. 18 this volume) there is general agreement that, by definition, the approach does not specify exercises, activities and tasks that were required to be followed, but presents them as exemplary rather than compulsory in teaching texts and training sessions. Such examples were shown as deriving from the philosophy of the approach rather than from specified work plans. In a widely read paper, Finocchiaro and Brumfit (1983) contrasted the major distinctions in philosophy of the Audiolingual Method and the Communicative Approach. The features of the Communicative Approach as cited here represented at least one statement of the tenets of Communicative Language Teaching and subsequently, Task-Based Language Teaching and Content-Based Instruction. A sample of these 'features' is shown below in Table 1 (with the original numbering retained).

Throughout, one sees the prioritisation of communication in action and the minimisation of structure study (i.e. 'grammar') in preferred modes of language learning and teaching. Communicative feature #13, that the target system will be learned best as a consequence of 'struggling' to communicate, not by conscious attention to that system, has been a cornerstone of all attempts to implement CLT, although many advocates might balk at the notion of this process as 'struggling'. And this notion of 'struggling' with communicative output as the ultimate path to linguistic system mastery subsequently conflicted with Krashen's view that such system mastery would be naturally and effortlessly acquired by exposure to comprehensible input in a minimum stress ('low affective filter') atmosphere According to Krashen, the learners' role is to "lose themselves in activities involving meaningful communication" and their capacity to do so will determine "the amount and kind of acquisition they will experience and the fluency they will ultimately demonstrate" (Krashen 1985). Following this 'Natural Approach', the teacher seeks to make input comprehensible by contextual support of one kind or another in the form of continuous talk, focusing on objects in the classroom and using pictures and gestures. When learners are ready to begin talking in the new language, the teacher

Table 1. Features of the Communicative Approach

AUDIO-LINGUALISM	COMMUNICATIVE APPROACH
1. Attends to structure and form more than meaning	Meaning is paramount
4. Language learning is learning structures, sounds, or words	Language learning is learning to communicate
7. Native-speaker-like pronunciation is sought	Comprehensible pronunciation is sought
9. Communicative activities only come after a long process of rigid drills and exercises	Attempts to communicate encouraged from the beginning
13. The target linguistic system will be learned best through the overt teaching of the patterns of the system	The target linguistic system will be learned through the process of struggling to communicate
14. Linguistic competence is the desired goal	Communicative competence is the desired goal
16. The sequence of units is determined solely by principles of linguistic complexity	Sequencing is determined by any consideration of content, function or meaning that maintains interest
18. "Language is habit" so errors must be prevented at all costs	Language is created by the individual, often through trial and error
19. Accuracy, in terms of formal correctness, is a primary goal	Fluency and acceptable language is the primary goal; Accuracy is judged not in the abstract but in context
21. Students are expected to interact with the language system, embodied in machines or controlled materials	Students are expected to interact with other people, either in the flesh, through pair and group work, or in their writings
22. Intrinsic motivation will spring from an interest in the structure of the language	Intrinsic motivation will spring from an interest in what is being communicated by the language

(Finocchiaro and Brumfit 1983: 91–93)

provides comprehensible language and simple response opportunities. Learner responses could be "Yes" or "No", class members' names, lower order numbers, simple colour identification of indicated objects, etc. There is a gradual progression from Yes/No questions, through either-or questions, to 'Acquisition Activities' that focus on meaningful interpersonal communication rather than on language form. A compendium of activities designed to support Natural Approach instruction of this kind is to be found in Brown and Palmer (1988).

The continuing tussle over the roles of input and output in language acquisition and language teaching have been maintained by debates in print, principally between Krashen (1994) and Swain (1995). Regardless of one's 'output' or 'input' preference or preference for a balance between the two, proponents of CLT (and its offshoots TBLT and CBI) persevered in the faith that 'focus on meaning' should take primacy over 'focus on form' on the grounds that structural/grammatical mastery derives from communication not as a prelude to it.

The following can be taken as a representative statement of the tenets of CLT (my glosses in parentheses):

- The focus is on process rather than product (the communicative interaction rather than the linguistic forms used in that interaction)
- Basic elements are purposeful activities and tasks that emphasise communication and meaning (rather than linguistic units or structures)
- Learners learn language by interacting communicatively and purposefully while engaged in the activities and tasks (rather than by studying grammatical form or forms)

(Feez 1998: 17)

3.2. Task-based language teaching (TBLT)

As we have seen, the main underlying principle of CLT was that classroom activities should focus primarily on the achievement of meaning on the assumption that this would lead to the acquisition of the forms that functioned naturally in this achievement. In TBLT, attention shifts more specifically to the kinds of activity that should be designed to that end (Nunan 2004; Müller-Hartmann and Schocker-v. Ditfurth 2008). It followed from the main CLT principle that classroom activities were not to be concerned with drills and exercises which focused on the language itself but with problems that needed a use of language to solve. Such problem-solving activities, or tasks, were an intrinsic part of communicative methodology (Widdowson 1978; Rodgers 1984; Prabhu 1987). Over the past two decades, the profession has seen a major and increasing focus of professional attention directed to establishing well founded principles upon which task design might be based.

Task-Based Language Teaching (TBLT) refers to an approach based on the use of 'tasks' as the core unit of planning, instruction, research and assessment in language teaching (see Bygate, Ch. 15 this volume). TBLT is considered by most language educators to be the logical development, but a pedagogically better defined version, of communicative language teaching (e.g. Willis 1996; Skehan 1998a, b). The question arises as to what kind of development it represents, and in what respects it provides more definite guidance for teaching. One difficulty in answering this question is that has been the lack of consensus on what does and does not comprise a task. Ellis 2003 cites no less than nine different definitions.

Skehan, whose research has provided much of the theoretical underpinning of TBLT, sets out the design features that define a task as follows:

> [...] a task is regarded as an activity which satisfies the following criteria:
> Meaning is primary.
> There is a goal which needs to be worked towards.
> The activity is outcome-evaluated.
> There is a real-world relationship. (Skehan 1998b: 268)

Another definition cited in Ellis runs as follows:

> A task is (1) a classroom activity or exercise that has: (a) an objective obtainable only by the interaction among participants, (b) a mechanism for structuring and sequencing interaction, and (c) a focus on meaning exchange; (2) a language learning endeavour that requires learners to comprehend, manipulate, and/or produce the target language as they perform some set of workplans. (from Lee 2000)

There would seem to be an agreement here that a task is designed to have a goal or objective and that its success is to be evaluated in terms of its outcome. What is less clear is what this outcome should be. One could argue that in the real world that Skehan refers to, it does not matter how a task is tackled so long as its objective is achieved. There is no requirement that something is learned from doing it. But in the language classroom, this requirement is central since the very objective of the task, as Lee would seem to suggest, is to induce learning. Both definitions refer to the primacy of meaning in accordance with CLT principles, but there is no indication in either case as to what kind of meaning is intended. Lee seems to associate a focus on meaning with the comprehension and manipulation of language, which might be taken to imply that it is semantic meaning he has in mind – the meaning that is inscribed in linguistic form. Skehan makes no reference to language at all but if what is primary is the meaning that relates the task to the real world, it would seem to be pragmatic meaning. The difficulty here is that the closer the real world relationship, the less focus on meaning in language, semantic meaning, there will tend to be.

What emerges from a consideration of these definitions is the familiar problem referred to earlier of how a focus on meaning is to be related to, or reconciled with, a focus on form. A third definition, proposed by Nunan, while in some ways echoing Lee, seeks to bring about such reconciliation:

> My own definition is that a pedagogic task is a piece of classroom work that involves learners in comprehending, manipulating, producing or interacting in the target language while their attention is focused on mobilising their grammatical knowledge in order to express meaning (Nunan 2004: 4)

Nunan's definition identifies the task as a pedagogic construct and there is no mention of a 'real world relationship'. This allows for the possibility of getting learners to put language to purposeful use, without this having to resemble normal or natural 'real world' pragmatic uses of the language. And this would not necessarily preclude a focus on form – indeed one of the chapters of his book is entitled 'Focus on form in task-based language teaching'.

There have been multiple attempts to classify (as well as to define) LT tasks. In the literature on TBLT, a number of systems have been made to group tasks into categories as a basis for their design.

Pica, Kanagy and Falodun (1993) classify tasks according to the type of interaction that occurs in task accomplishment:

1. jigsaw tasks: these involve learners combining different pieces of information to form a whole (e.g. three individuals or groups may have three different parts of a story and have to piece the story together)
2. information-gap tasks: tasks in which one student or group of students has one set of information and another student or group has a complementary set of information. They must negotiate and find out what the other party's information is in order to complete an activity. (A particularly good discussion of activities and attendant research studies of information gap tasks is given in Pica 2005).
3. problem solving tasks: students are given a problem and a set of information. They must arrive at a solution to the problem. There is generally a single resolution of the outcome.
4. decision-making tasks: students are given a problem for which there a number of possible outcomes and they must choose one through negotiation and discussion
5. opinion exchange tasks: learners engage in discussion and exchange of ideas: they don't need to reach agreement.

In her proposed framework for and examples of TBLT, J. Willis (1996) proposes six task types built on more or less traditional knowledge hierarchies. She labels her task examples as:

1. listing: e.g. listing international English words, e.g. in sport, in pop songs.
2. ordering and sorting: e.g. rank ordering 10 LT exercises by student preference.
3. comparing: e.g. comparing reports of same event from different news sources.
4. problem solving: e.g. giving response to an inquiry in a newspaper advice column.
5. sharing personal experiences: e.g. recalling early impressions from childhood.
6. creative tasks: e.g. creating a picture from a story or vice versa.

Other ways of distinguishing kinds of task have been proposed (see, for example, Richards and Rodgers 2001).

When looking at these different ways of classifying task types, it becomes even more difficult to identify what makes a task distinctive as a classroom activity. It would appear that any activity that engages learners in a purposeful use of language counts as a task, with different tasks being classified according to how the purpose and the language used are variously regulated to bring about a learning outcome. When an activity focuses primarily on the communicative purpose (focus on pragmatic meaning) it gets more task-like, and when the focus is primarily on the language to be used (focus on form), it gets to be more like an exercise of the traditional kind. One might indeed conclude that:

> A simple and brief practice exercise is a task […]. All materials designed for language teaching […] can be seen as compendia of tasks. (Breen 1989: 187).

However tasks are defined and classified, it is clear that they have to be pedagogically designed to meet language learning requirements: situations, purposes, problems have to be contrived to induce a use of language that is both appropriate as use and effective for learning (Ellis 2003). An alternative to such contrivance is to make use of situations, purpose and problems that already exist elsewhere in the curriculum, and link the learning of language directly with the content and procedures of other subjects. We come to the idea of Content-Based Instruction (CBI) and its more recent manifestation Content and Language Integrated Learning (CLIL).

3.3. Content-based instruction (CBI)

The approach is essentially founded on the faith that language proficiency can be achieved as a corollary of an engagement with content.

> It is the teaching of content or information in the language being learned with little or no direct or explicit effort to teach the language itself separately from the content being taught (Krahnke 1987: 65)

Instead of inventing content as an enabling factor in the acquisition of language, as is typical in task-based teaching, the idea here is that language would be acquired as a natural function of engaging with content as provided by other curriculum subjects. The move towards focusing language instruction more on subject content and less on formal language structure is a quest which links subject area teachers and language teachers. Teaching would therefore involve:

> […] the integration of content learning with language teaching aims […] the concurrent study of language and subject matter, with the form and sequence of language presentation dictated by content material (Brinton, Snow and Wesche 1989: vii).

Various educational initiatives in the last 40 or so years have emphasised the principle of acquiring content through language rather than the study of language for its own sake. They bear labels such as Language across the Curriculum, Immersion Education, Immigrant On-Arrival Programs, Programs for Students with Limited English Proficiency, Language for Specific Purposes (LSP), and more recently, Content and Language Integrated Learning (CLIL) (see Caspari et al. 2007; Dalton-Puffer 2007; see also Wolff, Ch. 20 this volume). Discussion of how thinking along CBI lines relates to language study at the university level is to be found in the papers in Krueger and Ryan (1993). At school levels, claims (and counter claims) are made for the particular advantages of the various standard school subject areas of mathematics, science, social science and language/literature as optimal content sources to support language acquisition.

The general case was made by Widdowson over thirty years ago:

> The kind of language course that I envisage is one which deals with a selection of topics taken from the other subjects: simple experiments in physics and chemistry, biological processes in plants and animals, map-drawing, descriptions of historical events and so on. [...] It is easy to see that if such a procedure were adopted, the difficulties associated with the presentation of language use in the classroom would, to a considerable degree, disappear. The presentation would essentially be the same as the methodological techniques used for introducing the topics in the subjects from which they are drawn. (Widdowson 1978: 16)

At the university and adult education levels, CBI courses have been organised on several different bases. Shih (1986) identifies a variety of university types of CBI: Theme-based, Sheltered, Adjunct, Team-Teach and Skill-based approaches. As Met notes, these varied configurations lie on a continuum, bounded by content-driven curricula at one end and language-driven curricula at the other (Met 1998).

Teachers and lecturers operating within CBI consciously and unconsciously make modifications in the language they use in teaching, in order to make the content they are focusing on more comprehensible to their students. These modifications include:

- simplification (e.g. use of shorter T units and clauses),
- well-formedness (e.g. using few deviations from standard usage),
- explicitness (e.g. speaking with non-reduced pronunciation),
- regularisation (e.g. use of canonical word order),
- redundancy (e.g. highlighting important material through simultaneous use of several linguistic mechanisms, etc.).
  (Stryker and Leaver 1993)

The particular instructional activities employed in CBI will be determined by the specific content area of instruction and the input and output varieties of content data and processing anticipated. However, activity types can be classified generally according to their instructional focus. Stoller (1997) classifies CBI activity focus types as:

- language skills improvement,
- vocabulary building,
- discourse organisation,
- communicative interaction,
- study skills,
- synthesis of content materials and grammar.

Several general types of instructional activities which are claimed to span all content subject areas are project work, academic vocabulary development and knowledge of and facility with knowledge structures. All have been employed in various subject matter studies linked to second language development.

Despite extensive discussion, written explication and some practical experience with CBI programs, a number of problems with such programs have been identified by those most closely associated with promotion of CBI.

The CBI premise that "The language being taught could be used to present subject matter, and the students would learn the language as a by-product of learning about real-world content" (Krahnke 1987) has proved largely illusory (see e.g. Norris and Ortega 2003). Stoller cites a number of other problems associated with current CBI models and practices. These are (summarised from Stoller in press):

- Lack of L2 content materials and staff time and expertise to construct such materials on site.
- Difficulties selecting and sequencing materials which align content foci with language structures.
- Difficulties matching CBI materials with student motivations, ages, cognitive levels and educational expectations.
- Institutional problems in faculty support, student self-perceived needs, administrative encouragement and adequate funding.
- Language teachers lacking content depth; content teachers lacking experience in addressing student language needs.
- Little research or curricular work exploring simultaneous accommodation of content and language requirements.
- Lack of teacher training programs or models that incorporate CBI instructor requirements.
- Miss-match in institutional status and pedagogical practices of language and subject matter teachers.
- Negative or uninformed attitudes of learners and parents in CBI programs.
- Confounding of assessment measures of academic progress, language learning, and content learning.
  (see also Stoller 2008)

4. Methodological principles

Shortcomings in implementation of TBLT and CBI such as those noted above have, in part, led to further explorations into other ways in which language teaching methodology might be conceived. One major direction such explorations have taken is an attempt to define universal 'principles' on which to base L2 instruction.

Brown (1994) in his attacks on methods suggests a set of principles as an alternative basis for pedagogical practice. Teachers are invited to consider these principles as the basis for their teaching and to devise classroom activities and teaching practices and behaviours to represent these principles. Alternative sets of such 'principles' are offered by Bailey (1996), Doughty and Long (2003), and Kumaradivelu (1994) outlines a set of Macro-strategies and accompanying Micro-strategies in the same vein. All of these proposals arose out of an explicit rejection of methods and other prescribed procedures and each, in its own way, claims to be based "on current theoretical, empirical, and pedagogical insights that will enable teachers to theorise what they practice and practice what they theorise." (Kumaradivelu 1994: 27).

These principles, or macro-strategies, are typically presented without a research base and with an 'understood' rather than explicit theoretical rationale. Since these all claim to be based on what is known and agreed upon in language teaching pedagogy, it is interesting to compare the content of each of these recommendations and the implications for choice and design of teaching activities that might follow.

Macro-strategies:

1. Maximise learning opportunities.
2. Facilitate negotiated interaction.
3. Minimise perceptual mismatches.
4. Activate intuitive heuristics.
5. Foster language awareness.
6. Contextualise linguistic input.
7. Integrate language skills.
8. Promote learner autonomy.
9. Raise cultural consciousness.
10. Ensure social relevance.

(Kumaradivelu 1994)

Principles:

- Engage all learners in the lesson.
- Make learners, and not the teacher, the focus of the lesson.
- Provide maximum opportunities for student participation.

- Develop learner responsibility.
- Be tolerant of learners' mistakes.
- Develop learners' confidence.
- Teach learning strategies.
- Respond to learners' difficulties and build on them.
- Use a maximum amount of student-to-student activities.
- Promote cooperation among learners.
- Practice both accuracy and fluency.
- Address learners' needs and interests.

(Bailey 1996)

'Ten Commandments':

1. Set a personal example with your own behaviour.
2. Create a pleasant, relaxed atmosphere in the classroom.
3. Present the tasks properly.
4. Develop a good relationship with the learners.
5. Increase the learner's linguistic self-confidence.
6. Make the language classes interesting.
7. Promote learner autonomy.
8. Personalise the learning process.
9. Increase the learners' goal-orientedness.
10. Familiarise learners with the target language culture.

(Dörnyei and Csizér 1998)

Principles 1:

- Lower inhibitions
- Encourage risk-taking
- Build students' self-confidence
- Help students develop intrinsic motivation
- Promote cooperative learning
- Encourage students to do right-brain processing
- Promote ambiguity tolerance
- Help students use their intuition
- Get students to make their mistakes work for them
- Get students to set their own goal

(Brown 2002)

Principles 2:

Activities

MP1 Use tasks, not texts, as the unit of analysis.
MP2 Promote learning by doing.

Input
- MP3 Elaborate input (do not simplify; do not rely solely on 'authentic' texts).
- MP4 Provide rich (not impoverished) input.

Learning processes
- MP5 Encourage inductive ('chunk') learning.
- MP6 Focus on form.
- MP7 Provide negative feedback.
- MP8 Respect 'learner syllabuses'/ develop-mental processes.
- MP9 Promote cooperative/collaborative learning.

Learners
- MP10 Individualise instruction (according to communicative needs, and psycholinguistically).

(Doughty and Long 2003)

The identification of general principles of this kind is, as indicated earlier, motivated by a reaction against prescriptivism, and this may account for the lack of instructional examples offered as representative of the principles as given. The assumption is that the particular classroom realisation of these principles is best left to be worked out by teachers and learners rather than handed down by researchers and textbook writers.

There are obviously a number of similarities among these sets of principles – aside from the fact that they all run to about ten in number and are all phrased in the imperative voice. There are some notable differences as well. Some similarities, such as the encouragement of cooperative learning, appear prominently in all four of them. Cooperative learning activities in language learning have been well-detailed in a variety of sources (e.g. Jacobs, Power and Loh 2002b). Activities that encourage 'Language Awareness' (LA) or 'Consciousness Raising' (CR) are recommended specifically or implied in the various statements of principles (see also Edmondson, Ch. 7 this volume). These represent ways of bringing to learner attention various features of language form without direct instruction. For example, the so-called 'garden-path technique' encourages learners to produce grammatical errors through overgeneralization or mistranslation, with instructors then providing immediate corrective feedback. Van Lier (1995) overviews LA and CR, providing inventories of activity types. The full range of both implicit and explicit 'form focusing' techniques and their reported effectiveness are reviewed in Norris and Ortega (2000). Promotion of learner autonomy, self-confidence, responsibility is another common theme in these sets of principle statements. Translating these themes such as learner autonomy into classroom activities to underwrite the aspirant goals is a bit more problematic. For example, strategy training (sometimes referred to as 'learning to learn') is a core proposal aimed at the promotion of learner autonomy. Skimming, scanning and search reading are considered sub-strategies of one category of learner strategies labelled Cognitive strategies.

However, issues of strategy definition, instruction and application are still a matter for debate and activity guidelines for teachers wishing to encourage learner autonomy are still very much 'under construction' (See Cohen and Macaro 2007 for discussion).

5. Current and controversial issues

One can trace in this survey how ideas about methodology have changed over the years with a gradual shift away from the prescription of particular ways of teaching, assumed to be applicable to all classrooms, to the adducing of more general pedagogic principles that need to be interpreted in different ways according to local circumstances.

This shift has also led to a reconsideration of the very nature of second language instruction and the roles of teacher and learner as participants in the process. Previously the tendency was to think of learning as teacher-directed, with the learners required to conform and their success measured by how far their intake corresponded with the teaching input. Gradually, however, has come the recognition that learners need to be active, and indeed interactive, participants and be granted some degree of autonomy so that they can take the initiative themselves in the learning process.

What kind of learner interactivity is effective for learning, and how it can be induced in classrooms, have become prominent issues in recent thinking about methodology, although it has been a concern in language pedagogy since the 1980s. Rivers in her *Interactive Language Teaching*, for example, has this to say:

> Students achieve facility in *using* a language when their attention is focused on conveying and receiving authentic messages (that is, messages that contain information of interest to both speaker and listener in a situation of importance to both). This is *interaction*. (Rivers 1987: 4)

The notion of interactivity has been linked to the teaching of reading and writing as well as listening and speaking skills. Carrell, Devine and Eskey (1988) use the notion of 'interactivity' to refer to the simultaneous use by effective readers of both top-down and bottom-up processing in reading comprehension as well as, elsewhere, to the relationship between reader and writer. Interactivity is frequently used to refer to a dialogic approach to the teaching of composition in which "we make decisions about *how* to proceed in composition as a result of an imagined dialogue with the reader we are writing *to*" (Robinson 1987).

Although there has been much enthusiasm for 'interactivity' as a defining notion in language teaching there has been some lack of clarity about just how this interactivity is to be pedagogically defined. Amongst the goals of current second language interaction research has been that of providing better data samples of (particularly classroom) conversational interaction, to offer deeper analyses of on-going 'normal' conversational interaction and to be able to direct these data and analyses to classroom pedagogy. Achievement of the last goal, it is hoped, would better enable students to reach their desired levels of communicative competence. With these goals in mind, SLA researchers have turned increasingly to consideration of pedagogical implications of linguistic research analyses emerging out of current research studies involving Conversational Analysis (CA) and Classroom Interaction (CI). How is achievement of these goals progressing?

Both CA and CI research traditions developed outside of a linguistic or SLA perspective. Conversational analysis, as a research tradition, is traced to the work of sociologist Harvey Sacks (e.g. Schegloff and Sacks 1973) and developed within a tradition which came to be known as ethnomethodology. As Hutchby and Wooffitt (1998: 14) note "CA is only marginally interested in language as such; its actual object of study is the interactional organisation of social activities." Ultimately, linguists and applied linguists took up an interest in CA. A special issue of the Modern Language Journal (88 (4), 2004) entitled *Classroom Talks* was devoted to tracing this interest and melding it with classroom-based studies. A parallel interest stimulated Seedhouse to take a CA perspective on his study of what he calls "the interactional architecture of the language classroom" (Seedhouse 2004).

Similarly, CI work was pioneered not by those in language pedagogy but by those within general education. Flanders (1960) developed one of the first instruments for analysing classroom interaction, an instrument used for analysis of interaction in classrooms independent of the classroom subject. Dissatisfactions with the Flanders' instrument gave rise to a host of counterproposals, ultimately stimulating publication of an occasional journal, *Mirrors of Behavior*, devoted exclusively to the presentation of scores of alternative models of classroom interaction. When SLA researchers sought to analyse the interactional patterns of second language classrooms, a similar plethora of competing models arose. Chaudron (1988) compared 26 models devoted to analysis of interaction patterns in second language classrooms. Earlier studies were focused primarily on features of teacher questions, teacher error correction, quantity of teacher speech, teacher explanations and teacher wait-time for student responses. Somewhat more recent classroom studies have looked at teacher/student and student/student interaction in respect to topic nomination, question/answer patterns and control mechanisms in the classroom. At least one classroom interaction analytical model, i.e. COLT (see e.g. Allwright and Bailey 1991), was devoted to examining the presence or absence of putative markers of outcomes of communicative language teaching methodology.

The most influential subsequent studies of the conversations of classroom interaction were intended to illuminate and test the Interaction Hypothesis. A host of research studies beginning with those of Wagner-Gough and Hatch (1975) and continuing to the present were designed to test various versions of this hypothesis. Long (1996) summarised a recent version of the Interaction Hypothesis as follows:

> *Negotiation for meaning*, and especially negotiation work that triggers *interactional* adjustments by the NS or more competent interlocutor, facilitates acquisition because it connects input, internal learner capacities, particularly, selective attention, and output in productive ways. (Long 1996: 451–452).

Critics of the Interaction Hypothesis note the 'considerable criticism' of the above interaction hypothesis (summarised in Ellis 1994: 278), much of it targeting the reasoning cited above and the current consensus appears to be that the hypothesis is unproven and unprovable (Seedhouse 1999).

Recent SLA studies have sought to temper the overly psycholinguistic treatment of interaction with a more socio-cultural view (Seedhouse 2005). Sfard (1998) contrasted the psycholinguistic vs. the social views of language learning as built around either the 'acquisition metaphor' or the 'participation metaphor' and cautions that both perspectives are necessary. The perspectives and metaphors have been multiplying since Sfard's characterisation. Byrnes (2007) concludes that language learning might "better be understood as socially embedded choices by individual language learners in a particular communicative context of situation that in turn resides within a larger context of culture"(Byrnes 2007).

Nunan takes a slightly different cut at summarising the current crop of multiple perspectives on instructed language learning:

> Researchers have begun to realise that there are social and interpersonal as well as psychological dimensions to acquisition, that input and output are both important, that form and meaning are ultimately inseparable, and that acquisition is an organic rather than a linear process [...]. The results seem to indicate while task variables appear to have an effect on the amount of negotiation for meaning, there appears to be an interaction between task variables, personality factors and interactional dynamic [which] underlines the complexity of the learning environment, and the difficulty of isolating psychological and linguistic factors from social and interpersonal ones.

Byrnes would probably concur with Nunan's summary statement that "Current SLA research orientations can be captured by a single word: complexity." (Nunan 2001: 91).

The quest for some kind of validation or legitimatisation for pedagogic proposals and practices brings up the general question of how far research into language and language learning can, or should, inform classroom methodology. As the closing quote above might suggests, there is no clear and easy pathway leading from current SLA research findings and theoretical positioning to recommendations for activities and tasks.

In one of his few direct statements about pedagogy, for example, Seedhouse contrasts CA data dialogs with those typically invented for LT materials. He cites a study in which Wong (2002) collected samples of American English telephone conversations and noted four sequence types which typically occur.

(summons-answer, identification-recognition, greeting, and *how are you*?) When examining invented, inauthentic phone conversations in ESL textbooks, Wang found these typical sequences to be "absent, incomplete or problematic" (Wong cited in Seedhouse 2004: 228.) Seedhouse suggests that such CA research findings "can be fed into future language-teaching materials design".

The assumption here is that naturally occurring language use is necessarily pedagogically appropriate as language for learning. This advocacy of authenticity, the use of 'real' language in classrooms has become a prominent feature of current thinking about language teaching methodology. Particularly now that corpus linguistics has made the facts of actual native speaker usage available, there is, it is argued, no excuse now for teachers to mislead their students by presenting them with invented examples. Such a view has not gone unchallenged (Widdowson 2003 and Ch. 8 this volume).

What we find here is the contemporary recurrence of an issue that, as we have seen, has always posed an unresolved problem for methodology: namely the relationship between the language that is needed to activate the process of learning, and that which has ultimately to be attained as the goal. The CLT injunction that there should be a focus on meaning and communication in the classroom because communicative competence must be the goal of learning has led latterly to the idea that this must involve the use of language attested as authentically produced by native speakers. But on the other hand, the process of learning may require for its activation some contrivance, some selection of language to learn from, some focus on form, and this will involve some degree of modification or distortion, some 'unnaturalness' of language use as compared with norms of native speaker behaviour.

It might be said indeed that although the methodological procedures reviewed in this chapter differ in many ways, and are supported by different assumptions, all of them are kinds of pedagogic contrivance, various attempts to manipulate learner behaviour in the classroom to activate the process of learning.

References

Adamson, Bob
2004 Fashions in language teaching methodology. In: Alan Davies and Catherine Elder (eds.), *The Handbook of Applied Linguistics*, 604–622. Oxford: Blackwell Publishing.

Allwright, Dick and Katherine Bailey
1991 *Focus on the Language Classroom*. New York: Cambridge University Press.

Bailey, Katherine
1996 The best-laid plans: Teachers' in-class decisions to depart from their lesson plans. In: Katherine Bailey and David Nunan (eds.), *Voices from the Language Classroom*, 15–40. New York: Cambridge University Press.

Beckett, Gulbahar H. and Paul H. Miller (eds.)
2006 *Project-Based Second and Foreign Language Education: Past, Present, and Future*. Greenwich, CT: Information Age Publishing.

Breen, Michael
1989 The evaluation cycle for language learning tasks. In: Johnson (ed.): 187–206.

Brinton, Donna and Christine Holten
1997 Into, through, and beyond. A framework to develop content-based material. *Forum* 35 (4): 10–15.

Brinton, Donna, Marjorie A. Snow and Marguerite Wesche
1989 *Content-Based Second Language Instruction.* New York: Newbury House.

Brooks, Nelson
1964 *Language and Language Learning: Theory and Practice.* 2nd edition. New York: Harcourt Brace.

Brown, H. Douglas
1994 *Principles of Language Learning and Teaching*. Englewood Cliffs, NJ: Prentice-Hall Regents.

Brown, H. Douglas
2002 *Strategies for Success: A Practical Guide for Learning English.* White Plains, NY: Pearson Education.

Brown, J. Marvin and Adrian Palmer
1988 *Listening Approach: Methods and Materials for Applying Krashen's Input Hypothesis.* Harlow, UK: Longman.

Brumfit, Christopher J. and Keith Johnson
1979 *The Communicative Approach to Language Teaching*. Oxfod: Oxford University Press.

Byrnes, Heidi
2007 Language acquisition and language learning. In: David G. Nicholls (ed.), *Introduction to Scholarship in Modern Languages and Literatures*, 3rd edition, 48–69. New York: Modern Language Association.

Carrell, Patricia, Joanne Devine and David Eskey
1988 *Interactive Approaches to Second Language Reading*. Cambridge: Cambridge University Press.

Carter, Ronald and David Nunan
2001 *The Cambridge Guide to Teaching English to Speakers of Other Languages.* Cambridge: Cambridge University Press.

Caspari, Daniela, Wolfgang Hallet, Anke Wegnerand and Wolfgang Zydatiß (eds.)
2007 *Bilingualer Unterricht macht Schule. Beiträge aus der Praxisforschung.* Frankfurt a. M.: Lang.

Chaudron, Craig
1988 *Second Language Classroom: Research on Teaching and Learning.* Cambridge: Cambridge University.

Christison, Mary Ann
2005 *Multiple Intelligences and Language Learning: A Guidebook of Theory, Activities, Inventories, and Resources*. Burlingame, CA: Alta Book Center.

Cohen, Andrew and Ernesto Macaro
2007 *Language Learner Strategies: 30 Years of Research and Practice*. Oxford: Oxford University Press.

Cook, Guy and Barbara Seidlhofer (eds.)
1995 *Principle and Practice in Applied Linguistics: Studies in Honour of H. G. Widdowson.* Oxford: Oxford University Press.

Cummins, Jim P.
2000 *Immersion Education for the Millennium: What We Have Learned from 30 Years of Research on Second Language Immersion.* www.iteachilearn.com/cummins/immersion2000.html.

Dalton-Puffer, Christiane
2007 *Discourse in Content and Language Integrated Learning Classrooms.* Amsterdam and Philadelphia: John Benjamins.

DeKeyser, Robert (ed.)
2007 *Practising in a Second Language: Perspectives from Applied Linguistics and Cognitive Psychology.* Cambridge: Cambridge University Press.

Doughty, Catherine J. and Michael H. Long
2003 Optimal psycholinguistic environments for distance foreign language learning. *Language, Learning and Technology* 7 (3): 50–80.

Dörnyei, Zoltan and Kata Czisér
1998 Ten commandments for motivating language learners: Results of an empirical study. *Language Learning Research* 2 (3): 203–229.

Ellis, Rod
1994 *The Study of Second Language Acquisition.* Oxford: Oxford University Press.

Ellis, Rod
2002 Does form-focused instruction affect the acquisition of implicit knowledge? A review of the literature. *Studies in Second Language Acquisition* 24: 223–236.

Ellis, Rod
2003 *Task-Based Language Learning and Teaching.* Oxford: Oxford University Press.

Feez, Susan
1998 *Text-Based Syllabus Design.* Sydney: National Centre for English Teaching and Research.

Finocchiaro, Mary and Christopher J. Brumfit
1983 *The Functional-Notional Approach: From Theory to Practice.* New York: Oxford University Press.

Flanders, Ned A.
1960 *Interaction Analysis in the Classroom: A Manual for Observers.* Ann Arbor: The University of Michigan Press.

Freeman, Donald
1992 Collaboration: constructing shared understandings in a second language classroom. In: David Nunan (ed.), *Collaborative Language Learning and Teaching*, 56–80. Cambridge: Cambridge University Press.

Freeman, Donald and Jack C. Richards
1993 Conceptions of teaching and the education of second language teachers. *TESOL Quarterly* 27 (2): 193–216.

Gattegno, Caleb
1972 *Teaching Foreign Languages in Schools: The Silent Way.* 2nd edition. New York: Educational Solutions.

Hammerly, Hector
1991 *Fluency and Accuracy*. Clevedon, UK: Multilingual Matters.
Harmer, Jeremy
1997 *The Practice of English Language Teaching*. Harlow, UK: Longman.
Harmer, Jeremy
1998 *How to Teach English*. London: Longman.
Howatt, Anthony P. R.
2004 *A History of English Language Teaching*. 2nd edition. Oxford: Oxford University Press.
Hutchby, Ian and Robin Wooffitt
1998 *Conversation Analysis: Principles, Practices and Applications*. Cambridge, MA: Polity Press.
Jacobs, George M., Michael A. Power and Wan I. Loh
2002 *The Teacher's Sourcebook for Cooperative Learning: Practical Techniques, Basic Principles, and Frequently Asked Questions*. Thousand Oaks, CA: Corwin Press.
Johnson, Keith (ed.)
1989 *The Second Language Curriculum*. Cambridge: Cambridge University Press.
Kelly, Louis
1969 *25 Centuries of Language Teaching*. Rowley, Mass.: Newbury House.
Krahnke, Karl
1987 *Approaches to Syllabus Design for Foreign Language Teaching*. Englewood Cliffs: Prentice-Hall.
Krashen, Stephen D.
1985 *The Input Hypothesis*. London: Longman.
Krashen, Stephen D.
1994 The input hypothesis and its rivals. In: Nick Ellis (ed.), *Implicit and Explicit Learning of Languages*, 421–453. London: Academic Press.
Krueger, Merle and Frank Ryan (eds.)
1993 *Language and Content. Disciplin- and Content-based Approaches to Language Study*. Lexington, Mass.: D.C. Heath and Co.
Kumaravadivelu, B.
1994 The postmethod condition: (E)merging strategies for second/foreign language teaching. *TESOL Quarterly* 28 (1): 27–48.
Kumaravadivelu B.
2001 Toward a postmethod pedagogy. *TESOL Quarterly* 35 (4): 537–560.
Larsen-Freeman, Diane
2000 *Techniques and Principles in Language Teaching*. 2nd edition. Oxford: Oxford University Press.
Lee, James F.
2000 *An Introduction to Task-Based Instruction*. New York: McGraw-Hill.
Lewis, Michael
1993 *The Lexical Approach*. London: Language Teaching Publications.
Lewis, Michael
1996 Implications of a lexical view of language. In: Willis and Willis (eds.): 10–16.

Long, Michael
1996 The role of the linguistic environment in second language acquisition. In: William Ritchie and Tej K. Bhatia (eds.), *Handbook of Second Language Acquisition*, 413–468. San Diego: Academic Press.

Lozanov, Georgi
1979 *Suggestology and Outlines of Suggestopedy*. New York: Gordon and Breach.

Mackey, William F.
1965 *Language Teaching Analysis*. London: Longman.

Met, Myriam
1998 *Content-Based Instruction: Defining Terms, Making Decision*. Washington, DC: National Foreign Language Centre Report.

Müller-Hartmann, Andreas and Marita Schocker-v. Ditfurth (eds.)
2008 *Aufgabenorientiertes Lernen und Lehren mit Medien: Ansätze, Erfahrungen, Perspektiven in der Fremdsprachendidaktik*. Frankfurt a. M.: Lang.

Neuner, Gerhard and Hans Hunfeld
1993 *Methoden des fremdsprachlichen Unterrichts. Eine Einführung*. Berlin: Langenscheidt.

Norris, John and Lourdes Ortega
2000 Effectiveness of L2 instruction: A research synthesis and quantitative meta-analysis. *Language Learning* 50 (3): 417–528.

Nunan, David
1991 *Language Teaching Methodology*. London: Prentice Hall International.

Nunan, David
1997 Language Teaching and Research. Education Resources Information Center Document (ED415692).

Nunan, David
2001 Second language acquisition. In: Carter and Nunan: 87–92.

Nunan, David
2004 *Task-Based Language Teaching: A Comprehensively Revised Edition of Designing Tasks for the Communicative Classroom*. Cambridge: Cambridge University Press.

Oller, John W. and Patricia Richard-Amato
1983 *Methods That Work: A Smorgasbord Of Ideas For Language Teachers*. Rowley, Mass.: Newbury House Publishers.

Ortner, Brigitte
1998 *Alternative Methoden im Fremdsprachenunterricht*. Ismaning: Hueber.

Pica, Teresa
2005 Classroom learning, teaching, and research: A task-based perspective. *The Modern Language Journal* 89: 339–352.

Pica, Teresa, Ruth Kanagy and Joseph Falodun
1993 Choosing and using communication tasks for second language instruction and research. In: Graham Crookes and Susan M. Gass (eds.), *Tasks and Language Learning. Integrating Theory and Practice*, 9–34. Clevedon: Multilingual Matters Ltd.

Pica, Teresa, Hyun-Sook Kang and Shannon Sauro
2006 Information gap tasks: Their multiple roles and contributions to interaction research methodology. *Studies in Second Language Acquisition* 28: 301–338.

Prabhu, N. S.
1987 *Second Language Pedagogy.* Oxford: Oxford University Press.
Revell, Jane and Susan Norman
1997 *In Your Hands: NLP in ELT.* London: Saffire Press.
Richards, Jack C.
1984 The secret life of methods. *TESOL Quarterly* 18 (1): 7–23.
Richards, Jack C. and Willy A. Renandya
2002 *Methodology in Language Teaching: An Anthology of Current Practice.* Cambridge: Cambridge University Press.
Richards, Jack C. and Theodore S. Rodgers
2001 *Approaches and Methods in Language Teaching.* Cambridge: Cambridge University Press.
Rivers, Wilga M.
1968 *Teaching Foreign Language Skills.* Chicago: University of Chicago Press.
Rivers, Wilga M. (ed.)
1987 *Interactive Language Teaching.* Cambridge: Cambridge University Press.
Robinson, Peter
1987 Projection into dialogue as a composition strategy. *ELT Journal* 41 (1): 30–36.
Rodgers, Theodore S.
1984 Communicative syllabus design and implementation: Reflection on a decade of experience. In: John A. S. Read (ed.), *Trends in Language Syllabus Design*, 28–51. Singapore: Singapore University Press.
Savignon, Sandra
2003 Teaching English as communication: A global perspective. *World Englishes* 22: 55–66.
Schiffler, L.
1991 *La Suggestopédie et le Superlearning – Mise à l'Épreuve Statistique*. Paris: Didier Erudition.
Schegloff, Emanuel A. and Harvey Sacks
1973 Opening up closings. *Semiotica* 8 (4): 289–327.
Seedhouse, Paul
1999 Task-based interaction. *ELT Journal* 53 (3): 149–156.
Seedhouse, Paul
2004 *The Interactional Architecture of the Language Classroom. Language Learning Monograph.* London: Blackwell Publishers.
Sfard, Anna
1998 On two metaphors for learning and the dangers of choosing just one. *Educational Researcher* 27: 4–13.
Shih, May
1986 Content-based approaches to teaching academic writing. *TESOL Quarterly* 20 (4): 617–648.
Skehan, Peter
1996 Second language acquisition research and task-based instruction. In: Willis and Willis (eds.): 17–30.
Skehan, Peter
1998a *A Cognitive Approach to Language Learning*. Oxford: Oxford University Press.

Skehan, Peter
1998b Task-based instruction. *Annual Review of Applied Linguistics* 18: 268–286.

Stevick, Earl W.
1980 *Teaching Languages: A Way and Ways*. Rowley, Mass.: Newbury House.

Stoller, Fredericka L.
1997 Project work: A means to promote language and content. *English Teaching Forum* 35 (4): 2–9.

Stoller, Fredricka L.
2008 Content-based instruction. In: Nelleke Van Deusen-Scholl and Nancy H. Hornberger (eds.), *Encyclopedia of Language and Education*, 2nd edition, 59–70. Heidelberg: Springer.

Stoller, Fredricka L.
(in press) Promoting the acquisition of knowledge in a content-based course. In: J. A. Crandall and D. Kaufman (eds.), *Content-Based Instruction in Tertiary Settings: Case Studies in TESOL*. Alexandria, VA: TESOL.

Stryker, Stephen B and Betty Lou Leaver
1993 *Content-Based Instruction in Foreign Language Education: Models and Methods*. Georgetown: Georgetown University Press.

Swain, Merrill
1995 Three functions of output in second language learning. In: Cook and Seidlhofer (eds.): 125–144.

Swain, Merrill
1985 Communicative competence: Some roles of comprehensible input and comprehensible output in development. In: Susan Gass and Carolyn Madden (eds.), *Input in Second Language Acquisition*, 235–256. Rowley, Mass.: Newbury House.

Ur, Penny
1997 *A Course in Language Teaching: Practice and Theory*. Cambridge: Cambridge University Press.

van Lier, Leo
1995 *Introducing Language Awareness*. London: Penguin Books.

Wagner-Gough, Judy and Evelyn Hatch
1975 The importance of input data in second language acquisition studies. *Language Learning* 25 (2): 297–308.

Widdowson, Henry G.
1978 *Teaching Language as Communication*. Oxford: Oxford University Press.

Widdowson, Henry G.
1990 *Aspects of Language Teaching*. Oxford: Oxford University Press.

Widdowson, Henry G.
2003 *Defining Issues in English Language Teaching*. Oxford: Oxford University Press.

Willis, Jane
1996 *A Framework for Task-Based Learning*. London: Longman.

Willis, Jane and Dave Willis (eds.)
1996 *Challenge and Change in Language Teaching*. London: Heinemann.

Wong, Jean
2002 "Applying" conversation analysis in applied linguistics: Evaluating dialogue in English as a second language textbooks. *International Review of Applied Linguistics* 40: 37–60.

Recommended readings

Bausch, Karl-Richard, Herbert Christ and Hans-Jürgen Krumm (eds.)
2007 *Handbuch Fremdsprachenunterricht.* 5th edition. Tübingen. Francke.

Bygate, Martin, Peter Skehan and Merill Swain (eds.)
2007 *Researching Pedagogic Tasks. Second Language Learning, Teaching and Testing*. Harlow: Longman.

Byram, Michael (ed.)
2000 *The Routledge Enclopedia of Language Teaching and Learning*. London: Routledge.

Edmondson, Willis J. and Juliane House
2006 *Einführung in die Sprachlehrforschung*. 3rd edition. Tübingen: Francke.

Hinkel, Eli (ed.)
2005 *Handbook of Research in Second Language Teaching and Learning.* Mahwah, NJ: Lawrence Erlbaum Associates

Howatt, Anthony P. R.
2004 *A History of English Language Teaching*. 2nd edition. Oxford: Oxford University Press.

Housen, Alex and Pierrard, Michel (eds.)
2005 *Investigations in Instructed Second Language Acquisition* Berlin: Walter de Gruyter

Kubanek-German, Angelika
1998 Primary foreign language teaching in Europe – trends and issues. *Language Teaching* 31:193–205

Kumaravadivelu, B.
2006 *Understanding Language Teaching: From Method to Post-Method.* Mahwah, NJ: Lawrence Erlbaum Associates

Larsen-Freeman, Diane
2000 *Techniques and Principles in Language Teaching*. 2nd edition. Oxford: Oxford University Press.

McCafferty, Steven G., Jacobs, George M. and Ana Christina DaSilva Iddings. (eds)
2006 *Cooperative Learning and Second Language Teaching.* Cambridge: Cambridge University Press.

Richards, Jack C. and Willy A. Renandya
2002 *Methodology in Language Teaching: An Anthology of Current Practice.* Cambridge: Cambridge University Press.

Richards, Jack C. and Theodore S. Rodgers
2001 *Approaches and Methods in Language Teaching.* 2nd edition. Cambridge: Cambridge University Press.

Tucker Richard and David Corson (eds.)
1997 *Second Language Education.* Volume 4 of David Corson (ed.), *Encyclopedia of Language and Education*. Dordrecht: Kluwer.

Widdowson, Henry G.
1990 *Aspects of Language Teaching*. Oxford: Oxford University Press.

Willis, Jane and Dave Willis (eds.)
1996 *Challenge and Change in Language Teaching*. London: Heinemann.

14. Autonomous language learning

Lienhard Legenhausen

"We can decide what to do. It is not Leni
[the teacher]
who decides. OK? But it us and *Leni who decide"*
(15-year-old boy in an interview)
"You are respons[ible]. So – if you don't do anything, you don't learn anything."
(15-year-old girl in an interview)[1]

1. Introduction

The late 1970s witnessed the emergence of the notion of autonomy in language learning. Many of its basic principles, however, have a century-old tradition and are deeply rooted in humanistic philosophy and education. It was largely due to the initiatives of the Council of Europe that the promotion of learner autonomy was boosted, resulting in the seminal text by Henry Holec ([1979] 1981) according to which autonomy implies that learners take charge of their own learning, that is, in Holec's words:

- to have, and to hold, the responsibility for *all* the decisions concerning *all* aspects of learning, i.e.:
- determining the objectives;
- defining the contents and progressions;
- selecting methods and techniques to be used;
- monitoring the procedure of acquisition properly speaking (rhythm, time, place, etc.)
- evaluating what has been acquired. (1981: 3)

Apart from rekindling discussions on good pedagogical practices, this definition also invited a host of misinterpretations and misunderstandings, the most apparent of which was that it opens up space for an 'anything goes'-approach to language learning. Ensuing discussions gave rise to related and competing concepts such as 'independent learning', 'self-directed learning', 'self-instruction' and also 'self-access learning', most of which can be distinguished from autonomous language learning on basically three accounts. First, in contrast to autonomous language learning, they highlight organisational aspects of the learning undertaking. Secondly, they tend to exclude vital conditions of social learning. Thirdly, they do not properly acknowledge the indispensable role of the teacher.[2]

Many misinterpretations seem to have been triggered by the very fact that the notion of learner autonomy is a highly complex and multifaceted construct which cannot as yet be moulded into a unified theory. Today's discourse on autonomy draws upon and is informed by diverse strands of European humanistic philosophy, anthropological theory, critical education and psychology, the most important of which will be briefly sketched out in the following section.

2. Theoretical and historical background

Although core ideas and principles can be traced as far back as to the political liberalism of the Age of Enlightenment with its proposals for more democratic action, the more immediate impact on contemporary educational thinking and on the shaping of autonomous learning has been exerted by educators and psychologists of the 20th century – among them John Dewey, Carl Rogers, Paulo Freire, Ivan Illich, George Kelly, and Lev Vygotsky. Working within different socio-political contexts and pursuing diverse goals geared to their respective social contexts, they all – in one way or another – provided persuasive arguments for the promotion of learner autonomy.

2.1. Anthropological and developmental arguments

Anthropological justifications for learner autonomy stress basic human needs which include the need for gaining control over environmental contingencies, thus assuring human survival. In order for the individual to be able to cope with the challenges and exigencies of life, he or she must first develop a cognitive distance from the environment, for which, in turn, a high degree of self-awareness and self-determination is a prerequisite. Anthropological arguments thus combine with self-determination theories, which are also constitutive for motivational justifications (cf. below).

Little, furthermore, argues that autonomy is an inbuilt phenomenon of all developmental and experiential learning. The cognitive view of child development, for example, includes the hypothesis that "the child is autonomous in the sense that the stimulus to develop comes from within itself and the process of development is not subject to external control." (1991: 15).

Since developmental processes are notoriously highly successful, insight into these processes might also inform methodological approaches in formal educational settings. However, what can all too often be observed in educational settings is a discontinuity or discrepancy between developmental and experiential processes, on the one hand, and traditional educational procedures, on the other. The result is the learners' alienation from their developmental-acquisitional needs as well as from their motivational needs. This classroom dilemma has been succinctly encapsulated in Barnes' often-quoted distinction between 'action knowledge' and 'school knowledge':

> School knowledge is the knowledge which someone else presents to us. We partly grasp it, enough to answer the teacher's questions, to do exercises, or to answer examination questions, but it remains someone else's knowledge, not ours. If we never use this knowledge we probably forget it. In so far as we use knowledge for our own purposes however we begin to incorporate it into our view of the world, and to use parts of it to cope with exigencies of living. Once the knowledge becomes incorporated into that view of the world on which our actions are based I would say that it has become 'action knowledge'. (1976:81)

By trying to reduce the gap between 'living' and 'learning' the autonomous classroom seeks to promote forms of experiential learning which lead to action knowledge.

2.2. Socio-political arguments

The Council of Europe's initiative was clearly motivated by political considerations. It explicitly intended to promote the individual's awareness of democratic values and saw the promotion of autonomy as a means towards greater political freedom and emancipation, which would allow citizens to engage actively and creatively in the shaping of community policies and thus to become responsible members of society. Cf. Holec (1981: 1): " ... the innovatory proposals relating to adult education policy [...] all have one thing in common; they insist on the need to develop the individual's freedom by developing those abilities which will enable him to act more responsibly in running the affairs of the society in which he lives." Holec thus subscribes to Janne's concept of adult education as "an instrument for changing the environment itself. From the idea of man 'product of society' one moves to the idea of man 'producer of society'". (Janne 1977, qtd. in Holec 1981:1).

The political agenda has a long tradition, and can, for instance, also be said to lie at the heart of Kant's moral philosophy. Here autonomy of the will is placed within the context of moral choices, the discussion of which also included the legitimacy of constraints. Several political philosophers have, moreover, linked personal autonomy to the right of individuals to exercise their own choices and characterised it as a source of human dignity. This is also a major concern of Paolo Freire's educational thinking. Individuals should be in a position to conduct their own affairs and be free from control by others. Freire tried to promote emancipation and empowerment of the less privileged through social collaboration and interactive participation. Another remarkable feature of his pedagogy was that he tried to rebalance the hierarchical nature of the teacher/learner relationship by perceiving teachers also in the roles of learners and learners in the roles of teachers, a principle that has also been repeatedly stressed in the more recent literature on learner autonomy (cf. Dam 2003).

2.3. Psychological arguments

For educationists working towards the implementation of principles of learner autonomy, the most appealing arguments derive from cognitive and motivational psychology.

It is mainly constructivist psychologies which have informed the discourse on learner autonomy. Constructivists hold that individuals create their own meaning systems for interpreting and organising their experiences, which implies that new knowledge is also constructed rather than discovered. This view severely limits the possibilities of transmitting new knowledge – or 'teaching' language, for that matter – since it is the learners themselves who have to construct their subjective versions of reality – or of a target language (cf. also Wolff 1996). Constructivist psychologies come in many shapes and forms, the most important of which for the theoretical underpinning of autonomous learning being Kelly's Personal Construct Theory (cf. Kelly 1955; Raskin 2002). Kelly's 'person-as-scientist' metaphor closely parallels the 'learner-as-researcher' view sometimes proposed in the language learning and teaching literature (cf. Breen 1983; Legenhausen and Wolff 1992), and Kelly's focus on personal agency, self-determination and free choice links up with cognitive theories of motivation (Deci 1980, 1996).

The relationship between motivation theories based on self-determination and autonomous language learning has been extensively explored by Ushioda (1996). She claims that "it is the engagement of the learner's own *intrinsic motivation* that must provide the foundation for autonomous language learning" (1996: 40). In order, however, for learners to be intrinsically motivated they must feel free from pressures and be able to exercise free choices in self-determined ways. In other words, "intrinsic motivation will be operative when action is experienced as autonomous" (Deci and Ryan 1985: 29).

In subsequent publications Ushioda qualifies and complements Deci and Ryan's and her own arguments by also highlighting processes of social mediation for the development of motivational attitudes (cf. Ushioda 2003). Apart from the intimate and inseparable link between intrinsic motivation and autonomy, she sees a need to acknowledge that "there is an equally intimate relationship between autonomy and internalisation of extrinsic goals" (Ushioda 2006: 285). This means that autonomous learners are also characterised by valuing and endorsing goals as defined for example in curricular guidelines and as agreed upon in classroom negotiation processes. If the importance of the social context for the development of motivational attitudes in autonomous classrooms is thus also emphasised, then this will contribute to resolving the apparent paradox between the individual's freedom of choice and self-determination on the one hand, and the collaborative social nature of *all* learning, on the other, as expounded in Vygotsky's sociocultural psychology.

Vygotsky's theory – with its focus on the interactive-social conditioning of learning – has to be acknowledged as another important influence on the 'autonomous discourse'. Vygotsky argued that all higher cognitive functions are the product of social interactions:

> Any function in the child's cultural development appears twice, or on two planes, first it appears on the social plane, and then on the psychological plane, first it appears between people as an interpsychological category, and then within the child as an intrapsychological category. (1981: 163)

In social interactions with adults or more knowledgeable peers, children – if given proper assistance – will be able to carry out tasks and solve problems which they could not have coped with on their own. However, adults need to be acutely aware of the child's developmental stage and thus be sensitive to his or her needs and readiness, in order to successfully guide and support the child's behaviour. This feature of Vygotskian psychology is summed up in the often quoted definition of the so-called 'Zone of Proximal Development' (ZPD), which is "the distance between the actual developmental level as determined by independent problem solving and the level of potential development as determined through problem solving under adult guidance or in collaboration with more capable peers." (Vygotsky 1978: 86)

2.4. Educational arguments

It is a trivial statement to claim that language pedagogy draws on all of the above disciplines and principles when defining its educational goals and methodological approaches.

For example, the concept of a ZPD, in which guidance plays a dominant role, has given rise to the metaphor of scaffolding in Jerome Bruner's theory of education. "One sets up a game, provides a scaffold to assure that the child's ineptitudes can be rescued or rectified by appropriate intervention, and then removes the scaffold part by part as the reciprocal structure can stand on its own." (Bruner 1983: 60)

In the context of second language acquisition, scaffolding has been defined along the following lines: "This concept [...] states that in social interaction a knowledgeable participant can create, by means of speech, supportive conditions in which the novice can participate in, and extend, current skills and knowledge to higher levels of competence." (Donato 1994: 40)

As a discourse strategy, scaffolding is of course a crucial feature of all classrooms relying on communicative interaction as the catalyst for language development. Here it is essentially the teacher's responsibility to modify her speech in ways that facilitate learners' comprehension, and thus ensure their participation in the interaction.

If, however, the classroom is characterised by self-selected activities in which learner-learner interactions in small groups dominate, then the idea of also explicitly introducing the concept of scaffolding to learners and make them aware of scaffolding techniques almost suggests itself (cf. Thomsen 2003). In Thomsen's study the learners were "given the opportunity of *consciously* [emphasis mine] trying to scaffold one another's learning [...]. Groups were asked to supply the class with further good examples of how 'to put up good scaffolds' and thus provide linguistic support" (Thomson 2003:39).

In this way processes and procedures in the classroom are made the content of instruction, a crucial feature that will be taken up again further below.

The learner's existing prior knowledge as the starting point for effective pedagogical interventions is another axiom of educational thinking as can be seen in Barnes' seminal statement: "To learn is to develop relationships between [what the learner knows already and the new system being presented to him], and this can only be done by the learner himself" (Barnes 1976: 81).

This tenet also provides the rationale for a differentiated approach to teaching/learning in general, and as realised in autonomous language learning in particular. In other words, it implies a rejection of teacher-fronted classrooms in which a class of heterogeneous learners is to work with the same content and is subjected to the same procedures.

One of the most immediate influences on educational goal setting as promoted within autonomous language learning derives from Carl Rogers' writing – notably *Freedom to Learn* (1969). This influence derives not only from the importance he attaches to self-actualisation, but also from statements like the following, which can be considered agenda-setting for process-oriented, autonomous approaches to learning:

> The only man who is educated is the man who has learned how to learn; the man who has learned how to adapt and change; the man who has realized that no knowledge is secure, that only the processes of *seeking* knowledge gives a basis for security. Changingness, a reliance on *process* rather than upon static knowledge, is the only thing that makes sense as a goal for education in the modern world. (1969:21)

This need for life-long learning based on the procedural knowledge of how to learn has by now become a statement of the obvious in the educational literature at large and has also been reiterated in John Trim's foreword to the Council of Europe's 1988 report on *Autonomy and Self-directed Learning: Present Fields of Application* (ed. H. Holec).

Rogers also tried to define the role of the teacher in formal settings, and he claimed that "teaching is a vastly over-rated function" (1969: 26). He saw the teacher's role as one of a facilitator of learning who provides the conditions for meaningful learning, and who is responsible for setting up a community of learning. Thus, by implication, he also emphasised the social nature of all learning.

3. Autonomy – a multifaceted construct

Given the complex relationship with humanistic philosophies and psychologies as well as critical educational theories, it is small wonder that autonomous language learning can neither be traced to any coherent body of thinking, nor has research managed to lead to a generally accepted theory of autonomous learning. Learner autonomy must be seen as a highly complex construct whose systematic description can be approached from various perspectives.

Benson (1997), for example, distinguishes three basic dimensions or versions of autonomy: the technical, the political and the psychological. The technical view of learner autonomy, which refers to the learners' ability to learn on their own outside institutional contexts, can be excluded from further discussion, since it is an extremely reductionist concept, and cannot be related to any of the above-mentioned foundational principles. It is, though, frequently mentioned in historical overviews, since the proliferation of the new technologies and the rise of self-access centres have stimulated discussions on learner-centredness and autonomy (cf. Gremmo and Riley 1995).

The political and – closely linked with it – the philosophical perspectives have the longest ancestry, as indicated above. When Kant discussed the legitimacy of constraints limiting the individual's freedom and autonomy, then he touched upon an issue which is as topical today as it was then. For obvious reasons the restrictions on autonomy have been a subject of continuing debate when attempting to implement principles of learner autonomy within a formal institutional framework. The political version of learner autonomy thus highlights the tension between constraints imposed on autonomy by the sociocultural context, including curricular guidelines and the freedom of others, on the one hand, and personal control over learning content, individual objectives etc., on the other, thus addressing by implication the power balance between educational authorities, teachers and learners. In traditional, transmission-oriented classrooms the locus of control is clearly placed outside the learners, i.e. rests with the teachers who in turn have to follow and interpret curricular guidelines. In the autonomous classroom, by contrast, 'negotiables' within the institutional constraints are first identified and then used to define the operating space for teachers and learners alike. The ensuing negotiation process between the teacher and learners – as well as between the learners – will result in decisions about content, approaches and evaluative procedures. This negotiation process thus allows for a significant shift of control towards the learners.

The political notion of control needs to be seen as closely related to responsibility, which brings the psychological dimension of learner autonomy to the fore. David Little's authoritative definition of learner autonomy belongs here:

> Essentially, autonomy is a *capacity* – for detachment, critical reflection, decision-making, and independent action. It presupposes, but also entails, that the learner will develop a particular kind of psychological relation to the process and content of his learning. (1991:5)

The Bergen definition of learner autonomy, agreed upon by participants of the 5th Nordic Workshop on Learner Autonomy held in 1989, combines psychological core features with the need for locating autonomy within a social learning context

> Learner autonomy is characterised by a readiness to take charge of one's own learning in the service of one's needs and purposes. This entails a capacity and willingness to act independently *and* in co-operation with others, as a social, responsible person. An autonomous learner is an active participant in the social processes of learning, but also an active interpreter of new information in terms of what she/he already and uniquely knows. (Trebbi 1990: 102)

In contrast to Holec's definition (cited above), here it is not only a capability which underlies autonomy, but also the willingness to take responsibility for one's own learning. This entails that learners have developed and can sustain positive motivational attitudes towards the learning task as indicated above.

4. Principles of autonomous language learning and their implementation

The principles of autonomous language learning can be described on three hierarchically ordered levels, i.e. as underlying, guiding and procedural principles.

4.1. Underlying principles

Underlying principles include the view that language learning is a 'creative construction process' – a concept that is in keeping with constructionist theories of learning.[3] It entails the view that the teachability of languages is severely constrained – a point which has been given empirical support also within Pienemann's processability theory (cf. Pienemann 1998). Learners have to construct their own rules of the language to be learned on the basis of the language they are exposed to and interact with. Although these rules are initially implicit by nature, awareness-raising activities will support the process of growing consciousness and contribute to structuring the learning content (cf. below). The driving forces of the acquisition process are, however, authentic communicative interactions, and in this respect the autonomous approach is also informed by the interactionist hypothesis of language learning.

This concept has a long tradition and can even be said to reach back to John Locke, who wrote as early as 1693: " ... the right way of teaching that [foreign] Language [...] is by talking it into Children in constant Conversation, and not by Grammatical Rules" (1989: 216). Almost three hundred years later, Evelyn Hatch comes to a similar conclusion: "One learns how to do conversation, one learns how to interact verbally, and out of this interaction syntactic structures develop" (Hatch 1978: 404). However, it was not until Michael Long (1996) provided some more theoretical justification to the claims that the interactionist hypothesis gained wider acceptance.

4.2. Guiding principles

The underlying principles provide the rationale for the guiding principles at the next lower level. It is here that autonomy in the sense of shifting responsibility and control towards the learner combines with the maxims of awareness-raising and authenticity. These are interdependent concepts, and together they form – in van Lier's words – 'a triad' which is foundational for the development of a language curriculum. Autonomy, awareness and authenticity are basic "constants which themselves cannot be further reduced or grounded, since they constitute what I consider essential properties of the educational enterprise" (van Lier 1996: 3). Although the complementary maxims of awareness and authenticity have for the last decades played a major role in ELT discussions at large, they take on a special significance in autonomous classrooms.

4.2.1. Awareness-raising

The discussion of awareness-raising was triggered by Hawkins (1984), who largely confined it to language awareness. He focused on language across the curriculum and also intended to improve mother tongue instruction. Ever since the concept has been extended and has become widely accepted also in foreign language teaching methodology. Despite its great appeal, however, it has so far eluded precise definitions and characterisations of its functions in the learning process (cf. Knapp-Potthoff 1997).

The need for awareness-raising in formal learning settings can be said to also result from the limited effects of teacher-directed, knowledge-transmissive techniques, which has made it an attractive concept in the discourse of autonomous language learning. Although the learners' language and language learning awareness might also develop 'naturally' as a concomitant to the learning process, it is here that one of the main responsibilities of teachers lies. Their task is to systematically try to get learners to reflect on the way they go about their learning and to stimulate awareness-raising by introducing tools and activities which facilitate the processes.

Awareness-raising applies to all aspects of the educational enterprise, notably to 'language as a system', 'communication as a process' as well as 'learning processes and conditions' as such (for an overview cf. Knapp-Potthoff 1997).

Awareness-raising of formal-structural aspects of the target language by and large replaces the 'grammar teaching' of more orthodox approaches. The emphasis on it, however, also means that the role of explicit analytic knowledge for the shaping of the learning process and the development of the learners' interlanguage in institutional contexts is acknowledged within autonomous language learning. The notion 'language as a system' not only refers to the target language, but also includes the learner's interlanguage, the awareness of which is a prerequisite for 'noticing' the discrepancies with regard to target language norms. It is here that the pedagogical concept of awareness-raising combines with (gap)-noticing as discussed in the literature on SLA research (cf. Schmidt 1990; Hulstijn and Schmidt 1994).

Awareness-raising and at the same time avoiding the pitfalls of knowledge transmission, i.e. teaching, is one of the pedagogical challenges in the language classroom. Tools facilitating noticing might, for example, include concordancing programs operated by the learners. The learners' own texts and corresponding L1 texts can easily be compared and contrasted by means of 'keyword in context' (KWIC) concordances and by using automatically generated frequency information for the identification of search arguments (cf. Johns 1986; Legenhausen 1996). This will allow learners to approach their learning task with the attitude of researchers (cf. Kelly's 'person-as-scientist' metaphor mentioned above).

The process of noticing structural features of the target language is also facilitated by having learners work with text types which include non-standard features – such as nursery rhymes in beginning classes, literary representations of dialectal forms at later stages (cf. Legenhausen 1995) or 'authentic' non-standard texts as discussed by Gnutzmann 1995.

Since classroom procedures and activities are largely based on small group interactions, the idea of getting learners to reflect upon and evaluate features of communication processes and what constitutes good group work suggests itself. The illustrative example in (1) is taken from a Danish mixed ability class after about three and a half years of learning English. The learners were asked to answer the question: What is good group work? One of the students came up with the following answer:

(1) "A good group work is work everybody take part in, and discuss everything, and they like each other. Everybody has to talk English all the time. Everybody has to do something for the group. When you learn something from the group." (qtd in Dam 2006: 276)

The focus on group interactions and reflecting on them is also likely to make the learners more aware of conversational strategies which will allow them to cope with more problematic communicative situations, including intercultural encounters.

What distinguishes autonomous classrooms, however, from most traditional approaches is the priority attached to making learning processes and learning conditions a topic of reflection and discussion. This feature is often discussed in the educational literature under the heading 'learning to learn' (cf. Ellis and Sinclair 1989). An emphasis on awareness of learning techniques and strategies is intended to support the learners' independence and to promote the learners' capacity for life-long intentional learning. This feature is succinctly expressed in an evaluation at the end of year 9 (i.e. after five years of English) from a learner of the same mixed ability class as the one mentioned above:

> (2) "I already make use of the fixed procedures from our diaries when trying to get something done at home. Then I make a list of what to do or remember the following day. That makes things much easier. I have also via English learned to start a conversation with a stranger and ask good questions. And I think that our 'together' session has helped me to become better at listening to other people and to be interested in them. I feel that I have learned to believe in myself and to be independent." (qtd in Dam 2006: 281)

Since awareness-raising as regards language systems, communication and learning processes has to be enacted as a genuinely interactive undertaking, they become *authentic topics* of discussion in the foreign language classroom. In other words and as indicated above, processes become essential learning content in the autonomous classroom.

4.2.2. Authenticity

The notion of authenticity in autonomous language learning, however, goes far beyond the question of topic authenticity and/or authentic materials (cf. Legenhausen 2000). According to some implementations of autonomous learning principles, the teacher, for example, would not ask any questions to which she could supply the answers herself (cf. Dam 2001). This tenet has far-reaching consequences for the type of interactions between teachers and learners and bars all forms of display questions from the classroom.

The notion of authenticity – according to van Lier – needs to be grounded in an existentialist concept. "An action is authentic when it realises a free choice and is an expression of what a person genuinely feels and believes. An authentic action is *intrinsically motivated* (1996: 6). This implies that a learner can authenticate any action and activity in the classroom, even those which conventional pedagogic wisdom would exclude from the inventory of suitable activities. However, criteria for good activities which the teacher would explicitly support include:

- the degree of learner involvement in setting up the activity
- the activation of the learners' existing knowledge
- the accommodation of learner differentiation
- the flexibility and openness of the task
- the promotion of creativity
- stimulation of self-discovery and self-awareness
- stimulation of social awareness of group dynamics and social management skills

etc.

4.3. Procedural principles

The implementation of the above-mentioned foundational principles in the autonomous classroom can take various forms, one of which has been developed and described in detail by Dam 1994 and 1995, and the following descriptions will be based on Dam's approach. The basic ideas as regards the organisation and the procedures of the autonomous classroom can be summarised in the following figure (cf. Legenhausen 2003).

The work cycle has to start out from a planning phase in which teacher and learners negotiate possible working procedures against the background of syllabus requirements. They can draw on a bank of ideas for activities to which

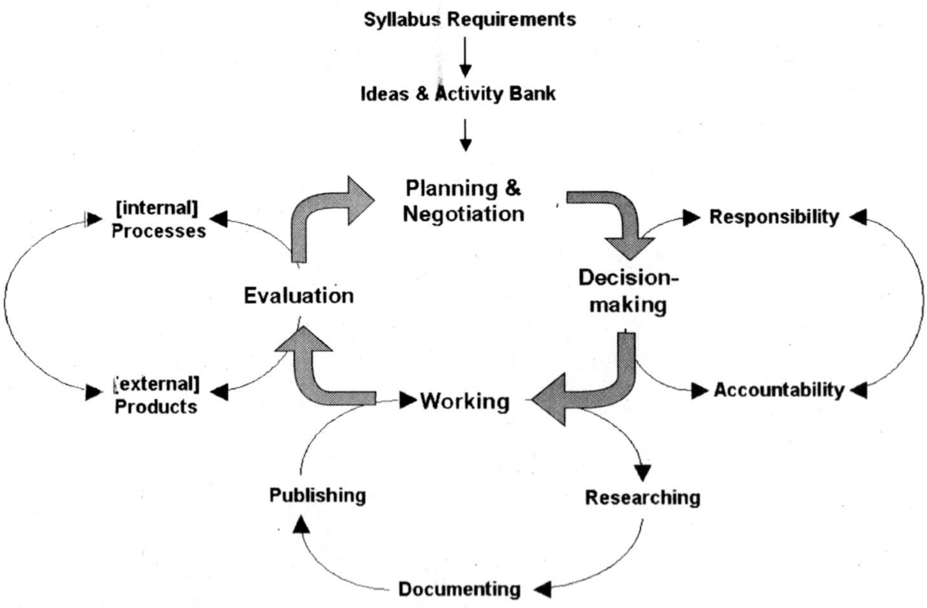

Figure 1. Work cycle

the teacher as well as the learners continuously contribute in the course of a school year. The planning and negotiation phase will result in learner decisions for which they will be held accountable. The standard procedure is that learners decide on projects – in the widest sense of the word – which they will work on in pairs or small groups. The above-mentioned 'person-as-scientist' metaphor applies here as well. This means that learners – with the help and support of the teacher – try to collect data and materials needed for carrying out their plans. It is essential that the working processes are documented and learning outcomes made available to other members of the class. Log books, portfolios and posters are considered essential tools for the documentation process.

The following illustration from a log book shows the learner's planning of future work in which tasks for other group members are specified. This division of labour is the result of previous negotiation phases. The data are also taken from the same Danish mixed ability class when learners were in grade 8:

(3) "1. Share homework with Lars. Lars had read in his book called 'The Soul …'. he has also found some pretty good ideas for our play.
2. Work on the play with my group. – Discuss the contents of our play. – Started to write the play down in 'Play-book'. […]
3. What to do tomorrow: Karsten + Lars writes on scene 1 + 2. Emrah + Anders writes on scene 3.
4. Homework: read in 'Peanuts'"

(qtd in Dam 2006: 273).

The crucial phase of the work cycle is reached with the obligation to evaluate working processes as well as project outcomes. It not only marks the end of a longer work cycle, but will also form a constitutive element of each lesson. In beginning classes it may just take the form of a simple linear scale on which learners mark whether they thought the lesson was 'good' or 'bad'. At more advanced stages evaluation provides an important topic of discussion as well as a writing impetus for the log book. A log book typically contains a section: 'Comments on today's work'. For example, one learner's entry after four years of English reads like this:

(4) "See a programme called, 'From princess to queen' about princess Elizabeth.
Comments: I think it was a little boring, but quite easy to understand, that was good."

(Workshop handout Dam 1999).

A detailed end-of-term evaluation after three years of English might require learners to answer a questionnaire with the following questions:

Objectives/plans

What were your objectives/plans for this term?

Outcomes

What did you achieve? If possible state why.

Learner's role

What do you feel you have been responsible for this year?

Did you live up to this responsibility? Why/Why not?

Materials/activities

Write down good activities or good materials you have worked with this year. State if possible why you liked them.

Evaluation

Which type of evaluation have you made use of? (diaries, whole-class talks, talks with teacher, talks with friends)

How do you judge the usefulness of the various types? (Good? Bad? In between? Don't know?) Why?

Teacher's role

Positive things?

Negative things?

Ideas for next term?

(Dam 1995: 53)

The essential role of the teacher when developing learner autonomy is to mediate between curricular requirements, on the one hand, and learner needs and interests, on the other. In this mediating role she has to strike a balance between, on the one hand, 'letting go' of control, while at the same time guiding learners through the various steps towards more autonomy (cf. Dam 2003: 139). This implies that she is responsible for setting up a learning environment in which negotiation can play a crucial role, and in which learners can exercise their own choices within the constraints of the curriculum.

It goes without saying that the negotiating space varies according to the specificity of the curricular guidelines. However, no matter how detailed the official demands and the objectives have been formulated, there is always a certain freedom or manoeuvering space when it comes to deciding how to achieve the objectives. It is essential that the guidelines are taken into class and – again – made a topic of discussion. In all likelihood they contain passages which are open to interpretation, and given the complexity of the learning task only certain aspects can be predefined by guidelines anyway. As regards the impact of syllabus guidelines on what is going on in classrooms, Breen (1984) claimed that they undergo various reinterpretations during the implementation process.

> Although, as teachers, we may follow a predesigned syllabus, every teacher inevitably interprets and reconstructs that syllabus so that it becomes possible to implement it in his or her classroom. Similarly, learners create individual learning syllabuses from their own particular starting points and their own perceptions of the language, learning, and the classroom. [...] The classroom is therefore the meeting place or point of interaction between the predesigned syllabus and individual learner syllabuses. This interaction will generate the *real* syllabus. (Breen 1984: 50)

The range of classroom decisions that are negotiable within process syllabuses is discussed and exemplified in Breen and Littlejohn (2000).

5. Profiling the autonomous learner

The development of learner autonomy is intertwined with the development of self-esteem. On the one hand, self-esteem is to be regarded as a prerequisite, and on the other hand, it will be fostered and promoted in the developmental process. A "robust sense of self" (Breen and Mann 1997) is, for example, needed in order for the learner to be able to engage in communicative interactions and reassert his or her stance in negotiations with teachers and peers.

The following open list of features might give additional clues as to what it means to be an autonomous learner. It will also partly reflect results from research on the 'good language learner' (cf. Naiman et al. [1978] 1995), since – as Little reminds us – "[learner autonomy] has existed for as long as there have been successful learners" (1999: 13). This is to say that autonomous learners

- have developed a desire to learn the language and are thus either intrinsically motivated or have endorsed extrinsic goals
- have accepted that it is necessary to take charge of their own learning
- have developed a metacognitive awareness of what the learning undertaking implies
- are actively involved in constructing the conditions of their own learning, i.e. are active agents in the learning process and show initiatives when planning and selecting working procedures
- have developed a strategic learning competence which they can also bring to bear on other domains than language learning
- manage to adapt their learning strategies to the requirements of the task
- actively seek opportunities for practising the language also outside the educational context
- have developed criteria for the evaluation of processes and procedures, and show a high degree of competence in self-assessment

etc.

6. The effectiveness of autonomous language learning

The number of case studies on the effectiveness of autonomous classrooms, especially as regards their linguistic outcomes, is as yet limited (cf. Benson 2001: Chpt.16). One of them, the so-called LAALE project (*Language Acquisition in an Autonomous Learning Environment*), is concerned with the linguistic development of the above-mentioned mixed ability class of Danish learners attending a comprehensive school. This class started learning English in year 5 when the learners were eleven years old, and the documentation of their learning progress ended after four years, when most of them left the school. During this four-year period the class was subjected to various data collection procedures, which included an array of different test formats. In order to be able to interpret the findings, most of the tests were also administered at identical intervals in a class of learners in the same Danish school and with learners from a German *Gymnasium*. The linguistic results of the 'autonomous class' compare extremely well with the classes who follow a textbook-based communicative syllabus (for further details cf. Dam and Legenhausen 1996; Legenhausen 1999, 2001, 2003).

It is not only as regards their conversational abilities and pragmatic competence that the autonomous learners excel, but also form and accuracy focussed test results convincingly show that the learners acquire complex grammatical structures without being explicitly taught. The following illustrative example relates to the acquisition of a grammatical core chapter in the beginning years of English, i.e. the acquisition of *do-support questions*. The mother tongues of both Danish and German learners – referred to as AG/Autonomous Group and TG/Traditional Group in the tables below – form questions by inversion, which implies that the learning difficulty must be regarded as very similar for both groups. The data in the tables derive from conversational interactions after one and half years of learning English when the learners were asked to talk for about five minutes about a chosen topic of interest.

Although overall accuracy figures for questions requiring do-support seem to indicate slightly better results for the traditional group (74 %) than for the autonomous learners (70 %), the figures misrepresent the degree of creative mastery of this structure. The very fact that more than half of the questions requiring do-support in the TG corpus are constructed with the verbs *like* and *live* (f = 83) points to the formulaic character of these questions. They are practised intensively in the textbook, and learners seem to have automatised them to a large extent. If questions with *like* and *live* are subtracted from Table 1, the accuracy rate drops in both corpora, however, much less so in the AG corpus (cf. TG: 74 % => 46 %; AG: 70 % => 63 %).

Table 1. Do-support in questions

	Frequencies	Well-formed Questions		Ill-formed Questions	
	Total	f	%	f	%
TG	135	100	74	35	26
AG	142	99	70	43	30

Table 2. do-support without the verbs *like* and *live*

	Frequencies	Well-formed Questions		Ill-formed Questions	
	Total	f	%	f	%
TG	52	24	46	28	54
AG	103	65	63	38	35

The main learning outcome, though, might be said to lie beyond the linguistic achievements. The 'autonomous' learners have not only kept up their motivation, but have become consciously aware of their learning abilities and needs (cf. the quotes introducing this article).

7. Controversial issues in autonomous language learning

7.1. The problem of cultural relativity

The question of whether or not the notion of autonomy is to be regarded as a Western construct has been hotly debated for some time now. Smith, for example, talks about "an ongoing debate regarding the validity of learner autonomy in Asian settings" (2001: 70). On the one hand, there is the view that autonomy is "yet another version of the free, enlightened, liberal West bringing one more form of supposed emancipation to the unenlightened, traditional, backward and authoritarian classrooms of the world" (Pennycook 1997: 43). Adherents of this view see autonomy as deeply embedded in Western philosophy and education, and any transfer to non-Western contexts will be perceived as a form of cultural imperialism. On the other hand, there are plenty of references to Chinese philosophy – and not just to Confucius – in which views are expressed that are in accord with autonomy (cf. Pierson 1996). Pierson argues that "there is an ancient Chinese pedagogical tradition congruent with and consistent with the best practice of autonomous learning" (1996: 54). He quotes several ancient Chinese philosophers to substantiate his view that the notion of autonomy is also deeply rooted in Chinese educational thinking.

7.2. The question of innateness

Closely linked to the question of cultural relativity is the debate on whether autonomy is an inborn and thus universal construct, or whether it is socially mediated. Holec, for example, claims that "[t]his ability is not inborn, but must be acquired by 'natural' means or (as most often happens) by formal learning, i.e. in a systematic, deliberate way" (1981: 3). By contrast, versions of constructivism start out from the premise that autonomy is an inborn capacity (cf. Candy 1989). This hypothesis is supported by Little, who claims that "autonomous language learning is the kind of learning for which we are fitted by nature" (1994: 441). In other words, it is "a general human behavioural capacity" (1999: 17). Little furthermore forcefully argues that autonomy is not only the goal, but also the outcome of all developmental learning (cf. Little 1994, 1999).

Since it is a common experience, though, that in formal learning contexts students do not – and often cannot – exercise their underlying capacity for autonomous learning, this would have to be interpreted in terms of suppression, suffocation or mutation of a 'natural' predisposition. This latter view would also be compatible with the concept of autonomy as a socially mediated construct.

7.3. Individual learner agendas, co-learners and the curriculum

If autonomy is largely based on the possibility of exercising free choices which serve one's personal needs, then this concept has to be perceived as mainly 'individual-centred'. This view raises the obvious question of how the personal learning agendas can be reconciled with the agendas of co-learners and with the external demands of curriculum specifications.

In this context reference to learners as 'social beings' seems to be obligatory, and the obvious point is stressed that all learning – no matter whether developmental or not – is socially determined and the result of interactions. It is here that the above-mentioned sociocultural theory, in which the interdependence between learners, co-learners and more knowledgeable adults is emphasised, comes in as a theoretical underpinning. Many authors include the belief that 'autonomy entails individualism' under the heading of misconceptions (cf. Aoki and Smith 1999). It thus becomes obvious that "genuine autonomy has to be exercised in an interdependent way" (Breen 2000: 22; cf. also Little 1991: 6) – a concept which places interactive negotiation processes in the centre of the educational undertaking. There is, furthermore, a necessity for mediation between various personal learning agendas and the curriculum which defines the borderline between negotiables and non-negotiables, as also indicated above.

7.4. The potential conflict between guidance and instruction and the role of strategy training

The teacher's task and responsibility includes the identification of negotiables in order to be able to map out the route of learning together with her students. She thus plays a crucial role in the negotiations and has to strike a balance between guiding and supporting her students, on the one hand, and avoiding the pitfalls of imposing her own agenda by resorting to instructional techniques, on the other. This potential conflict finds expression in the debate on whether it is desirable –

and feasible – to 'train' learners to become more independent learners and thus 'teach' learning strategies, or whether this approach runs counter to the very principles of autonomous learning.

Ellis and Sinclair (1989), for example, devised a "course in learner training" to be used together with a coursebook. It contains a two-stage programme, the first stage of which is to "prepare students for language learning" and the second stage provides activities and suggestions for "skill training". Wenden (1991) also devised detailed action plans with guidelines for teachers to select content for learner training. Wenden's chapter on strategy training includes the following guidelines:

- *Informed* Strategy training should be informed. The purpose of the training should be made explicit and its value brought to the students' attention.
- *Self-regulation* Students should be trained how to regulate or oversee the use of strategy, i.e. when it is appropriate to use it; the difficulties they have implementing it; and its effectiveness.
- *Contextualized* Strategies should be contextualized. Training should be in the context of the subject matter content and/or skill for which it is appropriate. It should be directed to specific language learning problems related to the learners' experience (Wenden 1991: 105).

Additional criteria refer to interactive and diagnostic features of strategy training. Wenden suggests series of activities which, for example, are "to train students to use 'inferencing', a cognitive strategy" (1991: 97). With reference to research results, Wenden emphasises the significance of transmissive techniques in strategy training, i.e. expository modes of strategy teaching:

> Research has shown that giving students information about the value of a strategy, i.e. about where and how often it may be used, greatly enhances the positive outcomes of training studies [...]. Brown and Baker (1984) consider that informed training is, in effect, training for lateral transfer. When students are given information about where a strategy can be used, it will be more likely that they will use it not only in the training context but in a variety of other appropriate settings. (Wenden 1991: 105)

In this statement a contrast between training contexts and real-life communicative settings is also evoked, which many researchers and practitioners in autonomous language learning would try to avoid. For example, Little states that "... the concept of autonomous language learning is closely associated with the desire to remove the barriers that often exist between learning and life" (Little 1991: 45). The title of one of Dam's articles reads: "Bridging the gap between real life and the language classroom – principles, practices and outcomes" (Dam 2001).

What the proposals by Ellis and Sinclair and Wenden have in common is the view that learner autonomy can be systematically promoted by teacher-initiated and teacher-controlled explicit strategy training. Thus the tenet of the limited effects of instruction, which for many educationists is a compelling argument for subscribing to autonomous principles, is considered less decisive when it comes to strategy training. A contrasting view is expressed by Esch, who makes the point that "the first misconception concerning the promotion of autonomous language learning is to reduce it to a series of techniques to train language learning skills leading to the display of 'autonomous behaviour'" (Esch 1997: 165).

If the limited effects of explicit teaching have been shown – say – in grammar instruction, then the same arguments also hold with regard to strategy training. "Control by the teachers, if it returns through the back door, will produce some short-term language learning gains but will not help learners reap the benefits of taking charge of their own learning" (Esch 1997: 175).

At the university level Esch would also provide students with systematic guidance as regards their strategic approaches by offering 'language strategy courses'. However, the crucial difference would be that attendance is voluntary, and the activities are student-initiated and -controlled.

The alternative to 'training' in classroom settings is to set up a learning environment in which learners are given the opportunity to try out various strategic approaches which are then reflected upon and discussed within the learning community. The teacher's role is to trigger these reflections and support the awareness-raising process.

8. Concluding remarks

The current state of play is far from allowing us to formulate a theory of autonomous language learning, although it would be desirable for reasons including diagnostic purposes in educational contexts. A unified theory might, for example, lead to more principled decisions as regards the type and timing of pedagogical interventions, and provide clearer guidelines to teachers when walking the tightrope between guidance and instruction.

Furthermore, a theory of autonomous language learning would also counteract the growing tendencies to dilute and misinterpret essential principles of autonomy, thus preventing the term from becoming as de-semanticised as the term 'communicative' has become in ELT. As early as 1981 Holec noted the "almost anarchical use" of the term. However, it would probably be realistic to accept Breen and Mann's stance (1997) that – given the multi-dimensionality of the construct – a unified theory might not be feasible. They even see definite advantages in the lack of a theory by suggesting

> that a diversity of interpretations is actually preferable to some consensus definition, even if such were feasible. This diversity allows the innovation in action to reflect variability in cultural interpretations and classroom practices and, thereby, generating a multiplicity of alternative realizations. (1997: 149)

Since it is obvious that there is not just one path to more autonomy in educational contexts, research is confronted with a host of unsolved questions. In applied linguistics they include the clarification of the relationship between language acquisition and the many variables of an autonomous learning environment. So far the autonomous learners' superiority as regards their proficiency development has not been established beyond doubt, although several studies point in that direction. However, from a pedagogical point of view this question might not be the crucial one, since more global educational objectives relating to the learners' self-esteem, their ability for life-long learning and their willingness as well as readiness to act as responsible members of the community they live in might turn out to be more relevant.

Notes

1 Learner quotes from the video edited by Dam, L. and Lenz, J. (1998). "*It's up to yourself if you want to learn. Autonomous language learning at intermediate level*". Danmarks Lærerhøjskole (DLH): Copenhagen.

2 For this reason the 'Learner Independence' Special Interest Group of IATEFL (International Association of Teachers of English as a Foreign Language) was renamed the 'Learner Autonomy' Special Interest Group in 2006.

3 The term was coined by Dulay and Burt in the 1970s (cf. Dulay and Burt 1974).

References

Aoki, Naoko and Richard C. Smith
1999 Learner autonomy in cultural context: The case of Japan. In: Cotterall and Crabbe (eds.), 19–27.

Barnes, Douglas
1976 *From Communication to Curriculum.* Harmondsworth: Penguin.

Benson, Phil
1997 The philosophy and politics of learner autonomy. In: Benson and Voller (eds.), 18–34.

Benson, Phil
2001 *Teaching and Researching Autonomy in Language Learning*. Longman: Harlow.

Benson, Phil and Peter Voller (eds.)
1997 *Autonomy and Independence in Language Learning*. London: Longman.

Breen, Michael P.
1983 How do we recognise a communicative language classroom? In: B. Coffey (ed.), *Teacher Training and the Curriculum.* The Dunford House Seminar, 133–153. London: The British Council.

Breen, Michael P.

1984 Process syllabuses for the language classroom. In: Christopher F. Brumfit (ed.), *General English Syllabus Design. Curriculum and Syllabus Design for the General English Classroom*, 47–60. (ELT Documents 118.) Oxford: Pergamon.

Breen, Michael P. and Andrew Littlejohn (eds.)

2000 *Classroom Decision-Making. Negotiation and Process Syllabuses in Practice*. Cambridge: Cambridge University Press.

Breen, Michael P. and Andrew Littlejohn

2000 The significance of negotiation. In: Breen and Littlejohn (eds.), 5–38.

Breen, Michael P. and Sarah J. Mann

1997 Shooting arrows at the sun: Perspectives on pedagogy for autonomy. In: Benson and Voller (eds.), 132–149.

Bruner, Jerome S.

1983 *Child's Talk: Learning to Use Language*. New York: Norton.

Candy, Philip C.

1989 Constructivism and the study of self-direction in adult learning. *Studies in Education of Adults* 21: 95–116.

Cotterall, Sara and David Crabbe

1999 *Learner Autonomy in Language Learning: Defining the Field and Effecting Change*. Frankfurt a.M.: Peter Lang.

Dam, Leni

1994 How do we recognize an autonomous classroom? *Die Neueren Sprachen* 93: 503–527.

Dam, Leni

1995 *Learner Autonomy 3: From Theory to Classroom Practice*. Dublin: Authentik.

Dam, Leni

2001 Bridging the gap between real life and the language classroom – principles, practices and outcomes. In: Johannes Wagner (ed.). *Pædagogik og læring i fremmed- og andetsprog. Odense Working Papers in Language and Communication* 22: 43–64.

Dam, Leni

2003 Developing learner autonomy: The teacher's responsibility. In: Little, Ridley and Ushioda (eds.), 135–146.

Dam, Leni

2006 Developing learner autonomy – looking into learners' logbooks. In: Markus Kötter, Oliver Traxel and Stephan Gabel (eds.), *Investigating and Facilitating Language Learning*, 265–282. Trier: Wissenschaftlicher Verlag.

Dam, Leni and Lienhard Legenhausen

1996 The acquisition of vocabulary in an autonomous language learning environment – the first months of beginning English. In: Pemberton, Li, Or and Pierson (eds.), 265–280.

Dam, Leni and Jette Lenz

1998 *It's up to yourself if you want to learn. Autonomous language learning at intermediate level*. Video. Danmarks Lærerhøjskole (DLH): Copenhagen.

Deci, Edward L.

1980 *The Psychology of Self-Determination*. Lexington, Mass.: D.C. Heath.

Deci, Edward L. and Richard Flaste
1996 *Why We Do What We Do: Understanding Self-Motivation.* New York: Penguin.

Deci, Edward L. and Richard M. Ryan
1985 *Intrinsic Motivation and Self-Determination in Human Behavior.* New York: Plenum Press.

Dewey, John
1933 *How We Think.* Boston: D.C. Heath.

Dewey, John
1938 *Experiences of Education.* New York: Collier Press.

Donato, Richard
1994 Collective scaffolding in second language learning. In: James P. Lantolf and Gabriela Appel (eds.), *Vygotskian Approaches to Second Language Research,* 33–56. Norwood, N.J.: Ablex Publishing Corporation.

Dulay, Heidi and Marina Burt
1974 A new perspective on the creative construction process in child second language acquisition. *Language Learning* 24: 253–278.

Ellis, Gail and Barbara Sinclair
1989 *Learning to Learn English: A Course in Learner Training.* Cambridge: Cambridge University Press.

Esch, Edith M.
1996 Promoting learner autonomy: Criteria for the selection of appropriate methods. In: Pemberton, Li, Or and Pierson (eds.), 35–48.

Esch, Edith M.
1997 Learner training for autonomous language learning. In: Benson and Voller (eds.), 164–175.

Freire, Paolo
1970 *Pedagogy of the Oppressed.* New York: Herder and Herder.

Gnutzmann, Claus
1995 Sprachbewußtsein ('Language Awareness') und integrativer Grammatikunterricht. In: Claus Gnutzmann and Frank G. Königs (eds.), *Perspektiven des Grammatikunterrichts,* 267–284. Tübingen: Narr.

Gremmo, Marie-Jose and Philip Riley
1995 Autonomy, self-direction and self access in language teaching and learning: The history of an idea. *System* 23: 151–164.

Hatch, Evelyn
1978 Discourse analysis and second language acquisition. In: Evelyn Hatch (ed.), *Second Language Acquisition – a Book of Readings,* 401–435. Rowley, Mass.: Newbury House.

Hawkins, Eric
1984 *Awareness of Language*, London: Longman.

Holec, Henry
[1979] 1981 *Autonomy and Foreign Language Learning.* Oxford: Pergamon. First published Strasbourg: The Council of Europe.

Holec, Henry (ed.)
1988 *Autonomy and Self-directed Learning: Present Fields of Application.* Strasbourg: Council of Europe.

Hulstijn, Jan H. and Richard Schmidt (eds.)
Consciousness in Second Language Learning. AILA Review 11.

Janne, H.
1977 *Organization, Content and Methods of Adult Education.* Report CCC/EEC 77: 3.

Johns, Tim
1986 Micro-Concord: A language-learner's research tool. *System* 14: 151–162.

Kelly, George
1955 *The Psychology of Personal Constructs.* New York: Norton.

Knapp-Potthoff, Annelie
1997 Sprach(lern)bewußtheit im Kontext. *Fremdsprachen lehren und lernen* 26: 9–23.

Legenhausen, Lienhard
1995 Abweichungsphänomene als Unterrichtsgegenstände. Zum systematisch-bewußten Umgang mit Grammatikfehlern und interimsprachlichen Regeln. In: Claus Gnutzmann and Frank G. Königs (eds.), *Perspektiven des Grammatikunterrichts*, 285–302. Tübingen: Narr.

Legenhausen, Lienhard
1996 The identification of over- and underrepresentation in learner languages through frequency lists and concordancing. In: Bernd Rüschoff and Dieter Wolff (eds.), *Technology-enhanced Language Learning in Theory and Practice,* 222–238. Szombathely: Balogh and Co.

Legenhausen, Lienhard
1999 The emergence and use of grammatical structures in conversational interactions – Comparing traditional and autonomous learners. In: Bettina Mißler and Uwe Multhaup (eds.), *The Construction of Knowledge, Learner Autonomy and Related Issues in Foreign Language Learning*, 27–40. Tübingen: Stauffenberg.

Legenhausen, Lienhard
2000 Principles of authenticity and the autonomous classroom. In: Ingo Plag and Klaus P. Schneider (eds.), *Language Use, Language Acquisition and Language History,* 200–212. Trier: Wissenschaftlicher Verlag.

Legenhausen, Lienhard
2001 Discourse behaviour in an autonomous learning environment. *AILA Review* 15: 65–69.

Legenhausen, Lienhard
2003 Second language acquisition in an autonomous learning environment. In: Little, Ridley and Ushioda (eds.), 65–77.

Legenhausen, Lienhard and Dieter Wolff
1992 STORYBOARD and communicative language learning. Results of the Düsseldorf CALL Project. In: Merryanna L. Swartz and Masoud Yazdani (eds.), *Intelligent Tutoring Systems for Foreign Language Learning,* 9–23. Berlin: Springer.

Little, David
1991 *Learner Autonomy 1: Definitions, Issues and Problems.* Dublin: Authentik.

Little, David
1994 Learner autonomy: A theoretical construct and its practical application. *Die Neueren Sprachen* 93: 430–442.

Little, David
1996 Learner autonomy: Some steps in the evolution of theory and practice. *Teanga. The Irish Yearbook of Applied Linguistics* 16. 1–13.

Little, David
1999 Learner autonomy is more than a Western cultural construct. In: Cotterall and Crabbe (eds.), 11–18.

Little, David, Jennifer Ridley and Ema Ushioda (eds.)
2003 *Learner Autonomy in the Foreign Language Classroom.* Dublin: Authentik.

Locke, John
1989 *Some Thoughts Concerning Education.* Oxford: Clarendon Press. First published 1693.

Long, Michael H.
1996 The role of the linguistic environment in second language acquisition. In: William C. Ritchie and Tej K. Bhatia (eds.), *Handbook of Second Language Acquisition,* 413–468. San Diego: Academic Press.

Naiman, Neil, Maria Fröhlich, Hans H. Stern and Angie Todesco
[1978] 1995 *The Good Language Learner.* Clevedon: Multilingual Matters. First published Toronto: Ontario Institute for Studies in Education.

Palfreyman, David and Richard C. Smith (eds.)
2003 *Learner Autonomy Across Cultures: Language Education Perspectives.* Houndmills, Basingstoke: Palgrave Macmillan.

Pemberton, Richard, Edward S. L. Li, Winnie W. F. Or and Herbert D. Pierson (eds.)
1996 *Taking Control: Autonomy in Language Learning.* Hong Kong: Hong Kong University Press.

Pennycook, Alastair
1997 Cultural alternatives and autonomy. In: Benson and Voller (eds.), 35–53.

Pienemann, Manfred
1998 *Language Processing and Second Language Development.* Amsterdam: Benjamins.

Pierson, Herbert D.
1996 Learner culture and learner autonomy in the Hong Kong Chinese context. In: Pemberton, Li, Or and Pierson (eds.), 49–58.

Raskin, Jonathan D.
2002 Constructivism in psychology: Personal construct psychology, radical constructivism and social constructivism. *American Communication Journal* 5: 3.

Ratner, Nancy and Jerome S. Bruner
1978 Games, social change and the acquisition of language. *Journal of Child Language* 5: 391–401.

Rogers, Carl R.
1969 *Freedom to Learn.* Columbus. Ohio: Charles E. Merrill.

Schmidt, Richard
1990 The role of consciousness in second language learning. *Applied Linguistics* 11: 129–158.

Smith, Richard C.
2001 Group work for autonomy in Asia: Insights from teacher-research. *AILA Review* 15: 70–81.

Thomsen, Hanne
2003 Scaffolding target language use. In: Little, Ridley and Ushioda (eds.), 29–46.

Ushioda, Ema
1996 *Learner Autonomy 5: The Role of Motivation*. Dublin: Authentik.

Ushioda, Ema
2003 Motivation as a socially motivated process. In: Little, Ridley and Ushioda (eds.), 90–102.

Ushioda, Ema
2006 Motivation and autonomy in language learning. In: Markus Kötter, Oliver Traxel and Stephan Gabel (eds.). *Investigating and Facilitating Language Learning*, 283–295. Trier: Wissenschaftlicher Verlag.

van Lier, Leo
1996 *Interaction in the Language Curriculum: Awareness, Autonomy and Authenticity*. London: New York.

Vygotsky, Lev S.
1978 *Mind in Society: The Development of Higher Psychological Processes*. Boston: Harvard University Press.

Vygotsky, Lev S.
1981 The genesis of higher mental functions. In: James V. Wertsch (ed.), *The Concept of Activity in Soviet Psychology*. Armonk, N.Y.: Sharp.

Wenden, Anita
1991 *Learner Strategies for Learner Autonomy*. London: Prentice Hall.

Wolff, Dieter
1994 Der Konstruktivismus: Ein neues Paradigma in der Fremdsprachendidaktik? *Die Neueren Sprachen* 93: 407–429.

Recommended Readings

Benson, Phil
2001 *Teaching and Researching Autonomy in Language Learning*. Longman: Harlow.

The most comprehensive survey of theoretical as well practical issues in autonomous language learning. Chapter 18 includes useful references to journals, websites, e-mail lists and professional associations.

Breen, Michael P. and Andrew Littlejohn (eds.)
2000 *Classroom Decision-Making. Negotiation and Process Syllabuses in Practice*. Cambridge: Cambridge University Press.

Apart from describing the rationale of process syllabuses, the authors have accumulated a host of practice reports and research studies of learner-centred classrooms. The book provides a framework for teachers which might encourage them to try out autonomous principles in their own institutional settings.

Dam, Leni
1995 *Learner Autonomy 3: From Theory to Classroom Practice.* Dublin: Authentik.
Dam gives a detailed account of her classroom practices, beginning with the first year of English. Dam's approach is widely considered the most innovative implementation of autonomous learning principles. Because of its rich documentation it can be used as guide for teachers who are interested in trying out steps towards more autonomy.

Holec, Henry
[1979] 1981 *Autonomy and Foreign Language Learning.* Oxford: Pergamon. First published Strasbourg: The Council of Europe.
A seminal publication which can be considered the foundational document of autonomous language learning.

Little, David
1991 *Learner Autonomy 1: Definitions, Issues and Problems.* Dublin: Authentik.
A concise and most insightful characterisation of the theoretical underpinning of autonomous language learning which also outlines practical issues in the implementation of autonomy.

van Lier, Leo
1996 *Interaction in the Language Curriculum: Awareness, Autonomy and Authenticity.* London: Longman.
This book provides an innovative theory of foreign language education in which the interdependence of autonomy, awareness and authenticity is focused upon. The book draws upon a wide variety of sources in philosophy, cognitive science and sociology.

Websites

http://www.havo.nl/autonomybibliography.php
A regularly updated website on autonomy and related issues. It includes the most comprehensive bibliography on autonomy with about 1000 entries compiled by Phil Benson and Hayo Reinders.

http://www.learnerautonomy.org
The website of the IATEFL Learner Autonomy Special Interest Group. Its basic idea is to share news and resources related to learner autonomy. IATEFL is short for 'International Association of Teachers of English as a Foreign Language'.

http://ld-sig.org
The website of the JALT Learner Development Special Interest Group. Its members have an interest in developing and researching practices that aim to support autonomous learning and teaching. JALT stands for 'Japan Association for Language Teaching'.

http://www2.warwick.ac.uk/fac/soc/celte/research/circal/dahla/
This is the home page of the DAHLA project, coordinated by Richard Smith. DAHLA stands for 'Developing an Archive and Histories of Learner Autonomy'.

15. Teaching the spoken foreign language

Martin Bygate

1. Introduction

Describing the participants studied in a recent research project, Ortega wrote: "All speakers [...] evaluated their motivation for learning and speaking Spanish as high, and their language-learning abilities as above average." Yet, despite high motivation and self-confidence, "remarks about feeling self-conscious when speaking in Spanish were frequent":

> [...] when it comes to communication, I feel lacking [laughs] [...] quite a bit, although I'm sure everybody [in my class] feels like that. We don't do a lot of speaking and everybody feels very awkward when they speak. I think that if you are only doing it two or three hours a week [attending Spanish class] it's really difficult to feel comfortable speaking. (Ortega 2005: 79).

Speaking is not necessarily an easy part of language learning. People might read and write quite effectively, and learn successfully through the written word, but the ability to speak does not always follow. In some ways, speaking is a different kind of engagement with the foreign language, and hence requires different kinds of learning activity. That is, learning the spoken foreign language can be a challenge in its own right. Ortega's own turn of phrase suggests that this is not only a problem for students. A few lines earlier, she reports that the students "were in a foreign language context with little access to the L2 outside the classroom". In fact, the key facility that might well have been hard to access was spoken Spanish. And this is a central problem in conceptualising the teaching and learning of speaking. When a teacher enters the classroom, what kinds of purpose, topic and interaction patterns can be usefully set in motion? How are the alternatives described? What procedures can teachers use? Answers to these questions depend on having appropriate conceptual frameworks. But to develop such frameworks, it can be hard to disentangle the different dimensions of foreign language speaking.

One key quality is perhaps its immediacy. Teachers can exploit speaking to obtain direct evidence of learner uptake and of any need for correction. Hence it has often been used as the default medium for learning and teaching. At the same time, because of that same sense of immediacy, speaking is also highly enmeshed in an individual's expressions of personal identity, both as learner and as second language user. This can make it hard for learners to separate the business of coming to grips with the oral use of the language from issues of identity, face and human relationships. Teachers can therefore be understandably hesitant in providing oral briefing or correction. Furthermore, although it can constitute a motivating aspect and medium of language learning, communicative talk can also be frustrating, in its transience as well as in its unpredictability. How do we teach speech, when it is not clear what features of speech are going to be produced? And if talk is transient, how can we chart the kinds and features of talk that can be usefully taught and learnt? And how can the processes of learners' uptake and mastery of talk be best understood? Technologically, compared with written language, research into spoken discourse is labour-intensive, and hence expensive. In contrast then, learning through the written word can seem safe territory.

As a result, answers to these questions are slow to emerge. And indeed, over the past 30 years, few book length studies have explored oral language pedagogy (exceptions are Brown and Yule 1983; Bygate 1987; Byrne 1976; Littlewood 1992; Riggenbach 1999). Those researching the speech of learners are mainly divided between those considering speech as a window on language learning (for example Boxer and Cohen 2004), those mapping the linguistic features of NS talk through analysis of corpora (such as Carter and McCarthy 1997) or NNS oral discourse (such as Jenkins 2000) and those exploring a particular pedagogy, such as the use of oral tasks (Bygate 2000; Bygate, Skehan and Swain 2001; Ellis 2005). So despite the importance attributed to speech within language development (see for example Ellis 1994), relatively little space has been devoted specifically to studies of the teaching of speaking.

This chapter, then, explores a troubled area of language pedagogy. In what follows we survey the history of the teaching of a speaking in a foreign language. We then report major aspects of the current state of the art of oral language teaching, and conclude by a consideration of a range of research issues that arise from this account.

2. History of the topic

The teaching of speaking has had a chequered history. Classic grammar-translation approaches to language teaching have long organised teaching and learning around written texts (see for example Whitney 1977, 1st ed 1944, later to be incorporated into the long running 'Colloquial Language' series published by Routledge). Grammar-translation (GT) techniques have been a major resource throughout the history of second language pedagogy – the reading of texts in the L2, translating them into the L1, exercises in translating L1 sentences structured around particular grammatical problems, and exercises in translating L1 texts into the L2. In GT approaches, speaking activities tended to involve working on L1 or L2 texts or sentences. The 19th century Reform Movement (Howatt 1984) brought a revolt against this paradigm. Its proponents argued that fluent second language use was generally best achieved without constant transfer to or from the L1, and indeed without explicit reference to the L1. The development of fluency and the mapping of grammar and meaning were seen as generally impeded by the activities used in GT approaches. Instead speech was to be made central in the teaching of language. But historically the qualities of speech favoured the exploitation of particular teaching procedures, since speech also offers a valuable channel for language learning: the fact that it occurs in the here and now of real time between two interlocutors means that it is well suited to enabling direct links between language and its referents through the use of ostensive techniques. And the same real time quality also makes it ideally suited for the use of pedagogical techniques of imitation and correction, and for enabling the automation of language processing.

These in-built qualities of oral language processing led a series of approaches and methods to exploit speech as a basic medium for learning by using it to enable immediate learner response, instant correction and rapid repetition. This was characteristic of various approaches, such as the Direct Method, Audiolingual (AL) Methods (for instance, Lado and Fries 1952, 1958; English Language Services 1964; Alexander 1967) and Audio-visual Methods. Its use as a medium for face-to-face interaction also led speaking to become for many the main embodiment first of 'functional' approaches to language teaching and more or less at the same time, of Communicative Language Teaching (CLT). Despite the fact that within linguistics, the term 'functional' refers to all aspects of language whether spoken or written (Halliday 1994) and was indeed used in this sense in some 'functional' language materials (such as White 1978, 1979), the term was quickly re-appropriated to refer particularly to the pragmatic functions of speech (for example, Morrow and Johnson 1979). 'Functional' approaches to language teaching, then, came to be seen as principally focused on the teaching of pragmatic expressions.

The term 'communicative' also became very widely interpreted to mean 'oral' or 'face-to-face', despite the fact that major groundbreaking work in CLT such as that of Widdowson (1978) and Swales (1990) in fact focused far more on written than on spoken discourse. This development may have been mainly motivated by the opportunity the face-to-face dimension of oral communication offered for personalising language learning in general, a facet of CLT noted by Brumfit (1984).

This 'personal' aspect of speech was also an important resource in the development of 'humanistic' approaches. These approaches (Stevick 1996) emphasised the importance of personal communication, respect for the individuality of the learner and for learners' individual learning processes in approaches such as the Silent Way, and Community Language Learning. The dimension of individual negotiation of learning associated with face-to-face oral interaction is strikingly congruent with these methodologies. Indeed a similar congruence can be found with the more recent concerns of those adopting interactionist or socio-constructionist approaches to language learning. In such approaches, speech is prized as a medium for negotiated learning: developing oral skills is less of a methodological challenge in its own right.

Hence over the past 130 years or so, speech has been particularly implicated in the development of general language teaching methodology rather than being the focus of syllabus development – even paradoxically much of the famous audiolingual (AL) approach. Of course it has to be acknowledged that this has not been a one-way process of identification: if speech has been drawn on for the realisation of new generations of approaches to the teaching of language, this may have been partly because developments in the teaching of languages have been illuminated by perceptions of the qualities of speech, and of the role of speech in language acquisition. A major limitation however in the development of the teaching of oral language is that innovation in foreign language methodologies has tended to be shaped as much by reactions against the overall straightjacket imposed by earlier methodologies as by perceptions of the nature of talk. Particular features of talk (such as automation) had been identified as posing significant challenges to previous methodologies; or else new methodologies had perhaps been over-interpreted in terms of aspects of talk (such as corrective feedback, or their potential for personalised learning). Rarely have we stood back from the development of generic language teaching methodologies and asked the question: what might constitute an appropriate methodology for the teaching of oral language as a sub-domain? Hence despite the various developments sketched out above, we have yet to see the emergence of an integrated methodology for the development of oral language skills.

This is reflected in research over the past 30 years. There is a long tradition of research into the learning and teaching of written skills, which has consistently emphasised the importance for pedagogy of focusing on written genres as well as on developing relevant processing capacities through learning activities (e.g. Alderson and Urquart 1984; Swales 1990; Urquart and Weir 1998 on reading, and Swales 1990; Grabe and Kaplan 1996; Hyland 2003 for writing). In contrast relatively few research monographs have focused explicitly on the pedagogy of oral skills (Bygate 1987; Littlewood 1992; Hughes 2002). In other words, speaking is often seen in terms of how it can contribute to language acquisition in general. Alternatively some writers have emphasised the importance of genre (for example Carter and McCarthy 1997; Hughes 2002; McCarthy and O'Keefe 2004) while neglecting the dimension of processing capacities. And others have concentrated on the aspects of the quality of speech such as dimensions of fluency, accuracy and complexity, but ignored the overall nature of spoken discourses. On the whole, neither type of research has been explicitly linked to a syllabus or to a range of pedagogical activities. And generally these approaches on the whole fail to examine questions such as: What types of speaking need teaching? How do they develop? How can they be taught? What learning problems do they pose in their own right? And how can they be dealt with?

However, in spite of these limitations, progress has been made. The emergence of the above publications, for instance, reflects a recognition that the learning of spoken language does present particular challenges, which deserve attention in their own right. The next section considers more closely some of the major ways in which oral language pedagogy has been explored.

3. State-of-the-art

In focusing on what is particular to the teaching of speaking, it is helpful to distinguish two main themes, first perspectives on the nature of spoken language, and second, the range of pedagogical responses. Consideration of the nature of spoken language can be usefully divided into a) the formal patterns of spoken language as product; b) the socio-psychological processes involved in generating spoken language; and c) the internal qualities of spoken language. In turn, pedagogical procedures can be reviewed in terms of a) activities and their exploitation; and b) approaches to the oral second language syllabus. In what follows, we consider each of these topics in turn.

3.1. The nature of spoken language

3.1.1. The formal patterns of spoken language

Over the last 20 years, research – especially corpus based research – has revealed more and more clearly many of the major characteristics of spoken language. In 1985 Chafe proposed that speech and writing differed in terms of lexical density, syntactic integration (vs. fragmentation), and personal involvement. Although these parameters are not of the same kind, his theorising has been largely supported by others. For example, drawing on the Longman Spoken and Written English Corpus, Biber, Conrad and Leech (2002) identify numerous features that are characteristic of conversation, which they group under contextual features (see Table 1).

This list is not exhaustive (for example interruptions are presumably a feature of the interactive nature of talk). Features can also be cross-classified – for example some kinds of real time features, such as repairs ('other-repairs' for instance) are interactive; real time features such as reduced forms are likely to be closely associated with avoidance of elaboration, and with features occurring under 'shared context' such as ellipsis; stance and vernacular are likely to be particularly closely related. The list is however consistent with Chafe's (1985)

Table 1. Contextual features of conversational talk (after Biber, Conrad and Leech 2002)

Shared context
Use of ellipsis; pro-forms
Deictic features
Avoids elaboration
Frequent use of pronouns
Less noun phrase modification
Frequent use of primary and modal verbs
Frequent use of *that-* and *wh-* complementation
Considerable use of vague language
Interactiveness
Use of negatives
Initiation-response pairs
Attention signalling
Vocatives
Stance
Endearments (or the opposite)
Interjections
Exclamations
Evaluative predicative adjectives
Stance adverbials (or 'disjuncts')
Real time
Dysfluencies – e.g. repairs
Reduced forms
Restricted and repetitive repertoire
Vernacular
Style and dialect variation

categories: 'lexical density' reflects the relative frequency of pro-forms, and the relatively low level of modification of head nouns; 'fragmentation' reflects the interactive real time nature of the production of talk; and Chafe's category of 'personal involvement' accounts largely for vernacular, stance and indeed for features such as vocatives and attention signalling. It has to be acknowledged that written language can have all of these features, just as oral language can take on the characteristics of written language. The value of the above characterisation though is that it reflects the relative frequency of the features in speech, and the fact that they are less typical of written language.

This account is not simply a descriptive matter: these characteristics can be closely related to the socio-psychological circumstances of language use. Working under the typical conditions of speech, that is, with processing having to be managed on the fly, it is likely to be easier to produce and listen to language shaped with the above characteristics, than written language, with its density, its integrated grammar, and its lack of personal involvement. The shape of spoken language then is related to its processing, which is the focus of the next section.

3.1.2. Socio-psychological processes of spoken language

One of the outstanding models of spoken language processing is that of Levelt (1989, 1999). Although developed to describe L1 use, his account is also helpful in discussing L2 speech processing. He proposes four key phases of language processing: conceptualisation, in which the speaker marshals intentions and meanings to be expressed; formulation, where speakers seek and sequence lexical elements, add morpho-syntactic features, and prepare a phonological speech plan (see Dalton and Seidlhofer 1994 and Celce-Murcia, Brinton and Goodwin 1996 for discussion of the psychological representation of speech sounds); articulation, which is the point where speakers convert their speech plan into the stream of sounds; and finally monitoring, which is the process whereby speakers check that their plans and production of speech match their intentions, and are accessible to their interlocutors within the relevant socio-psychological context. The four processes can be reasonably easily distinguished, and taken together provide an account of speaking which has the virtue of integrating the processing of pragmatics, lexico-semantics, morpho-syntax, phonology and phonetics within a complex multi-level capacity.

The model also allows for a complex relationship between the processes. For example, parts of the processing capacity are controlled (or consciously managed) while other parts are automated, with the automated phases generally accessible to controlled processing where necessary. The account also explains why it is normally difficult to use controlled processing for all aspects of speech production (for example, it is impossible for most of us to speak normally while attending to all the details of phonetic articulation): automation of the phases that require the least complex conceptual decisions lightens the load and speeds things up. Levelt's account also allows for the possibility of parallel processing, with conceptualisation forging ahead while formulation takes place, with articulation in turn lagging slightly behind. Only the monitoring capacity seems to range simultaneously across the phases.

Although Kormos (2006) sees Levelt's model as currently the strongest of those that have been elaborated, it has been criticised for lacking both an interactive and a pragmatic dimension (Hughes 2002) and for presenting an essentially steady state account of language production (de Bot 1992; Kormos 2006). De Bot also points out that the model was developed for L1 speakers, hence failing to elucidate the place of L1 knowledge in L2 production. Regarding the interactive pragmatic dimension, although it is true that this is not his major concern, Levelt does nevertheless devote a chapter to the elaboration of a pragmatic dimension to his account, illustrated via a series of interactive examples. Despite the fact that the model is largely a 'steady state' model, meaning that it does not explain change, Levelt does nonetheless discuss how increased experience of a speech activity can lead to changes in the speakers capacity to manage the demands. Further research into changes in speakers' production capacities, for example through task repetition designs (e.g. Bygate and Samuda 2005; Larsen-Freeman 2006; Lynch and Maclean 2001) suggest one way in which it may be possible to explore the model within a dynamic context.

The main criticism of Levelt's model is that it appears not to take much account of the interpersonal collaborative nature of talk. To do that requires a model in which different interlocutors jointly plan, track, adjust and contribute to the shape of the talk. Although Levelt does illustrate the processes of collaborative talk in his account of the joint management of reference, others such as Clarke and Wilkes-Gibbs (1986), Wilkes-Gibbs (1997), and Yule and Tarone (1991) take this further. In studying communication strategies – the strategies by which a speaker resolves problems of communication – whereas previous studies (e.g. Paribakht 1985; Poulisse 1987; Bongaerts and Poulisse 1989; Bialystok 1990) had largely framed this in terms of the adjustment strategies individual speakers adopt unilaterally when confronted by communication problems, Dobao (2004) shows how communication strategies are in fact jointly negotiated by speaker and listener. Either speaker or interlocutor may spot the need for rephrasing; either can provide an effective reformulation; and a communication strategy cannot be used without both interlocutors ratifying the strategic reformulation before the talk moves on. Seen in this light, the use of communication strategies depends on the joint identification and resolution of a problem with speaker and listener effectively plotting the direction of the discourse, and each anticipating upcoming meanings and appropriate ways of expressing them.

It is this joint charting of the discourse which has been particularly explored by Wilkes-Gibbs (1997). In a series of studies she demonstrates how speakers do not merely formulate their messages in terms of conceptualisations that they have privately established. Rather, messages are selected and formulated in the light of what they consider their interlocutor needs to understand. Hence they take bearings on their interlocutor's likely relevant knowledge states and where possible on the interlocutors' own pragmatic intentions or purposes. This will in particular influence the content and the degree of explicitness or vagueness which the speaker will judge necessary to build in to her talk. This can be researched by careful task construction and briefing of the participants. We will return to this issue later in this section.

3.1.3. Qualities of spoken language

The term 'quality' is being used here to refer to features commonly associated with performance, such as fluency, complexity and accuracy (see for example Skehan 2001). Since the realisation of both accuracy and complexity can be related to the construct of fluency, in what follows we will focus principally on fluency.

The term 'fluency' Segalowitz (2003: 384) defines as "an ability in the second language to produce or comprehend utterances smoothly, rapidly, and accurately". Fluency is mainly of interest because it is related to communicative effectiveness. Just as effective reading depends in part on the reader achieving a necessary speed of word recognition sufficient to ensure that the last part of a clause is understood before the first part has faded from working memory (Nation 1993, 2001), so for speech to be effective both for speaker and listener depends on the speaker being able to access words and phrases sufficiently fast. Hence it not only "improves the quality of performance" – it also "facilitates communication" (Segalowitz, 2003: 401).

Fluency is reflected in the rate of delivery of the stream of speech. Rate of delivery can be divided into speed, and what might be termed 'regularity', meaning the amount and distribution of pausing. The interest in rate of delivery derives from the assumption that all things being equal, both speed and regularity change as a function of proficiency.

Speed of delivery is generally measured in terms of number of syllables per minute. However speed is only one facet of fluency: there is also the matter of how pausing is distributed throughout the speech. There are two kinds of measure used to assess this aspect of fluency. One is Mean Length of Run (MLR) with length of run defined as a stretch of speech uninterrupted by pauses. That is, as proficiency increases, speakers become better able to produce stretches of talk without pausing to select or access the next word or phrase within an utterance. A second measure focuses on the relative frequency of pausing within utterances and at utterance boundaries. As with MLR, the expectation is that all things being equal, as speakers become more proficient they will pause relatively less within utterances. In addition, Pawley and Syder (1983) have shown that NS pause patterns differ according to the nature of the talk. More socio-cognitively demanding talk would involve proportionally more clause-internal pausing than clause-external pausing compared with less demanding talk. Furthermore, the more demanding types of talk would manifest more clause-external pausing. Hence speakers' pause patterns need to be assessed in the light of the nature of the speech event. But since a learner's level of proficiency will also affect the level of demand, it follows that, keeping task constant, both the proportion of clause-internal planning and the overall amount of clause-external planning will drop as proficiency increases.

Finally Skehan and Foster (2005) distinguish between two further kinds of dysfluency: "breakdown fluency", which is the kind of interruption aimed at creating additional processing time, which is conventionally associated with pausing; and "repair fluency", the kind of interruption which arises in order to correct some aspect of formulation or articulation.

The aspects of fluency that are described here imply that fluency is not simply a surface phenomenon. Rather they suggest that fluency is a reflection of the effectiveness with which speakers manage their pragmatic purposes, which itself will be a function of the discourse type and interactional purpose. To promote fluency, then, the question we need to ask is 'fluency in doing what?'. This will almost certainly imply the use of more than decontextualised drills and exercises. It is also likely to be aided by familiarisation both with the language and with the content of talk.

3.1.4. Summary

The relevance of the points made in this section so far is that the teaching of speech production has to enable learners to engage with the social and psychological processes of speech production, in real time, so that the following features occur:

- Learners link intention, formulation and articulation
- Learners relate their intentions and understandings to those of their interlocutors
- Learners produce speech under real time pressures
- Learners' speech is normally shaped differently from written language

Drawing also on Levelt's (1989) and (1999) schemas, this account can be represented via a modified version of a figure presented in Bygate (1987, cf. Figure 1).

This schema illustrates three key points. The first is the fact that speech production involves the four kinds of basic process: conceptualisation, formulation, articulation and monitoring. The second point is that during speech, each process in fact draws on stored knowledge, represented by the two columns, and the block arrows interrelating the processes and knowledge stores. The third point is the overall importance of speech purpose, against which the processes are mapped such that the speaker can check that conceptual planning is on track, that formulation is meeting the speakers' overall pragmatic intentions, and that articulation meets necessary standards of comprehensibility. A systematic approach to oral second language pedagogy has to take these different facets into account. The next section considers this aspect of the state of the art.

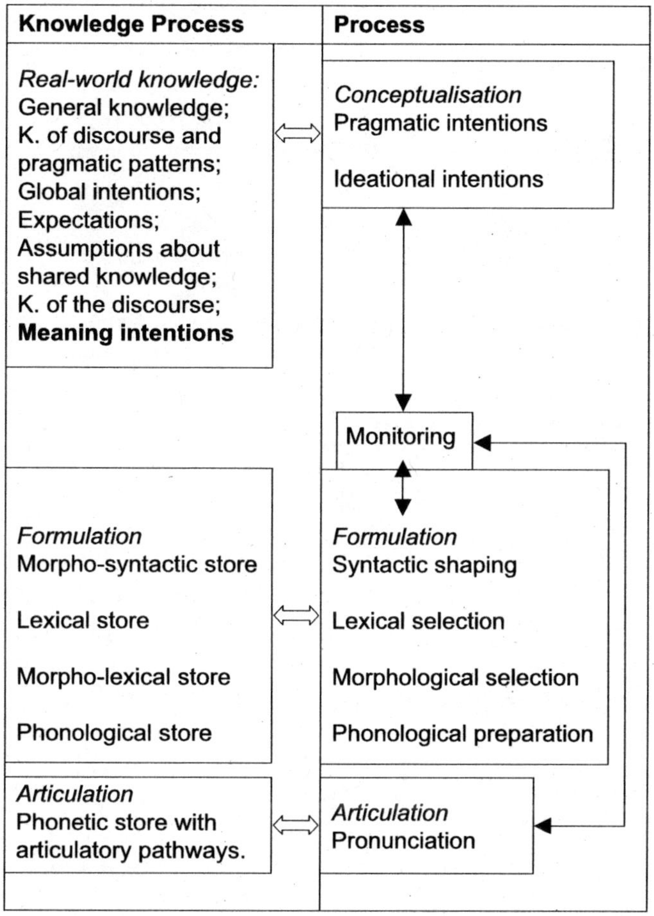

Figure 1. Elements of oral language processing (after Bygate 1987 and Levelt 1989)

3.2. Pedagogical responses

This section is divided into two parts. The first discusses developments in the design of oral activities, and the nature of the repertoire of activities that this has generated. The second part considers approaches to the teaching of speaking, that is, the main pedagogical strategies for developing speaking skills that have been elaborated in recent years.

3.2.1. Pedagogical activities

In a paper published in 1981, Abbott critically reviewed ten oral fluency exercises (1981: 116–129). To make clear the technical nature of his argument, he only considered material which he had written himself. His main conclusions were that different activities can be designed and used in order to target different aspects of oral language use, that all can have their uses within a language programme, and that critiquing exercises in terms of what they fail to do can be useful in pushing forward the parameters of materials design. A sample of the exercises appears in Table 2. The dates are of the original publication of each exercise, and the comments after each are paraphrases of Abbott's own. Abbott's earliest exercises (1961, 1969, not exemplified in Table 2) were essentially drills. Abbott points out that these can free up attention by limiting learners' memory load, and can help improve speed of articulation, and fluency in accessing lexico-grammatical items. However the language does not have the features typical of speech, and students don't have to attend to the overall meaning of their speech, though they may have to select an appropriate verb in light of the earlier part of the sentence. This same point lies behind Dalton and Seidlhofer's (1994) distinction between sentence-based and discourse based pronunciation activities.

Abbott points out that exercises such as 3 and 5 can help speech activity by limiting learners' memory overload, and can help improve their speed of articulation, and fluency in accessing syntactic structures, relevant lexical items, and their appropriate forms. However, they fail to offer learners the opportunity to engage in normal discourse processing. That is, learners can still produce the appropriate utterance without having to plan the meaning of the utterance, and without following the narrative. In other words, these activities engage learners in part of the overall discourse activity of speech, but not in the whole process of speech production. In contrast, we recognise exercise 9 (one of three examples provided by Abbott) as what became known as an 'information gap' activity, a development which can be seen as something of a technological revolution in activity design for its time. Indeed Abbott himself describes this type of activity as using a different 'technique' from the previous exercises: on the one hand, learners' language focus can be narrowed (as in the detective puzzle), while also retaining two key features of normal speech processes: i) speakers have to attend to the content as well as the form of utterances; and ii) collaborative dialogue is essential for the activity to be completed. Overall then Abbott's survey illustrates that the design of activities can be used to modify the extent to which learners engage in using all or only part of the language processing hierarchy.

The information gap activity can be seen as just one kind of communication task. Legutke and Thomas illustrate several other major types of possible communication task (1991: Chapter 4). Littlewood (1981, 2004) explores more broadly the range of possible oral activities. He distinguishes different types of pedagogical activity according to the extent to which they lead learners to focus on form or on meaning. Of course arguably no language activity can function without at least some reference to both form and meaning. But for Littlewood,

Table 2. Examples of evolution in the design of oral activities (after Abbott 1981)

Exercise 3 (1971)

EXAMPLE: A: *How's your mother?*
B: *Not very well, I'm afraid. She's going to a new doctor.*
A: *Oh? What's he like?*
B: *Well, she says he's very capable.*

Repeat the dialogue substituting the items below:

X	Y
Dentist	*clever*
Specialist	*knowledgeable*

Comments: i) imposes a big memory load, leading students to need written support
ii) does have features of oral language – a dialogue format, and language typical of speech (markers and exclamations: *well*', *Oh*; pronouns: *she*; ellipsis:*she's, not very well*)
iii) doesn't require students to plan the content of what they wish to say

Exercise 5(1975)

Aim To practise questions beginning with HOW.
Note Usually Daddy tells little Bobby a bedtime story about a spy called Captain Wonder. Last night, Daddy didn't finish the story, so Mummy (A) is finishing the story. But little Bobby (B) keeps asking questions.

Listen to these examples.
e.g. a) A *Captain Wonder escaped from his cell.*
B *How did he escape from his cell?*
A *Well, I'll tell you.*
b) A *He dug a tunnel.*
B *How did he dig a tunnel?*
A *With his spoon.*

Now you ask the questions.
1. A *He made a rope.*
B *How did he make a rope?*
A *By tying two sheets together.*
2. A *Then he reached the border.*
B *How did he reach the border?*
A *Oh, I forgot to tell you something.*
3. A *First, he got a car.*
B *How did he get a car?*
A *He stole one, and he drove it to the border.* Etc....

Comments: i) This is recognisable as a single dialogue on a single topic.
ii) It contains features of oral language (interjections, ellipsis, reference to addressee, etc.)
iii) Student has to provide appropriate structural transformation
iv) The whole drill is contextualised within a story, providing narrative interest.
v) Abnormal in that questions would normally use ellipsis.
vi) Simple imitation is required, involving no more than rote learning

Exercise 9 (1980)

Name	*Eyes*	*Hair*	*Age*	*Height*
Anderson	brown	Fair	40	Very tall
Jackson	(blue)	fair	20	Very tall
Johnson	blue	(fair)	39	Very short
Richardson	blue	fair	(41)	Very tall
Robinson	blue	white	70	(very tall)

Providing a model:
The table is originally empty except for the parenthesised items. Also on BB is the problem:
One of these men is a murderer. The police know that he is very tall, is about forty years old and has blue eyes and fair hair. Which man is the murderer?
T: *What colour is Mr Jackson's eyes?* C: *Blue*, etc.

Providing practice:
Pupils ask teacher – or other pupils who have been given the information. At the appropriate times, teacher encourages pupils to say, e.g.:
– *It can't be Mr Anderson, because he's got brown eyes.*
– *It might be Mr Jackson because he's got fair hair.*
– *It must be Mr Richardson!*

Comments:
i) The problem-solving element is motivating.
ii) Well suited to the practice of questions.
iii) Dialogue occurs naturally
iv) Features of oral language occur naturally.
v) 'Working column by column (vertically) and across (horizontally) elicits two forms of textuality':
Vertical: *What colour are Mr Anderson's eyes?*
And what about Mr Jackson's?
Horizontal: *What colour are Mr Anderson's eyes?*
And what about his hair?

some activities can vary in the extent to which they engage attention to meaning or to form; to be properly completed, some tend to require learners to attend more heavily to meaning than others. Littlewood (2004: 322) ranks a set of five types of activity, along a cline from form-focused to meaning-focused, as follows:

- *non-communicative learning* activities focus learners on understanding and mastering the formation and meanings of structures;
- *pre-communicative language practice* activities engage learners in "practising language with some attention to meaning, but not communicating new messages to others" as for instance in question-answer practice;
- *communicative language practice* activities "practise pre-taught language in a context where it communicates new information" as in information gap activities;

- *structured communication* activities are activities in which learners use "language to communicate in situations which elicit pre-learnt language but with some unpredictability" such as role-play or "simple problem-solving" activities;
- *authentic communication* activities are activities in which learners use "language to communicate in situations where the meanings are unpredictable", such as creative role play, more complex problem-solving, and discussion. (Littlewood, 2004: 322).

This typology reflects and builds on the historical evolution which Abbott described. For example, his account distinguishes structured and authentic communication activities in two ways; firstly, in terms of whether the learners use 'pre-learnt language with some unpredictability' (in structured activities) or whether they are expected to communicate 'unpredictable' meanings' (in authentic activities); and secondly in terms of 'simple' as opposed to 'complex' problem-solving activities. As he acknowledges, some (e.g. Samuda and Bygate 2008) would argue that the five activities are more fundamentally distinguished according to whether or not the learners have to communicate information that is new to the hearer, those that do being termed 'tasks' and those that don't being classed as 'exercises'. On this criterion, Littlewood's first two types of activity, non-communicative, and pre-communicative, can be labelled types of 'exercise', while the latter three, communicative language practice, structured and authentic communication activities, could be labelled varieties of 'task'.

The justification for distinguishing the five types of activity is that a) they genuinely do work differently from each other, and b) that it is pedagogically useful to distinguish between them because of the different contributions each can make to language learning. The same argument of course applies to any distinction between categories of activity, such as between exercises and tasks: the classificatory distinction is worth making if the activities do genuinely work differently, and if those differences are pedagogically useful. Conceptually, task-type activities seem to engage socio-linguistic, psycholinguistic and linguistic processes, whereas 'exercises' seem to exclude socio-linguistic processes and the conceptual level of communication, and some aspects of the psycholinguistic processes. In the remainder of this chapter, I will make the twofold distinction between task and exercise, although it is probably useful in some contexts to distinguish the five subtypes, and, as Littlewood (2004) points out, it remains a matter of consensus and empirical investigation which distinctions are adopted and used. Before reviewing alternative approaches to the teaching of spoken language, we briefly consider the possibility that oral tasks can themselves be distinguished – not through their relative focus on form or meaning, but in terms of the parameters used to design them.

Various frameworks have been developed for distinguishing between task types. Samuda, Johnson and Ridgway (2000) note four kinds of categorisation that have been used: *discourse types* which students use to navigate the tasks (e.g. monologic or dialogic, question and answer or joint construction, of narrative, argumentation, description) (see, for instance, Bygate 1987; Samuda and Bygate 2008); *processes* which students might be expected to engage in while carrying out a task (such as sorting, matching and prioritising) (for example, Willis 1996); *task-configuration* (e.g. one-way, two-way, open or closed) (e.g. Pica, Kanagy and Falodun 1993); and synopses of *overall formats*, categorising whole tasks, including instructions, as types (e.g. picture differences, prioritising) (see also Samuda and Bygate 2008). The types of category can apply to any task, and three of them can be associated with the aspects of speech processing considered earlier, as shown in Table 3.

Table 3. Type of task and type of processing

Processes:	socio-cognitive intentions and processes, such as brainstorming, prioritising, sequencing, persuading, problem-solving, either individually or jointly, task management
Discourse types:	ideational and interactive patterns of discourse, such as monologic or dialogic, question-answer or joint construction of narrative, description, personal talk, argumentation, hypothesising, direction, summarising.
Task-Configuration:	one-way or two-way, open or closed, leading to more or less negotiation for meaning

The categorisation in terms of processes, then, reflects the *socio-cognitive* intentions and processes which serve to motivate and orient language use. The categorisation by discourse type relates to the *ideational and interactive patterns of discourse* which students engage in to achieve their intentions. *Task-configuration*, such as whether the task is designed to be a one-way or two-way task, or an open or closed task, essentially bears on subcategories of discourse patterns: different task configurations have been of interest in light of the potential pedagogical value of the kinds of interaction they are thought to promote (such as negotiation for meaning).

Intersecting with this classification scheme is a second parameter, *task demand*, which relates to performance conditions. This reflects Levelt's (1978), and subsequently Johnson's (1996), Skehan's (1996) and Laufer and Hulstijn's (2001), observations that procedural tasks can be made more or less demanding by varying the pressures on students undertaking them. Although various kinds of task demand might be usefully exploited in the classroom, including that of the relative level of personal stress in performing the task, or degree of interlocutor familiarity, motivation, and personal involvement (see for instance

Laufer and Hulstijn 2001), studies have concentrated principally on three main types: *complexity*, which reflects the load and organisation of content information to be managed by the learners (e.g. Brown and Yule 1983; Robinson 2001; Skehan 2001); *planning, structure and familiarity*, which broadly concerns the extent to which learners are attuned to the nature of the information and the task (e.g. Ellis 2005); and *time pressure* (notably Yuan and Ellis 2003). Findings suggest that task complexity and pre-task planning can affect speakers' linguistic complexity and fluency, and that on-task planning and time pressure can affect speakers' fluency and accuracy. While more research is needed to see how learners of different levels of proficiency might be influenced by these aspects of tasks, and by different types of task, the overall message is that performance conditions can be expected to interact fairly consistently with the different categories of task.

Generally, then, we can conclude that there is a wide repertoire of different types of oral activities that can enable different kinds of oral language activity. This includes both 'exercises' (such as Abbott's first five exercises (1981), or Littlewood's first two activity types (2004)), and a potentially rich range of communicative activities (what we have been calling 'tasks'), with task demand a factor that can be varied in pedagogically interesting ways. Relating this account to the figure introduced at the end of the first part of this section enables us to map different types of activity onto the schema of oral language processing, as in Figure 2 below.

The diagram illustrates the basic claim that all communication-based activities engage conceptual processing, with its pragmatic socio-linguistic dimensions, as well as the levels of formulation and articulation. In contrast, exercises by definition only involve activating formulation and articulation procedures, and monitoring their operation in the light of conceptual plans made by the teacher or course book writer. The diagram shows that monitoring is needed for both communication and non-communication exercises, but that in the case of non-communicative exercises, monitoring is limited to checking that lexico-grammatical selection and performance matches what the course book or teacher intended. Also important to note that the diagram illustrates graphically how exercises activate part rather than all of the ability.

Following this review of descriptions and classifications of oral language activities, we next consider the main types of overall *approach* that have been adopted in the teaching of oral language.

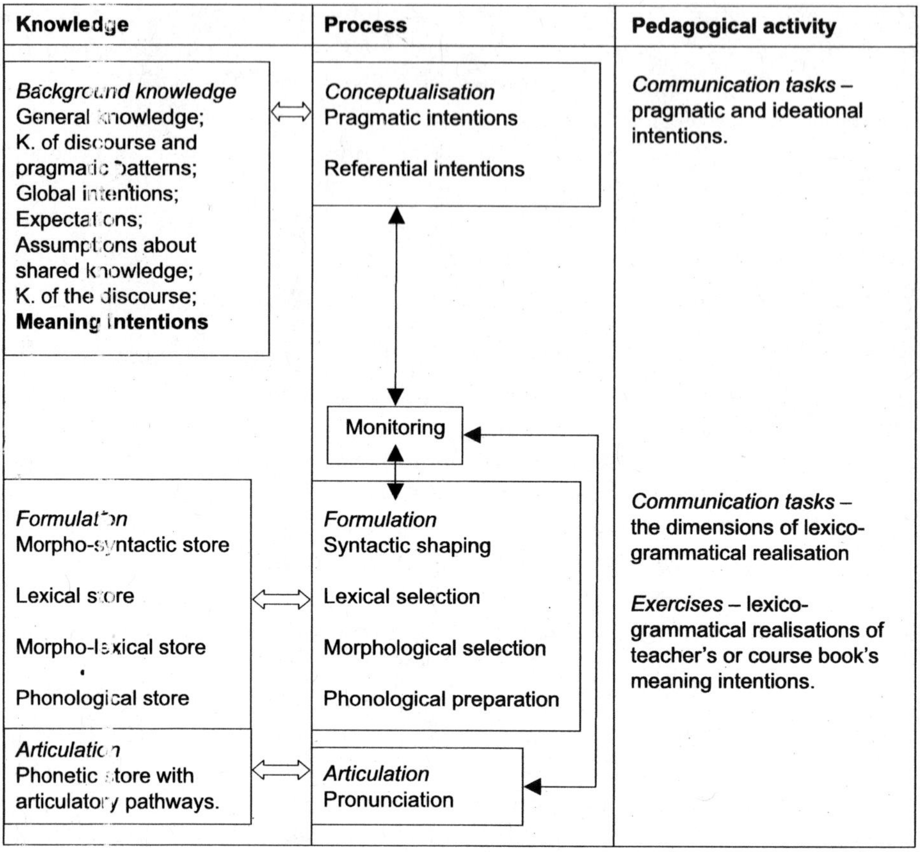

Figure 2. Relating pedagogical activities to aspects of oral language processing

3.2.2. *Approaches to the teaching of second language speaking*

The main kinds of approach to the teaching of speaking can be defined in terms of firstly the overall aims of the curriculum – the 'macro' level – , and secondly the ways in which the aims are most effectively achieved – the 'micro' level of the lesson or scheme of work, the level where teachers need to sequence and balance the procedures they use in order to achieve a given objective through one or a series of lessons.

At the level of curriculum, Brumfit 1984 signalled one major area of choice when he proposed that language courses should have two essentially distinct focuses, one of developing accuracy, and the other of promoting fluency. By fluency he meant the ability in students to autonomously manage the meaningful use of language. In his view, these two focuses were each sufficiently important to figure separately within a syllabus, and sufficiently distinct to require separate pedagogical treatment. In contrast, various authors, such as George (1972), Long (1985), Stevick (1996), VanPatten (1996), Doughty and Williams (1998) propose essentially that some kind of attention to meaning should always be intimately linked with the learning of form. This insistence on the importance of building attention to meaning into the curriculum reflects what in this chapter is termed 'holism'. That is, it is no longer sufficient for courses to focus on the learning of the parts of the language, without students either learning to link those parts to meaningful use, or developing their broader capacities to manage language meaningfully. Hence holism becomes an enduring challenge for the development of approaches to language pedagogy.

A curriculum can be more or less holistic. For example, historically within the GT approach, curricula were not holistic in the sense that they focused on accuracy, and on grammar and vocabulary, or on oral translation, and generally excluded fluency, discourse or TL meaning-focused activities. Similarly, an AL approach would not be described as holistic, because it tended to focus heavily on the production of sentences around a constant grammatical pattern, and ignored the dimension of pragmatic interactive use of language which is the basis for normal language production. It also had no interest in dealing with a range of different types of oral discourse. Similar points can be made about the relatively non-holistic curricula in notional-functional materials (e.g. Morrow and Johnson 1979), and arguably about pedagogies such as the Silent Way. In contrast, communicative approaches, comprehension based approaches such as Total Physical Response (Krashen and Terrell 1988), Input Processing (VanPatten 1996), and Task-based approaches (Ellis 2003; Samuda and Bygate 2008) would by definition be classified as essentially holistic. In the terms of this chapter, provided that the meaningful processing of discourse forms part of the curriculum, the approach counts as holistic.

However while curriculum is one important aspect of an approach, this does not of itself characterise the nature of the learning experience. To do this, we need to consider how the curriculum is navigated through the different kinds of learning activities that are available, within lessons or schemes of work. Here teachers have another choice. On the one hand they can start by concentrating on learners' initial mastery of details of the skill and building up from that towards the ability to manage the whole skill, an approach that we might call 'syncretic' (or additive). Alternatively teachers can work from the whole to the parts and back to the whole, thereby adopting what we might call a 'global' approach.

Johnson (1996) conceptualises these alternatives using the concepts of procedural knowledge (PRO), that is, the ability to use language in meaningful discourse, and declarative knowledge (DEC), which refers to the ability to recognise, interpret, and possibly produce individual items of language accurately. Johnson points out that a cycle of teaching could start from either type of knowledge and move to the other. So for instance, a DEC>PRO progression would start by developing knowledge of detailed items (vocabulary, grammar or pronunciation), and work towards learners being able to use them in discourse. This approach essentially starts with the 'small things' first. A PRO>DEC sequence on the other hand would start by activating language in meaningful discourse, and then highlighting the formal properties of targeted individual elements. This approach starts a cycle with the 'big things first', that is discourse meanings (Wong Fillmore 1979).

Brumfit (1979) described the communicative approach as essentially a reversal of the P>P>P sequence: first students communicate on a topic as far as possible; then the teacher teaches what is needed; then the students practice what is taught. One variant of this is to use the PRO focus as the basic activity throughout the cycle of work, with periodic interruptions to adopt a DEC focus followed by a return to the PRO activity. An example is Samuda's (2001) classroom-based study, in which an oral task is used to activate students' use of a domain of language, before alternating between explicit focusing on the language and subsequent further engagement in the task. This is one version of a task-based approach to teaching, the task providing an on-going reference point throughout the scheme of work, and a context for the learners to develop awareness and control of new features. It should be noted that the possible focus on either PRO or DEC capacities does not imply that teachers and learners will necessarily shift from one to the other. That is, it is quite possible for teacher and students to adopt a PRO>PRO>PRO, or just as easily a DEC>DEC>DEC focus. For instance, teachers basing their approach on Krashen's Input Hypothesis would assume that comprehension is all that is needed for acquisition to take place. As a result they might well adopt a PRO>PRO>PRO approach. Contrastingly, teachers who present and practice but fail to engage an active production phase (PP without the third P) would find themselves developing a DEC>DEC>DEC cycle. Finally, as noted above Brumfit (1984) argued that the PRO and DEC parts of the curriculum could be effectively kept separate, with teachers and learners having no need to systematically interrelate the two. Needless to say, the approach that a given teacher adopts will depend on their perception of the relative importance of focused attention to form, of the importance of procedural engagement, and of the relative merits of using either a procedural or declarative focus as the initial reference point for a cycle of teaching/learning.

The argument in this chapter is that procedural activities are essential to engage the 'whole' socio-cognitive activity of speaking. However, in order to use them we need some kind of course structure which will make oral activities relevant, and we consider one example in the next section.

3.2.3. Topic- and text-based approaches

Burns (2006) suggests that there are two main ways of structuring an oral curriculum: either by organising the course around topics, or else by basing it on what she calls 'text types'.

Focusing first on a topic-based approach, Burns doesn't provide a definition of 'language events' but illustrates the concept around the theme 'booking a flight'. A 'booking a flight' event might be made up of a sequence of episodes as in Table 4:

Table 4. Language events in a flight booking topic

"Discuss a good travel agent with friends
Consult directory pages for telephone number
Make initial request for brochures by phone or in person
Read brochures
Consult the travel agent on cheaper options
Fill in booking forms and make the payment
Describe plans to family, friends or neighbours" (Burns, 2006: 250)

The topic sequence has many of the hall marks of a task-based unit of work, with an overarching task composed of a series of related subtasks. Presumably additional episodes could be added, such as discussing the options with a friend, or checking websites for alternative offers. Burns proposes that this would be used by a teaching procedure including activities such as the following in Table 5:

Table 5. Teaching procedures for the flight booking topic

Pre-teaching some key vocabulary [...]
Providing newspaper article or advertisements for travel agents [...]
(Re)teach alphabetic referencing skills [...]
[Learners] practice finding agents' numbers and addresses [...]
Introduce structure, vocabulary, and typical expressions [...]
[Learners] undertake out of class interaction tasks, bringing material back into the classroom [...]
Learners [...] brainstorm relevant questions and [...] practice discourse strategies [for consulting the travel agent] [...]
Practice [relevant] reading and writing skills [...]
Practice explaining their plans to different people, where the status of their relationships and therefore the register choices they might make would vary
(Burns 2006: 250)

The sequence of teaching procedures illustrates a way in which activities can alternate between procedural tasks with a clear meaning focus, and declarative tasks focusing on formal features of language. In order to generate material for a topic-based sequence of activities, Burns notes a possible cycle of preparatory design procedures such as: "1) identifies the broad topic [...] 2) identifies a real-life task within the scope of that topic; 3) records one or more spoken interactions related to the task [...]; 4) identifies the genres, the stages and the grammatical patterns of the interactions; 5) selects classroom activities that extend the learners' knowledge of the topic and the text" (Burns 2006: 251).

Whereas the topic based approach works around a chain of language events, each in turn generating a range of PRO and DEC activities, a text-based approach uses samples of discourse as a basis for generating learning activities, as outlined in Table 6.

Table 6. Generating activities via a text-based approach

1)	Preparation activities, which "aim to prepare learners for the type of spoken interaction they will be focusing on"
2)	Discourse activities, in which "learners are introduced to specific generic structural features and provided with practice in becoming speaker// listener participants", including activities that "aim to focus attention on how speakers begin, progress and end interactions, take up their roles as speakers and listeners, and use specific discourse strategies and markers to maintain the interaction"
3)	Language activities, which "draw attention to the main language patterns and features associated with a particular genre", such as "relevant vocabulary and the grammatical structures foregrounded in the genre"
4)	Interaction activities offering "practice in producing whole sustained interactions or parts of interactions" and "provide opportunities for teachers and learners to (self)evaluate and gain feedback on performance"
	(Burns, 2006: 252–253)

Evaluation of the alternatives is beyond the scope of this chapter. However both illustrate ways of dovetailing the teaching of oral language with the broader language programme. Examples have of course been available in textbooks for some time (for instance *Challenges* by Abbs and Sexton 1978), and in monographs on pedagogy (such as Legutke and Thomas 1991). They echo the principles of the content-based language teaching movement (e.g. Brinton, Snow and Wesche 1989; Snow and Brinton 1997). However, we should note here that these frameworks do not specify the kinds of oral socio-linguistic or discourse factors that need to be addressed by a language programme, or indeed about how this might be done.

Part of this issue of coverage relates to the balance between input and production activities. In Burns' schema, three of the four phases under the text-based approach seem to focus on exposure rather than production, as do four of the five phases of the topic-based approach. This balance resembles that proposed by Riggenbach (1999), and partly echoes the views of those like Van-Patten (1996) who argue that input is a key pre-requisite for the development of the ability to use language. Riggenbach outlines an approach to the teaching of oral skills in which students are encouraged to undertake ethnographic style investigations into the patterns of talk of native or expert speakers. For her, five of six steps focus essentially on data collection, analysis, and self-evaluation. One step involves a 'generative' activity, but even here, learners either "*discuss* the target structure *or* produce the target structure in its appropriate context [emphases mine]" (1999: 63). There are similarities here too with Willis' (1996) proposed use of oral tasks, whereby students first observe native speakers carrying out a parallel task, before engaging in a similar one themselves. However an issue for consideration is the relationship between observation type activities, and production activities, the former aimed at providing learners with exposure to the features of the target discourse type, and the latter at encouraging uptake. There is an interesting empirical question to ask here (not unrelated to Krashen's hypothetical silent period) about how much exposure and how much time learners need before being able to activate discourse for themselves.

We should also note that the approach based on language events makes no clear distinction between exposure and production activities. None of Burns' three approaches are specifically associated with the teaching of particular aspects of oral discourse, whether socio-linguistic, psycho-linguistic, or just linguistic. That is, the problem of how to match the features of oral language to task type, and how to adjust attention to form and/or meaning within both receptive and productive activities are pedagogical issues which remain to be addressed.

The points emerging from the previous section can be used to set up a pedagogical framework which links aspects of spoken language (the oral second language syllabus), with types of pedagogical focus (the programme). The different levels of the oral programme could appear as outlined in Table 7.

Table 7. Linking spoken language and pedagogy in the curriculum

Syllabus//curriculum context: Language event, topic, or text

Macro learning cycles: observation activities and production activities,

Micro-learning cycles: both observation and production activities shifting between:

holistic (PRO or 'task'-type) activities, grounded in interpersonal socio-linguistic processes, notably joint negotiation of understanding, and associated holistic psycholinguistic process, including the development of fluency, and

analytic (DEC or 'part' practice) activities, focusing more narrowly on understanding and using systemic aspects of the language.

These latter focus on:

Discourse features: discourse patterns, strategic patterns, lexico-grammatical patterns, pronunciation.

This kind of framework suggests directions for future research and development, although not without leaving areas of continuing controversy. Some of these we consider in the following section.

4. Some controversial issues

4.1. The problem of ascertaining and selecting norms

Identifying relevant pedagogical norms is perhaps the single most contentious issue. Starting from an educational perspective, the very basis of the construct of 'learning' is that learners have to adjust in some way to an item of information or a pattern of behaviour which is new to them. This involves socio-psychological changes, both conceptual and behavioural, in the learners themselves. Learners cannot do this without reference to some 'norm' or standard. At the same time, the object of learning – in our case, the spoken language – has to be appropriated from the outside world. That is, learners have to make it their own. Much as every cook makes their own version of a standard recipe, or every musician produces their own version of a known piece of music, in appropriating the object of learning, learners will change it in some way. Hence the status of norm finds itself at the centre of a tension within education.

The situation is made more complicated in language learning because of the complex nature of language norms. Languages themselves are subject to dialectal variation – no single speaker performs their dialect quite like any other speaker; languages are in a state of perpetual change; and most importantly, where major international languages such as English are concerned, the learners may already be users of some actual or emerging dialect of the language. All this clearly sheds a very particular light on the issue of what norm to choose. It also has implications for how teachers will handle error. Not to invoke a norm or identify errors could confer an indeterminacy to the object of learning which learners could find unmanageable. On the other hand, to use norms in ways that are insensitive to what is acceptable in existing dialects would amount to teaching learners in ways that could be seen as contradicting the facts of language that they are already – or will soon be – exposed to. A final twist to the problem is Jenkins' (2002) argument that many features which till now have been legitimately identified as learners' errors (e.g. George 1972) may be becoming features of an emerging Lingua Franca (though the problem is not restricted to spoken language). This perspective opens up the possibility that a number of non-normal features of English are or are about to become features of a new norm. This issue can never be fully resolved, though it may be eased as the documentation of English as a Lingua Franca becomes more substantial as more descriptive facts become available through such initiatives as the VOICE project (see Seidlhofer 2004; http://www.univie.ac.at/voice/). Meanwhile it is possible that the fundamental educational tension between accommodation and appropriation will always remain an issue.

4.2. Approaches to oral language: clarifying the syllabus

A second major problem is to map out an oral language syllabus. Although oral language syllabuses appear in a range of general language course books, the underlying coherence of the curricula they propose is rarely elaborated on. Key issues to be addressed are the range of discourse types to be included, such as narrative, descriptive, argumentative; the kinds of interaction patterns which are to be encouraged (such as monologue or dialogue, and interview or open discussion); and the kinds of topic that would be appropriate for those types of discourse. Relatively little so far has been done in this area.

4.3. Approaches to oral language: syncretic or global?

The third problem to note is the issue of better understanding how development in the management of oral discourse can be optimally related to learning of analysed features of language, that is, the PRO>DEC or DEC>PRO problem.

4.4. The problem of identifying helpful teaching/learning procedures (via materials design, and implementation)

A fourth challenge is to assess the differential and complementary contributions to learning of a range of kinds of classroom procedure – teacher-class activities, group or pair activities or tasks – to oral language development. Brown and Yule (1983), and more recently Robinson (2001) have shown ways in which designers can vary the complexity of activities, for instance in terms of the numbers of features that need mentioning in an activity such as a description or a story, the number of contrasting features that need taking into account, and the number of here-and-now elements. Samuda (2005) illustrates how by adjusting the distribution of information, activities can also be varied in terms of the number and roles of the interlocutors. Johnson (1996) has suggested that activities can be varied in terms of the time pressures that might be placed on learners. As noted above, research into planning, (e.g. Mehnert 1998; Foster 2001;Yuan and Ellis 2003), shows apparent effects on speakers' fluency and accuracy, and its pedagogical relevance could be explored in the teaching of oral language. Finally Bygate (2006) has pointed out ways in which communicative repetition can be exploited in oral activities. This can be done through the internal design of individual activities, such as survey interview-type tasks, or what Lynch and Maclean (2001) call a 'poster carousel' activity; it can be done through some form of repetition of entire activities, for example by re-running the same activity in different pairings or grouping; by moving an activity from pair/group arrangement to whole class talk; or else it can be done by re-using a familiar activity on another occasion in a very slightly altered guise.

Exploring these options in the context of an oral language syllabus would shed light on how a range of activities and conditions can be used to develop oral second language abilities. However little of the research reported here has been carried out within the context of ongoing teaching programmes. The key question then is how far research and practice can productively interface.

4.5. The problem of engaging and documenting development

A further area of contention is our relatively limited overall idea of how language develops orally. This is not to say that we lack oral learner language data. However oral language data have generally been gathered in order to investigate underlying processes of language acquisition – for example many of the studies reported in Ellis (1994) or Tarone (1988) were based on oral data. The problem is that they were usually concerned with studying morpho-syntactic or pragmatic variation and error, rather than on the development of spoken discourse. There are exceptions. For instance Tarone and Parrish (1987) analysed the impact of task on accuracy in article usage; Bardovi-Harlig and Hartford (1990) studied the use of pragmatic strategies within the discourse context of academic advising sessions; Yule and Macdonald (1990) explored the relationship between speaker proficiency and discourse role in the successful completion of complex map reading tasks.

These kinds of studies open a window on the problems posed by different discourse activities, at particular levels of proficiency. What we are missing is a sense of how students' abilities on such activities develop, and as a result, we are still in the dark as to how their development can best be assisted. Is a focus on form or on meaning useful for learners (Ortega 2005)? Do repeated experiences of tasks or different levels of task demand affect their performance, and if so, how? How useful are explicit instruction and feedback?

4.6. The problem of obtaining learners' perceptions

Breen (1987) (and for general learning, Salmon 1980) argued that learners' perceptions of tasks are bound to have a significant impact on how they perform them. Evidence for this has been provided in general by various studies. For instance Willing (1988) pointed out that learners' strategies can be influenced by their preferred learning styles. Ortega (2005) found that the planning strategies students' used were related to their proficiency and to their perceptions of the tasks. Yet apart from Ortega's study, little work has been done on student perception of oral activities (exceptions being Murphy 1993 and Garrett and Shortall 2002). Further research would enable us to adjust task designs or the choice of tasks, help us to use them more sensitively in relation to learner perceptions, to review and evaluate the briefing students are given, and modify our expectations for task performance.

4.7. The problem of providing appropriate and timely modelling and feedback

A further problematic area of oral language teaching is the provision of modelling and feedback. Historically feedback on oral language learning has been explored in four main ways: first as the third 'reinforcement' phase in audio-lingual approaches; secondly as 'follow-up' in the classic 'Initiation>Response> Follow-up' pattern of teacher talk; thirdly as the closing 'ratifying' move in negotiation for meaning exchanges; and fourthly in the shape of teacher's 'recasts' – that is, communicatively supporting moves by the teacher carrying corrective re-phrasings of the learner's utterance.

It might change our perception if we consider the issue in terms of the classic problem of whether feedback is best provided on-line or off-line (see Johnson 1996 for some discussion of this). There are advantages and disadvantages to both on-line and off-line feedback, in terms of their impact on accuracy, transparency, disruptiveness and processability of the feedback. On-line feedback is likely to be more accurate and transparent, whereas off-line feedback is likely to be less disruptive to performance and easier for the recipient to process than during performance (Reed 1968). A further issue is the difficulty of responding to simultaneous performances in class. With improved computer and recording technology, we may well be able to develop a wider range of methods for providing oral feedback than have been exploited up to now.

4.8. The problem of assessing progress within the classroom

Associated with the previous point is the challenge for classroom teachers of assessing learners' oral language performance reliably. Students will often undertake speaking activities either in pairs and groups, often somewhat out of reach of the teacher, or else in the rather more formal less representative context of plenary teacher-class interaction. There are three striking practical difficulties here. One is simply to find the time to assess oral language when working with classes bigger than fifteen or so. The second is to obtain an appropriate sample of speech in normal class time. A third difficulty is that of finding the resources to carry out an adequate assessment. These three problems can perhaps be resolved at least in part through the availability of adequate technical and theoretical teacher expertise, but in most contexts this is likely to remain a challenging responsibility.

4.9. The problem of developing an appropriate account of teacher talk

The final problem links to the previous one: the teaching and assessment of oral language implies certain relevant oral language skills on the part of the teacher. The teacher's use of oral language is clearly important, whether we are working from a relatively socio-cultural (e.g. Mercer 1995; Nassaji and Wells 2000; van Lier 1996) or dialogic perspective (e.g. Barnes 1976; Barnes and Todd 1995; Alexander 2001, 2006) or instead adopting a more cognitive approach (e.g. Bialystok 1990; Yule and Tarone 1991; Johnson 1996; Doughty and Williams 1997; Skehan 1998). For instance the issue of teacher talk has been the subject of controversy over the role and importance of recasts: how far should teachers aim to provide language oriented feedback in a way which provides interactive support for the communication flow, and why and in what ways?

From a socio-cultural or dialogic perspective the quality of the teacher's talk has considerable importance. For instance, the kinds of questions teachers ask and how they formulate them seems to have an impact on how learners talk – and the same applies also to the shape and content of follow-up moves (Nassaji and Wells 2000). Cognitivists would probably hold similar views. For instance, to consider the role of communication strategies in managing talk, Yule and Tarone's (1991) argument that communication strategies in fact have to be *negotiated* interactively bears out the point: it is no good expecting a pupil to use communication strategies when speaking with the teacher, if the teacher does not allow learners to negotiate them. And the dialogic relationship also affects teacher's talk: – a teacher who does not allow the students to provide negotiated feedback is going to find it extremely difficult to use their own communication strategies in making accessible their classroom talk (Anani Sarab 2003): for without meaningful student feedback, teachers will remain in the dark as to whether they have been understood or not. Similarly if we consider the functioning of recasts (Doughty and Williams 1998), the teacher will be 'recasting in the dark', one might say, unless students feel in a position to indicate whether the recast makes sense or not.

So the effective functioning of students' talk depends at least in part on the teacher's own effective use of communication. Otherwise it will be an uncertain context for the teacher to make assessments of the learners' oral proficiency or of their progress. The problem then is, what are the features of teachers' talk which can help students ' talk, and how can they be promoted? Maybe these – rather than the question of the value of recasts – are the issues which need attention.

5. Contributions of Applied Linguistics

What then of the contribution of Applied Linguistics to this area of pedagogy? There seem to be three main areas of enquiry. The first major concern is the need to undertake research contextualised within the context of taught programmes. The eight problematic issues explored above can only really be effectively studied within the context of ongoing programmes of instruction. Assuming this kind of research context, perhaps the four most significant issues to explore within taught programmes are: a) the design and use of different procedures and activities; b) learners' and teachers' perceptions and uses of different activities; c) the patterns of learner development across levels of proficiency; and d) the dimension of teacher talk and teacher feedback in relation to learners' oral language.

Each of these areas of investigation focuses on the same fundamental applied linguistic question: what is the relationship between professional actions, and language use and learning? Exploring this generic question requires the use of concepts and categories of analysis capable of offering some purchase on the different aspects of the various professional decisions involved (such as aspects of the curriculum, and classroom procedures and activities), as well as on relevant aspects of learners' and teachers' oral language. Features of oral language to be studied could be expected to include discourse types, discourse features, and qualitative aspects of individual and interactive talk such as measures of fluency, accuracy, and co-construction.

6. Broader research perspectives

In addition to these basic applied linguistic issues, there are wider perspectives for researching the teaching of spoken language. Firstly, with the increases in mobility, populations from different language backgrounds are increasingly coming into face-to-face contact. The ability to manage speech in another language with a satisfactory degree of cross-cultural sensitivity is therefore certain to be important, whatever the language under consideration (see 4.1 above). The proximity of target-like language proficiency will not be everyone's objective. Yet for both fundamental and applied reasons, pedagogical expertise must include amongst its concerns the need to understand how target-like proficiency can be achieved. Secondly, while written language can be self-taught in adulthood, speaking in a second language is hard to master without support, and difficult to engage with at most stages of life. Hence a grasp of how to teach it is important. Thirdly for many learners, second language speech is important not only in its own right, but as an attractive mode of language learning: many students given no opportunity to learn the spoken language will find the foreign language learning experience impoverished. Fourthly, there is an absorbing applied linguistic puzzle in teaching spoken language via designed procedures: while the materials for teaching written language can exploit the same typographical resources as the focus of learning in order to engage with learners, the materials and procedures for teaching speaking involve a fascinating interplay between the written medium of the designs, and the intangible oral medium which is being developed. So oral second language pedagogy occupies a rich terrain, intersecting the socio-political issues of inter-community communication, the socio-psychological issues of oracy in classroom learning, and the technical design-implementation issues implied in pedagogical development.

This then opens a rich range of potential research themes, including the following:

a) what are the roles of speaking in a SL within and between societies, for inter-cultural inter-community communication, whether communal, professional, service, social, or business? What status should learners and teachers accord to native-like accuracy, fluency, and idiomaticity?
b) What are the roles of speaking for learning within the SL classroom?
c) What are the linguistic dimensions of the relationship between procedural design and implementation?
d) How can design and implementation be related to the emerging proficiency of learners?

In 1987 I suggested that oral language pedagogy raised some non-trivial questions, relating to curriculum, syllabus and materials, proficiency, and development. The quotation from Ortega's student at the start of this chapter suggests that despite the intervening years, there are still plenty of questions that remain unanswered.

References

Abbott, Gerry
1981 Oral fluency. In: Gerry Abbott and Peter Wingard (eds.), *The Teaching of English as an International Language*, 111–138. Glasgow: Collins.

Abbs, Brian and Malcolm Sexton
1978 *Challenges.* Harlow: Longman.

Alderson, J. Charles and A. H. Urquhart (eds.)
1984 *Reading in a Foreign language.* London: Longman.

Alexander, Louis
1967 *First Things First.* Harlow: Longman.

Alexander, Richard
2001 *Culture and Pedagogy.* Oxford: Blackwell.

Alexander, Richard
2006 *Towards Dialogic Teaching: Rethinking Classroom Talk.* 3rd edition. Thirsk, North Yorkshire: Dialagos.

Anani Sarab, Mohammad R.
2003 *Communication strategies in second language teacher talk with special reference to Iranian teachers of English.* Unpublished Ph.D. thesis, University of Leeds.

Bailey, Katherine M.
2005 *Practical English Language Teaching: Speaking.* New York: McGraw-Hill.

Bialystok, Ellen
1990 *Communication Strategies: A Psychological Analysis of Second-Language Use.* Oxford: Basil Blackwell.

Bardovi-Harlig, Kathleen and Beverley S. Hartford
1990 Congruence in native and nonnative conversations: status balance in the academic advising session. *Language Learning* 40 (4): 467–501.

Barnes, Douglas
1976 *From Communication to Curriculum.* Harmondsworth: Penguin.

Barnes, Douglas and Frankie Todd
1995 *Communication and Learning Revisited.* London: Heinemann.

Biber, Douglas, Susan Conrad and Geoffrey Leech
2002 *Longman Student Grammar of Spoken and Written English.* Harlow: Pearson Education.

Bongaerts, Theo and Nanda Poulisse
1989 Communication strategies in L1 and L2: Same or different? *Applied Linguistics* 10: 253–268.

Boxer, Diane and Andrew D. Cohen (ed.)
2004 *Studying speaking to inform second language learning.* Clevedon, Avon: Multilingual Matters Ltd.

Breen, Mike P.
1989 The evaluation cycle for language learning tasks. In: B. Keith Johnson (ed.), *The Second Language Curriculum*, 187–206. Cambridge: Cambridge University Press.

Brinton, Donna, Marguerite A. Snow and Marjorie B. Wesche
1989 *Content-Based Second Language Instruction.* New York: Newbury House.

Brown, Gillian and George Yule
1983 *Teaching the Spoken Language*. Cambridge: Cambridge University Press.
Brumfit, Christopher J.
1979 'Communicative' language teaching: an educational perspective. In: Christopher J. Brumfit and Keith Johnson (eds.),*The Communicative Approach to Language Teaching*, 183–191. Oxford: Oxford University Press.
Brumfit, Christopher J.
1984 *Communicative Methodology in Language Teaching*. Cambridge: Cambridge University Press.
Burns, Anne
2006 Teaching speaking: a textbased syllabus approach. In: Esther Uso-Juan and Alicia Martinez-Flor (eds.), *Current Trends in the Development and Teaching of the Four Language Skills*, 235–258. Berlin: Mouton de Gruyter.
Burns, Anne, Helen Joyce and Sandra Gollin
1996 *'I See What You Mean'. Using Spoken Discourse in the Classroom*. Macquarie University: NCELTR.
Bygate, Martin
1987 *Speaking*. Oxford: Oxford University Press.
Bygate, Martin (ed.)
2000 Special issue: 'Tasks in language pedagogy'. *Language Teaching Research* 4 (3): 185–192.
Bygate, Martin
2005 Oral second language abilities as expertise. In: Keith Johnson (ed.), *Expertise in Second Language Learning and Teaching*, 104–127. London: Palgrave.
Bygate, Martin
2006 Areas of research that influence L2 speaking instruction. In: Esther Uso-Juan and Alicia Martinez-Flor (eds.), *Current Trends in the Development and Teaching of the Four Language Skills*, 159–186., Berlin: Mouton de Gruyter.
Bygate, Martin and Virginia Samuda
2005 Integrative planning through the use of task repetition. In: Ellis (ed.), 37–74.
Bygate, Martin, Peter Skehan and Merrill Swain (eds.)
2001 *Researching Pedagogic Tasks: Second Language Learning, Teaching and Testing*. Harlow: Pearson Education.
Byrne, Donn
1976 *Teaching Oral English*. London: Longman.
Carter, Ron and Michael McCarthy
1997 *Exploring Spoken English*. Cambridge: Cambridge University Press.
Celce-Murcia, Marianne, Donna M. Brinton and Janet M. Goodwin
1996 *Teaching Pronunciation: a Reference for Teachers of English to Speakers of Other Languages*. Cambridge: Cambridge University Press.
Chafe, Wallace L.
1985 Linguistic differences produced by differences between speaking and writing. In: David R. Olson, Nancy Torrance and Angela Hildyard (eds.), *Literacy, Language and Learning: The Nature and Consequences of Reading and Writing*, 105–122. Cambridge: Cambridge University Press.
Clark, Herbert and Deborah Wilkes-Gibbs
1986 Referring as a collaborative process. *Cognition* 22: 1–39.

Dalton, Christine and Barbara Seidlhofer
1994 *Pronunciation.* Oxford: Oxford University Press.
de Bot, Kees
1992 A bilingual production model: Levelt's "speaking" model adapted. *Applied Linguistics* 13: 1–24.
Dobao, Ana. M., Fernandez
2004 The use of communication strategies by Spanish learners of English. A study of the collaborative creation of meaning, language and linguistic knowledge. Unpublished Doctoral thesis, University of Santiago de Compostela.
Doughty, Catherine and Jessica Williams (eds.)
1998 *Focus on Form in Classroom Second Language Acquisition.* Cambridge: Cambridge University Press.
Ellis, Rod
1994 *The Study of Second Language Acquisition.* Oxford: Oxford University Press.
Ellis, Rod (ed.)
2005 *Planning and Task Performance in a Second Language.* Amsterdam: John Benjamins.
English Language Services
1964 *English 900. Book One.* New York: The Macmillan Company.
Foster, Pauline
2001 Rules and routines: a consideration of their role in the task-based language production of native and non-native speakers. In: Bygate, Skehan and Swain (eds.), 75–94.
Garrett, Peter and Terry Shortall
2002 Learners' evaluations of teacher-fronted and student-centred classroom activities. *Language Teaching Research* 6 (1): 25–58.
George, Herbert V.
1972 *Common Errors in Language Learning.* Rowley, Mass.: Newbury House.
Grabe, William and Robert Kaplan
1996 *Theory and Practice of Writing.* Harlow: Pearson Education.
Halliday, Michael A. K.
1994 *Introduction to Functional Grammar.* 2nd edition. London: Arnold.
Howatt, Anthony P. R. and Henry G. Widdowson
2004 *A history of English language teaching.* 2nd edition. Oxford: Oxford University Press.
Hughes, Rebecca
2002 *Teaching and Researching Speaking.* Harlow: Pearson Education.
Hyland, Ken
2003 *Teaching and Researching Writing.* Harlow: Pearson Education.
Jenkins, Jennifer
2002 A sociolinguistically based, empirically researched pronunciation syllabus for English as an international language. *Applied Linguistics* 23 (1): 83–103.
Johnson, Keith
1996 *Language Teaching and Skill Learning.* Oxford: Blackwell.
Kasper, Gabriele and Eric Kellerman (eds.)
1997 *Communication Strategies. Psycholinguistic and Sociolinguistic Perspectives.* Harlow: Longman.

Kormos, Judit
2006 *Speech Production and Second Language Acquisition.* Mahwah, NJ: Lawrence Erlbaum.
Kramsch, Claire
1996 *Context and Culture in Language Teaching.* Oxford: Oxford University Press.
Krashen, Stephen D. and Tracy D. Terrell
1988 *The Natural Approach: Language Acquisition in the Classroom.* Hemel Hempstead: Prentice Hall.
Lado, Robert and Charles C. Fries
1945 *Teaching and Learning English as a Foreign Language.* Michigan: The University of Michigan Press.
Lado, Robert and Charles C. Fries
1958 *English Sentence Patterns. Understanding and Producing English Grammatical Structures: An Oral Approach.* Michigan: The University of Michigan Press.
Larsen-Freeman, Diane
2006 The emergence of complexity, fluency and accuracy in the oral and written production of five Chinese learners of English. *Applied Linguistics* 27 (4): 590–619.
Laufer, Batia and Jan Hulstijn
2001 Incidental vocabulary acquisition in a second language: The construct of task-induced involvement. *Applied Linguistics* 22 (1): 1–26.
Legutke, Michael and Howard Thomas
1991 *Process and Experience in the Language Classroom.* Harlow: Longman.
Levelt, Willem J. M.
1989 *Speaking. From Intention to Articulation.* Cambridge: MIT Press.
Levelt, Willem J. M.
1999 Language production: A blueprint of the speaker. In: Colin Brown and Peter Hagoort (eds.), *Neurocognition of Language,* 83–122. Oxford: Oxford University Press.
Littlewood, William
1981 *Communicative Language Teaching: An Introduction.* Cambridge: Cambridge University Press.
Littlewood, William
1992 *Teaching Oral Communication.* Oxford: Basil Blackwell.
Littlewood, William
2004 The task-based approach: some questions and suggestions. *ELT Journal* 58 (4): 319–326.
Lynch, Tony and Joan Maclean
2001 'A case of exercising': effects of immediate task repetition on learners' performance. In: Bygate, Skehan and Swain, 119–140.
McCarthy, Michael
1998 *Spoken Language and Applied Linguistics.* Cambridge: Cambridge University Press.
McCarthy, Michael and Anne O'Keefe
2004 Research in the teaching of speaking. *Annual Review of Applied Linguistics* 24, 26–43.

Mehnert, Uta
1998 The effects of different lengths of time for planning on second language performance. *Studies in Second Language Acquisition* 20 (1): 83–108.

Mercer, Neil
1995 *The Guided Construction of Knowledge.* Clevedon, Avon: Multilingual Matters Ltd.

Morrow, Keith and Keith Johnson
1979 *Communicate 1.* Harlow: Longman.

Murphy, Dermot
1993 Evaluating language learning tasks in the classroom. In: Graham Crookes and Susan M. Gass (eds.), *Tasks in a Pedagogical Context: Integrating Theory and Practice,* 139–161. Clevedon, Avon: Multilingual Matters Ltd.

Nassaji, Hossein and Gordon Wells
2000 What's the use of 'triadic dialogue'? An investigation of teacher-student interaction. *Applied Linguistics* 21 (3): 376–406.

Nation, Paul
1993 Using dictionaries to estimate vocabulary size: essential, but rarely followed, procedures. *Language Testing* 10: 27–40.

Nation, Paul
2001 *Learning Vocabulary in Another Language.* Cambridge: Cambridge University Press.

Ortega, Lourdes
2005 What do learners plan? Learner-driven attention to form during pre-task planning. In: Ellis (ed.), 72–110.

Paribakht, Tahereh
1985 Strategic competence and language proficiency. *Applied Linguistics* 6: 132–146.

Pawley, Andrew and Frances H. Syder
1983 Two puzzles for linguistic theory: nativelike selection and nativelike fluency. In: Jack C. Richards and Richard W. Schmidt (eds.), *Language and Communication*, 191–227. Harlow: Longman.

Pica, Teresa, Ruth Kanagy and Joseph Falodun
1993 Choosing and using communication tasks for second language instruction. In: Graham Crookes and Susan M. Gass (eds.), *Tasks and Language Learning. Integrating Theory and Practice*, 9–34. Clevedon, Avon: Multilingual Matters Ltd.

Poulisse, Nanda
1987 Problems and solutions in the classification of compensatory strategies. *Second Language Research.* 3: 141–153.

Poulisse, Nanda
1993 A theoretical account of lexical communication strategies. In: R. Schreuder and Berti Weltens (eds.), *The Bilingual Lexicon*, 157–189. Amsterdam: John Benjamins.

Reed, G. F.
1968 Skill. In: Eric A. Lunzer and J. F. Morris (eds.), *Development in Human Learning*, 104–43. London: Staples Press.

Riggenbach, Heidi
1999 *Discourse Analysis in the Language Classroom. Volume 1. The Spoken Language.* Ann Arbor: The University of Michigan Press.
Riggenbach, Heidi (ed.)
2000 *Perspectives on Fluency.* Ann Arbor: The University of Michigan Press.
Robinson, Peter
2001 Task complexity, task difficulty and task production: Exploring interactions in a componential framework. *Applied Linguistics* 22 (1): 27–57.
Salmon, Phillida (ed.)
1980 *Coming to Know.* London: Routledge and Kegan Paul.
Samuda, Virginia
2001 Guiding relationships between form and meaning during task performance: the role of the teacher. In: Bygate, Skehan and Swain (eds.), 119–140.
Samuda, Virginia and Martin Bygate
2008 *Tasks in Second Language Learning.* Basingstoke: Palgrave.
Samuda, Virginia, Keith Johnson and Jim Ridgway
2000 *Designing language learning tasks: a guide. Vol.1.* Working Papers on Task Design, Department of Linguistics and English Language, Lancaster University.
Seidlhofer, Barbara
2004 Research perspectives on teaching English as a lingua franca. *Annual Review of Applied Linguistics* 24: 209–239.
Skehan, Peter
1998 *A Cognitive Approach to Language Learning.* Oxford: Oxford University Press.
Skehan, Peter
2001 Tasks and language performance assessment. In: Bygate, Skehan and Swain (eds.), 167–185.
Skehan, Peter and Pauline Foster
2005 Strategic and on-line planning: the influence of surprise information and task time on second language performance. In: Ellis (ed.), 193–216.
Snow, Marguerite A. and Donna Brinton (eds.)
1997 *The Content-Based Classroom: Perspectives on Integrating Language and Content.* New York: Addison Wesley.
Stevick, Earl
1996 *Memory, Meaning and Method.* 2nd edition. Boston: Heinle and Heinle.
Swales, John
1990 *Genre Analysis.* Cambridge: Cambridge University Press.
Tarone, Elaine
1983 Some thoughts on the notion of 'communication strategy'. In: Claus Faerch and Gabriele Kasper (eds.), *Strategies in Interlanguage Communication*, 61–74. Harlow: Longman.
Tarone, Elaine
1988 *Variation in Interlanguage.* London: Arnold.
Tarone, Elaine and Betsy Parrish
1988 Task-related variation in interlanguage: the case of articles. *Language Learning* 38: 21–44.

Urquhart, A. H. and Cyril J. Weir
1998 *Reading in a Second Language; Process, Product and Practice.* Harlow: Longman.
van Lier, Leo
1996 *Interaction in the Language Curriculum: Awareness, Autonomy and Authenticity.* Harlow: Longman.
VanPatten, Bill
1996 *Input Processing.* Norwood, NJ: Ablex.
White, Ronald V.
1978 *Functional English I.* London: Nelson.
White, Ronald V.
1979 *Functional English II.* London: Nelson.
Whitney, Arthur H.
1977 (1st ed. 1944) *Colloquial Hungarian.* London: Routledge & Kegan Paul
Widdowson, Henry G.
1978 *Teaching Language as Communication.* Oxford: Oxford University Press.
Wilkes-Gibbs, Deborah
1997 Studying language use as collaboration. In: Kasper and Kellerman (eds.), 238–274.
Willing, Ken
1988 *Learning Styles in Adult Migrant Education.* Adelaide, Australia: National Curriculum Resource Centre.
Willis, Jane
1996 *A Framework for Task-Based Learning.* Harlow: Addison Wesley Longman Ltd.
Yuan, Fangyuan and Rod Ellis
2001 The effects of pre-task planning and on-line planning on fluency, complexity and accuracy in L2 monologic oral production. *Applied Linguistics* 24 (1): 1–27.
Yule, George and Doris Macdonald
1990 Resolving referential conflicts in L2 interaction: the effect of proficiency and interactive role. *Language Learning* 40 (4): 539–556.
Yule, George and Elaine Tarone
1991 The other side of the page: Integrating the communication strategies and negotiated input in SLA. In: Roger Phillipson, Eric Kellerman, Larry Selinker, Michael Sharwood Smith and Merrill Swain (eds.), *Foreign/Second Language Pedagogy Research,* 162–177. Clevedon, Avon: Multilingual Matters Ltd.

Recommended readings

Brown, Gillian and George Yule
1983 *Teaching the Spoken Language.* Cambridge: Cambridge University Press.
Burns, Ann, Helen Joyce and Sandra Gollin
1996 *'I See What You Mean'. Using Spoken Discourse in the Classroom.* Macquarie University: NCELTR.

Bygate, Martin
1987 *Speaking*. Oxford: Oxford University Press.
Byrne, Don
1976 *Teaching Oral English*. London: Longman.
Hughes, Rebecca
2002 *Teaching and Researching Speaking*. Harlow: Pearson Education.
Kasper, Gabriele and Eric Kellerman (eds.)
1997 *Communication Strategies. Psycholinguistic and Sociolinguistic Perspectives*. Harlow: Longman.
Kormos, Judit
2006 *Speech Production and Second Language Acquisition*. Mahwah, NJ: Lawrence Erlbaum.
Littlewood, William
1992 *Teaching Oral Communication*. Oxford: Basil Blackwell.
Riggenbach, Heidi
1999 *Discourse Analysis in the Language Classroom. Volume 1. The Spoken Language*. Ann Arbor: The University of Michigan Press.
Riggenbach, Heidi (ed.)
2000 *Perspectives on Fluency*. Ann Arbor: The University of Michigan Press.
Samuda, Virginia and Martin Bygate
2008 *Tasks in Second Language Learning*. London: Palgrave.

16. Teaching the written foreign language

William Grabe and Fredricka L. Stoller

1. Introduction

This survey examines major themes in foreign language instruction involving the written language. For the purposes of this overview, the term 'foreign language' refers to research and instruction in second, foreign, and additional languages. Research on the teaching of the written foreign language, from both reading and writing perspectives, is mostly derived from English first language (L1) instruction. However, this early foundation for both reading and writing instruction is no longer so easily recognised with the increasing amount of research being carried out by applied linguists on reading and writing development and on effective instructional practices in foreign language (FL) contexts. This survey provides an overview of early research on reading and writing in L1 (English and, in some cases, Dutch L1) and FL contexts, followed by a summary of more current (1990–present) research in the same areas. The survey then examines common instructional practices in both reading and writing that are supported by research and its implications. Finally, it considers instruction that integrates reading and writing.

An overview of FL written language instruction must take into account who the students might be. There is, in fact, an extraordinary range of settings and contexts for FL reading and writing instruction. In North America, as an illustration, language-minority students in kindergarten through 12th-grade classrooms may be generally fluent in the spoken second (or third) language, the dominant language of the educational system, but have a wide array of difficulties in reading and writing. More recent immigrant students may have a range of language-knowledge limitations as well as little exposure to reading and writing in the dominant instructional language. Both groups of students need to develop second language reading and writing abilities to succeed in their schooling. Other student groups, most commonly international students in university contexts, need to read and write for more advanced academic purposes (through doctoral studies). In addition, many secondary-school and university-level students begin to learn to read and write in a FL, though most will not go beyond two or three years of instruction nor will they ever read more than a language textbook or write more than a simple essay in the FL. Finally, there are adult learners who may not be literate in their native tongues or in a FL but who need basic reading and writing skills in the FL.

A similarly broad array of student populations and contexts can be identified for almost every other region of the world, indicating the complexity of any survey of FL reading and writing instruction. For example, in Europe, there are students at all levels of instruction who are learning to read and write a FL while studying select content areas (e.g., history, geography) in CLIL (Content and Language Integrated Learning) classrooms. Such CLIL classrooms represent a formalised response to the European Union's plurilingual education agenda (e.g., Dalton-Puffer 2007; Dalton-Puffer and Smit 2007; Fruhauf, Coyle, and Christ 1995; Grenfell 2002; Maljers, Marsh, and Wolff 2007; Marsh and Wolff 2007; Wilkinson 2004 see also Wolff; Ch. 20 this volume).

As diverse as these student groups may be, there are sets of teaching and learning principles and practices related to FL reading and writing that are pertinent across many instructional settings. Nonetheless, to provide coherence and present usefully detailed comments in this overview, we limit ourselves to a subset of FL learners, specifically those learning a FL for academic purposes, specific purposes, and research purposes. We anticipate that several of the issues raised and suggestions made are relevant to other FL learning contexts, both in North America and elsewhere.

2. A brief overview of early reading and writing research and instruction

Until the early 1970s, reading and writing were viewed as linguistically driven skills that could be learned by means of traditional reading comprehension questions and standard writing activities based on model texts that students were assigned to read. However, the rise of cognitive psychology in the late 1960s placed greater emphasis on the mental resources of the learner (as opposed to the learner as tabula rasa). This view of the learner, engaged actively in reading and writing processes, significantly influenced instruction in both skills. Cognitive psychology focused on the mental processing and knowledge representation abilities of individuals and sought explanations for a range of cognitive skills that assumed mental processing capabilities: learning, memory, attention, language, reading, writing, reasoning, problem solving, among others. The resulting research over the past 40 years has demonstrated overwhelmingly that complex cognitive abilities, such as reading and writing, are composed of a number of critical component skills and knowledge resources (Anderson 2005; Joshi and Aaron 2006; Kintsch 1998; Snowling and Hulme 2005; Traxler and Gernsbacher 2006). Building on the work of cognitive psychologists, reading researchers began to explore the resources that learners bring to the reading task. In particular, research on the component cognitive abilities of readers has demonstrated that a number of component abilities (e.g., word recognition skills, vocabulary knowledge, text structure knowledge, background knowledge resources, working memory skills) contribute to reading comprehension, both in L1 and FL contexts.

At about the same time, in the late 1970s, writing researchers broke away from the more traditional assumptions of learning that involved replicating models of differing modes of discourse (e.g., expository, argumentative, and narrative) and different patterns of discourse organisation (e.g., cause and effect, comparison and contrast, chronological timeline, extended definition/description, classification, problem-solution, analysis). A number of writing researchers introduced the notion that writing is better understood as a process than as a product and that writing research and instruction needed to focus on the process of writing as well as the development of abilities that support the writing process (Flower and Hayes 1977, 1981; Grabe and Kaplan 1996; Graves 1983, 1984; Johns 2005). The writing process was seen as comprising the cognitive processes of planning, generating, organising, using long-term memory resources, producing text, monitoring, reviewing, rereading, evaluating, and editing. These processes were not carried out serially but in cycles and not in any specific order after the process had been initiated (Bereiter and Scardamalia 1987; Flower and Hayes 1981; Graham 2006b; Hayes 1996, 2006).

As a consequence of these shifting views, reading and writing instruction began to change. Reading instruction, rather than being defined solely by sets of comprehension questions, expanded to incorporate pre-reading tasks and a wide range of post-reading activities and extensions, as well as the beginnings of reading strategy instruction. Writing moved from single-draft assignments, which provided students with practice in patterns of discourse organisation and opportunities to correct surface errors, to multiple drafts of paragraphs and essays, to the conception of writing errors as reflections of developmental steps, and to explorations of personal topics and self-expression. In both reading and writing, the emphasis shifted from the outcomes of reading and writing processes to comprehension and production processes themselves. By the mid 1980s, both reading and writing instruction were moving toward a cognitive-research foundation based on component-skills processes, though in differing ways.

In the 1980s, reading research began to focus heavily on the component cognitive processes involved in reading comprehension. After some period of controversy, a growing consensus emerged among cognitive and educational psychologists that reading abilities required the development of a number of component skills, including phonological awareness, word recognition, a large recognition vocabulary (i.e., words that readers can comprehend but not necessarily use on their own), main idea comprehension, knowledge of discourse structure, inferencing skills, and a range of strategies that support appropriate goals for reading (Ashby and Rayner 2006; Block and Pressley 2002; Gambrell, Morrow and Pressley 2007; McCardle and Chhabra 2004; Perfetti 1985, 1999; Perfetti, Landi and Oakhill 2005; Pressley 2006; Rayner and Pollatsek 1989; Stahl and McKenna 2006; Stanovich1980, 2000).

By the mid 1980s, most reading researchers had moved away from the knowledge-driven theories of Ken Goodman's Psycholinguistic Guessing Game Model of reading and Frank Smith's strong top-down assumptions (metaphorical views, widely accepted in the 1970s, characterising the reader as someone who had a set of expectations about text information and who sampled enough information from the text to confirm or reject the hypothesised expectations). Although researchers abandoned these views at this time, most teachers and teacher trainers would not make this shift for another 15–20 years. These changes in reading research through the 1980s are well documented (e.g., Adams 1990; Barr et al. 1991; Just and Carpenter 1987; Rayner and Pollatsek 1989; Snow, Burns and Griffin 1998), and major contemporary reference resources on reading research make no references to Goodman or Smith (e.g., Joshi and Aaron 2006; Kintsch 1998; McCardle and Chhabra 2004; Snowling and Hulme 2005; Traxler and Gernsbacher 2006).

Also during the 1980s, reading strategies and reading strategy instruction were explored in research and in various teaching formats. Pressley et al. (1989) outlined reading strategies that were reasonably well supported by research studies including the use of imagery, text structure awareness, inferencing, comprehension monitoring, summarising, and question formation. These strategies were further supported, and additional strategies noted, by research reported by the National Reading Panel (2000), Pressley and Afflerbach (1995), and Trabasso and Bouchard (2002). Strategy instruction has gained considerable support since that time and now represents a major focus of reading instruction (Block and Pressley 2007; Pressley 2002, 2006).

During this same period (the 1980s, into the 1990s), FL reading research was just beginning to develop research themes and ideas that extended beyond L1 reading research. Perhaps the most notable distinctions in FL reading research were the greater attention given by applied linguists to the importance of vocabulary and grammar knowledge, the need for additional reading experience (i.e., extensive reading), the support provided by reading strategies in FL comprehension, and the emerging role of L1 influences on FL reading (Bernhardt 1991; Grabe 1991; Koda 1994).

Research on writing in the 1980s was dominated by investigations of the writing process, in particular, the theories of Flower and Hayes (1981, 1984) and Bereiter and Scardamalia (1987). Flower and Hayes employed think-aloud procedures while students were engaged in various writing tasks and then analysed the think-alouds to create their model of the writing process. This model, based on extensive think-aloud data, proposed six major components that work together as part of the writing process: planning, production, review, long-term memory resources, the task environment, and monitoring. In the mid 1980s, the cognitive process oriented view was extended through a survey of writing research by Hillocks (1986) and the research program of Bereiter and Scardamalia

(1987), which showed that better writers engaged in more planning time, gave more consideration to the goals of the writing task, made revisions that could lead to a reorganisation of the text, and paid greater attention to the main emphases of the task. Throughout the 1980s and 1990s, FL writing research was heavily dependent on L1 writing research for its research questions and research methods; instructional implications followed closely behind L1 writing instruction practices.

3. Reading and writing research since 1990

Since the 1990s, L1 reading research has emphasised the importance of word recognition, vocabulary knowledge, syntactic parsing, text comprehension processes, inferencing, strategic reading in learning contexts, reading motivation, reading fluency, and extensive reading (Block and Pressley 2002; Kintsch 1998; Kuhn and Stahl 2003; National Reading Panel 2000; Snowling and Hulme 2005; Stanovich 2000). This current research represents extensions of productive and insightful research on the component skills of reading that began in the early 1980s. In both L1 and FL contexts, a growing area of research has centred around the similarities and differences in reading in different languages (Cook and Bassetti 2005; Joshi and Aaron 2006; Koda 2005, 2007; Snowling and Hulme 2005). It is now evident that orthographic, morphological, and syntactic differences across languages lead to differences in reading comprehension processes. At the same time, there is strong evidence that certain reading abilities are consistently required across languages (Koda 2007; Perfetti 2003; Perfetti, Liu, and Tan 2005).

For example, it is now well documented that all reading in all languages makes use of phonological processing during reading, and grapheme-sound correspondences represent a crucial resource for all readers, no matter their L1. Similarly, all readers make use of a range of reading strategies, use working memory resources in similar ways, and use syntactic, morphological, lexical, and discourse knowledge resources while reading. Differences in reading across L1s include differing attention to (a) orthographic units because of the varied L1 orthographies involved, (b) morphological knowledge (e.g., English, Spanish, Hebrew, and Chinese), and (c) syllable knowledge (e.g., English, Japanese, and Korean). Differences in the regularity of orthographic-sound correspondences (e.g., Finnish, Turkish, Spanish, English, Arabic, and Chinese) are a further source of variance across L1s (see Cook and Bassetti 2005; Frost 2005; Grabe 2009; Joshi and Aaron 2006; Koda 2007).

FL reading research has similarly moved toward a recognition of the importance of component reading skills (see above) and the need for extensive reading (Alderson 2000; Anderson 1999; Grabe and Stoller 2002; Koda 2005). The work of Dutch applied linguists has been particularly important in the study of component skills (Fukkink, Hulstijn, and Simis 2005; Schoonen, Hulstijn, and Bossers 1998; van Gelderen et al. 2004, 2007). Applied linguists from a variety of perspectives have also recently been emphasising differences between L1 and FL reading processes, distinct FL research perspectives, and important implications for instruction and assessment (Bernhardt 2005; Grabe 2009; Grabe and Stoller 2002; Koda 2005, 2007; Wang, Koda, and Perfetti 2003). Obvious differences between L1 and FL reading include (a) the weaker linguistic resources of FL readers at various stages of proficiency, (b) less exposure to print (i.e., fewer FL reading experiences), (c) varied social and cultural background assumptions, and (d) differing experiences with various text genres in the L1 and FL. Differences arising from the dual-language nature of the FL reader account for other L1–FL distinctions (Grabe and Stoller 2002; Koda 2005, 2007).

Writing research has taken a somewhat different path, at least in North American contexts. Much of the collaboration between psychologists and English department composition researchers ceased in the 1990s. Influenced greatly by rhetoric and literature colleagues, many North American composition researchers have, for the most part, come to believe that experimental research violates current post-modernist orientations to writing development. As a result, efforts to establish a continuing empirical base for writing research and instructional practices have been left primarily to educational psychologists and applied linguists, from whom have emerged four predominant orientations: (a) significantly revised models of the writing process (Graham 2006b; Hayes 1996, 2006), (b) strong psychology-based perspectives by European researchers (Allal, Chanquoy, and Largy 2004; Olive and Levy 2002; Ransdell and Barbier 2002; Rijlaarsdam and van den Bergh 2006; Rijlaarrsdam, van den Bergh, and Couzijin 2005; Torrance and Galbraith 1999), (c) empirical research by FL writing researchers, most often reported in the *Journal of Second Language Writing* (Ferris and Hedgcock 2005; Manchon and Roca de Larios et al 2008; Sasaki 2000) and (d) ongoing work in education and educational psychology (Graham 2006a; Graham, Harris, and Mason 2005; MacArthur, Graham, and Fitzgerald 2006). This research base has been strongly supported by European researchers, particularly in England, France, and the Netherlands.

These four approaches maintain the research assumption that writing, as a complex cognitive ability, is best understood and explained in terms of component-skill abilities. For example, the revised writing process model of Hayes (1996, 2006) retained many of the earlier component abilities of the writing process, but also now draws on research findings to emphasise the roles of working memory, reading, and motivation in the writing process. At the same time, his model refines depictions of planning and revision processes. From a European perspective, Rijlaarsdam and van den Bergh have carried out empirical studies of writing process tasks over the past 15 years. In a recent synthesis (Rijlaarsdam and van den Bergh 2006), they report that 11 categories of writing processes account for 76% of students' writing quality. As another example, empirical research studies by FL writing researchers have sought to understand better the roles of planning, revision, and feedback on FL student writing development (Ferris and Hedgcock 2005; Hyland and Hyland 2006).

In FL settings, there has been an increasing recognition of the differences between L1 and FL writers (see Grabe 2001; Silva, Leki, and Carson 1997). At the same time, FL research by applied linguists has continued to explore issues in writing and grammar, the importance of error correction, the role of FL language proficiency, the influence of L1 culture and text structuring on FL writing, the impact of differing instructional expectations, and the importance of genre orientations in writing instruction (Ferris and Hedgcock 2005; Hedgcock 2005; Hyland 2004; Johns 2002; Kroll 2003; Leki, Cumming and Silva 2008; Reynolds 2005; Sasaki 2004). The linkages between cognitive and social foundations for writing development have been explored effectively by Johns (1997) and Kern (2000). Again, important FL writing research has been carried out by Dutch researchers (Schoonen et al. 2003; Snellings, van Gelderen, and de Glopper 2002).

Foreign language writers differ from L1 writers in a number of ways that parallel L1–FL differences in reading. Most FL writers do not command the same levels of language proficiency as do L1 writers. Furthermore, they do not have the same levels of exposure to L1 texts, genres, and types of writing tasks that L1 students have. FL writers have a range of social and cultural experiences with writing that are likely to vary in multiple ways from the social and cultural factors influencing most L1 writers (Grabe 2001; Silva 1993; Silva, Leki and Carson 1997).

There has also been a growing awareness of the importance of combining reading and writing instruction to improve both reading and writing abilities (Belcher and Hirvela 2001; Langer and Flihan 2000; Shanahan 2006). Most commonly, integrated-skills instruction has been explored from the writing perspective, though reading researchers have long recognised the importance of writing for learning information from texts (e.g., summarising practice). A heightened interest in and emphasis on content-based instruction, the development of strategic learners, and genre-based approaches to writing have led to increased instances of reading and writing integration at classroom and curricular levels, thereby reinforcing the benefits of combining the two literacy skills instructionally (Graham 2006b; Guthrie, Wigfield, and Perencevich 2004; Shanahan 2006). Similar perspectives and approaches have been developed in FL contexts by applied linguists (Belcher and Hirvela 2001; Ferris and Hedgcock 2005; Kern 2000).

4. Goals for teaching FL reading

From research on reading processes and reading instruction emerges a set of goals that can inform reading instruction more generally and suggest effective instructional activities more specifically. Reading instruction for FL students who need to become reasonably fluent readers for academic purposes can be developed around a set of component skills supported by research (Anderson 1999; Block and Pressley 2002; Gambrell, Morrow and Pressley 2007; Grabe 2009; Grabe and Stoller 2001; Guthrie, Wigfield, and Perencevich 2004; National Reading Panel 2000; Perfetti, Landi and Oakhill 2005; Pressley 2006; Stanovich 2000). The component skills identified as critical for reading comprehension abilities include grapheme-sound correspondences, word recognition efficiency, vocabulary knowledge, syntactic knowledge, main idea recognition, discourse knowledge awareness, strategic responses to text comprehension, fluency skills, extensive exposure to text (amount of reading), and reader motivation. From these research findings emerge a number of straightforward goals for reading instruction (see Grabe 2009), as summarised in Table 1.

Table 1. Goals for reading instruction

To support the development of requisite language knowledge bases and processing skills, reading instruction should help students do the following:

1. Build a large recognition vocabulary
2. Develop reading fluency and build rapid and efficient word recognition
3. Process syntactic information from written texts efficiently
4. Identify main ideas in reading passages
5. Develop sophisticated inferencing skills
6. Develop discourse processing skills and awareness of text structuring
7. Develop strategies for effective comprehension processing and metacognitive awareness of reading goals
8. Use relevant background knowledge effectively

To achieve these goals, the single most important recommendations for reading instruction are engaging students in extensive reading, building and maintaining student motivation for reading, and combining reading and writing instruction.

Students must read a lot if they are to become good academic readers who can read large amounts of material and use the information from the readings for meaningful purposes. Direct instruction that targets many of the other goals for instruction improves reading comprehension abilities, but extensive reading is a means to develop a wide range of the research-supported goals at the same time. Increasing the amount of reading that a learner engages in directly supports every goal for reading listed in Table 1. The amount of reading must be considerable and carried out over an extended period of time for the positive effects to take hold.

Day and Bamford (1998) and Grabe (2009) suggest ways to promote extended reading in a reading curriculum, including the introduction and availability of many attractive reading materials (including graded readers), the development of a good class library, time for sustained silent reading, and many opportunities to read both in and out of class. More specific instructional options for teachers include reading interesting material to students, finding out what students like to read and why (and sharing what teachers themselves like to read and why), creating ways to interest students in reading topics, recording students' reading progress and creating incentives for students to start reading, asking students to take books and magazines home, and having students share and recommend reading material.

To support students' progress toward becoming more effective readers, with improved comprehension abilities, reading extensively is not sufficient. A number of more specific teaching practices should be integrated into reading instruction. The most straightforward feature of effective reading instruction involves engaging students in challenging but interesting texts and building their vocabulary knowledge and comprehension skills. Most well-designed comprehension instruction is organised around sets of pre-, during-, and post-reading activities. Pre-reading activities focus on previewing the text, tapping background knowledge, setting purposeful goals for reading, predicting the contents and organisation of the text, learning (and/or identifying) key vocabulary, developing concepts and ideas important to the main ideas of the text, and practising a set of strategies that are important for maintaining and monitoring comprehension. It is during pre-reading stages when students often survey classmates about relevant information as a way to build background knowledge and when teachers encourage engagement with the topic of the reading. During-reading activities involve clarifying complex ideas, predicting upcoming information, comparing text information to other information, taking appropriate notes, exploring attitudes, and interpreting alternative meanings of the text. Post-reading activities clarify and extend main ideas, require the use of newly encountered vocabulary, support strategy learning, create opportunities for recycling, promote critical interpretations and inferencing, and oblige students to use text information to engage in speaking and writing tasks of various kinds (see Anderson 1999; Fitzgerald and Graves 2004; Grabe and Stoller 2001).

Vocabulary learning is an important part of reading development; a subset of key vocabulary should be introduced and taught explicitly. Other vocabulary is introduced briefly, then noted, collected, used, practised, and recycled. Less common or less central vocabulary is acquired gradually through incidental contact, guessing word meanings, using word internal clues, and consulting the dictionary. Overall, approaches to vocabulary learning require that teachers select and introduce key words, recycle texts and vocabulary, and create vocabulary-rich learning environments so that students can practice vocabulary, develop word learning strategies, collect words, and use words in multiple and varied ways (e.g., Beck, McKeown, and Kucan 2002; Nation 2001; Stahl and Nagy 2006).

Another major component of an effective FL reading curriculum is fluency development. Fluency, for practical purposes, involves rapid word recognition, the ability to read a text at a reasonably rapid rate with appropriate comprehension, efficient skills in reading a text aloud while maintaining comprehension, and the ability to read a text for extended periods of time while maintaining comprehension. Fluency is often overlooked or viewed as unimportant in many FL contexts. However, it is receiving greater attention in both L1 and FL settings, and it is increasingly seen as a critical part of reading comprehension efficiency, particularly for students who are expected to read subject-area material in a foreign language (see National Reading Panel 2000; Rasinski 2003). Fluency practice in pre-, during-, and post-reading activities requires word recognition practice, paired readings, read-along activities with a teacher or an audiotape, reader's theater (in which students write a script, and then perform a scene, from a story that they are reading), timed readings, rereading texts and recycling through previously read texts, and extensive reading (see Anderson 1999; Grabe 2009; Rasinski 2003).

Students in academic settings need to develop an awareness of strategies to support reading comprehension. For example, the ability to recognise text organisation – that is, how texts signal the organisation of information, how texts present information in expected ways (comparisons and contrasts, problems and solutions, causes and effects, etc.), and how main ideas are highlighted – is useful for both reading and writing. Such discourse structure awareness is inextricably linked to becoming a strategic reader. Strategic readers use a range of strategies for text comprehension, often in combination, including forming goals for reading, predicting textual organisation and upcoming information, clarifying complex information, making appropriate inferences, monitoring comprehension in various ways, identifying sources of difficulty, summarising information, synthesising information, and critically evaluating information. The development of strategic reading requires explicit instruction, continual reminders and support from teachers, and repeated opportunities for practice and reflection (Anderson 1999; Dymock and Nicholson 2007; Pressley 2002, 2006).

Another important aspect of reading curricula, and writing curricula as well, is the need to develop strong student motivation for learning and practising literacy skills. Motivation represents a willingness to devote energy to learning, to persist in activities that lead to reading improvement, and a positive association with reading abilities. It provides a foundation for the development of the component skills outlined earlier. Although motivation is commonly viewed as a personal trait, there are multiple ways to help students maintain interest, persist in a task, and experience a sense of achievement and control (Dörnyei 2001; Grabe 2009; Guthrie,Wigfield, and Perencevich 2004). A classroom context can promote student motivation by developing group cohesiveness and communities of learners (with, for example, cooperative learning) who support each other's learning, efforts with challenging tasks, and increasing expectations for success. Teachers can promote student motivation by developing good lead-ins to texts and tasks that build initial interest, matching student skills with challenge, building curricular relevance, and giving students some control over topics, texts, and tasks. Additional teacher actions that can build student motivation include having students share their interests, thereby promoting learners as active participants so that learning is stimulating and enjoyable, and develop real levels of expertise in reading topics. Student success with more complex content and integrated reading and writing tasks also provides strong motivation for continued engagement with reading and writing (Guthrie, Wigfield, and Perencevich 2004; Pressley 2006; Pressley et al. 2003).

5. Goals for teaching FL writing

Foreign language writing instruction in academic settings falls into two general areas: writing for general academic purposes (e.g., note taking, multiple-paragraph essays) and writing for specific academic or professional task requirements (e.g., term papers and extended reports, tests, response papers, book reports, data collection notes, lab reports). The abilities required for these different types of writing can be developed through instruction centred on a number of goals supported by research, as explained below.

Most current approaches to FL writing instruction, particularly in academic contexts, combine a multiple-draft writing process, a genre-based approach, a socioliteracy perspective, a strategic orientation, and the use of content-driven resources (primarily reading texts) to inform writing (Ferris and Hedgcock 2005; Hyland 2004; Kroll 2003). Almost all writing instruction now assumes that students will engage in cycles of planning, information gathering, organising, generating, revising, and editing. A genre approach requires that students recognise and analyse the types of texts that they are expected to simulate or produce, understand why texts are organised and formatted in specific ways, and become sensitive to specific purposes for writing as well as the typical audiences for such genres (Hyland 2004; Paltridge 2001). A socioliteracy perspective extends the genre approach, highlighting inquiry into the genre forms themselves, the value systems (and communities) that support the genres, and the goals that are accomplished through these genres. Students learn to analyse, understand, produce, and critique genres relevant to their instructional contexts and educational goals (Johns 1997, 2005). Together the genre approach and socioliteracy perspective promote a strategic awareness about writing and strategic actions to achieve appropriate task outcomes. Both orientations (strategic awareness and strategic actions) support the use of content resources to inform writing; this view of academic writing instruction has contributed to the greater emphasis now placed on integrated reading and writing instruction (Ferris and Hedgcock 2005; Graham 2006a, 2006b; Hyland 2003; Johns 2005; Kern 2000; Leki and Carson 1994, 1997; Shanahan 2006).

From research on writing and writing instruction, it is possible to specify goals (see Table 2) that can inform writing instruction more generally and suggest effective instructional activities more specifically (Ferris and Hedgcock 2005; Graham 2006a, 2006b; Hyland 2003; Johns 1997; Paltridge 2001).

Table 2. Goals for writing instruction

For students to become effective writers in academic settings, they need to be able to do the following:

1. Recognise purposes for writing and the importance of establishing writing goals
2. Analyse writing tasks appropriately and develop plans for writing
3. Recognise genre constraints and analyse tasks in light of genre expectations
4. Write from textual resources and other sources
5. Engage in an ongoing cycle of brainstorming, collecting information (from various external sources, as appropriate), writing, reading and rereading, revising, seeking feedback, and editing
6. Build well-established routines for generating appropriate words, phrasings, paragraphs, and genre/structure
7. Develop writing strategies that improve writing outcomes
8. Make use of a variety of feedback options effectively as they become available
9. Write fluently

Like with reading, teachers can assist students in developing these abilities by building and maintaining student motivation for writing, providing students with consistent practice in specific writing tasks that have well-defined academic and professional purposes, and integrating reading and writing tasks.

Based on these goals, writing instruction – whether based on readings and other resources or carried out independently of reading resources – can be structured around the development of basic production skills, strategic approaches to writing tasks, practice with relevant genres, a writing process that works, and a range of feedback on writing in progress (e.g., Ferris 2002; Goldstein 2005; Grabe and Kaplan 1996). Much as with reading, writing develops more effectively over the long term through continual practice. Moreover, writing abilities develop in the specific types of writing that are practised. For example, beyond basic skills, writing narratives that recount past activities do not help students in presenting complex and sometimes conflicting information about the world or in writing persuasive arguments involving the effective use of evidence. Similarly, journal writing does not develop the more complex synthesis and evaluation skills required for producing problem-solution essays. The need to focus writing practice on tasks that complement students' real writing needs highlights the importance of genre-based approaches to writing (Hyland 2004; Johns 2002).

Genre-based approaches provide practice with relevant types of writing tasks in school and professional settings (e.g., Flowerdew 2000; Hyland 2004; Paltridge 2001). For example, to prepare students for academic contexts, students need to practice timed essays based on school subject matter if they are to become skilled at this task. Similarly, they need repeated opportunities to write responses to literary texts if they are to become skilled at drawing on literary text resources to craft such responses. They need to practice summary writing if summary writing is seen as a useful component of explanatory reports or persuasive writing. They need to write case-study analyses if they are to become skilled at analysing alternative solutions, selecting best options, and explaining outcomes in writing. All of these more specific skills take time to develop and require consistent practice (and motivation to persist). Much as with reading, specific activities can be integrated into an overall writing curriculum to assist students in developing such skills.

Genre-based writing instruction directs students to analyse the types of writing that they need to be able to produce for specific courses, disciplines, audiences, and purposes. Students need to learn how to examine writing tasks and identify exactly what is expected and why. Students and teacher should gather relevant examples of genres and critically examine these texts for their organisational patterns, attention to audience, consistent formal aspects (grammar, vocabulary, format, organisation), and other outstanding features (Johns 2002, 2005). A further critical aspect of the genre approach guides students in asking why such genres exist, what communities privilege these genres, and how the genres can or cannot be adapted to meet students' goals. As part of the approach, students gather authentic examples of writing tasks that lead to the production of key genres. From this point on, a genre approach follows most of the same goals for writing instruction described above.

A strategic approach to writing instruction (see Graham 2006a; Harris and Graham 1996) is important because most aspects of writing are open to strategic reflection and appropriate strategic actions. Almost all writing begins with reflection and inquiry about the purposes and goals for writing, a careful assessment of the writing task, and an understanding of the genre expectations associated with the task. Moreover, students need to consider, as part of strategic practice, ideas and resources useful for the writing task, ways to brainstorm and organise information, and plans for generating the text and later revising it. As one example of strategy-driven writing instruction, specific writing activities can be used to develop a stronger awareness of how discourse is structured. These activities can include identifying main (or important) idea sentences, determining the purpose of a sequence of paragraphs, recognising cause and effect segments in problem-solution texts (usually part of the 'problem'), locating markers of comparison-contrast structuring, and specifying types of evidence and types of arguments in persuasion texts (Graham 2006a, 2006b).

Writing, as a complex cognitive activity, requires extended and extensive practice not only with writing itself, but also with the related skills and resources required for good writing. One important early step is to establish specific goals for writing. These goals can be developed by asking students to specify reasons for the writing task, analyse the writing tasks themselves in some detail, and examine previously completed responses to the writing assignment. A second important starting point requires students to generate ideas and information to be used in the writing task, by, for example, reviewing text resources, relating background knowledge to the texts and task, developing a semantic map of the topic, and comparing ideas with others in a group.

Other aspects of writing development require specific attention as well. Writing fluency in academic settings involves more than fluent mechanics; it requires the ability to organise and generate texts efficiently (e.g., having effective procedures for generating supporting information and organising information effectively). Furthermore, it requires the awareness of strategic actions and options, and the development of useful writing routines for generating text through consistent practice with specific writing tasks. Writing also requires locating willing readers and seeking feedback. Finally, writing requires an ability to revise and edit. Techniques for revision include narrowing the focus of topical development, adding appropriate and relevant examples, removing extraneous information, outlining the organisation of a text after it has been drafted, incorporating appropriate and effective transitions to link sections of the text, and soliciting assistance from peer readers (Grabe and Kaplan 1996). Editing instruction and practice may involve reading the text aloud after it is revised; identifying weak vocabulary and finding better word choices; searching for overly long or complex sentences; recognising and removing strings of prepositional phrases; locating and changing repeated words and phrases; recognising and restructuring overused lists, conjoined words, and phrases; and focusing on one or two weaknesses previously identified (Grabe and Kaplan 1996).

6. Implications for integrated reading and writing instruction

In many FL reading and writing settings, instruction focuses on either reading or writing; much less commonly are the two skills combined and integrated on a consistent basis. In discrete-skill courses, reading instruction may cover a range of skill-development activities, but generally it is not extended to writing practice based on a reading. In writing courses, students commonly engage in writing tasks that draw on students' personal experience and background knowledge. The ability to write from information supplied by a text, or multiple texts, is often seen as an unnecessary complication. However, the integration of reading and writing in a single course has much greater academic validity. In secondary and tertiary content-area courses, most assignments that require a demonstration of learning involve a combination of reading and writing activities (Grabe 2001; Leki and Carson 1997). In writing-focused instruction that combines reading and writing, students are required to make use of textual information in writing tasks. Two major kinds of writing from texts can be identified: using text resources for creative expression and using text resources for disciplinary writing.

A range of literary texts can be used to support creative expression. A poem or a short essay can be cut into pieces and rearranged, accompanied by a written (or oral) explanation for the solution proposed. A literary excerpt can be continued to create an original extension, or a short excerpt can have parts, up to a sentence in length, left blank for students to fill in. Two poems or two prose excerpts can be compared for linguistic features and a written (or oral) analysis can be offered (see Widdowson 1992). Students are frequently asked to respond to specific features of literary texts and suggest how these features contribute to textual interpretation. Such features can include the use of specific details in descriptions, the use of quotations and dialogue, the way time is portrayed in narratives, alternative psychological orientations indicated by characters or narrator, and the use of symbolism and metaphor to convey multiple levels of meaning. Finally, students can convert a story or poem into a script for a dramatic scene, or craft a description of a character, or even the author, based on the segment provided.

Students can be prepared to use informational texts for subject-area writing through a variety of tasks, some of which are straightforward and common, others being more advanced and subject specific. The most common practice is summary writing. Though often overlooked, summary writing is a useful skill for a variety of academic purposes (Grabe 2001). Students can also write simple responses to prompts that oblige them to synthesise, explain, or react to a reading, or that prepare them for an upcoming reading by tapping background knowledge or guiding them in the consideration of new ideas that will be introduced in the text. Students can also be asked to connect new texts to previously read texts through speed writes, free writes, essay questions, and jigsaw activities. For example, in speed writes, students are given a topic, a statement, or a quote and have 10 minutes to write a response. In free writing, students can be asked to write daily for 10 minutes on a topic of their choice; the only requirement is that they write continuously. Jigsaw activities require students to work in groups with three different texts; then groups re-form so that each person in the new group reports on a different text. The new groups then assemble a full explanation in response to a writing task. In addition, students can extend tables, graphs, or figures, or fill in outline structures based on readings; students can then use these graphic representations to develop more extended prose (Grabe and Kaplan 1996).

Specific responses to texts can be explored and developed in multiple ways. Students can write about personal experiences related to a given text before and/or after reading. Students can form questions that might be answered in the text and then write out a response to at least one question answered by the text. Students can take a position on a text and refer to another text for support or they can compare readings that present different viewpoints. Students can generate a list of ideas from a text, prioritise the list by level of importance, prioritise lists in groups, and then develop some form of visual representation (map, outline, diagram) to be shared with the class. Activities such as these build the academic writing skills needed to produce academic genres (Belcher and Hirvela 2001; Grabe and Kaplan 1996; Kroll 2003).

A further way to understand reading and writing relationships is to consider how writing can enhance reading comprehension. Though this direction of interaction is less commonly discussed than reading to write, writing activities can develop students' reading expectations. Students can write out predictions based on a title or an initial skimming of the text. They can anticipate the next chapter or section of a text and write their own version of the next part, or they can write a brief response to a posed question that is central to an upcoming reading. Finally, before reading a text, students can create a survey (individually or in groups) to gather reading-related information. In a more extended context, students can write an essay and then be given reading resources to be used as further support and/or examples in an expanded written work (Ferris and Hedgcock 2005).

Beyond reading and writing interactions in the classroom, at advanced levels of writing development, students need assistance with discipline-specific genres. The genres that need to be read and written at advanced levels of study (e.g., graduate studies) are rarely addressed in FL classes. They can, however, be addressed in advanced writing support courses (e.g., Robinson et al. 2008; Swales and Feak 2004). At graduate levels, students may be asked to read and write research papers, grant proposals, conference abstracts, letters of various types, posters, and other professional reports. Such writing tasks go beyond the scope of this review, but they nonetheless represent a skill level required of a fair number of foreign language students (Swales 1990, 2004).

References

Adams, Marilyn
1990 *Beginning to Read: Thinking and Learning about Print*. Cambridge, MA: MIT Press.

Alderson, Charles
2000 *Reading Assessment*. Cambridge: Cambridge University Press.

Allal, Linda, Lucile Chanquoy and Pierre Largy (eds.)
2004 *Revision: Cognitive and Instructional Processes*. New York: Kluwer.

Anderson, John R.
2005 *Cognitive Psychology and its Implications*. 6th edition. New York: Worth Publishing.

Anderson, Neil
1999 *Exploring Second Language Reading: Issues and Strategies*. Boston, MA: Heinle and Heinle.

Ashby, Jane and Keith Rayner
2006 Literacy development: Insights from research on skilled reading. In: David Dickinson and Susan Neuman (eds.), *Handbook of Early Literacy Development*, Vol 2, 52–63. New York: Guilford Press.

Barr, Rebecca, Michael Kamil, Peter Mosenthal and P. David Pearson
1991 *Handbook of Reading Research*. Vol. 2. New York: Longman.

Beck, Isabel, Margaret McKeown and Linda Kucan
2002 *Bringing Words to Life: Robust Vocabulary Instruction*. New York: Guilford Press.

Belcher, Diane and Alana Hirvela
2001 *Linking Literacies: Perspectives on L2 Reading-Writing Connections*. Ann Arbor, MI: University of Michigan Press.

Bereiter, Carl and Marlene Scardamalia
1987 *The Psychology of Written Composition*. Hillsdale, NJ: Lawrence Erlbaum.

Bernhardt, Elizabeth B.
1991 *Reading Development in a Second Language: Theoretical, Empirical and Classroom Perspectives*. Norwood, NJ: Ablex.

Bernhardt, Elizabeth B.
2005 Progress and procrastination in second language reading. *Annual Review of Applied Linguistics* 25: 133–150.

Block, Cathy and Michael Pressley (eds.)
2002 *Comprehension Instruction: Research-Based Best Practices*. New York: Guilford Press.

Block, Cathy and Michael Pressley
2007 Best practices in teaching comprehension. In: Gambrell, Morrow and Pressley (eds.), 220–242.

Cook, Vivian and Benedetta Bassetti (eds.)
2005 *Second Language Writing Systems*. Buffalo, NY: Multilingual Matters.

Dalton-Puffer, Christiane
2007 *Discourse in Content and Language Integrated Learning (CLIL)*. Amsterdam: John Benjamins.

Dalton-Puffer, Christiane and Ute Smit (eds.)
2007 *Empirical Perspectives on CLIL Classroom Discourse*. Frankfurt, Main: Lang.

Day, Richard R. and Julian Bamford
1998 *Extensive Reading in the Second Language Classroom*. New York: Cambridge University Press.

Dörnyei, Zóltan
2001 *Motivational Strategies in the Language Classroom*. New York: Cambridge University Press.

Dymock, Susan and Tom Nicholson
2007 *Teaching Text Structure*. New York: Scholastic.

Ferris, Dana R.
2002 *Treatment of Error in Second Language Student Writing*. Ann Arbor, MI: University of Michigan Press.

Ferris, Dana R. and John Hedgcock
2005 *Teaching ESL Composition*. 2nd edition. Mahwah, NJ: Lawrence Erlbaum.

Fitzgerald, Jill and Michael Graves
2004 *Scaffolding Reading Experiences for English-Language Learners*. Norwood, MA: Christopher-Gordon.

Flower, Linda and John Hayes
1977 Problem-solving strategies and the writing process. *College English* 39: 449–461.

Flower, Linda and John Hayes
1981 A cognitive process theory of writing. *College Composition and Communication* 32: 365–387.

Flower, Linda and John Hayes
1984 Images, plans and prose: The representation of meaning in writing. *Written Communication* 1: 120–160.

Flowerdew, Lynne
2000 Using a genre-based framework to teach organizational structure in academic writing. *ELT Journal* 54: 369–375.

Frost, Ram
2005 Orthographic systems and skilled word recognition. In: Snowling and Hulme (eds.), 272–295.

Fruhauf, Gianna, Do Coyle and Ingeborg Christ (eds.)
1995 *Teaching Content in a Foreign Language: Practice and Perspectives in European Bilingual Education*. Alkmaar, The Netherlands: European Platform for Dutch Education.

Fukkink, Ruben G., Jan Hulstijn and Annegien Simis
2005 Does training in second-language word recognition skills affect reading comprehension? An experimental study. *Modern Language Journal* 89: 54–75.

Gambrell, Linda, Lesley Morrow and Michael Pressley (eds.)
2007 *Best Practices in Literacy Instruction*. New York: Guilford Press.

Goldstein, Lynn M.
2005 *Teacher Written Commentary in Second Language Classrooms*. Ann Arbor, MI: University of Michigan Press.

Grabe, William
1991 Current developments in second language reading research. *TESOL Quarterly* 25: 375–406.

Grabe, William
2001 Reading-writing relations: Theoretical perspectives and instructional practice. In: Diane Belcher and Alan Hirvela (eds.), *Reading and Writing Relations in L2 Contexts*, 15–47. Ann Arbor, MI: University of Michigan Press.

Grabe, William
2009 *Reading in a Second Language: Moving from Theory to Practice*. New York: Cambridge University Press.

Grabe, William and Robert B. Kaplan
1996 *Theory and Practice of Writing*. New York: Longman.

Grabe, William and Fredricka L. Stoller
2001 Reading for academic purposes: Guidelines for the ESL/EFL teacher. In: Marianne Celce-Murcia (ed.), *Teaching English as a Second or Foreign Language*, 3rd edition, 187–203. Boston: Heinle and Heinle.

Grabe, William and Fredricka L. Stoller
2002 *Teaching and Researching Reading*. New York: Longman.

Graham, Steve
2006a Strategy instruction and the teaching of writing: A meta-analysis. In: MacArthur, Graham and Fitzgerald (eds.), 187–207.

Graham, Steve
2006b Writing. In: Patricia Alexander and Philip Winne (eds.), *Handbook of Educational Psychology*, 2nd edition, 457–478. Mahwah, NJ: Lawrence Erlbaum.

Graham, Steve, Karen Harris and Linda Mason
2005 Improving the writing performance, knowledge, and motivation of struggling young writers: The effects of Self Regulated Strategy Development. *Contemporary Educational Psychology* 30: 207–241.

Graves, Donald
1983 *Writing: Teachers and Children at Work*. Portsmouth, NH: Heinemann.

Graves, Donald
1984 *A Researcher Learns to Write*. Portsmouth, NH: Heinemann.

Grenfell, Michael (ed.)
2002 *Modern Languages across the Curriculum*. New York: Routledge Falmer.

Guthrie, John, Allan Wigfield and Kathleen Perencevich (eds.)
2004 *Motivating Reading Comprehension: Concept-Oriented Reading Instruction*. Mahwah, NJ: Lawrence Erlbaum.

Harris, Karen and Steve Graham
1996 *Making the Writing Process Work: Strategies for Composition and Self-Regulation*. Cambridge, MA: Brookline Books.

Hayes, John R.
1996 A new framework for understanding cognition and affect in writing. In: Michael Levy and Sarah Ransdell (eds.), *The Science of Writing: Theories, Methods, Individual Differences, and Applications*, 1–27. Mahwah, NJ: Lawrence Erlbaum.

Hayes, John R.
2006 New directions in writing theory. In: MacArthur, Graham and Fitzgerald (eds.), 28–40.

Hedgcock, John
2005 Taking stock of research and pedagogy in L2 writing. In: Eli Hinkel (ed.), *Handbook of Research in Second Language Teaching and Learning*, 597–613. Mahwah, NJ: Lawrence Erlbaum.

Hillocks, George
1986 *Research on Written Composition: New Directions for Teaching*. Urbana, IL: National Conference on Research in English.

Hyland, Ken
2003 *Second Language Writing*. Cambridge: Cambridge University Press.

Hyland, Ken
2004 *Genre and Second Language Writing*. Ann Arbor: University of Michigan Press.

Hyland, Ken and Fiona Hyland (eds.)
2006 *Feedback in Second Language Writing*. New York: Cambridge University Press.

Johns, Ann
1997 *Text, Role, and Context: Developing Academic Literacies*. New York: Cambridge University Press.

Johns, Ann (ed.)
2002 *Genre in the Classroom: Multiple Perspectives*. Mahwah, NJ: L. Erlbaum.

Johns, Ann
2005 English for academic purposes: Issues in undergraduate writing and reading. In: Paul Bruthiaux, Dwight Atkinson, William Eggington, William Grabe and Vaidehi Ramanathan (eds.), *Directions in Applied Linguistics*, 101–116. Buffalo, NY: Multilingual Matters.

Joshi, R. Malatesha and P. Aaron (eds.)
2006 *Handbook of Orthography and Literacy*. Mahwah, NJ: Lawrence Erlbaum.

Just, Marcel and Patricia Carpenter
1987 *The Psychology of Reading and Language Comprehension*. Boston: Allyn and Bacon.

Kern, Richard
2000 *Literacy and Language Teaching*. Oxford: Oxford University Press.

Kintsch, Walter
1998 *Comprehension*. New York: Cambridge University Press.

Koda, Keiko
1994 Second language reading research: Problems and possibilities. *Applied Psycholinguistics* 15: 1–28.

Koda, Keiko
2005 *Insights into Second Language Reading*. Cambridge: Cambridge University Press.

Koda, Keiko
2007 Reading and language learning: Crosslinguistic constraints on second language reading development. In: Keiko Koda (ed.), *Reading and Language Learning* (Special issue of *Language Learning Supplement* 57), 1–44.

Kroll, Barbara (ed.)
2003 *Exploring the Dynamics of Second Language Writing*. New York: Cambridge University Press.

Kuhn, Melanie and Steven Stahl
2003 Fluency: A review of development and remedial practices. *Journal of Educational Psychology* 95: 3–21.

Langer, Judith and Sheila Flihan
2000 Writing and reading relationships: Constructive tasks. In: Roselmina Indrisano and James Squire (eds.), *Perspectives on Writing: Research, Theory, and Practice*, 112–139. Newark, DE: International Reading Association.

Leki, Ilona and Joan Carson
1994 Students' perceptions of EAP writing instruction and writing needs across the disciplines. *TESOL Quarterly* 28: 81–101.

Leki, Ilona and Joan Carson
1997 "Completely different worlds": EAP and the writing experiences of ESL students in university courses. *TESOL Quarterly* 31: 39–69.

Leki, Ilona, Alister Cumming and Tony Silva
2008 *A synthesis of research on second language writing in English.* New York: Routledge.

MacArthur, Charles A., Steve G. Graham and Jill Fitzgerald (eds.)
2006 *Handbook of Writing Research*. New York: Guilford Press.

Maljers, Anne, David Marsh and Dieter Wolff (eds.)
2007 *Windows on CLIL: Content and Language Integrated Learning in the European Spotlight*. The Hague: European Platform for Dutch Education.

Manchon, Rosa and Julio Roca de Larios
2007 On the temporal nature of planning in L1 and L2 composing. *Language Learning* 57: 549–593.

McCardle, Peggy and Vinita Chhabra (eds.)
2004 *The Voice of Evidence in Reading Research*. Baltimore, MD: Brookes Publishers.

Marsh, David and Dieter Wolff (eds.)
2007 *Diverse Contexts – Converging Goals: CLIL in Europe*. Frankfurt: Peter Lang.

Nation, Paul
2001 *Learning Vocabulary in Another Language*. New York: Cambridge University Press.

National Reading Panel
2000 *Teaching Children to Read: An Evidence Based Assessment of the Scientific Research Literature on Reading and its Implications for Reading Instruction*. Washington, D.C.: National Institute of Child Health and Human Development.

Olive, Thierry and C. Michael Levy (eds.)
2002 *Contemporary Tools and Techniques for Studying Writing*. Dordrecht, The Netherlands: Kluwer.

Paltridge, Brian
2001 *Genre and the Language Learning Classroom.* Ann Arbor, MI: University of Michigan.

Perfetti, Charles
1985 *Reading Ability*. New York: Oxford University Press.

Perfetti, Charles
1999 Comprehending written language: A blueprint for the reader. In: Colin Brown and Peter Hagoort (eds.), *Neurocognition of Language*, 167–208. Oxford: Oxford University Press.

Perfetti, Charles
2003 The universal grammar of reading. *Scientific Studies of Reading* 7: 3–24.

Perfetti, Charles, Nicole Landi and Jane Oakhill
2005 The acquisition of reading comprehension skill. In: Snowling and Hulme (eds.), 227–247.

Perfetti, Charles, Ying Liu and Li Hai Tan
2005 The lexical constituency model: Some implications of research on Chinese for general theories of reading. *Psychological Review* 112: 43–59.

Pressley, Michael
2002 Metacognition and self-regulated instruction. In: Alan Farstrup and S. Jay Samuels (eds.), *What Research Has to Say about Reading Instruction*, 3rd edition, 291–309. Newark, DE: International Reading Association.

Pressley, Michael
2006 *Reading Instruction that Works*. 3rd edition. New York: Guilford Press.

Pressley, Michael and Peter Afflerbach
1995 *Verbal Protocols of Reading*. Mahwah, NJ: Lawrence Erlbaum.

Pressley, Michael, Sara Dolezal, Lisa Raphael, Lindsey Mohan, Alysia Roehrig and Kristen Bogner
2003 *Motivating Primary-Grade Students*. New York: Guilford Press.

Pressley, Michael, C. J. Johnson, S. Symons, J. A. McGoldrick and J. A. Kurita
1989 Strategies that improve children's memory and comprehension of text. *The Elementary School Journal* 90: 3–32.

Ransdell, Sarah and Marie-Laure Barbier (eds.)
2002 *New Directions for Research in L2 Writing*. Dordrecht, The Netherlands: Kluwer.

Rasinski, Timothy
2003 *The Fluent Reader: Oral Reading Strategies for Building Word Recognition, Fluency, and Comprehension*. New York: Scholastic.

Rayner, Keith and Alexander Pollatsek
1989 *The Psychology of Reading*. Englewood Cliffs, NJ: Prentice Hall.

Reynolds, Dudley W.
2005 Linguistic correlates of second language literacy development: Evidence from middle-grade learner essays. *Journal of Second Language Writing* 14: 19–46.

Rijlaarsdam, Gert and Huub van den Bergh
2006 Writing process theory. In: MacArthur, Graham and Fitzgerald (eds.), 41–53.

Rijlaarsdam, Gert, Huub van den Bergh and Michel Couzijin (eds.)
2005 *Effective Teaching and Learning of Writing*. 2nd edition. Amsterdam: Kluwer.

Robinson, Marin S., Fredricka L. Stoller, Molly Costanza-Robinson and James K. Jones
2008 *Write Like a Chemist: A Guide and Resource*. New York: Oxford University Press.
Roca de Larios, Julio, Rosa Manchon, Liz Murphy and Javier Marin
2008 The foreign language writer's strategic behaviour in the allocation of time to writing processes. *Journal of Second Language Writing* 17: 30–47.
Sasaki, Miyuki
2000 Toward an empirical model of EFL writing processes: An exploratory study. *Journal of Second Language Writing* 9: 259–291.
Sasaki, Miyuki
2004 A multiple-data analysis of the 3.5-year development of EFL student writers. *Language Learning* 54: 525–582.
Schoonen, Rob, Jan Hulstijn and B. Bossers
1998 Language-dependent and language-independent knowledge in native and foreign language reading comprehension: An empirical study among Dutch students and grades 6, 8, and 10. *Language Learning* 48: 71–106.
Schoonen, Rob, Amos van Gelderen, Kees de Glopper, Jan Hulstijn, Annegien Simis, Patrick Snellings and Marie Stevenson
2003 First language and second language writing: The role of linguistic knowledge, speed of processing, and metacognitive knowledge. *Language Learning* 53: 165–202.
Shanahan, Tim
2006 Relations among oral language, reading, and writing development. In: MacArthur, Graham and Fitzgerald (eds.), 171–183.
Silva, Tony
1993 Toward an understanding of the distinct nature of L2 writing: The ESL research and its implications. *TESOL Quarterly* 27: 657–677.
Silva, Tony, Ilona Leki and Joan Carson
1997 Broadening the perspective of mainstream composition studies. *Written Communication* 14: 398–428.
Snellings, Patrick, Amos van Gelderen and Kees de Glopper
2002 Lexical retrieval: An aspect of fluent second language production that can be enhanced. *Language Learning* 52: 723–754.
Snow, Catherine, M. Susan Burns and Peg Griffin
1998 *Preventing Reading Difficulties in Young Children*. Washington, DC: National Academy Press.
Snowling, Margaret J. and Charles Hulme (eds.)
2005 *The Science of Reading: A Handbook*. Malden, MA: Blackwell.
Stahl, Katherine and Michael McKenna (eds.).
2006 *Reading Research at Work: Foundations of Effective Practice*. New York: Guilford Press.
Stahl, Steven and William Nagy
2006 *Teaching Word Meanings*. Mahwah, NJ: Lawrence Erlbaum.
Stanovich, Keith
1980 Toward an interactive-compensatory model of individual differences in the development of reading fluency. *Reading Research Quarterly* 16: 32–71.

Stanovich, Keith
2000 *Progress in Understanding Reading*. New York: Guilford Press.

Swales, John M.
1990 *Genre Analysis*. New York: Cambridge University Press.

Swales, John M.
2004 *Research Genres*. Cambridge: Cambridge University Press.

Swales, John M. and Christine B. Feak
2004 *Academic Writing for Graduate Students: Essential Tasks and Skills*. 2nd edition. Ann Arbor, MI: University of Michigan Press.

Torrance, Mark and David Galbraith (eds.)
1999 *Knowing What to Write: Conceptual Processes in Text Production*. Amsterdam: Amsterdam University Press.

Trabasso, Tom and Ellen Bouchard
2002 Teaching readers how to comprehend texts strategically. In: Block and Pressley (eds.), 176–200.

Traxler, Matthew and Morton Gernsbacher (eds.)
2006 *Handbook of Psycholinguistics*. 2nd edition. San Diego: Academic Press.

Van Gelderen, Amos, Rob Schoonen, Kees de Glopper, Jan Hulstijn, Annegien Simis, Patrick Snelling and Marie Stevenson
2004 Linguistic knowledge, processing speed, and metacognitive knowledge in first- and second-language reading comprehension: A componential analysis. *Journal of Educational Psychology* 96: 19–30.

Van Gelderen, Amos, Rob Schoonen, Reinoud Stoel, Kees de Glopper and Jan Hulstijn
2007 Development of adolescent reading comprehension in language 1 and language 2: A longitudinal analysis of constituent components. *Journal of Educational Psychology* 99: 477–491.

Wang, Min, Keiko Koda and Charles Perfetti
2003 Alphabetic and non-alphabetic L1 effects in English semantic processing: A comparison of Korean and Chinese English L2 learners. *Cognition* 95: 129–149.

Widdowson, Henry G.
1992 *Practical Stylistics*. Oxford: Oxford University Press.

Wilkinson, Robert (ed.)
2004 *Integrating Content and Language: Meeting the Challenge of a Multilingual Higher Education*. Maastricht: Maastricht University Press.

Wolff, Dieter
2009 Content and language integrated learning. See chapter 20 in this volume.

Recommended Readings

Journals Dedicated to Reading and Related Issues

Journal of Research in Reading
Reading and Writing
Reading in a Foreign Language
Reading Psychology
Reading Research Quarterly
Scientific Studies of Reading

Journals Dedicated to Writing and Related Issues

Journal of Second Language Writing
TEXT
Written Communication

Journals that Report Studies Related to Reading and Writing (and Other Topics)

Applied Linguistics
Applied Psycholinguistics: Psychological Studies of Language Processes
The Canadian Modern Language Review
English for Specific Purposes Journal
Foreign Language Annals
Journal of Educational Psychology
Language Learning: A Journal of Research in Language Studies
The Modern Language Journal
Studies in Second Language Acquisition
System
TESOL Quarterly

IV. Approaches to foreign language teaching

17. Principles of approach

Anthony P. R. Howatt

1. Introduction

The starting point for this paper is the dramatic change of direction taken by language pedagogy in the late nineteenth century which transformed the aims and methods of language teaching both to school pupils and adult learners. However, as well as discussing what the reformers were trying to achieve, we also need to be aware of what they were reacting against, namely the tension between the classical languages, which had been deeply entrenched in the grammar schools and their European equivalents for centuries, and modern foreign languages, which, at the end of the eighteenth century, after a long and reasonably successful mixture of autodidacticism and private-enterprise tuition, had staked a claim for a serious educational role in a new post-Enlightenment world. The initial response to this conflict had been a methodological compromise known to us as the Grammar Translation Method which retained most of the negative features of traditional language teaching while at the same time refusing to give modern languages what they most needed – a central role for the spoken language. Unsurprisingly, it failed.

When the bow-wave of dissatisfaction broke in the early 1880s there were essentially two ways forward: one was a new approach in the commercial adult sector, which had seen a number of innovative ideas during the century, and the other a greatly improved approach to provision in the schools where, it has to be said, change could not be expected to go too far. Apart from the other teachers (particularly in the classics departments), there were parents, examiners and of course the pupils themselves. One source of optimism, however, was an increase in the number of trained non-native speaker teachers since 1800 giving a greater sense of continuity than in the past when the maintenance of provision had been at the mercy of peripatetic native-speaking foreigners with varied talents.

As the following overview shows, language pedagogy has progressed through three very broadly defined phases since 1880:

Phase 1: 1880–1920; Reform and the Direct Method
A period of change which reformed the teaching of modern languages in schools and introduced the innovation we know as the Direct Method.

Phase 2: 1920–1970; The Oral/Structural Approach
A serious attempt to provide a scientific basis for language pedagogy which produced the Oral Method (1921) in the UK, the Oral Approach (1945) in the US, and, from the mid-1950s onwards, the Structural Approach.

Phase 3: 1970 onwards; Communicative Language Teaching
A number of initiatives under the umbrella-label Communicative Language Teaching (CTL) which aimed to include the use of language for communicative purposes in the pedagogical process.

Before moving on, we need a coherent intellectual framework which will allow us to clarify and compare methodological principles and practices as they emerge from the narrative. This framework has both external and internal features which have affected the subject in different ways. From the outside there have been influences at work which derive from the so-called 'underlying disciplines' of language pedagogy, namely linguistics (including phonetics) and the psychology of learning. These are alluded to in the paper, but there are enough excellent sources available now to excuse the absence of detail here.

The internal structure of the subject on the other hand has traditionally received rather less attention. The proposal here rests on a primary contrast between two 'macro-principles' of language pedagogy which arise from the nature of the task. The first of these (the *mimetic* principle) has its origins in the conviction that the processes of learning foreign or second languages are repeated instances of 'natural' human capacities, which are first made manifest in infancy but are available for use throughout life. If this is the 'nature' macro-principle which accords with the intuitive procedures of upbringing, then the second is its 'nurture' counterpart (the *mathetic* principle) which is moulded by the procedures of education that are rooted in the human desire to prepare and train each succeeding generation to assume conscious responsibility for the cognitive and cultural resources needed to understand and master its environment.

2. The mimetic/mathetic contrast

Language learning and language teaching are frustratingly asymmetrical in the sense already noted above that human beings have always been able to acquire foreign or second languages successfully without the assistance of instruction, though with varied results. Attempts to use pedagogical resources to emulate the success of first language acquisition have motivated many methodological proposals the key principle behind which has been the notion of replication. It is believed that if we recreate the conditions for successful language acquisition that obtained in infancy, we will enjoy the same success, because language learners are human beings and human beings are 'made that way'. In that sense the motivation is mimetic even if it is not necessarily imitative in all respects.

As we shall see, the practical results of this mimetic principle have been mixed. Everyday life does not flow through classrooms, so language teachers have had to find ways of mimicking selected aspects of it in the hope that they will turn out to be the relevant ones. The simplest strategy has been to create scripts purporting to be slices of linguistic life (i.e. dialogues), and then get the students to assimilate these samples and create similar ones for themselves. This is mimesis in its most obvious 'theatrical' form and it is probably helpful to those learners who have reasonably predictable language needs.

A recent alternative, which may be closer to the heart of the mimetic argument, has been to get learners to participate in activities or tasks that require the communicative use of language, sometimes in genuine interaction, sometimes in improvised exchanges, but whatever form the mimetic principle takes, there are two further principles which accompany it in the language classroom as in 'real life'. The first is the spoken language principle which recognises the fact that languages are naturally acquired through spoken interaction (this is not to deny written language a later role) and the second the utilitarian principle which provides the primary motivation for instruction.

This last point helps to explain why virtually all the successful instances of the mimetic paradigm have involved adult learners with practical reasons for learning foreign languages rather than school pupils for whom the supposed 'utility' of a foreign language may be too vague or lie too far in the future to count for much. In school, and particularly at secondary level, foreign languages need to fit into a broader pattern of educational provision in the form of a curriculum structured round an array of 'subjects'. This perception of language as a 'subject' to be 'mastered' rather than as a set of skills to be practised is the key feature of a mathetic pedagogy. Moreover, subjects are deemed to enjoy an autonomous existence 'outside' the individual learner who must submit to their demands as defined in the acknowledged sources (grammars, etc.).

The mathetic principle dominated the teaching of languages for millennia by virtue of the socially potent role assigned throughout the world to classical languages which have to be taught as subject matters that belong in books rather than in the streets of living cities. In the Latin west this dominance remained in force long after it could be justified by any convincing utilitarian arguments and it was wielded with some force to control the way that modern languages could be taught in schools. For instance, attempts to introduce 'natural' features such as the speech of everyday life were rejected in favour of a 'properly' mathetic account of the rules and conventions of correctly composed text.

Despite this prejudice, the spoken language is not necessarily excluded from mathetically-oriented classrooms, but it depends on what is meant by 'speech'. There is an important contrast here between intuitive spoken interaction, and consciously wrought spoken language which has its ultimate roots in written scripts. David Abercrombie was among the first to note this distinction in a paper published in 1963 where he called the former "conversation" and the latter "spoken prose". After pointing out how dependent language teaching is on the presentation of textual material (texts, dialogues, drills and exercises, etc.), he concluded his paper by observing: "it is worth remembering that when we, as language teachers, claim we are teaching the spoken language, most of the time what we are teaching is spoken prose" (Abercrombie [1963] 1965: 9). Things have moved towards genuine conversation since 1963, but the point still has some force.

We can now summarise this framework in the form of two 'paradigms' as in Table 1 with the proviso that it is usually more helpful to see them in terms of contrast rather than in terms of outright opposition. It is quite possible for instance to find them combined within a single programme of study.

Table 1. Features of mimetic / mathetic approaches

The mimetic paradigm	The mathetic paradigm
learning principles: imitation; language learning is a natural process; practice.	*learning principles:* study; a foreign language is a subject matter to be mastered; understanding.
language principle: interactive spoken language is primary; *conversation.	*language principle:* written language is primary; *spoken prose.
teaching principle: utilitarian objectives are paramount. *(according to Abercrombie 1963)	*teaching principle:* educational objectives are paramount.

3. The background to 1880; the Grammar Translation Method

As we have already noted, it is not always realised that until the late 1700s the only languages taught in European schools were the two classical languages while the study of modern foreign languages was largely autodidactic, sometimes with the help of private tutors, typically native speakers living in the local community. However, as the demands made on education started to reflect the increasingly diverse skills required in a society encountering the early effects of industrialisation, some schools began to respond to these new priorities. In the UK for instance, there were so-called 'English' (as opposed to 'Latin') schools which taught a modern curriculum based on the mother tongue including useful subjects like accountancy, navigation and foreign languages, but they never achieved the prestige of their Latin rivals.

There were stirrings elsewhere which also suggested a realignment of linguistic priorities in favour of the vernacular. In Britain, for instance, after a slow start in Scotland around 1730, the universities had moved decisively towards the rejection of Latin as the medium of instruction, bringing to an end the last utilitarian argument in favour of its presence on the school curriculum. From then onwards the classics had to rely on rather vague arguments about 'mental discipline' plus the contributions they claimed to make to the study of the mother tongue (etymology, etc.).

However, none of these practical developments had any serious impact on the prestige enjoyed by the traditionalists. The most that modern languages could expect was a condescending acceptance of the suggestion that 'some pupils' might like to take courses in 'optional' subjects such as French and German if time could be found for them, i.e. they cost extra and were time-tabled at unsocial hours. At the High School of Edinburgh, for instance, the first teacher of French was not hired until 1834 and of German twelve years later (both were native speakers), and their classes were scheduled with other option courses during the dinner break or after school. To be fair on the school, however, this action almost certainly represented the priorities of the middle-class parents who no doubt applauded the Prize-Giving Day oration in 1839 by the city's Lord Provost (equivalent to an English Lord Mayor) who, after commending the school for providing "studies which are more immediately concerned with the practical pursuits of life" (this included mathematics as well as French), waxed lyrical over "the study of the immortal languages of Greece and Rome [which] occupies a large portion of the time of the pupils [...] [about two-thirds in fact] [...] and whatever be the value of other studies, I hope never to see the day when the study of these noble languages should be discouraged as a waste of time", (Steven 1849: 254). Modern languages had a mountain to climb.

Given this background of disapproval, echoed throughout western Europe in one form or another, none of the existing foreign language textbooks serving utilitarian purposes such as conversation manuals, guides to letter-writing, dialogues, etc. were deemed suitable for use in academically reputable schools like Edinburgh High School. They had to be replaced by something better suited to the mathetic traditions of such establishments, which stressed the memorisation of grammar rules and vocabulary lists followed by the translation of 'worthwhile texts'. Modern linguists had to accept that grammar and translation were not negotiable, but they could influence the way in which the material was presented and taught to make it more palatable and effective. Traditional textbooks for Latin, some of which had been in continuous use for centuries, did no more than offer a continuous text (most of it also in Latin) and it was left to teachers to decide how much should be learnt by heart at any one time, though there were also some more adventurous authors who copied the catechistical question-answer technique used by the church. Exercises in the modern sense were unknown and the set passages were 'heard' and tested later by the teacher (this could be a brutal process, see Locke 1693).

A new textbook design did in fact emerge in Germany in the early 1780s and it was widely copied throughout Europe, eventually becoming the new standard model known to us as the Grammar Translation Method (though this label did not appear until a century or more later). The new author was a teacher of French in Frankfurt called J. V. Meidinger and his textbook, *Praktische französische Grammatik* (1783), consisted of a series of separate lesson units each with a few grammatical rules and paradigms, plus vocabulary lists for use with exercises in the form of sentences to translate into the foreign language. This was a genuinely innovative idea which was later extended to include sentences for translation into the native language. Most teachers at this time paid lip-service to the spoken language and may have included some pronunciation practice, but speech was a sensitive issue lest it should encourage scornful comments about 'tourist trivia' from the classical camp.

From the middle of the nineteenth century onwards the numbers taking modern languages in schools began to rise – partly because they were popular subjects with the increasing number of girls in full-time education – and the modest compromise represented by grammar-translation methods might have worked had it not been for the impact of public examinations which further raised the temperature of the competition with the classics. In practice the 'washback' effect of the exams was to promote an anxious defensiveness lest the teaching should be thought 'incomplete' and hence an almost neurotic concern for detail: grammar rules became finicky, word lists included increasingly rare words (particularly if they were 'exceptions'), exercise sentences packed in more grammar than sense and translation passages were designed to contain tricks and traps of all kinds. The time had come for modern languages to reject the role assigned to them as 'soft' versions of Latin and Greek and make a stand for radical reforms which would seek to reconcile the mathetic ideology of the secondary schools with the priorities of living as opposed to dead languages.

The key issue was obvious, namely a leading role for the spoken language, and this became the basic aim of the so-called Reform Movement which began to form across Europe after the publication in 1882 of Wilhelm Viëtor's famous pamphlet with its strongly worded title demanding a complete 'turn around' (*Umkehren*) in language teaching methodology (*Der Sprachunterricht muss umkehren!*). It was published under a pseudonym (later removed) which reflected the controversy surrounding the issue and Viëtor's anxiety lest his intervention might damage his career prospects.

4. Phase 1: 1880–1920; Reform and the Direct Method

The appearance of the Reform Movement and the Direct Method at more or less the same time was not entirely fortuitous. Despite their differences, they shared at least two concerns. One was of course the evident need for an improvement in language teaching which we have already touched on. The other was less obvious, namely to respond positively to the needs of learners who had hitherto been neglected because it was believed that foreign languages were 'beyond' them.

4.1. The Reform Movement

To pick up this last point about new categories of learner, it is interesting to note that Viëtor was not in the first instance addressing the highest level of the German school system, i.e. the so-called Gymnasien (grammar schools) which taught only French in addition to the classics. He was an anglicist as well as a phonetician and in the 1880s English was still excluded from the top schools because it was thought to be too easy. Before teaching at the university he had worked in 'lower level' schools known as Realgymnasien – and he was not alone among reformers in this respect (cf. Klinghardt 1888 for English and Walter 1888 for French). It also helped the Movement in general because there was less resistance to 'experimentation' than there would have been among the high flyers.

As we have seen, there were serious deficiencies in language teaching all over western Europe and reform spread quickly to France (Passy 1899), Britain (Widgery 1888; Sweet 1899), Scandinavia (Jespersen 1904) and elsewhere. But were these deficiencies merely details that could be put right with a little common sense, or did they represent a serious challenge to the mathetic principle itself? The answer lay somewhere between the two, as may be seen from the following summary of four major issues of principle that emerged from the Viëtor pamphlet and other sources:

1. The spoken language is primary in all foreign language study, and correct pronunciation is a top priority.
2. Lessons should be based on connected texts, printed in phonetic transcription, which must be presented orally by the teacher (i.e. no preparatory homework) and form the basis for question-and-answer work followed by extended speaking (e.g. re-tells) or writing (e.g. composition).
3. New grammar points should be drawn inductively out of texts which have already been studied in class.
4. The foreign language should be used as the medium of instruction wherever possible.

If the spoken language principle (1) is taken together with the connected text principle (2), then it is quite clear that what was intended was spoken prose in the Abercrombie sense and not conversation, a point further reinforced by the use of phonetic transcription. The traditionalists should have had no fears on this account – the new approach was as mathetic in intention as the old one – the reformers (many of them phoneticians) wanted to teach pronunciation properly, not to introduce 'chat', and there was no disagreement between the two camps about literature. The extended oral work in class was text-dependent and for the most part under the teacher's control (unpredictable utterances which may be difficult to monitor correctly are especially unpopular with non-native teachers). The inductive principle (3) was not an insuperable obstacle, particularly as grammar lessons were to be in the mother tongue.

So far, so good, but the foreign-language-only principle (4) was controversial, and not only for publicly admissible reasons. It also caused anxiety for teachers who lacked the necessary fluency but who could not admit this in public. This was a fair point at a time when teacher training was still inadequate, but embarrassing nonetheless. While there was a broad consensus that 'translation exercises and tests' should be avoided, being forced to explain all new words without glossing them (cf. Franke 1884) seemed excessive to many.

Setting the translation issue on one side, the reforms proved acceptable enough to most teachers, many of whom who were happy to discard some of the old techniques, e.g. teaching rules in isolation from texts, but there was inevitably a lot of variation. Once the Movement had run its course, there was little cause for further change in the schools until much later in the twentieth century when provision was expanded to include new categories of learners, including primary school children.

There was, however, a residual problem, namely nomenclature. The reformers did not settle on a name for their new approach ('reformed' did not make much sense after twenty years or more), with the result that it became confused with the Direct Method – even professionals like Harold Palmer assumed they were "generally synonymous" (Palmer [1917] 1968: 230) – and therefore with extreme anti-translation views which, as we have seen, they did not hold.

4.2. The Direct Method

Contrary to what many people think, Berlitz did not invent anything called the 'Direct Method' – in fact he stuck very closely to his own in-house label, the 'Berlitz Method' – but there is no doubt that he devised the methodology known by that name (there is possibly a French connection, cf. Passy 1899), and in doing so he provided a simple and practical set of principles and procedures which for the most part achieved their stated objectives. Above all he aimed to teach foreign languages to people who had been led to believe they could not learn them – the ordinary men and women in the street who would have run a mile from a grammar book or dictionary. Developments in the outside world meant that such people needed more than ever to speak foreign languages but the schools had failed them. In a Berlitz class they could at least make a practical start with some useful words and phrases (cf. Howatt 2004: 223–226).

The Direct Method was the first to bring to world prominence a mimetic approach to foreign language teaching, i.e. one that set out to emulate the way in which infants acquire their mother tongue: "the Berlitz Method is an imitation of the natural process by which a child learns its mother tongue" (Berlitz [1898] 2000: 1). Similar calls for a 'natural' approach to teaching languages had been common in the past (see Howatt 2004: chap.15) particularly since the attacks by Rousseau and Pestalozzi on the artificiality of all traditional language instruction intended for young children, even reading (Rousseau [1762] 1991). A more recent example was Claude Marcel, a French educationist who summed up his two-volume study in a set of principles ('axioms'), the first being: "The method of nature is the archetype of all methods, and especially of the method of learning languages" (Marcel [1853] 2000: 1, ii, iii, 216). Finally, there was Lambert Sauveur, a French contemporary of Berlitz in America, who devised a conversation-based approach described in his book: *I. Introduction to the Teaching of Living Languages without Grammar or Dictionary. II. Causeries avec mes élèves* ([1874] 2000) in which he presented 'transcripts' of these 'causeries' ('chats') which constituted his French lessons. It was later known in America as the 'Natural Method' (Kroeh 1887: 178–183). Berlitz, however, was the first to make ideas of this kind generally available by opening a chain of schools, beginning in Providence, Rhode Island in 1878, and the following is a checklist of the principles on which his work was based (Berlitz [1898] 2000), all of which are consistent with the Direct Method:

1. The primary aim of all language teaching is to teach the spoken language, understood as ordinary everyday conversation.
2. The foreign language must be used in the classroom at all times (the 'don't translate' principle). Meaning should be taught in the first instance by demonstration techniques which forge a 'direct' relationship between the foreign language word and its referent. The use of context and word definition come later.
3. The written language should play a subordinate role, and should not be introduced until the students have acquired the basics of pronunciation.
4. Grammar should be avoided.
5. Homework should never be used for advance preparation.
6. Learning a language should be like visiting the country where it is spoken, only more effective because "the language has been methodically and systematically arranged" (Berlitz [1898] 2000: 3).

There was no sign of a mathetic principle anywhere: no grammar, no translation, and no reading until after the introductory oral work was over. Conversation in the Abercrombie sense was taken as the proper aim for all foreign language learning and conversation could only be learnt through imitation and practice – an objective that was assisted by the Berlitz policy of employing only native speaker teachers who ideally should not be able to speak the learners' mother tongue. Classes were kept small, and the teachers were under strict instruction to avoid conventional schoolroom 'language lessons'. Berlitz lessons typically began with short exchanges led by the teacher, e.g. *'Is the table brown? – Yes, it is ... Is it black? – No, it is not'* (Berlitz [1898] 2000: 10) expanded into: *Is the table black? – No, it is not, it is brown,* etc. Later in the course, however, the method moved to a more text-based, question-and-answer format which resembled the Reform Movement.

"Translation is entirely abandoned" (Berlitz [1898] 2000: 1) was the most famous of the Direct Method principles and the most mimetic in intention. It was uncompromising but Berlitz defended his position by going beyond the obvious 'naturalistic' point to a more rational linguistic argument: "a knowledge of a foreign language acquired by translation is necessarily defective and incomplete; for there is by no means for every word of the one language, the exact equivalent in the other" (Berlitz [1898] 2000: 2).

The Direct Method was designed for adult learners and most attempts to take it into schools failed. One reason for this was its support for utilitarian objectives, though Berlitz always avoided explicit 'tourist talk', as the content of his lessons shows (it might be called a 'notional syllabus' today): "Lesson 1: objects and colours; Lesson 2: dimensions; Lesson 3: clothing, parts of the body; Lesson 4: place and position" etc. (Berlitz [1898] 2000: 9).

Finally, Berlitz made two further comments which link his work directly with what followed. The first is a specific, if informal, reference to habit formation: "the student forms the habit of using the foreign tongue spontaneously and easily" (Berlitz [1898] 2000: 3). And the second is the claim in Point 6 above that "the language has been methodically and systematically arranged [for the Berlitz student]" (Berlitz [1898] 2000: 3). Investigating the full implications of both these points provided the basis for much of the work in the subject over the next fifty years.

5. Phase 2: 1920–1970; The Oral/Structural Approach

5.1. The Oral Method (Harold E Palmer)

During the middle decades of the twentieth century an increasingly professionalised group of language teachers devoted their talents and energies to the search for a theoretical foundation for the scientific development of effective language pedagogy. As we have already noted, this search was focused on two issues raised by the Direct Method, namely, (a) that language learning is essentially the acquisition of a set of well-rehearsed speech habits, and (b) that these habits can be accounted for by a systematic study of the structure of language. The title of this section of the paper ('the Oral/Structural Approach') was devised to reflect these concerns.

The work began on a small scale at the University of London during the First World War with thc publication of a book with a title that summed up the pre-occupations of the whole period, namely *The Scientific Study and Teaching of Languages* by Harold Palmer, a former Direct Method teacher of English as a foreign language in Belgium who, on the outbreak of war, came to work with Daniel Jones in the Phonetics Department of University College. *The Scientific Study* (Palmer [1917] 68) was the first of three major works on the subject, the others being *The Oral Method of Teaching Languages* ([1921a] 2003), and *The Principles of Language-Study* ([1921b] 2003).

We shall be concerned mainly with the *Principles* in this paper, but we start with a preliminary comment on the *Oral Method* which drew on twelve years' teaching experience and gave Palmer a personal understanding of the strengths and weaknesses of the method, lending his work an authority that was unique in its day.

The Oral Method is a short manual for language teachers (not just teachers of English) which, as he says in the Preface (Palmer [1917] 1968: 191), arose from a suggestion by a colleague that he should write a book called *How to Conduct a Conversation Course*. It provides a coherent programme of oral practice based on a framework of categories that moves logically from 'conventional' to 'normal' conversation. The result is an attempt to make practical sense of the slippery notion of conversational interaction; it does not solve all the problems but it takes Berlitz's little exchanges *What's this? It's a book* into areas of the grammar which the Direct Method had never touched before.

It is clear from the *Oral Method* that the core of Palmer's work lay within the mimetic paradigm as outlined earlier. This is made even more explicit at the outset of *The Principles of Language-Study* ([1921b] 2003) where he advanced his theory of language acquisition claiming that "we are all endowed by nature with capacities for assimilating speech [which] are not limited to the acquiring of our mother-tongue, but are also available for one or more languages in addition." (Palmer [1921b] 2003:13). He calls these capacities 'spontaneous' and associates them with the spoken language. By contrast we need what he called our 'studial' capacities to cope with language instruction that requires deliberate, conscious study, including the written language ("nature alone will not teach us how to read or write." (Palmer [1921b] 2003: 15)).

Palmer's contrast is not unlike the more recent distinction between 'acquisition' and 'learning' (e.g. Krashen 1985), but it is more broadly drawn. We can also see connections between Palmer and Abercrombie i.e. 'spontaneous'/'conversation' and 'studial'/'spoken prose'. Also like Abercrombie, Palmer warns us not to assume that all spoken language is spontaneous and he goes out of his way to stress that most forms of oral practice are essentially 'studial' because they are designed to make us "conscious of the words and constructions we are using" (Palmer [1921b] 2003: 13).

Principles then goes on to list "nine essential principles of language-teaching":

"1. Initial preparation.
2. Habit-forming
3. Accuracy
4. Gradation
5. Proportion
6. Concreteness
7. Interest
8. Order of progression
9. Multiple line of approach" (Palmer [1921b] 2003: 79).

The idea behind Principle 1 ('Initial Preparation'), i.e. "the training of [the student's] spontaneous capacities for assimilating spoken language" (Palmer [1921b] 2003: 19), was an original one. Few if any course writers had ever taken the trouble to prepare students for the demands of learning a foreign language. Palmer believed it was essential and he included activities like ear-training, articulation exercises and some highly innovative work in listening comprehension.

Principle 2 ('Habit-forming') was crucial as the definition of the key concept of spontaneity: "we speak and understand automatically as the result of perfectly formed habits" (Palmer [1921b] 2003: 20). Assuming this to be true, drills and exercises would result in well-practised fluency provided Principle 3 ('Accuracy') was also observed: "*the student shall have no opportunity for making mistakes until he has arrived at the stage at which accurate work is reasonably to be expected*" (Palmer [1921b] 2003: 22 italics in the original).

Of the remaining six principles, the first four relate to the design of teaching programmes: Principle 4 ('Gradation') calls for "an ever-increasing rate of progress" while Principle 5 ('Proportion') requires that everything should be given equal attention. Principles 6 and 7 underline the importance of language lessons that focus on examples rather than rules and keep the student's interest.

With his last two principles Palmer returns to broader issues. Principle 8 compares modern approaches favourably with traditional ones: "the ancient school said: first learn how to form words, then learn how to form sentences, then pay attention to the 'idiomatic' phenomena, and lastly learn how to pronounce and to speak. The modern school says: first learn to form sounds, then memorise sentences, then learn systematically how to form sentences, and lastly learn how to form words," (Palmer [1921b] 2003: 28). Only the latter provides a 'rational' approach which, he claimed, would be confirmed by 'psychologists'. The list ends with Principle 9 ('The Multiple Line of Approach') which is a plea for what he describes as "judicious eclecticism" so that we can "adopt every good idea and leave the door open for [...] all that is likely to help us in our work", (Palmer [1921b] 2003: 29–30).

To follow the terminology used in the present paper, Palmer's old order, which "teaches us much about the language and its theory", is clearly mathetic, while his modern order, which "teaches us how to *use* a language", (Palmer [1921b] 2003: 29) reminds us that the mimetic approach has moved on from simplistic conversations to the more ambitious aim of 'using' a foreign language, but we need more than drills to teach us how to do that.

One final point concerns what Palmer didn't mention, namely the centrality of the text. He re-stated the case for sentences (disguised as 'habits') but in doing so jettisoned a key principle of the Reform Movement. It is not clear whether he noticed this himself at this stage, but when his Oral Method with its heavy reliance on drills ran into problems when he was teaching English in Japan in the 1920s, Palmer was persuaded to modify his approach and bring texts back centre stage.

This modification led to a new research interest in vocabulary control, a popular topic at the time in both Europe and the USA. In the mid-1930s he formed a partnership with three others: Michael West, a British colonial education officer who had recently completed a major study of reading needs in English as a second language in India (West 1926), Lawrence Faucett, an American teacher of English resident in China, and the leading American in the vocabulary field E. L.Thorndike (e.g. Thorndike 1921), and together they constructed a wordlist for use in preparing materials for the teaching of reading (Faucett et al. [1936] 2003; see also Bongers 1947). It was eventually published after the war as *A General Service List of English Words* (West 1953).

5.2. The Oral Approach (Charles C. Fries)

During the Second World War the focus of research and development in language teaching shifted from Europe to the United States which was the home of the two dominant theories that had influenced Harold Palmer in the 1920s and 30s. The first was structural linguistics which was of course the source of his dependence on sentences (later he adopted the term 'patterns') and the other the behaviourist school of psychology with it belief in the central role of habit formation. The same structuro-behaviourist partnership informed all the important American work in the field at this time such as for instance Charles C. Fries's Oral Approach (1945) and, a year or two earlier, the famous wartime project the Army Specialized Training Program (ASTP; Angiolillo 1947).

The ASTP (1943–1944) was set up by the US Army to teach a practical spoken command of 17 of the combatant languages to specially selected personnel with the appropriate academic background (ca. 15,000 altogether). The courses consisted of short, highly intensive periods of drill-and-dialogue work run by two-man teaching teams. The senior members of the team were college men with a linguistics background (in effect the first applied linguists) who prepared the teaching materials (there were no suitable oral materials, even in the 'big' languages). The other man was a native speaker with two functions: one was to act as the informant for the teaching materials and the other was to introduce them to the students and act as a so-called 'drillmaster'.

The methodology attempted to combine mimetic and mathetic approaches with two components over two days. Day 1 was devoted to a 'dramatised' presentation of the new dialogues followed by intensive drilling so that the material was mimicked and memorised (the 'mim-mem' approach as it was dubbed). On Day 2 the teaching shifted to a mathetic model for the teaching of grammar and 'background'. There was also a set book on methodology, namely Bloomfield's (1942) *Outline Guide for the Practical Study of Foreign Languages* which was originally intended as a fieldwork manual, but contains typically sensible and robust advice, e.g. "practice everything until it becomes second nature" and "remember always that a language is what the speakers do, not what someone thinks they ought to do" (Bloomfield 1942: 16). Quotes like these show how close American and British thinking were at the time, and it comes as no surprise to see Palmer's *Principles of Language-Study* on Bloomfield's reading list (the two men had in fact held a number of successful meetings when Palmer was on a US tour in 1931–1932).

The second major project, which took place at the same time, was the establishment of the English Language Institute (ELI) at the University of Michigan in 1941. The Director, Charles C. Fries, worked out an approach to teaching foreign languages which used many of the same ideas as Palmer, but gave them stronger roots in the kind of structurally-oriented descriptive linguistics associated with Bloomfield (Fries 1948). Fries's modification of Oral Method to Oral Approach reflected a looser and perhaps more mature relationship between theory and practice (cf. Anthony 1963). In 1945, however, Fries seemed to intend the phrase to be taken literally: students should approach (i.e. move towards) the task of acquiring a new language by following an intensive programme of purely oral practice which would last "throughout at least the first stage of language learning" (Fries 1945: 7), even if the eventual aim was a reading knowledge. It is also possible that Fries's personal antipathy to the term 'method' encouraged his use of 'approach' which focused as much on linguistic principles as on classroom procedures. For Fries his first responsibility was the provision of "satisfactorily selected and organised materials" (Fries 1945: 3).

Although the principles of the Oral Approach and the Oral Method shared the same theoretical roots, they contrasted in two significant respects. The first was right at the start where Palmer wanted a period of 'initial preparation', Fries insisted on a short (ca. 3 months) period of intensive pattern practice (to use the ELI term, cf. Lado and Fries 1954). Like Palmer ([1921b] 2003: 101), Fries was well aware that boredom was likely to be the Achilles heel of the approach, but practice was essential: "one must not become *impatient* to expand his vocabulary and attain fluency. Accuracy of sound, of rhythm, of intonation, of structural forms, and of arrangement, within a limited range of expression, must come first and become automatic habit before the student is ready to devote his chief attention to expanding his vocabulary." (Fries 1945: 3).

The second contrast arose from two different views of the impact of the mother tongue. Palmer did not discuss the issue in great detail, but he seemed to accept the Direct Method belief that 'natural methods' of learning meant that the new language would be acquired as a 'parallel' system to the old one; Fries on the other hand saw the old system as 'interfering' with the new one, e.g. "learning a second language after having developed great skill in the habits of our native language is a very different matter from learning our first language when no such habits had been set up."(Fries 1959: 44). To solve the problem Fries developed what he called "contrastive analysis" where the habit structures of the two languages were contrasted. Where they differed, it was predicted there would be learning difficulties needing special care and attention in the course materials. In practice, however, differences did not always predict difficulties.

During the 1950s the term 'Oral Approach' was dropped in favour of 'Structural Approach' thus highlighting the role of applied linguistics. The boredom issue, however, did not go away and the addition of recording technology in the form of the language laboratory did not help as much as was hoped (Stack 1960). This last version of structuralism was known as the Audiolingual Method (Brooks 1960), and consisted almost entirely of drills and exercises.

Table 2. Principles of the Structural Approach

1. Basic paradigm:	– mimetic
2. Learning principle:	– habit formation; accuracy
3. Language principle:	– structural patterns + controlled vocabulary; contrastive analysis
4. Teaching principles:	– new material presented in dialogues; pattern practice.

5.3. The post-war world and the return of meaning

The ideas and principles of the Oral/Structural Approach continued to embody 'the modern approach' to foreign language teaching until the end of the 1950s and on into the 60s partly because the theories of structural linguistics and behaviourist psychology on which they rested remained in circulation though criticisms had already begun by 1960 (e.g. Chomsky 1959). The 1950s was also the last decade of the old world so far as language teaching in schools was concerned and foreign languages were still largely reserved for the 'more gifted' secondary school pupils, which prolonged the legacy of the Reform Movement. There was, however, a light breeze of change blowing which grew into a wind by 1970, namely a new concern for the teaching of meaning. No longer was the teaching of form given the automatic priority which it had enjoyed since the links between 'habits' and 'structures' were formed back in the inter-war decades.

An early straw in the new wind appeared in Britain in 1950. At first it seemed little more than minor adjustment, but, with hindsight, it turned out to be much more than that. While it had always been accepted that patterns and structures had to be 'contextualised', this usually meant their inclusion in texts or dialogues. With the new concept of 'language in situations' (cf. Firth [1950] 1957), however, came the notion of using the resources of the classroom (plus pictures, if available) in order to dramatise the meaning of structures in a more memorable manner. The best-known example is the tense sequence: *I am going to open the window ... I am opening the window ... I have opened the window,* presented with the appropriate actions. Exercise routines like this were in the spirit of the Direct Method which most teachers of English as a foreign/second language followed at the time, and the Situational Approach (Hornby 1950) became popular. In India, for instance, it attracted the mnemonic label 'the SOS (Structural-Oral-Situational) Method' (Prabhu 1987: 10).

Then, around 1960 the concept of situation was enriched further in a totally new method that arrived from France towards the end of the 1950s. It was known as the Audio-Visual Method and 'method' was the appropriate term for a set of procedures which had to be learnt at special training courses run by their inventors at CREDIF in St Cloud near Paris. At the heart of the method was a situation presented as a sequence of pictures (originally on filmstrips but later in textbooks, cf. Alexander 1967) which also conveyed something of the social background to the new language (the original learners were new immigrants to France from overseas). When the situation was established, the learners listened to a tape-recorded dialogue which depicted an event or narrative that was taking place in the situation. The classroom work consisted of learning the dialogues by heart and there were also some structure exercises.

This new approach was an interesting extension of the mimetic paradigm through the use of technology (cf. Corder 1966). At first, however, the concept of situation was interpreted in a rather broad sense and research on whether the pictures could be used to predict the meaning of the language on the tape was not very convincing. Once again, the theatre metaphor of dialogues proved unsatisfactory and what was needed was a radically new principle which incorporated the notion that language is 'used' in order to get something done – not an easy notion to apply in the average classroom, but that was the direction in which the new wind was blowing.

6. Phase 3: 1970 onwards, Communicative Language Teaching

Before 1970 the only thing that mattered in learning languages was 'getting it right'. Accuracy had been a moral imperative for the old school ('following the rules') and a necessary objective for the modernists ('forming the correct habits'). One predictable result had been uniformity – all the grammar-translation textbooks contained essentially the same material, and the structuralist courses offered a highly standardised language with a controlled vocabulary, 'correct' pronunciation and so on. Gradually, however, uniformity began to give way to a new principle of diversity and new buzzwords emerged such as 'variation', 'appropriacy' and 'relevance'.

Some of the pressure for the recognition of diversity came from the proliferation of learner groups and learning purposes all of which meant the acceptance of variation and a relevant response to the ubiquitous word 'need' (e.g., Richterich 1972) so that each teaching programme could in principle be tailored to fit each requirement. Of course it could not work like that in practice, but the demands were real enough and the days of standardised provision and orthodoxy were over.

Diversity was also a major theme in the background disciplines, and particularly in the development of sociolinguistics during the 1960s promising at last a response to Palmer's remark back in 1921: "the modern order teaches us to *use* a language" (Palmer 1921b: 29). In the new functionalist world, the mimetic principle underlying the concept of 'use' meant that speaking or writing 'properly' required more than fidelity to the grammar, it also required fidelity to the way that language can be manipulated to create texts which are appropriate to the relevant conventions of discourse or, to repeat Hymes's famous dictum, to obey "rules of use without which the rules of grammar would be useless" (Hymes 1972: 278). After more than 50 years in a structural wilderness of sentence patterns, the connected text was once again paramount, but it was a connected text with implications for use – hence the interest people showed in so-called 'authentic' texts – if they wanted more than arbitrary illustrations of usage (Widdowson 1978: chap.1).

In the context of 'rules', the new Zeitgeist encouraged the view that the concept of 'error' itself should be revised to take account of the notion that, given the opportunity, learners try their new language out in order to discover what the rules are (not necessarily consciously), and in doing so make errors which should be seen as markers of (as yet incomplete) progress rather than of forgetting or 'carelessness'. In fact, if learners continue to gain experience of using the language, many errors disappear of their own accord (cf. Corder [1967] 1981). The theoretical background to Corder and Hymes was Chomsky's (1965) characterisation of language acquisition in terms of a growing intuitive knowledge of the rules of a (mental) grammar ('competence'). It was this notion that

Hymes (1972) alluded to when talking of 'rules of use' and which lay behind his hugely influential (if not always understood) expression 'communicative competence' – the source, perhaps, of the adjective in the new label: 'communicative language teaching' (CLT).

In language teaching terms this new concept of 'relevance-to-purpose' threatened to create an unwieldy number of different courses (rather like Fries's 'contrastive analysis' notion back in the 1940s), but as a first step it was possible to draw a line between lower-proficiency learners who needed 'everything' and higher-proficiency students whose needs were increasingly specific. This 'line' became the centrepiece of a major project in foreign language teaching commissioned by the Council of Europe which might be said to have set the CLT ball rolling in 1971–1972. Under the label 'The Threshold Level' and its equivalents in the other project languages, the line identified those below it as the intended audience for the project: all west European adults needing basic foreign language communication skills suitable for limited trips abroad. This in turn presupposed that at a basic level it was possible to claim that 'western Europe' was a sufficiently homogeneous category to allow course designers to use the same set of communicative categories starting from an analysis of the familiar concept of 'situation' (which we have already met above).

The outcome was an inventory of semantic (notional) and functional categories which provided material for syllabuses, teaching materials, assessment schemes, etc. across the continent (cf. Wilkins 1976). Given its mimetic orientation, it is not too surprising that the concept did not transfer easily into the secondary schools where, as we have noted before, learners do not readily see themselves as potential language users (tourists, and the like) but as actual language students. What this meant in effect is that they would turn a communicative inventory into a novel species of 'grammar' which they could then study mathetically (*if I need to ask for information in Spanish, I say* ... etc.). This may seem odd, but it makes sense in the circumstances.

What concerns school pupils most has little to do with utilitarian values, but it has everything to do with 'doing well' as the school system happens to define it at any particular time. This may help to explain the relative success of the Council of Europe categories as 'objectives' (Harding, Page and Rowell 1980).

Moving above the intermediate 'Threshold Level' line takes us into a more complex area where the main principle of generalisation did not lie in the content of communication so much as in the manner of study. This became known in language teaching circles as 'study skills' where training programmes focused on one or more of the so-called 'four skills' not for its own sake so much as a component of a professionally relevant activity, the most obvious being academic studies.

All the instances of CLT so far have including the communication of meaning as an important element in the pedagogical design of course and lesson structures, the (mimetic) aim being to prepare students to handle similar communicative events for themselves. There is, however, a different role that communication can play in a language teaching programme which is also mimetic, but in a much stronger sense. It is not enough merely to copy or imitate what people appear to be doing when they communicate – it is also necessary to do it yourself.

Contrary to what is sometimes claimed, real communication actually happens in foreign language classes all the time, but it happens accidentally and it is not always recognised because it tends to occur in a fragmented way in the interstices of other kinds of activity. It is possible that more is acquired in these moments than in much more highly organised events, but in recent times there has been an attempt to provide sustained opportunities for genuine communication (and therefore genuine acquisition) by setting up sequences of challenges or problems, usually in the form of 'tasks'. The reality principle is satisfied if the communicative challenge is met (and it can be very limited in scope and does not necessarily require speaking) – in which case the task goes on; otherwise it doesn't. Ideas along these lines were pioneered in the Bangalore Project ('Communicational Teaching Project') in the early 1980s (Prabhu 1987) and they have been expanded since.

Perhaps the most important feature of 'tasks' is that they move on from what we have called the 'theatre principle' in foreign language teaching which has been there for a long time ('situational dialogues' were, for instance, among the earliest materials for teaching French as a foreign language in England in the late 14th century, Howatt 2004: chap 1). The theatre principle tells you exactly what to say; improvisation tells you the kind of thing to say; only genuine communication forces you to work out what to say. And only genuine communication helps to push the acquisition boulder a little further up the hill.

References

Abercrombie, David
[1963] 1965 Conversation and spoken prose. *English Language Teaching* 18 (1): 10–16. (Reprinted in: David Abercrombie (ed.) 1965 *Studies in Phonetics and Linguistics*, 1–9. Oxford: Oxford University Press.)

Alexander, Louis G.
1967 *First Things First*. London: Longman.

Allen, John P. B. and Henry G. Widdowson (eds.)
1974 *English in Focus*. Oxford: Oxford University Press.

Angiolillo, Paul F.
1947 *Armed Forces Foreign Language Teaching: Critical Evaluation and Implications*. New York: Vanni.

Anthony, Edward M.
1963 Approach, method, and technique. *English Language Teaching* 17 (2): 63–67.

Axtell, James L. (ed.)
1968 *The Educational Writings of John Locke: a Critical Edition with Introduction and Notes.* (The 1705 edition of Locke's essay 'Some Thoughts Concerning Education'. Orig. publ. 1693) Cambridge: Cambridge University Press.

Bates, Matthew and Tony Dudley-Evans (eds.)
1976 *Nucleus.* London: Longman.

Berlitz, Maximilian D.
[1898] 2000 *The Berlitz Method for Teaching Modern Languages. English Part.* First Book. European Edition. 10th revised edition. Berlin et al.: Cronbach et al. (Reprinted in: Howatt and Smith (eds.) 2000, Vol. 5, Part III.)

Bloomfield, Leonard
1942 *Outline Guide for the Practical Study of Foreign Languages.* Baltimore: Linguistic Society of America.

Bongers, Herman
1947 *The History and Principles of Vocabulary Control.* Woerden: WOCOPI.

Brooks, Nelson
1960 *Language and Language Learning.* New York: Harcourt, Brace and World.

Chomsky, Noam
1959 A review of B.F. Skinner's "Verbal Behavior". *Language* 35 (1): 26–58.

Chomsky, Noam
1965 *Aspects of the Theory of Syntax.* Cambridge, Mass.: MIT Press.

Corder, S. Pit
1966 *The Visual Element in Language Teaching.* London: Longman.

Corder, S. Pit
[1967] 1981 The significance of learners' errors. *IRAL* 5 (4): 161–170. (Reprinted in: S. Pit Corder (ed.) 1981 *Error Analysis and Interlanguage*, 5–13. Oxford: Oxford University Press.)

CREDIF (Centre de Recherche et d'Etude pour la Diffusion du Français)
(various dates, ca. 1960) Courses: *Voix et images de France* (adults), *Bonjour Line* (children). Paris: Harrap-Didier.

Dakin, Julian
1973 *The Language Laboratory and Language Learning.* London: Longman.

Dunham, Fred S.
1944 The teaching of foreign languages in the army specialized training program. *University of Michigan School of Education Bulletin* 16 (1): 9–13.

Faucett, Lawrence W., Harold E. Palmer, Edward L. Thorndike and Michael P. West (eds.)
[1936] 2003 *Interim Report on Vocabulary Selection for the Teaching of English as a Foreign Language.* London: King. (Reprinted in part in: Smith (ed.) 2003, Vol. 5, 381–503.)

Firth, John R.
[1950] 1957 Personality and language in society. *The Sociological Review* 42: 37–53. (Reprinted in: 1957 *Papers in Linguistics 1934–1951*, 177–189. London: Oxford University Press.)

Franke, Felix
[1884] 2000 *Die praktische Spracherlernung auf Grund der Psychologie und der Physiologie der Sprache dargestellt.* Heilbronn: Henninger. (Reprinted in: Howatt and Smith (eds.) 2000, Vol. 2, 91–136.)

Fries, Charles C.
1945 *Teaching and Learning English as a Foreign language*. Ann Arbor: University of Michigan Press.
Fries, Charles C.
1948 As we see it. *Language Learning* 1 (1): 12–16.
Fries, Charles C.
1959 Preparation of teaching materials, practical grammars and dictionaries, especially for foreign languages. *Language Learning* 9 (1/2): 43–50.
Harding, Ann, Brian Page and Sheila Rowell
1980 *Graded Objectives in Modern Languages*. London: Centre for Information on Language Teaching and Research.
Hornby, Albert S.
1950 The situational approach in language teaching. A series of articles in *English Language Teaching* 9.
Hornby, Albert S., Edward V. Gatenby and H. Wakefield (eds.)
1952 *An Advanced Learner's Dictionary of Current English*. London: Oxford University Press.
Howatt, Anthony P. R. and Henry G. Widdowson
2004 *A History of English Language Teaching*. 2nd edition. Oxford: Oxford University Press.
Howatt, Anthony P. R. and Richard C. Smith (eds.)
2000 *Foundations of Foreign Language Teaching: Nineteenth Century Innovators*. London: Routledge.
Howatt, Anthony P. R. and Richard C. Smith (eds.)
2002 *Modern Language Teaching: the Reform Movement*. London: Routledge.
Hymes, Dell
1972 On communicative competence. In: John B. Pride and Janet Holmes (eds.), *Sociolinguistics: Selected Readings*, 269–293. Harmondsworth: Penguin.
Jespersen, Otto
[1904] 2002 *How to Teach a Foreign Language*. London: Swan Sonnenschein. (Reprinted in: Howatt and Smith (eds.) 2002, Vol. 4, 459–658.)
Klinghardt, Hermann
[1888] 2002 *Ein Jahr Erfahrungen mit der neuen Methode*. Marburg: Elwert. (Reprinted in: Howatt and Smith (eds.) 2002, Vol. 3, 13–104.)
Krashen, Stephen D.
1985 *The Input Hypothesis: Issues and Implications*. London: Longman.
Kroeh, Charles F.
1887 Methods of teaching modern languages. *Transactions and Proceedings of the Modern Language Association of America* 3: 169–185.
Lado, Robert and Charles C. Fries
1954–1958 *An Intensive Course in English*. Ann Arbor: University of Michigan Press.
Locke, John
1693 see Axtell (ed.1968)
Marcel, Claude
[1853] 2000 *Language as a Means of Mental Culture and International Communication*. London: Chapman and Hall. (Reprinted in: Howatt and Smith (eds.) 2000, Vol. 2/3.)

Meidinger, Johann V.
1783 *Praktische französische Grammatik.* Frankfurt.

Palmer, Harold E.
[1917] 1968 *The Scientific Study and Teaching of Languages.* London: Harrap. (1917. Republished by Oxford University Press, edited by D. Harper, 1968.)

Palmer, Harold E.
[1921a] 2003 *The Oral Method of Teaching Languages.* Cambridge: Heffer. (Orig. publ. 1921. Second impression (1922) reproduced in: Smith (ed.) 2003, Vol. 2, 187–334.)

Palmer, Harold E.
[1921b] [1964] 2003 *The Principles of Language-Study.* London: Harrap.1921. (Republished by Oxford University Press, edited by R. Mackin, 1964.
Reproduced in: Smith (ed.) 2003, Vol. 2, 1–186. [Page references derive from Smith (ed. 2003). Mackin (ed.1964) re-orders the introductory Synopsis (the source of many references) to the end of the book.])

Passy, Paul
[1899] 2002 *De la Méthode Directe dans l'Enseignement des Langues Vivantes.* Paris: Colin. (Reprinted in Howatt and Smith (eds.) 2002, Vol. 3, 485–517)

Prabhu, N. S.
1987 *Second Language Pedagogy.* Oxford: Oxford University Press.

Richterich, René
1972 *A Model for the Definition of Language Needs of Adults Learning a Modern Language.* Strasbourg: Council of Europe.

Rousseau, Jean-Jacques
[1762] 1991 *Emile, or on Education.* London: Penguin.

Sauveur, Lambert
[1874] 2000 I. *Introduction to the Teaching of Living Languages without Grammar or Dictionary.* II. *Causeries avec mes élèves.* Boston: Schoenhof and Moeller et al. (Reprinted in: Howatt and Smith (eds.) 2000, Vol. 5)

Smith, Richard C. (ed.)
2003 *Teaching English as a Foreign Language 1912–1936: Pioneers of ELT.* London: Routledge.

Stack, Edward M.
1960 *The Language Laboratory and Modern Language Teaching.* New York: Oxford University Press.

Steven, William
1849 *The History of the High School of Edinburgh.* Edinburgh: Maclachlan and Stewart.

Sweet, Henry
[1899] [1964] 2002 *The Practical Study of Languages: a Guide for Teachers and Learners.* London: Dent. (Republished by Oxford University Press, 1964, edited by R. Mackin. Reprinted in: Howatt and Smith (eds.) 2002, Vol. 4, 143–438)

Thorndike, Edward L.
1921 *The Teacher's Word Book.* New York: Teachers' College, Columbia University.

Viëtor, Wilhelm
[1882] 2002 *Der Sprachunterricht muss umkehren! Ein Beitrag zur Überbürdungsfrage.* (Under pseudonym 'Quousque Tandem'. Heilbronn: Henninger. Second edition, under his own name, in 1886, reprinted in: Howatt and Smith (eds.) 2002, Vol. 2, 1–40).

Walter, Max
[1888] 2002 *Der französische Klassenunterricht auf der Unterstufe: Entwurf eines Lehrplans.* Marburg: Elwert. (Second edition (1906) reprinted in: Howatt and Smith (eds.) 2002, Vol. 3, 105–194).

West, Michael
[1926] 2003 *Bilingualism (with Special Reference to Bengal).* Calcutta: Government of India. (Reprinted in: Smith (ed.) 2003, Vol. 3, 1–392).

West, Michael (ed.)
1953 A *General Service List of English Words.* London: Longmans/Green.

Widdowson, Henry G.
1978 *Teaching Language as Communication.* Oxford: Oxford University Press.

Widgery, William H.
[1888] 2002 *The Teaching of Languages in Schools.* London: Nutt. (Reprinted in: Howatt and Smith (eds.) 2002, 1–82).

Wilkins, David A.
1976 *Notional Syllabuses.* Oxford: Oxford University Press.

Recommended Readings

Not a great deal of reading is available in the history of language teaching per se but there are local sources covering the history of educational change in different parts of the world which will include details on the role of languages. It is likely that these narratives will parallel the one outlined above where the study of written texts in classical languages gave way to the acquisition of a practical spoken command of one or more modern languages. In addition to the general sources listed above, e.g. Stern (1983) and Howatt (2004), there is L.G. Kelly's deservedly famous thematic study 25 Centuries of Language Teaching (1969) which contains a substantial bibliography, and two more recent works with more specific objectives, namely Brumfit and Johnson's (1979) collection of foundation articles relating to Communicative Language Teaching and Richards and Rodgers' (1986) account which describes less well-known methods such as the 'Silent Way'. The facsimile collections listed earlier by Howatt and Smith (eds. 2000, 2002) and, more particularly, Smith (ed. 2003) give a vivid picture of what was actually being said and done at particular times. Finally, most language teaching journals, including *English Language Teaching Journal*, publish historical articles from time to time. The new references which do not appear in the main bibliography are:

Brumfit, Christopher J. and Keith Johnson (eds.)
1979 *The Communicative Approach to Language Teaching.* Oxford: Oxford University Press.

Kelly, Louis G.
1969 *25 Centuries of Language Teaching, 500 BC–1969.* Rowley, Mass.: Newbury House.

Richards, Jack C. and Theodore S. Rodgers
1986 *Approaches and Methods in Language Teaching: a Description and Analysis.* Cambridge: Cambridge University Press.

18. Communicative language teaching

Michael Byram and Marí del Carmen Méndez García

1. Introduction

Communicative Language Teaching (CLT) is often called an 'approach' and this indicates that there arose in the last few decades of the 20th century a certain mistrust of 'methods'. From the beginning of the modern age of foreign language teaching, marked by Viëtor's famous call for language teaching to start afresh (*Der Sprachunterricht muß umkehren*) in 1882, there have been many methods attempting to respond to the need to teach languages for purposes of communication. The major challenge has been to teach spoken language, since those who already learnt languages for purposes of reading the literature, philosophy and other cultural products of a country by studying grammar and practising translation could easily adapt their skills to writing. New methods often revealed their emphasis on spoken language by their titles – 'oral method', 'audio-lingual method' – but failed to recognise adequately the differences between spoken and written language and continued to make grammar the main focus and the acquisition of grammatical knowledge and skill the main task for learners. The focus of CLT changed the emphasis from almost exclusive attention to grammatical competence by identifying other competences which are crucial in communicating through speech. In this sense, the most outstanding by-product of CLT has been a change in the 'object' that is taught and learnt.

2. History of communicative language teaching

According to Brumfit and Johnson (1979: 24–25), there are three main areas of enquiry which have played an important part in CLT:

- The sociolinguistic, with Hymes, Gumperz and Goffman, among others working on ethnography of speaking, ethnomethodology and anthropology.
- The philosophical, with language philosophers like Grice, Austin and Searle emphasising 'speech acts'.
- The linguistic, with Ross, Fillmore and Lakoff reacting against Chomsky's centrality of syntax and their development of generative semantics, and with Halliday, McIntosh and Strevens (1964) and Crystal and Davy (1969) on discourse analysis.

In contrast, Savignon (1997: 10) differentiates between two broad areas, one theoretical and one practical: "The former comes from the discussions in psychology, linguistics, and communication theory; the latter comes from pedagogical needs and concerns". More comprehensively, Stern (1992: 11–13) points to two scientific and three pedagogic sources:

- Numerous linguistic studies which were ultimately adopted in second language teaching: sociolinguistic by Hymes and Labov, philosophical on the part of language philosophers such as Grice, Austin and Searle and purely linguistic like Firth's and Halliday's. The communicative approach originates, among others, from the pedagogic proposals, on the basis of these purely linguistic sources, of Widdowson and Candlin in the United Kingdom.
- Research in foreign language teaching which came to the conclusion that a more flexible and individualised approach is needed given that the learner builds his/her own competence in the foreign language independently and not necessarily according to the gradation of the syllabus.
- The Council of Europe Modern Languages Project with a clear emphasis on foreign language teaching according to learners' needs and its attempts to build a situational, notional and functional syllabus, with van Ek, Alexander and Wilkins conducting most of the studies in this area.
- The presence of a communicative curriculum that results from Canadian experiments of linguistic immersion in French.
- The humanistic approaches in the United States which advocate the role of human relationships in the teaching and learning process versus the previous all-important and impersonal teacher-centred approaches.

It is evident therefore that the history of CLT is under some dispute at least with respect to the emphases given to different sources of change.

2.1. Theories of language and communication

The differences among the sources cited above may be a consequence of the fact that the evolution of CLT has taken place in various forms in Europe and North America, two strands which have been surprisingly independent. On the one hand, in the USA the development can be traced from the critique by Hymes of Chomskyan, and ultimately Bloomfieldian, perspectives on language learning. In Europe, the origins can also be traced to the work of anthropologists and linguists (particularly in Britain, with a long linguistic tradition), but also to the work of the Council of Europe and the *Common European Framework of Reference* establishing different levels of second and foreign language proficiency to cater for the linguistic needs of an increasingly influential new population of immigrants and guest workers (Savignon 2000).

The introduction of the terms 'competence' and 'communicative competence', their evolution and the debate they have given rise to constitute one of the most important contributions of general linguistics to applied linguistics and, through the latter, to the pedagogy of foreign languages in the last third of the twentieth century.

It was the North-American linguist Noam Chomsky who, when defining the object of study of general linguistics, coined the term 'competence' in opposition to 'performance': "We thus make a fundamental distinction between competence (the speaker-hearer's knowledge of his language) and performance (the actual use of language in concrete situations)" (1965: 3–4). In doing so Chomsky alludes to a similar distinction made by the Swiss linguist Ferdinand de Saussure a few decades before. However where Chomsky places the distinction within the individual, Saussure argues that language has a social dimension 'langue' and an individual dimension 'parole', that together they are 'langage' and that the two are interdependent:

> "un côté individuel et un côté social. Le côté individuel du langage serait représenté par la parole. La parole précéderait la langue et permettrait son établissement. En retour, la langue serait nécessaire pour que la parole soit intelligible et produise tous ses effets" (Saussure[1916] 1972: 24).

Both Chomsky and Saussure suggest that linguistics should ignore the idiosyncrasies of the individual, and Chomsky does this by the idealisation implicit in the concept of the speaker-listener's competence since, as he argues,

> "Linguistic theory is concerned primarily with an ideal speaker-listener, in a completely homogeneous speech-community, who knows its language perfectly and is unaffected by such grammatically irrelevant conditions as memory limitations, distractions, shifts of attention and interest, and errors (random or characteristic) in applying his knowledge of the language in actual performance" (Chomsky 1965: 3).

The American anthropologist Hymes' reaction to Chomsky's definition of 'competence' initiated a heated debate upon language and the study of language which, in the long run, culminated in CLT. Hymes (1972: 272) draws a parallel between the 'perfection' linked to the notion of competence or, as he calls it, the 'Garden of Eden view', and the 'imperfection' of performance. He emphasises (1972: 277) that a theory of language should not only include grammaticality but also acceptability. This introduced the social dimension which Chomsky had ignored, since acceptability involves utterances by one person being accepted by another. As a consequence Hymes' definition of 'competence' incorporates both knowledge and ability for use:

> "I should take competence as the most general term for the capabilities of a person [...] Competence is dependent upon both (tacit) knowledge and (ability for) use. Knowledge is distinct, then, both from competence (as its part) and from systemic possibility (to which its relation is an empirical matter)" (Hymes 1972: 283).

He thus emphasises the inclusion of two spheres 'the linguistic and the cultural' in a theory of 'communicative competence', an expression he coins and defines as "That aspect of our competence that enables us to convey and interpret messages and to negotiate meanings interpersonally within specific contexts" (Brown 1994: 227). However, despite the original statement, the emphasis on the cultural took second place to emphasis on the functional and as Roberts et al. (2001: 25) argue, a more recent return to the cultural involves a critique of CLT, as we shall see below.

On the other side of the Atlantic, the British linguist Halliday worked on a different but related area, the relationship between grammatical structure and discourse. In a joint publication with Hasan (1976), Halliday highlights the role of cohesion as a binding element in discourse, the interpretation of one element depending on the interpretation of the others. Individually, one of the most notable contributions of Halliday is his definition of language as 'meaning potential' or "sets of options, or alternatives, in meaning, that are available to the speaker-hearer" (1979: 27). Savignon (2000) draws a parallel between Hymes' communicative competence and Halliday's meaning potential for the emphasis both put on language as social behaviour. Halliday's theory of communicative competence explicitly deals with the functions of language and explores language use in its context of situation, a term taken from the British anthropologist Malinowski, and Savignon (1997: 18–19) suggests that both Hymes and Halliday are in debt to Malinowski and Firth. Malinowski (1923, 1935) worked on little known languages and the problems of meaning equivalence in translation, and his term 'context of situation' was then expanded and applied by the British linguist Firth (1930, 1937). More recently, Widdowson has argued that Hymes and Halliday when referring to 'functions' were talking about different things. In the case of Halliday, the focus is on the potential for making meanings which are inherent in "the functions that (a language) has evolved to serve" and which are part of the language system (Widdowson 2007: 216). In the case of Hymes, function refers to the pragmatic realisation of meaning, including its appropriateness which is dependent on the particular circumstances, not the language system itself. What is deemed appropriate, in Widdowson's view, is not a matter of what native speakers – a term difficult to define in itself (Davies 2003) – have produced in the past, but what language learners can do with language in their own right, a view also found in Kramsch (1993).

Other language philosophers like Grice (1957), Austin (1962) and Searle (1969) followed Wittgenstein's analysis of language games by focusing on rules beyond the grammatical that account for the interpretation of discourse in society. Austin's (1962) subtly titled book *How to do things with words* emphasises that language has many more functions than the descriptive. Yet it is description which was the main function present in use of language in the foreign language classroom. Austin's theory of speech acts stated that rather than representing the world in their talk, people do something, and when listening, they expect something to be done with language. The success of talk rests not so much on its truth but more on the appropriacy of speech acts in a given time and place of interaction with others. This emphasis on 'speech acts', to use the title of Searle's influential book (1969), lies behind the development by Wilkins (1979a, 1979b) and others of a language syllabus for learners which identified the functions they might need language to serve and the notions they might need language to express for them.

In Germany, the concept of communicative competence is more readily associated with the work of Jürgen Habermas. Habermas (1970) builds on Austin's work and identifies different kinds of effects – or, as they would be termed in the Anglo-Saxon tradition, functions – that can be achieved by speakers and hearers. Acceptability of language is the extra dimension which Hymes added to Chomsky's criteria for judging utterances, but Habermas extends this to the notion of rationality in a community of communication. Successful communication depends on a shared understanding of the validity of the truth claims implicit in what is being said, although some claims cannot be tested by providing evidence since they are evaluative and reflect different values of different social groups. Thus although rationality in communication is fundamental and potentially universal, in the application of a theory of rational communication, there is a need for a meeting halfway between different value and moral positions (Warnke 1995). Habermas's work thus offers a potential for introducing a moral perspective into language teaching, but unfortunately this has not been recognised in the dominant versions of CLT which have stemmed from the two main strands discussed above.

Howatt summarises these changes in the understanding of language behind developments in language teaching by saying that language is not independent in itself but part of a theory of human communication: "Language, in other words, plays a role in a broader theory of communication. The starting-point is sociological: the roles people adopt, their rights and obligations, and the unspoken contracts they enter into to preserve communication" (1984: 276–277).

2.2. Theories of learning and teaching

At the same time as research on language from different but related fields such as linguistics, sociolinguistics and the philosophy of language was being conducted in Europe and America, new studies on psychology revealed that human learning, including language learning, cannot be explained by patterns of stimulus-response, but require a much more complex process in which the mind is actively processing information, establishing connections between old and new information and, in short, re-discovering and re-categorising the world (Howatt 1984: 284). The behaviourist theory of language learning which had been famously criticised by Chomsky (1965) was replaced by a cognitive constructivist view of human learning. However, the impact on language teaching of the fast growing field of Second Language Acquisition research remained and remains negligible, also in the realisation of the communicative approach, and one of its proponents has suggested that there is little to be taken into the classroom from SLA (Long 2000).

On the other hand, a theory of the relationship between 'acquisition' and 'learning' promoted by Stephen Krashen (1987, 1988) has been accepted by many methodologists, leading to the view that language cannot be learnt but only acquired in favourable circumstances, and this implies that language cannot be 'taught' but only 'caught' in the classroom. The role of the teacher is therefore merely to provide appropriate circumstances. Although considered by some SLA specialists to be simplistic and a poor theory because it is not verifiable, it is precisely because of its attractive simplicity that Krashen's 'monitor model' has been linked to CLT. Teachers seeking to promote communicative competence thus place more emphasis on activities which draw learners' attention to content rather than form in language, to 'doing things with words' as Austin (1962) might say.

The most developed version of this is in immersion education where children are educated in a foreign language, most well known in the programmes developed in Canada but in fact also well established in a number of European countries for many years, not least in Central and Eastern European countries such as the Czech Republic, Hungary and Bulgaria. A modified version of this, where only some subjects are taught through a foreign language and specific teaching techniques are being developed, has become common in western European countries in the form of 'Content and Language Integrated Learning' (CLIL).

2.3. Methodology

The contribution of different disciplines to CLT was an achievement in itself, an interdisciplinary framework evolving slowly in language teaching until the 1960s–70s. This was in Howatt's view new: "In the past, the diffusion of new ideas into the teaching profession from contributory theoretical disciplines such as linguistics had been relatively slow" (1984: 273). Widdowson in particular was influential in English Language Teaching, a field which was nurtured by a world-wide interest in the power of English, and which was then followed by practitioners of other languages. He underscored the necessity of studying language not with the sentence as the ultimate unit of meaning, but with discourse, understood as how sentences combine in texts and how they are used to 'perform communicative acts': "in general, language teachers have paid little attention to the way sentences are used in combination to form stretches of connected discourse. [...] Once we accept the need to teach language as communication, we can obviously no longer think of language in terms only of sentences" (1979: 49–50).

The echoes from theories outlined in the previous section are clear and, as far as methodology is concerned, the communicative approach was also a reaction to previous approaches, in particular structural methodology, methods and syllabuses, that failed to present and explore language for communication. Structural approaches, such as the audio-lingual method, carefully graded linguistic structures that were practised in intensive oral drills and had error avoidance as one of their chief aims. Repetition, followed gradually by substitution, aimed at creating a set of automatic and correct responses on the part of the learner. This approach was grounded in behaviourism which defined language learning as a set of habits (responses) conditioned and cued by certain words or phrases or situations (stimuli). In addition to the criticisms of behaviourism, two of the most evident methodological drawbacks of the approach were that audio-lingual gradation, at its best for beginners, presented serious obstacles in intermediate and advanced material (Allen and Widdowson 1979: 123) and that the teacher became the centre of the classroom activity (Savignon 1997: 25).

There were two strands in the development of CLT methodology: the definition of objectives and syllabuses, the 'what' of language teaching, and the determination of appropriate methods, the 'how'.

Wilkins (1979a: 82) believes that most textbooks produced until the 1970s had a grammatical syllabus as their basis. The grammatical syllabus, emerging from grammar-translation, audio-lingual, audio-visual and other methods, presents disadvantages such as the difficulty of applying the grammatical knowledge to communication acts, the low motivation observed in language learners, the inefficiency of teaching "the entire system regardless of the fact that not all parts of the system will be equally useful for learners", or the emphasis on the grammatical form, to which the meaning is subordinated (Wilkins 1979a: 82–83).

Alternative definitions of what is to be learnt, and corresponding syllabuses, started from the notion of communication. On the one hand, situational syllabuses appeared at the end of the 1960s and clearly departed from grammatical structures as the main criteria in syllabus design. Wilkins acknowledges the significance for communication purposes of considering the context of situation – the concept introduced by Firth, as pointed out above. A situational syllabus "is based upon *predictions of the situations in which the learner is likely to operate* [emphasis ours] through the foreign language" (1979a: 83). However, even though the situational syllabus can enhance learners' motivation, it is possible to predict all the situations a learner may need at best only in courses of Languages for Specific Purposes where some success was achieved. On the other hand, in general language courses, in schools and universities, the impossibility of prediction rules out situational syllabuses. As Howatt puts it, "there was no future in continuing to pursue the chimera of predicting language on the basis of situational events" (1984: 280).

In contrast, the notional syllabus was seen as productive for CLT. For Wilkins (1979a), grammatical syllabuses answered the question 'how' to produce language, whereas situational syllabuses answered the questions 'when' and 'where', and what was needed was a syllabus that considered "the *content* of probable utterances and from this it will be possible to determine which *forms* of language will be most valuable to the learner. The result will be a *semantic* or *notional syllabus*, which establishes the grammatical means by which the relevant notions are expressed" Wilkins (1979a: 86–89). The value of such a syllabus resides in the consideration of the communicative power of the language taught. Wilkins (1979a: 86–89) identifies two types of notional category: semantico-grammatical categories (time, quantity, space, matter, case and deixis), and categories of communicative function (modality, moral, suasion, argument, rational enquiry and exposition, personal emotions, emotional relations and interpersonal relations). The notional approach is based upon the view that languages realise differently the same underlying notions, and on this basis, van Ek (1979: 105–113) proposed a framework of language learning components that have to be specified for each syllabus: a) situations, b) social roles, c) psychological roles, d) settings, e) topics, f) language functions. Thus to the category of 'specific notions', lists of 'language functions' are added, which gives this approach the name notional-functional (Howatt 1984: 282).

Nonetheless, as Wilkins sees it, the knowledge of the grammatical system is the only one which allows the study of language systematically and "if a notional and functional approach is to be a serious alternative to either of these, it must be able to offer generalizations of equal or greater power" (Wilkins 1979b: 92). As we shall see below, this remains an un-resolved problem and weakness of teaching based exclusively on a notional-functional syllabus, and has led to a search for syllabuses and teaching which integrate the notional-functional and the grammatical. The issue is acknowledged in van Ek and Trim's *Threshold Level 1990*, which has become the basis for the many 'Threshold Levels' for different languages developed by the Council of Europe (www.coe.int/lang), and *Threshold Level 1990* contains an appended 'Grammatical summary' which characterises the "resources required for the realisation of the range of functions" (van Ek and Trim 1991: 129).

In addition to this strand of thinking which helps teachers and others to determine 'what' is to be taught, there is a need to reflect on the techniques of teaching the 'how'. This starts with the analysis of what competences learners need. On the theoretical arguments outlined earlier, the relationship between language, sociocultural aspects and communicative competence began to be explored by methodologists. The most influential formulation of the sub-competences making up an overarching communicative competence was put forward by Canale and Swain (1980) and Canale (1983). Canale and Swain made explicit the rationale underlying their fourfold components of communicative competence:

> Following Morrow (1977), we understand communication to be based in sociocultural, interpersonal interaction, to involve unpredictability and creativity, to take place in a discourse and sociocultural context […] We assume with Candlin (1978) that the relationship between a proposition (or the literal meaning of an utterance) and its social meaning is variable across different sociocultural and discourse contexts. […] We also agree with Palmer (1978) that genuine communication involves the 'reduction of uncertainty' on behalf of the participants. (Canale and Swain 1980: 29)

For Canale and Swain (1980: 7–11) the individual able to communicate successfully by means of language, that is to say, the individual who possesses communicative competence, should exhibit:

- Grammatical competence: "Knowledge of lexical terms and rules of morphology, syntax, sentence-grammar, semantics, and phonology".
- Sociolinguistic competence: "This component is made up of two sets of rules: sociocultural rules of use and rules of discourse".
- Discourse competence: "This type of competence concerns mastery of how to combine grammatical forms and meanings to achieve a unified spoken or written text in different genres. […] Unity of a text is achieved through cohesion in form and coherence in meaning".
- Strategic competence: "This component will be made up of verbal and non-verbal communication strategies that may be called into action to compensate for breakdowns in communication due to performance variables or to insufficient competence".

The Council of Europe's work, on the other hand has been based on a slightly different definition by van Ek, which includes, in addition to the ones in Canale and Swain's list:

- sociocultural competence: every language is situated in a sociocultural context and implies the use of a particular reference frame which is partly different from that of the foreign language learner; sociocultural competence presupposes a certain degree of familiarity with that context (van Ek 1986: 35)
- social competence: involves both the will and the skill to interact with others, involving motivation, attitude, self-confidence, empathy and the ability to handle social situations (van Ek 1986: 65)

Techniques for providing the learning environment in which all these competences can be acquired, as well as techniques for making learners conscious of what they are learning, have proliferated ever since. One such is the creation of a 'communication gap' where learners, usually in pairs, have to share information in order to solve a problem and in doing so have their attention directed to the information rather than the language forms in which it is couched. There is however a lack of principles to which such techniques refer, other than the importance of paying attention to the meaning potential of language, as in the information gap technique, and the belief that there has to be a combination of unconscious acquisition and conscious learning.

In summary, the history of language teaching in the modern age reveals a search for a theory of language, a theory of language learning and a related methodology/theory of teaching whose source lies in the need to use language for both oral and written interaction with speakers and writers (and their texts) expressing themselves in a foreign language. CLT is thus a continuation – some would say the culmination – of that search and one of the most recent and influential responses to the demands of the Reform Movement in the late 19th century for a fresh start. It now has a history of development over several decades and a consolidated position, but has also begun to be criticised. In the next sections we will present the current situation and the controversies which are beginning to arise.

3. State of the art

The consolidation of CLT began in the 1980s and in 1981 Littlewood, in an influential book on methodology, saw CLT as facilitating not only the study of language forms, but also "what people *do* with these forms when they want to communicate with each other", together with the development of "strategies for relating these structures to their communicative functions in real situations and real time" (1981, x–xi). Thus, four broad domains constitute an individual's communicative competence: linguistic competence, communicative functions, skills and strategies for using language in concrete situations and the social meaning of language forms (Littlewood 1981: 6).

More recently, Savignon (1997: 14) links communication with "expression, interpretation and negotiation of meaning" and considers communicative competence as a dynamic concept dependent on participants' degree of involvement in the communication process. With the language class in mind, Savignon defines communicative competence as "the ability of classroom language learners to interact with other speakers, to make meaning, as distinct from their ability to recite dialogues or perform on discrete-point tests of grammatical knowledge" (2000: 125). Savignon, too, emphasises the need to go beyond linguistic competence and to develop learners' communicative competence also in terms of strategic and sociolinguistic competence.

3.1. Current principles

The following is a summary of the main principles of the communicative approach as stated by Savignon (1972, 2000), Widdowson (1978), Canale and Swain (1980), Littlewood (1981), Canale (1983), Brown (1994), Bestard and Pérez (1992), and Ur (1996):

3.1.1. *Goal*

The main goal of the communicative approach is to favour the individual's development of communicative competence, a complex framework in which psychological, sociocultural, physical and linguistic elements come into play.

3.1.2. *Syllabus design*

Without excluding grammar, the need for the inclusion of a not exclusively formal organisation of the content is stressed. Additionally, the syllabus has to be built on elements such as general knowledge about language and its possibilities for communication, specific linguistic knowledge of the target language and sociocultural aspects linked to it.

3.1.3. *Methodology*

To reach communicative competence the learner has to be given the opportunity to practise and internalise not only grammatical structures but also discourse, sociocultural or strategic factors. Interpersonal communication, mutual interaction and understanding among learners and between learners and the teacher, is at the heart of the teaching and learning process. Communicative activities intend likewise to improve learners' motivation and to allow natural learning.

All the activities respond to learners' communicative needs and have to make sure that the interaction they lead to reflects genuine communication. Authentic materials, creativity and unpredictability play a significant role. Although the activities have the communicative use of the language, and not linguistic manipulation, as their main aim, the mastering of the linguistic rules is viewed as equally necessary and, therefore, facilitated through contextualised activities.

Such a methodology requires learners' development of coping strategies such as asking for information, seeking clarification, using circumlocution, in short, all the means required for a real negotiation of meaning. Communicative competence, hence, depends on the cooperation of the participants.

3.1.4. *Techniques*

In addition to established techniques for presentation and practice of new language items, opinion and information gap techniques are used with a view to arousing learners' interest, whereas role play and drama (Fleming 2000) aims at promoting interaction within the classroom in a way similar to what takes place outside it.

3.1.5. Language

Acceptability and fluency are given priority over grammatical accuracy, which means that the learner is encouraged to prioritise meaningful over grammatically correct utterances.

Authentic discourse in the target language, both in its oral and written form and in its situational, social and cultural context, becomes not only the object of study, but also a privileged tool in itself since its use within the classroom contributes to increasing learners' communicative competence.

Language use is creative and allows for the expression of meaning in a gamut of choices. As part of a wider focus on social interaction, language use depends on the participants, the situation and the goal of the communication.

3.1.6. Teachers and learners

Needless to say, teachers themselves have to be communicatively competent in the target language although, apart from a source of knowledge, teachers are mainly considered facilitators to help learners develop their communicative competence.

As a result, the learner, as the individual ultimately responsible for their learning, becomes the central figure of the process, which requires a high degree of involvement and participation. Consequently, learners' needs and interests require careful consideration, and the approach becomes 'learner-centred' with the pursuit of 'learner autonomy' being a preferred aim (Gremmo and Riley 1995)

3.1.7. Error correction and assessment

Errors are explicitly dealt with when they interfere in communication but if they do not interfere in communication, they are only pointed out if the learner makes them regularly. Errors are a necessary part of an evolving 'interlanguage' (Selinker 1992).

In terms of assessment, both learners' knowledge and the way it is put into practice in communication have to be given consideration with fluency rather than grammatical accuracy as the main assessment criterion. Therefore, the assessment is based on criteria such as fluency, comprehensibility, effort and interaction in improvised communicative tasks. Testing tools such as essay writing, in-class presentations and learners' portfolios (poems, reports, stories, videotapes, etc.) are considered to encapsulate and reveal learners' communicative competence.

3.2. Dissemination

The endorsement of CLT by influential theorists and teacher trainers in English Language Teaching led to a rapid dissemination of the principles, and reference to the aims of CLT can be found in language education policy statements throughout the world. In languages other than English the development was a little slower but followed essentially the same path. Unlike the resistance to the demands of the Reform Movement at the end of the 19th century, and consequent compromises in methods developed in the first half of the twentieth century, (Schilder 2000; Hüllen 2005: 104–109), the welcome for CLT has been warm and widespread. There are however criticisms and controversies, not least of the inappropriateness of CLT in certain education traditions, of the impracticality in some classrooms, and of the limitations it places on the purposes of foreign language as education.

4. Controversial issues

The contributions of the communicative approach to foreign language teaching are widely acknowledged. However, from the last two decades of the twentieth century, different critiques of CLT have given way to what has been termed a 'post-communicative' or 'post-methodological' period.

4.1. The significance of 'communication'

The term 'communicative approach' itself is labelled as a 'misnomer' by Nunan, who makes clear that there is not a unique communicative framework, but rather a family of approaches, each member of which claims to be 'communicative' (in fact, it is difficult to find approaches which claim not to be communicative!). There is also frequent disagreement between different members of 'the communicative family' (1989: 12). Like Nunan, Stern seems to imply that, like many preceding methods and approaches, the term 'communicative' runs the risk of being a passing fashion: "While some years ago everything in language pedagogy was 'audiolingual' and 'structural', 'communication' and 'communicative' have taken over the dubious privilege of being the fashionable terms today" (1992: 11).

An extreme view is presented by Swan (1985a), who considers the communicative approach to be, like its predecessors, a dogma with a limited contribution to language teaching and scarce novelty in its standpoints:

"Along with its many virtues, [...] it over-generalises valid but limited insights until they become virtually meaningless; it makes exaggerated claims for the power and novelty of its doctrines; it misrepresents the currents of thought it has replaced; it is often characterised by serious intellectual confusion; it is choked with jargon." (Swan 1985a: 2).

With more differentiation, Howatt coins the terms 'weak' and 'strong' version of the communicative approach to refer, respectively, to whether the language is learnt to be used, or whether we use the language to learn the language:

> the weak version [...] stresses the importance of providing learners with opportunities to use their English for communicative purpose and, characteristically, attempts to integrate such activities into a wider programme of language teaching [...] the 'strong' version of communicative teaching, on the other hand, advances the claim that language is acquired through communication, so that it is not merely a question of activating an existing but inert knowledge of the language, but of stimulating the development of the language system itself. (1984: 279, 286–287).

Dealing with the issue of the appropriacy of CLT in the many countries to which it has spread, Holliday (1994: 160) makes a distinction between BANA (Britain, Australasia and North America) and TESEP (Tertiary English and Secondary English Programs, State institutions in the rest of the world), and argues that even the weak version is not adaptable to every situation in the world (1994: 169), that it is specific to BANA English language education. Holliday (1994: 170–171) illustrates this with various examples, specific ones such as the fact that the paramount importance given to students' oral participation would encounter Japanese students' opposition, who prefer not to initiate in the classroom; more generally, pair work and group work encounter problems in large monolingual classes. For Holliday, the strong version on the other hand allows the learner to discover how language works in discourse and, in this sense, the student mainly interacts with an oral or written text and produces hypotheses about language. The use of a foreign language to teach other subjects (CLIL, Content and Language Integrated Learning) is one important manifestation of this.

One of the most controversial issues is the theoretical framework of communicative competence itself. Initially intended as a theoretical basis for the empirical description of the competences of monolingual native speakers, a simple and accurate transfer to foreign/second language teaching raises problems. Transfer leads to the proclamation of a certain degree of bilingualism or biculturalism as a goal, but this, it can be argued, is unrealistic in both theory and practice. Lightbown (1983) for example argues that comparison of first and foreign language learning shows that such bilingualism/biculturalism is not practical because the child up to the age of six devotes between 12,000 and 15,000 hours to the learning of the L1, which far exceeds the teaching hours in the second/foreign language classroom. In a similar vein, Savignon (2000) argues that the goals of communication and negotiation of meaning are very broad and seem to have frustrated numerous teachers who also find it difficult to design and implement a reliable approach to assessing learners.

Furthermore, Savignon cites studies which claim that language acquisition is to a large extent unaltered by classroom instruction since oral development "seemed to follow a similar morphosyntactic sequence regardless of learner age or context of learning" (2000: 127). It is clear from such remarks that the lack of a sound theory of language acquisition in classrooms, as opposed to natural settings, remains a weakness of CLT, and Swan's (1985a, 1985b) argument that a shortcoming of the communicative framework is the lack of attention to the individual's knowledge, skills and experience as speaker of his/her mother tongue is another dimension of this problem. This is especially evident with respect to the proliferation of inappropriate skills and strategies for foreign language teaching such as predictions about the topic or familiarity with the speaker or writer, which are already mastered by learners in their first language and which are easily transferable to the second or foreign language. Holliday is even more categorical; for him, the courses that "ignore the existing competence which the student brings to the classroom" are "*not* communicative" (1994: 169).

4.2. Grammar

Perhaps as a consequence of a lack of learning theory, a further controversial issue is the role of the teaching and learning of grammar. In spite of the originally heated debate on the exclusion of grammar from the communicative paradigm, nowadays there seems to be an agreement on the need to incorporate a focus on form, although always integrated with a parallel focus on meaning, for the individual's development of a global communicative competence in which discourse features, appropriacy and communication are also an integral part (see, for example, Canale and Swain 1980; Savignon 1972, 2000; Littlewood 1981). Nonetheless the relationship between grammar and semantics in the planning of teaching remains unclear.

In syllabus design, the change of emphasis from teaching the language to teaching language for communication posed an initial problem. The demand that communicative activity be "at the heart of the language lesson", highlights the problems in syllabus design of a traditional kind, but "building a course syllabus round interactive communication is, however, more problematical" (Howatt 1984: 277–279). The communicative approach has indeed generally been restricted to the notional/functional approach but has been criticised given that the grammatical syllabus constitutes the only gradation based on a logical order which is widely accepted by practitioners (Paulston 1974; Brumfit 1980, 1981). Howatt, however, deems this equation to be a misconception and makes the point that the communicative approach can be promoted on the basis of any syllabus, grammatical included, as long as "the linguistic material is suitably selected, presented and exercised" (1984: 287).

Littlewood also states that "a communicative approach to the content of a course need not involve abandoning the use of structural criteria for selection and sequencing" (1981: 77) and puts forward different possibilities for the organisation of a communicative course content: functional-structural organisation (conjunction of structural grading and language functions), functional organisation (exclusive focus on language functions, such as 'offering'), notional organisation (emphasis on general and specific notions, such as 'quantity'), topic based organisation (consideration of the topics learners have to be able to deal with, such as 'houses') and a combination of any of these. Similarly, and unlike Paulston and Brumfit, Swan (1985b: 78–81) considers that the structural-functional dichotomy in syllabus design should be superseded in favour of a more comprehensive syllabus which contemplates and integrates, at least, eight complementary elements: functional, notional, situational, thematic, phonological, lexical, structural, and related to the skills.

4.3. Methodology

Looking back over the decades of CLT, Savignon (2000) argues that some of the myths ascribed to CLT are not in themselves principles or practices of such an approach. Far from being exclusively concerned with oral interaction, CLT similarly stresses written communication. This also discharges the communicative approach from the falsely assumed exclusiveness of pair work and small group work as one of the main teaching standpoints. As far as textbooks and materials are concerned, Savignon (2005: 645) argues no one book can embody the communicative approach: "CLT cannot be found in any one textbook or set of curricular materials inasmuch as strict adherence to a given text is not likely to be true to the processes and goals of CLT", and this must be remembered when criticisms are made.

Swan, for example, has suggested that the notion of communicative 'appropriacy' has been over-emphasised (1985a: 6–7) for, even though certain utterances are appropriate under given circumstances, a large part of the lexicon of a language is unmarked for either social or situational appropriacy. Moreover, both Ur (1996) and Swan (1985b: 84–85) question the prominence given to authentic materials due to the fact that their degree of difficulty may be extremely high. They emphasise the pedagogic value of good quality non-authentic material. As a by-product of the communicative approach, the 'fallacy of real life', as Swan calls it, has to be questioned given that any kind of learning implies a certain distancing from real life.

Holliday also challenges "the myth of learner-centredness" (Holliday 1994: 174–175). The CLT claim to be a learner-centred approach is questioned. By nature, Holliday says, all approaches and methods are language-centred, the learner having always been the indisputable 'recipient' of the learning process. As to the other protagonist of the teaching and learning process, the teacher or instructor, and in spite of the potential of the teacher's role advocated by the communicative approach, the instructor could possibly still be considered as the central figure (Lee and VanPatten 1995: 11). In order for a true revolution to take place, both the teacher's and the learner's role have to change in unison.

What is more, the implementation of communicative techniques such as information and opinion gap (Cook 1991; Swan 1985b) may not be motivating for some students. In spite of their pedagogic potential, in order to be successful, these activities have to be based on an interesting content or information: a map of Liverpool, Swan reminds us, may not be motivating at all for a learner who is never going to be in such a city. As to pair work, it may not result in true communication but in exercises that resemble the pattern of audiolingual drills, that is to say, the question and answer pattern (Lee and VanPatten 1995: 11).

The controversial use of the foreign language in the classroom, with the exclusion of learners' mother tongue in the strong version of the communicative approach, was criticised by Ur (1996), who claimed that foreign language teaching benefits from first language use, for example, in practical issues such as classroom instruction. Similarly, Swan (1985b: 85–86), states that there is no foreign language learning without translation from and to the first language, and more recently Widdowson has argued for the rehabilitation of translation both on grounds of language learning theory and pedagogy and also for educational reasons (2003: 160). For, as Widdowson reminds us, "Language teachers are teachers, and what they teach is not just a language but a subject on the whole curriculum" (2003: 8).

Not all activities implemented in the communicative language class should be considered 'communicative' since not all of them encapsulate social meanings, but rather exploit linguistic patterns (Paulston 1974: 374). Littlewood (1981: 86) makes a distinction between pre-communicative activities, those that have a structural basis, and communicative activities, those with a functional basis and which consist in real social interaction tasks; pre-communicative activities should precede communicative activities and should lead to them. At that point, too, there is need for differentiation, since the teacher and the learner have to bear in mind that there may exist several target cultures associated with one language, with different sets of rules (Savignon 1997: 31).

In short, as Stern says, it is important to consider the limitations of the different approaches and methods, the communicative approach included, because of the nature of approaches and methods themselves, emerging from an emphasis on a particular notion:

> 'As for the communicative approach, the reliance on a single overriding concept, 'communication', is a disadvantage which prevents communicative language teaching from being entirely satisfactory as a theoretical framework. In order to account for all varieties and aspects of language teaching we either stretch the concept of communication so much that it loses any distinctive meaning, or we accept its limitations and then find ourselves in the predicament of the 'method' solution: an excessive emphasis on a single concept.' (Stern 1992: 14)

In fact, even after several decades, and in spite of the theoretical developments of the communicative approach, its current implementation in language classrooms may not be as effective as it may seem: "In short, although CLT may have caused a major revolution in the way that some people *thought* about language teaching, no major revolution occurred in the day-to-day *practice* of most language teachers" (Lee and VanPatten 1995: 8). Perhaps, this is more evident in what Holliday (1994: 160) terms TESEP, zones and countries other than Britain, Australasia and North America. Checa Marín corroborates this view; for him, the Communicative Approach has not been as determining for language teaching in Spain as it may appear because its implementation embodies 'serious obstacles' and 'tremendous difficulties' (2002: 27) for primary and secondary school teachers who find it almost impossible to apply its chief tenets to their teaching practice. This may be indicative of a more general malaise about the application of what was originally a scheme for adults. When van Ek produced a version of the European Threshold Level for schools, he pointed out that the characterisation of the target group in a threshold level for adults seemed to fit school learners too:

1. they would be temporary visitors to the foreign country […]; or:
2. they would have temporary contacts with foreigners in their own country;
3. their contacts with foreign language speakers would, on the whole, be of a superficial, non-professional type;
4. they would primarily need only a basic level of command of the foreign language

(van Ek 1977: 10)

This may seem to teachers in general education too narrow. But he also points out that "the present objective cannot be offered as *the* objective for foreign language teaching" (1977: 17), and that as an objective for communication it should be one part of a more comprehensive approach to foreign language education. What has often happened however is that those responsible for designing and implementing curricula have focused only on communication.

The broader perspective on the purposes of language teaching which van Ek hints at takes us to another issue. The difficulties of setting the native speaker as a model for learning have already been mentioned but even if the definition were clear, it can also be argued that it is undesirable and inappropriate to encourage learners to model themselves on native speakers when one considers the purposes of language teaching. The purpose should not be the imitation of native speakers but the creation of a capacity to 'mediate', to understand the relationships and differences among languages and cultures, to act as interpreter from one to the other, to gain a perspective which allows a richer, critical understanding of other cultures and one's own. As a contrast to 'the native speaker', the term 'intercultural speaker' was coined (Byram and Zarate 1997; Kramsch 1998), and a description of what competences are required to be intercultural has been developed (Byram 1997). There are links here with work outside general education, where the majority of language teachers work, to the sphere of 'cross-cultural/intercultural training' mainly focused on preparation of people in business and commerce for cooperation with people of other countries (Müller-Jacquier 2000; Landis and Bhagat 1996).

As was pointed out earlier, Hymes had already laid the ground for attention to the cultural and therefore the moral dimension of language teaching which arises when the intercultural speaker is postulated as the purpose of language teaching, and Widdowson, too, has recently emphasised the educational purposes of language teaching (2003). From this perspective, language teaching takes its place in schools and universities as a contribution to the education of learners, to the development of their understanding of themselves and their world (Guilherme 2002). More specifically, language education can be a contribution to education for citizenship and bring to the usual emphasis on citizenship in a particular country, an international, intercultural dimension which takes into account the economic and social changes in the contemporary world (Byram 2007, 2008).

5. Research perspectives

Howatt (1984: 289) summarises the relevance of the communicative approach:

> The overall impact of the communicative approach has been to enrich and extend the traditions of language teaching initiated by the reformers at the end of the last century. [...] Finally, the monolingual principle, the unique contribution of the twentieth century to classroom language teaching, remains the bedrock notion from which the others ultimately derive. If there is another 'language teaching revolution' round the corner, it will have to assemble a convincing set of arguments to support some alternative (bilingual?) principle of equal power.

Holliday is even more categorical in his assertion. For him, CLT is not one more approach to choose, but the only option for foreign language teaching. Its limitations, he affirms, can only be surpassed by further developments and new insights on the communicative approach: "Once this breakthrough is appreciated, it is no longer possible to go back to choose an earlier method if communicative language teaching does not appeal. What is needed is a further development of the communicative approach." (Holliday 1994: 166)

Howatt confers on applied linguistics the all-important role of being the main source from which our current understanding of English Language Teaching, and, consequently we could also say Language Teaching in general, originates: "If there is one single source which has been responsible for stimulating innovation and activity, it is (in one or another of its various guises) applied linguistics. It has not performed miracles, but as a focus of enquiry, critical self-examination, and new ideas, it has enriched the profession at least as much as it has irritated it" (1984: 226).

Savignon (2000) is of the opinion that the communicative methodology would benefit from a real understanding of sociocultural differences in learning styles. What is more, curricular design seems to profit from the creation of local materials in which process local teachers take part actively.

We have suggested earlier that a major lack in CLT has been a sound basis in learning theory and that Second Language Acquisition theory has not supplied such a basis. Work on language acquisition in the classroom is gradually developing (Mitchell and Myles 2004).

Research on the intercultural dimension has also been slow to develop (Byram and Feng 2004) and much that is reported is small scale research with limited generalisability.

It is also important to clarify the purpose of research. On the one hand, there is research which will help teachers to understand the causal relationships among factors in their classrooms, and this is where more research on language acquisition is important.

Equally important however is the recognition that language teaching has certain purposes and that the realisation of these purposes requires development of teaching and learning which are suitable for those purposes. This has become much more evident since the introduction of an intercultural dimension since the values implicit in all teaching cannot be ignored. When language teaching appeared to be a value-neutral activity – and this has been questioned in analysis of the social power relations in and beyond the classroom (Pennycook 1994, 1998) – researchers might focus only on the efficacy of particular methods, including CLT. Researchers thus need to be more aware of their own stance, as investigators or advocates (Byram and Feng 2004).

References

Allen, John P. B. and Henry G. Widdowson.
1979 Teaching the communicative use of English. In: Brumfit and Johnson (eds.), 122–142.

Austin, John
1962 *How To Do Thing with Words*. Oxford: Clarendon Press.

Bestard Monroig, Juan and María C. Pérez Martín
1992 *La Didáctica de la Lengua Inglesa. Fundamentos Lingüísticos y Metodológicos*. Madrid: Síntesis.

Brown, H. Douglas
1994 *Principles of Language Learning and Teaching*. Englewood Cliffs, New Jersey: Prentice-Hall.

Brumfit, Christopher J.
1980 *Problems and Principles in English Teaching*. Oxford: Pergamon.

Brumfit, Christopher J.
1981 Notional syllabuses revisited: a response. *Applied Linguistics* 2: 90–92.

Brumfit, Christopher J. and Keith Johnson (eds.)
1979 *The Communicative Approach to Language Teaching*. Oxford: Oxford University Press.

Byram, Michael
1997 *Teaching and Assessing Intercultural Communicative Competence*. Clevedon: Multilingual Matters.

Byram, Michael
2007 Developing a concept of intercultural citizenship. In: Geof Alred, Michael Byram and Michael Fleming (eds.), *Education for Intercultural Citizenship: Concepts And Comparisons*, 109–130. Clevedon: Multilingual Matters.

Byram, Michael
2008 *From Foreign Language Education to Education for Intercultural Citizenship*. Clevendon: Multilingual Matters.

Byram, Michael and Aanwei Feng
2004 Culture and language learning: teaching, research and scholarship. *Language Teaching* 37: 149–168.

Byram, Michael and Geneviève Zarate
1997 Defining and assessing intercultural competence: some principles and proposals for the European context. *Language Teaching* 29: 14–18.

Canale, Michael
1983 From communicative competence to communicative language pedagogy. In: Jack C. Richards and Richard W. Schmidt (eds.), *Language and Communication*, 2–27. London: Longman.

Canale, Michael and Merrill Swain
1980 Theoretical bases of communicative approaches to second language teaching and testing. *Applied Linguistics* 1: 1–47.

Checa Marín, Antonio
2002 Communicative language teaching in secondary education. Myths and realities. In: Antonio Bueno González, Gloria Luque Agulló, Francisca Molina

Navarrete, Ana María Ortega Cebreros and María L. Pérez Cañado (eds.), *Studies in Applied Linguistics and English Teaching,* 11–30. Jaén: Servicio de Publicaciones de la Universidad.

Chomsky, Noam
1965 *Aspects of the Theory of Syntax.* Cambridge, Massachusetts: MIT Press.

Cook, Vivian
1991 *Second Language Learning and Language Teaching.* Sevenoaks: Edward Arnold.

Crystal, David and Derek Davy
1969 *Investigating English Style.* London/Harlow: Longman.

Davies, Alan
2003 *The Native Speaker: Myth and Reality.* Clevedon: Multilingual Matters.

Firth, John R.
1930 *Speech.* London: Benn.

Firth, John R.
1937 *Tongues of Men.* London: Watts.

Fleming, H.
2000 Drama. In: Michael Byram (ed.) *Routledge Encyclopedia of Language Teaching and Learning,* 185–187. London: Routledge.

Gremmo, Marie-Jose and Philip Riley
1995 Autonomy, self-direction and self-access in language teaching and learning: the history of an idea. *System* 23: 151–64.

Grice, Herbert P.
1957 Meaning. *The Philosophical Review* 64: 377–388.

Guilherme, Manuela
2002 *Critical Citizens for an Intercultural World.* Clevedon: Multilingual Matters.

Habermas, Jürgen
1970 Toward a theory of communicative competence. In: H. Dreitzel (ed.), *Recent Sociology* Vol. 2, 115–148. London: Collier-Macmillan.

Halliday, Mak A. K, Angus McIntosh and Peter Strevens
1964 *The Linguistic Sciences and Language Teaching.* London: Longman.

Halliday, Mak A. K. and Ruqaiya Hasan
1976 *Cohesion in English.* London: Longman.

Halliday, Mak A. K.
1979 Towards a sociological semantics. In: Brumfit and Johnson (eds.), 27–45.

Holliday, Adrian
1994 *Appropriate Methodology and Social Context.* Cambridge: Cambridge University Press.

Howatt, Anthony P. R.
1984 *A History of English Language Teaching.* Oxford: Oxford University Press.

Hüllen, Werner
2005 *Kleine Geschichte des Fremdsprachenlernens.* Berlin: Erich Schmidt Verlag.

Hymes, Dell
1972 On communicative competence. In: John B. Pride and Janet Holmes (eds.), *Sociolinguistics,* 269–293. Harmondsworth: Penguin Books.

Kramsch, Claire
1993 *Context and Culture in Language Teaching*. Oxford: Oxford University Press.

Kramsch, Claire
1998 The privilege of the intercultural speaker. In: Michael Byram and Michael Fleming (eds.), *Language Learning in Intercultural Perspective: Approaches through drama and ethnography*, 16–31. Cambridge: Cambridge University Press.

Krashen, Stephen D.
1987 *Principles and Practice in Second Language Acquisition*. New York: Prentice-Hall International.

Krashen, Stephen D.
1988 *Second Language Acquisition and Second Language Learning*. New York: Prentice-Hall International.

Landis, Dan and Rabi S. Bhagat (eds.)
1996 *Handbook of Intercultural Training*. Thousand Oaks, CA.: Sage.

Lee, James F. and Bill VanPatten.
1995 *Making Communicative Language Teaching Happen*. New York: McGraw-Hill, Inc.

Lightbown, Patsy
1983 Exploring relationships between developmental and instructional sequences in L2 acquisition. In: Herbert W. Seliger and Michael H. Long (eds.), *Classroom-oriented Research in Second Language Acquisition*, 217–245. Rowley, Mass.: Newbury House.

Littlewood, William
1981 *Communicative Language Teaching*. Cambridge: Cambridge University Press.

Long. Michael
2000 Second Language acquisition theories. In: Michael Byram (ed.) *Routledge Encyclopedia of Language Teaching and Learning*, 527–534. London: Routledge.

Malinowski, Bronislaw
1923 The problem of meaning in primitive languages. Supplement to Charles K. Ogden and Ivor A. Richards (eds.), *The Meaning of Meaning: a Study of the Influence of Language upon Thought and the Science of Symbolism*, 451–510. London: Routledge/Kegan Paul.

Malinowski, Bronoslaw
1935 *Coral Gardens and their Magic*. London: G. Allen and Unwin.

Mitchell, Rosamund and Florence Myles
2004 *Second Language Learning Theories*. London: Arnold.

Müller-Jacquier, Bernd
2000 Intercultural training. In: Michael Byram (ed.), *Routledge Encyclopedia of Language Teaching and Learning*, 300–303. London: Routledge.

Nunan, David
1989 *Designing Tasks for the Communicative Classroom*. Cambridge: Cambridge University Press.

Paulston, Christina B.
1974 Linguistic and communicative competence. *TESOL Quarterly* 8: 345–362.
Pennycook, Alastair
1994 *The Cultural Politics of English as an International Language*. London: Longman.
Pennycook, Alastair
1998 *English and the Discourses of Colonialism*. London: Routledge.
Roberts, Celia, Michael Byram, Ana Barro, Shirley Jordan and Brian Street
2001 *Language Learners as Ethnographers*. Clevendon: Multilingual Matters.
Saussure, Ferdinand de
[1916] 1972 *Cours de Linguistique Générale*, édition critique préparée par Tullio De Mauro. Paris: Payot.
Savignon, Sandra J.
1972 *Communicative Competence: an Experiment in Foreign-Language Teaching*. Philadelphia: Center for Curriculum Development.
Savignon, Sandra J.
1997 *Communicative Competence. Theory and Classroom Practice*. New York: McGraw-Hill.
Savignon, Sandra J.
2000 Communicative language teaching. In: Michael Byram (ed.), *Routledge Encyclopedia of Language Teaching and Learning*, 124–129. London: Routledge.
Savignon, Sandra J.
2005 Communicative language teaching: strategies and goals. In: Eli Hinkel (ed.), *Handbook of Research in Second Language Teaching and Learning*, 635–651. Mahwah, NJ/London: Lawrence Erlbaum Associates.
Schilder, Hanno
2000 Reform Movement. In: Michael Byram (ed.), *Routledge Encyclopedia of Language Teaching and Learning*, 511–513. London: Routledge.
Searle, John
1969 *Speech Acts: an Essay in the Philosophy of Language*. New York: Cambridge University Press.
Selinker, Larry
1992 *Rediscovering Interlanguage*. Harlow: Longman.
Stern, Hans H.
1992 *Issues and Options in Language Teaching*. Oxford: Oxford University Press.
Swan, Michael
1985a A critical look at the communicative approach (1). *English Teaching Journal* 39: 2–12.
Swan, Michael
1985b A critical look at the communicative approach (2). *English Teaching Journal* 39: 76–87.
Ur, Penny
1996 The communicative approach revisited. *GRETA Revista para profesores de Inglés* 4: 5–7.
Van Ek, Jan A.
1977 *The Threshold Level for Modern Language Learning in Schools*. London: Longman.

Van Ek, Jan A.
1979 The threshold level. In: Brumfit and Johnson (eds.), 103–116.

Van Ek, Jan A.
1986 *Objectives for Foreign Language Learning. Volume 1: Scope*. Strasbourg: Council of Europe.

Van Ek, Jan A. and John L. M. Trim
1991 *The Threshold Level 1990*. Strasbourg: Council of Europe.

Warnke, Georgia
1995 Communicative rationality and cultural values. In: Stephen K. White (ed.), *The Cambridge Companion to Habermas*, 120–142. Cambridge: Cambridge University Press.

Widdowson, Henry G.
1979 Directions in the teaching of discourse. In: Brumfit and Johnson (eds.), 49–60.

Widdowson, Henry G.
2003 *Defining Issues in English Language Teaching*. Oxford: Oxford University Press.

Widdowson, Henry G.
2007 Un-applied linguistics and communicative language teaching. *International Journal of Applied Linguistics* 17: 214–220.

Wilkins, David A.
1979a Grammatical, situational and notional syllabuses. In: Brumfit and Johnson (eds.), 82–90.

Wilkins, David A.
1979b Notional syllabuses and the concept of a minimum adequate grammar. In: Brumfit and Johnson (eds.), 91–98.

Recommended readings

Brumfit, Christopher J. and Keith Johnson (eds.)
1979 *The Communicative Approach to Language Teaching*. Oxford: Oxford University Press.

Byram, Michael
1997 *Teaching and Assessing Intercultural Communicative Competence*. Clevedon: Multilingual Matters.

Holliday, Adrian
1994 *Appropriate Methodology and Social Context*. Cambridge: Cambridge University Press.

Language Teaching. Cambridge: Cambridge University Press.

Littlewood, William
1981 *Communicative Language Teaching*. Cambridge: Cambridge University Press.

Savignon, Sandra J.
1997 *Communicative Competence. Theory and Classroom Practice*. New York: McGraw-Hill.

Stern, Hans H.
1992 *Issues and Options in Language Teaching*. Oxford: Oxford University Press.
Widdowson, Henry G.
1978 *Teaching Language as Communication*. Oxford: Oxford University Press.
Widdowson, Henry G.
2003 *Defining Issues in English Language Teaching*. Oxford: Oxford University Press.

19. Language for specific purposes vs. general language

Claus Gnutzmann

1. Introduction: What is specific about languages for specific purposes?

1.1. Definition and teaching aspects

When discussing Languages for Specific Purposes (LSP) it is worth bearing in mind that in the vast majority of cases one is, in fact, talking about English for Specific Purposes (ESP) and, also, to a considerable extent, about the use of English in scientific, academic and business communication. This is not surprising in view of the dynamic development of English as a medium of world-wide communication affecting more or less all domains of peoples' lives and activity, especially if these have a non-regional and transnational impact. The latter is particularly applicable to the areas of science and technology, where it has been estimated that almost 85 % of all scientific and technological information in the world is written in English (Kaplan 2001: 12). In the natural sciences, for example, over 90 % of all publications are in English (Ammon 1998: 152), and now almost similar figures hold true for the social sciences. Thus, 'anglophony' has become the communicative norm in these disciplines throughout the world, i.e. also for books and journals published outside English-speaking countries.

The scope of LSP has been described as referring to "language research and instruction that focuses on the specific communicative needs and practices of particular social groups" (Hyland 2007: 391). This definition partly overlaps with the field of professional communication and the development of communities of practice (Candlin and Sarangi forthcoming) although the latter's research focus is less on language and more on the process of social learning that takes places when people cooperate and communicate in professional contexts, e.g. in doctor-patient communication, counselling interviews, sales talks etc. It is rather typical of Anglo-American approaches to LSP that they very much concentrate on the teaching and learning dimension whereas Continental-European views tend to be broader and are also concerned with standardisation of terminology, translation, intelligibility and critical linguistics as additional areas of application (for a comprehensive overview of international LSP research cf. Hoffmann, Kalverkämper, and Wiegand 1998). It is particularly the Leipzig school of LSP research (cf. Gläser 1979, 1990, 1995; Hoffmann 1985, 1988, 1989) which has to be credited with laying the linguistic-communicative foundations of the teaching of LSP (cf. also Weise 2007). Although there seems to be no universally accepted definition of LSP, a typical definition usually makes reference to the users and uses as well as to the linguistic characteristics of LSP, which serve as a platform for its pedagogical implementation. Thus, criteria such as the following are usually listed: LSP is employed by specialists, it is used in written and spoken communication within one professional field and across professional fields, and it is utilised publicly and supra-regionally. Additionally, LSP texts do not have a grammar of their own but rather exhibit a specific selection, use and frequency of morpho-syntactic features of the general language; also there exist strong tendencies towards a standardisation of terminology and discourse structure (cf. Gnutzmann 2006a: 196–197). The *special* language component in LSP has sometimes implied a potential contrast to the *general* language, although in the literature the connection of LSP to the general language is usually emphasised: "Special languages are semi-autonomous, complex semiotic systems based on and derived from general language; their use presupposes special education and is restricted to communication among specialists in the same or closely related fields" (Sager, Dungworth, and McDonald 1980: 69).

Looking at ESP primarily from a pedagogical perspective Dudley-Evans (2001: 132) identifies three "absolute characteristics" of ESP and four "variable characteristics" (similarly Dudley-Evans and St John 1998: 4–5), which due to their generality can also be applied to the whole field of LSP. Starting from the premise that ESP should above all be concerned with teaching language, discourse and the appropriate communication skills by making use of topics as well as the underlying methodology of the target discipline to achieve such aims, Dudley-Evans arrives at the following absolute characteristics of ESP: (1) the specific needs of the learners determine the design of the ESP course; (2) the specific purpose the language is taught for is reflected in the use of the underlying methodology and activities of the related discipline and (3) the course focuses on the language (grammar, lexis, register), skills, discourse and genres which are appropriate to these activities. The variable characteristics relate to the absolute characteristics and address aspects of teaching ESP on a more practical and concrete level: (1) ESP may be connected to specific disciplines or designed for them; (2) the teaching methodology may differ from that applied in general language teaching; (3) ESP courses are usually intended for adult learners who are taught at tertiary-level institutions or during their professional career, although courses may also be designed for learners at secondary school level; (4) as a consequence, for most ESP courses basic knowledge of the language is required and so the courses are generally planned for intermediate or advanced students.

The characteristics of teaching and learning specific languages, as outlined above, include primarily all the learner's dispositions, the methodology and the special language as absolute characteristics. Other features distinguishing the learning and teaching of LSP/ESP from learning and teaching the general language comprise the role of the teacher, the relationship between learner and teacher, the content and the teaching materials. The content, i.e. subject knowledge, is related to the specific purpose the language is learned for and the linguistic-communicative properties of the special language itself. All of these features will be dealt with in detail later in this chapter.

1.2. LSP and the general language

The most prominent difference of special languages compared to the general language lies in their terminology, which very often consists of words derived from other languages such as Latin or Greek. Specialised vocabulary also includes words from the general language, which are then used with a clearly defined and technical meaning, but there can also be a transfer of words from LSP back into the general language, which may result either in greater precision of a communicative event or even cause a communicative barrier.

The general language provides the basis for LSP terminology in the humanities and social sciences. This is largely due to the fact that terminology in these disciplines needs to be flexible to represent connections between human activities. This flexibility is an essential feature of the vocabulary of the general language, in line with Wittgenstein's well-known assertion that the meaning of a word is its use. A further reason for the use of terms derived from the general language is the public demand for comprehensible accounts of research results in the humanities and social sciences since, in general, there are no visible or tangible outcomes as can be found, for example, in the technological disciplines (Knobloch 1987: 57). Since the meanings of words in the general language do not allow precise definitions in a technical sense, terms derived from the general language need to be (re)defined according to the context and their specific meaning in LSP. Therefore some words have two sets of meanings: one in the general language and another in LSP, e.g. *role* and *group* in sociology. Terminological standardisation as in the natural and technological sciences would be counterproductive in the humanities and social sciences because communication and progress in these fields of enquiry are very often the result of dismissing or modifying existing concepts and terms and coining new ones (Gnutzmann 1996: 3).

In addition to terminology, there are also grammatical features as well as phonetic and graphemic characteristics, which distinguish LSP from the general language (for a compact survey of 'language issues in ESP' cf. Dudley-Evans and St John 1998: 74–94). These tend not to be grammatical constructions which are unique to LSP, although such special expressions can be found, for instance, in mathematics:

(1) "If *D* is the domain of a variable in an open sentence, the process of finding the truth set is called **solving the open sentence over D**" (cf. Halliday 2005: 75, emphasis in the original).

On the whole, grammatical properties of LSP are more aptly characterised as entities resulting from the specific selection, use and frequency of linguistic features belonging to the general language. They include, for example, the use of passive constructions, nominalisations and (complex) nominal groups, which seem to be 'universal' features of LSPs across languages. Although the proportion of passives is higher in LSP than in other genres it is also true that active constructions always outnumber passives. According to Swales (1990: 58), "[a] genre comprises a class of communicative events, the members of which share some set of communicative purposes". Agentless passive constructions in LSP are used in order to emphasise the result of an action or process and to avoid repetition of the subjects *I* and *we*. In English, passive constructions are most frequently used to express the impersonal and neutral quality of a statement; other possibilities to express the detachment of the writer are offered, for instance by constructions beginning with introductory *it* (e.g. *It has been noted with concern that the stock of books in the library has been declining alarmingly*, cf. Leech and Svartvik 1994: 32). Nominalisations and nominal groups are favourably used in LSP because of their precise and dense mode of expression and their syntactic flexibility, i.e. they can be used as subject or object and can be positioned within a sentence according to their relative importance. On the other hand, if a nominal construction turns out to be extremely dense it may be difficult even for specialists to understand, as in:

(2) "The model rests on *the localized gravitational attraction exerted by rapidly oscillating and extremely massive closed loops of cosmic string*" (cf. Halliday 2005: 76, italics mine).

The high frequency of the simple present tense in scientific texts is due to the fact that this tense is used in LSP to express general truths and repeated actions. Therefore, the simple present offers itself as a highly appropriate tense for definitions, descriptions and observations in science and technology.

On the morphological level, the adaptation and borrowing of Latin and Greek words and with them the rules of word formation used in these languages result in a greater number of affixes used in special languages than in the general language. The use of affixes in LSP differs from the general language because they are often used with restricted meanings and functions, for example: "The suffixes *-ic* and *-ous* have a special meaning in chemistry which they do not have in general language, e.g. *forensic*, *populous*" (Sager, Dungworth, and McDonald 1980: 253).

The frequent use of modals such as *could, may, might, would* and verbs such as *appear, seem, tend,* as well as verbs like *suggest* (instead of *demonstrate, show*) is a further characteristic of LSP texts. The use of these expressions, which is generally referred to as hedging, serves to express the degree of certainty which a writer attributes to statements in his text (cf. Dudley-Evans and St John 1998: 76–77). Thus, the use of different hedging devices allows a writer to signal strong commitment, neutrality, detachment, scepticism or even refusal of what she/he reports in an article.

Features which are used only with a very low frequency in LSP are contracted verb forms like *I've*, *you're*, *they'll*, etc. because these are characteristics of the spoken language and are very often not considered appropriate for written ESP. Acronyms, which are formed from the initial letters of multi-word expressions, enter the vocabulary as independent one-word units, for example: *radar* = ***ra**dio **d**etecting **a**nd **r**anging* and *hifi* = ***hi**gh **fi**delity*. The previous words also illustrate how technical terms, and in this case even abbreviations, come into the general language and are used across languages.

LSP enters the general language in different ways, but mostly via the mass media, popular scientific literature and advertisements. The vocabulary of the general language has grown immensely, due to new developments and inventions, especially in the fields of science, technology, engineering, politics and economics (e.g. *DNA*, *franchise*, *global player*, as well as terms from the new technologies, such as *Internet*, *e-mail*, *download* or @). This development influences the vocabulary used at work, in vocational and academic training and even in leisure activities.

1.3. Central problems of LSP

Central problems of LSP obviously derive from the specific purpose the language is learned and taught for, e.g. whether the focus is on spoken or written communication, the degree of abstractness required by the learners. Although it is generally assumed that LSP learners are intermediate or advanced users of the language, the demands of the learners with regard to their LSP objectives may vary enormously depending on, for example, whether they are looking for help in spoken communication in a lab context or for advanced written communication in the drafting of a research paper. This considerable heterogeneity as regards meeting the needs of learners in many different professional and academic fields and communication contexts makes it extremely difficult, if not impossible, to educate LSP teachers to cater for all these requirements. Therefore the role of LSP teachers, their education, qualification and recruitment, the relationship between teacher and learners as well as the methodology of LSP are central issues which have to be addressed (cf. 3.3.).

2. Origins and developments

Traditional LSP research, at least in Continental Europe, started out in the 19th century as a historical-philological discipline aiming to preserve the specific lexis of crafts and trades that were in the process of becoming obsolete. Modern LSP research, however, is one of the disciplines of applied linguistics using an integrative approach to account for facts and problems arising from the interplay of language and subject. It was probably in the nineteen-seventies and eighties when, due to growing internationalisation in the fields of economy, trade and education, the teaching and learning component of LSP became more and more important. As a consequence, the instrumental function of LSP designed to support the process of international cooperation on a communicative-practical level prevailed to the exclusion of others, for example those approaches taking a critical look at the dominant role of English as a global language (e.g. Pennycook 1994; Phillipson 2003).

The history of LSP research has identified a sizeable number of approaches to the study of LSP, of which only a representative selection can be dealt with here (cf. Hoffmann 1984; Hyland 2007). Very much in line with the historical origins of LSP, it was above all lexicological and terminological approaches that were initially at the centre of research and practice. According to Hoffmann (1984: 29) scientific terms must "satisfy rigorous claims and quality requirements", such as specialisation, conceptuality, exactitude, monosemia and one-to-one relationship between content and form, and it is the primary aim of terminological work to meet these requirements (cf. Arntz, Picht, and Mayer 2004: 3). Terminological work does not so much deal with individual terms, but rather takes into consideration terminological systems and subsystems of specific disciplines. With regard to LSP classes it has repeatedly been pointed out that the mediation of terminology in the strict sense is not really part of the responsibilities of the LSP teacher, mainly because this is basically teaching the subject. In register analysis, which evolved during the 1960s and early 1970s, the analysis of LSP texts is taken beyond the level of terminology. The aim is to identify lexical and grammatical characteristics of registers which are subsequently used to develop syllabuses for students of LSP. Register analysis has shown that the specific selection of certain grammatical structures, as mentioned in the previous section, such as the passive voice, nominal groups and the present simple tense, are characteristic features of specific languages.

With regard to the discourse and communicative functions of texts the Prague School of Linguistics (cf. Luelsdorff 1994; Scharnhorst and Ising 1976) has exerted a considerable influence on LSP research. Viewed from a functional perspective, four 'functional languages' (1. communicative, 2. specialised practical, 3. theoretical, 4. poetic) are distinguished. LSP texts can be classified as a practical and theoretical language depending on their level of abstractness and with regard to their linguistic-communicative features. Functional speech analysis allows for classifications of texts according to the following criteria (Hoffmann 1984: 30):

1. Sphere of communication combined with the topic of the message (e.g. technical)
2. Degree of specialisation (popular vs. academic)
3. Medium or technique of communication (spoken vs. written)
4. Treatment of the topic (e.g. descriptive, evaluative)

Each of these criteria represents a cluster of features and is employed to identify the complex structure of texts. Functional stylistics is a component of functional speech analysis, which focuses on functional styles and classifies them according to their communicative function. Distinctions are made between: 1. Official communication, 2. science, 3. journalism, 4. conversation, 5. literature.

The description of scientific styles underscores features such as exactitude, simplicity and clarity, objectivity, abstractness, generalisation, density of information and use of technical terms, symbols and figures (cf. Hoffmann 1984: 31). All in all, these features are understood as typical indicators of a highly impersonal, detached, abstract and more traditional mode of scientific communication, which has been challenged recently by bringing in the cultural component of LSP (cf. Clyne 1991 and the anthology by Danneberg and Niederhauser 1998) and by invoking individual, subjective and emotive aspects of LSP authors (Baumann 2004).

Another communicative approach on the functional analysis of scientific texts is (rhetorical) discourse analysis: scientific texts are analysed to show how sentences are used to perform communicative acts. Studies incorporate the analyses of whole texts and text segments according to features such as the organisation of information and rhetorical techniques employed by the author (cf. Trimble 1989: 2). The results of these analyses provide the basis for teaching materials and syllabuses for teaching LSP – and especially ESP – to non-native speakers of that language. In order to define the aims more precisely needs analysis or target situation analysis is applied in LSP classes. The objective is "to take the existing knowledge and set it on a more scientific basis, by establishing procedures for relating language analysis more closely to learners' reasons for learning" (Hutchinson and Waters 1987: 12).

So far, then, it has emerged that modern research on LSP developed from a linguistic perspective focusing on the various aspects of structure and use of language to a learner-centred and needs-oriented approach relating directly to the learning and teaching of LSP. The learning-centred approach on ESP as described by Hutchinson and Waters (1987: 19) "is an approach to language teaching in which all decisions as to content and method are based on the learner's reason for learning". The concept of current needs analysis (cf. Dudley-

Evans and St John 1998: 121–144) and its implementation in LSP teaching is based on various types of information about the learners, e.g. professional, personal, their present language proficiency, as well as general language learning information and information about the environment in which the course is taught (means analysis).

In contrastive text linguistics and discourse analysis, texts encoded in two different languages are analysed and classified according to their function and structure (cf. Adamzik 1998) as well as to their cross-cultural differences (e.g. Connor 1996; Mauranen 1993). Research in the contrastive analysis of LSP originates from linguistic and pedagogic interest. Linguistic research interest focuses on the formal linguistic structure and communicative function of texts and on questions of text typology (Arntz 2004: 294); didactic interest evolved from mounting evidence that the success of technical communication depends to a large extent on the knowledge of appropriate text types and their structure (Gnutzmann and Oldenburg 1991: 103). In this approach differences and similarities in communication structures within articles in different languages, e.g. English and German, are analysed, compared and adapted for the teaching of LSP. Whole texts, though more often semi-autonomous parts of texts such as the abstract, introduction and conclusion, form the basis of studies to empirically identify cultural differences and similarities in scientific discourse across languages. The analysis of such text segments is often preferred as an alternative to analysing entire texts, since mainly the former yield manageable results that are suitable for pedagogical application. Thus, the aim of such descriptions with regard to teaching LSP is to develop a list of criteria for creating and evaluating teaching materials (Ludwig 1999: 32–33; cf. also Kretzenbacher 1990; Oldenburg 1992; Seidlhofer 1995 for detailed analyses of conclusions and abstracts).

Drawing on insights into Functional Sentence Perspective (FSP) provided by the Prague School, recent research on information structure has reemphasised that the communicative structure of sentences is signalled through concepts such as theme and rheme. The constituent carrying the information which is already known (theme) is usually followed by the constituent providing the greatest part of new information (rheme). Violations of this principle can lead to difficulty in understanding the meaning of a sentence (cf. Göpferich 2004: 221–229 for examples from LSP) or in understanding the intention of the author. The phenomenon of theme and rheme is one of the key issues with regard to the organisation of information in texts, which is the main focus of FSP as an essential constituent of the grammaticality of a text (cf. Daneš 1974: 106). Although the notions of theme and rheme give valuable information on the thematic structure of sentences, it has been criticised that the terms have not been properly defined. As an alternative Gülich and Raible (1979: 75–76) suggest an approach by which the macro-structure of a text can be analysed according to *Gliederungsmerkmale* ('linguistic-organisational characteristics'), which enable the reader or hearer to differentiate between different parts of a text. This approach is obviously based on the idea that each text segment has distinct formal characteristics and can therefore be classified accordingly.

In accordance with the idea that scientific communication should be objective, neutral and dispassionate LSP research on the whole showed very little interest in the study of topics that did not seem to fit these criteria. It was therefore only very recently that LSP researchers started to become interested in the individual style of authors and the representation of emotions in scientific texts as opposed to the impersonal quality traditionally assigned to scientific texts (Laurén, Myking, and Picht 2004). The main idea of research on authors' individual style is that behind every text there is an individual human being whose personality in some way influences the way he or she writes. Furthermore, academic communication can also be viewed as a process of *persuading* other scholars of the validity of one's own arguments and convictions. As a consequence, it has been argued that to do this effectively the rhetorical conventions used in particular social and cultural contexts by certain academic communities should be observed (Hewings 2006: 10). Although scientific texts, in traditional definitions, are considered to be emotionally neutral, emotions can in fact be involved in the cognitive processing of scientific discourse in different functions. They can, for example, help to focus attention on specific information, control access to the different parts of memory, influence the hierarchy of cognition and restrict the amount of cognitive information (Baumann 2004: 97).

3. Central concepts and approaches

3.1. Content and Language Integrated Learning/Bilingual education

Content and Language Integrated Learning (CLIL) is an interdisciplinary approach to bilingual education (cf. Wolff, Ch. 20 this volume), which is mostly practised at secondary schools. Even though, in principle, all school subjects can be taught in and through a foreign language it is mainly subjects related to the social sciences rather than science subjects and mathematics which have been at the centre of CLIL. However, owing to the dynamic increase of English medium study courses in Europe and world-wide (cf. Ammon and McConnell 2002; Maiworm and Wächter 2002) it can be expected that the latter subjects are likely to benefit from this development and will become more popular as CLIL subjects. What is most characteristic of CLIL is that the acquisition of subject knowledge and of language proficiency are interconnected. The focus of CLIL teaching is undoubtedly on the content of the subject, and the acquisition of additional language competency is seen as a result of exposure to and use of the foreign language on the basis of authentic and motivating materials in (quasi-)natural settings.

Since the linguistic focus of CLIL is on the foreign language, it has been emphasised that learners' use of the mother tongue should not be totally excluded from CLIL classes, and that students should also master the relevant subject terminology in their mother tongue. On a critical note, it has been argued that an increase in CLIL and therefore an increase in English-taught subjects could result in a possible decline of the status and significance of the national language as the language of education at schools and in higher education.

3.2. English for Academic Purposes

English for Academic Purposes (EAP) is a sub-branch of ESP which is concerned with the identification of students' (special) communication needs and study skills in (pre-)tertiary education as well as with the analysis of linguistic and discoursal structures used in academic texts. In contrast to LSP, EAP does not so much deal with the forms and functions of language in certain disciplines but mainly with language and academic skills which enable learners to communicate in a greater variety of contexts and subjects. Therefore, a general approach to an EAP course does not concentrate on the topics and issues of a particular field but puts more emphasis on the teaching of overall study skills such as listening to lectures, reading, note-taking and writing (cf. Hamp-Lyons 2001: 126–127). Thus, EAP-learners' ability to communicate outside the 'specialist' communities is not restricted, as might be the case with other LSP learners who may find it difficult to communicate in the general language.

In line with the spread of English world-wide EAP is used in English-speaking countries as well as in countries where English is spoken as a second or official language (ESL) and as a foreign language (EFL). Dudley-Evans and St John (1998: 35) suggest a distinction according to four types of situation:

"1. An English-speaking country, such as UK or USA.
2. An English-as-a-Second-Language (ESL) situation, where English is the official language of education and is widely spoken, […].
3. A situation in which certain subjects, such as medicine, engineering or science, are officially taught in English, while for other subjects and at other levels of education the national language is used.
4. A situation where all subject courses are taught in the national language, but English may be important for ancillary reasons."

The skills required by learners may differ depending on the type of linguistic situation. When foreign students intend to study at a university or college in an English-speaking country the whole range of skills will probably be needed. However, if they study a subject in their native language in their home country, it may be sufficient to concentrate on the acquisition of skills for reading academic texts. Not surprisingly, many EAP programmes concentrate largely on reading and writing whereas in general English courses more attention is usually paid to speaking and listening (Hamp-Lyons 2001: 126–127). The fact that the vast majority of all scientific and technological information is in English means that skills in English are essential in order to learn about new developments and to participate in scientific discourse. Reading and writing skills are imperative for the everyday work of researchers, scientists and students.

Due to the increasing number of international students at universities in English-speaking countries the interest in EAP courses has been growing as well. As international students have to pay much higher tuition fees than home students (and EU students in Europe) universities try to raise the number of overseas, especially non-EU students to improve their financial situation. However, a considerable number of non-native speakers of English enter the universities of Ireland and Great Britain with the help of European exchange programmes like ERASMUS.

Within EAP a distinction is made between English for General Academic Purposes (EGAP) and English for Specific Academic Purposes (ESAP) (Blue 1988). EGAP focuses on skills essential to academic activities in general, such as writing essays, dissertations and reports, which involves forming accurate sentences, structuring ideas and the ability to quote correctly. Reading articles and textbooks entails the capacity of scanning for specific information, evaluating a writer's point of view, understanding the main ideas and distinguishing the supporting details from the main ideas (Dudley-Evans and St John 1998: 96–98).

In ESAP, the focus is on the particular academic subject, including the language and discourse structure, terminology, the subject-specific skills and the individual academic conventions. Jordan (1997: 5) points out two problems concerning the teaching of EAP to students whose mother tongue is not English. The first problem is that these students may already possess advanced academic skills in their L1 and need help to transfer these skills into English. Students, however, may also need help with other characteristics of EAP, e.g. phraseology and style, which makes it difficult for the teacher to precisely define the aims of an EAP course. The second issue involves students from countries with educational systems which differ from those in the UK, Australia or North America. These students may need extensive help both with the skills of EGAP and in the field of ESAP if they intend to study in those countries.

3.3. Teaching LSP: Differences to general language teaching

Whereas the learning of a foreign language in general can be conceived of as a quest starting from very little, perhaps even zero competence in the target language and progressing to increasing proficiency in it, typical LSP learners usually have some grounding in the foreign language as such. They require special knowledge and proficiency to cope with challenges arising from communicative needs in a certain discipline or working environment. As a consequence, LSP learners are perhaps more adequately described as learners who make needs based special language choices, which due to the mutual relationship between general and special language are likely to further increase their general language proficiency. In the following section, some of the major factors of general language and LSP teaching will be outlined and exemplified: contents and aims, methods, materials, assessment, learner and teacher.

The learners' individual aims are usually considered to serve as the basis for the planning of LSP courses. However, since learners quite often seem to be uncertain about their aims it is necessary for both teachers and learners to find out about the specific demands collaboratively in order to be able to plan the lessons and define the aims accordingly (Fearns 2003: 171). Klein (1988: 191) emphasises that learners' needs should be analysed repeatedly during a course in order to adjust them to possible changes in the learners' development and perspectives. The contents of the course as well as the materials and methods used should then be adjusted repeatedly to the aims identified in the continued needs analysis.

3.3.1. Contents and aims

Although terminology is obviously an outstanding characteristic of LSP, this does not imply that the teaching of terminology should be at the centre of LSP classes. Since technical terms, terminology and terminological subsystems are constitutive components of a discipline, their mediation should be the prerogative of the subject teacher unless the LSP teacher also happens to be a specialist in the respective subject. Instead, LSP teaching tends to give special attention to subject-overriding phenomena exhibiting a high frequency of occurrence such as passive constructions, nominalisations and nominal groups. These structures can be made accessible to the students by textual analysis and they should be practised in the writing of texts. Hutchinson and Waters (1987: 13) stress the importance of skills and strategies, which they define as common reasoning and interpreting processes. Such a skills-centred approach is said to underlie all language use, irrespective of the surface forms, and to enable learners to access meaning from discourse. Following from this, the authors recommend that LSP teaching should not so much concentrate on the surface forms of the language or the specific subject register but rather focus on the underlying interpretive strategies, because they can help learners to cope with the surface forms, for example guessing the meaning of words from context. Although the teaching of written skills is generally given higher priority in LSP courses, listening comprehension and speaking have received more attention recently (cf. Kelz 1996: 511). This tendency towards spoken communication may appear to be in contrast to what has been stated for EAP in the previous section, but can easily be explained because the significance of skills varies in the different disciplines: The ability to deal with spoken language is generally considered to be of lesser importance in the natural sciences; whereas in the discourse of economics and business competency in listening comprehension and speaking are regarded as more essential. Methods and materials need to be selected accordingly.

3.3.2. Methods

Keeping in mind that in LSP courses it is not uncommon that students have a greater subject knowledge than their teachers it is advisable that learners should be actively involved in planning the course and in selecting the teaching methods. On the other hand, there are certain general methodological principles and work approaches such as authenticity, problem-solving, task-based learning, project work and learning by doing which are always highlighted as being relevant (cf. also Jordan 1997: 124). Since methods are chosen according to the specific necessities of the learners and the contents of the course, teachers ought to be familiar with a variety of methods in order to apply the most appropriate. Specific methods for teaching LSP include, for example, applications of guessing techniques to extract meaning from texts and the interpretations of diagrams and charts.

3.3.3. Materials

In order to prepare learners for situations they will actually encounter in their academic studies and in their profession materials used in LSP classes should be authentic, as far as this is possible. There may be limits to text authenticity with regard to the origin of such materials because it is also important to observe the principle of learner authenticity, which means that the learners must be in position to be able to interact appropriately with the material and generate a positive psychological reaction. Therefore, texts and materials employed in class involve the use of suitable scientific and technical texts commensurate with the participants' abilities at the time. This way, learners are encouraged to practise and produce written texts such as reports, abstracts as well as products of verbal communication like business negotiations or presentations (cf. Fluck 1992: 204–205; Kelz 1996: 509–510). Again, the key defining feature of ESP is that "its teaching and materials are founded on the results of **needs analysis**" (Dudley-Evans 2001: 131, emphasis in the original).

Due to the specific and individual character of LSP classes teaching materials quite often consist of photocopied manuscripts or collections of material gathered by the teachers since the more specific the purpose for which the language is taught, the less interesting it is for commercial publishers to produce these specific teaching materials. Since the Internet provides the opportunity to get the latest information on almost all kinds of topics, it is widely used as an important source for new LSP materials. However, not all web sources are equally well suited for LSP purposes, either because they may be unreliable or they may require a level of competence in the language and/or the specific field which is not available to the learners as yet. Several types of teaching materials can be distinguished: subject-specific materials, materials for several – usually related – subjects and materials which are neutral with regard to a subject. These materials can be further differentiated according to their function: for example *kurstragend* ('determining the course as a whole'), *kursstützend* ('supporting the course'), *kursbegleitend* ('accompanying the course') or *Selbstlernmaterialien* ('self-study materials') (cf. Fluck 1992: 215–216).

3.3.4. *Assessment*

Tests designed for the assessment of LSP classes have varying degrees of specificity, depending on the contents and the aims of the class. Two characteristics are usually mentioned which distinguish LSP tests from those for general language classes: authenticity of task and interaction between language knowledge and specific purpose content knowledge (Douglas 2000: 2). Both aspects are also mentioned by Fluck (1992: 209) when he states that testing procedural knowledge, i.e. being able to communicate within the field of the specific purpose and to actually perform in a foreign language, is more important in LSP than testing declarative knowledge about a language. A further desirable requirement for effective LSP testing is that experts of the specific field should be involved in designing the tests and that tests should be drawn up according to the contents and the tasks which were used in class (Fluck 1992: 210). Ineffectiveness of tests can be caused by the use of specialised vocabulary or language structures the learners have not come across in class and which prevent them from performing according to what they were in fact able to learn in class. Different uses of terms in different disciplines can also be a source of confusion in setting tasks and planning tests: In mathematics, for example, *discuss/discussion* refers to comparing and assessing mathematical problems, whereas in other subjects it is mainly related to the comparison and appraisal of arguments (cf. Fluck 1992: 212).

3.3.5. *Learners*

On the whole, learners in LSP courses are more involved in defining the aims of the course than general language learners are, because the former can make use of their specialist knowledge, which – due to the interaction between subject and language – ought to be conducive to their learning the special language. In this way, such learners may and should take responsibility for their learning process as early as possible, which could also help them with regard to motivation.

Students who start learning a special language with very little subject knowledge are much less in a position to participate in developing the aims for the course than professionally experienced learners. Students with very limited subject experience need LSP training largely to access specialised subject knowledge, starting at a fairly basic level and to build up their linguistic skills. On the other hand, professionally experienced learners need LSP training mainly to expand their linguistic skills as they are already skilled in their profession. Therefore, it would be highly advantageous if LSP teachers know about the learners' subjects or could receive some specialist help in designing the course particularly when designing a course for (prospective) university or college students (cf. Kelz 1996: 508).

3.3.6. Teacher

It will have become clear by now that with regard to the various tasks an LSP teacher has to fulfil she/he can be located somewhere between a foreign language teacher and a subject specialist. However, considering that we identified the teaching of terminology as a genuine assignment for subject teachers we can further conclude that an LSP teacher is probably more of a language teacher than a subject specialist. This statement is also reflected in the training and education of LSP teachers, who generally start their LSP career with a background in languages. Obviously, LSP teachers need to go far beyond the teaching of linguistic skills in the narrow sense of the word, since students are presumably more in need of comprehension strategies and techniques not only for language details but also for a text as a whole including methodology, aims, structure of argumentation (cf. also Wildegans 1997: 28). The advantages that LSP teachers with appropriate subject and language teaching qualifications hold have been convincingly pointed out in a case study by Mühlhaus and Lawlor (1999: 54) using the example of teachers with specialist knowledge of law: "Prior to the delivery of the introduction to law, the tutors have been able to plan the necessary lexical and conceptual input, and these have been practised in the language class." This content and language integrated approach avoids confronting students with specialised texts they are not yet able to understand, but prepares them to meaningfully apply their new, subject-embedded linguistic knowledge in class.

Ideally, LSP teachers should possess qualifications in the following areas:

- Very high proficiency in the target language, on the level of general but also special uses
- Theoretical and descriptive knowledge of LSP pertaining in particular to terminology, syntax, pragmatics as well as intercultural differences in the discourse structure of genres

- Subject knowledge (at least of a basic nature) of the academic discipline(s) whose special languages she/he teaches
- Ability to select and prepare LSP material in consideration of the requirements and aims of a particular class

3.3.7. The relationship between teacher and learner

Since teachers tend to be specialised in language rather than in the subject and it is not uncommon for learners to know more about the subject than their teacher, the relationship between teacher and learners is different from that in general language teaching as teachers quite often need to draw on the specialist knowledge of the learners to determine the aims and the content of the course. Such distribution of knowledge and competency as well as the shared interest in the aims of the course by teachers and learners and how to achieve them, the mutual exchange of information on learners' dispositions as well as the teachers' expertise and the institutional possibilities offer good potential for a balanced and constructive relationship between teachers and learners.

The different professional and language backgrounds of learners and teachers can also be a source of misunderstandings in LSP classes. Some learners may give very short answers, sometimes only single-word ones, whereas the teacher may expect the learner to answer more fully in a complete sentence. A possible reason for single-word answers could be the learner's lack of linguistic proficiency or it could also be that the (spoken) discourse conventions used in a certain field may demand very short contributions. For that reason it seems necessary that teachers acquire an understanding of the potentially different ways of thinking and communicating in different subject contexts and discourse communities, which have been defined as "special interest groups" (Swales 1990: 24) who use and help to develop a particular kind of discourse.

Learners' difficulties in understanding their teachers can be caused by a lack of linguistic proficiency but also by restricted subject knowledge. Therefore, it seems to be important for teachers of LSP to have at least a basic knowledge of the learners' subject in order to locate the source of their difficulties in class. This can also help to prevent misunderstandings and may further contribute to a respectful relationship between learner and teacher.

4. Current issues and perspectives

Apart from the inherently problematic issue of the requirement profile of LSP teachers, who should ideally possess language and subject competence, other concepts of LSP (cf. section 3.3.) relating to learner, methodology etc. have not been objects of fundamental discussions for some time, which suggests that they seem to be 'well under control'. The bulk of research into the linguistic description and the pedagogical applications of LSP has shown that the history of the discipline of LSP to a great extent mirrors that of Applied Linguistics, particularly in its narrow sense, i.e. relating to language teaching and learning. For instance, with regard to foreign language teaching, early LSP methodology was largely based on insights from linguistics and less so on ideas coming from education and learning psychology. However, this has changed subsequently, as can be seen from the shift of emphasis towards learner orientation and needs analysis as more recent guiding principles for LSP research and practice. With regard to the content and aims of ESP courses, it has been common practice for native speaker norms of British and/or American English to serve as more or less undisputed reference models for the teaching of ESP. Similarly, the stylistic conventions of Anglo-American discourse were – and still are – practically taken for granted as desirable targets in the acquisition of ESP writing skills. Concerning the cultural determination of academic texts Mauranen (2006: 53–54) has convincingly argued that editors of academic journals apprehend the cultural dimension of texts, and, following from this, that ways of academic writing should be developed "which are widely accessible and not constrained by any one cultural norm such as the Anglo-American".

The largely uncritical acceptance of English is perhaps not surprising in view of the omnipresence of English, especially American English, in written scientific and academic communication. However, from the perspective of the very high number of non-native participants in these kinds of discourses it may be somewhat astonishing that this state of affairs has lasted so long and is only now being discussed on a broader level.

4.1. The ambivalence of English in global communication

Despite and because of its ubiquity, the role of English and its significance in academia have been perceived in quite opposite ways. In the discourse of "anglophone" subjects (Skudlik 1990: 210–218), i.e. where English is used as an exclusive medium of communication, such as the natural sciences, mathematics and medicine, the use of English as a world-wide lingua franca for LSP communication is generally welcomed as a most valuable and indispensable medium for global communication (Gnutzmann 2006b). The situation is, however, different in disciplines such as law, the social sciences and the humanities. These academic domains are strongly associated with language and culture, and since their objects of investigation are very much embedded in particular languages and cultures, the latter are very often assumed to play a natural and constitutive role in the research processes in these areas. It is for this reason that researchers, especially from the humanities, dismiss 'English monolingualism' in academia as an inadequate concept, because they see it above all as being associated with an Anglo-Saxon idea of science and in conflict with European science communication, which can only be "successful by strengthening the European science languages and the development of scientific multilingualism" (Ehlich 2004: 182).

4.2. English as a lingua franca: a linguistic variety in its own right?

In order to counterbalance the dominance of English and the alleged cultural and ideological baggage associated with it, several approaches including the acquisition of plurilingual competence, which is favoured by the Council of Europe (2001), have been advanced. One of the most promising has been to profile and establish English as a Lingua Franca (ELF) as a form of English in its own right, and ultimately as a linguistic variety of the language. It is particularly the work of Seidlhofer (e.g. 2002, 2006, 2007), Jenkins (2000), House (2003), Knapp and Meierkord (2002) and others, which has to be given credit for offering new perspectives on the structures and functions of ELF and treating such usage no longer as deficient occurrences of the language but as a form of English that will more and more derive its norms of correctness and appropriateness from its own usage rather than native British or American English. It has consequently been argued that given the identification of ELF as a linguistic variety "it should be possible to describe it systematically, and eventually also to provide a codification which would allow it to be captured in dictionaries and grammars and to be taught, with appropriate teaching materials to support this teaching" (Seidlhofer 2001: 14).

An important start for the description of ELF uses and structures has been made through the VOICE project, by "providing a sizeable, computer-readable corpus of English as it is spoken by this non-native speaking majority of users in different contexts" (http://www.univie.ac.at/voice/, last accessed 15/04/09). One of the major research objectives of VOICE, which is directed by Barbara Seidlhofer, is to provide a linguistic basis of ELF for teaching and learning purposes. From a communication perspective of ELF world-wide the inclusion of a reference section "English as a Lingua Franca" in the latest edition of the *Oxford Advanced Learner's Dictionary* is certainly quite remarkable and may have far-reaching consequences for the future in terms of codification (Seidlhofer 2005).

The concept of lingua franca is usually referred to as a medium of communication between people each speaking different mother tongues. Thus a lingua franca is an auxiliary, a third language. According to this definition native speakers of English could not be part of lingua franca communication in English. However, in view of the global spread of English, in which, obviously, many native speakers also participate, the original definition has been expanded and can also include native speakers, in particular if the cause and topic of the communication are of a non-native nature and are situated in neither of the communicators' country of origin, i.e. on neutral territory.

ELF is a kind of English which is commonly used by non-native speakers of the language and which can serve many different purposes ranging from the use of very formal and academic written English to very mundane spoken communication. Since not all ELF speakers make use of the whole range of purposes it can be assumed that they constitute a very heterogeneous group. When necessary, ELF speakers employ a range of communicative strategies such as simplification, paraphrasing and summons-answer sequencing. It is also reported that ELF communication is generally characterised by cooperation, transparency and consensus amongst its participants (cf. Beier 2006: 133). On the other hand, in an empirical study investigating the communicative behaviour of students in a competitive ELF situation Knapp (2002: 241) has shown that these characteristics did not apply there and were replaced by an uncooperative and diverging style. Since 'cooperation' depends significantly on what is at stake in an ELF communication, the context of situation will have to be taken into account for an adequate analysis of lingua franca talk.

The investigation of ELF as a variety in its own right has almost exclusively been devoted to the study of oral communication. However, linguistic standardisation is very much tied up with the written language. The process of linguistic standardisation generally involves the selection of a specific variety from a set of varieties that are used in a speech community. Thus, it seems doubtful whether this process can actually be applied to the various forms and uses of ELF. ELF communications cover such a wide range of topics and user competencies – from very broken to highly elaborate – that it is difficult to gauge all these uses for the purposes of selection. After all, ELF communication is transitory, ephemeral, heterogeneous, i.e. characterised by features that do not really contribute to stabilisation: "It is a temporary, potentially variable and/or unstable linguistic phenomenon, and in contrast to territorialised Englishes it is devoid of any conventional speech community identity value" (James 2005: 136–137). In order to limit the enormous range of variation in ELF communication, which makes it impossible to yield usable research results, it is necessary that research should focus on ELF in specific contexts, e.g. academic communication (Mauranen 2003: 525). In view of the considerable variability of ELF it is hard to imagine that ELF can justifiably reach the stage of codification. Furthermore, the focus of research (e.g. of the VOICE project) has been almost entirely on spoken, intelligibility-driven ELF communication. Thus, the teaching of ELF would obviously prevent learners and students from becoming familiar with more than a basic reading and writing competence. This may be acceptable for certain very restricted communication purposes, but it would not be generally compatible with the requirements of many ESP learners, especially those who are involved in a degree course in the natural sciences, engineering or economics and have to do a lot of reading in English and submit papers, project reports and dissertations in English.

The possible exclusion of the native speaker as a linguistic reference norm and as a model for the non-native users is seen as a major – socio-political – asset by proponents of ELF as a variety in its own right. This is an argument which should be taken seriously because successful ELF communication very much depends on the ability of the participants to negotiate meaning, which does not necessarily rely on native speaker norms. Furthermore, in the context of teaching English to non-native speakers, an insensitive enforcement of native speaker rules has generally demotivated students and has caused them to become taciturn in the foreign language. Obviously greater tolerance towards errors in foreign language teaching is needed.

4.3. Which teaching model for the English language classroom?

A principal question in the recent discussion has been whether, in view of the global spread of English, there is an emerging alternative to a Standard English or native speaker based model in ELT. Although there have been numerous suggestions in favour of non-native ELF-based models it is difficult to accept that the linguistic and pedagogical prerequisites for introducing a new paradigm can be met at present (cf. Gnutzmann 2005): in order to function as a teaching model, especially for the written language, the linguistic variety in question should be regarded as authoritative, which above all includes codification in grammars and dictionaries. It should be accepted by its users – native and non-native – and it should cover a wide range of communicative situations, from informal to formal ones. As a result, a suitable teaching model should also have a written manifestation in order to encode texts of a more formal nature and to serve as a reference model and as a model of orientation for learners. In no way does this imply that learners have to strictly adhere to native speaker norms to be successful users of the language.

Despite the controversies surrounding the developments towards a possible new ELF paradigm it can be confirmed that a great deal has been achieved: It has enhanced the self-esteem and optimism not only of non-native learners, but also of teachers and researchers, consolidated the use of ELF as a legitimate and functional mode of oral and intercultural communication and shown that communicative success is not necessarily dependent on linguistic correctness (cf. Gnutzmann 2007: 328). In line with the origin of a lingua franca, ELF research has so far focused almost exclusively on spoken communication, its conceptualisation and the identification of grammatical characteristics. Considering the importance of literacy in LSP but also in general language teaching it would be highly desirable for the textual and discourse dimensions of writing to receive more attention in the future.

References

Adamzik, Kirsten
1998 Methodische Probleme kontrastiver Textsortenstudien. In: Danneberg and Niederhauser (eds.), 103–130.

Ammon, Ulrich
1998 *Ist Deutsch noch internationale Wissenschaftssprache? Englisch auch für die Lehre an den deutschsprachigen Hochschulen*. Berlin/New York: Mouton de Gruyter.

Ammon, Ulrich and Grant McConnell
2002 *English as an Academic Language in Europe*. Frankfurt am Main: Lang.

Arntz, Reiner
2004 Der Vergleich von Fachsprachen. In: Baumann and Kalverkämper (eds.), 285–312.

Arntz, Reiner, Heribert Picht and Felix Mayer
2004 *Einführung in die Terminologiearbeit*. Hildesheim: Olms.

Baumann, Klaus-Dieter
2004 Emotionen in der Fachkommunikation – ein kommunikativ-kognitiver Untersuchungsansatz. In: Baumann and Kalverkämper (eds.), 83–119.

Baumann, Klaus-Dieter and Hartwig Kalverkämper (eds.)
2004 *Pluralität in der Fachsprachenforschung*. Tübingen: Narr.

Beier, Rudolf
2006 Englisch als fachliche Lingua franca in Vorlesungen. In: Werner Forner and Stephan Habscheid (eds.), *Sprachliche und fachliche Kompetenzen: Zwei Seiten eines Blattes?*, 131–149. Frankfurt am Main: Lang.

Blue, George M.
1988 Individualising academic writing tuition. In: Pauline Christina Robinson (ed.), *Academic Writing: Process and Product*, 95–99. (ELT Documents 129.) London: Modern English Publications.

Candlin, Christopher and Srikant Sarangi (eds.)
forthcoming *Handbook of Communication in Organisations and Professions*. (HAL Vol. 3.) Berlin/New York: Mouton de Gruyter.

Carter, Ronald and David Nunan (eds.)
2001 *The Cambridge Guide to Teaching English to Speakers of Other Languages*. Cambridge: Cambridge University Press.

Clyne, Michael
1991 The sociocultural dimension: The dilemma of the German speaking scholar. In: Schröder (ed.), 49–67.

Connor, Ulla
^{2}1996 *Contrastive Rhetoric: Cross-Cultural Aspects of Second-Language Writing*. 2nd edition. Cambridge: Cambridge University Press.

Council of Europe (ed.)
2001 *A Common European Framework of Reference for Languages: Learning, Teaching, Assessment*. Cambridge: Cambridge University Press. Online-document: http://www.coe.int/t/dg4/linguistic/Source/Framework_EN.pdf (last accessed 15/04/09).

Cummins, Jim and Chris Davison (eds.)
2007 *International Handbook of English Language Teaching: Part One*. New York: Springer.
Daneš, František
1974 Functional sentence perspective and the organisation of text. In: František Daneš (ed.), *Papers on Functional Sentence Perspective*, 106–128. The Hague: Mouton.
Danneberg, Lutz and Jürg Niederhauser (eds.)
1998 *Darstellungsformen der Wissenschaften im Kontrast: Aspekte der Methodik, Theorie und Empirie*. (Forum für Fachsprachen-Forschung 39.) Tübingen: Narr.
Douglas, Dan
2000 *Assessing Languages for Specific Purposes*. Cambridge: Cambridge University Press.
Dudley-Evans, Tony
2001 English for specific purposes. In: Carter and Nunan (eds.), 131–136.
Dudley-Evans, Tony and Maggie Jo St John
1998 *Developments in English for Specific Purposes: A Multi-Disciplinary Approach*. Cambridge: Cambridge University Press.
Ehlich, Konrad
2004 The future of German and other non-English languages for academic communication. In: Andreas Gardt and Bernd Hüppauf (eds.), *Globalization and the Future of German*, 173–184. Berlin/New York: Mouton de Gruyter.
Fearns, Anneliese
2003 Fachsprachenunterricht. In: Karl-Richard Bausch, Herbert Christ and Hans-Jürgen Krumm (eds.), *Handbuch Fremdsprachenunterricht*. 4th edition, 169–174. Tübingen: Francke.
Fluck, Hans-Rüdiger
1992 *Didaktik der Fachsprachen*. Tübingen: Narr.
Gläser, Rosemarie
1979 *Fachstile des Englischen*. Leipzig: VEB Enzyklopädie.
Gläser, Rosemarie
1990 *Fachtextsorten im Englischen*. Tübingen: Narr.
Gläser, Rosemarie
1995 *Linguistic Features and Genre Profiles of Scientific English*. Frankfurt am Main: Lang.
Gnutzmann, Claus
1996 Linguistische Fachsprache und wissenschaftsgeschichtlicher Kontext: Dargestellt am amerikanischen Strukturalismus und seinen Weiterentwicklungen. *Fachsprache/International Journal of LSP* 18 (1/2): 2–9.
Gnutzmann, Claus
2005 'Standard English' and 'World Standard English': Linguistic and pedagogical considerations. In: Gnutzmann and Intemann (eds.), 107–118.
Gnutzmann, Claus
2006a Fachsprachen und fachbezogener Fremdsprachenunterricht. In: Udo O. H. Jung (ed.), *Praktische Handreichung für Fremdsprachenlehrer*. 4th edition, 196–204. (Bayreuther Beiträge zur Glottodidaktik 2.) Frankfurt am Main: Lang.

Gnutzmann, Claus
2006b Fighting or fostering the dominance of English in academic communication?. *Fachsprache/International Journal of LSP* 28 (3/4): 195–207.

Gnutzmann, Claus
2007 Teaching and learning English in a global context: Applied-linguistic and pedagogical perspectives. In: Sabine Volk-Birke und Julia Lippert (eds.), *Anglistentag 2006 Halle: Proceedings*, 319–330. Trier: Wissenschaftlicher Verlag Trier.

Gnutzmann, Claus and Frauke Intemann (eds.)
2005 *The Globalisation of English and the English Language Classroom.* Tübingen: Narr.

Gnutzmann, Claus and Hermann Oldenburg
1991 Contrastive text linguistics in LSP-research: Theoretical considerations and some preliminary findings. In: Schröder (ed.), 103–136.

Göpferich, Susanne
2004 Die funktionale Satzperspektive und ihre Relevanz für die Textproduktion. In: Baumann and Kalverkämper (eds.), 217–242.

Gülich, Elisabeth and Wolfgang Raible
1979 Überlegungen zu einer makrostrukturellen Textanalyse. In: Elisabeth Gülich, Klaus Heger and Wolfgang Raible, *Linguistische Textanalyse: Überlegungen zur Gliederung von Texten*, 73–126. Hamburg: Helmut Buske.

Halliday, Michael A. K.
2005 Some grammatical problems in scientific English. In: Michael A. K. Halliday and James R. Martin, *Writing Science: Literacy and Discursive Power*, 69–85. London/New York: Routledge.

Hamp-Lyons, Liz
2001 English for academic purposes. In: Carter and Nunan (eds.), 126–130.

Hewings, Martin
2006 Introduction. In: Martin Hewings (ed.), *Academic Writing in Context: Implications and Applications: Papers in Honour of Tony Dudley-Evans*, 9–16. London/New York: Continuum.

Hoffmann, Lothar
1984 Seven roads to LSP. *Fachsprache/International Journal of LSP* 6 (1/2): 28–38.

Hoffmann, Lothar
1985 *Kommunikationsmittel Fachsprache: Eine Einführung*. Tübingen: Narr.

Hoffmann, Lothar
1988 *Vom Fachwort zum Fachtext: Beiträge zur Angewandten Linguistik*. Tübingen: Narr.

Hoffmann, Lothar
1989 Fachsprachenlinguistik und fachbezogene Fremdsprachenausbildung: Positionsbestimmungen aus Sicht der Leipziger Schule. *Die Neueren Sprachen* 88: 448–462.

Hoffmann, Lothar, Hartwig Kalverkämper and Herbert Ernst Wiegand
1998 *Fachsprachen: Ein internationales Handbuch zur Fachsprachenforschung und Terminologiewissenschaft*. (Handbücher zur Sprach- und Kommunikationswissenschaft 14.1.) Berlin: Mouton de Gruyter.

House, Juliane
2003 English as a lingua franca: A threat to multilingualism? *Journal of Sociolinguistics* 7 (4): 556–578.

Hutchinson, Tom and Alan Waters
1987 *English for Specific Purposes: A Learning-Centred Approach*. Cambridge: Cambridge University Press.

Hyland, Ken
2007 English for specific purposes: Some influences and impacts. In: Cummins and Davison (eds.), 391–402.

James, Allan
2005 The challenges of the lingua franca: English in the world and types of variety. In: Gnutzmann and Intemann (eds.), 133–144.

Jenkins, Jennifer
2000 *The Phonology of English as an International Language*. Oxford: Oxford University Press.

Jordan, Robert R.
1997 *English for Academic Purposes: A Guide and Resource Book for Teachers*. Cambridge: Cambridge University Press.

Kaplan, Robert B.
2001 English – the accidental language of science?. In: Ulrich Ammon (ed.), *The Dominance of English as a Language of Science: Effects on Other Language Communities*, 3–26. Berlin/New York: Mouton de Gruyter.

Kelz, Heinrich P.
1996 Fachsprachenunterricht. In: Hans Goebl, Peter H. Nelde, Zdenek Starý and Wolfgang Wölk (eds.), *Kontaktlinguistik: Ein internationales Handbuch zeitgenössischer Forschung*, 507–515. Berlin/New York: Mouton de Gruyter.

Klein, Eberhard
1988 Wenn Lehrer und Lerner die Rollen tauschen: motivationsfördernde Aspekte der Interaktion im fachbezogenen Fremdsprachenunterricht. In: Claus Gnutzmann (ed.), *Fachbezogener Fremdsprachenunterricht*, 189–204. Tübingen: Narr.

Knapp, Karlfried
2002 The fading out of the non-native speaker: Native speaker dominance in lingua-franca-situations. In: Knapp and Meierkord (eds.), 217–244.

Knapp, Karlfried and Christiane Meierkord (eds.)
2002 *Lingua Franca Communication*. Frankfurt am Main: Lang.

Knobloch, Clemens
1987 Esoterik und Exoterik: Über Begriffsmoden in den Humanwissenschaften. In: Clemens Knobloch (ed.), *Fachsprache und Wissenschaftssprache*, 55–70. Essen: Die blaue Eule.

Kretzenbacher, Heinz L.
1990 *Rekapitulation – Textstrategien der Zusammenfassung von wissenschaftlichen Fachtexten*. (Forum für Fachsprachen-Forschung 11.) Tübingen: Narr.

Laurén, Christer, Johan Myking and Heribert Picht
2004 Sprache, Domäne und Domänendynamik. *Fachsprache/International Journal of LSP* 26 (1/2): 5–13.

Leech, Geoffrey and Jan Svartvik
1994 *A Communicative Grammar of English*. London: Longman.
Ludwig, Heidrun
1999 *Methoden und Ziele der Fachtextlinguistik*. Marburg: Tectum.
Luelsdorff, Philip A. (ed.)
1994 *The Prague School of Structural and Functional Linguistics: A Short Introduction*. (Linguistic and Literary Studies in Eastern Europe.) Amsterdam: Benjamins.
Maiworm, Friedhelm and Bernd Wächter (eds.)
2002 *English-Language-Taught Degree Programmes in European Higher Education: Trends and Success Factors*. Bonn: Lemmens.
Mauranen, Anna
1993 *Cultural Differences in Academic Rhetoric: A Textlinguistic Study*. Frankfurt am Main: Lang.
Mauranen, Anna
2003 The Corpus of English as a Lingua Franca in academic settings. *TESOL Quarterly* 37 (3): 513–527.
Mauranen, Anna
2006 Descriptions or explantations? Some methodological issues in Contrastive Rhetoric. In: Martin Hewings (ed.), *Academic Writing in Context*, 43–54. London/New Xork: Continuum.
Mühlhaus, Susanne and Teresa Lawlor
1999 Languages for specific purposes for undergraduate and postgraduate courses: A case study. *Fachsprache/International Journal of LSP* 1 (2): 53–60.
Oldenburg, Hermann
1992 *Angewandte Fachtextlinguistik: "Conclusions" und Zusammenfassungen*. (Forum für Fachsprachen-Forschung 17.) Tübingen: Narr.
Pennycook, Alastair
1994 *The Cultural Politics of English as an International Language*. (Language in Social Life Series.) London/New York: Longman.
Phillipson, Robert
2003 *English-Only Europe? Challenging Language Policy*. London/New York: Routledge.
Sager, Juan C., David Dungworth and Peter F. McDonald
1980 *English Special Languages*. Wiesbaden: Brandstetter.
Scharnhorst, Jürgen and Erika Ising (eds.)
1976 *Grundlagen der Sprachkultur: Beiträge der Prager Linguistik zur Sprachtheorie und Sprachpflege*. Berlin: Akademie-Verlag.
Schröder, Hartmut (ed.)
1991 *Subject-Oriented Texts*. Berlin/New York: Mouton de Gruyter.
Seidlhofer, Barbara
1995 *Approaches to Summarization: Discourse Analysis and Language Education*. (Language in Performance 11.) Tübingen: Narr.
Seidlhofer, Barbara
2001 Towards making "Euro-English" a linguistic reality. *English Today* 17: 14–16.
Seidlhofer, Barbara
2002 The shape of things to come? Some basic questions about English as a lingua franca. In: Knapp and Meierkord (eds.), 269–302.

Seidlhofer, Barbara
2005 English as a Lingua Franca. In: Albert S. Hornby (ed.), *Oxford Advanced Learner's Dictionary of Current English*, R92. Oxford: Oxford University Press.

Seidlhofer, Barbara
2006 English as a lingua franca in the expanding circle: What it isn't. In: Rani Rubdy and Mario Saraceni (eds.), *English in the World: Global Rules, Global Roles*, 40–50. London: Continuum.

Seidlhofer, Barbara
2007 Common property: English as a lingua franca in Europe. In: Cummins and Davison (eds.), 137–153.

Skudlik, Sabine
1990 *Sprachen in den Wissenschaften: Deutsch und Englisch in der Internationalen Kommunikation*. Tübingen: Narr.

Swales, John M.
1990 *Genre Analysis: English in Academic and Research Settings*. Cambridge: Cambridge University Press.

Trimble, Louis
1989 *English for Science and Technology: A Discourse Approach*. Cambridge: Cambridge University Press.

Weise, Günter
2007 *Struktur und Funktion englischer Wissenschaftstexte*. (Allgemeine Literatur- und Sprachwissenschaft 9.) Essen: Die blaue Eule.

Wildegans, Gotthard
1997 Fachverstehen und Sprachverstehen. In: Armin Wolff and Walter Schleyer (eds.), *Fach- und Sprachunterricht: Gemeinsamkeiten und Unterschiede. Studiengänge Deutsch als Fremdsprache: Von der Theorie zur Praxis*, 21–29. Regensburg: Fachverband Deutsch als Fremdsprache.

Wolff, Dieter
2009 Content and language integrated learning. See chapter 20 in this volume.

Recommended Readings

Bibliographies

Bierbaumer, Peter and Anja Burkert (eds.)
1997 *Englisch als Fachsprache. Kommentierte Bibliographie. Sonderheft Fachsprache 2*. Wien: Braumüller.

An LSP-bibliography entitled "Kleine Bibliographie fachsprachlicher Untersuchungen" has appeared regularly and biannually in the Austrian journal *Fachsprache. International Journal of LSP* since the publication of its first volume in 1976 until today. This very useful bibliography, presently compiled by Ines-A. Busch-Lauer, is arranged under the topic headings, 'bibliographies', 'anthologies', 'LSP in general', 'terminology', 'translation of LSP texts', and 'LSP teaching'.

Handbooks, overviews, general literature

Brieger, Nick
2006 *Technical English: Vocabulary and Grammar.* 2nd edition. München: Langenscheidt.

Buhlmann, Rosemarie and Anneliese Fearns
2000 *Handbuch des Fachsprachenunterrichts: Unter besonderer Berücksichtigung naturwissenschaftlich-technischer Fachsprachen.* 6th edition. Tübingen: Narr.

Engberg, Jan
2007 *New Directions in LSP Teaching.* Bern: Lang.

Flowerdew, John
2001 *Research Perspectives on English for Academic Purposes.* Cambridge: Cambridge University Press.

Friedrich, Patricia
2008 *Teaching Academic Writing.* London: Continuum.

Gavioli, Laura
2005 *Exploring Corpora for ESP Learning.* Amsterdam: Benjamins.

Gotti, Maurizio and Davide Giannoni
2006 *New Trends in Specialized Discourse Analysis.* Bern: Lang.

Harding, Keith
2007 *English for Specific Purposes.* Oxford: Oxford University Press.

Hartley, James
2008 *Academic Writing and Publishing: A Practical Handbook.* London: Routledge.

Herzog, Gottfried
2007 *Normen für Übersetzer und technische Autoren.* 2nd edition. Berlin: Beuth.

Hoffmann, Lothar, Hartwig Kalverkämper and Herbert Ernst Wiegand (eds.)
1998 *Fachsprachen/Languages for Special Purposes. Ein internationales Handbuch zur Fachsprachenforschung und Terminologiewissenschaft/An International Handbook of Special-Language and Terminology Research (Handbücher zur Sprach- und Kommunikationswissenschaft/Handbooks of Linguistics and Communication Science, 14(2)).* Berlin/New York: Mouton de Gruyter.

Horn-Helf, Brigitte
2007 *Kulturdifferenz in Fachtextsortenkonventionen: Analyse und Translation; ein Lehr- und Arbeitsbuch.* Frankfurt am Main: Lang.

Hüttner, Julia Isabel
2007 *Academic Writing in a Foreign Language: An Extended Genre Analysis of Student Texts.* Frankfurt am Main: Lang.

Hyland, Ken
2007 *English for Academic Purposes: An Advanced Resource Book.* 2nd edition. London: Routledge.

Hyland, Ken and Marina Bondi (eds.)
2006 *Academic Discourse Across Disciplines.* Frankfurt am Main: Lang.

Koester, Almut
2007 *The Language of Work.* 2nd edition. London: Routledge.

Leki, Ilona
2007 *Undergraduates in a Second Language: Challenges and Complexities of Academic Literacy Development*. New York: Erlbaum.

McCarthy, Michael
2008 *Academic Vocabulary in Use: 50 Units of Academic Vocabulary Reference and Practice; Self-Study and Classroom Use*. Cambridge: Cambridge University Press.

Pickett, Nell Ann
2000 *Technical English: Writing, Reading, and Speaking*. 8th edition. New York: Longman.

Roelcke, Thorsten
2005 *Fachsprachen*. 2nd edition. Berlin: Erich Schmidt Verlag.

Williams, Ivor
2007 *English for Science and Engineering*. Boston: Thomson.

Young, Dona
2008 *Business English: Writing for the Global Workplace*. New York, NY: McGraw-Hill.

Journals

English for Specific Purposes
Fachsprache. International Journal of LSP
Journal of English for Academic Purposes
System, an international journal of educational technology and applied linguistics
Terminology. International Journal of Theoretical and Applied Issues in Specialized Communication

20. Content and language integrated learning

Dieter Wolff

1. Introduction

Until recently politicians, language planners and educationalists were ready to believe in the myths propagated by economists and industrialists who argued that one international language – namely English – is sufficient to cater for the communicative needs of our globalised society. This tendency has changed considerably in recent years: the European Union can serve as an example. Although it always was the language policy of the European Commission to accept the national languages of its member states, to protect European minority languages and to encourage multilingual communication, the need to enable European citizens to speak at least two languages apart from their mother tongue was recognised only fairly recently. Now the European member states begin to realise that one single language which in the global context is always a minority language and a second or foreign language for most of the people using it, will not suffice as the only tool for communication within the Union.

Although politicians and educationalists seem to have recognised the necessity of learning other foreign languages the latter have not reached agreement yet as to the most efficient methodological approach. When analysing the results of foreign language teaching in our schools it becomes clear that only few students acquire the linguistic competence necessary for their future life. This is true for all the languages they learn including the first foreign language. These findings prove that our present-day methodological approaches to foreign language teaching and learning do not lead to the desired results: proficiency in two foreign languages, which enables learners to interact competently in their profession and in everyday life.

Although the so-called communicative approach proved much more successful than all the former grammar-oriented approaches to language learning it does not seem efficient enough to reach the language teaching and learning goals which have been set up in the context of the new language policy. New approaches which are more content- and process-oriented have been brought forward and seem to be better suited to attain these goals. One of these is *Content and Language Integrated Learning*, an approach which will be focussed upon in this chapter.

2. Outline and History of Content and Language Integrated Learning (CLIL)

Content and Language Integrated Learning (CLIL) as an educational approach was developed in Europe and is, therefore, very strongly European-oriented. It is based on the well-known assumption that foreign languages are best learnt by focussing in the classroom not so much on language – its form and structure – but on the content which is transmitted through language. Compared to other content-based approaches the specific novelty of this approach is that classroom content is not so much taken from everyday life or general content of the target language culture but rather drawn from content subjects or academic viz. scientific disciplines.

This different notion of content which is the most typical feature of the approach is of great interest in the current discussion on improving foreign language competence. First, the approach can be adapted to all levels of language teaching: primary, secondary and tertiary, for all curricula include academic content: primary curricula contain content areas on a very basic level, secondary curricula more specifically in content subjects (History, Geography, Mathematics), and tertiary curricula consist of academic subjects (Information Technology, Physics, Engineering, Sociology, Arts, Design etc.) which can at least partially be integrated into the students' language studies. And second, teaching content and language in integration saves time within the overall curriculum. If content and language are learnt and taught in integration and not in isolation the time available for the teaching/learning process of a content subject and a foreign language doubles; length of study time both for language and content subject can thus be reduced considerably, and as a consequence, more languages can be introduced into the curriculum and more time can be devoted to the study of each language.

2.1. A definition of CLIL

Content and Language Integrated Learning (CLIL) has been introduced recently as a common term for a number of similar approaches in Europe to teach content subjects through a foreign language. Other terms used are *Bilingual Content Teaching*, *Bilingual Subject Teaching* or *Content-Based Language Teaching*. The term CLIL is now the most commonly used, however, especially since it describes the approach better than any of the other terms and since a definition has been found which seems to be acceptable to everybody:

> Content and language integrated learning (CLIL) is a generic term and refers to any educational situation in which an additional language and therefore not the most widely used language of the environment is used for the teaching and learning of subjects other than the language itself (Marsh and Langé 2000: iii).

There are at least three points which are essential in the context of this general definition. The most important one is that CLIL must not be regarded simply as an approach to language teaching and learning but that it is concerned both with content and language. Many scholars tend to believe that within the CLIL paradigm content subjects are taught in a foreign language only to improve the students' foreign language competence. But this is not the intention of this approach, which is geared towards content learning as much as towards language learning. Recent research (which will be dealt with more extensively in part 6 of this paper) has made it clear that although foreign language proficiency is improved within CLIL even when the most traditional methodology is used, the content subject benefits as much from such an approach. From what we know now about content subject learning in a foreign language we can conclude that learners learn faster and are more motivated than those in traditional content subject classrooms. It has also been shown that learners look at content from a different and broader perspective when it is taught in another language.

The second point is equally important: within a CLIL framework content and language are learnt in integration. The two subjects – a language and a content subject like History or Geography – are related to each other and dealt with as a whole. This does not take place within the traditional school or university framework, where learners have difficulties in establishing relationships between subjects (cf. Hallet 1998). It is a pedagogical principle, however, in primary schools.

The last point in the definition we would like to highlight has something to do with the way language is dealt with in the classroom. In our definition it is made clear that another language is used to teach and learn content subjects, i.e. that it is the medium of instruction. This does not mean, however, that language as such should not be focused upon in the classroom. Language is both content and medium in the CLIL classroom. This distinguishes CLIL from what is usually called immersion (for a definition of the term cf. for example Genesee 1986, 1987) in language teaching methodology. On the other hand, in the CLIL classroom language is not taught in the same way as in a traditional classroom – it is focused upon when it is necessary and important for the understanding of a specific aspect of the content subject or the academic discipline. (Methodological aspects of CLIL are dealt with in 3.2. in more detail)

2.2. Variants of CLIL

CLIL as an educational concept is not homogeneous; a rather large number of different variants can be distinguished. Variation depends on a number of factors of which the school type – primary, secondary, tertiary – is the most important. A CLIL approach varies independent of a specific educational system or other factors, according to whether it takes place in primary, secondary or tertiary education. Other factors responsible for variation are country-specific, i.e. environmental. They depend on the specific educational system and on the wider socio-linguistic context in which the approach is embedded. In the following a distinction is made between variants induced by typology and by the specific environment.

2.2.1. *Typologically induced variants*

The number of *primary schools* which have adopted some kind of CLIL approach is surprisingly high. A distinction must be made between at least two types of primary CLIL schools:

(1) The first type of primary CLIL schools exists in bilingual border regions, in France for example in Alsace, in Italy in Southern Tyrol or in the Aosta Valley. In Germany we find primary CLIL schools of this type also in large industrial centres, for example in Berlin, where primary classes, in a non-CLIL context, include learners of often up to eight different mother tongues. In France and Italy the minority languages (German and French) are used as languages of instruction, in the CLIL classrooms in Berlin one of the larger minority languages is the language in which part of the content is taught. This can be Turkish, Greek, Spanish, Italian or Russian. So, this type of primary CLIL is often but not always a combination of additive and maintenance bilingual education (cf. Baker 1996); learners maintain their family language while they are also acquiring a higher language competence in the society they live in.

(2) But purely additive bilingual education is common as well at primary level, for example when learners in Spain are taught part of their content curriculum in English, French or German. Here the language of instruction is neither the language spoken in the country or the learners' mother tongue. Often primary CLIL branches of this type are the outcome of parents' initiatives, based on private bilingual kindergarten and pre-schools.

The holistic methodological approach which is characteristic of primary education makes it necessary to integrate the foreign language into the subject areas taught in the classroom. The larger subject areas are Language (mother tongue and foreign language), Natural Sciences, Social Sciences, Arts and Sports; they are taught partly in the majority language and partly in the minority or foreign language chosen. In the 14 primary CLIL schools in Berlin non-German children are chosen according to their first language and brought together with an equal number of German speaking children, so that we have Turkish-German, Spanish-German or Greek-German classes. Children have separate language classes, both in the mother tongue and in the foreign language, and content areas are taught half in German and half in the other language. Native speakers of both languages teach mother tongue and foreign language classes, content is often taught in tandems. In these classes, for the non-German children

CLIL is both maintenance and additive bilingual education, for the German children the main goal is the addition of another language. (Zydatiß 2000)

From a survey which was undertaken recently (cf. Marsh, Maljers and Hartiala 2001) some important information was gathered as to organisational and structural aspects of CLIL in *secondary schools* in Europe. Although CLIL has developed differently in different European school systems there are a number of similarities which are mentioned here in order to make the approach more transparent as an educational framework.

In general, CLIL schools or CLIL branches are organised in such a way that one or more content subjects (in general from the Humanities and Social Sciences) are taught in a foreign language for at least four years. The content subjects most frequently chosen are History, Geography and Social Sciences. The most frequently used languages are English and French, German ranking third. In general, it can be estimated that in secondary CLIL schools the age span of learners can reach from ten to eighteen years. The number of schools offering preparatory language classes for CLIL is fairly small; if Germany is excluded, where preparatory courses are compulsory, not more than 15 percent of the schools make such an offer. It is interesting to note that maintenance education is not so important in secondary CLIL.

In *tertiary education* it is mainly vocational schools which have opted for teaching content through a foreign language. In these schools the content subjects are, in general, different from secondary schools, ranging from Information Technology to Economics and Business Studies, from Agriculture to Mechanics. In some of the smaller European countries like Finland or the Netherlands management or professional schools exist which educate their students entirely in a foreign language, usually English. In colleges and universities, however, CLIL is only rarely used as a methodological approach to language and content teaching. Apart from academic subjects like *English or French Studies* or teacher training programmes geared at future teachers of English or other languages which are at least partly taught in English or other respective languages, the number of academic subjects taught in a foreign language is still comparatively low. Even if languages are part of a university curriculum they are learnt separately and not in integration with the content of the academic subject. This is true even for the initiatives taken by university councils in Germany and similarly in France to offer entire university programmes in English in order to attract foreign students from other, especially Asian countries.

2.2.2. *Environmentally induced variants*

We will now discuss the so-called environmental parameters which are responsible for the development of different forms of CLIL in different countries. A distinction can be made between five environmental parameters:

1. *Interpretation of the concept*: Despite the fact that CLIL as a general educational concept is quite homogeneous in those countries in which it has been introduced, variation in its interpretation can be observed. Variation can be represented on a scale which reaches from pure foreign language teaching on the one end to a form of content teaching in which the focus on language is almost non-existent, and the foreign language is predominantly used as a working language. The former interpretation could also be called a language-learning, the latter a content-learning interpretation. CLIL as a language learning approach is seen mainly as an innovative form of language teaching, and the potential available for content subject learning is less taken into account. It is assumed that by applying the CLIL concept the foreign language competence of the learner is improved. It is quite natural that on the basis of such an interpretation teaching is being influenced methodologically by foreign language teaching concepts; in some way this type of interpretation can be classified as foreign language teaching using other contents than traditional foreign language teaching contents. The other interpretation in which the foreign language is used as a working language leads to a different, content-oriented methodology which is strongly influenced by mother-tongue content subject teaching. In its purest form this concept strongly relies on the immersion idea, which assumes that learners inductively pick up the foreign language while working with content. Most CLIL specialists locate themselves on this scale more towards its content-oriented end, although most of them do not believe that learners can tackle the difficult task of learning the foreign language purely inductively; they plead for an integration of language and subject teaching in order to use the full potential of the integrative approach.

2. *Choice of subjects*: From the very beginning this parameter has led to much discussion. Traditionally, subjects included in the Social Sciences or the Humanities were taught in a foreign language. Statistically, subjects like History, Geography or Social Sciences are the most common. In some countries Natural Science subjects like Mathematics or Biology are taught – often still experimentally – in a foreign language. In primary schools where subjects are usually included into larger content fields the Social Sciences field in which children first encounter historical, geographical and sociological aspects is the most popular. The discussion on the suitability of certain subjects or content fields with respect to teaching them in another language has not gone very far yet. It is fairly certain, however, that subjects belonging to the Humanities are more suitable when it comes to the promotion of interculturality, as they are characterised by culture-specific features which by contrast lead to consciousness-raising with respect to the cultural particularities of the target language culture. (cf. however the research positions discussed with respect to intercultural learning in part 6 of this paper). When looking at the countries which have implemented CLIL (cf. the new Eurydice report prepared by the European

Commission) it can be seen that in almost all of them subjects from the Humanities are usually the natural choice while in some countries Natural Sciences subjects are also taught, at least experimentally.

3. *Exposure time*: It is only plausible that a decision about the time a learner should be exposed to content-subject learning in a foreign language leads to variation in the CLIL approach which is being developed. The varieties are characterised in particular by the number of subjects which are taught in the foreign language, and by the time (in months or years) learners are exposed to this teaching process. The time span lasts between exposure for several years (maximum seven years according to my knowledge) and only a few weeks. It is quite common that up to three content subjects are taught in a foreign language. Closely related to this and also influencing exposure time is the use of both native and foreign language in the classroom, i.e. a certain amount of content might be taught in the foreign and the rest in the learner's native language. Whereas in some countries a change of language of this kind is quite common, in others teachers tend to use the foreign language only in the classroom. This aspect will also be discussed in the chapter on methodology (cf. 3.2.) in which we will introduce the concept of functional bilingualism. A specific type of change between languages is related to the term modular CLIL which we will discuss in the next paragraph (cf. 2.3.).

4. *Curricular integration*: Different variants of CLIL are also influenced by the decision to really implement this approach into the curricular and evaluative structure of an educational system. If no curriculum exists for CLIL in a specific country the approach takes a certain arbitrary character which does not only influence its quality but can also lead to its being offered only irregularly which usually will be followed by its disappearance. And if, furthermore, the CLIL concept does not rely on examinations and certification which are recognised by the educational system as such it will not be accepted. At present, a number of approaches are highly arbitrary seen from this angle, others are fully integrated into the educational system and even lead to diploma which are recognised by other countries.

5. *Linguistic situation*: One of the most influential parameters influencing CLIL is the linguistic situation in which this approach is embedded. This becomes particularly clear when looking at the situation in Europe. It is well known that Europe is a geographical unit which can be characterised language-wise by two observable facts: linguistic variation within its boundaries and, additionally, linguistic variation within many of its states. For the latter it is typical that the different languages spoken in one country are related differently to one another[1]. This complex linguistic situation contributes to the development of different types of CLIL. In some cases it is the language which is the other official or officially recognised language which determines the choice of the CLIL language. In other cases the language of the neighbouring country is chosen as

the CLIL language. This is quite common in regions which have a political border with the other country. In Germany, for example, the CLIL language of most federal states bordering France (Rhineland-Palatinate, Sarre, Baden-Württemberg) is French. It is understandable that in such linguistic contexts specific variants of CLIL develop, especially because learners are often in contact with this language in their extra-school life.

2.3. Modular CLIL

As mentioned above, CLIL has been introduced recently in many schools especially in the European Union. Implementing this approach in all schools is a very costly affair, however. This is the reason why a number of European states are experimenting with a variant of CLIL which could be introduced fairly quickly in all schools. This variant which is already quite common in secondary schools in Germany is called modular CLIL.

Modular CLIL can be defined as an approach to teaching content in a foreign language in non-language subjects over shorter periods of time. A History teacher who decides to teach part of the curriculum in the students' mother tongue and another part in a foreign language might serve as an example. He/she might wish to teach the history of the Nazi period in Germany in German or the French Revolution in French. Similarly, a Mathematics teacher could decide to teach the theory of probabilities in French, the first foreign language of his/her students. The rest of the curriculum would, however, be taught in the students' mother tongue. The content elements which the teacher chooses are usually called modules, they could also be called projects or thematic units. It is easy to see that although modular CLIL could be implemented theoretically in all schools it is subject to a number of conditions which often cannot be fulfilled. First, the teacher has to have the linguistic competence in a foreign language to be able to teach content. Second, the students' linguistic competence in the CLIL language must be sufficient to follow instruction. If the teacher is not a content but a language teacher it is important to ensure that he/she knows enough about the content subject to be able to teach it. Teachers who have a dual qualification in content and language teaching are, of course, best suited to teach CLIL modules. As we will discuss in more detail later, these teachers are quite common in the German-speaking countries where dual qualifications are the rule at least in secondary education.

The learning objectives of modular CLIL are slightly different from regular CLIL. In a way, modular CLIL is an incentive to make learners understand how important a foreign language can be in comprehending a content subject. Like regular CLIL it is a helpful tool to learn language registers which are useful in professional life. It is the language-for-specific-purposes aspect which is particularly attractive although learners will not be as competent as regular CLIL learners at the end of their studies. But in dealing with the foreign language within a content subject context they better understand the use of foreign languages in their education. This usually has a highly motivating effect for their language learning processes.

In modular CLIL competent teachers are responsible for the choice of the thematic units and/or the project themes they intend to work on in the foreign language. There are a number of topics which are particularly suited for use in modular CLIL. First, in the Humanities and Social Sciences there are topics which are specifically related to the foreign language culture, for example historical or geographical themes, e.g. the Spanish Civil war (in Spanish), the geographical structure of Italy (in Italian). Second, themes which can be dealt with from one's own and the foreign culture's perspective are interesting with respect to the development of multiperspectivity, for example discussing Nazism and the Second World War, using native German and English or French documents. Seen from a materials' perspective topics for which a large amount of interesting and not too difficult foreign language materials exist are quite suitable for modular CLIL as well.

On the whole, modular CLIL is a useful concept to help implementing the CLIL idea into our school systems. It certainly cannot replace CLIL as such but it can serve as a bridge between traditional language teaching on the one hand and regular CLIL on the other.

2.4. Some historical remarks on CLIL

When looking at European history we can easily see that in medieval as well as in early modern and modern societies multilingualism was more or less the rule and monolingualism the exception. This statement is true, of course, only for the higher social classes, the nobility, the clergy and later on the bourgeoisie. It is still astonishing, however, to read that at Frederick II' court French was the vernacular language, that the Austrian emperors spoke up to twelve different languages or that the diplomats at the European courts could interact with one another without using an interpreter. The question arises how these people could develop such a high competence in other languages. It is certain that many learned a second or even a third language the natural way like children learn their mother tongue. But institutional language learning, especially when the language to be learned was Latin, was quite common even during the Middle Ages. Often Latin was not only the content but also the medium of instruction especially with respect to content subjects. And at quite an early stage we can find forms of integrated content and language learning, for example in the education of the children of the nobility by private teachers and gouvernantes who used their mother tongues (which were foreign languages for their protegés) to teach them content subjects.

The first schools in which modern foreign languages were used as working languages were founded in the 18th century. An interesting example is the first French-speaking Hugenot school in Berlin, the *Gymnasium zum Grauen Kloster* which still exists as a Franco-German school. In the beginning of the 20th century we find schools of this type in many European, African, American and Asian capitals, their number has increased considerably after the second world war, especially due to the European integration. Nowadays the European Union has founded such schools in all the cities in which a European institution has its place. In these European schools and also in International Schools it is not uncommon that three or even more foreign languages are used as working languages. It is clear that these schools whether they are German, English or French schools abroad or European schools are not CLIL schools in the strict sense of the term although they make use of the most important methodological principle of CLIL, the use of a foreign language to teach content.

The history of CLIL in Germany during the last century can serve as a good example to understand what distinguishes CLIL from the European school model. Integrated language and content education which fits the working definition of CLIL has quite a long history in the German school system. Already in the first half of the 20th century private and mostly elitist schools existed which made use of the main principle of CLIL, i.e. using another language to teach a limited number of content subjects. After the second world war the number of these schools increased. Most of them were grammar schools in which CLIL branches were founded after the Franco-German friendship treaty was concluded in 1963. And they were normal state schools which, apart from traditional subject-specific education, implemented so-called bilingual branches or wings in which up to three subjects and a language were taught in integration. For more than ten years French used to be the only CLIL language in this type of school. In the eighties more and more grammar schools included bilingual branches in which English was the language of instruction. During that time other secondary schools ('Realschulen', 'Hauptschulen') also introduced mainly English-based CLIL. Nowadays CLIL schools can be found in all the 'Länder' of the Federal Republic.

It is important to note that the history of CLIL in Germany reflects a development from elitist CLIL to a form of CLIL available for all secondary students. In a way, the implementation of CLIL in all school types has led to a kind of democratisation of language learning and of the school system.

3. Psychological, methodological and curricular considerations

In the following we will give an overview of some of the psychological, methodological and curricular considerations which played an important role in recent discussions on CLIL. Psychologically, our interest is focussed on the learner and the added value of CLIL for the classroom. Methodologically, we will discuss the CLIL approach as compared to traditional language and content teaching approaches. And from a curricular point of view we will look at aspects of curricular development from a CLIL perspective.

3.1. Psychological considerations

It was already mentioned that foreign language teaching is not as successful as it should be. Lack of motivation, enthusiasm and interest are common with learners in many classrooms. Foreign language teaching is regarded as difficult; learners do not see any use in dealing with another language. The situation is similar in content teaching. Lack of motivation and interest seem to be less marked, however, than in language teaching. In recent discussions it is maintained that CLIL offers opportunities to improve this situation. In the following we will discuss some of the arguments from a learning psychological angle.

CLIL theoreticians and teachers alike claim that the learning environment created by CLIL increases the learner's general learning capacities and also his/her motivation and interest. The integration of content subject and language, they say, creates a learning environment which cannot be set up within isolated subject or language teaching. A CLIL classroom which is set up according to modern educational principles is a kind of workshop in which learners are not simply inundated with school knowledge but in which the reality of the school is connected with the reality of the world outside. The fictional world of the language classroom is substituted by something more real which interlinks with the world outside (cf. Barnes 1976). Although these claims are not yet empirically validated they can be found in most reports available on CLIL classrooms.

CLIL theoreticians also focus on the learner. They argue that in CLIL the separate roles of the learner as a foreign language learner and a content subject learner merge into one role. He/she acquires the concepts and schemata of the content subject first in another language; this process is similar to first language acquisition where the child acquires the linguistic signs and the underlying concepts at the same time. Especially for the higher-ranking scientific facts and processes he/she builds up new concepts which are not influenced by everyday concepts developed in the learner's mother tongue. In CLIL the learner's concepts are foreign language based, the mother tongue concepts build on these foreign language concepts because the learner gets into contact with specific parts of the world around him first via the foreign language.

The learner's linguistic development is also influenced positively in a CLIL environment. The complex concepts which he develops help him to express himself adequately in the foreign language with respect to the contents of the content subject. And the fact that content subject learning has a scientific character contributes to the learner's developing an academic competence in the foreign language (cf. Cummins 1987)[2]. In CLIL the learner acquires linguistic competencies which do not only extend beyond communicative competence but also relate much more to the use of the foreign language in professional life later on.

Another added value which is being discussed by CLIL theoreticians but also by teachers and concerns both content subject and language relates to the content component. The content subject deals with content which is appropriate to the learner's state of cognitive development, i.e. content he/she would also be taught in his mother tongue classroom at that time. Motivation, curiosity and involvement can therefore be raised much better through CLIL than through the contents of the traditional foreign language classroom (cf. Wolff 1997a).

3.2. Methodological considerations

For many years, when CLIL played only a minor role in institutionalised teaching and learning, methodological aspects were neglected to a large extent. In general, teachers taught their content subject in the foreign language just as they would have taught it in their mother tongue. Similarly, language teaching and learning in the CLIL classroom took place according to traditional language teaching methodology. In a way, the content of the content subject simply replaced the traditional content of the language classroom, and apart from this the CLIL classroom looked like a traditional teacher-centred language or content subject classroom.

The situation has changed considerably in recent years. Educationalists and practising teachers have realised that the pedagogical potential of CLIL is higher than they had anticipated, and a number of more innovative advocates of CLIL insist that a specific CLIL methodology should be developed. (Wolff 1997b; Thürmann 2000; Abendroth-Timmer et al. 2004) The development of such a methodology is under way now for secondary CLIL; the methodological discussion centres around three general issues: promoting reading comprehension, focus on writing, developing methods in which language sensitive teaching and learning plays a central role. There can be no doubt that these issues reach far beyond the typical methodological discussions in language and content teaching.

Reading and reading skills are regarded as highly important in the CLIL classroom. Most of the acquisitional processes are related to reading comprehension: learners work with documents and other sources in order to acquire knowledge in the content subject. Although reading strategies play an important role in all learning contexts, in CLIL they decide on the students' success or failure. A specific CLIL methodology has to take this into account: thus the promotion of reading strategies plays an important role in all methodological discussions. And it must not be forgotten that content subject work also includes specific reading skills: e.g. working with graphs, maps, charts etc. Specific processing strategies have to be acquired which help learners to process the information contained in these materials. In a way, the focus on processing strategies in the CLIL classroom is characteristic of a new methodological approach, which is not only language- but also content-based. Learners do not read texts in order to learn language but in order to acquire knowledge in the content subject. This makes the whole learning process more skill-oriented both with respect to language and to content.

This is also true of the productive skills. Whereas in the communicative language classroom the promotion of oral skills is regarded as being particularly important, in CLIL classrooms writing skills take up a highly significant role. From very early on learners have to use the foreign language to write down the results of what they have studied: they compose reports, definitions, compile results of observations etc. Content subject language competence is to a large extent text competence (cf. Portmann-Tselekas 2002), and a CLIL methodology must be a methodology geared towards writing proficiency in the foreign language.

The most important point in the discussion is, however, the integration of content and language in the CLIL classroom. It has become clear from the experience we have had with communicative and other related language learning approaches that purely meaning-focused language learning is not very successful: focus on form is as important, especially in institutionalised learning contexts. This is the reason why CLIL teachers opt for an approach which is content-oriented but at the same time language-sensitive. It is the content of the content subject which is in the centre of the learning-teaching process, but in order to deal with the content in the foreign language learners have to acquire both knowledge and skills which are necessary to manipulate this content. In the classroom this works according to the language-across-the-curriculum principle, i.e. language is focused upon whenever necessary.

Three aspects of language work have been discussed in some detail in recent years. One is terminology which has lost its overwhelming importance in the CLIL classroom. Especially in the early CLIL years teachers believed that content teaching could only work if students had the precise terminology in the foreign language at their disposal. Language work during the sixties and seventies simply consisted of learning lists of terminological expressions. Nowadays it is emphasised that the terminological inventory of a content subject can be differentiated into more general and more specific terms. As quite a number of CLIL specialists (for example Krechel 1995) have put it, in CLIL one should begin by providing more general content subject-oriented terminology and should then slowly move towards more and more specific vocabulary.

The second aspect is more skill-oriented and concerns classroom discourse. Because of its content orientation classroom discourse plays a much more important role in CLIL than in a traditional language classroom. According to Thürmann (1999) discourse skills in a CLIL classroom can be analysed as consisting of two sets: one more general functional set consisting of speech acts like identify – classify/define – describe – explain – conclude/argue – evaluate and one more specific set which differs according to content subjects or groups of subjects, for example making inductions/stating laws – describing states and processes – working with graphs, diagrams, tables etc. – interpreting – writing reports. These pragmatic categories are also regarded as the building stones for vocabulary and vocabulary work in the classroom.

The last language-oriented methodological aspect to be mentioned here is concerned with the use of language in the classroom. Like in a modern communicative language classroom the foreign or CLIL language is used as frequently as possible. But in a CLIL classroom in which intercultural learning is based on the principle of contrastivity it can also be useful to work with first language materials. When looking, for example, at a historical event like the First World War from a French and a German perspective this multiperspectival view can only be developed in the students if they work with French and German materials, i.e. foreign language and mother-tongue texts. Methodologically, the CLIL classroom should not be characterised by monolingualism (i.e. using the foreign language exclusively) but rather by functional bilingualism, i.e. using the mother tongue and mother tongue materials when it is necessary to promote a multiperspectival, contrastive and integrated view of content. This approach is fairly new compared to the theories brought forward in foreign language teaching methodology where the exclusive use of the foreign language is seen as mandatory (cf. Otten and Wildhage 2003).

3.3. Curricular considerations

As was mentioned earlier, CLIL as a new integrated subject in primary, secondary and tertiary education can only continue to exist in the long run if programmes or curricula are developed which clarify the aims, the contents and the procedures of such an approach. Curricula should be developed under the responsibility of the educational system, although programmes set up by single schools when they introduce CLIL can be helpful.

Curricular work for CLIL is still in its early stages even in countries where the approach has been in existence for many years. Naturally, all countries which have introduced CLIL have issued regulations which are, in general, of an administrative nature only. These regulations lay down issues like the number of years CLIL should be administered in the respective system, the CLIL languages, the content subjects, entrance exams and certification. The only official curricula we know of were developed by the federal state of North-rhine-Westfalia in Germany where almost 200 CLIL schools are in existence. These curricula which are officially called *recommendations* are organised according to categories common to all curricula: aims, contents, methodology and evaluation. For each combination of language and content subject officially accepted by the school administration a specific curriculum exists, for example English–Social Sciences, Italian–History, French–Geography. There are altogether 12 such curricula (cf. for example Ministerium für Schule und Weiterbildung, Wissenschaft und Forschung NRW 1994).

The learning objectives of all Northrhine-Westfalian curricula are defined in a similar way. They include the development of subject-specific learning, the promotion of general communicative skills and abilities, the development of the ability to work with subject-specific materials (study skills), and the development of content-oriented skills and abilities. In the recommendations for content issues the curricula emphasise two aspects: that CLIL learners should, at the end of their school career, have approximately the same knowledge of the content subject as mother tongue learners, and that content, especially in the Humanities and the Social Sciences, should be related to the culture or the cultures of the CLIL language. Undoubtedly, these criteria are not easy to fulfil; that is the reason why the curricula also recommend to have a close look at the mother tongue content curricula and to decide what contents in these curricula can be dealt with in more detail with respect to the target language culture. They also recommend to include a comparative or contrastive element into their teaching and to use native and CLIL language texts.

The methodological approach recommended is characterised by contrast and comparison (at least with respect to the Humanities and Social Sciences). Two examples from Social Sciences may suffice: (1) Viewing an event from different perspectives (example: the Irak war and the 11th of September from a German and an American perspective. (2) Viewing national events from an international perspective (German views and attitudes to xenophobia, American views and attitudes to xenophobia). Other aspects mentioned with respect to methodology are learner orientation and the use of both source and target language. There are, as yet, no specific recommendations with respect to evaluation. So far, they relate to the general evaluative regulations valid within the educational system.

In the autonomous region of Andalusia in Spain educational authorities set up during the last three years the first fully-fledged CLIL curriculum in Europe. This curriculum which was developed with the help of the Goethe Institute in Madrid is concerned with the integration of German as the CLIL language and Social Sciences ('Sciencias sociales') as a content subject. German is a language which is used quite commonly in Southern Spain, especially in tourism, so it is not surprising that a number of primary and secondary schools has taken to CLIL as a means to promote the German language and culture. The curriculum is structured according to principles similar to the ones adopted in the recommendations in Northrhine-Westfalia. It has not yet been published, more information can be obtained from the Goethe Institut in Madrid.

4. Controversial issues

In the first three parts of this paper we have drawn a positive, admittedly almost idealistic picture of CLIL as a new educational approach. In the following we will focus on a number of controversial issues which have been discussed over the last years and have not been solved yet. These issues concern the learner and learning psychological aspects on the one hand and more practical issues like teacher education, materials and certification on the other.

4.1. The learner

There are a number of controversial issues related to the learner in a CLIL learning context. The first one has to do with the learners' language competence in their mother tongue. Learners who are taught content subjects during their school career in another than their native language are exposed to the academic registers of their first language for a shorter time than learners who are learning content in their native language. Experts argue that this might have negative effects on the development of the learner's native language. This problem should not be neglected; in most contexts, however, CLIL is operated in a way which reduces the inherent danger to a large extent. First, the number of the content subjects which are taught in another language are reduced to two or maximal three, i.e. the larger part of the content subjects is still taught in the learner's first language. Second, integrated content and language teaching is organised methodologically in such a way that the foreign language is not used without at the same time referring to the learner's native language: while dealing with a content subject topic structures and lexemes are worked out contrastively which leads to the promotion of the learner's first language as well. In this context it was found that language awareness of learners who are instructed in such an integrated context is more developed than when language teaching takes place in isolation. An impoverishment of first language competence can be regarded as rather exceptional; it should be ensured, however, that only a limited number of content subjects are taught in the foreign language. This distinguishes CLIL from immersion programmes where usually all subjects are taught in the foreign language.

Specialists (cf. Baker 1996) argue as well that there is a danger of impoverishment with respect to the learner's knowledge of the content subject, when it is taught only in a foreign language. This problem must be taken seriously, especially if school authorities demand at the same time that the learner's knowledge in the content subject should be as extensive as that of the 'normal' mother-tongue learner. The problem is one of definition. If we understand by historical knowledge merely the historical facts listed in a text book (declarative knowledge) it is easily possible to define it. If, however, we also include procedural knowledge, i.e. knowledge on how to deal with historical content, it will be much more difficult to define it. In modern content subject learning it is difficult to define content quantitatively and therefore equally difficult to define a learner's content subject knowledge.

The central problem of multilingual education in the context of CLIL, however, seems to lie in a societal phenomenon which is typical of most of the industrialised countries in the world and especially of Europe and the European Union. Especially in the large Western European countries but increasingly also in Southern Europe large groups of migrants have settled down whose children have learned two languages at a very early stage, their first or family language – Turkish, Arabic, Hindi, Russian, Croatian etc. – and the vernacular language of the country they live in. In general, these children have learnt their family language only orally; they can only rarely read or write it. At the same time, children of the migrant population have enormous problems with the vernacular language, whether it is German, French, Italian, English etc. They learn these languages only inadequately, especially as they are not specifically promoted in school, in particular with respect to the academic skills of reading and writing. In using Cummins' (1987) distinction between BICS (= Basic Interpersonal Communicative Skills) and CALP (= Cognitive Academic Language Profiency) one could say that these children are fairly proficient with respect to BICS but that they have large deficits with respect to CALP. It is well known that the children of the migrant population more often fail in school because they lack academic proficiency (cf. Gogolin 1994), and it is therefore easy to conclude that they would have even greater difficulties if they were taught content in another language. The comparatively small number of migrant children in German CLIL classes is a clear indication that their parents are being dissuaded by teachers and the school authorities to send their children to this kind of instruction.

One could argue at this stage that academic failure of migrant children is an important reason why CLIL can never become an educational approach from which all children benefit. Although this is a very strong argument against democratising CLIL, we believe that if we find the right way, it is still possible to integrate such problematic groups into a CLIL learning environment. Canadian research on immigrant children could lead us the way. Already during the seventies of last century it was shown in Canada and in the United States that immigrant children failed in school if they had not learned to read and to write in their family language. (Grosjean 1982: 70) At that time the Canadian government set up so-called 'heritage language programmes' in which immigrant children were promoted in their family language and also learned to read and to write in this language. These programmes still exist, and it became clear in the accompanying research that children who participate in them attain the same or even better academic results than English-speaking children (Danesi 1991; Cummins 1992). It is absolutely necessary that other countries where these problems exist follow the Canadian example. In some European countries such programmes exist as well but they are not sufficient in number to prepare all bilingual migrant children for a school system in which they will be confronted at an early stage with yet another language. If the world's industrial countries manage to offer extensive language programmes in which migrant children are promoted in their first language it will not be dangerous but rather advantageous to introduce CLIL into our respective school systems.

4.2. The school

Problems related to integrating CLIL into the school are not uncommon; we will discuss a few general issues here, but there are others typical for specific educational systems which cannot taken up here (for more details cf. Marsh 2002).

One central problem related to implementing CLIL on a larger scale is the lack of teachers capable of teaching CLIL professionally. Apart from the German-speaking countries both in the European context and world-wide the type of teacher who is qualified in only one subject dominates. The additional training in the subject – a foreign language or a content subject – is quite a costly endeavour for a country which intends to implement CLIL. And even in Germany and Austria where a dual qualification at least for secondary schools exists it is necessary to provide additional training to teach in an integrated context. A way to resolve this problem could be to make use of native speakers who have studied a content subject in their respective mother tongue country. Such a solution would, however, necessitate foreign language teacher training.

A second problem which concerns the teaching and learning context has something to do with the materials used. Only in a few countries materials exist which were developed exclusively for CLIL. Text books do not exist, the materials available are usually booklets with text collections relating to the content subject. Many teachers develop their own materials, they exchange them with other teachers or use native-language textbooks for the content subject in their courses. In general, adaptations are necessary, however, although some teachers use these materials without adapting them. Publishers still hesitate to edit their own materials or textbooks. It is possible to solve this problem, however. In some European countries, for example, teacher associations have been founded in which teachers co-operate who teach content subjects in a foreign language. Such associations create databases in which teachers will find adequate materials.

Certification is another unsolved problem. Students who have gone through a CLIL course usually do not get a special diploma; the fact that they have done part of their studies in a foreign language is just mentioned in their school leaving certificate. A Europe- or even world-wide agency which distributes such diploma would be welcome. It could control the standards of CLIL in the respective countries and could deliver specific CLIL diploma which are valid in other countries as well and give students access to further education in these countries.

5. Contribution of applied linguistics

Content and language integrated learning is a new educational approach to language and content learning. It is an approach which was not developed first in theory and then applied in a practical everyday teaching context, but rather originates from everyday teaching practice. This does not exclude, however, that in order to confirm the underlying educational principles CLIL has taken recourse to research in a number of applied sciences, including Applied Linguistics. In a way, CLIL as an educational approach is at the interface of a number of academic disciplines: apart from Applied Linguistics and its sub-disciplines other sciences have become important like learning theory and the Psychology of Knowledge (cf. Mandl and Spada 1988; Strohner 1995). In the following we will give an overview of the different disciplines related to CLIL beginning with Applied Linguistics.

The most important fields of Applied Linguistics related to CLIL are Second Language Acquisition Research (SLA), Research on Bilingualism, Foreign Language Learning (FLL) and Applied Psycholinguistics.

Within SLA a number of different theoretical constructs have been developed which attempt to explain acquisitional processes both of natural and instructed language learners. In our opinion neither the Universal Grammar nor the Monitor Model have enough explanatory power to make us understand why and in what way language learning takes place in a CLIL setting. The only theory which seems powerful enough is the so-called interactionist position. The main idea behind it is that second language acquisition takes place through conversational interaction. Researchers like Hatch (1992), Long (1983) and Pica (1994) argue that what Krashen (1982) calls *comprehensible input* is necessary for language learning, but that in order to understand the effect interaction has on the learning process the question must be answered how input is made comprehensible. Interactionists claim that this takes place through negotiation of meaning. Interaction involves negotiation of meaning and this entails modification of input which in turn makes input comprehensible. So actually what promotes acquisition is interactional modification. Later on, in the development of the theory, a more far-reaching argument was added (cf. Platt and Brooks 2002). Through modification, it was claimed, the learner's attention is focussed on a specific linguistic structure of the target language which is thus taken in and learned. There can be no doubt that these ideas constitute an interesting theoretical construct in order to understand why in a CLIL classroom language learning takes place although the learner's attention is focussed on content.

Naturally, research on bilingualism has always been an important source in order to understand what is going on in the CLIL classroom and within the CLIL learner. The development of the bilingual learner's cognitive abilities as compared to the monolingual child play an important role in the general discussion on bilingual education and also on CLIL. The psycholinguistic research dealing with the storage of a bilingual's two languages in the brain was also discussed for some time in the educational and also in the CLIL context. And last but not least, research which has dealt with different types of bilingual children (simultaneous vs. consecutive, elitist vs. enforced) and has shown in what way these types of bilingualism influence the learning of other languages has become an important reference source in setting up new bilingual programmes. Societal bilingualism and research on bilingual groups plays a role in CLIL when it comes to choosing CLIL languages and specific methodological approaches (cf. Baker 1996).

Research on foreign language learning in an instructed context has always been a central concern in reflecting on CLIL. When CLIL became more popular, foreign language teaching had entered already into its communicative phase. So many of the methodological considerations in the CLIL context were and are still influenced by this foreign language teaching approach. Another source of influence is tasked-based learning which as an FL teaching approach includes an element of content. Recently, autonomous learning and CLIL were discussed in a number of papers (cf. for example Wolff 2003) and it was argued that CLIL offers some advantages compared to other institutionalised frameworks and learning environments within which the promotion of learner autonomy has been attempted. More than other, more isolated approaches CLIL provides a rich learning environment in which language and content are equally important and in which learners can work with content in a motivating way, focusing on language – its form and structure – whenever it is necessary.

Applied Psycholinguistics is a discipline within Applied Linguistics which deals with the psycholinguistic abilities and skills from a learner's perspective. It centres around the question what first and second language learners should learn in order to master the psycholinguistic strategies and processes which constitute speaking and listening, writing and reading. It also deals with the question in what way these strategies and processes can be promoted. Applied Psycholinguistics' research is very important for CLIL. As mentioned already, both content and language learning in CLIL is based on highly developed reading, writing, speaking and listening skills, and CLIL practitioners have drawn on quite a number of the research results provided by Applied Psycholinguistics (on Applied Psycholinguistics cf. Wolff 2002).

The fact that CLIL is concerned with teaching both language and content has led theoreticians to focus not only on language but also on content. The question was asked whether general learning theory and general theories of knowledge can give more insight into the learning of content in integration with language. The most discussed general learning theory is based on ideas of constructivist philosophy and cognitive psychology. This theory, constructivism, has considerably influenced learning in institutionalised contexts in recent years and is also being discussed within the CLIL field. According to this theory content learning and language learning is, in the largest sense of the term, acquisition of knowledge. Constructivism of which the Psychology of Knowledge is a part deals with questions of how people acquire knowledge, how they store knowledge in their memory, how they restructure and automatise it to have it ready for use. The Psychology of Knowledge makes a distinction between declarative and procedural knowledge, i.e. factual knowledge and knowledge about the processes underlying all our actions. This distinction plays an equally important role in this theory as the schema concept , which explains in what way we have stored knowledge in our memory and how we can call upon it. Similar to SLA research which looks at the acquisition of language as a constructive process, the Psychology of Knowledge regards all acquisitional processes as constructive. The results of all constructive processes whether related to language or to content are concepts and schemata (cf. Strohner 1995).

6. Research perspectives

Research on CLIL is, unfortunately, still in its infancy. This has something to do with the fact, that CLIL is a practically oriented educational approach in which, until recently, researchers did not show much interest. It has also something to do with the small number of CLIL classes which were available for observation and study. But it seems as if now a number of research projects have gone off the ground which are mainly conducted by young PhD researchers in the European context. The large number of CLIL schools especially in Germany and Austria have led to this growing research interest as well as the interest of the European Commission to promote this approach in order to foster multilingualism. Most of the research money comes from national agencies and from the European Union.

When looking at the first research results published in Germany recently (cf. for example Bonnet and Breidbach 2004) it can be seen that there are five general fields of interest on which this research centres:

(1) Research on the acquisition of linguistic competence in a CLIL classroom.
(2) Research on the acquisition of content subject competence in a CLIL classroom.
(3) Research on the acquisition of intercultural competence in a CLIL classroom.
(4) Research focusing on content subject methodology in a CLIL context.
(5) Research on the evaluation of CLIL by teachers and learners.

Naturally, the first research field has by far been the most popular in recent years. Especially in the context of second language acquisition research conducted by Henning Wode for more than twenty years (cf. for example Wode 1999), some studies were published which looked at the linguistic development of kindergarten and primary school children. Although these studies are comparable to the Canadian studies on immersion children they show that small children are well capable of learning a foreign language in contexts in which content is not simply games, songs and play but which have an academic character. Wode's and his collaborators' research also shows that small children exposed to another language (in their case English) for some twenty to twenty-four hours a week learn this language according to the developmental principles discovered by SLA research (cf. Pienemann 1989). Wode's research was criticised by a number of people especially because he only looks at the linguistic development of children and does not see it in relationship with the development of content. A second critical aspect mentioned has something to do with the fact that the children analysed learn language in an immersion context which is not a context characteristic of CLIL.

Other research on the development of linguistic competence rather centres on the question in what way language learning through language use really works. Unfortunately, most of this research is of a fairly eclectic nature and consists mainly of reports by CLIL teachers. It becomes clear, however, in most of these reports that language learning only works in language use when learners are involved in the content with which they deal in the foreign language (cf. Wolff 2004). This might be one of the reasons why CLIL works so well with respect to language learning.

Research on the acquisition of content subject competence is fairly new. The reason for this is probably that most researchers are linguists or Applied linguists and do not know much about the academic disciplines underlying content subjects. A very interesting research projects which will be published soon, was conducted by Lamsfuß-Schenk (for a short description of the project see Lamsfuß-Schenk 2002). This researcher was interested in the question whether there were differences in the learning of History content when learners were instructed in their mother tongue or in a foreign language. Lamsfuß-Schenk taught two parallel classes for one school year in History, one in German, the children's mother tongue, and one in French. After having analysed the results she tentatively comes up with the hypothesis that the children who have learnt the content subject in the foreign language develop more precise concepts to discuss historical content. Other research shows that CLIL learners do learn content equally well as learners who are instructed in their mother tongue.

It should be mentioned as well that in the context of developing content subject competence researchers in general mention the difficulties they have in differentiating between linguistic and content subject development. Language is inherent in all content subjects, it is "across the curriculum" as has been claimed many years ago.

Research on the development of intercultural competence is of a fairly theoretical nature. The question whether intercultural competence can be better developed in a CLIL classroom has not yet been tackled empirically: most researchers assume that intercultural competence and intercultural understanding are an outcome of the learning situation in a CLIL classroom (cf. de Florio-Hansen 2003). There are researchers, however, who claim that it is absolutely necessary to develop a new definition of interculturality in a CLIL context before intercultural competence can be investigated in such a classroom. Hallet (2004) points out that there are at least three definitions of culture in modern cultural theory which have to be taken into consideration[3], and that scientific and academic disciplines represent cultures as well which might be fairly independent of the cultures we usually deal with. Seen from this angle intercultural competence in CLIL must be regarded as a multiperspectival competence which allows learners to understand the different cultural perspectives underlying scientific approaches in different cultures. (An interesting example are the different ways of looking at history in French and German historiography). There can be no doubt that it will be very difficult to set up empirical research based on these theoretical reflections.

Research on content subject methodology in a CLIL context is interested in the question whether established content subject methodologies must be altered substantially in such a context. The empirical research on History and CLIL published by Helbig (2001) is influenced by foreign language teaching approaches and does not answer this question entirely, other research (cf. Hoffmann 2004) comes to the conclusion that the content subject approach to CLIL must be seen rather as a prototype of how to deal with school subjects in an interdisciplinary way.

Research on the evaluation of CLIL by teachers and learners belongs to a fairly new qualitative research paradigm within which researchers try to gain information about the attitudes teachers and learner have about CLIL. This research is done with the help of structured interviews and classroom observations. Researchers argue that CLIL teachers but also learners know a lot about CLIL, about CLIL methodology and about the use of CLIL. The research available now (Dirks 2004; Viebrock 2004) shows that the naïve attitudes towards CLIL especially by students often coincide with the concepts developed in theory.

Notes

1 In some European countries two or more official languages exist like in Belgium, in Switzerland or in Finland; in other countries other languages might be officially recognised like in Great Britain where Welsh is officially recognised. In quite a number of countries several not officially recognised languages are spoken by parts of the population like Turkish in Germany or Arabic in France.

2 Cummins coined the term CALP = 'cognitive academic language proficiency' for this competence.

3 In this paper a distinction is made between culture as construction (Stuart Hall 1997), culture as standardisation and programme (Hansen 2000) and culture as webs of significance (Clifford Geertz 1993).

References

Abendroth-Tiommer, Dagmar, Andreas Bonnet, Stephan Breidbach, Reinhard Hoffmann, Ernst Kirchner, Lutz Küster, Jutta Rymarczyk, Helmut J. Vollmer, Wolfgang Zydatiß
2004 Didaktiken im Dialog: Für eine integrative Didaktik des bilingualen Unterrichts. In: Bonnet and Breidbach (eds.), 13–27.

Baker, Colin
1996 *Foundations of Bilingual Education and Bilingualism.* Clevedon: Multilingual Matters.

Barnes, Douglas
1976 *From Communication to Curriculum.* Harmondsworth: Penguin.

Bonnet, Andreas and Stephan Breidbach (eds.)
2004 *Didaktiken im Dialog: Konzepte des Lehrens und Wege des Lernens im bilingualen Sachfachunterricht.* Frankfurt, Main: Lang.

Cummins, Jim
1987 Bilingualism, language proficiency and metalinguistic development. In: Peter Homel, Michael Palij and Doris Aaronson (eds.), *Childhood Bilingualism: Aspects of Linguistic, Cognitive and Social Development*, 57–73. Hillsdale, NJ: Erlbaum.

Cummins, Jim
1992 Heritage language teaching in Canadian schools. *Journal of Curriculum Studies* 24: 281–86.

Danesi, Marcel
1991 Revisiting the research findings on heritage language learning: three interpretive frames. *Canadian Modern Language Review* 47: 650–659.

De Florio-Hansen, Inez
2003 Inhaltsbasiertes Fremdsprachenlernen. Bilingualer Unterricht auf dem Prüfstand. *Praxis des neusprachlichen Unterrichts* 50: 11–19.

Dirks, Una
2004 Kulturhüter oder Weltenwanderer? Zwei ideale Realtypen bilingualen Sachfachunterrichts. In: Bonnet and Breidbach (eds.), 129–140.

Geertz, Clifford
1993 *The Interpretation of Cultures.* London: Harper Collins.

Genesee, Fred
1986 The baby and the bath water or what immersion has to say about bilingual education: Teaching and learning in bilingual education – Significant immersion instructional features. *NABE Journal* 10: 227–254.

Genesee, Fred
1987 *Learning Through Two Languages*. Cambridge, Mass.: Newbury House.

Gogolin, Ingrid
1994 *Der monolinguale Habitus der multilingualen Schule*. Münster: Waxmann.

Grosjean, Francois
1982 *Life with Two Languages: An Introduction to Bilingualism*. Cambridge, Mass.: Harvard University Press.

Hall, Stuart
1997 *Representation. Cultural Representations and Signifying Practices*. London: SAGE.

Hallet, Wolfgang
1998 The Bilingual Triangle. Überlegungen zu einer Didaktik des bilingualen Sachfachunterrichts. *Praxis des Neusprachlichen Unterrichts* 45: 115–125.

Hallet, Wolfgang
2004 Bilingualer Sachfachunterricht als interkultureller Diskursraum. In: Bonnet and Breidbach (eds.), 141–152.

Hansen, Klaus P.
2000 *Kultur und Kulturwissenschaft: Eine Einführung*. Tübingen: Francke.

Hatch, Evelyn
1992 *Discourse and Language Education*. Cambridge: Cambridge University Press.

Helbig, Beate
2001 *Das bilinguale Sachfach Geschichte. Eine empirische Studie zur Arbeit mit französischsprachigen (Quellen-) Texten*. Tübingen: Stauffenburg.

Hoffmann, Reinhard
2004 Geographie als bilinguales Sachfach: Fachdidaktische Grundsatzüberlegungen. In: Bonnet and Breidbach (eds.), 207–220.

Krashen, Stephen
1982 *Principles and Practice in Second Language Acquisition*. Oxford: Pergamon.

Krechel, Hans-Ludwig
1995 Inhaltsbezogene Spracharbeit im bilingualen Sachfach Erdkunde. In: British Council/CREDIF/Goethe Institut (eds.), *Triangle 13*, 95–112. Paris: Didier.

Krechel, Hans-Ludwig
2003 Bilingual island-hopping: Bilinguale Module. In: Manfred Wildhage and Edgar Otten (eds.), *Praxis des bilingualen Unterrichts*, 192–211. Berlin: Cornelsen.

Lamsfuß-Schenk, Stefanie
2002 Geschichte und Sprache – Ist der bilinguale Geschichtsunterricht der Königsweg zum Geschichtsbewusstsein? In: S. Breidbach, Gerhard Bach and Dieter Wolff (eds.), *Bilingualer Sachfachunterricht: Didaktik, Lehrer-/Lernerforschung und Bildungspolitik zwischen Theorie und Empirie*, 191–206. Frankfurt, Main: Lang.

Long, Michael H.
1983 Native/non-native speaker conversation and the negotiation of comprehensible input. *Applied Linguistics* 4: 126–41.
Mandl, Heinz and Hans Spada (eds.)
1988 *Wissenspsychologie*. München/Weinheim: Psychologie Verlags Union.
Marsh, David
2002 *CLIL/EMILE – The European Dimension: Actions, Trends and Foresight Potential*. Bruxelles: The European Union.
Marsh, David, Anne Maljers and Aini-Kristiina Hartiala
2001 *Profiling European CLIL Classrooms – Languages Open Doors*. Jyväskylä: University of Jyväskylä.
Marsh, David and Gisella Langé
2000 *Using Languages to Learn and Learning to Use Languages*. Jyväskylä: University of Jyväskylä.
Ministerium für Schule und Weiterbildung, Wissenschaft und Forschung NRW (eds.)
1994 *Empfehlungen für den bilingualen deutsch-englischen Unterricht – Sekundarstufe I: Biologie, Erdkunde, Geschichte, Politik*. Frechen: Ritterbach.
Otten, Edgar and Manfred Wildhage
2003 Content and Language Integrated Learning: Eckpunkte einer kleinen Didaktik des bilingualen Sachfachunterrichts. In: Manfred Wildhage and Edgar Otten (eds.), *Praxis des bilingualen Unterrichts*, 12–45. Berlin: Cornelsen.
Pica, Teresa
1994 Research on negotiation: What does it reveal about second language acquisition? Conditions, processes, and outcomes. *Language Learning* 44: 493–527.
Pienemann, Manfred
1989 Is language teachable? Psycholinguistic experiments and hypotheses. *Applied Linguistics* 10: 52–79.
Platt, Elisabeth and Frank B. Brooks
2002 Task engagement: A turning point in foreign language development. *Language Learning* 52: 365–400.
Portmann-Tselikas, Paul R.
2002 Textkompetenz und unterrichtlicher Spracherwerb. In: Paul R. Portmann-Tselikas and Sabine Schmölzer-Eibinger (eds.), *Textkompetenz. Neue Perspektiven für das Lehren und Lernen*, 13–43. Innsbruck: StudienVerlag.
Strohner, Hans
1995 *Kognitive Systeme: Eine Einführung in die Kognitionswissenschaft*. Opladen: Westdeutscher Verlag.
Thürmann, Eike
1999 Eine eigenständige Methodik für den bilingualen Sachfachunterricht? In: Gerhard Bach and Susanne Niemeier (eds.), *Bilingualer Unterricht: Grundlagen, Methoden, Praxis, Perspektiven*, 75–93. Frankfurt,Main: Lang.
Viebrock, Britta
2004 Elemente einer subjektiven didaktischen Theorie: Was ein Lehrer über fremdsprachliches Lernen und Konzeptbildung im bilingualen Erdkundeunterricht denkt. In: Bonnet and Breidbach (eds.), 167–178.

Wode, Henning
1999 Immersion teaching: A European perspective. In: Federica R. Garotti (ed.), *l'immersione Linguistica: Una Nuova Prospettiva*, 78–94. Mailand: Franco Angeli.

Wolff, Dieter
1997a Content-based bilingual education or using foreign languages as working languages in the classroom. In: David Marsh, Bruce Marsland and Tarja Nikula (eds.), *Aspects of Implementing Plurilingual Education: Seminar and Field Notes*, 51–64. Jyväskylä: University of Jyväskylä.

Wolff, Dieter
1997b Bilingualer Sachfachunterricht: Versuch einer lernpsychologischen und fachdidaktischen Begründung. In: *Initiativen für den Fremdsprachenunterricht an Hamburger Gymnasien*. Hamburg: Amt für Schule, 45–53.

Wolff, Dieter
2002 *Fremdsprachenlernen als Konstruktion: Grundlagen für eine konstruktivistische Fremdsprachendidaktik*. Frankfurt, Main: Lang.

Wolff, Dieter
2003 Content and language integrated learning: a framework for the development of learner autonomy. In: David Little, Jennifer Ridley and Ema Ushioda (eds.), *Learner Autonomy in the Foreign Language Classroom: Teacher, Learner, Curriculum and Assessment*, 211–222. Dublin: Authentik.

Wolff, Dieter
2004 Integrating language and content in the language classroom: Are transfer of knowledge and of language ensured?. In: *Proceedings of the GERAS*. Paris: GERAS

Zydatiß, Wolfgang
2000 *Bilingualer Unterricht in der Grundschule: Entwurf eines Spracherwerbskonzepts für zweisprachige Immersionsprogramme*. Ismaning: Hueber.

Recommended readings

Baetens Beardsmore, Hugo
1993 *European Models of Bilingual Education*. Clevedon: Multilingual Matters.

Baker, Colin and Sylvia P. Jones
1998 *Encyclopedia of Bilingualism and Bilingual Education*. Clevedon: Multilingual Matters.

Dalton-Puffer, Christiane
2007 *Discourse in Content and Language Integrated Learning (CLIL) Classrooms*. Amsterdam: John Benjamins

Gajo, Laurent
2007 Linguistic knowledge and subject knowledge: how does bilingualism contribute to subject development? *The International Journal of Bilingual Education and Bilingualism*. 10(5), 563–581.

Jansen O'Dwyer, Esther
2007 *Two for One: Die Sache mit der Sprache*. Bern: h.e.p. Verlag

Kroschewski, Annette, Anja Schuenemann and Dieter Wolff
1998 *A Resource Base for Bilingual Educators.* Jyväskylä: University of Jyväskylä.

Lamsfuß-Schenk, Stefanie
2008 *Fremdverstehen im bilingualen Geschichtsunterricht: Eine Fallstudie.* Frankfurt/Main: Peter Lang.

Marsh, David, Bruce Marsland and Anne Maljers
1998 *Future Scenarios in Content and Language Integrated Learning.* Jyväskylä: University of Jyväskylä.

Marsh, David and Dieter Wolff, (eds.)
2007 *Diverse Contexts – Converging Goals: CLIL in Europe.* Frankfurt/Main: Peter Lang.

Mehisto, Peeter, David Marsh and Maria Jésus Frigols
2008 *Uncovering CLIL: Content and Language Integrated Learning in Bilingual and Multilingual Education.* Oxford: MacMillan

Zydatiß, Wolfgang
2007 *Deutsch-englische Züge in Berlin (DEZIBEL): Eine Evaluation des bilingualen Sachfachunterrichts an Gymnasien.* Frankfurt/Main: Peter Lang.

21. Computer assisted foreign language learning

Kurt Kohn

1. Introduction – setting the scene

To prepare the ground, I would first like to sketch out an idealised 'best practice' scenario illustrating typical (and available) computer-based tasks and activities and how they can be pedagogically embedded in realistic contexts of language learning and teaching. The fictitious scenario is characteristic of the German context in particular as regards the implied educational system and the general availability of technological infrastructures.

One evening, Katharina Olsen, aged 17 and an 11th grade student at a German Gymnasium, has just finished 'skyping'[1] with her French tandem friend Florence in Avignon. Besides personal matters, it was a mixed bag of German and French language problems they talked about, mostly questions regarding appropriate phrases in connection with recent written assignments in school. They both keep a diary of problems for their weekly 'meetings'. A welcome side effect of their encounters is the possibility to practise oral proficiency. Communication is usually fairly smooth: whenever production in the respective foreign language is too difficult, they switch to their native languages to avoid comprehension problems.

Right now, Katharina is busy with online learning activities available on the educational school server. *Couleur des Choses* is a multimedia package offering a set of video-based tasks: listening and reading comprehension, practising words and phrases, grammar in context. Her teacher has recommended that she focus in particular on grammatical problems and related exercises. Usually, she finds grammar somewhat boring but in this case the video topic is in sync with her biology lesson, which motivates her.

After Katharina is finished with *Couleur des Choses*, she has to prepare a few questions for tomorrow's monthly chat conference with a school in Montpellier. Because of poor typing skills, not all students are in favour of the chat. Language-wise it is also quite a challenge since the level of the students' French and German foreign language proficiency is not always up to what they want to communicate. After the first meetings, it has become clear to everybody that more careful preparation is needed.

The chat conference is part of a European school network cooperation. It requires a fair amount of organisational work, which is shouldered by a 'steering committee' consisting of the two teachers in charge and a few students from both schools. In the future, the plan is to furthermore explore the potential of internet-based videoconferencing. The technological infrastructure still remains a problem, both in terms of equipment and access. But then, most of the e-learning activities are carried out at home. The computer lab is mainly used for introducing the students to new software and best learning practice and for special events like tomorrow's chat.

Bernd Olsen, Katharina's father, is a teacher of English and Geography at a Gymnasium some 40 km from home. When e-learning was introduced in his school about a year ago, he was rather sceptical. These new technologies were unfamiliar and seemed to reduce his personal pedagogical contact with his students and thus to threaten what he loved most about being a teacher. After a series of teacher training seminars, however, he began to understand better the pedagogical nature and diversity of e-learning – from language practice with ready-made packages to task-based learning with authentic material to peer communication in a discussion forum or chat room; not to forget tailor-made online testing and self-assessment. All in all, he has learned to appreciate the potential of e-learning to support autonomous and collaborative learning, and to help teachers to provide pedagogical support outside and beyond the classroom.

In the meantime, Bernd Olsen has developed his personal pedagogical preferences of blending e-learning activities with more traditional approaches. However, not everything he would love to do is feasible. He has soon realised that the new technologies easily create a Catch-22 – it is possible to do things which are pedagogically desirable but clearly impossible to achieve single-handedly. The obvious answer is to cooperate across individual teachers and institutions.

Recently, Bernd Olsen has joined a European networking community of language teachers. They discuss problems and approaches, share an Open Source course portal and are now busy setting up a joint pool of corpus-based language learning and assessment resources for several European school languages. The idea is to develop all this as a by-product of their daily work; however, the going is rougher than expected. It helps having three university-based applied linguistics centres on board as part of a school-university cooperation scheme. Their task is to provide theoretical and methodological guidance as well as content development and technological networking support. The project is beneficial to both sides: the school members use the networking facilities to solve their Catch-22 problem, which is even greater for 'less widely taught languages' with only occasional support from educational publishers; the university members enjoy the advantage of having direct and flexible access to real-life pedagogical scenarios to carry out evaluation and research studies following an action research approach.

Today, Bernd Olsen is among the 'beneficiaries'. In the language learning corpus he has located video interviews with people in the Santa Fe area. He has chosen an interview with a city councillor that is recommended for listening comprehension. Content-wise, the interview is particularly interesting because of its reference to the water issue in Santa Fe. This makes it relevant for his geography lesson as well, which is held in English as part of a bilingual classroom scheme. He uses an authoring tool to create a few additional online tasks in the question and answer format, which are designed to help his students understand the issue and practise new terms and phrases. He also decides to prepare a forum activity, due next week, which requires his students to explore and discuss water problems in other parts of the world. This will develop common ground for discussions in class.

Susanne Olsen, Bernd's wife, is chief executive of TexCom, a medium-sized German textile company. Tonight she is in a hotel room in Milan, occupied with final preparations for an important business meeting tomorrow afternoon with potential distributors mainly from Italy, Greece, France and Spain. At the meeting, she wants to present her company and explore possibilities for expanding into new markets. Communication will be mostly in English, which is still quite a challenge to her – but this is the way things are being handled in Europe and world-wide.

Having gone through her Powerpoint presentation, Susanne Olsen is now giving her Business English a final brush up. Three weeks ago, she analysed her meeting-specific language problems with David White, a business communication expert assigned to her by the training institute that organises all language and communication-related training activities for her company. When the fixed series of face-to-face training sessions with David was over, they continued to use the content and communication facilities of an e-learning portal for keeping up a needs-based coaching contact. For her trip to Milan, David had recommended a multimedia package, *The Language of Meetings*, which can be used both offline and online. They had gone through the dialogue-based modules, and Susanne Olsen had selected two that were of particular interest to her: *Making your voice heard* and *Getting your point across*. She started practising about a week ago – mainly listening and speaking with a special focus on relevant communicative moves and expressions. Although not the real thing, these activities make her feel more comfortable, and she is looking forward to the 'field test' tomorrow.

With these 'scenes from the language learning frontier' in mind, I will now take a closer look at the special symbiosis between the human and the technological factor in CALL. The guiding assumption is that technology has a supporting and enhancing role, which can not be properly understood and exploited without understanding and taking into account the human nature of language learning and teaching. It will therefore be necessary to make references to the development and achievements of applied linguistic research on a frequent basis.

2. Evolution of CALL

2.1. Opening moves

In the early days of CALL, the picture was much simpler (cf. Levy 1997; Chapelle 2001). It all began in the mid-1960s and 70s at North American universities with systems like PLATO and TICCIT, exploiting the then available mainframe technology for the development and implementation of language courseware (cf. Hart 1981; Jones 1995). The main pedagogical intention behind the development of these systems was to supply teachers with something they could use as an add-on to regular language classes from English as a second language to several foreign languages like French, German, Italian, and Arabic. Following the prevailing behaviourist/audio-lingual model of the day, focus was very much on drill-type and question/answer activities. However, the potential of the computer was also used to reach out beyond the restrictions of the traditional language laboratory by integrating authoring templates, audio, and feedback.

With the advent of the PC in the early 1980s, processes of democratisation and diversification were set in motion: CALL became feasible for a larger number of educational institutions and projects with smaller budgets for development and maintenance. CALL-related research was soon gaining ground in the Applied Linguistics community as is witnessed by the foundation of professional organisations from the AILA *Educational Technology Commission* in 1976 to CALICO (USA) in 1982 and EUROCALL (Europe) in 1986. Scientific journals of the first hour include *ReCALL*, *The CALICO Review*, *Computer Assisted Language Learning*, *On-CALL*, *CÆLL Journal*, and *Systems*.

Recognition and support also came from the Commission of the European Communities. To further promote and synchronise European projects in the field of technology-enhanced language learning and teaching, the LINGUA and DELTA programmes joined forces in the 1993 London conference *Foreign Language Learning and the Use of new Technologies* (European Commission 1993). In the same year, the DELTA Concerted Action *Technologies in Language Learning and Tutoring* was launched to carry out "a systematic review and assessment of the current range of technology developments with regard to their potential applications for second language learning" (Kohn 1994b: 2). For future research and technology development (RTD) projects the Concerted Action recommended the strategic incorporation of 'life/work-embedded learning', 'open integration of learning modes' and 'user-oriented technology'. About ten years later, these recommendations found more general recognition as the pillars of blended language learning (see chap. 3).

2.2. Technology and pedagogy

Right from the start, the evolution of CALL has been shaped by a certain tension between technology and pedagogy. The relationship between the two has never been without problems, in particular with regard to the question of who is, or should be, in the driving seat. In my experience, the general consensus has always been that pedagogical objectives and principles should take the lead (also see Felix 2003; Colpaert 2006). But the original motivation for using the computer for language learning and teaching purposes can not be separated from what computer technology has to offer. It is thus hardly surprising that, more often than not, technology seems to override pedagogical experience and creativity – and this works in both directions: either enthusiastic over-estimation of technology or blunt rejection. The attempt, however, to draw a fixed line of demarcation between a positive and a negative technology push would be beside the point. To a considerable degree, the solution is in the eye of the individual beholder, and its direction also depends on whether we are looking at CALL research or CALL practice.

It is worth noting that with regard to modern approaches to language learning pedagogical insights never really lagged behind technological innovation. When the 'multimedia PC' was heralded in the mid-1990s as the ultimate answer to all our pedagogical woes, the communicative paradigm shift had already taken place, in particular in the English language teaching community. In its wake, three key insights had a shaping influence on further pedagogical developments in general and best practice in CALL in particular:

First, learners were recognised as the real players and decision-makers as to what should go on in class, which led to a shift from teacher-centredness to learner-centredness and an emphasis on learner autonomy (cf. Holec 1981; Little 1995; Benson 2001). Second, it became clear that a more communicative approach also required more authenticity, in particular in reference to the authentication of learning materials and learning activities in meaningful and relevant discourse events (cf. Widdowson 1979: 159–167). And third, not surprisingly, communicative language learning was identified as an interactive and collaborative undertaking (cf. Nunan 1992). These insights were constitutive for more advanced versions of communicative language teaching (CLT) like task-based or project-based language learning (cf. Prabhu 1987); and they were later subsumed under the umbrella of constructivism and constructionist approaches to language learning (cf. Wolff 1994; Rüschoff 1999). As a consequence, and indeed independent of the development of computer technology, the objective and challenge of modern language teaching was seen in facilitating learner autonomy, authentication and collaborative interaction.

How does computer technology fit in?

The pedagogical attraction of the early desktop computers of the 1980s was their capability for fast data processing. This made it possible to develop a range of language practice tools – from vocabulary and grammar trainers to text programs – that helped support more extensive self-study activities and contributed to the promotion of more learner autonomy. From the very beginning, authoring functions were considered relevant by teachers who aimed at needs-driven and authentic language learning. *Gapmaster* and *Choicemaster* (Wida Software) as well as *Fun with texts* (Camsoft) and *Storyboard* (Wida Software) (cf. Legenhausen and Wolff 1992) were successful early examples that have been continually enhanced as computer technology moved on. From early on, communicative principles and requirements like autonomy and authenticity thus provided a framework of orientation for the pedagogically relevant deployment of the new technologies.

In the early and mid-1990s, multimedia technology became a serious option – first with laser videodiscs, later with CD-ROMs and multimedia LANs (local area networks). In the digital world, traditionally separate media – text, sound, image and video – all belong to the same type of data. This made it possible to weld different types of material into integrated multimedia packages – with a promising potential for autonomous and interactive communication-oriented practice activities involving listening and reading comprehension, speaking and writing, with both scripted and genuine material. However, a considerable drawback stood against these advantages: as long as multimedia learning material was only available on CD-ROM or in a LAN, content management in terms of maintenance, access and distribution were seriously restricted and handicapped. High updating costs and inconvenient delivery processes, along with organisational and technical difficulties involved in handling multimedia language packages in PC/LAN-based learning pools, were among the main reasons why the 'multimedia boom' of the mid-1990s in educational and training institutions fell dramatically short of initially high expectations. The advantages multimedia could have supplied education with were largely outweighed by practical difficulties. It is thus hardly surprising that, with the exception of the private CD-ROM consumer market, educational multimedia was not a commercial success (cf. Davies 2002).

A major breakthrough was achieved due to the internet, which has gradually become available to a wider learning and teaching community since the late 1990s. It is the medium for distribution and communication per se, and is thus well suited for supporting both language-focused and communication-focused learning activities. As regards language-focused learning, the internet/web has the advantage of open access to a rich variety of language learning and testing packages and authentic resource material from a wide range of knowledge areas. The great advantage of web-based content is that it can be accessed from anywhere and at any time, and can be regularly serviced and updated at reasonable costs. An initial weakness of online contents as regards language learning has to do with the textual origin of the web. The communicative learning potential of online contents very much depends on its multimedia power, i.e. its flexibly integrated exploitation of text, sound, image and video. A multimedia upgrading of the web was therefore of crucial importance. Impressive progress has been made in this respect over the last few years, regarding both functionality and processing capacity, so that language-focused online learning has long moved beyond simple clicking activities.

In terms of communication-focused language learning, the internet provides relevant facilities, both synchronous and asynchronous, including in particular e-mail, forum, chat, internet telephony, video conferencing, blogs and wikis. These online communication tools can be easily combined with each other – as they can (and should) be combined with language-focused activities – to support different pedagogical scenarios from online tutoring to collaborative learning in online groups. In the online environment, the once strict borderline between pedagogically designed learning activities and work/life-embedded communication is fading. New online opportunities for real and relevant contact are emerging, with a rich potential for incidental language learning through autonomous and authenticated communicative interaction in pairs or in groups (also see Felix 2001, 2003; O'Dowd 2006, 2007; Warschauer and Kern 2000). Internet/web-based language learning can thus be fully aligned with the major principles and requirements of communicative and constructivist language learning.

In addition to providing multimedia and web-based language learning contents and opportunities for online communication and interaction, the processing capabilities of the computer can also be used for guidance and control. Throughout the evolution of CALL, the possibility of intelligent CALL (ICALL) has attracted the interest and imagination of both researchers and practitioners (cf. Schwartz and Yazdani 1992; Holland, Kaplan, and Sams 1995). A general objective is to develop more individualised CALL environments that provide error feedback, learning material, and interactive tasks that are sensitive to the learner's level of proficiency and learning needs. Expert systems, intelligent tutoring systems, adaptive user modelling, natural language processing, and automated speech recognition have been used to provide 'intelligent' support in all relevant domains of language learning and practice from reading, writing, listening and speaking to grammar and vocabulary (for an overview see Gamper and Knapp 2002; Nerbonne 2003).

Again, the delicate relationship between pedagogy and technology needs to be considered. No doubt, notions like 'intelligent tutoring' had an immediate appeal for someone whose pedagogical preferences were shaped by the audio-lingual approach. In a way, intelligent tutoring seems to make the teacher-centred behaviouristic dream of programmed instruction (cf. Callender 1969) come true – which is quite the opposite of a pedagogical approach based on learner-centredness, communication and individual construction. It is thus hardly surprising that from a communicative and constructivist perspective the application of artificial intelligence (AI) in language learning was met with caution: “AI-based software, […] which assigns a tutoring function (and that is a teacher function) to the computer, should, if at all only play a marginal role in a language classroom” (Wolff 1993: 22–23).

But language learning is a complex matter. In particular, insights into the relevance of “pushed” output processing (cf. Swain 1985, 1995, 2005) have contributed to our appreciation of “some degree of focus-on-form” (Skehan 2003: 392) within communicative learning activities. In this context, a new non-behaviouristic justification for deploying intelligent language tutoring systems becomes possible (cf. Heift and Nicholson 2001; Toole and Heift 2002; Heift and Schulze 2003; Klenner and Visser 2003; Heift and Schulze 2007). The pedagogical focus is on facilitating individualised, form-oriented learning activities (restricted to controlled language domains) that can (and should be) embedded in communicative learning environments. It should be added, though, that progress in ICALL is still mainly confined to the field of research.

This is altogether different with regard to corpus linguistics, which has enjoyed practical relevance since the publication of the *Collins COBUILD English Language Dictionary* (Sinclair 1987). Throughout the 1990s, corpus-based lexicography flourished and was complemented by corpus-based grammar writing from the *Collins COBUILD English Grammar* (Sinclair 1990) to the *Longman Grammar of Spoken and Written English* (Biber et al. 1999), *An Empirical Grammar of the English Verb System* (Mindt 2000) and the *Chemnitz Internet Grammar of English* (cf. Heller 2005; Schmied 2006). Other pedagogical applications of corpora and corpus techniques (e.g. concordances) include the analysis and (critical) evaluation of ELT textbooks and grammars (cf. Mindt 1997; but compare Widdowson 2003: 111–133), the construction of targeted learning tasks based on ‘real’ language as well as autonomous data-driven learning explorations by learners themselves (cf. Tribble and Jones 1990; Johns and King 1991; Wichmann et al. 1997). Beyond the pedagogical deployment of native speaker reference corpora, new corpora have emerged whose very concept and design is motivated and influenced by pedagogical interests and considerations. The range goes from non-native speaker reference corpora of written and spoken learner English (ICLE and LINDSEI; cf. Granger, Dagneaux and Meunier 2002) to spoken English as a lingua franca (cf. VOICE: http://www.univie.ac.at/voice; ELFA: http://www.eng.helsinki.fi/elfa) and small ‘Do it yourself’ (DIY) corpora that focus on genres and topics of immediate relevance to a specific group of learners (cf. Tribble 1997; Aston 2002).

While these corpora provide a wealth of empirical information and help English language teachers and ELT content developers match their pedagogical decisions with real language, they share a serious drawback: corpora contain texts in the sense of surface manifestations of attested language use, bare of any contextual information (cf. Widdowson 2003: 75–91). And standard corpus techniques such as concordances, word lists and frequency counts are applied to these decontextualised data with the aim of studying primarily lexico-grammatical patterns and aspects of word meaning. Especially DIY corpora seem to offer possibilities for dealing with these limitations. Sabine Braun (2005, 2006, 2007) argues that the pedagogical potential of (DIY) corpora should be further increased by adapting them in more specific ways to pedagogical needs and purposes. In the case of ELISA (http://www.uni-tuebingen.de/elisa), a small interview corpus Braun uses to illustrate her points, this particularly concerns a thematic annotation as well as the incorporation of pedagogically relevant enrichment resources. Among them are audiovisual material, cultural and linguistic background information, corpus analysis results and ready-made tasks and exercises. The overall objective of ELISA is to help teachers and learners proceed from decontextualised textual data to context-embedded discourse interaction and thus to facilitate and promote learner autonomy and authentication (also see SACODEYL: http://www.um.es/sacodeyl; Hoffstaedter and Kohn 2009).

2.3. Stages in the development of CALL

A chapter on the evolution of CALL would not be complete without concluding remarks about the developmental stages in CALL. Concepts like 'traditional', 'explorative', 'multimedia' and 'web-based' have been used to inject a sense of order into the evolutionary flow of events. A more ambitious model is the one proposed by Mark Warschauer and Deborah Healey (cf. Warschauer 1996, 2000; Warschauer and Healey 1998); it is based on an analysis of the combined effects of five shaping forces: "technology", "English-teaching paradigm", "view of language", "principal use of computers", and "principal objectives". In its most recent version, the model distinguishes three main stages of CALL: "structural" (1970s – 1980s), "communicative" (1980s – 1990s) and "integrative" (21st century).

While the time reference clearly characterises these stages as temporal phases of development, Warschauer hastens to emphasise that he does "not want to suggest that these stages have occurred sequentially, with one following the other, from 'bad CALL' to 'good CALL'. At any time, any of these may be combined for different purposes." (Warschauer 2000) This statement reveals a fundamental dilemma since it remains unclear what we are supposed to understand by (temporal) 'stages' that are not sequential. It is thus hardly surprising that on closer inspection the model loses some of its descriptive validity. In his critical analysis of developmental models of CALL, Stephen Bax (2003) gives Warschauer credit for his deeper historical analysis, but he also points out terminological inconsistencies and unclear criteria. Bax argues that during the period of communicative CALL "there was relatively little pedagogically useful com-

Table 1. The three stages of CALL (based on Warschauer 2000)

Stage	1970s-1980s: Structural CALL	1980s-1990s: Communicative CALL	21st Century: Integrative CALL
Technology	Mainframe	PCs	Multimedia and Internet
English-Teaching Paradigm	Grammar-Translation and Audio-Lingual	Communicative Language Teaching	Content-Based, ESP/EAP
View of Language	Structural (a formal structural system)	Cognitive (a mentally constructed system)	Socio-cognitive (developed in social interaction)
Principal Use of Computers	Drill and Practice	Communicative Exercises	Authentic Discourse
Principal Objective	Accuracy	And Fluency	And Agency

munication going on in CALL" (2003: 18). In the case of integrative CALL, with its socio-cognitive emphasis on task-based and collaborative learning in online discourse communities, Bax criticises the somewhat fuzzy borderline to communicative CALL: "the use of language in authentic contexts had surely been stressed from the very beginnings of CLT […] – to imply that it is somehow 'post communicative' is odd" (Bax 2003: 19). Bax' criticism is further corroborated by Udo Jung's (2005) bibliometric analysis.

There is, however, another reason why the concept of communicative CALL in particular appears to be less valid. It all goes back to the question of what a communicative learning activity really is. A straightforward answer would be that only those activities merit the label 'communicative' that involve communicative interaction. But what about activities designed to contribute to the overall goal of acquiring communicative competence by focusing on one of its essential dimensions, e.g. grammatical competence (cf. Canale and Swain 1980)? Even if we do not want to call such activities 'communicative' when seen in isolation, they can nevertheless be pedagogically integrated in communicative learning scenarios, thereby acquiring a communicative value of 'second degree'. The debate around communicative CALL is much too centred on the technology aspect. If we isolate technology-based learning activities from the pedagogical context in which they are embedded, we will hardly be able to adequately understand their pedagogical nature. But then again, how we look at CALL – as a separate learning 'entity' or embedded in more comprehensive pedagogical scenarios – is in itself a matter of developing and changing views.

In his own stage model, Bax (2003) tries to avoid the pitfalls of the 'communicative CALL' debate by giving preference to more general classification criteria: restriction versus openness and isolation versus integration. On this basis, he identifies three broad stages of development: *restricted CALL*, *open CALL*, and *integrated CALL*.

Restricted CALL (1960s until 1980) is characterised by its fairly closed nature on all relevant levels:

- learning content mainly concerns aspects of the language system;
- learning tasks and activities are limited to drills and quizzes, text reconstruction, short questions and answers, and involve only minimal interaction with other learners;
- feedback emphasises correct/incorrect;
- teachers are mainly reduced to the role of a monitor, and they regard technology with an attitude of exaggerated fear and/or awe;
- CALL modules are self-contained units, shaped more by technology than pedagogy, and not really integrated into the syllabus;
- learning takes place in a separate computer lab not specifically equipped for language learning purposes.

In *open CALL* (1980s until today) the learning content is extended to communicative skills:

- learning tasks and activities also include games, simulations and computer mediated communication (CMC);
- feedback focuses on skills development; teachers act as monitors and facilitators, but their attitude toward technology is still one of exaggerated fear and/or awe;
- the pedagogical integration of CALL modules remains poor;
- the computer lab may be specially devoted to language learning requirements.

Integrated CALL, finally, differs from both restricted and open CALL in a fundamental way. The leading objective and characteristic is what Bax calls 'normalisation', i.e. a "stage when a technology is invisible, hardly even recognised as a technology, taken for granted in everyday life" (Bax 2003: 23; also see Chambers and Bax 2006)[2]. In integrated CALL, computer-based learning and communication activities seamlessly blend into the entire pedagogical environment and approach as required by the learners' needs; technological decisions are informed and shaped by pedagogical ones. Bax argues that most of integrated CALL is still in the future and successful implementation will eventually (need to) result in the extinction of CALL as a separate field.

Bax' model emphasises the fluid diversity that is characteristic of CALL development and prompts Jung to conclude that there are "no clear-cut phases or watertight periods in CALL or in the documentation thereof" (Jung 2005: 9). As regards the predicted extinction of CALL, one might want to take a more moderate view. It should be clear, however, that it is about high time that we come to see computer-assisted learning and teaching as something 'normal' and, what is more, as part of a larger pedagogical ensemble. We will not get the best out of CALL activities unless we learn to integrate and normalise them in more comprehensive pedagogical scenarios of blended language learning.

3. Blended language learning

3.1. Vision and reality

One thing is certain: the new technologies – multimedia, internet, intelligent tutoring systems – have not simplified the world of teaching and learning; on the contrary, they have made it more complex, varied and demanding. We are witnessing a process of pedagogical diversification: while we used to have lessons, books and cassettes/tapes, we now have lessons, books and CD-ROMs, and the web with online content and discussion forums and chats and blogs and wikis and podcasts.

The challenge of the day is blended language learning (cf. Kohn 2006; Neumeier 2005), i.e. the pedagogical integration of traditional forms of language learning and teaching with the new potential of e-learning[3]. The aim is to exploit the strengths and opportunities of the approaches involved without being handicapped by the disadvantages and weaknesses they have when used in isolation. At first glance, this does not sound particularly exciting. Language teachers have always combined different methods, materials and types of equipment, depending on their learners' needs and capabilities, depending on their own pedagogical experience and preferences, depending on available infrastructure. In a way, blended language learning is an old hat.

Why do we talk about it at all? To understand this, we need to go back a few years in recent CALL history. From the mid-1990s onwards, first multimedia and then e-learning were deemed capable of solving all our problems. Such was the dream of training managers; and language trainers were getting worried that they might lose their job. But neither of this materialised; and since about 2003, 'blended learning' has been advertised as the ultimate solution. The name was new, but in pedagogically minded circles of CALL the concept behind it had been around for quite a while – without, however, a commonly accepted label. An early suggestion was 'distributive integration':

> "This concept encapsulates a flexible and comprehensive learning approach which supports the selective combination and integration of different language learning modes in such a way that any restrictions and negative effects present in each single

> mode are neutralised and the learner is given maximum customised support [...]. A distributive integration approach may combine direct teaching with distance tutoring and autonomous self-access learning and is thus responsive to individual needs, aptitude, preferences and situational conditions." (Kohn 1994a: 33; also see Colpaert 2007)

A less opaque terminological variant was "pedagogical integration" (Kohn 1995, 2001). Also compare the European Telos project[4] (1996–98), which explicitly aimed at supporting the integration of classroom-type learning and teaching with autonomous multimedia-based self-study, customised learnware delivery and tele-tutoring. From a pedagogical perspective, it should have been 'blended' language learning right from the start. But CALL development was much too influenced by a 'digital divide'[5] between CALLists and non-CALLists; and too much attention was given to the question of whether a CALL approach was better than a traditional one.

The recently growing interest in blended language learning has an added value which can hardly be overemphasised: it brings into focus the fact that language learning and teaching is about human beings, about their communication and learning needs and purposes. Technology plays an ancillary role, which is determined and shaped by the human dimension. The key to success lies in integrating old and new ways of learning within a comprehensive approach of blended learning, so that people's requirements are adequately met. Only if we manage to embed the computer in a wider pedagogical context will we be able to benefit from its pedagogical potential.

According to an appealing vision, the concept of blended learning marks a turning point in human learning and teaching. And it is promoted with high hopes and great expectations: blended learning is said to offer

> "a real opportunity to create learning experiences that can provide the right learning at the right time and in the right place for each and every individual, not just at work, but in schools, universities and even at home. It can be truly universal, crossing global boundaries and bringing groups of learners together through different cultures and time zones. In this context Blended Learning could become one of the most significant developments of the 21st century". (Thorne 2003: 18)

But what about reality? Has the vision come true over the past few years? As regards language learning, the answer is no. So far, uptake has been slow. Blended language learning has not had an easy time of it. What are the forces that work against it?

A first factor that should be considered is the pedagogical validity and comprehensiveness of traditional ways of learning and teaching. There is nothing fundamentally wrong with NOT using the computer. And what's more, there are no 'empty spaces' in traditional approaches that wait to be filled with technology-based learning activities. Making the best use of the pedagogical potential of modern technologies is more than just adding something to what is already available. What is necessary is rather a more substantial re-organisation of the entire approach based on a new pedagogical design. This is a demanding task, somewhat like rebuilding a ship on high sea. And the task is made even more demanding by a second factor, the digital divide mentioned above, which makes many people see and experience e-learning in opposition to traditional ways of teaching and learning, rather than as something complementary – part and parcel of the same learning and teaching challenge. A third factor working against blended learning is closely connected with the motivation behind the recent 'discovery' of the concept itself. Blended (language) learning is first and foremost a response to the pedagogical limitations (and lack of commercial success) of an 'e-learning only' strategy. It is thus a convincing solution for those who have always believed in e-learning. All the others still need to be convinced – and for them the acid test is the pedagogical viability of e-learning activities.

3.2. E-learning and its language learning potential

So what then is the pedagogical added value of e-learning in a language learning context? Relevant criteria for answering this question should be derived from principles of best practice regarding autonomous learning, authentication, and collaborative learning (cf. chap. 2.2.). The pedagogical viability of e-learning activities for language learning purposes depends on their contribution (in blended learning scenarios) to the fulfilment of these principles. In the following, I will take a brief look at some of the tools that are around, with a special focus on open source or free-of-charge software; for a more extensive account, see Stockwell (2007) and Davies (2007).

E-learning activities require a pedagogical control centre, which can be a learning management system (LMS) such as *Moodle* (http://www.moodle.org). The pedagogical core functions of an LMS commonly include

- course editing and administration,
- authoring and integration of pedagogical instructions and multimedia learning resources,
- tutorial guidance through communicative contact (via e-mail, forum, and chat) as well as learning control support (via feedback, evaluation, and tracking statistics),
- facilitation of autonomous learning through a variety of learning activities, in particular forums and chats, written assignments and assessments, (collaborative) glossaries and wikis.

In each e-course unit, language and communication-focused learning resources and activities can be combined in a flexible manner, depending on learning goals and pedagogical preference. This enables teachers to provide their learners with materials and interactive communication tasks for individual and collaborative self study activities outside classroom hours – without releasing them from tutorial guidance. Autonomous learning can thus be facilitated and further developed; focus is on the learners' liberation from place and time constraints as well as on their being responsible for their own learning. To a large extent, the particular strength of an LMS depends on the core functions it provides and on its underlying pedagogical concept.

But there is also the advantage of incorporating external learning resources and tools to cater to more specific language learning requirements. As regards language-focused learning, this includes ready-made language courses and tests as well as open web resources. In addition, the deployment of programming-free authoring tools enables teachers to assume a more active role in the content process by creating and adapting language learning and testing materials geared to meet the 'local' needs of their learners. For instance, *Hot Potatoes* (http://web.uvic.ca/hrd/halfbaked/) and *Telos Language Partner* (http://www.sprachlern-medien.de) are authoring tools that can be embedded to further enhance the authoring capabilities of the LMS. Of increasing importance is the integration of pedagogically relevant corpora and corpus analysis tools because of their potential for authenticated learning. For communication-focused learning, social networking and online collaboration, the pedagogical potential of linking in multimodal communication facilities, like messenger and (video) conferencing systems, internet telephony applications or podcasts, blogs and wikis, can hardly be overestimated (cf. Warschauer and Kern 2000; O'Dowd 2006; O'Bryan and Hegelheimer 2007; Lomicka and Lord 2009). Such tools open up a broad range of possibilities for authentic communicative interaction and contribute significantly to making the LMS more tailored to language learning purposes.

We can thus conclude that e-learning provides an innovative potential for modern approaches to language learning and teaching. It is particularly suited to support communicative language learning objectives and methods, and shows a high level of compliance with the principles of learner autonomy, authentication, and collaborative learning. Relevant dimensions of language-focused learning (listening, reading, speaking and writing on the basis of multimedia materials, e.g. cultural or subject-specific texts and videos) can be pedagogically combined with written or spoken learning activities in forums, chats or voice/video conferences. All this makes e-learning a highly attractive pedagogical partner in blended language learning scenarios, in particular with regard to finding an answer to the crucial question of how to ensure continuity of learning in between classroom meetings. Concerning the 'right mix', however, there are no easy answers, no recipes. Ultimately and inevitably, it is up to the course designer and the teacher to make a pedagogical decision, taking into account the learning objectives, experiences and attitudes of the actors involved, the overall pedagogical approach, administrative and institutional framework conditions, and available technological infrastructures.

This leaves us with the question of the pedagogical validity of e-learning in a blended language learning context. In winter term 2000/01, a Business English course was piloted at the English Department of the University of Tübingen, Germany, to further explore this issue (cf. Hahn and Kohn 2001). Development and implementation of the course were supported by the European Leonardo da Vinci project TALL (*Teaching Autonomy in Language Learning*). The blended learning approach adopted placed a strong emphasis on home-based self-study activities with a CD-ROM package (*Executive English – Marketing* by McGraw-Hill Lifetime Learning), which combined listening and reading activities based on video scenes, specialised vocabulary exercises, and dialogue practice. An e-learning platform provided tutorial support including instructions for weekly CD-ROM activities, additional online exercises focusing on grammar and 'phrases of the day', online communication via e-mail, forum and chat and occasional phone contact with a tutor. Two classroom meetings were offered at the beginning and the end of the course. The meeting at the beginning included informal personal introductions, information about the pedagogical concept and learning strategies, technological information and practice and a language test (pre-test); the meeting at the end consisted mainly of a language test (post-test).

The CD-ROM and web-based language learning contents were created with *Telos Language Partner* (cf. Kohn 2008). The course went on for 8 weeks with a total learning effort of about 40 hours: 6 hours classroom, 18 hours CD-ROM, 8 hours online grammar, and 8 hours forum/chat. Participants were economics students with an intermediate level of general English (B1/B2), who were recruited from the University of Tübingen and universities in the surrounding area. The course had 14 participants, of whom 11 successfully completed the full programme, including the final test. Two tutors were involved in course development and implementation. Course evaluation was based on log sheets during the course as well as questionnaires and interviews after the course; evaluation data were elicited from both students and tutors.

Without any exception, the course was rated 'good' or 'very good'. The following aspects were deemed positive: the diversified learning concept, the variety and quality of the offline and online multimedia learning materials in general, the dialogue exercises on the CD-ROM in particular, the new learning experience with chat activities, being able to direct one's own learning process, flexibility of time and space, communication contact with other participants. On the whole, adjusting to the new and initially unfamiliar course format was judged unproblematic. Between pre-test and post-test, the error rate went down from 55 % to 20 %. Regarding attitudes, the initial values of 11 % enthusiastic, 89 % curious and 0 % sceptical had changed to 36 % enthusiastic, 55 % curious and 9 % sceptical at the end of the course. The students had fun, and all of them said they would take part in a similar course again, or recommend it to fellow students.

There were also negative aspects: technical problems, in particular, were mentioned as being time-consuming and therefore frustrating; the work-load was found to be (too) high; the possibility of self-organisation bore the risk of shallow learning activities; and there were also motivation problems around the middle of the course. The frequently expressed desire for more classroom phases fits into this picture. It underlines once more that giving learners enough room to breathe is not sufficient. Autonomous learning needs to be accompanied by suitable tutorial measures in the sense of 'guided autonomy'. In this respect, classroom phases can be of marked significance. To the extent that these are reduced, other means of guidance must be found.

Overall, the pilot course turned out to be successful. It demonstrated that autonomous language learning can be encouraged and facilitated in a blended learning environment, and tutors can further optimise their 'local' teaching activities by combining them with learning resources and communication tools 'globally' available in an LMS. Further empirical studies involving other blended learning designs are needed to gain deeper and generalisable insights into conditions for successful blended language learning (see also Neumeier 2005; Leakey and Ranchoux 2006).

4. Challenges and research perspectives

4.1. Teacher autonomy

The concept of learner autonomy has raised considerable attention in the CALL community. This has helped CALL research, development and practice to focus on their communicative and constructivist foundations, and has emphasised the role of teachers as tutorial guides and facilitators. All this is not new. What is new, however, are the challenges that arise with regard to teacher autonomy in CALL-enhanced blended learning settings.

In the 'old world', teachers are used to selecting their teaching and learning materials from published resources, in particular books, but also audio and video tapes; in addition, they integrate their own exercises based on materials from newspapers and magazines, broadcast and TV; the primary form of pedagogical communication and interaction is face-to-face contact in the classroom. In this way, teachers exercise their autonomy, which enables them to function as a pedagogical 'interface' between their learners' needs and purposes and available learning resources and opportunities. The same interface function needs to be fulfilled by teachers in blended learning settings. Regarding language-focused learning, teachers thus need to participate in collaborative authoring activities by selecting, adapting and expanding their own offline and online materials in addition to ready-made products provided by publishers; and regarding communication-focused learning, they need to support and monitor pedagogical communication and interaction in online learning spaces outside and beyond classroom meetings (cf. Kohn 2000, 2001).

But in blended language learning settings, it is a serious challenge for teachers to maintain their autonomy. Key requirements include teachers' open and positive attitudes toward e-learning, their familiarity with relevant e-learning technologies, their competence in analysing and judging the pedagogical potential of e-learning and how it can be creatively exploited to support communicative and constructivist principles of language learning and teaching, as well as their competence and motivation in networking with each other and sharing infrastructures, open learning resources and experiences. Teacher attitudes and competencies, however, are not sufficient. What is also needed are changes in institutional framework conditions regarding, in particular, collaborative teaching within and across institutions, availability of open source learning contents, flexible time arrangements outside class hours for customised content adaptation and e-moderation (cf. Salmon 2000) as well as incentives for continuous work-embedded teacher education.

Flexibility of working time is a prerequisite for the fulfilment of the other requirements. In terms of customisation of learning contents, for instance, most teachers find themselves in a Catch-22 bind. Easy-to-handle authoring tools, e.g. *Hot Potatoes*, *InGenio*, *MALTED* or *Telos Language Partner*, make it possible for them to adapt e-learning and e-testing contents to what is needed in a given blended learning situation (cf. Rüschoff 2004; Gimeno 2008; Kohn 2008). At the same time, however, teachers are usually deeply submerged in daily class routine and consequently have hardly any time for authoring CALL materials. A similar conflict between pedagogical reason and technological feasibility on the one hand and constraints imposed by traditional work definitions on the other can be identified with regard to teachers becoming involved as e-moderators. As long as the workload of teachers is mainly defined in terms of class hours, it will be difficult, if not impossible, for them to make the best use of what e-learning has to offer.

More teacher autonomy is clearly needed for the CALL scenarios depicted in the introduction to come true.

4.2. Teacher education

With the implementation of blended learning approaches, language teaching will be more demanding – and more rewarding. To make this happen, those teacher education measures need to be implemented that embrace the specific pedagogical conditions and requirements of e-learning and blended language learning. Over the past few years, a CALL perspective in teacher education has received growing interest, with a strong focus on the provision of training contents for ICT (Information and Communication Technologies) courses geared to language teachers' needs. Davies (2003: 196) discusses several offline and online initiatives and specifies four introductory course topics: using generic software in language learning and teaching, exploring the World Wide Web, CALL pedagogy and methodology, and CALL authoring tools. In a similar vein, a substantial body of textbook-type modules for in-service teacher training has been developed by the ICT4LT project (*ICT for Language Teachers*), initiated in 1998 and funded under the Socrates Program of the European Commission (http://www.ict4lt.org). The ICT4LT website (Davies 2007) is regularly updated and expanded and has become one of the first places to go for information and advice in the field.

A more course-oriented concept of ICT education for language teachers was pursued by the Socrates project TALLENT (*Teaching and Learning Languages Enhanced by New Technology*), also initiated in 1998 (http://www.solki.jyu.fi/tallent). The project website provides a learner needs analysis questionnaire along with content specifications, references and websites for nine course modules. This instrument is intended to be used for negotiating and designing residential ICT seminars and workshops for in-service teachers and trainers in European languages as a second/foreign language. In the European Leonardo da Vinci project LANCELOT (2005–07), the focus was on an online-only scenario. The objectives were to promote online language learning through the professional development of 'live online language teaching' in virtual classrooms via Internet. Project outcomes included practical guidelines for the live online language teacher, guidelines for the training of live online language teachers, as well as a certification procedure for documenting the qualification acquired (http://lancelot.univie.ac.at/).

Hubbard and Levy (2006a) present and discuss a broad range of research and practice-related topics and issues in teacher education in CALL. The volume is organised in five sections covering foundations of CALL teacher education, CALL degree programs, CALL pre-service courses, CALL in-service projects, courses and workshops, as well as alternatives to formal CALL training. Across the various contributions, five recurring themes provide additional cohesive links:

1. integration of technical and pedagogical training;
2. limits of formal training because of the speed of technological development;
3. authentic embedding of CALL education;
4. learning about CALL through the use of CALL;
5. permeation of the language teacher curriculum with a CALL perspective.

In their own contribution, the editors outline a descriptive role model approach to CALL education (Hubbard and Levy 2006b), operating with the distinction of two intersecting role dimensions: institutional (pre-service teacher, in-service teacher, CALL specialist and CALL professional) and functional (practitioner, developer, researcher and trainer). Each of the resulting institutional-functional role pairs, e.g. in-service teacher/developer, can then be characterised with regard to the technical and pedagogical knowledge and skills for CALL that are required for successful performance and thus provide the basis for determining final training objectives. As a future developmental step, they propose to further refine this role model approach and to extend it beyond CALL education to the study of CALL in general.

4.3. CALL research

CALL teacher education can only be as good as our understanding of the conditions and processes of (successful) computer-assisted language learning and teaching. This is where CALL research comes in. While there is not enough space to discuss the existing literature and its role in CALL practice more extensively (but see Levy 1997; Chapelle 2003; Kukulska-Hulme and Traxler 2005; Levy and Stockwell 2006; Mishan 2005; Trinder 2006), useful insights can be gained from studies trying to identify ways of optimal methodological practice in CALL research.

CALL effectiveness research (cf. Dunkel 1991; Levy 1997: 120–121, 28–30, 39–41; Chapelle 2001: 51–94; Jamieson, Chapelle and Preiss 2005), which has accompanied CALL development from early on, gives a good reflection of how CALL is generally conceptualised. The comparison studies of the 1980s were focused on the overall effectiveness of CALL, i.e. the question of whether computer-assisted learning was better than traditional learning. More recently, this broad view has been replaced by an interest in the "differential impact of CALL methods" (Felix 2005a: 16). To gain more profound insights into the impact of computer technology on language learning, Felix proposes meta-analyses that go beyond isolated studies and create "a series of systematic syntheses of findings related to one particular variable such as learning style or writing quality" (Felix 2005a: 17; also see Felix 2005b).

It should be noticed that besides the problem of comparing apples and pears, the meta-analysis approach seems to share with earlier effectiveness studies their conceptualisation of CALL as something separate from 'non-CALL'. With the emergence of the blended language learning paradigm for CALL practice, this view can no longer be upheld. To the extent that language learning and teaching with computers is designed as an integral part of a wider pedagogical environment, CALL research approaches need to be revised accordingly. As regards CALL effectiveness, for instance, the impact of a particular CALL solution on learners' attitudes and motivation, learning processes or learning outcomes might be positive in blended learning scenario A but negative in scenario B. What is thus required is the pedagogical contextualisation of CALL research through incorporation of a blended language learning dimension. Longitudinal field studies based on grounded-theory methodology can help provide orientation and an interpretative framework for focused experimental studies. In this way, CALL research can help us gain a deeper understanding of how computers can be used to facilitate human language learning as an autonomous, authenticated and collaborative construction process.

The driving force behind Mike Levy's approach to CALL research is to understand the specific nature of CALL. Based on a detailed qualitative analysis of an annotated corpus of 177 articles from CALL-related books and major CALL journals, all published in 1999, he aims at a deeper, theoretical conceptualisation from an inside perspective. In a first study, Levy (2000) places the analytical focus on a sub-set of 47 research-related articles. The themes most frequent in these articles are computer-mediated communication (CMC), CALL artefacts, CALL hybrids, CALL environments, teacher education, and technological effects on reading and writing. Following a thorough discussion of these themes, Levy concludes that CALL is a coherent and autonomous field of research "worthy of study as a body of work in its own right, not merely as an adjunct to research being undertaken in another, related field" (Levy 2000: 190). In a second study, Levy (2002) takes a closer look at critical issues of CALL design. 93 articles from the CALL-1999 corpus are analysed with regard to design as a principled approach to CALL (e.g. a learner-centred CALL model), design of CALL artefacts (e.g. websites and learning environments, courseware projects, and online courses), CALL design in relation to state-of-the-art technologies (e.g. automatic speech recognition, broadband videoconferencing), as well as design implications of authoring systems.

Against this background, he discusses the relationship between CALL design and underlying theory, emphasising the "need for theoretical pluralism" (Levy 2002: 71). With regard to the field of Second Language Acquisition (SLA) with its various linguistic (e.g. Universal Grammar), cognitive, functional/pragmatic, sociocultural and sociolinguistic models and approaches as a potential source of theory for CALL research, Levy refers to Mitchell and Myles' (1998) review of the relationship between SLA research and language education. While their account has a negative undercurrent, it remains somewhat inconclusive. On the one hand, they state that the "findings of SLA research are not sufficiently secure, clear and uncontested, across broad enough domains, to provide prescriptive guidance for the teacher (nor, perhaps will they ever do so)" (1998: 195); yet on the other hand, they emphasise the pedagogical value of SLA research and the "rich variety of concepts and descriptive accounts, which can help teachers interpret and make better sense of their own classroom experiences, and significantly broaden the range of pedagogical choices open to them" (1998: 195).

These two positions, however, are not irreconcilable. The seemingly ill match between SLA research and CALL stems rather from a false presupposition. The role of SLA research must not be misunderstood as providing 'prescriptive guidance' to teachers; there is no short-cut from SLA research to language pedagogy, regardless of whether CALL applications are involved or not. CALL research and practice need to be theory-based; and SLA theories seem to be natural candidates (cf. Chapelle 2005). Clearly, our thinking and talking about CALL research and practice are inevitably influenced by the way we think and talk about language and language learning; the question is not if, but rather how.

In addition to a normalisation of CALL practice in blended language learning settings, we thus need a normalisation of CALL research and the shedding of any historically evolved boundaries that might exist between SLA and CALL. But integration works in both directions. In so far as SLA is concerned with the conditions and processes underlying human language learning and teaching, it provides a general theoretical foundation for CALL. At the same time, however, CALL enriches and extends the range of conditions and processes for language learning and teaching; and the normalisation of CALL practice will itself require accompanying research activities. Normalisation places CALL research where it belongs – in the human context of language learning and teaching (cf. Chambers and Bax 2006: 466).

As a final point, it needs to be emphasised that CALL provides a highly productive methodological potential for researching key issues of second language learning and teaching (cf. Chapelle 2001: 132–156). Whether we look at self-directed and authenticated learning, communicative collaboration and trans-cultural interaction, linguistic competence and skills development or content and language integrated learning (CLIL) – CALL not only opens up new ways of learning, it also helps us to design language learning practices for focused research. In the future, this methodological enabling power will be a major contribution of CALL to second language learning and teaching research in general.

Acknowledgments

I wish to thank Michaela Albl-Mikasa, Julian Bishop, Sabine Braun, Linda Carlson and Petra Hoffstaedter for their support, and the anonymous reviewer for helpful comments on an earlier version of this paper.

Notes

1 Skype is an internet-based communication service (voice, video, instant massages), which can be used free of charge.
2 It is interesting to note that this opinion seems to echo what Warschauer and Healey wrote in 1998: "As our focus of attention gradually shifts from the computer itself to

the natural integration of computers into the language learning process, we will know that computer technology has taken its rightful place as an important element of language learning and teaching" (1998: 67–68).

3 In the following, I will use the term e-learning in a fairly broad sense to refer to the deployment of Information and Communication Technologies (ICT) for learning and teaching purposes. This includes multimedia, internet, intelligent tutoring systems und so forth. What exactly comes under ICT at a certain time is to some extent an open question and depends on the technological state of the art.

4 Funded by the European Commission in the Telematics Applications Programme (http://www.uni-tuebingen.de/telos).

5 The term has also been used more generally to refer to the gap between the "haves" and "have-nots" regarding ICT access. Also see Warschauer's (2003) work on the social contextualisation of ICT.

References

Aston, Guy
2002 The learner as corpus designer. In: Bernd Kettemann and Georg Marko (eds.), *Teaching and Learning by Doing Corpus Analysis*, 9–25. Amsterdam: Rodopi.

Bax, Stephen
2003 CALL – past, present, future. *System* 31 (1): 13–28.

Benson, Phil
2001 *Teaching and Researching Autonomy in Language Learning*. London: Longman.

Biber, Douglas, Stig Johansson, Geoffrey Leech, Susan Conrad and Edward Finegan (eds.)
1999 *Longman Grammar of Spoken and Written English*. Harlow: Pearson Education.

Braun, Sabine
2005 From pedagogically relevant corpora to authentic language learning contents. *ReCALL* 17 (1): 47–64.

Braun, Sabine
2006 ELISA: a pedagogically enriched corpus for language learning purposes. In: Sabine Braun, Kurt Kohn and Joybrato Mukherjee (eds.), *Corpus Technology and Language Pedagogy*, 25–47. Frankfurt, Main: Peter Lang.

Braun, Sabine
2007 Integratin corpus work into secundary education: From data-driven learning to needs-driven corpora. *ReCALL* 19(3): 307–328.

Callender, Patricia
1969 *Programmed Learning: Its Development and Structure*. London: Longman.

Canale, Michael and Merrill Swain
1980 Theoretical bases of communicative approaches to second language teaching and testing. *Applied Linguistics* 1: 1–47.

Chambers, Angela and Stephen Bax
2006 Making CALL work: towards normalisation. *System* 34: 465–479.

Chapelle, Carol A.
2001 *Computer Applications in Second Language Acquisition. Foundations for Teaching, Testing and Research*. Cambridge: Cambridge University Press.

Chapelle, Carol A.
2003 *English Language Learning and Technology. Lectures on Applied Linguistics in the Age of Information and Communication Technology*. Amsterdam/Philadelphia: John Benjamins.

Chapelle, Carol A.
2005 Interactionist SLA theory in CALL research. In: Joy Egbert and Gina M. Petrie (eds.), *Research Perspectives on CALL*, 53–64. Mahwah, NJ: Laurence Erlbaum Associates.

Colpaert, Jozef
2006 Pedagogy-driven design for online language teaching and learning. *CALICO Journal* 23 (3): 477–497.

Colpaert, Jozef
2007 Distributed language learning. *Computer Assisted Language Learning* 20 (1): 1–3.

Davies, Graham
2007 ICT4LT Homepage. In: Graham Davies (ed.), *Information and Communications Technology for Language Teachers (ICT4LT)*. Slough: Thames Valley University [Online]. Available from: http://www.ict4lt.org/en/en_home.htm [Accessed 10 August 2007].

Davies, Graham
2002 Beyond babel: language learning online. Review of Felix 2001. *TELL and CALL* 1. Available from: http://www.camsoftpartners.co.uk/FelixReview.htm [Accessed 10 August 2007]

Davies, Graham
2003 Perspectives on online and offline training initiatives. In: Uschi Felix (ed.), *Language Learning Online. Towards Best Practice*, 193–214. Lisse: Swets and Zeitlinger.

Dunkel, Patricia
1991 The effectiveness of research on computer-assisted instruction and computer-assisted learning. In: Patricia Dunkel (ed.), *Computer-Assisted Language Learning and Testing*, 5–36. New York: Newbury House.

European Commission (ed.)
1993 *Lingua-Delta: Foreign Language Learning and the Use of New Technologies. Conference Proceedings*. Brussels: Bureau LINGUA.

Felix, Uschi
2001 *Beyond Babel: Language Learning Online*. Melbourne: Language Australia Ltd.

Felix, Uschi
2003 Pedagogy on the line: identifying and closing the missing links. In: Uschi Felix (ed.), *Language Learning Online: Towards Best Practice*, 147–170. Lisse: Swets and Zeitlinger.

Felix, Uschi
2005a Analysing recent CALL effectiveness research – towards a common agenda. *Computer Assisted Language Learning* 18 (1/2): 1–32.

Felix, Uschi
2005b What do meta-analyses tell us about CALL effectiveness? *ReCALL* 17 (2): 269–288.
Gamper, Johann and Judith Knapp
2002 A Review of intelligent CALL systems. *Computer Assisted Language Learning* 15 (4): 329–342.
Gimeno, Ana M. (ed.)
2008 *Computer Assisted Language Learning: Authoring Tools for Web-Based CALL.* Valencia: Universidad Politécnica de Valencia.
Granger Sylviane, Estelle Dagneaux and Fanny Meunier
2002 *The International Corpus of Learner English.* Louvain-la-Neuve: Presses Universitaires de Louvain
Hahn, Stefanie and Kurt Kohn
2001 *Executive English – Marketing. Ein Evaluationsbericht zum Sprachenlernen mit Multimedia- und Webunterstützung.* Tübingen: Steinbeis-Transferzentrum Sprachlernmedien.
Hart, Robert S.
1981 The PLATO system and language study. *Studies in Language Learning* 3: 1–24.
Heift, Trude and Devlan Nicholson
2001 Web delivery of adaptive and interactive language tutoring. *International Journal of Artificial Intelligence in Education* 12 (4): 310–325.
Heift, Trude and Mathias Schulze
2003 Student modeling and 'ab initio' language learning. *System* 31 (4): 519–535.
Heift, Trude and Mathias Schulze
2007 *Errors and Intelligence in Computer-Assisted Language Learning: Parsers and Pedagogues.* New York: Routledge.
Heller, Isabel
2005 Learner experiences and CALL-tool usability – evaluating the Chemnitz Internet Grammar 1. *Computer Assisted Language Learning* 18 (1/2): 119–142.
Hoffstaedter, Petra and Kurt Kohn
2009 Real language and relevant language learning activities: insights from the SACODEYL project. In: Anton Kirchhofer and Jutta Schwarzkopf (eds.), *The Working of the Anglosphere. Contributions to the Study of British and US-American Cultures*, 291–303. Trier: WVT.
Holec, Henri
1981 *Autonomy in Foreign Language Learning*. Oxford: Pergamon Press
Holland, Melissa V., Jonathan D. Kaplan and Michelle R. Sams (eds.)
1995 *Intelligent Language Tutors: Theory Shaping Technology.* Mahwah, NJ: Lawrence Erlbaum Associates.
Hubbard, Philip and Mike Levy (eds.)
2006a *Teacher Education in CALL.* Amsterdam: John Benjamins.
Hubbard, Philip and Mike Levy
2006b The scope of CALL education. In: Hubbard and Levy (eds.), 3–20.
Jamieson, Joan, Carol A. Chapelle and Sherry Preiss
2005 CALL Evaluation by developers, a teacher, and students. *CALICO Journal* 23 (1): 93–131.

Johns, Tim and Philip King (eds.)
1991 *Classroom Concordancing*. Birmingham: University of Birmingham.

Jones, Randell L.
1995 TICCIT and CLIPS: the early years. *CALICO Journal* 12 (4): 84–96.

Jung, Udo O. H.
2005 CALL: past, present and future – a bibliometric approach. *ReCALL* 17 (1): 4–17.

Klenner, Manfred and Henriëtte Visser
2003 What exactly is wrong and why? Tutorial dialogue for intelligent CALL systems. *Linguistic Online* 17 (5): 81–98.

Kohn, Kurt
1994a Distributive language learning in a computer-based multilingual communication environment In: Heidrun Jung and Robert Vanderplank (eds.), *Barriers and Bridges: Media Technology in Language Teaching*, 31–43. Frankfurt, Main: Peter Lang.

Kohn, Kurt (ed.)
1994b *Technologies in Language Learning and Teaching. DELTA Concerted Action Report (DELTA Project 2101).* Brussels: European Commission, DG XIII.

Kohn, Kurt
1995 Perspectives on computer assisted language learning. *ReCALL* 7 (2): 5–19.

Kohn, Kurt
2000 Multimediales Sprachenlernen: Wo bleibt die Autonomie der Lehrenden? In: Erwin Tschirner, Hermann Funk and Michael Koenig (eds.), *Schnittstellen: Lehrwerke zwischen alten und neuen Medien*, 132–141. Berlin: Cornelsen.

Kohn, Kurt
2001 Developing multimedia CALL. *Computer Assisted Language Learning* 14 (3/4): 251–267.

Kohn, Kurt
2006 Blended Language Learning. Potential und Herausforderung. In: Udo O. H. Jung (ed.), *Praktische Handreichung für Fremdsprachenlehrer*, 4th edition, 286–292. Frankfurt, Main: Peter Lang.

Kohn, Kurt
2008 Telos Language Partner: "Do it yourself" authoring for content-based language learning. In: Gimeno (ed.), 157–174.

Krashen, Stephen D.
1985 *The Input Hypothesis*. London: Longman.

Kukulska-Hulme, Agnes and John Traxler (eds.)
2005 *Mobile Learning: A Handbook for Educators and Trainers*. London: Routledge.

Leakey, Jonathan and Alexandre Ranchoux
2006 BLinguA. A blended language learning approach for CALL. *Computer Assisted Language Learning* 19 (4/5): 357–372.

Legenhausen, Lienhard and Dieter Wolff
1992 STORYBOARD and communicative language learning: results of the Düsseldorf CALL project. In: Swartz and Yazdani (eds.), 9–23.

Levy, Michael
1997 *Computer-Assisted Language Learning: Context and Conceptualization*. Oxford: Clarendon Press.
Levy, Mike and Glenn Stockwell
2006 *CALL Dimensions: Options and Issues in Computer-Assisted Language Learning*. Mahwah, N.J.: Lawrence Erlbaum Associates.
Levy, Mike
2000 Scope, goal and methods in CALL research: questions of coherence and autonomy. *ReCALL* 12 (2): 170–195.
Levy, Mike
2002 CALL by design: discourse, products and processes. *ReCALL* 14 (1): 58–84.
Little, David
1995 *Learner Autonomy 1: Definitions, Issues, and Problems*. Dublin, Ireland: Authentik.
Lomicka, Lara and Gillian Lord (eds.)
2009 *The Next Generation: Social Networking and Online Collaboration in Foreign Language Learning*. CALICO Monograph Series, Volume 8.
Long, Michael
1983 Native speaker/non-native-speaker conversation and the negotiation of comprehensible input. *Applied Linguistics* 4 (2): 126–141.
Mindt, Dieter
1997 Corpora and the teaching of English in Germany. In: Wichmann, Fligelstone, McEnery and Knowles (eds.), 227–237.
Mindt, Dieter
2000 *An Empirical Grammar of the English Verb System*. Berlin: Cornelsen.
Mishan, Freda
2005 *Designing Authenticity into Language Learning Materials*. Bristol: Intellect Books.
Mitchell, Rosamond and Florence Myles
1998 *Second Language Learning Theories*. London: Arnold.
Nerbonne, John
2003 Natural language processing in computer-assisted language learning. In: Ruslan Mitkov (ed.), *The Oxford Handbook of Computational Linguistics*, 670–698. Oxford: Oxford University Press.
Neumeier, Petra
2005 A closer look at blended learning – parameters for designing a blended learning environment for language teaching and learning. *ReCALL* 17 (2): 163–178.
Nunan, David (ed.)
1992 *Collaborative Language Learning and Teaching*. Cambridge: Cambridge University Press.
O'Bryan, Anne and Volker Hegelheimer
2007 Integrating CALL into the classroom: the role of podcasting in an ESL listening strategies course. *ReCALL* 19 (2): 162–180.
O'Dowd, Robert
2006 *Telecollaboration and the Development of Intercultural Communicative Competence*. München: Langenscheidt.

O'Dowd, Robert (ed.)
2007 *Online Intercultural Exchange. An Introduction for Foreign Language Teachers*. Clevedon: Multilingual Matters.

Prabhu, N. S.
1987 *Second Language Pedagogy: A Perspective*. Oxford: Oxford University Press.

Rüschoff, Bernd
1999 Construction of knowledge as the basis of foreign language learning. In: Bettina Mißler and Uwe Multhaup (eds.), *The Construction of Knowledge, Learner Autonomy and Related Issues*, 79–88. Tübingen: Stauffenburg Verlag.

Rüschoff, Bernd
2004 Authenticity and the use of technology-enhanced authoring tools in language learning. In: Angela Chambers, Jean E. Conacher and Jeannette Littlemore (eds.), *ICT and Language Learning: Integrating Pedagogy and Practice*, 165–182. Birmingham: University of Birmingham Press.

Salmon, Gilly
2000 *E-Moderating. The Key to Teaching and Learning Online*. London: Kogan Page.

Schmied, Josef
2006 Corpus linguistics and grammar learning. In: Sabine Braun, Kurt Kohn and Joybrato Mukherjee (eds.), *Corpus Technology and Language Pedagogy. New Resources, New Tools, New Methods*, 87–106. Frankfurt, Main: Peter Lang.

Sinclair, John (ed.)
1987 *Collins COBUILD English Language Dictionary*. London: Collins.

Sinclair, John (ed.)
1990 *Collins COBUILD English Grammar. Helping Learners with Real English*. London: Collins.

Skehan, Peter
2003 Focus on form, tasks, and technology. *Computer Assisted Language Learning* 16 (5): 391–411.

Stockwell, Glenn
2007 A review of technology choice for teaching language skills and areas in the CALL literature. *ReCALL* 19 (2): 105–120.

Swain, Merrill
1985 Communicative competence: some roles of comprehensible input and comprehensible output in its development. In: Susan M. Gass (ed.), *Input in Second Language Acquisition*, 235–253. Cambridge, Mass.: Newbury House.

Swain, Merrill
1995 Three functions of output in second language learning. In: Guy Cook and Barbara Seidlhofer (eds.), *Principle and Practice in Applied Linguistics*, 245–256. Oxford: Oxford University Press.

Swartz, Merryanna L. and Masoud Yazdani (eds.)
1992 *Intelligent Tutoring Systems for Foreign Language Learning. The Bridge to International Communication*. Berlin: Springer-Verlag.

Thorne, Kaye
2003 *Blended Learning. How to Integrate Online and Traditional Learning*. London: Kogan Page.

Toole, Janine and Trude Heift
2002 The tutor assistant: an authoring tool for an intelligent language tutoring system. *Computer Assisted Language Learning* 15 (4): 373–386.

Tribble, Chris and Glyn Jones
1990 *Concordances in the Classroom: A Resource Book for Teachers*. Harlow: Longman.

Tribble, Chris
1997 Improvising corpora for ELT: quick-and-dirty ways of developing corpora for language teaching. In: Barbara J. Lewandowska-Tomaszczyk and Patrick J. Melia (eds.), *PALC-97: Practical Applications in Language Corpora*, 106–117. Lodz: Lodz University Press.

Trinder, Ruth
2006 *Language Learning with Computers: The Students' Perspective. A Theoretical and Empirical Investigation.* Frankfurt, Main: Peter Lang.

Warschauer, Mark and Deborah Healey
1998 Computers and language learning: an overview. *Language Teaching* 31: 57–71.

Warschauer, Mark and Richard Kern (eds.)
2000 *Network-based Language Teaching: Concepts and Practice*. Cambridge: Cambridge University Press.

Warschauer, Mark
1996 Computer assisted language learning: an introduction. In: Sandra Fotos (ed.), *Multimedia Language Teaching*, 3–20. Tokyo/San Francisco: Logos International.

Warschauer, Mark
1999 *Electronic Literacies: Language, Culture, and Power in Online Education.* Mahwah, NJ: Lawrence Erlbaum Associates.

Warschauer, Mark
2000 The death of cyberspace and the rebirth of CALL. *English Teachers' Journal* 53: 61–67.

Warschauer, Mark
2003 *Technology and Social Inclusion: Rethinking the Digital Divide*. Cambridge, Mass.: MIT Press.

Wichmann, Anne, Steven Fligelstone, Tony McEnery and Gerry Knowles (eds.)
1997 *Teaching and Language Corpora*. London: Longman.

Widdowson, Henry G.
1979 *Explorations in Applied Linguistics.* Oxford: Oxford University Press.

Widdowson, Henry G.
2003 *Defining Issues in English Language Teaching*. Oxford: Oxford University Press.

Wolff, Dieter
1993 New technologies for language teaching. In: European Commission (ed.), *Lingua-Delta: Foreign Language Learning and the Use of New Technologies. Conference Proceedings*, 17–27. Brussels: Bureau LINGUA.

Wolff, Dieter
1994 Der Konstruktivismus: Ein neues Paradigma für die Fremdsprachendidaktik? *Die Neueren Sprachen* 93 (4): 407–429.

Recommended readings

Chapelle, Carol A.
2001 *Computer Applications in Second Language Acquisition. Foundations for Teaching, Testing and Research*. Cambridge: Cambridge University Press.

Chapelle, Carol A.
2003 *English Language Learning and Technology. Lectures on Applied Linguistics in the Age of Information and Communication Technology*. Amsterdam/Philadelphia: John Benjamins.

Davies, Graham
2007 ICT4LT Homepage. In: Graham Davies (ed.), *Information and Communications Technology for Language Teachers (ICT4LT)*. Slough: Thames Valley University [Online]. Available from: http://www.ict4lt.org/en/en_home.htm [Accessed 10 August 2007].

Felix, Uschi
2001 *Beyond Babel: Language Learning Online*. Melbourne: Language Australia Ltd.

Heift, Trude and Mathias Schulze
2007 *Errors and Intelligence in Computer-Assisted Language Learning: Parsers and Pedagogues*. New York: Routledge.

Hubbard, Philip and Mike Levy (eds.)
2006a *Teacher Education in CALL*. Amsterdam: John Benjamins.

Kukulska-Hulme, Agnes and John Traxler (eds.)
2005 *Mobile Learning: A Handbook for Educators and Trainers*. London: Routledge.

Levy, Michael
1997 *Computer-Assisted Language Learning: Context and Conceptualization*. Oxford: Clarendon Press.

Levy, Mike and Glenn Stockwell
2006 *CALL Dimensions: Options and Issues in Computer-Assisted Language Learning*. Mahwah, N.J.: Lawrence Erlbaum Associates.

O'Dowd, Robert
2006 *Telecollaboration and the Development of Intercultural Communicative Competence*. München: Langenscheidt.

Warschauer, Mark
2003 *Technology and Social Inclusion: Rethinking the Digital Divide*. Cambridge, Mass.: MIT Press.

Warschauer, Mark and Richard Kern (eds.)
2000 *Network-based Language Teaching: Concepts and Practice*. Cambridge: Cambridge University Press.

Bibliographies

EUROCALL: CALL Bibliography. Available from: http://www.eurocall-languages.org/resources/bibliography [Accessed 10 August 2007].

Journals

ALSIC, Apprentissage des Langues et Systèmes d'Information et de Communication. Available from: http://alsic.u-strasbg.fr/ [Accessed 10 August 2007].

CALICO Journal. The Computer Assisted Language Instruction Consortium (CALICO), Duke University, Durham, NC. Available from: https://www.calico.org/p-5-CALICO%20Journal.html [Accessed 10 August 2007].

Computer Assisted Language Learning: An International Journal. Lisse: Swets and Zeitlinger. Available from: http://www.tandf.co.uk/journals/titles/09588221.asp [Accessed 10 August 2007].

Language Learning and Technology: A journal for second and foreign language educators. Available from: http://llt.msu.edu [Accessed 10 August 2007].

ReCALL. Cambridge: Cambridge University Press. Available from: http://journals.cambridge.org/journal_ReCALL [Accessed 10 August 2007].

Associations

EUROCALL. European Association for Computer Assisted Language Learning. Available from: http://www.eurocall-languages.org/ [Accessed 10 August 2007].

CALICO. The Computer Assisted Language Instruction Consortium. Available from: https://calico.org/ [Accessed 10 August 2007].

V. Evaluation in language learning and teaching

22. Principles of testing and assessment

Tim McNamara

1. Introduction

Language testing as an activity within applied linguistics has a distinctive character. It is practical in focus; building a test can be compared to building a road, and testers can be compared to engineers. Thus, language testing tends to be highly technical, as tests are very complex design objects, and many skills are involved in their construction. Tests like roads also need to be robust, and typically have to be constructed and to operate under circumstances that impose heavy practical constraints of time and money. And as with roads, the uses to which tests will be put may or may not meet with the approval of the constructor – just as roads can enable armies to march to war more effectively, so language tests can be used to discriminate against minorities. But testing is unlike engineering in that the material it is building with is cultural: language. And the uses of tests are also typically cultural and social. Moreover, these uses are not separate from but implicated in the technical character of test design.

As Spolsky (1995) has shown, language testing has a long history. Spoken language tests have been used since at least the middle ages. But in modern societies the role of testing has grown, and has become more central to social organisation in general. Language tests play a key role in managing the allocation of scarce resources within education systems, in controlling the movement of people across national boundaries, as gatekeeping procedures for educational and professional advancement, and in general as mechanisms for subjecting individuals to social power. Language tests have at the same time also become more technically complex and 'scientific', their technical qualities being one of the sources of their power.

Work in language testing finds its guiding principles in theories of validity and the validation of test score interpretations. Research on the validity of language tests has often focused on the solution of technical problems, and has had a confirmatory bias, in that it is carried out by the people who constructed the test, who may be thought to have a vested interest in the test emerging successfully from scrutiny. Critical thinking about language tests tends also to be inhibited ultimately by the fundamental requirement to produce workable language tests. This has meant that the social setting in which language tests have their meaning has been little discussed and some would even go so far as to oppose such discussion on the grounds that it is self-defeating if it weakens the ability to produce workable tests. There is a danger then of language testing remaining simply a highly technical and rather un-self-critical field where practical considerations are given priority over social significance. The situation is not helped by the isolation of language testing from other research fields within applied linguistics and in other areas of the humanities and education. There is a great need for more interdisciplinary work, although the apparently highly technical character of much work in language testing appears to militate against this. In fact, as we shall see, most of the fundamental concepts in language testing are quite straightforward and accessible. It is in the consideration of its social implications that greater complexity arises.

2. History of the field

The early history of the field of language assessment demonstrates a lively awareness of the social and political functions of tests. The idea that tests could be used to manage educational systems by tying funding to outcomes, the basis for contemporary national testing in the United Kingdom and the United States, has a very long history and can be found, for example, in 15th century Italy. In 19th century England, the payment by results policy (teachers were paid according to the achievement of their students) was the subject of vigorous public criticism, led by the educator and poet Matthew Arnold (Spolsky 1995; Madaus and Kellaghan 1992). It is interesting to note that though this system subsequently collapsed, it is making a come-back in contemporary society: educational funding, including the level of teachers' salaries, is being increasingly tied to the evidence of learning outcomes which are provided by tests, but without any acknowledgement or even perhaps recognition that the earlier experiment was a failure. The use of literacy tests in 19th century America directed at restricting the rights of recently freed African-American slaves and immigrants to vote was also the subject of controversy (Wiley 2005) and was eventually successfully opposed, although again, a return to such practices is being seen in many countries with growing immigrant populations, in the form of language tests for entry, residence and citizenship (see Hogan-Brun, Mar-Molinero and Stevenson 2009). The advent of modern scientific educational testing at around the time of the First World War, however, obscured the social and political functions of tests (Spolsky 1995). Language tests drew on theories of the measurement of cognitive abilities; this cognitive orientation meant that the focus was on the accuracy of measurement of individual abilities, and consideration of social issues was restricted to the fairness (accuracy, meaningfulness) of these measurements, not to the social policies in the service of which tests were commissioned. The focus was on test design, not on test use. At the time that modern language testing matured into a science, a branch of educational measurement, in the 1950s, the structuralist linguistics on which it drew was similarly asocial in that it viewed language as an abstract system of forms, which while shared, was stored in the individual mind; language use was not considered directly. Skills-based testing as a complement to discrete point testing of points of grammar and vocabulary made some concession to language use, but this kind of testing was mostly restricted to the testing of listening and reading, and the texts involved lacked many of the features of authentic language use. It was also argued (e.g. by Lado 1961) that the measurement of the productive skills of speaking and writing, which was expensive, time-consuming and not always reliable, depending as it did on human judgement, could be circumvented by measurement of knowledge of elements of the linguistic system (pronunciation, grammar, vocabulary). Thus the typical language test of the 1950s and 1960s became a test of grammar, vocabulary and pronunciation, with measures also of the skills of reading and (less often) listening; the assessment of writing was done if at all through an essay, and the assessment of speaking through an oral interview. In the 1970s, under the influence of Oller (1979), who emphasised the need for tests to take into account at least the immediate textual context of an utterance and introduced a psycholinguistic performance requirement for language tests (language needed to be produced under normal real-time conditions of use), the cloze test found a theoretical justification; because of its ease of construction and administration, it came to replace the reading test with questions, and was often seen as a replacement of the test of writing, too, because it was argued that it tapped the same underlying performance skill as writing.

The first challenge to the orthodoxy most clearly associated with Lado came from the advent of the communicative movement in the late 1960s, with the spread of Hymes's notion of communicative competence (Hymes 1972). From that time there were calls for language testing to reflect this more sociolinguistically oriented understanding of language proficiency, though even here, as Halliday (1978) pointed out, the focus remained essentially cognitive, focusing on individual competence, albeit in an expanded domain which included knowledge of the rules of interaction in a particular speech community. The version of communicative language teaching which developed in Europe in the 1970s was strongly influenced by the notional/functional syllabuses developed under the auspices of the Council of Europe, which emphasised pragmatic and functional skill in language, although still at a somewhat atomistic level (see Johnson, Ch. 13, this volume). An important paper by Morrow (1979) argued for a strong performance element in communicative language tests, focusing on whole communicative tasks, and this was strengthened by the growth of language teaching for specific purposes in the 1970s and early 1980s, where needs analyses focused on communicative roles and tasks at the level of activity rather than on individual notions and functions, and language tests for specific purposes, particularly for academic purposes, began to show a somewhat similar orientation. The development of several British English language tests for academic purposes, most notably the ELTS test, later revised as the IELTS test (Alderson and Clapham 1993; Clapham and Alderson 1997), showed a greater orientation to matching the design of the test to what was understood of the communicative demands of the particular target setting, in this case study in an English medium university. This work then spread to other areas of tests of English for specific purposes for example the testing of immigrant health professionals; one of the better known examples here is the Occupational English Test (OET) (McNamara 1996), which assessed the clinically relevant communication skills of immigrant health professionals to Australia through a test that was contextualised in the work settings of the professions involved.

These developments in Britain and Australia were not matched in the United States, which continued to focus on narrowly psychometric concerns of reliability, and tended towards more objectively scored formats for tests, particularly the use of multiple choice items. However, recent developments in the United States have seen the full scale adoption of communicative testing, for example in the new internet-based Test of English as a Foreign Language (TOEFL iBT) (Chapelle, Enright and Jamieson 2007), a test of English for Academic Purposes which is now fully contextualised in academic settings and has a high level of authenticity, without any loss of reliability. Conversely, British tests, which have traditionally been more communicative in their focus, and less concerned with technical quality considered in terms of psychometric orthodoxy (Alderson, Clapham and Wall (1995) speak of the tradition of hand-crafted British tests) are becoming more sophisticated in the attention they give to the psychometric qualities of tests. Another factor leading to similar approaches to assessment in both countries has been the adoption in both of policies requiring educational systems to report outcomes in terms of achieved proficiency standards (a development which is also found in the rest of Europe and in other countries around the world). This development will be discussed further below.

3. Central concepts and theoretical approaches: validity

Language assessment draws on theories of validity developed in the broader field of measurement to establish fundamental conceptual bases for language testing. Central to such theories is the notion that assessment involves using samples of behaviour to draw inferences about individuals being assessed. An assessment is designed on the principle that a clear relationship can be established between what we can claim about an individual and the procedures used to gather evidence in support of the claim. Such claims are today typically couched in practical, functionalist terms, reflecting the communicative tradition of language teaching and testing. For example, the widely used and very influential Common European Framework of Reference for languages (CEFR: Council of Europe 2001) represents an ordered set of claims, grouped into six levels (from lowest to highest: A1, A2, B1, B2, C1, C2) according to the complexity of the skills concerned. It is claimed, that a speaker at level A2 for example

> Can understand sentences and frequently used expressions related to areas of most immediate relevance (e.g. very basic personal and family information, shopping, local geography, employment). Can communicate in simple and routine tasks requiring a simple and direct exchange of information on familiar and routine matters. Can describe in simple terms aspects of his/her background, immediate environment and matters in areas of immediate need.

while a speaker at B1

> Can understand the main points of clear standard input on familiar matters regularly encountered in work, school, leisure, etc. Can deal with most situations likely to arise whilst travelling in an area where the language is spoken. Can produce simple connected text on topics which are familiar or of personal interest. Can describe experiences and events, dreams, hopes and ambitions and briefly give reasons and explanations for opinions and plans.

and a speaker at B2

> Can understand the main ideas of complex text on both concrete and abstract topics, including technical discussions in his/her field of specialisation. Can interact with a degree of fluency and spontaneity that makes regular interaction with native speakers quite possible without strain for either party. Can produce clear, detailed text on a wide range of subjects and explain a viewpoint on a topical issue giving the advantages and disadvantages of various options.
> (Council of Europe 2001: 24)

Such a statement of claims represents the test *construct*, the assumed view of language proficiency which is assessed in the test and which is the target of measurement in any individual case.

The design of an assessment begins by defining a relevant set of claims for the candidates to be assessed (relevant to some general level of required language ability or, more specifically, to the communicative setting in which they will be involved – academic, work related, and so on). Increasingly, these claims are dictated to us by policies governing teaching and assessment practices in educational systems. Policies typically dictate a statement of learning outcomes in terms of which achievement will have to be reported. This is the broad function of the Common European Framework of Reference for languages, for example, and educational systems are increasingly developing similar frameworks and statements of standards. Increasingly, too, any local standards need to be interpretable in terms of the dominant standards, particularly the CEFR, so that educational systems all over the world, for example in China,

Taiwan, Japan and Australia, are now orienting their statements of standards towards the CEFR, if they are not adopting it outright. This has advantages in terms of the interpretability of claims across settings – rather like having a common currency into which the local currency can be converted – but it has the disadvantage that whatever thinking about language, language learning and its goals is represented in the conceptualisation and wording of the dominant framework tends to assume a hegemonic status, with alternatives being excluded as not being interpretable in terms of the framework.

Once a set of claims has been determined, the next stage in test development is to consider the situations in which evidence for such claims might naturally occur, and whether performance in these situations might be considered directly, or how it might be replicated or at least represented in the design of test tasks. For example, where written or spoken performance naturally occurs in the course of instruction (students give talks, or produce written texts), such texts might be assembled and presented in a portfolio for assessment (Hamp-Lyons and Condon 2000). Evidence of ability in the receptive skills of reading and listening may also be available indirectly if the production of the written and spoken texts is dependent on reading and listening to material which will form input or act as a stimulus to the spoken or written production. Students in academic settings for example often find themselves listening to lectures and reading relevant materials which they then use as input for essays or class presentations. It is possible to think of a language assessment in such settings which relies on evidence which is accumulated in the normal course of instruction and which requires no formal separate test.

More typically, however, and especially where assessment is not tied to a particular course of instruction, a formal procedure, i.e. a test, will need to be developed for gathering the evidence on which to base the claims about students. Usually there are severe constraints on the time that a test will take, and on the time and resources that will go into its development, scoring and reporting. Decisions need to be made on several fronts: the range of skills to be assessed, the degree to which they will be integrated (that is, how far speaking and writing will depend on prior reading and/or listening), the length of the test, the format of tasks, the logistic requirements (equipment for the delivery of listening tests and tests of speaking), the selection and training of judges, the criteria by which performances will be judged, and so on. The decisions made will ultimately be recorded in a set of *specifications* for the test, rather like a recipe for the production of subsequent *test forms*, which will be subject to revision as experience with the test and investigation of its strengths and weaknesses proceeds. Once some draft specifications have been drawn up, pilot materials written to these specifications need to be prepared and tried out on a sample of test takers who resemble the target group in all important respects. Data from these *test trials*, including feedback from trial subjects, are then analysed and the materials revised. The aim is to improve the test quality as much as possible. Inconsistency in judgements about individuals being assessed is a typical threat to test quality, so estimates of this consistency, or the *reliability* of the test, are made, and need to meet agreed professional standards. The outcome of these developmental stages is an operational version of the test, ready for administration.

Despite all the efforts and care taken in the design and construction of the test, we cannot take for granted that an assessment procedure, no matter how carefully developed, will yield meaningful claims about the individuals being assessed. Validity theory insists that these claims be subject to interrogation – what evidence is there to support the truth or relevance of the claim in relation to any particular individual being assessed? We need to think through and anticipate threats to the meaningfulness of claims. For example, it has long been recognised that where there is some doubt as to whether a person should be categorised as, let us say, A2 or B1 on the CEFR scale, the categorisation of such a borderline candidate is likely to be determined as much by the characteristics of the person making the judgement (whether they are relatively harsh or lenient, whether they are consistent in their judgements with other judges, or even with themselves on different occasions) as it is by the characteristics of the person being assessed. If this reality is not understood and controlled for, the outcome of the assessment is in danger of becoming no more than a form of lottery, where the candidate's fate depends on who he or she happens to get as a judge. Validity theory is fundamentally concerned with investigating such threats to the meaningfulness of scores and the conclusions about candidates they represent, and is principally focussed on the *fairness* of the assessment, in this sense.

Current theories of test validity make a distinction between these procedures intended to provide a basis for assessing knowledge and skill, and the use of such procedures for making decisions about individuals. We can compare this with the distinction between the accuracy of a measuring tape and the use made of differences in measurement of different individuals. For example, in military recruitment, only individuals measured as being above a certain height are eligible for recruitment: the measuring instrument is used first to measure individuals, and then that measurement is used to make decisions about inclusion or exclusion. Validity theory has increasingly insisted that not only the measurement itself but also the uses to which the measurement is put are the responsibility of those involved in test development (see McNamara and Roever 2006, for a detailed account of these issues).

The most significant early theorist of test validity was Lee Cronbach (Cronbach and Meehl 1955; Cronbach 1971), who prioritised the issue of the interpretability of test scores. He understood that a test was a procedure for gathering evidence in support of an inference about the test taker, and understood that tests therefore necessarily involved interpretation of the evidence. As all interpretations involve judgement and uncertainty, the quality or validity of a test lay in the strength and defensibility of the procedures for drawing inferences about test candidates from the evidence of the candidate's performance on the test. Cronbach concluded that questions of validity would therefore involve the design of the test, the procedures used in scoring (particularly where, as with tests of speaking and writing, they involved human judgement), theories of the candidate abilities on which the test performance is presumed to draw, and confirmatory evidence from external sources (other people who have some independent knowledge of the candidate's abilities, performance by the candidate on other related tests, and so on). For Cronbach, "one does not validate a test, but only a principle for making inferences" (Cronbach and Meehl 1955: 297); "one validates not a test, but an interpretation of data arising from a specified procedure" (Cronbach 1971: 447)

In Cronbach's earlier discussions of tests, he did not address test use; but he also developed theory in a related field, the evaluation of educational programs. Here, he understood that program evaluation also involved interpretation, and that moreover interpretations of the worth and quality of a program would necessarily depend on questions of policy and values. In his later writings on tests he included the role of beliefs and values in validity arguments, which he saw as linking 'concepts, evidence, social and personal consequences, and values' (Cronbach 1988: 4). In this he may have been influenced by the work of the American validity theorist Samuel Messick, who brought together concern for the quality of inferences in tests and concern for the values implicit in test constructs, and the social and educational consequences of their use, in a unified theory of test validity. Messick (1989) saw the development of a validity argument as involving a number of aspects, which he set out in a famous validity matrix:

	TEST INTERPRETATION	TEST USE
EVIDENTIAL BASIS	Construct validity	Construct validity + Relevance/utility
CONSEQUENTIAL BASIS	Value implications	Social consequences

Figure 1. Facets of validity (Messick 1989: 20)

It may be helpful to gloss these rather abstract terms in the following interpretation of the matrix (McNamara and Roever 2006: 14)

	WHAT TEST SCORES ARE ASSUMED TO MEAN	WHEN TESTS ARE ACTUALLY USED
USING EVIDENCE IN SUPPORT OF CLAIMS: TEST FAIRNESS	What reasoning and empirical evidence support the claims we wish to make about candidates based on their test performance?	Are these interpretations meaningful, useful and fair in particular settings in which the test is to be used?
THE OVERT SOCIAL CONTEXT OF TESTING	What social and cultural values and assumptions underlie test constructs and hence the sense we make of scores?	What happens in our education systems and the larger social setting when we use tests?

Figure 2. Understanding Messick's validity matrix (adapted from McNamara and Roever, 2006: 14)

Developing a validity argument in support of the interpretation and use of test scores involves a number of aspects. First, we need to articulate a rationale for the design of the test and the reasonableness of the interpretation of test scores as indicators of candidate ability. This involves explaining the relationship of test tasks and test performance to the domain of ability or the future domain of communicative activity which the test is targeting. We also need to confront such a rationale with the evidence of test performance, where investigations using (for example) statistical analysis of test scores, or qualitative interpretations of candidates' reports of test taking processes, may cast doubt on or offer support for the interpretations we wish to make.

Messick (1989) sees two major sources of threat to the meaningfulness of test scores: *construct under-representation* and *construct-irrelevant variance*. Given the necessary complexity of judgements of the evidence of the productive skills of speaking and writing, the room for disagreement about the quality of a performance, and the need to train judges and provide ongoing monitoring of their work, test developers have sometimes attempted to substitute other more easily manageable measures in place of these: for example, for writing, tests of control of grammar and vocabulary, sometimes in the format of a cloze test. Such methods seriously under-represent the construct of writing, which requires writers to consider issues of audience and genre among other things, which are not represented in such test formats. In the testing of speaking, research in the last twenty years has taken us away from psycholinguistic models of speaking (with the focus on real-time coordination of the elements of grammar, vocabulary and pronunciation to produce an integrated performance) towards a sociolinguistic model where speaking is seen as resembling dancing, and requires the coordination of the work of both participants for it to happen successfully. The recognition that speaking sentences is not the same as saying utterances, the latter being an aspect of the reciprocal communicative ability of talking, is the basis for Widdowson's distinction between linguistic skill and communicative ability (Widdowson 1978). This distinction has not been taken up in the literature on language testing, which continues to use the terms 'skill' and 'ability' interchangeably in certain contexts.

As the role of the co-participants in the 'dance' of spoken interaction has been studied, so the influence of the interlocutor on impressions of the candidate's performance has emerged as an important issue, leading to criticism of the conventional interview format for speaking tests as under-representing the task of speaking where the interlocutor is not so skilled or experienced in eliciting a performance from the candidate. Such studies have also cast light on another source of construct-irrelevant variance in test scores, that is, where differences in scores attained by different individuals are the result of factors other than their own performance and the abilities that underlie it which are the target of measurement. In particular, in assessments of speaking and writing, the choice of task and the characteristics of the judge have been shown to exert a potentially large and distorting influence on test scores. Most research into language testing is aimed at understanding such threats to the interpretability of test scores.

A further aspect of a validity argument is that we need to take into account the setting in which a test is used. For example, well-established tests such as IELTS (International English Language Testing System), which were developed for the selection of students for university study in English-medium universities, have, because of their quality and reputation, increasingly been used in settings for which they were not initially designed, such as the certification of the clinically-relevant communication skills of health professionals, or for the assessment of learners as young as 14 or 15 entering English-medium high schools. All such uses need to be validated afresh, according to Messick.

Further aspects of the validity argument involve articulating and defending the values implicit in the test, and investigating their impact on the educational systems of which they are a part, and the wider society in which they find their place. These areas of validation are far less well established in language testing research which has tended to focus on the first of Messick's cells, but these areas are increasingly important given the growing importance socially and politically of language tests.

An example of the way values are present in tests can be found in the double role that language tests play in the assessment of abilities at the end of high school in several countries, where the scores gained are used for the dual purposes of demonstrating achievement at school, and of selection for university entry. On the one hand, following current communicative orthodoxy, such tests relate to a syllabus of study which aims at least in theory to develop communicative competence in the learner. Tests accordingly might be expected to focus on communicative tasks in speaking, reading, listening and writing. On the other hand, the scores from the tests may be used to determine university entrance, including entry to courses which are subject to extreme competition for places, and here, the relevant criteria for selection will not prioritise content knowledge but general intellectual and personal qualities such as self-discipline, perseverance and intelligence which are taken as indicators of aptitude for university study, especially given that the course followed at university may bear little relationship to the subjects studied at school which are the basis for university selection. The issue is not only that there is an inevitable gap between actual achievement as proficiency, 'competence', and the potential for further development, 'capacity' or 'capability' (see Widdowson 2003 for this distinction), but that the kinds of capability important for university selection are not necessarily seen as having any relation to those reflected in the more explicitly functionalist and practical communicative orientation of most current communicative syllabuses.

Thus, in some countries, the language test scores of students whose achievement is based simply on hard work and study are distinguished from the scores of those whose achievement is a reflection of home background in the language concerned or opportunity to spend time in a country in which the relevant language is spoken. For these latter students, their achievement may be valued less than those for whom the language proficiency achieved did not have the benefit of such experiences, the argument being that their scores are less indicative of the qualities of discipline, etc. which are the basis for university selection (Elder 1997). In Japan, the testing of speaking is neglected in the high school at all but the most junior levels because oral proficiency in a foreign language such as English is considered to be unrelated to the personal qualities of hard work and intelligence which are the target of the Japanese educational system, a reflection of deeply held Confucian educational values (Akiyama 2004).

The consequences of language tests have been most clearly understood in terms of the notion of *washback*, that is, the impact of a test on the teaching and learning with which it is associated (Cheng, Watanabe and Curtis 2004). Broader social consequences of tests are considered under the heading of test impact. The resulting social responsibility of language testers is also the subject of much current debate. Nevertheless, as we shall see in the next section, the use of language tests is still not adequately theorised.

Messick's work has set out most adequately to date the general scope of language test validation, but its generality and breadth has meant that it has proved difficult for test developers to implement confidently. What are the practical steps that need to be taken to engage appropriately with the dimensions of the validation task? Subsequent developments in the theory have involved articulating the stages of the development of a validity argument (Mislevy, Steinberg and Almond 2003; Kane 2001). This in turn has been interpreted for language testing by Bachman (see especially Bachman 2005).

4. The responsibilities of language testers

The most controversial issue facing language testing is the question of the responsibilities of language testers, as the uses of language tests have become more and more prominent in society and in politics, and in consequence have a pervasive influence on aspects of people's everyday lives. It is not only that tests have an effect on educational values, but they can have an immediate impact on fundamental issues of welfare and social justice.

Thus, in educational settings, in the United States, because of the bipartisan policy known as 'No Child Left Behind', some school authorities are facing a loss of control of the curricula and management of their schools because their students are not performing at prescribed levels on tests of English. As a result, too, bilingual education is suffering as schools spend increasing amounts of time and energy preparing students to meet these crucial English tests on which the fate of the whole school rests. The results of international comparisons of proficiency in reading in the mother tongue under an assessment scheme known as PISA (Program in Student Assessment), carried out by the Organisation of Economic Cooperation and Development (OECD), were have precipitaled significant changes in the education systems of countries such as Germany and Austria where students have not performed as well as expected on these tests.

In the area of employment, airline pilots in Korea and China are in danger of losing their jobs because of failure on a test of competence in English in the aviation workplace mandated from 2008 by the International Civil Aviation Organisation. In Britain, language tests are no longer required of health professionals from European Union countries, while those from elsewhere require rigorous assessment of their competence to communicate in English in professional settings.

And in the area of immigration and citizenship, language tests are playing an increasingly important role in the service of arguably discriminatory policies. In Sweden, Denmark and the Netherlands, the electoral fate of governments is tied to their stance on language tests for immigration and citizenship. Asylum seekers in Australia, the United Kingdom, Germany, the Netherlands and elsewhere face language tests as part of the authentication of their claims; the presumed link between geographical origin and accent is exploited in such tests, although how they are carried out and their accuracy and validity have been subjected to successful challenge in the courts. Intending immigrants to the Netherlands from Morocco are facing demanding tests in spoken Dutch before being granted a visa to join a prospective spouse who is a Dutch citizen. In the United Kingdom, Australia and elsewhere, intending citizens are facing new and demanding tests of English language proficiency and tests of knowledge of national history and political and social values; these latter tests are conducted in the main language spoken in the country concerned, and thus constitute in themselves demanding language tests.

In short, the political and social functions of language tests, and their role in employment, education, immigration, citizenship and the policing of identity, are increasingly prominent. There is a resulting shift of attention away from a focus on the cognitive dimensions of language assessment (the measurement of proficiency in the individual, isolated mind of the learner) to the political and social roles played by assessment, particularly in the context of globalisation, with the development of a field known as *critical language testing* (Shohamy 2001). The need to understand and evaluate the role of tests in social and political settings is presenting significant challenges to the world of language assessment research, which is ill-equipped theoretically to conceptualise and problematise such functions.

An important issue here is the question of the construct. Take the case of the widespread, and growing, practice of requiring demonstration of proficiency in the national language for the purpose of gaining entry to a society as an immigrant, or the right to reside there permanently once one has entered, or of subsequently gaining citizenship and thus the right to vote and to access to other social benefits (McNamara and Shohamy 2008). Legislation in Europe typically frames the proficiency requirement in terms of a level on the Common European Framework of Reference (CEFR, see above: Van Avermaet 2009). However, studies of the policy discourses in which the requirement has been formulated (e.g. Blackledge 2009; Horner 2009) make it plain that the construct in such tests is not about practical communicative skill; in fact, the measurement of language proficiency serves as a pretext for a deeper assessment, of (external) conformity to a national ideology. What standard of conformity is sufficient? In educational settings, the establishment of sufficient minimum standards involves dividing the continuum of scores into a number of categories; the score where one category ends and another begins is called a cut score. The setting of cut scores in language tests in such cases is necessarily subjective, and most procedures for establishing cut-points involve gathering multiple judgements of the sufficiency of various levels of performance in relation to a given criterion. In case of tests aimed at immigrants, however, the categories are two: acceptable and unacceptable, for the purpose of granting entry, residence or citizenship. Given that the underlying construct in this case is conformity to a set of socio-cultural values, as measured by a proxy measurement of language proficiency, rather than language proficiency for more clearly functional purposes, the question of 'how much' is not open to rational judgement, and standard procedures become irrelevant. It is not surprising, given the entirely political character of the assessments, that cut-points are determined not by language testers but by policy makers, and on purely political grounds. The wildly differing CEFR requirements in different countries noted by Van Avermaet (2009) is then explicable given the differing political settings in each of the countries concerned.

In summary, the construct of language proficiency in tests for immigration and citizenship is best understood in terms of ideology, not functional language proficiency. To what extent does language testing theory admit of this possibility? As we have seen, the articulation and critical examination of the values implicit in tests is part of Messick's framework, though as a matter of practice this is almost never done. Similarly, Kane (2001) sees the uses of tests as falling within the domain of test validation: in other words, test developers have a responsibility to articulate and defend the intended uses of tests. Underlying the discussions of both authors, and more explicitly in the work of Kane, is the assumption that the developers of tests will somehow determine and thus take responsibility for both the values expressed in tests and the uses to which they are put, assuming (as is the case for these tests for immigration and citizenship) that such uses are known or can be anticipated. This presents a dilemma for test developers. Both the nature of the test construct, and the uses to which the test is to be put, are not determined by the test developers, but are entirely externally determined as a function of policy and political processes. A further problem for language testers is that their very expertise in developing fairer tests is effectively politicised in such cases. The technical quality of tests becomes a means of enforcing power, as tests can disarm criticism, a point made by Shohamy (2009) and by McNamara and Roever (2006). On the general question of the responsibility and ethics of language testing, see McNamara and Shohamy (2008).

5. Recent developments

A number of developments in the practical design of language tests have attracted discussion recently. These include the use of technology in language tests, the integrated assessment of skills, particularly in the testing of English for academic purposes, and developments in the assessment of spoken language, including the assessment of English as a lingua franca. These will be discussed in turn, and the contribution of applied linguistics research considered in relation to each.

The increased capacity of digital technology is transforming the possibilities for language tests, particularly of spoken language, which are administered on a large scale. One of the most controversial developments is the use of matching technology for the purpose of systematic comparison of highly specific segmental and suprasegmental features of candidate spoken production with the same features analysed in a digital corpus of native speaker performances of the same material. A measure of the distance of the candidate performance from that of the native speakers is then used as the basis for an estimate of the overall spoken proficiency of the candidate. Such measures show impressively high correlations with more complex performance-based measures of spoken proficiency derived for example from face to face interviews. They are also very cost efficient, yielding scores for spoken proficiency at a fraction of the cost of more direct measures. These techniques have, however, proved controversial because the candidate is only required to produce very restricted samples of speech – the repetition of sentences, the provision of lexical opposites, and so on, as it is necessary that the candidate produce exactly the material that is contained in the electronic corpus of native speaker samples. This goes directly against current orthodoxy in relation to performance assessment, which stresses linguistic creativity, communicative context and so on; this technological advance appears to many to have the retrograde effect of focusing again on formal linguistic features associated with an approach to testing which as we have seen is now no longer in favour – a case of measuring what you can reliably measure rather than what is valid. It also represents a purely psycholinguistic view of spoken proficiency, as involving the real-time coordination of linguistic elements, and eschews any social or interactive perspective. The advantage of the method in terms of cost and ease of administration (the test can be taken over the telephone, and takes only a few minutes) is proving irresistible to testing agencies, despite the objections of advocates of communicative methods. It remains to be seen what the washback effect of such methods will be on teaching and learning, and whether performance on the test is coachable (that is, can be improved by developing test-wiseness without a corresponding improvement in underlying proficiency).

Developments in technology are also reflected in the long-awaited reform of the Test of English as a Foreign Language (TOEFL iBT: cf. Chapelle, Enright and Jamieson 2007), one of the two main international tests used to assess the academic language skills of international students wishing to study in English-medium environments, particularly in the United States. The test is delivered on the internet and the performances, including in speaking and writing, are collected digitally. The digital format of the spoken and written production allows easy distribution for scoring, and by enabling different parts of the performance to be distributed to different judges, has led to significant increases in reliability. The provision of an appropriate technological infrastructure for delivery of the test on the internet has continued to be a problem in certain countries, however; this will presumably resolve itself in time. Again, the advantages to be gained by technological innovation have their costs: internet delivery constrains the format of test tasks, particularly in the area of speaking, and thus raises questions of test validity.

TOEFL iBT is significant for a further reason, in that it is the first very large scale test to introduce *integrated assessment* of the skills of speaking, listening, reading and writing, which, since Lado (1961), have been assessed separately, despite the overwhelming evidence from surveys of academic environments showing that the skills are integrated in reality (students typically have to write or speak about material that they have heard or read). This is likely to have a productive impact on teaching and learning in preparation for the test. It raises important theoretical and technical issues, however, if we want to continue the practice of reporting on the separate skills, where performance in one skill is dependent on performance in another. For example, the writing skills of candidates may be assessed by requiring them to summarise and to respond to ideas which have been presented to them in a short lecture and a series of short written texts.

Spoken language has for long been tested in the context of a face-to-face interview; the best known example is the Oral Proficiency Interview (OPI), long a staple within British English language examinations, and widespread in the United States particularly in the testing of foreign languages following its adoption by the American Council on the Teaching of Foreign Languages (ACTFL) as part of its embrace of the communicative movement (American Council on the Teaching of Foreign Languages 1986). The special character of the interview format, and particularly the role of the interlocutor in such assessments (Brown 2003), has been the focus of much recent research, leading to questions over how possible it is to generalise from performance under such conditions to more naturalistic conditions of conversations among peers. An alternative to the interview has emerged, in which pairs or small groups of candidates interact, and the performance judged by non-participant examiners. A concern has been voiced about the impact of the interlocutor in such assessments – what difference does it make if a candidate is paired with someone of higher or lower proficiency, of the same or a different gender, with an outgoing or retiring personality type? The concern of much of this research has until recently been to remove the impact of what are considered to be construct-irrelevant factors (the interlocutor) and to assume some stable underlying independent proficiency trait. More recently, however, the pair or group oral has been looked at from another perspective, that of the need to assess English as a lingua franca (Seidlhofer, Breiteneder and Pitzl 2006). Given that typical communication situations in English increasingly do not involve interaction with native speakers exclusively, the character of the paired interaction can now be seen to have the advantage that it more closely resembles English as a lingua franca communication. In such situations, being able to cope with someone of differing proficiency or differing in their capacity to facilitate interaction is quite typical, and what were previously seen as construct-irrelevant factors can be seen as the construct-relevant. The task facing language testers is to develop criteria which reflect what is relevant to success in such settings, including such things as flexibility, being a good listener, being able to identify and overcome instances of misunderstanding or breakdown, and so on. Much research is needed to validate the use of such criteria in these kinds of assessments, and here ongoing work on the character of spoken interaction in other fields of applied linguistics is likely to continue to inform understanding of the construct.

References

Akiyama, Tomoyasu
2004 Introducing speaking tests into a Japanese Senior High School entrance examination. Unpublished Ph.D. thesis, The University of Melbourne.

Alderson, J. Charles and Caroline Clapham (eds.)
1993 *Examining the ELTS Test: An Account of the First Stage of the ELTS Revision Project – Research Report 2.* London: The British Council/University of Cambridge Local Examinations Syndicate.

Alderson, J. Charles, Caroline Clapham and Dianne Wall
1995 *Language Test Construction and Evaluation.* Cambridge: Cambridge University Press.

American Council on the Teaching of Foreign Languages
1986 *ACTFL Proficiency Guidelines.* New York: American Council on the Teaching of Foreign Languages.

Bachman, Lyle F.
2005 Building and supporting a case for test use. *Language Assessment Quarterly* 2(1): 1–34.

Blackledge, Adrian
2009 Being English, speaking English: Extension to English language testing legislation and the future of multicultural Britain. In: Hogan-Brun, Mar-Molinero and Stevenson (eds.), 83–107.

Brown, Annie
2003 Interviewer variation and the co-construction of speaking proficiency. *Language Testing* 20 (1), 1–25.

Chapelle, Carol A., Mary K. Enright and Joan M. Jamieson (eds.)
2007 *Building a Validity Argument for the Test of English as a Foreign Language.* Mahwah, NJ: Lawrence Erlbaum.

Cheng, Liying, Yoshinori Watanabe and Andy Curtis
2004 *Washback in Language Testing: Research Contexts and Methods.* Mahwah, NJ: Erlbaum.

Clapham, Caroline and J. Charles Alderson
1997 *Constructing and Trialling the IELTS Test – Research Report 3.* London: The British Council/University of Cambridge Local Examinations Syndicate/IDP Education Australia.

Council of Europe
2001 *Common European Framework of Reference for Languages: Learning, Teaching and Assessment.* Cambridge: Cambridge University Press.

Cronbach, Lee J.
1971 Validity. In: Robert L. Thorndike (ed.), *Educational Measurement*, Second edition, 443–597. Washington, DC: American Council on Education.

Cronbach, Lee J.
1988 Five perspectives on the validity argument. In: Howard Wainer and Henry I. Braun (eds.), *Test Validity*, 3–18. Hillsdale, NJ: Lawrence Erlbaum Associates.

Cronbach, Lee J. and Paul E. Meehl
1955 Construct validity in psychological tests. *Psychological Bulletin* 52: 281–302.

Elder, Catherine
1997 What does test bias have to do with fairness? *Language Testing* 14 (3): 261–277.

Halliday, Michael A. K.
1978 *Language as Social Semiotic: The Social Interpretation of Language and Meaning*. London: Edward Arnold.

Hamp-Lyons, Liz and William Condon
2000 *Assessing the Portfolio: Principles for Practice, Theory, and Research.* Cresskill, NJ: Hampton Press.

Hogan-Brun, Gabrielle, Clare Mar-Molinero and Patrick Stevenson (eds.)
2009 *Discourses on language and Integration: Critical Perspectives on Language Teaching Regimes in Europe.* Amsterdam/Philadelphia: John Benjamins.

Horner, K.
2009 Language, identity and citizenship in Luxembourg: unpacking the discourse of integration. In: Hogan-Brun, Mar-Molinero and Stevenson (eds.), 109–128.

Hymes, Dell
1972 On communicative competence. In: John B. Pride and Janet Holmes (eds.), *Sociolinguistics*, 269–293. Harmondsworth: Penguin.

Kane, Michael T.
2001 Current concerns in validity theory. *Journal of Educational Measurement* 38 (4): 319–342.

Lado, Robert
1961 *Language Testing: The Construction and Use of Foreign Language Tests.* London: Longmans Green and Co.

Madaus, George F. and Thomas Kellaghan
1992 Curriculum evaluation and assessment. In: Philip W. Jackson (ed.), *Handbook on Research on Curriculum*, 119–154. New York: Macmillan.

McNamara, Tim
1996 *Measuring Second Language Performance*. London/New York: Addison Wesley Longman.

McNamara, Tim and Carsten Roever
2006 *Language Testing: The Social Dimension*. Malden, MA/Oxford: Blackwell.

McNamara, Tim and Elena Shohamy
2008 Language tests and human rights. *International Journal of Applied Linguistics* 18 (1): 89–95.

Messick, Samuel
1989 Validity. In: Robert L. Linn (ed.), *Educational Measurement*, 3rd edition, 13–103. New York: American Council on Education and Macmillan.

Mislevy, Robert J., Linda S. Steinberg and Russell G. Almond
2003 On the structure of assessment arguments. *Measurement: Interdisciplinary Research and Perspectives* 1 (1): 3–62.

Morrow, Keith
1979 Communicative language testing: revolution or evolution? In: Christopher J. Brumfit and Keith Johnson (eds.), *The Communicative Approach to Language Teaching*, 143–157. Oxford: Oxford University Press.

Oller, John W.
1979 *Language Tests at School*. London: Longman.
Seidlhofer, Barbara, Angelika Breiteneder and Marie-Luise Pitzl
2006 English as a lingua franca in Europe. *Annual Review of Applied Linguistics* 26: 1–34.
Shohamy, Elena
2001 *The Power of Tests: A Critical Perspective on the Uses of Language Tests*. London: Pearson.
Shohamy, Elena
2009 Language tests for immigrants: Why language? Why tests? Why citizenship? In: Hogan-Brun, Mar-Molinero and Stevenson (eds.), 45–59.
Spolsky, Bernard
1995 *Measured Words*. Oxford: Oxford University Press.
Van Avermaet, Piet
2009 Fortress Europe? Language policy regimes for immigration and citizenship. In: Hogan-Brun, Mar-Molinero and Stevenson (eds.).
Widdowson, Henry G.
1978 *Teaching Language as Communication*. Oxford: Oxford University Press.
Widdowson, Henry G.
2003 *Defining Issues in English Language Teaching*. Oxford: Oxford University Press.
Wiley, Terrence G.
2005 *Literacy and Language Diversity in the United States*. 2nd edition. Washington, DC: Center for Applied Linguistics.

Resources

The International Language Testing Association (ILTA) publishes a useful bibliography of research on language testing, available online at http://www.iltaonline.com/ILTA_pubs.htm

Additional resources can be found at the Language Testing Resouces Website, http://languagetesting.info

A useful teaching resource is

Stow, Hardy
1996 *Mark My Words: Assessing Second and Foreign Language Skills* [video series]. Parkville, Victoria: Language Testing Research Centre and Multimedia Education Unit, University of Melbourne. Available at http://www.ltrc.unimelb.edu.au/resources/index.html

Recommended readings

Alderson, J. Charles
2000 *Assessing Reading*. Cambridge: Cambridge University Press.
Bachman, Lyle
1990 *Fundamental Considerations in Language Testing*. Oxford: Oxford University Press.
Bachman, Lyle and Adrian Palmer
2008 *Language Testing in Practice*. 2nd edition. Oxford: Oxford University Press.
Brown, James D. and Thom Hudson
2002 *Criterion-Referenced Language Testing*. Cambridge: Cambridge University Press.
Davidson, Fred and Brian K. Lynch
2002 *Testcraft: A Teacher's Guide to Writing and Using Language Test Specifications*. New Haven/London: Yale University Press.
Douglas, Dan
2000 *Assessing Languages for Specific Purposes*. Cambridge: Cambridge University Press.
Fulcher, Glenn
2003 *Testing Second Language Speaking*. London: Longman/Pearson Education.
Fulcher, Glenn and Fred Davidson
2007 *Language Testing and Assessment*. London/New York: Routledge.
Hughes, Arthur
2003 *Testing for Language Teachers*. 2nd edition. Cambridge: Cambridge University Press.
Luoma, Sari
2004 *Assessing Speaking*. Cambridge: Cambridge University Press.
McKay, Penny
2006 *Assessing Young Language Learners*. Cambridge: Cambridge University Press.
Purpura, James
2004 *Assessing Grammar*. Cambridge: Cambridge University Press.
Read, John
2000 *Assessing Vocabulary*. Cambridge: Cambridge University Press.
Shohamy, Elena
2001 *The Power of Tests*. Harlow, Essex: Longman/Pearson.
Elena Shohamy and Nancy H. Hornberger (eds.)
2007 *Language Testing and Assessment*. [Volume 7 of *Encyclopedia of Language and Education*. 2nd edition]. Dordrecht, The Netherlands: Springer.
Weigle, Sara C.
2002 *Assessing Writing*. Cambridge: Cambridge University Press.
Weir, Cyril
2005 *Language Testing and Validation: An Evidence-Based Approach*. Houndgrave, Hampshire, UK: Palgrave-Macmillan.

Journals

The main specialist journals in the field are *Language Testing* and *Language Assessment Quarterly*, as well as *Assessing Writing*. In addition, there is a refereed e-journal, *Melbourne Papers in Language Testing*, available on-line at http://www.ltrc.unimelb.edu.au/mplt/index.html

23. Issues in certification

Annelie Knapp

1. Introduction: The need for certification

"Do you speak English?" This seemingly simple question, asked thousands of times every day, is in effect quite hard to answer. Apart from diverging conceptions of what is meant by "English", there are three fundamental problems with this question: It suggests either "yes" or "no" as an answer, and it does not invite any differentiation with regard to varying degrees of knowledge. Furthermore there is a certain ambiguity in the verb "speak". Within the context of this question the tacit assumption is that the verb "speak" should not be taken literally as denoting ability for the oral production of utterances, but that "speak" should rather be regarded as a cover-term for something like general language proficiency – the everyday notion of "speaking a language". But what else – apart from producing oral utterances in a language – does "speaking a language" entail? Thus, depending on the situational context, the question "Do you speak English?" may mean many different things, e.g. "Is there a chance that you can understand me when I talk to you in English?" or "Can I take it for granted that you will be able to handle all business affairs via English as the medium of communication?" or even "Is English your mother tongue?" Last, but not least, any answer to this question will be a very subjective one, with individual people being likely to over- or underestimate their abilities.

It is obvious that for various reasons and purposes less ambiguity and a more precise and detailed specification of proficiency in a language is absolutely necessary. In other words, there is a need for valid and reliable measures that give objective information about a certain standard and allow for comparisons between individuals. Often there is also a need to certify the level of proficiency, usually on the basis of a test, as there are many situations in which individuals will want to or have to prove their proficiency in a foreign language to other people. Those situations can be grouped into three main categories: access to university in a foreign country, application for a job, where some competence in a foreign language is needed, or immigration to a foreign country, where a certain amount of proficiency in the official language of that country is a formal prerequisite for citizenship. It is a common feature of these types of situations that certification of language proficiency has a selective character and therefore a gate-keeping function. As an increasing number of people – for some reason or other – have the desire to pass that gate, certification has become a profitable business, too: normally test takers have to pay for their certificate – another gate to pass. Publishers in the language teaching business can take advantage of this situation as well. Materials for test preparation are needed as well as courses to prepare for the tests.

Up to now we have taken the concepts of "certification" and "proficiency" for granted, but they need to be more precisely defined. What exactly do we mean by "certification"? In the context of this article we define certification as a formal confirmation of a certain level of proficiency in a foreign language that places an individual in relation to other individuals with regard to this proficiency. This leaves us with the question of what is meant by "proficiency". As this is a rather problematic category, we will confine ourselves to a definition of "proficiency test" to start with.

The conventional classification of foreign language tests according to their purposes and functions distinguishes among achievement tests, proficiency tests, placement tests and diagnostic tests. As indicated by the term itself, placement tests are used to place language learners in appropriate language courses. Diagnostic tests are aimed at identifying specific problem areas of individual learners, with the intention to provide support for overcoming those problems. Achievement tests are supposed to measure what a foreign language learner has learned with regard to the goals of a particular course or series of courses he has attended. Proficiency tests are used to specify a learner's abilities in a foreign or second language, regardless of the goals of a particular course and even regardless of whether the learner has had any tuition at all or acquired the L2 in naturalistic contexts. This implies that in principle proficiency tests totally neglect how, when and why an individual has gained proficiency in a foreign language. Their orientation is clearly towards the future. The results of proficiency tests are used for making inferences about an individual's future performance in the foreign language: on the job, in university studies or as a member of a social community.

After this introduction, this article will continue with a brief historical overview of the development of certification in the field of foreign language proficiency (section 2). In section 3, different approaches to certification will be characterised in more detail. The main focus will be on the most widely used procedures for testing proficiency in English as foreign language, as – for reasons that will be explained below – English proficiency tests have very often been the pioneers that other languages have followed. Section 4 will focus on theoretical backgrounds of certification, dealing with the construct of language proficiency, with problems of finding appropriate scales and descriptors for assessment and with the "native speaker" as a point of reference. Section 5 is devoted to problems of using test results and – in this context – issues of equivalence between different types of test, and the final section 6 will specify some questions for further research.

2. History of the field

The development of proficiency tests and, as a consequence, of certification started in the academic field. Between the early 1950s and the early 1960s, the UK as well as the USA experienced an enormous increase in the number of overseas students from non-English speaking countries in higher education institutions – a development that has meanwhile spread to other English-speaking countries like Canada, Australia and New Zealand and that – to some extent – has also affected non-English speaking countries in the course of progressive internationalisation in higher education. It was soon realised both in the UK and in the United States that some kind of admission test was necessary to ensure adequate proficiency in the English language. "Otherwise, because of inadequate proficiency in English, the institutions and the students would waste time and effort" (Davies 2008: 3). By the mid-1960s English language proficiency tests were used in both countries. The fact that there were separate strands of development in the UK and in the USA led to considerable differences between tests in terms of content and the practice of test implementation (Davies 2008).

In the UK, the *English Proficiency Test Battery* (EPTB), a joint project of the University of Birmingham and the British Council and based on a predecessor, the *British Council subjective measure*, was the first proficiency test that was used for certification purposes on a large scale. Later developments led to the *English Language Testing Service* (ELTS), which was considered to be a paradigm shift towards a communicative approach to testing, and later on to the *International English Language Testing System* (IELTS). The EPTB was restricted to testing the receptive skills of reading comprehension and listening comprehension and was divided into a linguistic / system section and a work sample section. The ELTS replaced the *English Proficiency Test Battery* – a development that again the British Council was responsible for. With ELTS the idea that a test should be "authentic" or "relevant" came into play, which, as a consequence, led to a growing interest in English for Specific Purposes (ESP) and more generally Language for Specific Purposes (LSP). Proficiency testing was now considered as a means to measure in how far test takers could meet the communicative demands of specific situations, in this case, the demands of attending academic courses of different types and disciplines. These ideas are reflected in the modular part of the ELTS test, consisting of a study skills test, a writing test and an interview and taking into account the contents and skills relevant to particular fields of study. The ELTS test experienced various revisions, which finally resulted in a switch from ELTS to IELTS, which will be described in more detail below. With the change to IELTS, the *International Development Program* (IDP) of Australian Universities and Colleges joined the original ELTS, and "IELTS took on a truly international nature" (Milanovic and Weir 2008: x).

During the same period of time, work on developing other tests for assessing proficiency in the English language was going on at several universities in the UK. Among the well-known certificates that have emerged from this work are the certificates of the *University of Cambridge Local Examination Syndicate* (UCLES), such as the *Cambridge First Certificate in English*, the *Certificate in Advanced English* and the *Certificate of Proficiency in English*[1]. Compared to ELTS and IELTS, these certificates do not aim to document proficiency in Academic English, though, but rather the general language proficiency of students of English.

In the USA, the different versions of the TOEFL (*Test of English as a Foreign Language*) and later on its sister, the TOEIC (*Test of English for International Communication*), both developed and distributed by the *Educational Testing Service* (ETS) in Princeton, New Jersey, have dominated the scene[2]. Robert Lado's *Test of Aural Comprehension*, the *English Language Test for Foreign Students* and the *Michigan Test of English Language Proficiency* can be regarded as predecessors of the TOEFL. Until the 1990s, the TOEFL was definitely the world's most widely used English language test. The fact that the TOEFL was – and still is – a gate-keeping device for gaining access to US universities has certainly contributed to its success. Meanwhile however, other certificates, like IELTS, have come to be accepted in US universities as well. One major problem of the TOEFL was the lack of a speaking component. With the implementation of an internet-based version in 2006, this problem has been overcome to a certain extent[3]. The TOEIC was developed to meet the need for certification outside the university context, in particular in business life, but it is used in connection with immigration as well. It can be taken as a test of listening and reading and / or as a speaking and writing test.

Certification and proficiency testing in English as a foreign or second language can be regarded as pioneering work – but other languages have followed soon, mainly in the European context. The major tests in use for European languages other than English are the following:

- TFI (*Test du Français International*) and DELF / DALF (*Diplôme d'études en langue française* and *Diplôme approfondi de langue française)* for French[4]
- TestDaF (*Test Deutsch als Fremdsprache)*[5], DSH (Deutsche Sprachprüfung für den Hochschulzugang)[6], telc (European Language Certificate)[7], ÖSD (Austrian German Diploma)[8] for German
- CELI *(Certificado della Conoscenza della Lingua Italiana)*[9] for Italian
- DELE *(Diplomas de Español como Lengua Extranjera)*[10] for Spanish.

Meanwhile, the existence of a certificate in a certain language has become a matter of prestige. Since the (perceived) need for certification of proficiency in a specific language can also be seen as an indication of the importance of this language for international communication, the development and implementation of certification instruments has political implications as well. The launching of the Chinese proficiency certificates *Hanyu Shuiping Kaoshi* (HSK) in 1991[11] and CertChinLang (*Certificate of Chinese Language*, Hongkong)[12] is a case in point.

Apart from the increasing number of languages for which certification is available, another factor has contributed to the proliferation of certificates. Many decision-makers in the gate-keeping processes mentioned above seem to have felt the need for tests that were more accurately targeted at the linguistic and communicative demands in specific professional contexts. In other words, there was a demand for certificates that were based on tests with greater prognostic validity for future job performance. This caused further differentiation in the field, giving rise to many specialised certificates, initiated and / or issued mainly by Chambers of Commerce and Ministries of Education. From a theoretical perspective, and in line with considerations that dominated the IELTS debate, this development raises the question of the relationship between a construct like "general language proficiency" and domain-specific language proficiencies. From a practical perspective, the result of these developments is an extremely confusing / unclear situation with a multitude of different certificates targeting different types of addressees, characterised by diversity in terms of underlying concepts of proficiency, test contents, test tasks and testing procedures, and thus jeopardising the original idea of creating transparency and comparability.

As a response to this counterproductive diversity, attempts have been made to restore some kind of comparability and homogeneity. The *International Certificate Conference* (ICT) as well as the *Association of Language Testers in Europe* (ALTE), founded in 1990, tried to establish comprehensive systems of certification and a common definition of levels of proficiency.

The latest, most ambitious and most influential of these attempts was the development of the *Common European Framework of Reference for Languages: Learning, Teaching, Assessment* (CEFR) in 2001, in which ALTE members were involved in various stages. The CEFR defines descriptors for six levels of proficiency which are independent of any particular language and the knowledge of particular language structures and lexical items, but mainly focus on the ability to communicate successfully. A more detailed description will follow in section 3.

Whereas in the early phases of proficiency testing there was a strong emphasis on designing tests, attention to procedures of test administration and analysis has grown in recent times. In order to ensure reliability of the tests, the conditions under which the tests are administered are meticulously defined, testers have to undergo special training, and test takers are offered various possibilities (practice tests) to get acquainted with the testing procedure and in particular with its time constraints.

The growing demand for certification of language proficiency has had political and economic implications as well. Since the overwhelming majority of certificates is required for English as a foreign language, certification has made a substantial contribution to the spread of the English language, and to certain varieties of English in particular. In addition, this situation has enhanced the development of English language teaching as a global business. The fact that, along with the tests themselves, various sorts of materials, preparation books and practice tests, are offered for purchase to test takers and teachers / test administrators, is just the most obvious aspect of this development.

3. Current approaches to certification

In order to give a better insight into different approaches to certification, into the structure of proficiency tests and the dynamics (and sometimes confusion) in their development, this section is devoted to a more detailed discussion of a selection of the most widely used and most intensively discussed approaches to certification. The relatively strong focus on assessing proficiency in the English language in this section is a result of a corresponding strong focus on English in research and publications in the field of assessment and certification. It does not imply any kind of neglect of the relevance of proficiency tests in other languages.

3.1. TOEFL

The Test of English as a Foreign Language (TOEFL), in use since 1964, has developed from a paper-based test (PBT) to a computer-based version (CBT) and, since 2006, is also available as an internet-based test (iBT TOEFL), with relevant changes in content. The TOEFL is characterised on the official TOEFL website as a test that "measures the ability of non-native speakers of English to use and understand English as it is spoken, written and heard in academic settings"[13]. Offered by the ETS, it is now recognised as a certification of proficiency in the English language by more than 6,000 institutions in 110 countries. The ETS claims that this test is a highly reliable measure of English-language proficiency, built to the highest psychometric standards and validated by more than 40 years of world-class, scholarly research.[14]

The paper-based version consists of a "Listening Comprehension" section, a "Reading Comprehension" section, a "Structure and Language" section[15], and a 30-minute writing test (the "Test of Written English"). According to the ETS, the content of the test is authentic, consistent with the language used in everyday, real academic settings.

The total score of the paper-based test ranges on a scale from 310 to 677, with all three sections contributing equally to the total score. The "Test of

Written English" score is reported separately on a scale of 1 to 6 and is not added to the TOEFL score. The TOEFL scores are valid for two years from the test date. The TOEFL scale is purely descriptive. There is no criterion for passing or failing. Whether a certain score is sufficient or acceptable depends on the requirements of the respective institution.

The most relevant difference in the CBT version is – apart from the change in test administration procedures – the computer adaptive test strategy for the "Listening Comprehension" and the "Structure and Language" sections that the CBT TOEFL follows. Apart from that, the CBT differs in terms of test scores, 300 being the top score.[16]

With iBT TOEFL, far more fundamental changes were introduced. It has an additional focus on speaking and can be considered as a response to an increasing emphasis on developing communicative competence in foreign language teaching and, correspondingly, a growing awareness of the necessity to include a section for testing oral communicative ability. It aims at enhancing authenticity – and thereby predictive validity – by trying to simulate real university experience. The iBT TOEFL version can also be regarded as an attempt to keep up with test developments in Europe, in particular with IELTS and the CEFR. The test is divided into four sections: "Listening", "Reading", "Speaking" and "Writing", with integrated tasks for the productive skills, thus combining writing with reading and listening. The task-format is partly multiple choice and partly free production of language on part of the test takers. The new speaking section may serve to illustrate the types of task in more detail. It consists of two independent tasks, which require speaking on familiar topics, and four integrated tasks. The integrated tasks combine skills in reading and in listening to a conversation and a short lecture with the requirement to respond orally.

Again, a new scale of test scores is introduced: the maximum total score is 120, with the scores for each skill ranging from 0–30. Also in line with developments in Europe, score descriptors (also referred to as "competency descriptors") are available to give meaning to the numbers. For example, a score of 28–30 in the speaking section of the test is supposed to indicate that the test taker is very likely to be able to give prepared presentations in English and is likely to orally summarise information he / she has read in English. An elaborate description of iBT TOEFL and score comparison tables, relating the different versions of the TOEFL, is available on the internet.[17]

It is remarkable that in spite of these changes that have been introduced fairly recently, the general make-up of the TOEFL has remained very much the same for decades. Davies regards the "pervasive psychometric influence on all test development in the USA" (Davies 2008: 73) as one of the reasons for this situation, which he sees in sharp contrast with the dynamics of the development of assessment tools in Britain (and in Europe, one might add).

3.2. TOEIC and TFI

The TOEFL's pronounced focus on Academic English requires an alternative for other testing and certification purposes. Partly in accordance and partly in contrast with the TOEFL profile, the Test of English for International Communication (TOEIC) claims to measure the ability of non-native speakers of English to listen, read, speak and write in English in the global workplace.[18] The TOEIC measures proficiency in international business English, but it is also used in other contexts, e.g. by the UK Border and Immigration Agency, which requires the TOEIC Speaking and Writing test for visa purposes. There is also a demand for the TOEIC in academic contexts, albeit not normally for admission purposes, but rather for enhancing students' employment profile.

Launched in 1979, the TOEIC test is meanwhile used by over 9,000 organisations in more than 90 countries. It is available as a paper-based test with two sections, "Listening" and "Reading", covering 200 multiple choice questions. A "Speaking and Writing" test, delivered through the internet, has been added to the TOEIC product line to complement the "Listening" and "Reading" test. The test tasks are based on authentic interactions in the workplace.[19] In addition to a numerical score that ranges from 0 to 495 for each skill, a "Can-do-levels table" is available with descriptions intended to serve as guidelines to understanding the competence reflected in the scores. Six levels of competence are defined: Novice, Elementary, Intermediate, Basic Working Proficiency, Advanced Working Proficiency, and Advanced General Professional Proficiency. The descriptor for "Basic Working Proficiency in Listening" may serve as an example:

> "Can understand
> – explanations of work problems
> – requests for products on phone
> – discussions of current events by mother tongue speakers of English
> – headline news on radio"[20]

On the basis of Tannenbaum and Wiley (2004), ETS also offers a table which relates TOEIC sum scores and sub-scores in listening comprehension and reading comprehension to levels of the Common European Framework of Reference[21].

The TFI (Test de Français International), another ETS product, is a French language proficiency test for both academic and professional purposes. Up to now it is only available as a listening and reading test, and it closely follows the TOEIC "Listening and Reading" test in its format and scoring. Compared to the elaborate website for the TOEIC, there is only scant information about the TFI on the internet, however[22].

3.3. IELTS

IELTS, the International English Language Testing System[23], is available in more than 120 countries and recognised by more than 6,000 organisations. It competes with TOEFL for the position as the world's premier test of proficiency in English.

ELTS, the predecessor of IELTS, introduced a needs-based approach to assessment, proceeding from a definition of the communicative demands faced by foreign students coming to study in the UK (cf. Milanovic and Weir 2008: ix). As such needs were considered to differ according to the subject of study, a modular and subject-specific approach was chosen, with six modules corresponding to six different academic areas. In spite of its high face validity, an evaluation study revealed severe practical and theoretical difficulties with this approach. In particular, it turned out to be extremely problematic to successfully equate modules relating to different academic areas.

As a consequence and with the intention of paying greater attention to construct validity, the number of modules was reduced to three in the first version of the IELTS, launched in 1989. Apart from the General components ("Listening" and "Oral Interaction / Speaking") it contained modular components for "Reading" and "Writing" in three domain-specific variants: for Physical Sciences and Technology, for Life and Medical Sciences, and for Arts and Social Sciences, thus grouping different subjects of study into more general categories.

The development from a subject-specific to a more general construct of academic language proficiency as a basis for assessment continued with the revision of the first IELTS version in 1995.[24] As the separation into three different academic modules still proved to be problematic, IELTS is now offered in just two formats that test takers can choose between: an "Academic Module" and a "General Training Module". Whereas the "Academic Module" is intended for candidates who want to get access to universities and other institutions of higher education, especially in Australia, Great Britain, Ireland, New Zealand and South Africa, the "General Training Module" is intended for immigration purposes or for people who are going to an English-speaking country to work or train at below undergraduate level, such as vocational training courses or work experience. The two modules are identical in the "Listening" and "Speaking" sections, but they have different tests in the "Reading" and "Writing" sections. More precisely, the two types of reading tests differ with regard to the choice of texts and the level of difficulty of the test items. For writing, the "Academic" and "General Training" modules are differentiated in terms of the content and nature of the two writing tasks, the cognitive demands of the tasks and the contextual parameters of the tasks.

IELTS is available as a paper-based test and also as a computer-based test in many countries. Band scores, ranging from 1 to 9, with half-bands, are used for reporting each language skill as well as the total score.[25]

3.4. ALTE

The Association of Language Testers in Europe (ALTE) is an association of providers of foreign language examinations in Europe. It was founded in 1990 by eight European institutions, among them Cambridge University and the German Goethe-Institut. Since then membership has grown, so that in 2008 the ALTE website[26] lists 31 members, representing the testing of 26 European languages. These languages are (in alphabetical order): Basque, Bulgarian, Catalan, Danish, Dutch, English, Estonian, Finnish, French, Galician, German, Greek, Hungarian, Irish, Italian, Latvian, Lithuanian, Luxembourgish, Norwegian, Polish, Portuguese, Russian, Slovenian, Spanish, Swedish, and Welsh.

ALTE's orientation is not predominantly towards academic language. It rather reflects the need for "meaningful comparisons between qualifications gained in different states of the European Union", because "Employers need to know which particular language qualification it is realistic to demand when advertising a post, and employees have an interest in being able to rate their own present level of expertise and future training needs"[27]. The main objectives of ALTE are to establish common levels of proficiency that are comparable across languages, to establish common standards for all stages of the language testing process and to exchange ideas and know-how in joint projects, particularly in the ALTE Framework Project.

The ambitious goal of creating a common framework within which proficiency in various languages could be defined and described in the same format made it necessary to move away from a structure-oriented approach towards a communicative approach to foreign language testing, with descriptors of levels of proficiency being independent of any particular language. This development was in line with the growing emphasis on developing communicative competence in the field of foreign language teaching.

The ALTE framework distinguishes six levels of proficiency, which are characterised by a system of "Can-do" statements. In 2008 such "Can-do" statements exist for 13 languages. The ALTE system comprises about 400 "Can-do" statements, which are subdivided into 40 categories. It provides descriptors for "Overall general ability" and for three domain-specific abilities: for "Social and Tourist typical abilities", for "Work typical abilities" and for "Study typical abilities", thus taking a moderate stance with regard to the distinction between general and domain-specific language proficiency[28]. An example may serve to illustrate the character of "Can-do" descriptors: The "Overall general ability" B2 level in Listening / Speaking reads as "CAN follow or give a talk on a familiar topic or keep up a conversation on a fairly wide range of topics." The same level of proficiency in the "Work typical abilities" section is characterised by "CAN take and pass on most messages that are likely to require attention during a normal working day". For the "Study typical abilities" the B2 level is defined as "CAN give a clear presentation on a familiar topic, and answer predictable or factual questions."

3.5. The CEFR

The innovations initiated by ALTE prepared the ground for the *Common European Framework of Reference*, which – as an instrument of the Council of Europe to achieve greater unity among its members and, specifically, to promote plurilingualism in Europe – was recommended for setting up systems of validation of language competences in a European Union Council Resolution in November 2001. The goals associated with the CEFR are stated by the Council of Europe as follows: "The Common European Framework of Reference (CEFR) provides a basis for the mutual recognition of language qualifications, thus facilitating educational and occupational mobility. It is increasingly used in the reform of national curricula and by international consortia for the comparison of language certificates"[29]. These goals show a close resemblance to the ALTE goals, yet the CEFR has a much broader scope, which becomes obvious when considering the full name of the framework: *Common European Framework of Reference for Languages: Learning, Teaching, Assessment.* The CEFR focus is not reduced to testing and certification. It claims to be relevant for language testing and teaching alike:

> The Common European Framework provides a common basis for the elaboration of language syllabuses, curriculum guidelines, examinations, textbooks, etc. across Europe.
> (…)
> The Common European Framework is intended to overcome the barriers to communication among professionals working in the field of modern languages arising from the different educational systems in Europe. It provides the means for educational administrators, course designers, teachers, teacher trainers, examining bodies, etc., to reflect on their current practice, with a view to situating and co-ordinating their efforts and to ensuring that they meet the real needs of the learners for whom they are responsible.
> By providing a common basis for the explicit description of objectives, content and methods, the Framework will enhance the transparency of courses, syllabuses and qualifications, thus promoting international co-operation in the field of modern languages. The provision of objective criteria for describing language proficiency will facilitate the mutual recognition of qualifications gained in different learning contexts, and accordingly will aid European mobility (Council of Europe 2001: 1).[30]

In its relatively brief history the CEFR has had an enormous impact on foreign language teaching and testing in Europe and beyond. An increasing number of contemporary textbooks that are used in European countries specify the CEFR level they aim at. In addition, the Council of Europe encourages providers of examinations to situate their examinations in relation to the CEFR by offering a manual for relating language examinations to the CEFR (Council of Europe 2009). Even the scores of the American TOEFL and TOEIC have been mapped on the CEFR.

The CEFR does not offer any specific test, but rather a description of reference levels that tests and other forms of assessment in any language can refer to. The "Descriptive Schema" and the "Common Reference Levels" are the key components of the Framework. They provide descriptors of proficiency as "Can-do" statements on a global scale as well as on more specific scales of various levels, differentiating between domains of language use and kinds of communicative language activities.[31]

The CEFR defines six levels of proficiency, grouped into three broader categories: "Basic User" (Levels A1 and A2), "Independent User" (Levels B1 and B2) and "Proficient User" (Levels C1 and C2). In the course of development of the CEFR further differentiations have been made in specifying "plus-levels" (A2+, B1+ and B2+) in the middle section of the scale. With regard to the issue of domain-specific proficiency, the CEFR differentiates between the personal domain, the public domain, the occupational domain, and the educational domain.

The detailedness and complexity of the CEFR can be illustrated by taking oral production activities as an example. In addition to scale-related descriptors for "Overall spoken production", there are specific scales for "Sustained monologue: describing experience", "Sustained monologue: putting a case", "Public announcements" and "Addressing audiences". The CEFR is innovative in other ways as well: The proficiency descriptors also consider strategies employed in communicative activities, like compensating for deficiencies or repairing an imperfect utterance. The CEFR also extends the concept of assessment to include self-assessment and offers corresponding self-assessment grids.

The CEFR is a tremendous project, and in the context of this article we can by no means do justice to its complexities and the effort that has been invested in it by many people. As the "Can-do" descriptors and the proficiency scales are crucial elements of the CEFR, we will return to these issues in our discussion in section 4.

4. Theoretical background and controversial issues

4.1. Language proficiency

A key issue in the context of certification is the underlying concept of language proficiency. There are at least three sets of questions involved: First, how can we define the construct of "language proficiency", and should a distinction be made between "general language proficiency" and various domain-specific proficiencies? Second, how can we break down "proficiency" into smaller components?

Third, how can we describe different grades of proficiency, and how should scales of proficiency be conceptualised? Let us discuss each of these questions in turn.

4.1.1. The construct of language proficiency

The vagueness and fuzziness of the word "proficiency" as it is used in everyday language needs to be replaced by a clear definition for use in academic contexts. This statement is not as trivial as it might seem at first sight. It rather exemplifies a typical dilemma of Applied Linguistics: the need for unambiguousness and precision of terms on the one hand, and the need for comprehensibility and acceptance of these terms by the users of practical results of theorising and research on the other, in this case test takers and test administrators as well as those people who want to or have to base decisions about other people on the certificates they submit.

For scientific purposes, "proficiency" needs to be defined in distinction to similar concepts like "knowledge", "skill", "competence" and "ability" in particular, and of course, the relationship between "general cognitive proficiency" and "language proficiency" has to be specified. A review of the relevant literature shows a lot of inconsistency and confusion, which is no surprise in view of the fact that definitions of terms depend on underlying theories, in this case of theories of language and language acquisition. Definitions of "language proficiency" range from "what is meant when we say someone is proficient in a language is that that person can do certain things in that language" (Ingram 1985: 220) and "Language proficiency is what language tests measure" (Vollmer 1981: 152) to more detailed ones, which specify criteria for being proficient. One of the earliest attempts at specifying such criteria is that made by Spolsky (1989), who preferred to replace the term "proficiency" with "knowing a language":

> Proficiency: Knowing a language:
> Prefer to say that someone knows a second language if one or more criteria (to be specified) are met. These criteria are specifiable:
> a. as underlying knowledge or skills
> b. analysed or unanalysed
> c. implicit or explicit
> d. of individual structural items (sounds, lexical items, grammatical structures)
> e. which integrate into larger units
> f. such as functional skills
> g. for specific purposes
> h. or as overall proficiency
> i. productive or receptive
> j. with a specified degree of accuracy
> k. with a specified degree of fluency
> l. and with an approximation to native speaker usage
> m. of one or more specified varieties of language. (Spolsky 1989: 80)

Many definitions of proficiency share the idea that proficiency is something more than or something different from "competence" in the Chomskyan sense, i.e. something more than being in a mental state of knowing a language. Rather, the idea of *putting language to use* seems to be crucial to the concept of "proficiency". Conceptualisations of proficiency differ, however, with regard to the question in how far putting language to use requires further types of competence (or "competencies") in addition to grammatical competence and in how far it is mainly a matter of performance and behavioural realisation of underlying knowledge. In analysing Taylor's (1988) definitions of proficiency as "the ability to make use of competence" and performance as "what is done when proficiency is put to use" (Taylor1988: 166, quoted from North 2000: 47), North concludes that proficiency is here seen as something between competence and performance, other definitions varying with regard to closeness rather to the competence side or to the performance side.

One of the most influential attempts to specify the competence underlying language proficiency is the model of communicative competence developed by Canale and Swain (Canale and Swain 1980 and Canale 1983). They distinguish grammatical, discourse, sociolinguistic and strategic competence as sub-components of communicative competence. This model is still reflected in the design of many proficiency tests and in the CEFR as well.

Unfortunately, some scholars and institutions use the terms "competence" and "proficiency" without explaining how they relate to each other – which causes further confusion. Even the CEFR follows this practice. Although the Framework is supposed to define "levels of proficiency", and although "proficiency scales" have been developed, the discussion of the approach adopted in the CEFR (Council of Europe 2001: 9ff.) refers to "competences" and to "communicative language competences" in particular, without explaining the relation to the concept of "proficiency", which is one of the key terms of the CEFR, but remains undefined.

4.1.2. *General language proficiency and academic proficiency*

The notion of "language use" included in definitions of "proficiency" triggers a set of further theoretical and practical problems. As "use" manifests itself in real life situations, a fundamental decision that has to be made in designing proficiency tests is whether to measure "general proficiency" in using a language or rather proficiency in using the language for specific purposes, in a restricted, specified set of contexts – or both. As we have seen, different tests reflect different answers to this question, and such answers may be revised in the course of time[32]. Many tests show some kind of combination between general proficiency and domain-specific proficiency (e.g. academic proficiency or – even more specific – subject-related proficiency), trying to meet the demands for authenticity and relevance of the test tasks that the paradigm of communicative language testing had introduced. But what distinguishes "general" and "specific" proficiency? Vocabulary is certainly an important dimension, but why should the ability to use domain-specific vocabulary be part of an examination that takes place before the test takers have had access to this domain? What degree and amount of subject knowledge – in conjunction with subject-specific terminology – on the part of the test takers can be assumed?

Another approach to adapting assessment tools to the future communicative needs of the test takers in the context of certain domains is that of identifying typical situations and communicative tasks in those domains. For the construct of academic proficiency, such situations and tasks could be "listening to lectures", "writing summaries" etc. However, there are problems and pitfalls as well: which situations and communicative activities can be regarded as "typical" – or even "prototypical" – of the sub-type of proficiency that is to be measured? Moreover, teaching practices at universities, conceptions of the roles of teachers and learners, and, as a consequence, communicative practices in higher education vary with cultural context, and they change over time as well. Thus, with the exception of some "core activities" that are probably universally relevant for academic studies, like listening to lectures, it is difficult to decide upon activities which are "typical" in academic contexts, without creating a cultural bias – an issue that has hardly been taken into account up to now.

The development of ELTS / IELTS nicely illustrates changes in attitudes towards specific language proficiencies and their assessment as well as corresponding differences in the underlying constructs of academic proficiency. In tracing the history of IELTS, Davies characterises EPTB, the predecessor of ELTS, as an instrument that took a structuralist approach, focusing on linguistic features and learners' problems, and sampling the linguistic features of lectures, textbooks and articles. ELTS made a radical change towards a communicative approach, focusing on specific purposes and "offering texts, both spoken and written, from a range of so-called authentic academic discourses" (Davies 2008: 112), thus taking up the developments in the field of LSP with the shift of its main focus from terminology to discourse (see Gnutzmann, ch. 19 this volume). IELTS, then, moved away from *language uses* to *features of language use*, changing its focus from situations of subject-specific language use in academic contexts towards a more general and more abstract view of what constitutes academic discourse:

> [IELTS] is dedicated to presenting general features of academic language use in its texts from lectures and journals (for Listening and Reading) and in the cogent and coherent discourse which candidates are required to produce (for Speaking and Writing). That then is what characterises academic proficiency: it is the language of coherent argument, where implications are understood and inferences made. … Academic proficiency then is the ability to perform the appropriate discourse. And what is appropriate can indeed be generalised across subject disciplines (…): argument, logic, implication, analysis, explanation, reporting". (Davies 2008: 113).

One might question, though, whether proficiency as it is conceptualised in this statement is still a matter of language use or rather a blend of general cognitive abilities and linguistic competence.

4.1.3. *Skills*

Language can be used for production or for reception, in spoken or in written mode. The common distinction of four "skills" – listening comprehension, speaking, reading comprehension and writing – mirrors these basic forms of language use. The majority of language tests are organised according to skills. They either have separate sections for each of the skills the test is supposed to cover or – a more recent development – they combine two or more of these skills in integrative test tasks. In particular, the growing awareness of the co-occurrence and interrelatedness of speaking and listening in real life situations, together with increasing research activities in the fields of discourse analysis and conversation analysis, has led test designers to prefer a combined "Oral Interaction" section to individual "Speaking" and "Listening" sections (IELTS) or to differentiate between "Spoken Interaction" and "Spoken Production" as in the CEFR. The iBT TOEFL goes even one step further by combining oral and written skills in complex test tasks.[33]

Though widely accepted in practice, the constructs of the four skills are poorly defined. Much like "proficiency", the concept of "skill" itself is a fuzzy one. It can be defined as a psycholinguistic concept, referring to the "ability to process phonetic, lexical and grammatical information receptively and productively, accurately and online" (Hulstijn 2007: 665), or as a more comprehensive construct including knowledge about stylistic differences in spoken and written mode, strategies of inferring the meaning of unknown words etc. The skill of "Speaking" may serve to illustrate the various ways and the various degrees of complexity in which language skills are conceptualised and operationalised for assessment purposes. At one end of a scale of complexity we can find a concept of "Speaking" that is reduced to phonetic / phonological knowledge, as in Lado's (1961) claim to test pronunciation using paper and pencil techniques, a procedure that does not even require real oral expression, but rather the demonstration of knowledge about phonological similarities between words (that is, "online processing" is not even required for assessing this "skill"). At the other end of the scale we can find the detailed and complex set of descriptors for "Speaking" in the CEFR, including command of idiomatic expressions and colloquialisms, awareness of connotations, fluency, turn-taking, use of cohesive devices in discourse, using communication strategies, developing an argument, among others (Council of Europe 2001: 35f.).

Moreover it is by no means clear what any two "skills" have as a common core and what distinguishes them. Is it the same "ability to make use of competence" that these skills require, and are there theoretical grounds on which a practice of testing these skills separately can be justified? Do we have reasons to assume any kinds of implicational relations between skills, for example assuming that the ability to make receptive use of a language precedes the ability to use this language productively? Do oral and written modes of using the language require different kinds of knowledge? How do the structure-based categories of "Grammar" and "Vocabulary" relate to the skills categories? Additional problems result from the fact that each of the skills is affected by the conditions under which it is performed and by the constraints of the testing situation in specific ways. The scope of this article allows just for discussion of a few of these problems in more detail.

Obviously, skills can only be assessed by using verbal material that is characterised by a selection of grammatical structures and vocabulary. Therefore, any assessment of a "skill" is at the same time an assessment of lexical and grammatical knowledge. The selection of tasks and of verbal material that is used in these tasks as well as the performance standards that are set for these tasks allow for consideration of grammatical and lexical knowledge to various degrees. In practice, there seems to be a lot of uncertainty as to handling the relationship between skills and structure. On the German website of the TOEIC, for example, it is claimed for the original version of the TOEIC that it assesses listening, reading, and grammatical competence.[34] With the addition of the new "Speaking" and "Writing" components, however, grammatical competence is not mentioned any longer. The situation for the TOEFL seems to be even more undecided: The first PBT TOEFL was made up of five parts: "Listening Comprehension", "English Structure", "Vocabulary", "Reading Comprehension", and "Writing Ability". Descriptions of the contemporary version of the PBT vary between listing the categories "Listening Comprehension", "Structure and Written Expression", "Reading Comprehension" on the one hand, and "Listening", "Structure / Grammar", "Reading" and "Writing" on the other. In the CEFR, linguistic competences are part of communicative competences and, beside sociolinguistic and pragmatic competences, are included in the assessment of each skill[35]. This diversity of approaches indicates that it is by no means easy to decide which part of a predominantly skills-oriented assessment tool is suitable for measuring grammatical competence. On the whole, there seems to be a tendency to give up structure-related categories in the make-up and description of assessment tools and rather to integrate measurement of structural competence into the skills framework.

This leaves us with the question how an adequate representation of structural knowledge can be taken care of. The place where this can be done is in the selection of tasks and materials on which these tasks are based and in rating procedures.

In the context of a communicative skills approach to assessment the conditions under which test takers perform gain more importance than in structure-based tests. To mention just a few examples: Performing in the oral mode normally means less processing time and less chances for monitoring one's speech than performing in the written mode. Performance in listening comprehension may vary, e.g. with conditions of noise and with the accent of the speaker. Performance on oral interaction tasks in face-to-face situations may be dependent on the cooperativeness of the interlocutor and his / her adaption to the test taker's level of knowledge and skill.

In general, the assessment of productive skills poses more problems than the assessment of receptive skills, because it is more difficult to control responses in productive tasks. Closed test tasks, in particular multiple choice tasks, are hardly suitable for yielding valid results in assessing productive skills, and open tasks require skilled examiners and detailed guidelines for scoring. Reliability problems are much more severe with productive tasks, in spite of examiner training. The assessment of speaking skills requires, as an additional complication, individual administration or suitable electronic devices for recording spoken language. These practical reasons are responsible for dispensing with a "Speaking" section in some tests.

4.2. Grades of proficiency and proficiency scales

A basic assumption behind approaches to certification and attempts at measuring proficiency is the idea that there are degrees of language proficiency that can be arranged on a scale. In other words: some people are more proficient than others, and every individual can improve his / her proficiency and "move up the scale". The idea of scales, mostly conceived of as linear, is reproduced in the different sub-scales of proficiency.

Proficiency scales vary according to their functions and their addressees.[36] As such, they can be more or less constructor-oriented, assessor-oriented, or user-oriented (Alderson 1991 and CEFR 2001: 37–39). User-orientation has gained importance in recent times. Whereas the numerical scales used for many certificates have deficits in terms of user-orientation, since the numerical scores as such do not give any information about a test taker's proficiency profile, "Can-do" descriptors are regarded as much more transparent and suitable for assisting communication between stakeholders in the testing process and, above all, the interpretation of test results by non-specialists. Proficiency scales also differ with regard to whether they follow a top down approach, specifying degrees of approximation to a predefined standard, or rather a bottom up approach, which does not focus on the test takers' deficits, but rather on what they are able to do and thus on their growing proficiency.

The emerging consensus on distinguishing six levels of proficiency and certification makes it easier for users to build up concepts of what a particular level entails. Two things have to be noted, however: First, the six levels model is without any theoretical or empirical support. It seems to be a compromise – grown from practical experience – between the need for sufficient and meaningful differentiation among levels on the one hand and assumptions about the degree of complexity that can be handled by the users of test results on the other. Second, the six levels do not represent equidistant steps in the development of proficiency, as the authors of the CEFR have to admit (CEFR: 18), and it is by no means clear how the size of the steps can be measured. This in an unresolved issue that turns out to be particularly problematic when trying to map other scales on the CEFR (see below, section 5.1.).

The conception of proficiency scales raises some more fundamental questions. What does it mean to have improved in certain areas, i.e. to be better than before? Improvement can be interpreted in terms of *quantity*, meaning that someone knows or can do *more* things in a language than before. Improvement can also be interpreted in terms of *quality*, meaning that someone knows or can do things *better* than before. For the field of grammar, "improvement" may mean (for the productive skills) being able to produce a larger variety of syntactic structures than before, but it may also mean being able to produce the same limited set of syntactic structures more correctly than before, i.e. in accordance with native-speaker norms. The difference between "more" and "better" is also an important issue with regard to word knowledge: improvement may mean having gained in *breadth* of word knowledge (i.e. "knowing" more words) or having gained in *depth* of word knowledge (i.e. having more detailed knowledge about a word, e.g. regarding register restrictions, collocations, grammatical behaviour). These two kinds of improvement cannot be easily combined on a linear scale – and maybe they even should not. In his critical discussion of the CEFR, Hulstijn (2007), though appreciating the CEFR enterprise and its goals in principle, points to the problems resulting from scales of the mixed "What & How well" type: language learners may develop in the "what" and "how well" dimensions at different rates – a situation which a descriptor that combines both dimensions cannot represent.

Let us take the CEFR to exemplify another shortcoming of the "Can-do" scales: their implicational character and underlying implicit (and sometimes explicit) assumptions about sequential stages in the acquisition of the skills and competences the descriptors refer to. The following extract from the CEFR illustrates this problem:

> Each level should be taken to subsume the levels below it on the scale. That is to say, someone at B1 (*Threshold*) is considered also to be able to do whatever is stated at A2 (*Waystage*), to be better at what is stated at A2 (*Waystage*). That means that provisos attached to a performance placed at A2 (*Waystage*)for example *'provided speech is clearly and slowly articulated'* will have less force, or be non-applicable to a performance at B1 (*Threshold*)
> Not every element or aspect in a descriptor is repeated at the following level. That is to say that entries at each level describe selectively what is seen as salient or new at

> that level. They do not systematically repeat all the elements mentioned at the level below with a minor change of formulation to indicate increased difficulty. (Council of Europe 2001: 36f.)

Apart from the fact that the relations between different levels and their descriptors do not seem to follow a consistent pattern, assumptions about implications lack theoretical as well as empirical foundation. For example, there is no reason to assume that in the category of "Overall oral production" a learner necessarily has to pass through a stage in which he / she can produce phrases about people and places (level A1) before being able to describe daily routines and likes / dislikes (level A2; Council of Europe 2001: 58).[37]. Further drawbacks of "Can-do" scales result from their language-independent and context-free character and, as a result, from the need to describe language use without making reference to form, i.e. to particular syntactic structures and particular sets of lexical items. Most of the descriptors operate with vague terms, like "well-structured", "clear", "detailed", "simple", "short", "relevant", "limited" and the like, which are open to a wide range of interpretations. Alderson (2007: 661) detects "overlaps, ambiguities and inconsistencies in the use of terminology as well as important gaps in the CEFR scales".

Therefore, the criticism that has been brought forward against scales of language proficiency in the CEFR mainly refers to the limitations resulting from the language-independent framing of the CEFR, the merely intuitive character of the scales and descriptors and its unsatisfactory theoretical and empirical foundation (see for example Alderson 2007, Barkowski 2003, Hulstijn 2007, North 2000, and Quetz 2001 and 2003 in their critical comments on the CEFR).

4.3. The native speaker as a point of reference

Certification presupposes some kind of standard against which language learners' proficiency can be defined. A "natural" answer to this demand seems to be an orientation towards native speaker norms. This seemingly straightforward decision is not without problems, though. Firstly, native speakers of a language are far from being homogeneous with regard to their language proficiency. Rather, native speakers differ enormously as to the scope of their vocabulary, particularly so in domain-specific vocabulary, and even in grammatical terms there is some amount of variation. Carroll pointed out this problem as early as 1979 (Carroll 1979: 22–23). The situation is still more problematic when it comes to communicative competence. Quite a proportion of native speakers will not meet the highest level defined in a proficiency test, and even the more restricted notion of "educated native speaker" is only a vague specification (cf. the discussion in North 2000: 55.)

Secondly, the notion of "native speaker" itself is problematic as well. "Native speaker" has to be defined with respect to a certain variety of a language. A most obvious case is the difference between Standard British English and Standard American English. These two standard varieties of English are not the only alternatives for specifying "native-speakerness" of English, though. But in English proficiency testing there is little awareness of these issues. Take the TOEFL test as an example. It claims to measure "the ability of non-native speakers of English to use and understand English as it is spoken, written and heard in academic settings. It is an internationally accepted measure of Academic English proficiency".[38] This characterisation seems to take it for granted that everybody knows what is meant by "English". It disregards the fact that there are many different Englishes used in universities around the world, with only some of these Englishes having to be considered as native varieties. Pennycook, in his critical discussion of the predominant orientation towards an idealised native speaker, draws attention to the fact that "Maintaining the native speaker as the preferred model ... has clear implications for the maintenance of language standards derived from the central English-dominant nations" (Pennycook 1994: 176). In quoting Rampton, who states that "the supremacy of the native speaker keeps the UK and the US at the centre of ELT (Rampton 1990: 98)" (Pennycook 1994: 176), he adds further emphasis to the political and economic dimensions of decisions about "native-speakerness".

Apart from different standard varieties of a language, regional and social variation has to be taken into account. In deciding about how to handle language variation, the prognostic quality of the proficiency test should be the focus of interest: What kinds of inferences should be made for the test taker's ability to cope with what kinds of communicative situations? Will he / she have to communicate with people speaking different dialects of a language? In this case, at least some proficiency in aural comprehension of several varieties of a language will be necessary. This kind of criticism produced a half-hearted reaction on part of ETS in the redesigned 2007 version of the TOEIC, which integrates the use of different English accents, as spoken in the U.S., Great Britain, Canada and Australia. Incidentally, it should be noted that the notion of comprehensibility, which is a key concept in "Can-do" statements, turns out to be an extremely fuzzy and difficult one against this background.

Growing international mobility and – as a result – increasing multilingualism aggravates the problems of standards and comprehensibility. Paradoxically, one of the main the reasons for certification – giving access to another speech community – changes this speech community and increases its internal linguistic variability. Let us take the university context as an example. It would be naïve to assume that certification opens the door for just one student to get access to a predominantly monolingual university context. Since many students (and lecturers as well) do the same thing, communicative requirements change: students will have to communicate successfully in a lingua franca situation with different people speaking different learner varieties of a language. One might argue that, as a consequence, the ability to aurally comprehend various learner varieties should be included in a proficiency test for university entrance.

Thirdly, apart from the issue of variability, there is the question whether all language learners really aim at native speaker proficiency – whatever type of native-speakerness may be intended. For some reason or other, they may not even want to attain a native speaker profile, or they may regard such an aim as unrealistic for themselves. This situation makes it doubtful whether a "top-down" definition of proficiency scales, i.e. describing a language learner's proficiency as to certain degrees deficient compared with that of a native speaker, is the best way to proceed. The formulation of "Can-do" statements", rather a "bottom-up" process, as initiated by ALTE and elaborated in the CEFR, might be an alternative. Describing what a learner can do in a foreign language does not necessarily need a native speaker norm (cf. the discussion in North 2002). Quite in line with the concept of plurilingualism in Europe which is promoted by the Council of Europe, the authors of the CEFR explicitly disassociate themselves from native speaker norms as targets in formulating "Can-do" statements – instead of "Cannot-yet-do" statements. One has to be careful, though: even if the "Can-do" statements in the CEFR do not refer to native speaker norms in terms of grammatical and lexical accuracy, there may be a native-speaker orientation in the "Can-do" statements in other dimensions. Take as an example the following specification of "Text design" as part of Discourse competence in the CEFR:

> Text design: knowledge of the design conventions in the community concerning, e.g.:
> how information is structured in realising the various macrofunctions (descriptions, narrative, exposition, etc.);
> how stories, anecdotes, jokes, etc. are told;
> how a case is built up (in law, debate, etc.);
> how written texts (essays, formal letters, etc.) are laid out, signposted and sequenced." (Council of Europe 2001: 123)

In view of the enormous variation in culture-specific conventions of structuring texts, there is definitely a cultural / native speaker bias involved here. Krumm, discussing the use of the CEFR in the context of migration, e.g. for gaining citizenship, draws attention to the fact that the heterogeneous groups of migrants are totally different from the learners originally targeted by the CEFR and that most of the descriptors are far removed from their social and cultural contexts" (Krumm 2007: 668).

5. Certification in practice

Putting certification into practice leads to yet another set of unresolved issues, some of which will be discussed in this section.

5.1. Problems of equivalence

Given the diversity of approaches to certification, as outlined above, different people acquire different sorts of certificates, and different institutions require different sorts of certificates. As for various reasons this situation is not likely to change in the near future, there is a need for deciding about equivalences between certificates and between test scores in particular. The ETS invests an enormous amount of money in statistical procedures for establishing score equivalences (cf. Soltau 2008a and 2008b). See the following table as an example of comparisons between different test scores and level systems, published on the internet by the Vancouver English Centre (VEC)[39]:

TOEIC	**TOEFL Paper**	**TOEFL CBT**	**TOEFL IBT**	**IELTS**	**VEC Online Score**	**Approximate VEC Level**
0 – 250	0 – 310	0 – 30	0 – 8	0 – 1	0 – 34	2
	310 – 343	33 – 60	9 – 18	1 – 1.5	35 – 38	3
255 – 400	347 – 393	63 – 90	19 – 29	2 – 2.5	39 – 45	4 – 5
	397 – 433	93 – 120	30 – 40	3 – 3.5	46 – 53	6 – 7
405 – 600	437 – 473	123 – 150	41 – 52	4	54 – 57	8
	477 – 510	153 – 180	53 – 64	4.5 – 5	58 – 65	9 – 10
605 – 780	513 – 547	183 – 210	65 – 78	5.5 – 6	66 – 73	11 – 12
	550 – 587	213 – 240	79 – 95	6.5 – 7	74 – 81	13 – 14
785 – 990	590 – 677	243 – 300	96 – 120	7.5 – 9	82 – 100	15
Top Score	**Top Score**	**Top Score**	**Top Score**	**Top Score**	**Top Score**	**Top Level**
990	**677**	**300**	**120**	**9**	**100**	**15**

ETS provides "English Language Competency Descriptors" for the iBT TOEFL Test[40], descriptors for the "Writing Task"[41] and a table for mapping the iBT on the CEFR[42] to facilitate comparison. The Council of Europe, on the other hand, offers a manual for relating language examinations to the CEFR (Council of Europe 2009).

Although necessary and convenient for practical reasons, the procedure of comparing results from different kinds of test and of mapping a test to a common framework of reference is not without problems. Different approaches to testing and different underlying constructs of proficiency make it difficult to claim that having achieved a certain test score in test A implies the same kind and the same degree of proficiency as a certain test score in test B or even that it corresponds to a "Can-do" descriptor" of the CEFR. Thus, comparisons between test results can lead to no more than rough equivalences for formal gate-keeping purposes, establishing equivalences between test scores (or levels) of persons who are placed in approximately the same position on a scale relatively to other individuals having taken the same test. In particular, if a test result is matched with a level of the CEFR, this does not necessarily imply that the test taker "can do" what is indicated by the descriptors for that CEFR level.

Researchers of both IELTS and ETS are aware of the problems involved, as can be seen from the following quotations:

> As several writers in the field have pointed out, the mapping of any test to a framework such as the Common European Framework of Reference (CEFR) or the Canadian Language Benchmarks (CLB) is a complex and long-term endeavour involving the collection of evidence from a variety of sources, including logical argument and content analysis, as well as empirical validation and benchmarking studies. Work to align IELTS band scores (overall and modular) with the CEFR levels began some years ago and continues as part of a long-term research agenda for IELTS. Some of this work on alignment has already been reported and discussed".[43]

Another IELTS statement that can be found in the FAQ section of the IELTS website as an answer to the question "Is it possible to have both IELTS scores on the same scale as CEFR?" has the same sceptical tone:

> The answer to this question depends very much on what we mean by 'having both IELTS scores on the same scale of the CEFR'. We would need to take into account not just the fact that IELTS has both Academic and General Training variants but also that IELTS scores are reported as overall band scores and as individual skill-based modular scores (i.e. for Listening, Reading, Writing and Speaking). For these reasons we need to know what we mean by placing any of these scores on the CEFR scale, taking into account that the CEFR itself also operates a number of differentiated though supposedly related scales.[44]

In their TOEFL iBT Research Report *Linking English-Language Test Scores Onto the Common European Framework of Reference: An Application of Standard-Setting Methodology* Tannenbaum / Wylie express their reservations about such an endeavour:

> (…) it is important to point out that linking test scores to the CEFR is no mean feat, and doing so poses challenges from more than a methodological perspective. The concerns of Weir (2005) regarding the current state of the CEFR led him to report that 'it is not surprising that a number of studies have experienced difficulty attempting to use the CEFR for test development or comparability purposes' (p.283). But surely the imperfect nature of the CEFR is not the sole cause; any test is also an

> imperfect representation of its intended construct. Asking panelists to create an interpretative bridge between the CEFR and a test, particularly a test not designed a priori to measure the CEFR, should not be taken for granted, and should appropriately be considered and treated as a research-based question. (Tannenbaum and Wiley 2008: 4f.)

To make things even more unsatisfactory in practice, there seem to be enormous deficits in the correct application of the existing equivalence scores. In her detailed survey of how universities handle criteria for admission of international students, Soltau (2008a and 2008b) found that some institutions handle the issue of score equivalence very carelessly. Whereas some universities regard a TOEFL Score of 550 (paper version) as equivalent to an IELTS Band Score of 5.5, others require an IELTS result of 7.0 for the same TOEFL Score. In addition, some universities give only incomplete information about the required scores for admission, for example by just mentioning the test type, but not the score required for admission. Soltau also draws attention to the fact that – for whatever reason – some university programmes accept questionable tests as a basis for admission, thus counteracting the original purpose of making predictions about the linguistic prerequisites for successful completion of a course of studies.

5.2. Test implementation

As already mentioned in section 2, attention to means of test administration has grown in recent times. For most of the tests currently in use in international contexts, "Score User Guides" are available that give detailed information about test administration and use of test scores. The Score User Guide for the Computer-Based TOEFL, for example, is a 43 page brochure informing the users about test design, test scores, administration procedures, security, staff and faculty training and release of test results. It also gives guidelines for essay ratings and for using the test scores, along with concordance tables[45]. With increasing awareness of the need for supplementing multiple choice tasks with open tasks, i.e. for tests tasks that require language production on the part of the test takers instead of choosing from a given set of responses, scorer training gains importance to ensure inter-scorer reliability. For the writing section of the computer-based TOEFL, for example, prospective TOEFL readers are trained to interpret TOEFL standards, to score across multiple topics and to use specific software for scoring. Successful completion of an online test makes them certified readers, and they are allowed to score essays from the writing section, monitored by a scoring leader.

Still another factor affecting test implementation should be considered. An institution's facilities may influence the choice of instruments for certification in substantial ways. Lack of space, of electronic facilities, staff or financial resources may prevent an institution from implementing a test format that allows for oral production, and may lead to choosing a less adequate test instead, possibly with less predictive validity.

5.3. Economic issues

The natural desire of test takers to pass the test for certification with good results, the desire of institutions to admit applicants with good test results, and – last but not least – the interests of test providers in revenue has led to numerous additional services that are subject to charge: materials for test preparation, practice exams, entire language courses to prepare for successful certification. All these services have contributed to making certification and language testing a big business – a situation that may affect the quality of certification negatively. This article has pointed out a range of problems and gaps in the theoretical foundations of certification. The relevance of certification for individuals' lives and careers – particularly its function in gate-keeping processes – on the one hand, and the economic interests of the testing business in a competitive context on the other, make it necessary to build up confidence in the certification process and its quality. This situation poses obstacles to discussing the shortcomings of tests and certification procedures in forthright terms. The descriptions of tests and certificates on the internet and in brochures are written in the style of advertisements, playing down the drawbacks, and with growing acceptance of the CEFR test providers have hastened to show that their tests are compatible with this framework, sometimes at the cost of stretching the facts.

6. Research perspectives

As certification and, as a consequence, proficiency testing will remain an important issue for Applied Linguistics in the future, research in this area is necessary and will hopefully pay off in practice. This section summarises some of the key issues in certification that need further research.

6.1. Research into theoretical foundations

It should have become obvious in the course of this article that some of the key concepts underlying the certification of language proficiency are in need of being placed in a theoretical context and require a more precise definition. This pertains to the concept of language proficiency itself, including its relation to cognition, but also to sub-components of language proficiency and the theoretical concepts that seem appropriate for modelling them. In particular, the concept of "skill" requires a clearer outline, and the relationship between general proficiency and domain-specific proficiencies should be specified more clearly.

Following Hulstijn's (2007) ideas, a theory of proficiency that is to be used for the assessment of L2 proficiency should be based on a solid analysis of L1 proficiency and be subject to empirical validation. Taking into account our critical discussion of the native speaker as a point of reference for proficiency testing and certification in section 4.3., Hulstijn's suggestion might be supplemented by arguing for a solid analysis of what kind of proficiency is needed for successful L2 performance in lingua franca encounters.

6.2. Linking language assessment research to research on second language acquisition

Research on language proficiency assessment and on certification would certainly benefit from closer links to research in SLA. Although practices of assessing language proficiency have to a certain degree followed trends in foreign language teaching, they have not taken much advantage of research on second language acquisition so far. On the contrary: the development of frameworks such as the CEFR, beneficial as it definitely is, has rather contributed to a dissociation of assessment from SLA research. The CEFR is not based on empirical evidence taken from L2-learner data and on insights into developmental routes in language acquisition. Thus Alderson (2007: 661) calls for fundamental research into how proficiency in the main European languages develops over time.

Furthermore, proficiency tests do not take into account the dynamic character of second language acquisition / foreign language learning – neither in terms of progress nor in terms of language attrition processes. As a certain amount of predictive power is expected from proficiency tests, this is problematic indeed. The results of a proficiency test do not tell anything about the test taker's speed of language acquisition nor about potential fossilisation of his / her interlanguage – factors that will definitely influence the prospects for his / her future foreign language development.

A neglect of characteristics of learner language is also reflected in scoring procedures for closed test items. Closed test items are usually evaluated as either correct or incorrect, although – from the perspective of SLA – some "incorrect" responses are certainly better than others. This is not reflected in the scores, though. Other characteristics of learner language and of language learners' behaviour are disregarded as well: uncertainty about correctness – and avoidance of certain syntactic structures and lexical elements as a potential consequence – has been shown to be a characteristic of learner language. Again, a simple correct-incorrect dichotomy fails to capture this dimension of learner language. Trying to incorporate results of SLA research into research on proficiency testing would be a worthwhile, though challenging undertaking.

6.3. Finding alternatives to current native speaker standards

Further research is needed for adapting the design of tools for assessment and certification to the changing practices of language use in international communication. With an increasing number of nations recognising their right to speak their own variety of a language, in particular of the English language, a situation which Davies (2008: 110) characterises as the "anglo inner circle hegemony" should be replaced by a more tolerant approach, involving more English speaking countries in the development of assessment tools and integrating a broader range of varieties of English. At the same time the increasing use of English (and other languages) as a lingua franca (or linguae francae) should be reflected in assessment tools. Last but not least, an effort should be made to reduce the cultural bias in assessment tasks, acknowledging different standards of communication in different cultures.

6.4. Evaluation of practices in certification

This article has, among other things, pointed out some deficits in putting certification into practice, for example inconsistencies in establishing equivalence scores. The divide between intentions and practice might be made even more dramatic by the use of frameworks like the CEFR. Intended to be user-friendly, the scales and descriptors might nevertheless turn out to be applied inconsistently, due to ambiguity of the descriptors, to the complexity of the framework or to insufficient training of the users. This, too, is an important field for empirical research.

Although Davies (2008: 2) seems to welcome the development of the field of foreign language testing as a discipline that has confidence in itself, and has gained independence from fashions in linguistics, applied linguistics and language teaching studies, this development has to be regarded with some reservation. On the organisational level, this development is certainly to be appreciated in view of the growing importance of foreign language testing. It would be dangerous, though, to support processes of disconnecting the field of foreign language testing from theoretical underpinnings in linguistics and applied linguistics (including theories of L2 learning and teaching) or to leave it to the discretion of psychologists. On the contrary, the field of foreign language testing needs deeper insights into the nature of (foreign) language proficiency and into the mental processes that are involved in dealing with different sorts of language-related test tasks. In addition, the enormous backwash effect that testing has on teaching asks for close cooperation between the testing and the teaching sectors.

Notes

1 www.cambridgeesol.org
2 www.ets.org
3 For more details see section 3.1. below.
4 www.de.tfi-europe.com
5 www.testdaf.de
6 www.daad.de/deutschland/deutsch-lernen/wie-deutsch-lernen/00573.de.html
7 www.telc.net
8 www.osd.at
9 www.cvcl.it
10 cvc.cervantes.es/aula/dele/default.htm
11 The test began to be designed 1984 by the Beijing Language Institute and was launched abroad in 1991; see www.hsk.org.cn/english/Center_intro.aspx.
12 www.hku.hk/student/all/uregcourse/html1997/cerclang.htm
13 www.uk.toefl.eu/?iso=GB
14 www.ets.org
15 Note that the terminology on the TOEFL website is inconsistent here: The same section is sometimes called "Structure and Language" and sometimes "Structure/Written expression". For comments on inconsistency in this area see section 4.1.3.
16 The CBT TOEFL is no longer in use.
17 www.ets.org/Media/Tests/TOEFL/pdf/TOEFL_iBT_Score_Comparison_Tables.pdf
18 www.ets.org
19 It should be added that another test also belongs to the TOEIC family: the TOEIC Bridge Test for learners of English at beginner and intermediate levels. It focuses only receptive skills.
20 www.uk.toeic.eu/fileadmin/free_resources/UK%20website/UK_Current/TOEIC_Can-do_table.pdf)
21 www.uk.toeic.eu/toeic-sites/toeic-default/table-toeic-cecr/ . For a critical discussion of problems involved in establishing equivalences see below, section 5.1.
22 www.de.etsglobal.org/germany/tests/tfi-test/
23 http://www.cambridgeesol.org/exams/academic-english/ielts.html
24 For a detailed account of this development see Davies 2008.
25 www.cambridgeesol.org/assets/pdf/ielts-research-faqs.pdf
26 www.alte.org
27 www.alte.org/about_alte/index.php
28 See the description of the ELTS – IELTS development in section 3.3. and the discussion of the construct of language proficiency in 4.1.
29 www.coe.int/T/DG4/Linguistic/CADRE_EN.asp
30 www.coe.int/t/dg4/linguistic/Source/Framework_EN.pdf
31 The format of "Can-do" statements as descriptors has been adopted for the TOEIC as well.
32 As a consequence of the ELTS Validation Project, for example, the decision was made to move the 'Speaking' module from the specific to the general component of the test. 'Reading' and 'Writing' were considered to be the more formal skills for academic purposes, while 'Speaking' and 'Listening' were regarded as having a wider range, as these skills are also used in informal communication (Davies 2008: 62).

33 The CEFR adds "Mediating" as another skill (or rather: 'communicative activity' – a term that the CEFR prefers).
34 www.de.toeic.eu/toeic-sites/toeic-germany/ueber-toeic/was-ist-der-toeicR-test/
35 The authors of the CEFR prefer the term "communicative activity", thus avoiding the ambiguity of the term "skill".
36 For a detailed discussion of proficiency scales and problems of validation see North 2000.
37 See the argument presented by Hulstijn 2007: 666.
38 www.uk.toefl.eu/
39 secure.vec.bc.ca/toefl-equivalency-table.cfm
40 www.ets.org/Media/Tests/TOEFL/pdf/EngLangCompDescriptors.pdf
41 www.ets.org/Media/Tests/TOEFL/pdf/Independent_Writing_Rubrics_2008.pdf
42 www.de.etsglobal.org/uploads/tx_etsquicklinks/CEFR_Mapping_TOEFL_iBT_2008.pdf
43 www.cambridgeesol.org/assets/pdf/ielts-research-faqs.pdf
44 www.cambridgeesol.org/assets/pdf/ielts-research-faqs.pdf
45 www.ets.org/Media/Tests/TOEFL/pdf/989551.pdf

7. References

7.1. References quoted in the text

Alderson, J. Charles
1991 Bands and scores. In: J. Charles Alderson and Brian North (eds.), *Language testing in the 1990s*. London: British Council / Macmillan, Developments in ELT, 71–86.

Alderson, J. Charles
2007 The CEFR and the Need for More Research. *The Modern Language Journal* 91 (4), 659–663.

Barkowski, Hans
2003 Skalierte Vagheit – der europäische Referenzrahmen für Sprachen und sein Versuch, die sprachliche Kommunikationskompetenz des Menschen für Anliegen des Fremdsprachenunterrichts niveaugerecht zu portionieren. In: Karl-Richard Bausch, Herbert Christ, Frank G. Königs and Hans-Jürgen Krumm (eds.), *Der Gemeinsame europäische Referenzrahmen für Sprachen in der Diskussion*. Tübingen: Narr, 22–28.

Bausch, Karl-Richard, Herbert Christ, Frank G. Königs and Hans Jürgen Krumm (eds.)
2003 *Der Gemeinsame europäische Referenzrahmen für Sprachen in der Diskussion*. Tübingen: Narr.

Canale, Michael
1983 On Some Dimensions of Language Proficiency. In: John W. Oller (ed.), *Issues in Language Testing Research*. Rowley/ Mass.: Newbury House, 333–342.

Canale, Michael and Swain, Merrill
1980 Theoretical bases of communicative approaches to second language teaching and testing. *Applied Linguistics* 1/1, 1–47.

Carroll, John B.
1979 Psychometric Approaches to the Study of Language Abilities. In: Charles J. Fillmore, D. Kempler and D.-Y. Wang (eds.), *Individual Differences in Language Ability and Language Behavior.* New York: Academic Press, 13–51

Casper-Hehne, Hiltraud (ed.)
2004 *DSH und TestDaF als hochschulbezogene Prüfungssysteme für Deutsch als Fremdsprache.* Baltmannsweiler: Schneider-Verlag Hohengehren.

Council of Europe
2001 *A Common European Framework of Reference for Languages: Learning, Teaching, Assessment.* Cambridge: Cambridge University Press.

Council of Europe
2009 Relating Language Examinations to the Common European Framework of Reference for Languages: Learning, Teaching, Assessment (CEFR) – A Manual. Available at: http://www.coe.int/t/dg4/linguistic/Manual%20 Revision%20-%20proofread%20-%20FINAL.pdf

Davies, Alan
2008 *Assessing Academic English.* Testing English proficiency 1950–89: the IELTS solution. Cambridge: Cambridge University Press.

Hulstijn, Jan H.
2007 The shaky ground beneath the CEFR: Quantitative and qualitative dimensions of language proficiency. *The Modern Language Journal* 91 (4), 663–667.

Ingram, David E.
1985 Assessing Proficiency: An overview of some aspects of testing. In: Kenneth Hyltenstam and Manfred Pienemann (eds.) *Modelling and Assessing Second Language Development.* Clevedon: Multilingual Matters, 215–276.

Krumm, Hans-Jürgen
2007 Profiles Instead of Levels: The CEFR and Its (Ab)Uses in the Context of Migration. *The Modern Language Journal* 91 (4), 667–669.

Lado, Robert
1961 *Language Testing. The Construction and Use of Foreign Language Tests*: A Teacher's Book. London: Longman.

Milanovic, Michael and Cyril Weir
2008 Series Editor's note. In: Alan Davies, Assessing Academic English. Cambridge: Cambridge University press, ix–xii.

North, Brian
2000 *The Development of a Common Framework Scale of Language Proficiency.* New York etc.: Peter Lang.

Pennycook, Alistair
1994 *The Cultural Politics of English as an International Language.* London/ New York: Longman.

Quetz, Jürgen
2001 Der Gemeinsame Europäische Referenzrahmen. *Info DaF* 28/6, 553–563.

Quetz, Jürgen
2003 Monkey Teachers? In: Karl-Richard Bausch, Herbert Christ, Frank G. Königs and Hans-Jürgen Krumm (eds.), *Der Gemeinsame europäische Referenzrahmen für Sprachen in der Diskussion.* Tübingen: Narr, 178–188.

Rampton, M.B.H.
1990 Displacing the 'native speaker': expertise, affiliation and inheritance. *ELT Journal* 44 (2): 97–101.

Soltau, Anja
2008a Englischsprachige Masterprogramme in Deutschland: Qualitätssicherung in der akademischen Lingua-Franca-Kommunikation am Beispiel von sprachlichen Zulassungskriterien. In: Annelie Knapp and Adelheid Schumann (eds.), *Mehrsprachigkeit und Multikulturalität im Studium*. Frankfurt: Lang, 155–169.

Soltau, Anja
2008b Englisch als Lingua Franca in der wissenschaftlichen Lehre: Charakteristika und Herausforderungen englischsprachiger Masterstudiengänge in Deutschland (2008) http://www.sub.uni-hamburg.de/opus/volltexte/2008/3602/

Spolsky, Bernard
1989 *Conditions for Second Language Learning: Introduction to a General Theory.* Oxford: Oxford University Press.

Tannenbaum, Richard J. and Caroline E. Wylie
2004 *Mapping test scores onto the Common European Framework*: Setting standards of language proficiency on the Test of English as a Foreign Language (TOEFL), The Test of Spoken English (TSE), The Test of Written English (TWE), and The Test of English for International Communication (TOEIC). Princeton, NJ: Educational Testing Service.

Tannenbaum, Richard J. and Caroline E. Wylie
2008 *Linking English-Language Test Scores onto the Common European Framework of Reference: An Application of Standard-Setting Methodology*". TOEFL iBT Research Report (TOEFLiBT-06). Available at: www.ets.org/Media/Research/pdf./RR-08–34.pdf

Taylor, David S.
1988 The Meaning and Use of the Term 'Competence' in Linguistics and Applied Linguistics. *Applied Linguistics* 9 /2, 148–168.

Vollmer, Helmut
1981 Why are we Interested in 'General Language Proficiency?' In: Charles J. Alderson and Arthur Hughes (eds.) *Issues in Language Testing*. London: British Council, ELT Documents 111, 152–176.

Weir, Cyril J.
2005 Limitations of the Common European Framework for developing comparable examinations and tests. Language Testing 22, 281–300.

7.2. Internet sources (last access: Jan. 2009)

cvc.cervantes.es/aula/dele/default.htm
http://secure.vec.bc.ca/toefl-equivalency-table.cfm
www.alte.org
http://www.alte.org/cando/general.php
www.cambridgeesol.org
www.cambridgeesol.org/assets/pdf/ielts-research-faqs.pdf
www.cambridgeesol.org/exams/academic-english/ielts.html

www.coe.int/T/DG4/Linguistic/CADRE_EN.asp
www.coe.int/t/dg4/linguistic/Source/Framework_EN.pdf
www.cvcl.it
www.daad.de/deutschland/deutsch-lernen/wie-deutsch-lernen/00573.de.html
www.de.etsglobal.org/germany/tests/tfi-test/
www.de.etsglobal.org/uploads/tx_etsquicklinks/CEFR_Mapping_TOEFL_iBT_2008.pdf
www.de.tfi-europe.com
www.de.toeic.eu/toeic-sites/toeic-germany/ueber-toeic/was-ist-der-toeicR-test/
www.ets.org
www.ets.org/Media/Tests/TOEFL/pdf/989551.pdf
www.ets.org/Media/Tests/TOEFL/pdf/EngLangCompDescriptors.pdf
www.ets.org/Media/Tests/TOEFL/pdf/Independent_Writing_Rubrics_2008.pdf
www.ets.org/Media/Tests/TOEFL/pdf/TOEFL_iBT_Score_Comparison_Tables.pdf
www.hku.hk/student/all/uregcourse/html1997/cerclang.htm
www.hsk.org.cn/english/Center_intro.aspx
www.osd.at
www.telc.net
www.testdaf.de
www.uk.etsglobal.org
www.uk.toefl.eu/
www.uk.toefl.eu/?iso=GB
www.uk.toeic.eu/fileadmin/free_resources/UK%20website/UK_Current/TOEIC_Can-do_table.pdf
www.uk.toeic.eu/toeic-sites/toeic-default/table-toeic-cecr/

7.3. Additional readings

Alderson, J. Charles and Caroline Clapham and Diane Wall
1995 *Language Test Construction and Evaluation*. Cambridge: Cambridge University Press.

Alderson, J. Charles
2005 *Diagnosing Foreign Language Proficiency: The Interface between Learning and Assessment*. London: Continuum.

Bachman, Lyle F.
1990 *Fundamental Considerations in Language Testing*. Oxford: Oxford University Press.

Bachman, Lyle F.
2000 Modern language testing at the turn of the century: assuring that that what we count counts. *Language Testing* 17, 1–42.

Canale, Michael
1983 From communicative competence to communicative language pedagogy. In: Jack C. Richards and Richard W. Schmidt (eds.), *Language and Communication*. London: Longman.

Chapelle, Carol A., Mary K. Enright and Joan M. Jamieson (eds.)
2008 *Building a Validity Argument for the Test of English as a Foreign Language™*. New York: Routledge.

de Jong, John H.A.L. and Ludo Verhoeven
1992 Modelling and Assessing Language Proficiency. In: Ludo Verhoeven and John H.A.L. de Jong (eds.), *The Construct of Language Proficiency*. Amsterdam / Philadelphia: John Benjamin, 3–19.

Harley, Birgit, Patrick Allen, Jim Cummins and Merrill Swain (eds.)
1994[3] *The Development of Second Language Proficiency*. Cambridge: Cambridge University Press.

Hughes, Arthur
2003 *Testing for Language Teachers* (second edition). Cambridge: Cambridge University Press.

Jones, Neil
2002 Relating the ALTE Framework to the Common European Framework of Reference. In: Council of Europe (ed.), *Case Studies on the Use of the Common European Framework of Reference*. Cambridge: Cambridge University Press, 167–183.

Little, David
2007 The CEFR and Educational Policies in Europe. *The Modern Language Journal* 91, 669–672.

McNamara, Tim
2000 *Language Testing*. Oxford: Oxford University Press.

Park, Jae-Eun
(2007) Co-construction of Nonnative Speaker Identity in Cross-cultural Interaction. *Applied Linguistics*, 28(3), 339–360.

Spolsky, Bernard (1989)
Conditions for Second Language Learning: Introduction to a General Theory. Oxford: OUP.

Taylor, David S.
1988 The Meaning and Use of the Term 'Competence' in Linguistics and Applied Linguistics. *Applied Linguistics* 9 /2, 148–168.

Usó-Juan, Esther and Martínez-Flor, Alicia (eds.)
2006 *Current Trends in the Development and Teaching of the Four Language Skills*. Berlin/ New York: Mouton de Gruyter.

Westhoff, Gerard
2007 Challenges and Opportunities of the CEFR for Reimaging Foreign Language Pedagogy. *The Modern Language Journal* 91 (4), 676–679.

Young, Richard and Agnes W. He (eds.)
Talking and Testing. Discourse Approaches to the Assessment of Oral Proficiency. Amsterdam / Philadelphia: John Benjamins 1998.

24. Evaluation and learning in language programmes

Richard Kiely and Pauline Rea-Dickins

1. Introduction

Example of evaluation as a tool for learning

In an English for Academic Purpose (EAP) class for L2 undergraduate students in a British University, the teacher leads an evaluation of the programme. She carries out a structured group discussion in Week 5 of the 12-week programme, and administers a student satisfaction questionnaire in the final class. Evaluation, according to institutional policy, is a required activity at all levels of the university, and a learning opportunity for students, teachers and managers. In the EAP department this policy was implemented through a mid-course group discussion, a modified form of Nominal Group Technique (NGT), and an end of course questionnaire. The purposes of this aspect of the curriculum are the development of the programme to ensure that it meets students' learning needs, and quality assurance on the part of the institution, which is required to demonstrate both the quality of the learning experience of students, and its own capacity in monitoring this. The group discussion activity is a reflective, social activity, moulded ecologically to complement the teaching and learning activities, the teacher's persona and role, and the time resource available. The report, a brief list of strengths and suggestions for development compiled by the tutor after discussion with the students, is passed on to the coordinator for EAP programmes and then discussed as one of a batch of reports by the EAP team. Then, summarised and accompanied by other monitoring documentation such as external examiners' report and grade sheets, the evaluation report is received and considered by a series of institutional committees. Such reports, grounded in the learning experience of students, in classrooms and within programmes are posited as key evidence of the quality of teaching and learning when the subject area is inspected as part of the national Teaching Quality Assessment.

The impact of the evaluation within the programme was particularly significant for the students and teacher. Three related outcomes of the evaluation discussion contributed to the rest of the programme (though these did not feature in the summarised reports). First, a discussion about the strategy for dealing with the vocabulary demands of the long, challenging texts which were a core part of the teaching strategy led the teacher to reflect and then adapt her teaching to address student preferences. Second, a discussion about the length and difficulty of the reading texts and the nature of the comprehension tasks based on these proved a platform for engaging with the nature of critique, and the development of an academic voice. Third, an issue which did not emerge in the discussion in the classroom – the ways in which both 'strong' and 'weak' students felt the other shaped the learning opportunities on the programme in a way which disadvantaged them. The first two issues show the ways in which the evaluation can be considered to have added value to the programme. The third illustrates one way in which it fell short.

This example represents what might be seen as an ideal: evaluation embedded in the implementation of the programme, and engaging immediate stakeholders (students, tutor, and institutional managers) and more remote stakeholders (main programme tutors, inspecting and accrediting bodies and students' sponsors) in cycles of learning which have the potential to improve the programme. We discuss the challenges of realising this learning potential in the final sections of this chapter, with particular reference to the interplay between the practices of evaluation and research.

This brief account illustrates the context, nature and potential of evaluation as "a form of enquiry which describes the achievements of a given programme, provides explanations for these, and sets out ways in which further development might be realised" (Kiely 2009). The purposes of evaluation are development and accountability (Rea-Dickins and Germaine 1992). *Development* involves improvement of the programme, not only for future cohorts of students, but also for current students. It involves reflection on the learning materials used, changing teaching techniques and strategies, and underpinning these dimensions of practice, the teacher's own professional learning. *Accountability* involves explicit attention to the issues which students raise, so that they can see that their stake is recognised, and also documentation of these processes, so that more remote stakeholders within the institution and beyond (for example, professional accrediting bodies) can be assured that students are listened to, and that the development of the programme involves active attention to their experiences of learning.

The nature of the evaluation is framed by the ecology of the programme: activities which fit both the expectations of students, and the time resources available for data collection, analysis and reporting. Key strengths of this form of evaluation include this reflective engagement by students, and teacher learning regarding the validity of programme goals and the viability of various strategies to achieve these. There are also weaknesses which co-occur with these strengths. First, as an evaluation the exercise here is very different from the measurement and comparison approach which has characterised programme evaluation for much of the twentieth century. Thus the value of the evaluation process may be undermined by the lack of compliance with widely held norms. Second, evaluation activities may be viewed by teachers and students as bureaucratic and intrusive, and considered a distraction from the main business of instruction and learning. Third, the local ownership of the programme and evaluation (teacher and students) is difficult to realise, particularly in relation to balancing interests: key stakeholders such as subject tutors (on the main programmes of study of these EAP students) are not involved (they may, for a range of reasons, opt for non-involvement, or practical issues may limit opportunities in this area), and university managers and administrators only marginally so. Programme evaluation as exemplified here can be a powerful tool for learning, but can also be constructed as bureaucratic, limited or threatening, and thus marginalised in programme management processes.

We next explore these themes in contemporary programme contexts from historical and epistemological perspectives.

2. Language programme evaluation – outline and history

2.1. The social context of language programme evaluation

Language programme evaluation is a specialist area in the wider fields of educational and social programmes. The accountability rationale for evaluation has both democratic and ethical dimensions: where such programmes are provided as a public good, it is important to assess their effectiveness to ensure that they merit the investment of public and private funds. Social programmes involve specialist services, and users may not from the outset be in a position to assess their merits. Programme evaluation has an ethical remit to protect through providing high quality information to users and other stakeholders. These twin dimensions of accountability underpin the notion that evaluation processes should improve programmes. It is important that monitoring and scrutiny are not just ends in themselves, but support the development of the programme. Accountability and development feature as overarching purposes for programme evaluation across the social world.

Educational evaluation is a sub-field of the wider programme evaluation field. Key notions here are evaluation for curriculum development (Stenhouse 1975) and stakeholder evaluation (Weiss 1986). A particular complexity in educational evaluation is that effectiveness is due as much to implementation as it is to the design features of a particular programme or intervention. A key strategy for maximising the impact of good implementation is involvement of teachers and other stakeholders such as students and parents in evaluation, leading to learning from and use of evaluation findings. Evaluation in educational programmes has over recent decades become more integrated into practice both in terms of programme management and classroom teaching (Rea-Dickins and Germaine 1992; Norris 1998). It has meshed with action research, institutional self-assessment, and self evaluation for professional development purposes, in ways which indicate accountabilities through development and improvement, rather than alongside or as an outcome of these. Thus the case for effectiveness is not so much an outcome of an evaluation, as it is the process of monitoring, review and action-taking.

Language programme evaluation has increasingly become part of recent trends in educational evaluation – the work of Stenhouse and Weiss for example constitute reference points for such integration. There are two principal factors in the development of language programme evaluation: the influence of Second Language Acquisition (SLA) research and the role of foreign language programmes (particularly English) in social and economic development. The main contribution of SLA has been to provide a theoretical base for the elaboration of the instructional strategies to be implemented and evaluated. As far as the role of language in development is concerned, from the 1970s onwards, English language programmes have been implemented as a vehicle for social and economic development in countries in South Asia, Africa and Latin America and evaluations carried out to document their educational, social and economic impact (see Nuttall 1991; Alderson 1992; Kiely and Rea-Dickins 2005).

These two factors provided focus for the theory and policy levels of language programme evaluation. It was anticipated that the evaluations related to SLA would generate instructional strategies which in turn would inform teaching activities, materials and teacher education courses. With regard to policy, the expectation was that evaluations which tracked and measured impact would shape how aid would be directed for socio-economic development. However, in both cases the evaluations proved both expensive and of limited contribution to the development of theory and policy. More recently, language programme evaluation has emphasised the relevance of practice: programme improvement at classroom level through evaluation of various aspects of the curriculum (Rea-Dickins 1994; Pennington 1998; Lamie 2005; Kiely 2009); and at institutional level through a focus on quality management (Mackay 1994; Mackay, Wellesley and Bazergan 1995; Kiely 1998; Crabbe 2003; Norris 2006), or a focus on compliance with mandates (Blue and Grundy 1996; Thomas 2003; Ferguson and Donno 2003). These trends have seen language programme evaluation become part of an increasingly regulated domain of service provision, quality and effectiveness.

2.2. Components of language programme evaluation

There are many components in a language programme, and approaches to evaluation have typically focussed on methods, materials and teachers either as aspects of a comprehensive programme evaluation or as a focus for a particular evaluation process such as coursebook selection.

2.2.1. *Evaluation of teaching methods*

As stated above the evaluation of instructional methods characterised early language programme evaluations. These studies used experimental designs and focussed largely on measurement of learning outcomes. Later studies, following Long's (1984) call for process-product studies to advance both language learning research and language instruction, focussed on techniques such as teacher question types. Two recently published studies into instructional methods illustrate the enduring currency of both experimental design and measurement of learning outcomes in the evaluation of instructional methods. Klapper and Rees (2003) compare the impact of teaching based on Focus-on-Form (FonF) and Focus-on-Forms (FonFs) in a University German as a Foreign Language programme. The longitudinal study was carried out over four years (including one year residence abroad in Germany), and the data were largely test results from the various stages of the programme. Garrett and Shortall (2002) compare different activity types in EFL classrooms in Brazil. They focus on four classroom activity types – teacher-fronted grammar (TFG), student-centred grammar (SCG), teacher-fronted fluency (TFF) and student-centred fluency (SCF). The data involve a different form of outcome from test data: student satisfaction in terms of *learning value*, *interest* and *relaxation* of the classroom activities, as captured on a 5-point rating scale after the implementation of the activities. These studies provide valuable findings for language teaching professionals, but there is little to support a decision to opt, at a policy level, for either FonF or FonFs, or for an approach based on grammar or fluency.

There are two challenges to learning from evaluation through studies like these. First, they are motivated by theory development in the field of language learning within Applied Linguistics, and may not be connecting with the issues related to professional practice. Bygate (2004) addresses this problem in Applied Linguistics: for enquiry to have substantive impact on real-world language problems, it has to work with the agenda of 'the lay community' such as programme administrators and language teachers as well as Applied Linguistics researchers. Second, both Klapper and Rees (2003) and Garrett and Shortall (2002) describe ambitious studies in terms of the data required to inform on the instructional issues. In both cases the resources available do not afford a full description of programme processes. The combination of weak theoretical constructs in the area of instructional methods and insufficient research resources to describe the natural variability in classroom processes has lessened the learning opportunity, particularly for policy and practice of these studies.

The Klapper and Rees and Garrett and Shortall studies have been published as research studies, and constitute a trend in this area in the last decade. New perspectives on instruction, for example, task-based learning (Skehan 1998; Ellis 2003) and processing instruction (Van Patten 2002; Lee and Benati 2007) have been explored as research rather than as teaching methods evaluation, that is, in laboratory or small-scale settings. These instructional strategies have yet to be extensively implemented at policy level and evaluated. It is unlikely, however, that the evaluation process here will replicate that of methods evaluations in the past, where SLA-informed designs did not yield informative results. Rather, we envisage a growth of small scale studies, led by programme managers and groups of teachers, developed in context specific directions, and supported by local materials development and teacher development initiatives. Evaluations constructed in this way include the work on task-based learning of Van den Branden (2006) and on university French as a foreign language (Towell and Tomlinson 1999): these are longitudinal with a range of curriculum investigations carried out by teachers and programme consultants for a range of evaluative and developmental purposes. We envisage that future evaluation for the development of instructional strategies will involve accounts of implementation from contexts such as these, accounts of how decisions are taken, rather than 'branded' methods tested and quality-assured for replication in new contexts.

2.2.2. *Evaluation of language teaching materials*

The focus of materials development in the past has been either the development and use of checklists for the selection of suitable coursebooks and other materials (Cunningsworth 1995; Sheldon 1988; McDonough and Shaw 1993; McGrath 2002) or the development of constructs for the design of materials (Rea-Dickins and Germaine 1992; Tomlinson 1998, 2003). In terms of the three stage model set out in Breen (1987, see also Rea-Dickins and Germaine 1992) – *workplan* (design construct), *in use* (classroom application) and *outcomes* (learning gain) – the focus of materials evaluation has been at the workplan stage. One obvious reason for this is that a focus on materials at the selection stage is relatively easy to maintain, whereas in relation to materials in use, and as a dimension of outcomes, the particular contribution of the materials is shaped by decisions regarding instructional management and learning strategy of teachers and students. The three stage model remains a goal for materials evaluation. Of particular importance is the *in use* stage: the potential here is for understanding how teachers and students use materials, and how materials can add value to the pedagogy, i.e. engaging teachers and learners in learning activities they would otherwise not do.

We can view the current thinking about materials evaluation in terms of *construct* and *compliance* approaches. In construct approaches, the basis in language learning theory, the focus of the scrutiny of materials is their potential to promote the development of the particular language skills relevant to the programme. For example, in the evaluation of *Tour de France*, Parkinson, McIntyre and Mitchell (1982) developed criteria from communicative language teaching (CLT) theory, thus basing the materials evaluation on this construct. In the English for Academic Purposes (EAP) programme described above, a construct approach would examine the extent to which the materials used in the programme facilitate development of critical and information management skills as well as further language development at a systemic level. Recent research in EAP has outlined a range of descriptive approaches to the academic use of language (particularly English), such as genre and discourse analysis (Swales 1990); corpus analysis approaches (Charles 2006; Nesi and Gardner 2006); and critical EAP (Benesch 2001; Canagarajah 2002). The task of evaluation in this specialist field is to assess the extent to which these applied linguistics frameworks afford pedagogic models: to understand the contribution they make to teaching EAP (Watson Todd 2003). In both CLT and EAP constructs, notions of authenticity of language or language use are central, although the appropriate pedagogic articulation of this notion is still a matter of debate. Evaluations have the potential, as yet unexplored, to critically examine such constructs, to validate them as a basis for developing instructional strategies.

In a compliance approach to materials evaluation the focus is the degree of fit with language programme factors. In contexts where the curriculum has an examination preparation function, the evaluation of materials might consider the extent to which test formats were embedded in the coursebook. In addition we might envisage contextual features such as programme duration and lesson frequency; different starting points in terms of language level of students; differential use of programme supports such as computer-assisted learning opportunities; and different teacher skills and expectations as factors which shape materials evaluation. Thus materials not only have to support language development in a theoretically coherent way: they also have to fit the programme in terms of the organisational features and learning culture. Donovan (2003) and Denton (2007) describe how commercial publishers of language learning materials operationalise a compliance approach in order to fit with local curricula, examining traditions, and teachers' expectations on the one hand and to avoid cultural dissonance and offence on the other.

In the classroom, teachers and materials constitute potentially different beacons to guide the implementation of the learning programme. The literature on materials evaluation shows both how teachers can shape the learning potential of materials, and how materials can influence the teacher's classroom style and strategy (Allwright 1981; Ellis 1997). The ongoing task for this component of language programme evaluation is to describe this relationship: to better understand how teachers construct materials as a resource in different programme contexts; and how materials can constitute a resource which aligns effectively with teacher judgements about the needs of their classrooms and students.

2.2.3. *Evaluation of teachers*

A major issue which has emerged through the evaluation of methods and materials is the fidelity factor: the extent to which programmes were implemented and materials used as set out in the workplan. In the 1970s and 1980s this gave rise to a range of instruments for describing teaching (see Wallace 1991 for a comprehensive summary). The purpose of this enterprise was to monitor the ways in which teachers were implementing theoretically-generated instructional methods. A salient such instrument was the Communicative Orientation to Language Teaching (COLT) inventory (Spada 1987; Rea-Dickins and Germaine 1992). Such observation schemes were used for evaluation purposes, both in the context of evaluating innovative programmes (Mitchell 1989, 1990, 1992) and evaluating teacher performance, whether for awards and qualifications or for in-service professional development. A central aspect of this approach to classroom observation and evaluation is the positioning of teachers as programme components, such as materials, whose contribution to the programme can be managed, altered and adapted. More recently, the contribution of teachers has been viewed differently: they are programme designers in action, taking decisions based on professional assessment of the unfolding programme in order to construct and maximise learning opportunities (Graves 1996; Nunan and Lamb 1996; Breen et al. 2001; Murphy and Byrd 2001; Richards 2006). This role for teachers includes on-going self-evaluation and leading evaluation activities on behalf of the institution as the EAP teacher in the programme described above.

The overview of key trends in the evaluation of the components of language programmes shows two developments over recent decades. First, holistic views of programmes, where method, materials and teacher action are in a dynamic, mutually-shaping relationship, have come to prevail. Second, the shape of programmes, as illustrated in the example at the start of this chapter, is a matter of distributed agency: teachers and students determine activities within the programme; managers and committees within institutions play a role; and outside stakeholders, such as examining bodies and quality assuring agencies also contribute. All of these participants have access to research findings and contribute to policies on resources such as language centres. The result is a view of a language programme as a complex weave, where the task of evaluation is to extricate the different strands and consider their relationship. The next section explores this task in terms of *purpose* and *performance*. Purpose relates to the motivations for and investments in the evaluation process. Performance focuses on what is evaluated: the performance of the student, of the teacher, or of programme components such as a course book or a language centre.

2.3. Purpose and performance in language programme evaluation

Developments in language programme evaluation over recent decades can be represented as a search for effectiveness which relates to two overarching themes: i) purpose, in terms of monitoring and inspection, knowledge building and programme improvement; ii) performance, in terms of teacher action, learner achievement, and institutional quality. This framework addresses the complexity of contemporary language programme evaluation. The focus on purpose situates the analysis of local evaluation processes in the wider policy and social context. And through the notion of performance, attention to specific contributions and action is achieved. Table 1 lists a sample of language programme evaluations with an analysis of the purpose of each and the particular performance which is examined.

There are two important patterns in this table. First there is a development from the early evaluations to the later ones in terms of the purpose: the shift is from a focus on theoretical knowledge building, to implementation issues for the specific programme. Thus, there is a sense that the role of the evaluator is that of consultant or critical friend, who is an advocate for the success of the programme, and whose observations, findings and conclusions are as relevant to current practice as much as to future policy development.

Second, there is a sense in which an evaluation is part of a project, or curriculum development initiative. Thus it is increasingly difficult to separate the evaluation process from the curriculum implementation process. Harris and Conway (2002) for example, started the evaluation of the Primary Modern Language Project at the start of the project, and integrated a description of the innovation impact in project contexts into the evaluation remit. Byram's (2000) report on the Interculture Project is presented in part as a dialogue, a working document which presents observations of the external consultant and the response and accounts of action by the project participants in the different university departments.

Overall the trend in Table 1 represents a developing comprehensiveness in terms of evaluation purpose, which increasingly addresses the range of factors which affect programme implementation and eventually effectiveness of learning. There is evidence of ongoing engagement with programme participants and through this, evaluation findings contributing to critical debate and ameliorative action in classrooms, in the development of materials, and in the management of change within programmes (for example, student participation and management processes are key performances in evaluations since 2000). There are two potential problems with this generally positive picture. First, as evaluators become advocates for success and effectively programme 'insiders', there may be a new requirement for externality in the search for an 'objective' view: Kiely and Rea-Dickins (2005) examine the management requirement for 'externality' in evaluation processes. Second, the close integration of evaluation within programmes

Table 1.

Examples of programme evaluations	**Purpose**	**Performance**
Tour de France (Parkinson, McIntyre and Mitchell 1982) Focus: Course book evaluation	To determine the extent to which a particular coursebook generated communicative language teaching and learning	Interaction of teachers and students in classroom activities (systematic observation)
Expatriate English Language Teachers Scheme 1987–1989 Focus: Medium of instruction in EFL in Hong Kong (Kiely and Rea-Dickins 2005)	To determine the extent to which exclusive use of the target language provided enhanced opportunities for learning	Learning outcomes (a battery of tests) Teacher action (student and school manager questionnaires, and teachers' self-reports)
Science Across Europe 1999–2000 Focus: Content and Language Integrated learning (CLIL) (Kiely and Rea-Dickins 2005)	To determine the extent to which particular science materials facilitated integrated teaching of Science and English, and identify new directions for such materials development	Teacher action (student questionnaires, EFL and Science teachers' self-reports, systematic observation); Learning outcomes (teacher reports and student self-report)
Teachers' English Language competence Focus: (Kiely and Rea-Dickins 2005)	To determine the English language competence and related teaching skills To identify perceptions of and attitudes to the use of English as medium of instruction	Teachers' English language level (battery of tests) Teachers English language use in classroom (systematic observation)
English for Academic Purposes (Kiely 1998; 2001; 2003; 2004; Kiely and Rea-Dickins 2005)	To determine the quality of the programme, with specific attention to the perceived needs of students, and the teacher response to these needs.	Teacher action (ethnographic observation; materials analysis) Students' learning experience (ethnographic observation; interviews)
Language Centre Evaluation (Mackay 1994; Mackay, Wellesley and Bazergan 1995; Morrison 2005)	To determine the managerial and institutional contribution to university English language programmes	Quality management processes, including course design, staffing, teacher development and learning resources (questionnaire; interviews)

Resource centre evaluation (Kiely and Rea-Dickins 2005)	To determine effectiveness of ELT resource	Management processes (interviews, focus groups)
Primary Modern Language Programme (Ireland) (Harris and Conway 2002)	To determine the effectiveness of a primary school foreign language programme; To inform on management of innovation issues	Learning outcomes (battery of tests) Teacher action (questionnaires, systematic observation) Management processes (questionnaires)
Learning in English for Academic Purposes (LEAP) (Jacobs 2000)	To determine the effectiveness of an EAP programme To determine how an analysis of student needs might inform development of the programme	Management processes (interviews, questionnaires) Teacher action and materials (ethnographic observation) Learning outcomes (assessment tasks)
The Interculture Project (1997–2000) (Saunders 2000)	To determine the role of evaluation in developing project activities within the Interculture Project	Management processes (interviews, notes from meetings)
The Interculture Project (Byram 2000)	To determine the quality and usability of materials and learning activities	Review of materials, activities, and student work
Evaluation of a Virtual Learning Environment (VLE) (Timmis 2004; Kiely and Rea-Dickins 2005)	To determine the actual and potential contribution of a web-based learning resource	Students' participation patters and perceptions (discussion board review; focus groups) Teacher action (review of task types and discussion board)

may create limitations in knowledge transfer and opportunities for learning beyond specific programme contexts and evaluations. The increase in web-based dissemination of evaluation reports may alleviate this aspect of programme evaluation: the immediacy of communication here may lead to new opportunities for learning within and across programmes.

2.3.1. *Evaluation purpose*

Language programme evaluation has evolved over the last century in terms of stated purpose and objectives. Initially the function of evaluation processes was to monitor the curriculum and inspect specific aspects of it, such as classroom teaching and learner achievement. More recently, the focus has been on curriculum development. The stated purposes of the evaluations in Table 1, abstracted from the aims, objectives and terms of reference of these evaluations, illustrate how evaluations achieve such development through elaboration of a situated programme theory. The focus or starting point of development varies with the context, for example, the medium of instruction, the integration of content and language in the curriculum or the use of information and communication technology in programmes. The goal of understanding and constructing an effective learning experience remains constant. Norris (2006), for example, establishes assessment in language programmes as a starting point. But rather than using the test results to make assertions about programme effectiveness, he proposes internal programme investigation of the means of assessment – content and format of assessment tasks – and ongoing exploration of how this broad-based account of assessment practices and outcomes might be used to understand empirically the nature of the learning experience within the programme. This process of evaluation should inform on the development of a) language skills; b) critical knowledge informing language use; and c) thoughtful dispositions underpinning effecting language learning and use. The process also enhances teachers' pedagogic knowledge and skills and establishes a basis for accounting to internal quality stakeholders and external accrediting bodies (in this case, the American Council on the Teaching of Foreign Languages – ACTFL).

The example set out at the beginning of this chapter also shows the convergence of purposes in foreign language programme evaluation. In terms of knowledge-building, there is the task of learning about EAP pedagogy, of institutional provision in EAP, and individual teacher learning. In terms of the management function, evaluation enables the institution to base the development of its curriculum on the student experience, and to demonstrate to external accrediting bodies – in this case, the British Association of State English Language teaching (BASELT); British Association for Learning English for Academic Purposes (BALEAP); and the Quality Assurance Agency (QAA) – that the programme meets their standards and mandates. A key issue is the extent to which very different purposes can be achieved through the same enquiry process.

2.3.2. Performance

A programme evaluation at its most general level is a study of implementation. At this level a number of performances are involved, typically, those of the students who do the learning, the teachers whose task is to shape and facilitate the learning, and the institution which at various level contributes to the performance of students and teachers. Three stages can be discerned in the ways a focus on performance has been developed in language programme evaluation. First, in early evaluations the focus was on the teacher (Gitlin and Smythe 1989). This corresponds with a view of evaluation as a means of curriculum control. One area where this focus has been significant in language programme evaluation is the implementation of the communicative approach. For example, the Communicative Orientation of Language Teaching (COLT, Spada 1987) develops a focus on the teacher as a means of understanding the classroom process. Second, and more important in language education has been a focus on the performance of the learner. Typically this involved a measurement of learning outcomes, and use of these as part of an experimental, comparative design, to inform on the effectiveness of a particular programme or specific instructional techniques. This focus on the performance of learners has been a characteristic of landmark evaluations in the past such as the Colorado (Scherer and Wertheimer 1964) and Pennsylvania (Smith 1970) Projects in the United States; Primary French in Britain (Burstall et al 1974); the Communicational Teaching Project in Bangalore (Beretta and Davies 1985; Prabhu 1987); the Hong Kong Expatriate English Language Teachers Scheme (Kiely and Rea-Dickins 2005). Third, the emerging management perspective on programme evaluation has situated the performance of the institution as the focus of evaluation. The evaluation process, carried out by bodies such as BALEAP, ACTFL or the European Association of Quality Language Services (EAQUALS) scrutinises a wide range of aspects of language programmes, such as teacher qualifications, materials, and health and safety considerations, to determine whether they meet a minimum threshold required for recognition or accreditation.

The focus on performance in programme evaluation raises a number of data issues. Sound, credible evaluation processes and findings are dependent on quality data gathering and analysis procedures. The central issue in this regard for many programmes is that of resources. The development and validation of tests and questionnaires, the analysis of audio and video classroom data, the handling of student and electronic text data all require specialist, expensive skills which are likely to be unaffordable for many programmes.

3. State of the art

The preceding sections illustrate the broad range of activities which are currently within the programme evaluation framework. The historical development has been a cumulative one, such that now anyone contemplating or planning an evaluation has a range of conceptual and methodological options to consider. Key considerations have to do with stakeholder perspectives; assessment and evaluation processes; language learning; language teaching; and programme management.

3.1. Stakeholders in the evaluation process

Weiss (1986) sets out the challenge of a stakeholder perspective in programme evaluation: it can "improve the fairness of the evaluation, democratise access to data, and equalise whatever power knowledge provides" (1986: 144). This challenge has been taken up across the evaluation sector: in a review of the articles in the journal *Evaluation* and *American Journal of Evaluation*, the words 'stakeholder evaluation' occur in more that 10 % of abstracts. In language programme evaluation, stakeholder perspectives increasingly inform evaluation practice: Kiely and Rea-Dickins (2005) describe what is involved in 'stakeholder as participant' rather than a 'stakeholder as informant' approach. Among strategies currently used to facilitate greater engagement and participation by stakeholders are the analysis of stakes as part of the evaluation design (Murphy and Rea-Dickins 1999), collaboratively established terms of reference (Alderson and Scott 1992), agenda setting meetings (Kiely and Rea-Dickins 2005), and stakeholders such as students designing questionnaires (Kiely 2006). The EAP example set out at the beginning of this article illustrates in some ways how such an approach might be realised: the students and teacher work together to gather and interpret the data, and co-write the evaluation report which is considered by institutional committees, and subsequently becomes part of the documentation which can be scrutinised by external bodies.

3.2. Assessment and evaluation processes

As illustrated in section 2 above, programme evaluation has in the past meant assessment, reflecting the view that the effectiveness of a programme is evident from test results alone. The logic here has proved difficult to sustain. From a language assessment perspective, the view that language tests are neutral psychometric facts, has been eclipsed by a view which sees them as socially-situated and culturally-constructed assertions (Rea-Dickins 1997; McNamara 2000; Fulcher and Davidson 2007). McNamara's chapter in this volume (see Ch. 22) explores social aspects of testing from a validity perspective, drawing in particular on the work of Messick. The implication for programme evaluation is that it is unwise to rely on test results alone, but such results and details of the process which contribute to them (including formative and classroom-based assessment) are an essential data-set for any programme evaluation (Norris 2006, and section 2 above).

3.3. Language learning

A strength of language programme evaluation has been the focus on language learning: this has been a key argument for the validity of studies in recent decades. A weakness, however, has been the narrow base on which evaluation epistemologies have been constructed: the reliance on theoretical constructs from SLA research, translated directly into instructional techniques. New perspectives in recent years have developed more comprehensive accounts of language learning processes (Firth and Wagner 1997; Kramsch 2002; Block 2003). The challenge for evaluation is to understand language learning, not just through a cognitive lens, but through the range of development processes and identity perspectives that make up a programme, and determine the means by, and the extent to which language development occurs. The wider challenge of identity perspectives for programme evaluation set out in Lincoln (2001, in Kiely and Rea-Dickins 2005: 43) is reflected in identity-oriented accounts of language development (Norton 2000; Rea-Dickins, Kiely and Yu 2007), and in accounts of programmes as communities of practice (Wenger 1998).

3.4. Language teaching

The development of our understanding of language teaching has paralleled that of language learning in recent years. Teaching is no longer viewed as the delivery of a pre-planned programme, but rather the interpretation and realisation of a programme construct. This has particular implications for the notions of method and teaching materials: these are no longer viewed as blueprints which comprehensively encode the teaching task, but rather as outline constructs which gain their definition and character in classroom interaction. Breen et al. (2001) and Mann (2005) explore the contribution of pedagogic principles and teachers' cognitions to this task. Rampton (1999) illustrates the cultural and historical anchors of such principles and the practices they generate. Richards (2006) shows how each teacher performance in classroom interaction constitutes 'identity work': teachers carefully micro-manage their contribution to the programme. Yin (2006) illustrates the ways assessment practices shape classroom processes. These perspectives increase the complexity of the language programme evaluator's task, and point to the need to unpack the teacher's stake.

3.5. Evaluation and programme management

Two aspects of language programme management make use of evaluation processes. Internal management activities which have a focus on quality enhancement, teacher learning and curriculum development use evaluation feedback from students and others. External management, through quality benchmarks and mandates from accrediting bodies, are effected through specified reporting procedures and through inspection. The accreditation requirements of BALEAP set out in Table 2 illustrates how an external body can shape the management of a language programme.

Table 2. Evaluation procedures as accreditation requirements

BALEAP programme evaluation requirements
5.8.1 Effective mechanisms will exist to ensure the on-going evaluation of all aspects of the course, to enable both students and staff to provide regular feedback, and for any necessary improvements to be made during the course.
5.8.2 End-of-course questionnaires will be administered and/or evaluation sessions conducted for students and staff to provide meaningful feedback on the course.
5.8.3 Effective systems will be in place to formally monitor the subsequent academic achievement of students who have completed the pre-sessional programme. Such a follow-up exercise will be undertaken at regular intervals (at least once every three years) and will include consultation with past students and with staff in receiving departments.
5.8.4 The outcomes of on-going and end-of-course evaluation and follow-up exercises will be documented, and records will be kept of action taken in response to these outcomes. The Course Director will be able to provide evidence of the ways in which these evaluation procedures have informed the development of the course from year to year.
DOCUMENTARY EVIDENCE – *Information on evaluation procedures e.g. on-going, midcourse, end of course and post-course.* – *Samples of any questionnaires used, (including student and staff questionnaires), staff observation records, minutes of staff meetings.* – *Copies of completed student and staff questionnaires of previous courses.* – *Course reports and summaries of previous course evaluation exercises.* – *Evidence of follow-up exercise on students' progress in consultation with receiving departments.*
http://www.baleap.org.uk/accreditation/index.aspx

A key focus here is the explicit link between evaluation data and quality assurance and enhancement. Increasingly, external evaluation relates closely to internal processes – an effective programme is one which self monitors, and identifies measures to improve the curriculum and maximise opportunities for learning by all participants. Blue and Grundy (1996) provides an account of how the process of preparing for the BALEAP accreditation constitutes a stimulus for investigative focus on programme structure, materials and staff development.

3.6. Summary – ever increasing complexity

This set of features of current evaluation practice and debates has increased the complexity of the evaluation task. Programmes are individual and personalised, and teaching involves constructing the curriculum rather than just delivering it. The programme is managed internally by students and teachers, and also shaped by quality frameworks and mandates from external bodies. Evaluation has to develop in three ways to meet the needs of these factors. First, it has to work with distributed programme ownership, in ways which promote this as well as inform on its effectiveness. This means engaging with diverse stakeholders' interests, needs and expectations, for example, providing accrediting bodies and their stakeholders with accountability information, and assisting teachers and managers with analyses of problems in order to facilitate programme improvement. Second, evaluators have to view effectiveness in diverse ways. This might include some measurement of outcomes, satisfaction with the experience of the programme, opportunities for teacher and institutional learning, and insights into the operation of the curriculum, such as effectiveness of materials, assessment procedures, and administrative aspects of the programme. Third, new approaches to data collection and analysis are required to inform on the complex web of interactions which make up language programmes. This is not a question of supplanting tests, questionnaires and observation schedules: rather it is a case of augmenting these, so that a comprehensive account of the programme is established efficiently. Three strategies which enhance programme evaluation data merit particular attention here. First, group discussions – focus groups (Kreuger 1994); Nominal Group Technique (Kiely 2003) – are increasingly used to capture data on the programme experience. Second, administrative data collected routinely in programmes can be harnessed to provide information on patterns of participation, progress and achievement in programmes (Patton 1997; Kiely and Rea-Dickins 2005). Third, the use of computers to support teaching and learning in programmes provides opportunities for capturing tracking data which can provide detailed accounts and insights into interaction and use of programme learning resources (Kiely and Rea-Dickins 2005; Pennington 2004).

4. Controversial issues

4.1. Evaluation and research

As discussed in section 2 above, early conceptions of language programme evaluation focussed on generating generalisable knowledge: in the search for effective methods, second language learning theories were operationalised and evaluated to construct knowledge which would inform policy and practice. These initiatives failed to contribute substantially either to second language learning research or programme design and method of instruction, and as a result, enquiry into second language instruction issues has more recently taken place in a research frame rather than as programme evaluations. Instructional strategies such as task-based learning (TBL, Skehan 1998; Ellis 2003), Processing Instruction (Van Patten 2002; Benati and Lee 2007) Focus on Form/Focus on Forms (De Keyser 2003; Ellis 2001) are investigated not in actual programme contexts, but in short term, micro contexts where a range of what might be considered programme issues are not investigated. This is due in part to a recognition of the complexity of language programmes where a research focus on particular aspects of cognition or social interaction is difficult: a multitude of factors shape lesson development and classroom interaction, and participants (teachers and students) are constantly managing relationships and representations as well as learning goals.

There are two problems arising from this relocating of enquiry into second language instruction issues. First the research programmes tend to focus on learning issues from a particular theoretical perspective, such as cognitive processing, so the findings do not map onto the ways teachers act and make decisions. Such research neither clarifies curriculum policy issues, nor leads to evaluation designs which might generate an empirically supported pedagogy. Second, the alternative research paradigm, which looks at second language teaching in a more socially oriented way is largely data-based, responding in its analysis to a range of potentially interesting aspects of instruction arising in data from language classrooms, and drawing on a range of theoretical perspectives to develop explanations. Such research in the areas of classroom discourse analysis, conversational analysis, ethnography, identity and sociocultural aspects of learning is difficult to relate to the task of framing and evaluating instructional policies. In both cases, there is the problem of simultaneously pursuing a research agenda and communicating with teachers and other practitioners. A resolution of this problem may lie in longitudinal studies: see section 2 above for a discussion of multi-faceted curriculum research (Van den Branden 2006; Towell and Tomlinson 1999), which affords insights into programme evaluation purposes might derive from such an approach.

4.2. Evaluation and practice

Whereas the direction of development of research into second language instruction has been towards learning theory, the development of evaluation of practice has been towards programme management and quality assurance. The discussion in the preceding sections has demonstrated that the expectation that evaluations would generate firm recommendations for practice in classrooms has been largely unfilled. As Greenwood (1985) and Brumfit (1984) noted in commentaries on the Bangalore evaluation, a lack of engagement with the task of teachers meant that there was no basis for the wider implementation of Prabhu's instructional strategy. Evaluation and practice within language programme evaluation tend to come together in the area of quality assurance rather than teaching method. A key mechanism in this development has been through the elaboration and use of accreditation schemes and mandates (Kiely and Rea-Dickins 2005). While these evaluation frameworks serve both the profession and individual learners well, there are two potential problems with them. First, they can act as ceilings as well as thresholds. They prescribe practice in ways which can minimise creativity and innovation. A script is established and all development is in these terms. Second, they privilege learner satisfaction in ways which may not correspond to effective language learning. Thus programmes may position grammar or profile speaking and communication skills in order to meet expectations of learners, or prepare them for tests and examinations rather than to progress their language skills towards long-term proficiency.

These issues of positioning for language programmes represent controversies not so much in the sense of hotly-contested options and solutions, but rather in the sense of complex operations where the conceptual nature of the different components is still to be described, and the connections between these still to be mapped. The next section continues this mapping of complexity, by exploring the ways research in Applied Linguistics and other fields in the educational and social sciences might come together to generate an approach to language programme evaluation which contributed both to theory development and to practice in classrooms and programmes.

5. Contribution of Applied Linguistics and other research perspectives

Widdowson (2000) distinguishes between Applied Linguistics and Linguistics Applied. While the conceptual basis of the latter is clear, in so far as it derives from the discipline of Linguistics, the source of explanations for phenomena investigated as Applied Linguistics are by nature interdisciplinary. Language programme evaluation is a particularly apt demonstration of this view of Applied

Linguistics: not only does it have roots in a range of social and educational fields of enquiry, its development, as is evident from the discussion throughout this chapter, requires ongoing engagement with new tools and practices within programmes, and emerging theoretical concepts and explanations. Table 3 maps fields of enquiry which have informed the development of language programmes (Column 1). Columns 2 and 3 illustrates research topics in Applied Linguistics and other disciplines (with examples of key published work). The table illustrates the inherent interdisciplinarity of language programmes, and the range of perspectives which inform evaluations.

Table 3 shows that in relation to language learning and teaching (Rows 1 and 2) the constructs and evidence base have come from applied linguistics. In some fields key contributions have come from outside applied linguistics, from grounded analyses of practice (materials) or other disciplines (programme management). There are three aspects of language programmes with recognised contributions from both within and outside applied linguistics: assessment, syllabus design and teacher learning. In the field of assessment novel perspectives on assessment for learning by education researchers (e.g. Tunstall and Gipps 1996; Gardner 2006) have generated opportunities for new takes on second language assessment. In syllabus design, theoretically-generated syllabuses have been eclipsed by initiatives in the Stenhousian tradition: the focus on underlying syllabus models and teaching and learning approaches has been replaced by analyses of lived classroom experiences. Similarly the development of teachers' professional skills is increasingly informed by notions of reflective practice (Schön 1983) and exploratory practice (Allwright 2003), approaches which work with practitioner experience, rather than with constructs from Applied Linguistics as the basis for learning and programme improvement.

Applied Linguistics can contribute further to the development of language programme evaluation in three ways. First, it can continue to develop theoretical perspectives on the range of issues it currently focusses on in relation to language use and language learning. The findings of research studies may in time be elaborated and implemented in educational settings where programme evaluation processes can inform on 'real-world value' and adapt to fit local contexts. Even without such formal evaluations, findings from applied linguistics research can guide teachers, teacher educators and managers within programmes in ongoing cycles of implementation and evaluation to stimulate teachers and students and enhance learning. Second, Applied Linguistics as a discipline is developing novel conceptual analyses which can enrich language programme evaluation. In discourse studies, for example, Sarangi (2006) proposes an integrated analysis of institutional talk, professional action, and practitioner learning in the social context of health care interactions. This approach may be a way of exploring language classrooms to inform on teacher identity and professional development, programme design and the use of learning materials. Third, inno-

Table 3. Contributions to language programme evaluation from Applied Linguistics and other fields

Programme evaluation issues	Some contributions from Applied Linguistics	Contributions from other disciplines
Language learning	Task based learning (Skehan 1998; Ellis 2003) Grammar teaching (Van Patten 2002; Benati and Lee 2007) Socio-cultural perspectives (Lantolf 2000; Kramsch 2002) Motivation (Dornyei 2001) Autonomy (Benson 2001)	
Language teaching strategy	Teaching and context (Breen et al. 2001) Teaching as social practice (Holliday 1992; Richards 2006) Teaching as interaction (Walsh 2006)	
Syllabus design	Language generated syllabuses (Wilkins 1976; White 1988)	Teaching-generated syllabuses (Legutke and Thomas 1991; Graves 1996; Nunan and Lamb 1996)
Assessment strategies	Language testing (Rea-Dickins 2001; Leung and Rea-Dickins 2007; Ellis 2003; Weir 2004)	Assessment for Learning (Black et al. 2003; Gardner 2006)
Teacher learning	Teachers using Applied Linguistics concepts (Richards and Lockhart 1994)	Teacher thinking (Borg 2006; Burns 2005; Mann 2005)
Language learning materials		Materials selection (Cunningsworth 1995) Materials development (McGrath 2002; Tomlinson 2003)
Programme management		Quality management (Mackay 1994; Mackay, Wellesley and Bazergan 1995; Crabbe 2003) Management of change (Holliday 1992; Markee 1997; Lamie 2005)

vative research methods developed in Applied Linguistics can contribute to language programme evaluation. In the past the battery of psychometric tools from general educational measurement have played an important role. More recently in Applied Linguistics a wide interest in qualitative methods has generated tools for analysing classroom interaction data; interview and focus group data, and texts used as materials or produced by students.

In addition to contributions from Applied Linguistics we see a range of innovative perspectives from other contexts of programme evaluation can be drawn on to develop programme evaluation. Some examples of these are:

i) Investigation of overlaps and syntheses with other curriculum development strategies from the educational sciences. Action research (Burns 2005); Reflective practice (Richards and Lockhart 1994; Richards and Farrell 2006); Exploratory practice (Allwright 2003) all share a focus on curriculum development with language programme evaluation.
ii) Perspectives on evaluation design such as realist evaluation (Pawson and Tilley 1997; Pawson 2003a, 2003b); case study approaches (Stake 1995); ethnographic approaches (Fetterman 1988; Markee 1997), utilisation-focused approaches (Patton 199?) and constructivist evaluation (Guba and Lincoln 1989) which have not yet been extensively used in language programme evaluations.
iii) Fresh perspectives on the nature of language programmes and how they might be designed and managed to reflect current concerns with potentially contradictory trends such as autonomy and individualisation on the one hand and compliance with mandates and external frameworks on the other. Soft systems methodology (SSM) (Checkland and Scholes 1999; Kiely and Rea-Dickins 2005) is one example of a management perspective which might be developed to capture the complexities of a language programme in the context of programme evaluation.

We started this chapter with an example of programme evaluation practice, which highlighted the issues around learning from and through evaluation. This example also reflects the interdependency of evaluation and research processes. Many aspects of this evaluation were clarified through PhD research (Kiely 2000), and subsequent publications: Kiely (2001) examined the issue of evaluation as a catalyst for change, in particular as a context for teacher reflection, and re-assessment of the teaching strategy. Kiely (2003) examined the evaluation instrumentation, in particular the structured discussion technique which provided glimpses into the learning experience of the marginalised students most in need of an English for Academic Purposes programme (EAP), but which ultimately privileged the more articulate stronger students. Kiely (2004) explored the nature of the evaluation and – the programme construct that is both the focus of the evaluation and the key values of participants which give the programme its character in implementation. The research has two functions: it describes and validates the evaluation format and activities, and it relates aspects of the programme and its evaluation to the wider project of knowledge construction in EAP and Applied Linguistics.

Developments in the field will benefit from increased practice in the area of programme evaluation. It is evident from the discussion throughout this chapter that there has been a wealth of fresh and innovative ideas from a range of sources. Each of these ideas requires sustained implementation in contexts of practice so that over time an ecological fitness for purpose is established. The example set out at the beginning of this article illustrates how evaluation as a dynamic programme resource adapts to the context: the group discussion technique and the reporting aspect are adapted by the teacher and other members of the EAP team. Whereas earlier approaches to programme evaluation viewed on line adaptations of a preconceived workplan as deviant and problematic in terms of blueprint fidelity, current thinking would see them as reflecting ownership, agency and individualisation within programmes. Through practice, theoretical procedures change, new insights inform decisions, learning happens. Evaluation as part of this practice facilitates such change, allows tools to become processes, and empowers participants to maximise their own learning from the programme.

References

Alderson, J. Charles
1992 Guidelines for the evaluation of language education. In: J. Charles Alderson and Alan Beretta (eds.), *Evaluating Second Language Education*, 274–304. Cambridge: Cambridge University Press.

Alderson, J. Charles and Mike Scott
1992 Insiders, outsiders and participatory evaluation. In: J. Charles Alderson and Alan Beretta (eds.), *Evaluating Second Language Education*, 25–58. Cambridge: Cambridge University Press.

Allwright, Dick
1981 What do we want teaching materials for? *English Language Teaching Journal* 36: 5–18

Allwright, Dick
2003 Exploratory practice: Rethinking practitioner research in language teaching. *Language Teaching Research* 7: 113–141.

Benesch, Sarah
2001 *Critical English for Academic Purposes: Theory, Politics and Practice.* New Jersey: Lawrence Erlbaum Associates Inc.

Benson, Phil
2001 *Autonomy in Language Learning*. Harlow: Pearson Education.

Beretta, Alan and Alan Davies
1985 Evaluation of the Bangalore Project. *English Language Teaching Journal* 39: 121–127.

Black, Paul, Chris Harrison, Clare Lee, Bethan Marshall and Dylan Wiliam, D.
2003 *Assessment for Learning: Putting It into Practice.* Maidenhead: Open University Press.

Block, David
2003 *The Social Turn in Second Language Acquisition*. Edinburgh: Edinburgh University Press.

Blue, George and Peter Grundy
1996 Team evaluation of language teaching and language courses. *English Language Teaching Journal* 50: 244–253.

Borg, Simon
2006 *Teacher Cognition and Language Education*. London: Continuum.

Breen, Michael
1987 Learner contributions to task design. In: Christopher Candlin and Dermot Murphy (eds.), *Language Learning Tasks*, 23–46. Englewood Cliffs NJ: Prentice-Hall.

Breen, Michael, Bernard Hird, Marion Milton, Rhonda Oliver and Anne Thwaite
2001 Making sense of language teaching: Teachers' principles and classroom practices. *Applied Lingistics* 22: 470–501.

Brumfit, Christopher J.
1984 The Bangalore Procedural Syllabus. *English Language Teaching Journal* 38: 233–241.

Burns, Anne
2005 Action Research: An evolving paradigm? *Language Teaching* 38: 57–74.

Burstall, Clare, Mark Jamieson, S. Cohen and Marian Hargreaves
1974 *Primary French in the Balance*. Slough: National Foundation for Educational Research.

Bygate, Martin
2004 Some current trends in applied linguistics: towards a generic view. *AILA Review* 17: 6–22.

Byram, Michael
2000 *The Interculture Project: Evaluation Report*. The Interculture project. http://www.lancs.ac.uk/users/interculture/reports.htm Accessed September 2007.

Canagarajah, Suresh
2002 *Critical Academic Writing and Multilingual Students*. Ann Arbor: University of Michigan Press.

Celani, M Antonieta, John L. Holmes, Rosinda C. G. Ramos and Mike R. Scott
1988 *The Brazilian ESP Project: An Evaluation*. Sao Paulo: Editora de PUC-SP.

Charles, Maggie
2006 The construction of stance in reporting clauses: A cross-disciplinary study of theses. *Applied Linguistics* 27: 492–518.

Checkland, Peter and Jim Scholes
1999 *Soft Systems Methodology in Action*. Chichester: Wiley.

Crabbe, David
2003 The quality of language learning opportunities. *TESOL Quarterly* 37: 9–34.

Cuningsworth, Alan
1995 *Choosing your Coursebook*. London: Heinemann.

De Keyser, Robert
2003 Implicit and explicit learning. In: Catherine Doughty and Michael H. Long (eds.), *Handbook of Second Language Acquisition*, 313–348. Oxford: Blackwell.

Denton, E.
2007 To what extent does market research shape publishers' development of course books for secondary schools in Italy? Unpublished MSc TESOL paper, University of Bristol.

Donovan, Peter
2003 Piloting – a publisher's view. In: Brian Tomlinson (ed.), *Materials Development in Language Teaching*, 149–189. Cambridge: Cambridge University Press.

Dörnyei, Zóltan
2001 *Teaching and Researching Motivation*. Harlow: Longman.

Ellis, Rod
1997 The empirical evaluation of language teaching materials. *ELT Journal* 51: 36–42.

Ellis, Rod (ed.)
2001 *Form Focussed Instruction and Second Language Learning*. Malden, MA: Blackwell.

Ellis, Rod
2003 *Task-Based Language Learning and Teaching*. Oxford: Oxford University Press.

Ferguson, Gibson and Sarah Donno
2003 One-month teacher training courses: Time for a change? *English Language Teaching Journal* 27 (1): 26–33.

Fetterman, David M.
1988 *Qualitative Approaches in Evaluation in Education: The Silent Revolution*. New York: Praeger.

Firth, Alan and Johannes Wagner
1997 On discourse, communication, and (some) fundamental concepts in SLA research. *The Modern Language Journal* 81: 285–300.

Fulcher, Glenn and Fred Davidson
2007 *Language Testing and Assessment*. London: Routledge.

Gardner, John (ed.)
2006 *Assessment and Learning*. London: Sage.

Garrett, Peter and Terry Shortall
2002 Learners' evaluations of teacher-fronted and student-centred classroom activities. *Language Teaching Research* 6: 25–57.

Gitlin, Andrew and John Smyth
1989 *Teacher Evaluation: Educative Alternatives*. Lewes: Falmer Press.

Graves, Kathleen
1996 *Teachers as Course Developers*. Cambridge: Cambridge University Press.

Greenwood, John
1985 Bangalore revisited: a reluctant complaint. *English Language Teaching Journal* 39: 268–273.

Guba, Egon and Yvonna Lincoln
1989 *Fourth Generation Evaluation*. Newbury Park: Sage.

Harris, John and Mary Conway
2002 *Modern Languages in Irish Primary Schools – An Evaluation of the National Pilot Primary Project*. Dublin: Institiúid Teangeolaíochta Éireann.

Holliday, Adrian R.
1992 Tissue rejection and informal orders in ELT projects: Collecting the right information. *Applied Linguistics* 13 (4): 403–424.
Jacobs Cecilia
2000 The Evaluation of Educational Innovation. *Evaluation 6:* 261–283.
Kiely, Richard
1998 Programme evaluation by teachers: Issues of policy and practice. In: Pauline Rea-Dickins and Kevin Germaine (eds.), *Managing Evaluation and Innovation in Language Teaching*, 78–104. Harlow: Longman.
Kiely, Richard
2000 Program evaluation by teachers: An observational study. Unpublished PhD. University of Warwick.
Kiely, Richard
2001 Classroom evaluation – values, interests and teacher development. *Language Teaching Research* 5 (3): 241–261.
Kiely, Richard
2003 What works for you?: A group discussion approach to programme evaluation. *Studies in Educational Evaluation* 29: 293–314.
Kiely, Richard
2004 Learning to critique in EAP. *Journal of English for Academic Purposes* 3: 211–227.
Kiely, Richard
2006 Evaluation, innovation and ownership of language programmes. *The Modern Language Journal* 90: 597–601.
Kiely, Richard
2009 Small answers to the big question: Learning from language programme evaluation. *Language Teaching Research* 13:99–116.
Kiely, Richard and Pauline Rea-Dickins
2005 *Programme Evaluation in Language Education.* Basingstoke: Palgrave Macmillan.
Klapper, John and Jonathan Rees
2003 Reviewing the case for explicit grammar instruction in the university foreign language learning context. *Language Teaching Research* 7: 285–314.
Kramsch, Claire (ed.)
2002 *Language Acquisition and Language Socialization.* London: Continuum.
Krueger, Richard
1994 *Focus Groups: A Practical Guide*. London: Sage.
Lamie, Judith
2005 *Evaluating Change in English Language Teaching.* Basingstoke: Palgrave Macmillan.
Lantolf, James P. (ed.)
2000 *Sociocultural Theory and Second Language Learning.* Oxford: Oxford University Press.
Lee, James and Alessandro Benati
2007 *Second Language Processing: Theories, Problems and Solutions.* London: Continuum.

Legutke, Michael and Howard Thomas
1991 *Process and Experience in the Language Classroom.* Harlow: Longman.
Leung, Constant and Pauline Rea-Dickins
2007 Teacher assessment as policy instrument – contradictions and capacities. *Language Assessment Quarterly* 4: 6–36.
Long, Michael H.
1984 Process and product in ESL programme evaluation. *TESOL Quarterly* 18: 409–425.
Mackay, Ronald
1994 Undertaking ESL/EFL programme review for accountability and improvement. *English Language Teaching Journal* 48: 142–149.
Mackay, Ronald, Sally Wellesley and Etty Bazergan
1995 Participatory evaluation. *English Language Teaching Journal* 49: 308–317.
Mann, Steve
2005 The language teacher's development. *Language Teaching* 38: 103–118.
Markee, Numa
1997 *Managing Curricular Innovation.* Cambridge: Cambridge University Press.
McDonough, Jo and Christopher Shaw
1994 *Materials and Methods in ELT.* Oxford: Backwell.
McGrath, Ian
2002 *Materials Evaluation and Design for Language Teaching.* Edinburgh: Edinburgh University Press.
McNamara, Tim
2000 *Language Testing.* Oxford: Oxford University Press.
Mitchell, Rosamond
1989 Second language learning: Investigating the classroom context. *System* 17: 195–210.
Mitchell, Rosamond
1990 Evaluation of second language teaching projects and programmes. *Language, Culture and Curriculum* 3: 3–17.
Mitchell, Rosamond
1992 The 'independent' evaluation of bilingual primary education. In: J. Charles Alderson and Alan Beretta (eds.), *Evaluating Second Language Education*, 100–137. Cambridge: Cambridge University Press.
Morrison, Bruce
2005 Evaluating learning gain in a self-access language learning centre. *Language Teaching Research* 9: 267–293.
Murphy, Dermot F. and Pauline Rea-Dickins
1999 Identifying stakeholders. In: Veronica McKay and Carew Treffgarne (eds.), *Evaluating Impact*, 89–98. Serial No. 35. London: Department for International Development.
Murphy, John and Patricia Byrd
2001 *Understanding the Courses We Teach: Local Perspectives on English Language Teaching.* Michigan: University of Michigan Press.
Nesi, Hilary and Sheena Gardner
2006 Variation in disciplinary culture: University tutors' views on assessed writing tasks. In: Richard Kiely, Gerald Clibbon, Pauline Rea-Dickins and

Helen Woodfield (eds.), *Language, Culture and Identity in Applied Linguistics*, 99–118. London: Equinox Publishing.

Norris, John M.
2006 The why (and how) of student learning outcomes assessment in college FL education. *Modern Language Journal* 90: 576–583.

Norris, Nigel
1998 Curriculum evaluation revisited. *Cambridge Journal of Education* 28: 207–220.

Norton, Bonny
2000 *Identity and Language Learning: Gender, Ethnicity, and Educational Change*. Harlow: Longman/Pearson Education.

Nunan, David and Clarice Lamb
1996 *The Self-Directed Teacher: Managing the Learning Process.* Cambridge: Cambridge University Press.

Nuttall, D.
1991 *Evaluating the Effects of ELT. Dunford House Seminar 1991*. London: The British Council.

Parkinson, Brian, Donald McIntyre and Rosamond Mitchell
1982 An independent evaluation of 'Tour de France'. *Stirling Educational Monographs No* 11. Department of Education, University of Stirling.

Patton, M. Q.
1997 *Utilisation-Focussed Evaluation.* Thousand Oaks: Sage.

Pawson, Ray
2003a Evidence-based policy: in search of a method. *Evaluation* 8: 157–181.

Pawson, Ray
2003b Evidence-based policy: the promise of realist synthesis. *Evaluation* 8: 340–358.

Pawson, Ray and Nick Tilley
1997 *Realistic Evaluation*. London: Sage.

Pennington, Martha
1998 Designing language programme evaluations for specific purposes. In: Li Edward and Gregory James (eds.), *Testing and Evaluation in Second Language Education*, 199–213. Hong Kong: Hong Kong University of Science and Technology.

Pennington, Martha
2004 Cycles of innovation in the adoption of information technology: a view for language teaching. *Computer Assisted Language Learning* 17: 7–33.

Prabhu, N. S.
1987 *Second Language Pedagogy*. Oxford: Oxford University Press.

Rampton, Ben
1999 Dichotomies, difference, and ritual in second language learning and teaching. *Applied Linguistics* 20: 316–340.

Rea-Dickins, Pauline
1994 Evaluation and English Language Teaching. *Language Teaching* 27: 71–92.

Rea-Dickins, Pauline
1997 So, why do we need relationships with stakeholders? *Language Testing* 14: 304–314.

Rea-Dickins, Pauline

2001 'Mirror, mirror on the wall': identifying processes of classroom assessment. *Language Testing* 18: 429–462.

Rea-Dickins, Pauline and Kevin Germaine

1992 *Evaluation*. Oxford: Oxford University Press.

Rea-Dickins, Pauline, Richard Kiely and Guoxing Yu

2007 Student identity, learning and progression. In: *IELTS Research Report, Volume 7*, 59–136. Cambridge: Cambridge ESOL/The British Council/IDP Australia.

Richards, Keith

2006 Being the teacher: Identity and classroom conversation. *Applied Linguistics* 27: 51–77.

Richards, Jack C. and Thomas Farrell

2005 *Professional Development for Language Teachers*. Cambridge: Cambridge University Press.

Richards, Jack C. and Charles Lockhart

1994 *Reflective Teaching in Second Language Classrooms*. Cambridge: Cambridge University Press.

Sarangi, Srikant

2006 The conditions and consequences of professional discourse studies. In: Richard Kiely, Gerald Clibbon, Pauline Rea-Dickins and Helen Woodfield (eds.), *Language, Culture and Identity in Applied Linguistics*, 199–216. London: Equinox Publishing.

Saunders, Murray

2000 Report on the evaluation of Interculture Project Experience. *The Interculture project*. http://www.lancs.ac.uk/users/interculture/reports.htm [Accessed September 2007.]

Scherer, George A. C. and Michael Wertheimer

1964 *A Psycholinguistic Experiment in Foreign Language Teaching*. New York: McGraw-Hill.

Schön, Donald A.

1983 *The Reflective Practitioner*. Aldershot: Arena.

Sheldon, Leslie E.

1988 Evaluating ELT textbooks and materials. *English Language Teaching Journal* 42: 237–246.

Skehan, Peter

1998 *A Cognitive Approach to Language Learning*. Oxford: Oxford University Press.

Smith, P. D.

1970 *A Comparison of the Cognitive and Audio-Lingual Approaches to Foreign Language Instruction: the Pennsylvania Foreign Language Project*. Philadelphia: The Center for Curriculum Development, Inc.

Spada, Nina

1987 Relationships between instructional differences and learning outcomes: A process-product study of communicative language teaching. *Applied Linguistics* 8:137–155.

Stake, Robert
1995 *The Art of Case Study Research.* Thousand Oaks: Sage.
Stenhouse, Lawrence
1975 *An Introduction to Curriculum Research and Development.* London: Heinemann.
Swales, John
1990 *Genre Analysis.* Cambridge: Cambridge University Press.
Thomas, Helen
2003 The arguments for and the meaning of quality. *English Language Teaching Journal* 57: 234–241.
Timms, Sue
2004 *Evaluation of the TESOL Blackboard.* Unpublished report. University of Bristol/Institute for Learning and Research Technology.
Tomlinson, Brian
1998 *Materials Development in Language Teaching.* Cambridge, Cambridge University Press.
Tomlinson, Brian (ed.)
2003 *Developing Materials for Language Teaching.* London: Continuum.
Towell, Richard and Philip Tomlinson
1999 Language curriculum development research at university level. *Language Teaching Research* 3:1–32.
Tunstall, Pat and Caroline Gipps
1996 Teacher feedback to young children in formative assessment: a typology. *British Educational Research Journal* 22: 389–404.
Van den Branden, Kris
2006 *Task-Based Education: From Theory to Practice.* Cambridge: Cambridge University Press.
VanPatten, Bill
2002 Processing instruction: an update. *Language Learning* 52: 755–803.
Wallace, Michael J.
1991 *Training Foreign Language Teachers.* Cambridge: Cambridge University Press.
Walsh, Steve
2006 *Investigating Classroom Discourse.* London: Routledge.
Watson Todd, Richard
2003 EAP or TEAP? *Journal of English for Academic Purposes* 2: 147–156.
Weir, Cyril
2004 *Language Testing and Validation.* Basingstoke: Palgrave Macmillan.
Weiss, Carol H.
1986 Towards the future of stakeholder approaches in evaluation. In: House, Ernest R. (ed.), *New Directions in Educational Evaluation,* 186–198. Lewes: Falmer Press.
Wenger, Etienne
1998 *Communities of Practice: Learning, Meaning, and Identity.* New York: Cambridge University Press.
White, Ronald
1988 *The ELT Curriculum.* Oxford: Blackwell.

Widdowsen, Henry G.
2000 On the limitations of linguistics applied. *Applied Linguistics* 21:3–25.
Wilkins, David A.
1976 *Notional Syllabuses.* Oxford: Oxford University Press.
Yin, M.
2005 Teacher thinking in EAP classroom language assessment. Unpublished EdD dissertation, University of Bristol.

Recommended Readings

Kiely, Richard and Pauline Rea-Dickins
2005 *Programme Evaluation in Language Education.* Basingstoke: Palgrave Macmillan.
Lamie, Judith
2005 *Evaluating Change in English Language Teaching.* Basingstoke: Palgrave Macmillan.
Lynch, Brian
2003 *Language Assessment and Programme Evaluation.* Edinburgh: Edinburgh University Press.
McGrath, Ian
2002 *Materials Evaluation and Design for Language Teaching.* Edinburgh: Edinburgh University Press.
Rea-Dickins, Pauline and Kevin Germaine
1992 *Evaluation.* Oxford: Oxford University Press.

Websites

The following websites provide information on programme evaluation for both practitioners and researchers, including evaluation guidelines, research methods, bibliographies, book reviews and journal articles.

Foreign Language Program Evaluation Project
http://nflrc.hawaii.edu/evaluation/
Evaluation Handbook
http://www.ncela.gwu.edu/pubs/eacwest/evalhbk.htm
Evaluation Cookbook
http://www.icbl.hw.ac.uk/ltdi/cookbook/
CREATE (Consortium for research on educational accountability and teacher evaluation)
http://www.wmich.edu/evalctr/create/
Handbook for Mixed Method Evaluations
http://www.ehr.nsf.gov/EHR/REC/pubs/NSF97-153/START.HTM
CRESST (National Center for Research on Evaluation, Standards, and Student Testing)
http://www.cse.ucla.edu/
The West Michigan University Evaluation Center
http://www.wmich.edu/evalctr/

W.K. Kellogg Foundation Evaluation Handbook
http://www.wkkf.org/Pubs/Tools/Evaluation/Pub770.pdf
Guidance on evaluation and review for DFiD staff
http://www.dfid.gov.uk/aboutdfid/performance/files/guidance-evaluation.pdf
Evaluation Virtual Library
http://www.policy-evaluation.org/

Biographical notes

Janina Brutt-Griffler is Associate Professor of Foreign and Second Language Acquisition and Director of Polish Studies at the College of Arts and Sciences at the State University of New York, Buffalo, US. Prior to coming to the US, she taught on the graduate faculty at the University of York, England. Her research and graduate teaching focuses on sociolinguistics, language policy, second language acquisition and multilingual writing. She is the author of *World English: A Study of Its Development*, winner of the Modern Language Association's 2004 Kenneth W. Mildenberger Prize. Her other recent publications include *Bilingualism and Language Pedagogy* and *English and Ethnicity.*

Martin Bygate is Professor of Applied Linguistics and Language Education at Lancaster University, UK, and currently President of AILA (*Association Internationale de Linguistique Appliquée*). His main interests are educational applied linguistics, second language acquisition, oral second language proficiency, task based language teaching, and language in education. Publications include *Speaking* (1987), *Grammar and the Language Classroom* (co-edited with Alan Tonkyn and Eddie Williams, 1994), *Researching Pedagogic Tasks* (co-edited with Peter Skehan and Merrill Swain, 2001), and *Tasks in Second Language Learning* (co-authored with Virginia Samuda, 2008). He was co-editor of *Applied Linguistics Journal* from 1998–2004.

Michael Byram is Professor Emeritus of Education at the University of Durham, England where he was involved in language teacher training and teaching for higher degrees since 1980. Prior to that he was a teacher of French and German in secondary school, having studied Modern Languages at King's College, Cambridge.

Vivian Cook is known for developing the idea of multi-competence. He has written books on Chomsky, on the applications of SLA to language teaching, and on writing systems and spelling. His current research concerns bilingual cognition. He was a founder and first President of the European Second Language Association (EUROSLA) and is co-founder and co-editor of *Writing Systems Research*

Jean-Marc Dewaele is Professor in Applied Linguistics and Multilingualism at Birkbeck, University of London. He published on psycholinguistic, sociolinguistic, pragmatic and psychological aspects of multilingualism. He is member of the editorial boards of *Intercultural Pragmatics*, the *International Journal* *of Multilingualism, EUROSLA Yearbook, Estudios de Lingüística Aplicada Inglesa* and the *Canadian Modern Language Review*. He is Reviews editor for *Sociolinguistic Studies* and assistant editor of the *International Journal of Bilingualism*. He is President of the *European Second Language Association* (*EUROSLA*) and Convenor of the AILA research network *Multilingualism: Acquisition and Use*.

Willis Edmondson is Professor Emeritus of Sprachlehrforschung (Foreign Language Teaching Research) and Applied Linguistics at the University of Hamburg, Germany, and also taught from 2005 to 2007 at the University of Hebron (Palestine). He has published more than 120 articles and books on almost all aspects of Foreign Language Teaching Research and on various aspects of foreign language learning. His main research interests focus on discourse analysis, theories of second language acquisition, and variables affecting foreign language classroom learning.

Konrad Ehlich is Honorary Professor at the Freie Universität Berlin (since 2009), Professor at the Ludwig-Maximilans-Universität of Munich (Germany) (since 1992) and Honorary Doctor of the Aristotle-University Thessaloniki (Greece). His main research and teaching areas are linguistic pragmatics, discourse and text linguistics, communication in institutions, spoken language/data transcription, writing and written language, narratology, sociology of language and language politics, German as a foreign and as second language and ancient Hebrew.

Claus Gnutzmann is Full Professor of English Language and Applied Linguistics at the University of Braunschweig. He has previously held similar posts at the University of Paderborn and the University of Hanover; he was educated at the University of Kiel, University of Stuttgart, University College London and the City University of New York. He holds an MA degree in Modern English Language from London (1971), a Dr. phil. in Phonetics from Kiel and a second doctorate (»Habilitation«) in English Linguistics from Hannover. His main research interests lie in linguistic and pedagogical grammar, language awareness, contrastive linguistics and error analysis, languages for special purposes as well as the globalisation of English and its classroom applications. His recent publications include *English in Academia. Catalyst or Barrier?* (2008), *The Globalisation of English and the English Language Classroom* (edited with Frauke Intemann, 2008, second edition), *Fremdsprache als Arbeitssprache in Schule und Studium* (2007). He is one of the editors of the journal *Fremdsprachen Lehren und Lernen* (»Teaching and Learning Foreign Languages«), which publishes articles in German, English and occasionally in French.

William Grabe is Regents' Professor of English at Northern Arizona University where he teaches in the MA-TESL and PhD in Applied Linguistics programmes. He authored *Reading in a Second Language: Moving from Theory to Practice* (Cambridge, 2009), and he co-authored *Teaching and Researching Reading* (2002) and *Theory and Practice of Writing* (1996). He also served as editor of the *Annual Review of Applied Linguistics* (1990–2000).

Anthony P. R. Howatt was educated in Scotland and, after postgraduate studies in Applied Linguistics at Edinburgh University, he was appointed as a lecturer in the subject in the mid-1960s following some years teaching EFL abroad. He was a contributor to the Edinburgh Course in Applied Linguistics edited by J. P. B. Allen and S. P. Corder in the 1970s and his main publication – *A History of English Language Teaching* – first appeared in 1984 with a revised edition with H.G. Widdowson in 2004.

Britta Hufeisen is Professor at the Division of Multilingualism Research at Technische Universität Darmstadt where she teaches in a range of postgraduate programmes in Applied Linguistics. Her current interests include German as a Second Foreign Language, text competencies in L2, and blended learning.

Ulrike Jessner teaches mainly at the University of Innsbruck, Austria. She has published widely in the field of bilingualism and multilingualism with a special focus on the acquisition of English in multilingual contexts. She is the co-author of *A Dynamic Model in Multilingualism* (2002) and the author of *Linguistic Awareness in Multilinguals* (2006). She is also the co-editor of *International Journal of Multilingualism* and the book series *Trends in Applied Linguistics* published by Mouton de Gruyter.

Keith Johnson is Emeritus Professor of Linguistics and Language Education in the Department of Linguistics and English Language at Lancaster University. His recent publications include *An Introduction to Foreign Language Learning and Teaching* (Second Edition, 2008), *Expertise in Second Language Learning and Teaching* (edited collection, 2005), *Designing Language Teaching Tasks* (2003), and *Language Teaching and Skill Learning* (1996). He was founding editor of the journal *Language Teaching Research*, and his main research interest in recent years has been in language teaching expertise. He was a member of staff at Lancaster for thirteen years. Before that he worked at the Universities of Essex and Reading. He has travelled widely as lecturer and consultant.

Richard Kiely is Reader in Applied Linguistics and Education in the Graduate School of Education at the University of Bristol, UK. He coordinates the *Centre* *for Research on Language and Education* (*CREOLE*) and leads the doctoral programmes in TESOL / Applied Linguistics. He is currently researching identity and learning in graduate programmes, and the development of academic literacies in Applied Linguistics.

Annelie Knapp is Professor of Applied Linguistics and Foreign Language Teaching at the University of Siegen, Germany, where she is also head of the foreign language department in the university's Centre for General Academic Competences. Her research interests focus on foreign language teaching and intercultural communication. In these areas, she has published on error analysis, language awareness, intercultural communication and intercultural competence. She is currently leading a large scale research project on multilingualism and multiculturalism in university studies.

Karlfried Knapp is Professor of Applied Linguistics at the University of Erfurt, Germany, where he is also the director of the University's Language Centre, and Honorary Professor at Bejing Capital Normal University, China. His teaching, research and publications focus on the epistemology of Applied Linguistics, second language acquisition, intercultural communication, non-professional interpreting and the sociolinguistics of English as a Lingua Franca. He is senior editor of *Angewandte Linguistik – Ein Lehrbuch* (second edition 2007), series editor of the Mouton-de Gruyter *Handbooks of Applied Linguistics* and founding editor of the forthcoming *European Journal of Applied Linguistics*, also at Mouton-de Gruyters. From 2002 to 2008 he served as the Secretary General of the *Assocication Internationale de Linguistique Appliquée* (AILA) and is currently involved in a research project comparing lay theories of linguistic competence across different cultures and their respective consequences for language policies and testing.

Kurt Kohn is chair professor of Applied English Linguistics at the University of Tübingen and Director of the Steinbeis Transfer Centre *Sprachlernmedien / Language Learning Media* (http://www.sprachlernmedien.de). His research areas include second language learning and teaching, English as a Lingua Franca and translation studies. Since the early 1990s, he has been involved in European CALL projects focusing on content authoring, blended learning and pedagogic corpora. He is co-developer (with Petra Hoffstaedter) of the language learning and authoring software *Telos Language Partner* and has co-authored multimedia and web-based language learning packages.

Claire Kramsch is Professor of German and Affiliate Professor of Education at the University of California at Berkeley, U.S.A. She is past president of the *American Association for Applied Linguistics* and past co-editor of *Applied Lin-*

guistics. She has written extensively on discourse and culture in language study and is the author of *Discourse Analysis and Second Language Teaching* (1981), *Interaction et Discours dans la Classe de Langue* (1984), *Reden Mitreden Dazwischenreden* (1990), *Context and Culture in Language Teaching* (1993), *Language and Culture* (1998) and *The Multilingual Subject* (in press). She is the editor of *Redefining the Boundaries of Language Study* (1995) and *Language Acquisition and Language Socialization. Ecological perspectives* (2002) and co-editor of *Precis du Plurilinguisme et du Pluriculturalisme* (2007).

Lienhard Legenhausen is Professor Emeritus of Language Pedagogy and Applied Linguistics at the University of Münster, Germany. His research interests include the study of learner language, technology-enhanced language learning as well as learner-centred approaches to classroom learning / teaching.

Tim McNamara is Professor in the School of Languages and Linguistics at the University of Melbourne, where he is also active in the Language Testing Research Centre. His publications include *Language Testing* (2000) and *Language Testing: The Social Dimension* (with Carsten Roever, 2006). His main areas of research are language testing and language and identity.

Marí del Carmen Méndez García is Lecturer at the Departamento de Filología Inglesa (Department of English Philology), Universidad de Jaén (University of Jaén), Spain. She studied French and English at the University of Jaén and first taught English at private language schools from 1991. She was awarded a doctoral scholarship by the Spanish Ministry of Education (1997–2000) and since then has done research in the cultural component in EFL material and intercultural competence and intercultural communication.

Rosamond Mitchell is Professor of Applied Linguistics in the Centre for Applied Language Research, School of Humanities, University of Southampton, UK, where she teaches on a range of postgraduate programmes in Applied Linguistics. Her current interests include foreign language education in the primary school, and the use of learner corpora in second language acquisition research. She is co-author of *Second Language Learning Theories* (2004).

Pauline Rea-Dickins is Professor of Applied Linguistics in Education in the Graduate School of Education at the University of Bristol, UK, where she is Director of Research. She researches and writes in the areas of language testing and assessment, classroom-based assessment, and the role of language in school examinations taken in a second language.

Theodore Rodgers is Professor of Psycholinguistics (Emeritus) at the University of Hawaii. He has lived and taught in eight countries, most recently in the MATEFL program at Bilkent University in Turkey. He is co-author (with Jack Richards) of *Approaches and Methods in Language Teaching* (2001, second edition) and *Doing Second Language Research* (with J.D. Brown, 2003).

Barbara Seidlhofer is Professor of English and Applied Linguistics at the University of Vienna. Her teaching and research focus on applied linguistics, corpus linguistics, sociolinguistics, discourse analysis and pragmatics, in particular in their relevance for language teacher education. Her publications include the books *Pronunciation* (with C. Dalton), 1994; *Approaches to Summarization: Discourse Analysis and Language Education* (1995); *Principle and Practice in Applied Linguistics*, co-edited with G. Cook, (1995); *Language Policy and Language Education in Emerging Nations*, with R. de Beaugrande and M. Grosman, 1993 and *Controversies in Applied Linguistics,* 2003. She was also for several years editor of the *International Journal of Applied Linguistics*. She is the founding director of the Vienna-Oxford International Corpus of English (VOICE), which provides a basis for the linguistic description of English as a Lingua Franca – which is also the theme of her forthcoming book *Understanding English as a Lingua Franca.*

Fredricka L. Stoller is Professor of English at Northern Arizona University where she teaches in the Master's degree in Teaching English as a Second Language and PhD in Applied Linguistics programmes. She is interested in literacy skills development, content-based instruction, and disciplinary writing. She co-authored *Teaching and Researching Reading* (2002) with William Grabe and *Write Like a Chemist: A Guide and Resource* (2008) with Marin Robinson.

H. G. Widdowson began his academic career in 1969 as a lecturer in Applied Linguistics at the University of Edinburgh and in 1977 became Professor of Education at the University of London with particular responsibility for the Teaching of English to Speakers of Other Languages. He was also for several years concurrently Professor of Applied Linguistics at the University of Essex and subsequently Professor of English Linguistics at the University of Vienna. He was a founding editor of the journal *Applied Linguistics* and for thirty years acted as applied linguistics adviser to Oxford University Press. He has written extensively on a range of topics relating to applied linguistics including discourse analysis, the stylistics of literature and language teacher education. His most recent publications are *Defining Issues in English Language Teaching*, *Text, Context, Pretext* and *Discourse Analysis*. He now lives in (relative) retirement as Professor Emeritus, University of London, and Honorary Professor, University of Vienna.

Antje Wilton is Assistant Professor for English and Applied Linguistics at the University of Erfurt, Germany. In her MA thesis she investigated the translation abilities of untrained natural bilinguals. She wrote her PhD on humour in bilingual conversation. Her research interests include conversation analysis, native / non-native interaction, multilingualism in the history of English and lay theories of multilingualism.

Dieter Wolff is Professor Emeritus for Applied Psycholinguistics at the Bergische Universität Wuppertal (Germany). His main research interests are language processing in a second language, language teaching and learning in instructed contexts, and bilingual education. For six years he was Vice President of *AILA* (*Association Internationale de Linguistique Appliquée*). He was co-editor of three journals on Applied Linguistics and foreign language teaching. Currently, he is advisor to several European governments with respect to Content and Language Integrated Learning (CLIL). His list of publications includes ten books and more than 200 articles in scientific journals and similar publications.

Name index

H

M

N

Y

Z

Language index

Subject index

D

E